# Designs, Methods and Practices for Researc of Project Management

'Beverly Pasian's book is extremely important and timely. It is also ambitious, and we should commend her for undertaking this mission. The book integrates under one roof a tremendous collection of research lessons and experience on how to investigate project management and how to better understand it in the future. The book should be highly recommended to different groups of researchers and educators. Nice and very relevant undertaking!'

Aaron Shenhar, Technological Leadership Institute, SPLWIN, Rutgers and Tel Aviv Universities

'The field of project management has come a long way in the last quarter of a century in improving the quality of its research and the rigour of the research methodologies on which it is based. However, it stands accused of being very narrow now. Project management research is based on rigorous methodologies, but a very narrow range of methodologies are used. Having now built a firm base, project management research now needs to move out into new areas to broaden the topics that can be investigated and the ways they can be investigated. In that we can find new insights into the field. This book will make an extremely valuable contribution into opening up the research horizons of project management. I would also like to use chapters as readings on my research management courses.'

Rodney Turner, Professor of Project Management, Kingston Business School, UK

'This book is a tour de force on research designs, methods and practices. It covers a wide range of foundational aspects, general and specific research approaches, mixed methods strategies, unique environment settings and state-of-the-art tools, such as social media. All presented by renowned researchers. Clearly a must have for every project management researcher.'

Reinhard Wagner, IPMA Vice President for Research

'Project Management is an interdisciplinary discipline that adopts and integrates theories and practices from organization management/behavioral science and operations research/management science. A potpourri of different research approaches presented by top scholars in our field will help students, academics, and practitioners apply the appropriate research questions, designs, and methodologies whether they are working on a research manuscript or preparing for a professional report. This book is an excellent encyclopedia dedicated to research designs, methods, and practices for project management.'

Young Hoon Kwak, George Washington University School of Business, USA

'As project management researchers and academics, all of us, to some degree, are prisoners of the research traditions in which we were taught and originally practiced. Empiricists are encouraged to remain empirical; math modelers should continue to model; and case methodologists should remain firmly embedded in their case methods. But it doesn't have to be this way. The project management field is so rich in diversity – of both theory and research practice – that it offers virtually innumerable means for academics and practitioners alike to learn more about the discipline, to build new theory, and through clever research, to advance our knowledge apace. To simply say that this book, Designs, Methods and Practices for Research of Project Management, is "timely", is to sadly underappreciate what Beverly Pasian has here created. An edited work filled with the ideas of some of the best researchers and theorists that the project management field has to offer is a gem and should be part of the library of everyone who has a genuine interest in where the field is headed and the best methodological ways to get it there.'

Jeffrey K. Pinto, Penn State University, USA

'Designs, Methods and Practices for Research in Project Management edited by Beverly Pasian is a long overdue collection of papers by some of the best minds in project management research. In one complete edition, the editor skillfully weaves significant papers addressing key issues together to produce what I am sure will become the "go to" handbook for researchers in project management. This is an area in which many educators from traditional academic disciplines have a difficult time comprehending what there is to do. The study of project management casts a very broad net over a wide range of subjects, many of which are research areas having their own feet. The interests of our PhD students are quite diverse indeed. The book organizes information into seven parts: 1) Foundational issues; 2) Focusing your research effort; 3) Specific data collection and analysis techniques; 4) Examples of mixed methods strategies; 5) Unique environments for project management research; 6) Writing for a future researcher; and 7) Benefitting from experience: supervisors and publications. The book addresses what all young researchers need to know. We will make it mandatory reading for ours.'

John H. Cable, University of Maryland, USA

'This is the book I wish existed when I started my journey towards a PhD in Strategy, Programme and Project Management. With chapters written by management of projects researchers, it squarely addresses the issue of doing academically rigorous research in an area some academics regard as being not researchable. By providing management of projects context, this book is a valuable complement to the seminal texts on conducting research that one frequently refers to.'

James Szot, The University of Texas at Dallas, USA

# Designs, Methods and Practices for Research of Project Management

Edited by
BEVERLY PASIAN

GOWER

**Gower Applied Business Research**
Our programme provides leaders, practitioners, scholars and researchers with thought provoking, cutting edge books that combine conceptual insights, interdisciplinary rigour and practical relevance in key areas of business and management.

Published by
Gower Publishing Limited
Wey Court East
Union Road
Farnham
Surrey
GU9 7PT
England

Gower Publishing Company
110 Cherry Street
Suite 3-1
Burlington
VT 05401-3818
USA

www.gowerpublishing.com

Beverly Pasian has asserted her right under the Copyright, Designs and Patents Act, 1988, to be identified as the editor of this work.

**British Library Cataloguing in Publication Data**
A catalogue record for this book is available from the British Library.

    ISBN: 9781409448808 (pbk)
    ISBN: 9781409448815 (ebk – ePDF)
    ISBN: 9781472407993 (ebk – ePUB)

**The Library of Congress has cataloged the printed edition as follows**:
Designs, methods and practices for research of project management / [edited] by Beverly Pasian.
    pages cm
  Includes bibliographical references and index.
  ISBN 978-1-4094-4880-8 (pbk.) -- ISBN 978-1-4094-4881-5 (ebook) -- ISBN (invalid) 978-1-4724-0799-3 (epub) 1. Project management--Research. 2. Social sciences--Research--Methodology. I. Pasian, Beverly.
  HD69.P75D47 2015
  658.4'04072--dc23

2014029433

MIX
Paper from
responsible sources
FSC® C013985

Printed in the United Kingdom by Henry Ling Limited,
at the Dorset Press, Dorchester, DT1 1HD

# Contents

# List of Figures

# List of Tables

# List of Contributors

**Chivonne Algeo** is a Senior Lecturer and Course Director of Project Management at the University of Technology, Sydney, and has more than 20 years' experience in delivering a variety of projects for major financial, insurance and health organisations across the Asia Pacific. Chivonne's teaching covers a range of postgraduate project management subjects for students and government agencies. Her research is focused on how project managers exchange knowledge; the professionalisation of project management; the synergy and tension between project and change management; and gender bias in project management. Chivonne contributes to the project management sector as a Fellow and past Board Director of the Australian Institute of Project Management (AIPM), and through her connections with the Project Management Institute (PMI).

**Thomas Biedenbach** is an Assistant Professor of Management at Umeå School of Business and Economics at Umeå University in Sweden. He holds a PhD degree from Umeå University. His current research focuses on project portfolio management, universities' innovation support system, and effects of platform development on business models. His research has been published in journals such as the *International Journal of Project Management* (IJPM), *International Journal of Managing Projects in Business* (IJMPB), *Journal of Change Management* and *Project Management Journal* (PMJ). In addition to teaching various management courses at undergraduate and graduate levels, he has experience in teaching research methodology for business students.

**Marian Bosch–Rekveldt** is an Assistant Professor Project Management at Delft University of Technology, the Netherlands. She holds an MSc in mechanical engineering (1999) and a PhD in project management (2011). Before starting her PhD research in 2006, she worked as a project engineer and project manager at a large Dutch organisation for applied research. In 2011, she finished the PhD research titled 'Managing project complexity: A study into adapting early project phases to improve project performance in large engineering projects.' She is involved in teaching (BSc, MSc, DE graduate school and professional education) and research in the field of project management of large (infrastructure) projects.

**Spike Boydell** is a property theorist and emergent transdisciplinarian who has had the pleasure of engaging in doctoral supervision with scholars from a range of backgrounds – property rights, planning, construction, law and of course project management. Sharing in a diversity of research journeys has helped him evolve his understanding of research design and exposed him to a diversity of research modalities – albeit he finds qualitative and mixed method approaches more stimulating than quantitative or econometric models. He has worked at universities in the UK, Australia and the South Pacific. Spike is currently the Professor of the Built Environment at the University of Technology, Sydney, where he is also the Founding Director of the UTS: Asia–Pacific Centre for Complex Real Property Rights.

**Christophe N. Bredillet** is the Scientific Director, Société française pour l'avancement du Management de Projet (SMAP) and adjunct Professor at Queensland University of Technology, and specialises in the fields of Portofolio, Programme & Project Management (P3M). From 2012 to 2015, he was the Director of the QUT Project Management Academy. From 1992 to 2010, he was the Dean of Postgraduate Programmes and Professor of Strategic Management & P3M at ESC Lille. His main interests and research activities are in the field of Philosophy of Science and Practice in P3M, including dynamic of evolution of the field, bodies of knowledge, standards and their link with governance and performance. He has been Executive Editor of PMJ since May 2004.

**Naomi Brookes** is a Professor of Complex Project Management based in the School of Civil Engineering in the University of Leeds in the UK. Naomi has worked with a huge range of organisations to help them improve their project management practice as well as publishing a wide range of research contributions in the field of project management. She has a substantive track record in leading research projects and is currently the Chair of the MEGAPROJECT COST Action, a trans-European and cross-sectoral network of over 80 researchers investigating the design and delivery of megaprojects in the European Union (EU).

**Roslyn Cameron** is a Research Fellow with Curtin Business School at Curtin University in Australia and has been an avid yet critical supporter of mixed methods research (MMR) since she utilised a sequential mixed methods model in her own PhD thesis. Since then she has conducted numerous MMR plenary sessions and workshops for DBA students and RHD students at Doctoral symposia and academic conferences. She is currently Associate Editor of the *Electronic Journal of Business Research Methods* and is on the Editorial Board of the *International Journal of Multiple Research Approaches*. She is Co-convenor of the Australian and New Zealand Academy of Management (ANZAM) Special Interest Group (SIG) for MMR which was launched in December 2011. Roslyn has published widely on the use of MMR across several disciplines and is a strong advocate for developing research capacity in MMR amongst business and management doctoral students and novice and experienced researchers alike.

**James Connor** is a Senior Lecturer at the University of New South Wales Canberra at the Australian Defence Force Academy (ADFA). James lectures in project management, organisational behaviour and leadership and his view that we interact and exist through our emotional life informs all his research into emotions, sport and project management. James has presented key note speeches for the Norwegian Security Agency and Australian Defence Force on loyalty, emotion and culture. He has undertaken funded research for an Australian Federal Government agency on program management and holds a PMI Research Grant. James currently supervises a number of students working on military loyalty, military team work and formation, and portfolio management.

**Lynn Crawford** is Director of the Project Management Program at The University of Sydney. Through Human Systems International assists leading corporations and government agencies in assessing and developing organizational project management capability. Ongoing research includes competence and career paths and differences in project management practices across roles, project types and industries. Lynn is a Life Fellow of AIPM, Honorary Member of IPMA, Co-Vice Chair of PMI's Global Accreditation Center and received the 2011 IPMA Research Achievement Award.

**Robin Croft** is a reader in Marketing at the University of Bedfordshire in England. He has written extensively around a range of topics, mostly involving interpersonal communication, in politics, the arts and in general discourse. At the same time he has been studying how twenty-first-century tools of person-to-person communication, particularly social media, are forcing brands and consumers back into earlier narrative-based structures.

**Darren Dalcher** is Professor of Project Management at the University of Hertfordshire and Director of the National Centre for Project Management. He has built a reputation as a leader and innovator in the area of practice-based education and reflection in project management and has worked with many major industrial, commercial and charitable organisations and government bodies. He has written over 150 refereed papers and book chapters on project management and software engineering. He is the editor of a major new book series, Advances in Project Management, published by Gower Publishing. Darren is an Honorary Fellow of the Association for Project Management, and Chartered Fellow of the British Computer Society.

**Bob Dick** is an independent scholar, an occasional academic, and a consultant in community and organisational change. He has been a practitioner and an academic for most of the past 40 years and continues to work in both fields. In both he uses concepts and processes from action research, action learning and community and organisation development to help people improve their work, learning and life. As he does so he uses action research to improve his own practice. He resides in Brisbane's leafy western suburbs with the love of his life, Camilla.

**Carolyn Dickie** is Deputy Pro Vice Chancellor of Curtin Business School. Following a diverse career in management situations such as banking, finance and arts organisations, her university teaching and research interests focus on various aspects of global management including project, strategic and human-resource management. With an emphasis on cross-cultural management, Carolyn has supervised local and overseas students in higher degree by research studies, published articles in national and international magazines and written book chapters and textbooks on her discipline interests. She continues to hold chair/deputy-chair positions on boards of not-for-profit organisations to maintain her practical role in business improvement.

**James Ernest** has a PhD in Management from Curtin University and a Master's in Project Management (MPM) from the University of Sydney. He has lived and worked in a number of post-conflict countries (India, Kenya, Uganda, Rwanda, Kosovo, Nauru and Australia) and completed his doctoral degree whilst working with international aid organisations. A more effective strategic framework for aid agencies in post-war situations, and an operational framework to assist project management teams in the planning and implementation of development/reconstruction projects were proposed as a result of the study. James remains committed to improving project management practice in post-conflict situations.

**Leonardo Ensslin** has a post-doctoral position in Multicriteria Decision Aiding at Lancaster University (2000) and has a PhD in Industrial Systems from the University of Southern California (1974). Leonardo Ensslin is postgraduation professor and researcher in the Department of Business Administration of Universidade do Sul de Santa Catarina, Brazil. His degree is in mechanical engineering by Universidade Federal do Rio Grande do Sul and he has a Master's in Production Engineering from Universidade Federal de Santa Catarina. He is a consultant and lecturer in analysis and performance evaluation, organisational improvement systems, innovation and decision aiding processes.

**Sandra Rolim Ensslin** is performing Post-Doctoral fellow in University Management with focus on Performance Evaluation at the Universitat Valencia. She holds a doctorate (2002) and master's degree (1995) in Production Engineering from the Federal University of Santa Catarina (UFSC). She has a degree in Accounting from Catholic University of Pelotas (1991). She teaches in the graduate programme in Accounting and the programme in Production Engineering at UFSC. She has been the scientific editor of the journal *Revista Contemporânea de Contabilidade* (RCC) since

2004. Her research focuses on the themes of performance evaluation, Multicriteria Decision Aid–Constructivist (MCDA–C) Methodology, intangible assets, procedures and methods of scientific research.

**Nicole Ferdinand** is a Senior Lecturer in Events Management in the School of Tourism at Bournemouth University. Her current research projects focus on grass roots cultural event organisations in London. Her most recently completed research project is entitled 'Carnival Futures: Notting Hill Carnival 2020' which was supported by the King's Cultural Institute. She has been a Senior Lecturer at London Metropolitan University and a Visiting Lecturer for the Stenden University of Applied Sciences in the Netherlands and the Haaga Helia University of Applied Sciences in Finland. She is also a member of the European Tourism Futures Institute Network based in Leeuwarden in the Netherlands.

**Stella George** is a project management coach, mentor and researcher. She is the programme manager for the Advance Centre of Leadership in Business at the University of Calgary. Stella helped develop the Athabasca University Project Research Institute and was co-researcher on a PMI-sponsored research project into project management as a management innovation. Stella has written several book chapters including one in Clelland's *Project Management Circa 2025* and her work is published in the *Project Management Journal (PMJ)* and the *International Journal of Managing Projects in Business (IJMPB)*. Stella's coaching helps project managers integrate knowledge and develop mastery in their own project management practice. Stella received the 2014 IPMA research award for her work with Janice Thomas and Svetlana Cicmil on Pm as a management innovation.

**Deborah E. Gibbons** holds a bachelor's degree in Psychology and master's and doctoral degrees in organisational behavior and theory, with a statistics minor. As an Associate Professor at the Naval Postgraduate School, she teaches system dynamics, team-building, leadership, motivation, decision making and other managerial topics. Her research addresses inter-organisational networks that support collaboration, knowledge-sharing, and community-building; humanitarian aid and disaster response; concurrent effects of personality and social context on cognition and behavior; and diffusion of information, attitudes and behaviours in multi-cultural environments. Her work on network evolution and function has informed coordination and change in a variety of organisations.

**Markus Hällgren** is Professor in Management at Umeå School of Business and Economics, Umeå University, Sweden. Hällgren is focused on the everyday practice within temporary organisations with a particular interest in decisions, goals and team dynamics. Within that general framework he has, among other themes, studied the everyday practice of managing unexpected events in temporary organisations, the application and consequences of a practice-based approach to organisational research, and team dynamics and decisions in extreme environments. Markus is currently the principal investigator of the research environment Extreme Environments – Everyday Decision-making (www.tripleED.com). Markus has also received Umeå University's young researcher award, The Royal Skyttean research award in Social Science, and two highly commended paper awards from the Emerald Literati network.

**He Qinghua** is a Professor in the School of Economics and Management and a director of the lean construction research center in the Research Institute of Complex Engineering & Management in Tongji University. Dr He has devoted himself to researching management theory, method and means innovation of large-scale complex construction projects in China. In addition, Dr He is quite active in practice. He is a senior member of the Royal Institution of Chartered Surveyors (FRICS) and the Chartered Institute of Building (FCIOB), and has acquired International Project Management Professional Level A (IPMP – A). Dr He has conducted many complex construction management consulting services projects such as project management of Shanghai International Tourism Resort and Shanghai Expo.

**Patrick Healy**'s career has been as an academic in the Faculty of Design Architecture and Building of the University of Technology, Sydney. He served in various positions such as Head of Department of Building, Director of the Master of Project Management Program, and for 12 years (1994–2006) was a staff-elected member on the University's governing body. He lectured to a range of students including those in architecture, construction management and project management, and participated in the supervision of Master's and PhD students. He is the author of *Project Management: Getting the Job Done on Time and in Budget* (Butterworth Heineman, 1997). He has lived and worked in Ireland, England, Germany and Australia.

**Robert Hickey** is a Project Officer at the Applied Research and Communications Fund in Sofia, Bulgaria. His work there has focused on energy and environmental policy, citizen participation in policy-making, the evaluation of research and innovation systems and institutions, innovation and business support to the creative industries, and overcoming regional barriers to research collaboration. He is currently working towards his PhD on the economics of energy efficiency at the International Business School in Botevgrad, Bulgaria.

**Helgi Thor Ingason** holds a PhD in Process Metallurgy from the Norwegian University of Science and Technology (NTNU), MSc in Mechanical and Industrial Engineering from the University of Iceland and a Stanford Advanced Project Management Certification. He is an IPMA Certified Senior Project Manager. Dr Ingason is an Associate Professor at the University of Reykjavik and Head of the MPM programme at the University, and a colloquium keynote speaker at MOT and PM programmes at Bentley University in Boston. Dr Ingason is the co-author of seven books on project management, strategic planning, product development, project ethics and quality management. More information on Dr Ingason can be found on www.academia.edu.

**Haukur Jonasson** is an Assistant Professor in Leadership, Management and Organisation behaviour at the School of Technology and Engineering at Reykjavik University. He is the Director of the University's Master's course in Project Management (MPM). He holds a Cand. Theol. degree from the University of Iceland, and a PhD degree in Psychiatry and Religion from Union Theological Seminary in New York and has clinical certifications in pastoral counselling from The HealthCare Chaplaincy Inc., and in psychoanalysis from the Harlem Family Institute in New York. Mr Jonasson has also pursued business education at the Indiana University School of Business and the Heriot-Watt, Edinburgh Business School. He is the co-founder of the Nordica Consulting Group ehf Ltd., affiliated consultant at HLP-Hirzel und Leder Management Consultants in Frankfurt, Germany, and a research affiliate at the Cooper Union for the Advancement of the Sciences and the Arts. Haukur is the co-author of five books in Icelandic and Project Ethics (Gower/Ashgate, 2013).

**Juha-Matti Junnonen** is a Research Manager in Construction Management at Aalto University. He has been involved in teaching and research at university level for over 20 years. His research and teaching is focused on construction management, with particular emphasis on production systems, management of construction operations and whole-life performance of built assets and environments.

**Sami Kärnä** is a Doctor of Technology and a Master of Administrative Sciences at Aalto University. His doctoral thesis, published in 2009, was related to customer satisfaction in construction. He is currently working as a senior researcher in the Built Environment Services Research Group. Kärnä has published over 40 articles and other publications on customer satisfaction, service quality and customer relationship management in the construction and real estate business. He has focused on developing performance evaluation tools to serve the whole branch of business.

**Ole Jonny Klakegg**, MSc, PhD, has 25 years of experience in research, teaching and consulting within project management. In his current main position he is Professor in Project Management at the Norwegian University of Science and Technology, Department of Civil and Transport Engineering. He also holds a part-time position as R&D Director at Faveo Management – the biggest project management consultancy company in Scandinavia. Klakegg has experience in a large number of major projects in Norway in private and public sectors, including building, transport, health, and defence projects. His research interests include project governance and risk/ uncertainty management.

**Louis Klein** is an internationally-recognised expert in the field of Systemic Change Management. He is the founder of the international think and do tank SEgroup and has been its president since 2001. He holds a PhD in sociology. He is the chairman of the Focus Group on Social and Cultural Complexity at the International Centre for Complex Project Management (ICCPM) as well as a board member of the World Organisation of Systems and Cybernetics (WOSC). In 2010, he received the International Centre for Complex Project Management's research award.

**Rogério Lacerda** is Doctor in Production Engineering from Federal University of Santa Catarina (2012). He has a master's degree in Production Engineering from the Federal University of Santa Catarina (2009) and he graduated in Business Administration and postgraduate qualification in Information Engineering. Professor Lacerda is Professor and Researcher of the Business Administration Department of Federal University of Santa Caterina (UFSC/Brazil). Lacerda has spent many years helping large companies in Strategic Management, Project Management and Business Process Management. His research focuses on strategic management and performance measurement. He is a Project Management Professional and has contributed to the OPM3 standard of the PMI. Rogerio Lacerda can be contacted at: rogerlacerda@gmail.com.

**Liisa Lehtiranta** is a doctoral student at Aalto University, School of Engineering, Finland. The focus of her research work is on construction project processes, including risk management, collaborative work and procurement. Her dissertation aims to identify and systematise practical solutions for multi-organisational risk management in Finnish construction management projects.

**Li Yongkui** is an Associate Professor of Construction Project Management at the Research Institute of Complex Engineering and Management (RICEM) of Tongji University in China. His research interests lie in complex projects organisation, case studies of mega projects management and IT application in construction management (for example, Building Information Modelling, organisation network simulation and the integrated programme management platform), and is currently working on developing China's Mega Construction Projects Case Base. In addition, Dr Li is also a member of the Institute Chartered of Build, the Royal Institution of Chartered Surveyors and IPMA-B. Furthermore, he has served for many large and complex projects owners such as governments, real estate companies and private corporations.

**Paul Littau** is a PhD student and research member at the Institute of International Project Management at the University of Siegen, Germany. He holds a Diploma in Mechanical Engineering with a focus on International Project Management. His research interest lies in stakeholder management within projects and project organisations. He also gives lectures in Project Management at the University of Siegen, Germany, and plays an active role in the IPMA's Young Crew.

**Beverley Lloyd-Walker** has supervised over 15 candidates to successful completion of master's and doctoral-level theses over the last ten years. These candidates have researched areas such as emotional intelligence in project teams and contributing factors to international project team placement success. Her own areas of research include people in temporary organisations, project team skills and careers in project management. In particular, Beverley's recent research and publications have centred on people working in new relationship-based procurement forms and the areas of professional skill development required by project leaders and team members to adapt to these new delivery forms.

**Giorgio Locatelli** is a Senior Lecturer in Management, Economics and Industrial Engineering at the Lincoln School of Engineering and a core member of faculty of MIP, the Business School of Politecnico di Milano. He is an elected member of the Italian National Board of the Project Management associations (ANIMP) for the Transportation and Logistics section. Currently Dr Locatelli is furthering his research into megaprojects and sustainability of power plants projects. He has 60 plus international peer-reviewed publications.

**Harvey Maylor** is Associate Fellow and Cohort Manager for the Major Projects Leadership Academy, Said Business School, University of Oxford. Previously he was Director of the International Centre for Programme Management at Cranfield University, UK, a $4M five-year industry-funded collaborative research centre. His main research interests are in creating competitive advantage from projects, complexity and the (non)adoption of change. His latest publications include work in *Research Technology Management*, the *International Journal of Operations and Production Management*, the *International Journal of Management Reviews* and the *International Journal of Project Management*. Among his textbooks, *Project Management* (4th edition, FT Prentice Hall, 2010) is Europe's best-selling project management text, and *Researching Business and Management* (2nd edition, Palgrave, with Dr Kate Blackmon and Dr Martina Huemann) will be published in 2015.

**Dr Lawrence R. Monteilh** (DPA, La Verne University) is Senior Lecturer and Curriculum Developer at Fontbonne University – Eckelkamp College of Global Business & Professional Studies. St. Louis, Missouri, USA. His research interests are project management, cultural communication, logistics and supply change management. He has contributed to the *Emerging Markets Encyclopedia*, has other book chapters in development, and reviews manuscripts for the *Journal of International Business Studies*. Dr Monteilh presented at the Key West, Florida, USA International Multidisciplinary Academic Conference: 'Logistics – The complexities inherent in the business and military operation control systems and overall strategy imbedded in supply chain management'. Research completion 2013.

**Steven Nijhuis** (1965) earned a master's in Mathematics in 1989. Since then he has held various positions as project manager (steel making industry, building industry, consulting) on a variety of topics (for example, logistics, quality assurance, financial governance, ICT, education, simulation). In 2005 he became Head of the Project Management Office of the Applied Science department of the Utrecht University of Applied Sciences. While holding this position, he is doing research on how to develop project management competences.

**Dr Kersti Nogeste** is both a practising Program and Project Management Consultant and an Adjunct Professor at RMIT University, Melbourne, Australia. As such, Dr Nogeste brings together the practical relevance of managing clients' strategic initiatives and the academic rigour required to contribute to university endeavours. Dr Nogeste is particularly experienced in managing projects and programmes of work which enable improved business outcomes via information & communications technology (I&CT). Dr Nogeste's academic achievements include a Doctor of Project Management (DPM) degree which developed a stakeholder-driven method for defining expected project outcomes, the development and delivery of postgraduate courses (for RMIT University and as an EU Erasmus Mundus scholar for the Politecnico di Milano, Milan, Italy), the supervision of doctoral candidates, being the author and reviewer of journal articles and a highly regarded conference speaker.

**Mano Nugapitiya** is a Director of Endstate, a management consultancy he co-founded in 2002. As a project management practitioner with 25 years' experience, Mano developed an early interest in the soft skills and human interaction in projects and the effect of these on project outcomes. During his role as the project manager in the Alpine Way Reconstruction in Thredbo, Australia, following the 1997 landslide, Mano applied an auto-ethnographic approach to gain interesting insights into his own lived experience in that project. This inevitably became central to his PhD research. He continues to progress his research interests as an Honorary Associate of the University of Technology Sydney.

**Gloria Oliomogbe** has a master's degree from Coventry University and graduated with a prize for the overall performance in Engineering Project Management in 2008. Her undergraduate degree, BSc in Mechanical Engineering (honours) in 2005 was from the University of Lagos. She is currently a doctoral student in Civil Engineering at the University of Leeds. Her PhD research investigates the intangible benefits from project management deployment in organisations. She is also an Early Stage Researcher with the Megaproject Cost Action.

**Jill Owen** was a Senior Lecturer at the University of New South Wales Canberra at the Australian Defence Force Academy (ADFA). Jill lectured in project management, having previously taught at Monash University where she completed her PhD on the role of knowledge-based practices in the effective delivery of projects. She holds a Bachelor of Economics from Latrobe University and a Master's Prelim Information Management & Systems from Monash University. Prior to joining UNSW Canberra at ADFA, Jill worked across a wide range of industries including financial services, airline, health, insurance and credit, delivering business and information technology projects. Jill was a member of the Academic Member Advisory Group (AMAG) for the PMI. Sadly, Jill passed away in November 2013.

**Laura Pekuri** has graduated from Oulu Business School with a major in management accounting. Her master's thesis dealt with the validation issues related to the constructive research approach. She is now a PhD student in the Department of Industrial Engineering and Management at the University of Oulu. Her doctoral dissertation is focused on lean implementation and cultural change within construction companies.

**Blaize Horner Reich** is Dean and RBC Professor of Technology and Innovation at the Beedie School of Business, Simon Fraser University, Vancouver, Canada. She worked for 15 years in the IT industry before beginning her academic career. Her research focuses on IT Projects (knowledge perspectives, predicting success, theory of projects) and on IT governance. Her research has been published in a wide range of IT and Project Management journals and she is on the editorial board of the *Project Management Journal, International Journal of Project Management, Journal of IT, Information Systems Management* and *Journal of Strategic Information Systems* . Dr Reich speaks frequently to academic and practitioner audiences and her research team's website, www.PMPerspectives.org, makes project management research accessible to practice.

**Tracey Richardson** has experienced firsthand the dynamics of worldwide operations. During her 20 plus years in the United States Air Force, she visited 17 countries and over half of the United States, managing the same operations/logistics, limited resources, and regulation challenges facing large, global companies. In various capacities, working in aircraft maintenance, including sortie production and industrial manufacturing, she has acquired leadership skills in all aspects of project management, logistics and operations. She is currently an Assistant Professor of Project Management at Embry-Riddle Aeronautical University. Dr Richardson received her Doctorate in Organizational Leadership from Argosy University and is certified by the PMI as a Project Management Professional and PMI Risk Management Professional.

**Shankar Sankaran** is a Professor of Organizational Project Management at the School of the Built Environment at the University of Technology Sydney and a Core Member of the research centre titled the Centre for Management and Organization Studies. Shankar has supervised more than 25 doctoral students who have used a variety of methodologies including action research mixed-methods. Shankar has edited books, published book chapters and presented papers at international conferences, and has published refereed papers in international journals. Shankar and his co-researchers carried out a study of the use of mixed-methods in project management research that was presented at the EURAM 2012 conference in Rotterdam and is now being published by the *Project Management Journal.* Shankar is the Founding Editor of *Organisational Project Management,* and on the editorial board of the *International Journal of Project Management.*

**Miles Shepherd** is an active Research Supervisor with a number of Russell Group Universities in UK and lectures at universities in UK, Europe and USA. He holds significant posts with the Association for Project Management (APM) in UK and has served as President and Chairman of the International Project Management Association (IPMA) and is member of IPMA's Research management Board. He is also a Director of the PMI's Global Accreditation Center for Project Management (GAC). With more than 30 years of experience of project management, he has an international practice and has extensive experience in developing national and international standards including joint authorship of BS 6079, contributions to ISO 38500 (Governance of Project Management) and to various systems engineering standards. He was Chairman of the ISO Committee that developed ISO 21500 and is Chairman of the ISO Technical Committee responsible for extending international standards to programme and portfolio management.

**Gilbert Silvius** is an independent researcher and lecturer in the field of project management. His affiliations include universities in the Netherlands, Belgium, South Africa, Austria and Vietnam. Gilbert's research interests include the integration of the concepts of sustainability in project management. He has authored and edited several publications on this topic, including *Sustainability in Project Management* (Gower, 2012) and *Sustainability Integration for Effective Project Management* (IGI Global, 2013). Gilbert also has over 20 years of practical experience as a project manager or consultant in various projects. At Van Aetsveld, project and change management, he advises organisations on the development of their project managers and their project management capabilities.

**Jonas Söderlund** is Professor at BI Norwegian Business School and a founding member of KITE, Linköping University. He has researched and published widely on the management and organisation of projects and project-based firms, time and knowledge integration in projects, and the evolution of project competence. His recent work appears in *Advances in Strategic Management, International Journal of Management Reviews, Organization Studies, Human Resource Management,* and *R&D Management.* His most recent books are the *Oxford Handbook of Project Management* (Oxford University Press), *Human Resource Management in Project-based Organizations: The HR Quadriad Framework* (Palgrave), and *Knowledge Integration and Innovation* (Oxford University Press).

**Hedley Smyth** is Director of Research at The Bartlett School of Construction and Project Management, University College London. He is responsible for Enterprise Management of Project Organisations and his research interests are organisational culture, competency and capability development, particularly related to relationship management and trust, and to marketing and business development in project enterprises. He is particularly interested in the extent and character of the management of the project business–project interface in terms of organisational behaviour. He leads the PhD research programme in the School and is responsible for the provision of teaching on the management of project enterprises.

**Pau Lian Staal-Ong** works as a Senior Consultant for Audits & Evaluations at AT Osborne BV – a major Dutch consultancy specialised in project management in the building and construction environment. She is active as a quality manager, consultant, trainer and auditor in mostly large and mega projects in the Netherlands and abroad. Since 2006, Pau Lian has been involved in NETLIPSE, the European programme focusing on improving and disseminating project management knowledge in large infrastructure (transport) projects, the recent years as Programme Director. In 2013 Pau Lian joined the IPMA Project Excellence Awards Board, responsible for the yearly international project excellence awards.

**Janice Thomas** has 30 years of experience in the project management field as a practitioner, researcher and educator. She is the author of four books and over 100 conference, practitioner or academic articles. From 2004 to 2008 she co-led PMI's largest ever, ground-breaking research into the Value of Project Management. In 2006, she was recognised as one of the 25 most influential women in project management by the PMNetwork and, in 2010, Janice was awarded the Research Achievement Award by the PMI as 'an individual who has significantly advanced the concepts, knowledge, and/or practices of project management'.

**Craig Thomson** is a Lecturer in Sustainability and the Built Environment at Glasgow Caledonian University. He graduated with a Geography degree, and completed a MRes and PhD in Construction Management from the University of Dundee, focusing on looking at innovation within construction projects. He has strong research interests in project based environments considering areas of sustainability assessment; sustainability management; innovation and knowledge management and in professional learning, and has published over 25 academic papers in these areas. He has been involved in teaching and supervising postgraduate students since 2008 and he has been a Fellow of the Higher Education Academy since 2012.

**Michael Tong** is the Programme Leader for the Master's programmes in Construction Management and International Project Management at Glasgow Caledonian University; both accredited by the APM and the PMI. Prior to academia, he worked in a number of construction projects in the Far East, including Hong Kong Airport and Shanghai Times Square. His research interests are in project-based learning, supply chain management and relationship management. He has successfully organised and co-edited four international postgraduate research conferences. He currently teaches and trains in project management and research methods as well as actively supervising postgraduate students.

**Derek Walker** is Professor of Project Management at the School of Property, Construction and Project Management, RMIT University. He worked in various project management roles in the UK, Canada, and Australia for 16 years before commencing his academic career in 1986. He obtained a Master of Science from the University of Aston (Birmingham) in 1978, and a PhD in 1995 from RMIT University (Melbourne). He has written over 250 peer-reviewed papers and book chapters and supervised 24 doctoral candidates through to completion. His research interests centre on innovation, knowledge management, and project management project procurement systems. He is also editor of *The International Journal of Managing Projects in Business* for Emerald Insight.

**Christian A.P. Weiland** is an independent entrepreneur who accompanies change projects with a focus on team development, process building and social-complex project management. After completing his interdisciplinary studies, including political science, sociology and economics at the University of Cologne, Christian Weiland joined the cooperative SEgroup in 2012. Next to his change projects, he systemically reflects on his work and publishes in different academic fields.

**Hany Wells** is the Head of Postgraduate Development at the Business School, University of Hertfordshire. She is responsible for the development and management of key postgraduate strategies for a large portfolio of postgraduate programmes. Her research interests are in examining how project management methodologies are selected across varied business contexts and their overall influence upon project performance. Hany, in her role as the Head of Information Systems and Project Management, in the past seven years has established a successful project management unit at the Business School, pioneering the design and development of several popular programmes in project management delivered both on campus and on-line.

**Eddy Westerveld** works as Managing Consultant for Audits & Evaluations at AT Osborne. He is active as a project manager, researcher and consultant in large infrastructure and urban renewal projects in the Netherlands and abroad. He specialises in setting up project delivery organisations and auditing these projects to be able to learn and improve their management. Eddy completed his PhD thesis at the Erasmus University Rotterdam in 2010. Within this thesis he described how complexity is present in infrastructure projects, and how this complexity is managed in practice and affects project success.

**Nigel L. Williams** is the Senior Lecturer in Project Management at Bournemouth University and has previously worked at the University of Bedfordshire. Before joining academia, Nigel worked for 15 years as a Project Manager and Business Consultant for manufacturing organisations in the Caribbean Region. Nigel holds a PhD in Engineering from the University of Cambridge. He also holds a BSc in Mechanical Engineering and an MSc in Marketing from the University of the West Indies. His research interests include maturity models and the impact of online stakeholder engagement on projects.

**Yang Qing** is a master's student who is majored in Construction Engineering Management in School of Economics and Management, Tongji University. During her master's, she mainly researched on Project Management Maturity (PMM) from the perspective of Construction Consulting Services (CCS). Previously, she spent almost one year studying beam section and beam loading method optimisation. As a junior researcher, she published five articles in the construction domain, such as 'Review on Project Management Maturity in Construction Management Field'.

**Michael Young** is an award-winning project, programme and portfolio manager and plays an active leadership role in the project management profession both within Australia and internationally, including key roles in the AIPM, leading standards development and research. He is also the IPMA representative to the ISO Technical Committee. Michael has published numerous journal and conference papers as well as a number of book chapters. He is the co-editor for a new project management research monograph series. His research interests include project portfolio management, strategy implementation and maturity.

**Roxanne Zolin** is Associate Professor in the School of Management, Queensland University of Technology. She helped to develop and teaches the Executive Master's in Complex Project Management in Canberra. Roxanne has managed large and small projects in software development, new product development, enterprise development, advertising, marketing and promotions. Roxanne did her PhD in Construction Engineering Management at Stanford University, where she also holds a master's in Sociology. She researches the affects of complexity on project success and failure. As Assistant Professor at the Naval Postgraduate School in Monterey, CA, Roxanne developed the capstone course for the Executive Master's in Business Administration.

# List of Abbreviations

| | |
|---|---|
| 3BL | Triple Bottom Line |
| ACLO | Aboriginal Community Liaison Officer |
| ADFA | Australian Defence Force Academy |
| AHP | Analytic Hierarchy Process |
| AIPM | Australian Institute of Project Management |
| ANIMP | Italian National Board of the Project Management Associations |
| ANZAM | Australian and New Zealand Academy of Management |
| APM | Association for Project Management |
| AR | Action Research |
| BIM | Business Information Modelling |
| CCCPM | Cross-Cultural Complex Project Management |
| CCS | Construction Consulting Services |
| CF | Conceptual Framework |
| CIoB | Chartered Institute of Building |
| CMM | Capability Maturity Model |
| CoE | Centre of Excellence |
| CoI | Community of Interest |
| CoP | Community of Practice |
| CPM | Critical Path Method |
| CPMM | Construction Project Management Maturity |
| CYPRASS | Campaspe Young Persons Referral and Support Scheme |
| DEA | Data Envelopment Analysis |
| DPM | Doctor of Project Management |
| EC | European Commission |
| EFQM | European Foundation for Quality Management |
| EGOS | European Group of Organizational Studies |
| EJBRM | Electronic Journal of Business Research Methods |
| ES | Enterprise Software |
| EPSRC | Engineering and Physical Sciences Research Council |
| EU | European Union |
| EURAM | European Academy of Management |
| GAC | Global Accreditation Center |
| GRAMMS | Good Reporting of Mixed Methods Research |
| ICCPM | International Centre for Complex Project Management |
| ICT | Information and Communication Technology |
| IJMPA | International Journal of Multiple Research Approaches |
| IJMPB | International Journal of Managing Projects in Business |
| IJMRA | International Journal of Multiple Research Approaches |
| IJPM | International Journal of Project Management |
| IPAT | Infrastructure Project Assessment Tool |
| IPMA | International Project Management Association |
| IRM | Integrated Research Model |

| | |
|---|---|
| IRNOP | International Research Network on Organizing by Projects |
| IS | Information Systems |
| ISD | Information Systems Development |
| ISSS | International Society of Systems |
| IT | Information Technology |
| JCEM | Journal of Construction Engineering and Management |
| JCM | Journal of Change Management |
| KBPs | Knowledge-Based Processes |
| LIP | Large Infrastructure Project |
| MCDA | Multicriteria Decision Analysis |
| MIP | Politecnico di Milano School of Management |
| MMR | Mixed Methods Research |
| MPM | Master of Project Management |
| MRP | Material Requirement Planning |
| NDA | Non-Disclosure Agreement |
| NETLIPSE | Network of Large Infrastructure Projects in Europe |
| NGO | Non-Governmental Organization |
| NSERC | National Science and Engineering Research Council |
| OPM | Organised Project Management |
| P3M | Portfolio, Programme & Project Management |
| PCR | Post-Conflict Reconstruction |
| PERT | Program Evaluation and Review Technique |
| PIR | Post Implementation Review |
| PM | Project Management |
| PMBoK | Project Management Body of Knowledge |
| PMI | Project Management Institute |
| PMJ | Project Management Journal |
| PMM | Project Management Maturity |
| PMMM | Project Management Maturity Model |
| PMP | Project Management Professional® |
| PMO | Project Management Office |
| PMP | Project Management Professional |
| PMR | Project Management Research |
| PRINCE2 | **PR**ojects **IN C**ontrolled **E**nvironments |
| RCC | Revista Contemporânea de Contabilidade |
| RICEM | Research Institute of Complex Engineering and Management |
| SCMOI | Standing Conference of Management and Organizational Inquiry |
| SIG | Special Interest Group |
| SME | Subject Matter Expert |
| SNA | Social Network Analysis |
| SPM | Standardised Project Management |
| SSHRC | Social Sciences and Humanities Research Council |
| SSM | Soft System Methodology |
| TSE | IEEE Transactions on Software Engineering |
| WOSC | World Organisation of Systems and Cybernetics |
| YFHS | Youth-Friendly Health Services |

# Foreword

Research in project management has come a long way in the last 20 years. When I started my PhD journey there was very little academic research available on project management other than the beginnings of the Scandinavian School and a lot of work exploring critical path and queuing theory. Projects were not really considered a phenomenon worthy of study in management. Sometimes in operations management there was a little discussion of how best to develop a Gantt chart or critical path or identify critical success factors through some sort of computer simulations or survey methods. Today, projects, often termed temporary organisations, and studied using organisational research methods, are a hot topic even in the top management journals; a discussion of project management research is as likely to cover epistemology, ontology and methodology as any other social science.

However, until now, there has never been a single book that provides an introduction to these topics in the context of project management research. This book provides this starting point by delivering short introductions to relevant methodological issues. As such, it provides an important addition to the project management literature. You are lucky to have this book as a starting point for your research journey.

There are many ways to frame a research question and even more ways to answer it. The challenge with developing a methods book that addresses all the types of questions project management researchers are likely to want to tackle is that no one scholar has the breadth and depth of methods knowledge to bring to bear the expertise required to cover all the important research questions adequately. This book addresses this problem by leveraging the best (old and new) minds in project management to deliver a thoughtfully edited volume.

The book starts with an introduction to the BIG questions of research. How do you look at the phenomenon, what paradigm, ontology or epistemology are you coming from? The authors in the second section of the book walk you through the ethical and cognitive issues involved in 'moving from a hunch to a research question' to steal the title from one chapter. These authors also provide great guidance on how to move from reviewing the literature to a great critical review of the literature. The third section provides guidance on particular methods commonly used in project management research. The fourth section provides examples of how to apply a mixture of methods to understand the complex phenomenon of projects. The fifth section looks at the range of difficulties encountered in conducting research in specific and often difficult contexts. The book wraps up by discussing how to finish the research and get it published. All in all an illuminating introduction to most of the tough questions you need to answer as you set up for your first study.

The one thing we know about project management is that we don't know enough. Selecting a question and the appropriate methods to answer it is an important first step on the research journey. This book provides an introduction to all the relevant topics that will help you to select a question and get started on the methods side of your research.

I wish you well in your research endeavours and I look forward to meeting you at a research conference or reading your findings in the near future. I am sure you will owe thanks to these authors, and in particular to Beverly, for kick-starting this project and managing it through to completion.

Janice Thomas
Professor, Project Management, Athabasca University
Director, Project Research Institute, Athabasca University
2014 IPMA Research Award Winner
2010 PMI Research Award Winner
Author of these research monographs:
*Project Management Implementation as Management Innovation* (2013);
*Researching the Value of Project Management* (2008);
*Professionalization of Project Management* (2006);
*Selling Project Management to Senior Executives* (2002);
*Making Sense of Project Management* (2000)

# Introduction

Working through methods theory as a graduate student or new researcher is challenging work. Its abstractions, complex language and concepts can contribute to feelings of isolation and self-doubt that are difficult to overcome. It was only when I started teaching research methods for both undergraduate and graduate students that my appreciation – even enjoyment – of this domain grew. The origins of this book can be traced back to a difficult day in my own doctoral journey when I was struck by the thought that research might not be a collaborative effort, not a 'team sport' if you will. Since that day, my perspective and reality have changed ... and the result is this book.

The notion of research and, specifically, research design being a solo, isolating endeavour has been replaced for me with the certainty that it can be a highly creative exercise, necessitating the involvement of others. This book provides both evidence of that certainty and guidance on how you might approach such collaboration yourself.

## Who Are the Audiences for This Book?

Students and supervisors of project management research are the primary audiences for this book, but with methods instructors and other, more established researchers also benefiting.

- New researchers
  - Student or new researchers can be easily overwhelmed by the theory, practice and execution of original research. This feeling can be reinforced by isolation from supervisors or instructors who are new to their roles as research 'guides,' or uncertain of the issues and challenges specific to the domain of project management. Understanding the requirements of a clear, credible and executable research design is something achieved through the careful and repeatable visiting of appropriate theory and examples. New researchers shouldn't meet this challenge on their own – and they certainly don't have to. This book offers the voices of dozens of researchers who have themselves benefited from collaborating with others. They have not only experienced the research journey themselves but also are able to distill from this specific instruction and references of direct relevance to new project management researchers.
- Supervisors and tutors
  - As a key player in the research student's journey, supervisors have their own needs for information and instruction. Regardless of levels of experience or familiarity with the associated issues, all supervisors can benefit from the perspectives of others and, in this case, those specific to the project management domain. Each chapter is (co)written by someone with supervisory experience.
- Instructors/Lecturers
  - Some readers may be staff and/or faculty working within higher education responsible for teaching research methods for project management students (at both undergraduate and graduate levels) who may not have supervisory responsibilities. This book can be of

assistance as a textbook in courses at both levels and has been structured to walk an instructor through a basic teaching path.

Suggestions for following the book within the confines of a broad teaching plan are provided further on.

## The Structure of the Book

Several core sections separate the book's content and are presented to enable a researcher, student or supervisor to move through various stages of a research project from proposal to publication. The following are brief descriptions of each.

### SECTION DESCRIPTIONS

1. Foundational elements
   Positioning your research requires an understanding of conceptual issues upon which you can orient your research questions and design. This is not an easy task, and one certainly not unique to project management. Experienced researchers have provided insight and instruction in the opening chapters along with examples and references to hundreds of references. Of special interest is the fact that many of these are from across disciplines in management studies outside of project management.
2. Focusing your research effort
   Once you have identified a problem, phenomenon or curiosity of interest, bringing it into focus as an area of research suitable for investigation is the next step. This will be affected by many personal and professional influences as you wrestle with the demand to clearly articulate the question(s) your research will answer. Ultimately, however, you will need to position your interest amongst the work of existing research in the relevant fields. This section contains both instruction and examples.
3. Specific data collection and analysis techniques
   Both qualitative and quantitative methods, tools and techniques are shared in this section. Rather than introduce a strict demarcation between 'quant' and 'qual', I'll let the submissions speak for themselves. Taking a meta view of these chapters (along with those in Section 4), one could see a shift, perhaps, away from the quantitative approach to project management research that has been historically dominant.
4. Examples of mixed methods strategies
   Interest in the 'third movement' of methodological theory has been significant in project management – a reality demonstrated by the unexpectedly high number of submissions based on mixed methods strategies. This development warranted an entire section of such chapters.
5. Unique environments for project management research
   Building on the methodological issues of earlier chapters, this section includes examples of research designs successfully executed in various (and sometimes unusual) settings. Firmly believing in the value of case examples and the power of self-selection, these were included not just to instruct but to inspire.
6. Writing as a future researcher
   The use of social media has only begun to assist researchers identify and examine project management phenomenon. Early papers and presentations are thrilling as they reveal new

insights through the use of new techniques to pinpoint, analyse and explain data. This development shows the living nature of methodological theory and, is similar to the impact of multi/mixed methods design in creating new opportunities for data collection and analysis.

7. Benefitting from experience: supervisors and publications
The struggle with the abstractions of research can be alleviated when examples of their ultimate form are provided. Writing a journal article, for example, can be straightforward exercise when the structure, components and purpose of each are understood. The logic of a basic five or six-chapter structure of a master's or doctoral thesis (in the social sciences) can be more apparent when demonstrated by others. How such work can be translated into other publications is also a logical extension of a new scholar's work post-candidature and one that is made a little easier when, again, shown by others. These activities are common to new and emergent research scholars and certainly not unique to those in the project management domain. The purpose of this section is, however, to bring a focus to that area with the perspective of those who have achieved those results.

## CHAPTER ELEMENTS

Each chapter contains the same collection of elements, each with their own purpose and style.

- Motivation statement
  - Contributing authors joined the project by invitation or self-selection. In each case, I was curious as to why they wanted to be part of the effort and asked them to write a motivational statement. The voice, perspective and details vary with the authors themselves and, in doing so, might be encouraging to readers.
- Abstract
  - Each chapter begins with an abstract that provides a brief but focused description of the chapter with slight variations reflecting the type of chapter content (for example, original research, case study, commentary or more purely instructional). Differences exist amongst them, and readers are encouraged to consider how the tone, style and content introduce the content in each chapter.
- Chapter goals
  - Authors were asked to write specific goals that would provide both a focus and measurability to the reader's engagement with the material. Instructors and supervisors can also use these along with the 'tips' to creation sub-sections for specific guidance.
- Keywords
  - As a standard element of academic writing (and many textbooks), keywords identify the topics or sub-topics of significance in the chapter and support the larger index of the book. As was the case with the abstracts, readers are encouraged to consider the different approaches to this critical chapter element.
- Figures and tables
  - Visual content is an invaluable approach to teaching and learning and one that was encouraged amongst contributors. More than 100 original and previously-published figures and tables are included.
- Tips for supervisors
  - For each chapter, author(s) were asked to provide specific direction to the intended readers to focus their engagement on the material. Many of the chapters – especially in Sections 1 and 2 – contain abstract elements that might be used in different ways in the preparation of research proposal and/or the management of student activities. Each

'Tip' is intended to bring focus to your thinking, encourage group/peer discussion or interaction between supervisors and students.

- Tips for students
    - Familiarity with the topic of each chapter will certainly vary amongst readers but, as is the case with the supervisory tips, points have been provided for students. These can be used by students individually or in peer groups, and/or in combination with those provided for supervisors.
- Questions and/or exercises
    - Again with supervisory or peer engagement as a key goal, questions or exercises have been included in each chapter. Authors were free to include either element, so one might take a moment to consider why the material of a particular chapter lent itself to one or the other – is there a normative or formative distinction to be made or was it simply the author's disposition? Readers are encouraged to pause with each chapter and use these elements to challenge their understanding of the material. In many (if not most!) cases, there are no 'right' answers – a reality that reflects the inherent nature of project management as a social science.
- References and suggested readings
    - More than 1,000 individual references are provided throughout the book covering a range of topics and sources.

## Different Approaches to the Chapters

In anticipating the needs of readers, chapters have been categorised under different themes. Readers can, of course, follow the seven-section structure explained above, but the following groupings offer more focused guidance.

### ARTICULATING YOUR QUESTION

There's no avoiding the fact that 'The Question' will change multiple times over the course of a research project. For those new to this challenge, they often make this their first test and, unfortunately, perceive themselves to be failing. (Supervisors need to be especially supportive here, and counsel their candidates that this needn't be the case.) The language, purpose and impact of each question changes with each revision, and the following chapters help bring these issues into more manageable perspectives:

- Novel or incremental contributions: the construction of research questions (Chapter 9).
- Moving from hunches to a research topic: salient literature and research methods (Chapter 10).
- Moving from hunches to an interesting research topic: defining the research topic (Chapter 11).

### ENGAGING THE LITERATURE

Students or new researchers often approach their work either with a clear idea in mind or looking for inspiration. In both cases, existing literature is an invaluable resource, as the following chapters will demonstrate:

- Finding a way in the Broceliande Forest: the magic domain of project management research (Chapter 4).
- Moving from hunches to a research topic: salient literature and research methods (Chapter 10).
- Developing a critical literature review for project management research (Chapter 13).
- Critical engagement of previous research (Chapter 14).

## APPRECIATING THE FUNDAMENTALS

Philosophical and paradigmatic issues concerning the research question, topic and eventual thesis are challenging in any domain. Readers are fortunate to have scholars who have addressed these key fundamental issues in a project management context and offered their thoughts in the following chapters:

- Project management research: addressing integrative challenges (Chapter 1).
- Project management research: social dimensions and organisational context (Chapter 2).
- The paradigm as steering mechanism for new research endeavours (Chapter 3).
- Finding a way in the Broceliande Forest: the magic domain of project management research (Chapter 4).
- Ontology and epistemology (Chapter 5).
- Ethical considerations in project management research (Chapter 12).

## A TEACHING PATH

Instructors of research methods have an enormous selection of books to choose from, but for those teaching a project management context, course or program the following chapters can be a helpful sequence:

- Project management research: addressing integrative challenges (Chapter 1).
- Project management research: social dimensions and organisational context (Chapter 2).
- The paradigm as steering mechanism for new research endeavours (Chapter 3).
- Finding a way in the Broceliande Forest: the magic domain of project management research (Chapter 4).
- Research methods and success meaning in project management (Chapter 7).
- Novel or incremental contributions: the construction of research questions (Chapter 9).
- Moving from hunches to a research topic: salient literature and research methods (Chapter 10).
- Moving from hunches to an interesting research topic: defining the research topic (Chapter 11).
- Critical engagement of previous research (Chapter 14).
- An agile approach to the real experience of developing research methodology and methods (Chapter 19).
- The voice of experience: an interview with Lynn Crawford (Chapter 35).
- Supervisors and their sociological (and sometimes seemingly illogical) imagination (Chapter 36).
- Common flaws in project management research reports (Chapter 37).
- Publish or perish: transform your thesis into a tangible product (Chapter 38).

## TEAM-BASED PROJECT MANAGEMENT RESEARCH

Working with partners in project management research is an enormous opportunity for learning, publishing and networking. Each of the following chapters demonstrate research teams where this has successfully occurred:

* Enter or not: how to gain and sustain access to research sites (Chapter 21).
* The value of mixed methods (Chapter 23).
* Managing research in large collaborative teams (Chapter 24).
* An empirical research method strategy for construction consulting service projects (Chapter 27).
* A practical research method: the NETLIPSE case study (Chapter 28).
* Using multi-case approaches in project management research: the MEGA Project Experience (Chapter 29).

## USING CASE EXAMPLES

The best tool to provide instruction is often a case or experience. To this end, many are included that reflect different aspects of project management research in multiple team environments, organiaations and industries. You will find such content in the following locations:

| Chapter | Name |
| --- | --- |
| 6 | A current research example: CCCPM |
| 8 | Case: A commercial study |
| 10 and 11 | Case study: Dr Alejandro Arroyo (2009) |
| 16 | Considering case studies in project management |
| 17 | Vignette: combining action-oriented approaches in project management |
| 17 | Vignette: systems analyst using action research |
| 18 | Major AR cycle: the CYPRASS project |
| 20 | Alpine Way reconstruction in Thredbo, Australia |
| 21 | Site 1: engineering consulting organisation |
| 21 | Site 2: outsource provider in a government department |
| 23 | Example case: a mixed method project framework |
| 24 | Case context: the reality of a large team collaborative research |
| 25 | Doctoral research: engineering projects in Dutch process industry |
| 26 | Doctoral research: e-Learning in project management |
| 27 | Post-doctoral research: construction consulting services projects |
| 28 | The NETLIPSE case study |
| 29 | The MEGAPROJECT investigation |
| 30 | Challenges and complexities post-conflict societies (Kosovo) |
| 31 | Complexities of oil and gas exploration industries |
| 32 | Social network analysis of American public health programmes |
| 33 | Programme description: Love Luton Festival |

## About the Contributors

Project management researchers and practitioners from around the world have contributed to this book. You will find members of the academy, project management practitioners and professionals from all levels of government offering their insights into various elements of the research experience. Each of them has an active and direct connection to both the practice and research of project management. Please take a moment to review the List of Contributors.

# PART I
# FOUNDATIONAL ISSUES

One of the challenges of research is the extent to which you must work in abstractions. You might have a general idea of your research interest, problem or phenomenon you want to explore or situation you want to explain, but positioning this work on the foundational issues of ontology, epistemology, axiology and praxeology won't necessarily clarify things. Researching project management (PM) as a subject domain is difficult for several reasons, not the least of which is the struggle to position it within a specific context. It pushes boundaries because it can be positioned in multiple ways as its own field, within management studies and/or other applied sciences.

As a new or developing PM researcher, where does this leave you? How and where should you start positioning your research as a specific contribution on a foundation of abstractions? Answering these questions is difficult and necessary, but with the help of the following chapters, perhaps a little easier.

- Maylor and Söderlund share their thoughts on the importance of having a research strategy and to consider that PM theory, brought in from recognised disciplines, is essential in developing not only your research, but the field of as a whole.
- Young challenges current thinking about PM. He argues that researchers should broaden their perspectives from the reductionist, tools and techniques-based view of PM and explore other aspects of the domain – perhaps cultural dimensions?
- Biedenbach shows the value of utilising paradigms and articulating the research philosophy to effectively direct a new research endeavour. The benefits of doing this within the growing field of PM are discussed.
- Bredillet builds on the PM schools of thought and discusses the main aspects for research of paradigmatic PM science, ontological argument about the existence of projects and their management, and the relationship between theory and practice.
- Klakegg discusses how difficult it is to isolate the researcher from the research. This chapter identifies some of the most fundamental reasons for this within the context of PM research.
- Klein and Weiland look at research as both a process and a project with the experience of the Systems Excellence Group as a case study.

# 1

# Project Management Research: Addressing Integrative Challenges

Harvey Maylor and Jonas Söderlund

*We wrote this chapter to improve both the relevance and impact of PM research in the future and avoid remaining 'stuck in the middle' by making little contribution to the broader academy or practice.*

At one time, all that was needed to do 'good research' was something interesting to look into, and something interesting to say about it; and 'interesting' to anyone other than you was entirely optional. The requirements today for scholarship at all levels in business and management schools are entirely different. In this chapter, we provide a summary of a recently published article on research strategy, and focus on the implications for researchers. The main message is that theory, brought in from recognised disciplines, is essential in developing not only your research, but the field of PM as a whole. In addition, we underline the importance for researchers of developing *perspective awareness* alongside *contextual awareness* if your work is to meet the enduring requirements of relevance and impact.

At the end of this chapter, the reader can:

*   recognise five integrative challenges for business and management research and researchers;
*   demonstrate the centrality of developing perspective awareness and contextual awareness among scholars in PM;
*   understand the implications for their own work in the context of a rapidly developing academy.

Keywords: research, relevance, impact, context, perspective, theory, integrative challenges

## Introduction

Much has changed in the business and management academy in recent years. Business and management scholars struggle with a number of challenges. The challenges, initially set out in the article published in the *International Journal of Project Management* (IJPM), (Söderlund and Maylor, 2012), and now in short-form here, are not only strategic challenges for our field, but also for you as researchers. We wrote the original paper and this chapter, not to give answers, but to encourage debate.

## Five Integrative Challenges

Our point of departure is a consideration of the pressures driving the intellectual activity of business and management schools today. Those most germane to our discussion are the need to improve both the relevance of research and the currently limited impact of research on management practice generally. For the PM field, these two terms – relevance and impact – would appear to be very straightforward at first – PM as a research field is highly relevant to business and management today, and impact means our ability to influence practice (Pettigrew, 2011).

Yet whilst projects are ubiquitous undertakings, the relevance of the academy to modern practice is limited. For instance, the main standards for PM practice (including those of the Project Management Institute (PMI), and the Association of Project Management (APM) in the UK) have no direct research evidence in them or for them. The notions of engaged scholarship (Van de Ven, 2007) and Evidence-based Management (Rousseau, 2012) are rare in our field today. Impact, according to many schools, is where work from one of the top journals is seen to be impacting practice in some demonstrable manner. PM journals do not count as 'top journals'. On a 1–4 scale, where 1 is poor and 4 is the best, PM journals are all currently rated as 1 and 2 although their quality is improving steadily. There are few PM papers published in the better journals, and their impact on practice is at best minimal.

This is our challenge – our two strongest opportunities, relevance and impact, not being exploited. As a result PM research is often 'caught in the middle'; to many in the academy, anything to do with PM is 'too close to practice to be of academic interest', whilst practitioners find our outputs, particularly those highly valued journal articles, 'too abstract to be of value'. If we are to contribute to relevance and impact, our work has to be designed with our opportunities in mind.

We unpacked this situation further to identify five challenges. These are listed below, framed as a duality (interacting and reinforcing) between two aspects of that challenge:

- **Challenge I: Strategy and execution**. Strategy, as a discipline within management and business studies, has successfully demonstrated its value to the academy. However, much of what is published in the strategy field ignores any discussion of strategy implementation. Recent work has either called for (Whittington, 2006; Starkey and Madden, 2001) or contributed to dealing with this omission (Morgan, Levitt and Malek, 2007; Shenhar and Dvir, 2007). The opportunity is to pick up the approaches of strategy and to focus on aspects of execution. Impact and relevance are both possible from such work.
- **Challenge II: Business and technology**. Whilst some business and management schools have created significant competitive advantage by integrating business and technology (MIT Sloan is a good example), others today are contributing to the fragmentation of disciplines into increasingly trivial areas (Sandberg and Tsoukas, 2011). PM if viewed as an integrating function, rather than a functional discipline, has the opportunity to bring together domain knowledge from many areas, including that of technology, and to do so with benefit.
- **Challenge III: Hard and soft skills**. Hard skills include the administrative tasks of producing plans, creating reports and the use of PM toolsets. Soft skills enable working with and through other individuals and organisations. For PM research, a focus on 'hard skills' has limited both the relevance and impact of research. These are probably necessary, but certainly not sufficient for modern, complex projects. It is the integration of these subject areas that is a challenge and opportunity.
- **Challenge IV: Research and practice**. Rigour and relevance are the original 'double hurdle' of management research (Pettigrew, 1997). Rigour is a given requirement with all research, and will be explored further in the next section and in other chapters in this book. We have focused on the aspects of relevance and impact. However, 'relevance' has

already been shown to be problematic. As researchers, we can do research *on* individuals and organisations, or *with* them. *Co-production* is one means to do research with individuals and organisations, but this is very involved, and many scholars rightly prefer to rely on numerical datasets as their route to publication. Relevance then, requires that the researcher is deeply committed to seeing beneficial change happen. However, it is worth noting that in other industries, *research* (basic research which provides the knowledge foundation) is explicitly separated from *development* which can lead to bridging that relevance gap. We will consider this further in the next challenge.

- **Challenge V: Exploration and exploitation**. Ideally, research should 'build' over time, with the findings from one study adding to those from others, and increasing our level of knowledge and insight. PM as a field is not unique in failing to do this (Barnett, 2007). Indeed, project risk management is a case in point. Over 100 articles on project risk management were published in the PM journals from 2000 to 2011. The majority of authors redefined concepts, built new models and didn't question whether their work was contributing to anything. Indeed, this is a theme we will pick up below.

## From Challenges to Research Choices

There are many themes above that we could develop further, but we have limited the discussion to issues that we believe are most relevant to those of a doctoral researcher.

The main issue is avoiding that situation of being 'stuck in the middle' – producing research that is not valued by the academy or practitioners. A doctoral thesis should make a contribution to the subject knowledge directly (a summary of the requirements for doctoral work at many of the institutions where we have examined), and that the thesis needs to stand on its academic qualities. The practitioner book or articles can follow afterwards, with more appropriate language and addressing integrative challenges IV and V. Therefore, it is essential for the progress of you as a researcher (and the field as a whole) that your research has a sound theoretical basis against which to define its contribution. This might be through *extending*, *enhancing* or *adapting* theory.

This immediately provides a challenge for PM researchers. PM research for many years has been a-theoretical; much of it doesn't have a recognised basis (by this we mean 'recognised by the academy more generally'). However, this is rarely understood and, as a result, in too many research proposals we see mistaken references to 'the theory of PM'. Is there such a thing? If not, as we contend, how do you frame your research?

There are some good examples published in the PM literature, of work grounded in established theory. The application of the Resource Based View of the firm from the field of strategy (Jugdev, 2004), ambidexterity from organisational learning, (Liu and Leitner, 2012) and management innovation (Thomas, Cicmil and George, 2012) are all studies that have done just this. The literature they draw from is that of a *home discipline* (Economics and Strategy, for instance) and most importantly, they place projects as the *context* for their research. The research approach comes from that home discipline. The context is a special consideration that will draw from that theoretical perspective and then contribute to the enrichment of that perspective through the application in the context, as all of the above examples illustrate.

In contrast, project risk management is neither a discipline, nor a theory nor a context. It is an activity that takes place in projects. However, we could view this from many perspectives and use many alternative theorisations. For instance, we could consider the role of Prospect Theory (Kahneman and Lovallo, 2002) in the management of risk in projects. How managers respond to risks, the behaviours that they exhibit and their levels of risk tolerance, for instance, could be the subject of research carried out using this perspective. Another study attempting to reground uncertainty and risk is not needed. The application of theory from other fields is where such a study could be both relevant and impactful. This is where perspective awareness becomes a key attribute of the researcher.

## Developing Perspective Awareness

In a review of the field of PM, Söderlund (2011) identified seven different schools of thought in the mainstream literature. Each school shares a common view of projects, why they exist, why and how they differ and what is important in those projects and PM research (Söderlund, 2005). In addition, they provide quite different definitions of what determines success and failure. Based on this categorisation, we could argue that we already have established active perspectives of projects and the management of projects. In this respect, the field of PM research has begun to develop multiple perspectives for itself. This is an important development and it underlines that PM scholars should be more aware of their perspective.

As scholars, the home discipline from which you take your perspective (or view or theoretical lens) cannot be PM. PM does not meet generally accepted criteria for being a discipline (by the criteria of Fabian, 2000; applied in Harland et al., 2006). The home discipline could be economics and strategy, finance, organisational behaviour/theory, operations research/management or any other functional discipline within management and organisation studies. Less often we see that insight is obtained by bringing in a perspective from outside the standard business and management canon, as was done to some effect by those who 'imported' complexity theory.

The existence of many potential perspectives for your context, provide the researcher with a *conceptual toolbox* (Weick, 2012). This toolbox is needed to deal with non-trivial managerial and organisational problems, since there is no single 'best' research approach. What you will find is that different perspectives are applicable at different times and different theories offer different explanations to different parts of a problem.

Currently, the management of projects offers a plethora of interesting opportunities for research. This is just one of the reasons why it is growing both in popularity and in the pluralism of research approaches. However, increasing growth and pluralism of a research field bring their own challenges. In particular, the field might fragment with little possibility of fruitful debate and sharing of insights and ideas (Söderlund, 2011), evident in the current approaches to researching risk management. To avoid fragmentation there is a need to develop *contextual awareness*.

## Developing Contextual Awareness

Contextual awareness is knowing your area of application – having a good understanding of the field and the challenges that organisations and practitioners are facing. Your work can only have impact if what you are investigating has enduring interest for the field. Given that research can take many years, your challenge needs careful choosing. We need to make sure that the community of practitioners remain interested in our work.

It helps then if you can frame your context – your area of interest – in terms of *a phenomenon* – for instance, the phenomenon of managers over-stating benefits to get projects approved. Our experience with such phenomena is that they need to be:

1. *Identifiable* – not just a hunch that something is happening, where is the evidence that it is occurring? One research project we supervised included a preliminary phase of work which identified clearly that the phenomenon was not, contrary to popular belief in the

organisation, happening. There were some interesting areas identified during the phase however, which were shown to exist and were amenable to further analysis.

2. *Not already explained by existing work* – there is a gap in our understanding both in practical and theoretical terms. For instance, the phenomenon of 'there was chaos in the project' would be easily understood through knowledge of existing standards and processes, and be caused by 'absence of plans' for instance.

3. *Researchable* – we have recently encountered research topics including one that required interviewees to admit to criminal behaviour for the researcher to be able to carry out the research. This had to be discounted on research ethics grounds.

4. Once your phenomenon meets these criteria, there are many options for you to consider. To narrow your choices somewhat, we always recommend scanning a range of highly rated management journals and seeing which of the perspectives seems to 'fit' with your worldview. Please note, we suggested scanning, often best done with hard copies of journals, rather than sanitised through a search engine as this is prior to identifying keywords for a full search (for further details see Maylor, Blackmon and Huemann, 2015). Conference proceedings (the main PM conferences are International Research Network on Organizing by Projects (IRNOP) and PMI's Research and Education Conference; the European Academy of Management (EURAM) and the European Group of Organizational Studies (EGOS) all have project tracks) are also a good source. We cannot tell you which perspective will be the best for you – this is part of your conversation with supervisors and others.

*The following case illustrates how the use of a PM phenomenon was used as the subject for a piece of doctoral research.*

## Case Example

Noticing that organisations and individuals don't seem to learn from projects was the first step in Neil's doctoral journey. The phenomenon was well reported and therefore justifiable. The next step was to look at the existing descriptions of why this phenomenon occurred. These didn't appear to provide a comprehensive answer either practically or theoretically. Neil decided to use a theoretical framing from the organisational learning literature, which relied on the analysis of Intellectual Capital (Kang and Snell, 2009). Projects were the context for his exploration of Intellectual Capital and its impacts on the use of knowledge in organisations. His work extended theory into the projects context, and in doing so provided new insights into learning that hadn't been provided before. One benefit of such an approach (extending existing approaches), in addition to obtaining his doctorate, was the readiness for publication of the research outputs (for example, Turner, Swart and Maylor, 2013).

## A Final Note

Relevance and impact are two of the key opportunities facing our field that have not been successfully exploited to date. Neither can be taken as assumed, just because we are working in a field that is 'close to practice'. The main implication of this for researchers is the need to move from PM as discipline, to PM as context for our work. Using PM as context means we can draw on established theoretical approaches to both framing and executing research. This will improve the standing of PM research and researchers in the academy more generally, something that has to be beneficial for us all. Important in this development is perspective awareness and contextual awareness.

Indeed, perspective awareness and contextual awareness are synergistic. The researcher who is able to really uncover the interesting elements in a particular context has the potential to also develop new perspectives and ultimately new theories. Ultimately, this is when PM research will have the greatest impact – when it contributes to management and organisation studies in general.

## Tips and Questions

### TIPS FOR STUDENTS

- Build your statement of research in the clear terms of context and perspective. For example ... I am studying X in the context of projects, from the perspective of Y. For instance, I am studying strategy implementation through projects from the perspective of the resource-based view of the firm.
- If you are turning to research from your work as a project manager (or 'practitioner'), take a critical eye to your (past or current) practice to identify a researchable phenomenon and avoid 'being stuck in the middle'.
- Identify which of the integrative challenges are most relevant for your particular study and how this will form part of the unique contribution your work makes to PM research.

### TIPS FOR SUPERVISORS

- Separating out context and perspective can be challenging for new researchers. We have found it helpful to work through some of the articles cited as examples (Liu and Leitner, 2012; Thomas, Cicmil and George, 2012; Judgev, 2004) with students as a means to increase both contextual and perspective awareness.
- The 'home discipline' of your student will likely not be PM. Working with them – especially early when relevant literature is being identified – will require special attention.
- Framing a suitable topic can be based on identifying a phenomenon that is not already explained and clearly researchable. Your guidance needs to be creative and constructive.

### QUESTIONS

1. How do you see the five integrative challenges from your understanding of the PM literature?
2. What are the papers that you have admired in your reading so far, and what is their theoretical basis?
3. What is your phenomenon of interest? Does it meet the three criteria we have proposed?
4. What is your theoretical basis? What are the leading publications that support such an approach and what are the associated implications for research?

## References

Barnett, M. L. (2007). (Un)learning and (mis)education through the eyes of Bill Starbuck: An interview with Pandora's playmate. *Academy of Management Learning & Education*, 6(1), 114–127.

Fabian, F. H. (2000). Keeping the tension: Pressures to keep the controversy in the management discipline. *Academy of Management Review*, 25(2), 350–372.

Harland, C., Lamming, R., Walker, H., Phillips, W., Caldwell, N., Johnsen, T., Knight, L. and Zheng, J. (2006). Supply management: Is it a discipline? *International Journal of Operations and Production Management*, 26(7), 730–753.

Jugdev, K. (2004). Through the looking glass: Examining theory development in project management with the resource-based view lens. *Project Management Journal*, 35(3), 15–26.

Kahneman, D. and Lavallo, D. (2002). 'Timid Choices and Bold Forecasts: A Cognitive Perspectiveon Risk Taking' in Kahneman, D. and Tversky, A. (eds) *Choices, Values, and Frames*. Cambridge, UK: Cambridge University Press, pp. 393–413.

Kang, S. and Snell, S. A. (2009). Intellectual capital architectures and ambidextrous learning: A framework for human resource management. *Journal of Management Studies*, 46(1), 65–92.

Liu, L. and Leitner, D. (2012). Simultaneous pursuit of innovation and efficiency in complex engineering projects – A study of the antecedents and impacts of ambidexterity in project teams. *Project Management Journal*, 43(6), 97–110.

Maylor, H., Blackmon, K. and Huemann, M. (2015). *Researching Business and Management*, 2nd edition. Basingstoke, UK: Palgrave.

Morgan, M., Levitt, R. E. and Malek, W. (2007). *Executing Your Strategy: How to break it down and get it done*. Boston, MA: Harvard Business School Press.

Pettigrew, A. M. (1997). 'The Double-Hurdles for Management Research' in Clarke, T. (ed.), *Advancement in Organizational Behaviour: Essays in honour of D.S. Pugh*. London, UK: Dartmouth Press, pp. 277–296.

Pettigrew, A. M. (2011). Scholarship with impact. *British Journal of Management*, 22(3), 347–354.

Rousseau, D. (ed.) (2012). *The Oxford Handbook of Evidence-Based Management*. Oxford, UK: Oxford University Press.

Sandberg, J. and Tsoukas, H. (2011). Grasping the logic of practice: Theorizing through practical rationality. *Academy of Management Review*, 36(2), 338–360.

Shenhar, A. and Dvir, D. (2007). *Reinventing Project Management: The diamond approach to successful growth and innovation*. Boston, MA: Harvard Business School Press.

Söderlund, J. (2005). What project management really is about: Alternative perspectives on the role and practice of project management. *International Journal of Technology Management*, 32(3/4), 371–387.

Söderlund, J. (2011). Pluralism in project management: Research at the crossroad of specialization and fragmentation. *International Journal of Management Reviews*, 13(2), 153–176.

Söderlund, J. and Maylor, H. (2012). Project management scholarship: Relevance, impact and five integrative challenges for business and management schools. *International Journal of Project Management*, 30(6), 686–696.

Starkey, K. and P. Madan (2001). Bridging the relevance gap: Aligning stakeholders in the future of management research. *British Journal of Management*, 12(Special Issue), S3–S26.

Thomas, J. L., Cicmil, S. and George, S. (2012). Learning from project management implementation by applying a management innovation lens. *Project Management Journal*, 43(6), 70–87.

Turner N., Swart J. and Maylor H. (2013). Mechanisms for managing ambidexterity: A review and research agenda. *International Journal of Management Reviews*, 15(3), 317–332.

Van de Ven, A. (2007). *Engaged Scholarship*. New York: Oxford University Press.

Weick, K. (2012). *Making Sense of the Organization, Vol. 2: The Impermanent Organization*. New York, NY: Wiley.

Whittington, R. (2006). Completing the practice turn in strategy research. *Organization Studies*, 27(May), 613–634.

# 2

# Project Management Research: Social Dimensions and Organisational Context

Michael Young

*I wrote this chapter as a result of my repeated encounters with researchers, practitioners and consultants who are completely focused on examining new aspects of well-known and defined knowledge areas, such as risk management. My observation is that many researchers, practitioners and consultants are exploring how to build a better mousetrap yet none of them have taken a step back and considered whether we collectively have a mouse problem, or whether there is, in fact, a plague of rabbits. Much of the PM practice and research is largely focused on describing aspects of an individual project, yet there is little focus on how many projects interact in the wider organisational context where many projects are delivered concurrently.*

As an emerging profession, the field of PM continues to grow, adapt and evolve. PM faces new challenges as the tools, methods and approaches to management that comprise the discipline are applied to different domains, for different ends, in different cultures. This chapter is focused on the discipline of PM and how it has changed and evolved. Whilst initial developments occurred in specific techniques, such as critical path method, there now is a shift towards the use of PM in an enterprise or organisational context. There has also more recently been the incorporation of strategy and management concepts as well as a focus on governance. This chapter challenges researchers and students' current thinking about Project Management and is intended to broaden their perspectives from the reductionist, tools and techniques-based view of PM as it appears through the Project Management Body of Knowledge (PMBoK) lens. The desired outcome is that students question the existing PM paradigm and explore new areas of PM practice or application.

At the end of this chapter, the reader can:

- explore the history of PM and the current shift in thinking and paradigm that is underway;
- examine the shift in thinking in both research and application of PM in practice;

- identify new areas of PM practice or application to explore.

Keywords: paradigms, history of project management, schools of thought

    This chapter focuses on the discipline of PM and how it is changing and continues to evolve requiring fresh ontological and epistemological perspectives when undertaking research in this field. It examines these developments and highlights the initial focus on specific techniques such as the critical path method as well as the shift towards PM in an enterprise or organisational context. More recently there has been the incorporation of strategy and management concepts and a focus on governance, which is a change from the traditional engineering view. New research perspectives have also emerged exploring the notion of *complex projects*, based on developments in chaos theory and systems thinking. The implications for the choice of research paradigm and ontology are discussed in this context.

## Development of Project Management (PM) Tools

Despite the abundance of projects in earlier times, PM was not discussed as a concept or practice until the 1950s. The 'modern' PM era started in 1958 with the development of Critical Path Method (CPM) / Program Evaluation and Review Technique (PERT) (Snyder and Kline, 1987), followed by the development of other core PM tools such as Material Requirement Planning (MRP). With the advent of large computer systems, CPM/PERT would be easily calculated by specialised programmers working on large government and defence projects. At this time, project offices were established as 'brokers of information' and were staffed by a small number of skilled schedulers and estimators (Kwak, 2003).

    During the 1960s and 1970s, the United States Department of Defense, NASA, and large engineering and construction companies utilised PM principles and tools to manage large budget and schedule-driven projects (Kwak, 2003). During the 1980s and early 1990s, with the revolution of the information technology (IT) sector, a shift from using mainframe computers to multitasking personal computers occurred. In the mid-1980s, the Internet served researchers and developers, and local area networks and Ethernet technology started to dominate network technology (Kwak, 2003).

    PMBoK was published by the PMI in 1987 which attempted to codify, define and structure PM knowledge and practice. At the time, the manufacturing and software development sectors started to adopt and implement sophisticated PM practices and, by the 1990s, PM theories, tools, and techniques were widely received by different industries and organisations (Kwak, 2003).

    Arguably, with the exception of risk management, no new principles of cost, design or schedule control have been developed since Earned Value, Configuration Management, Value Engineering, Precedence Scheduling and Resource Allocation in the mid-1960s (Morris, 1994). However, as Weaver (2007) points out, new techniques such as Critical Chain, Earned Schedule and portfolio management tools have been developed in the 20 years following Morris's book.

    Two leading PM organisations, the APM Group and PMI, commissioned major studies only to conclude that PM tools have reached maturity (Sargeant, 2010). However, when such tools are used, their value cannot be conclusively demonstrated (Thomas and Mullaly, 2008). Whilst the development of specific tools and techniques has fuelled the growth and development of modern PM, the thinking and developments in management science have also played a significant role.

## Developments in Management Science

PM has evolved in its specialist area along very similar lines to general management theory and management science more broadly. In its infancy, PM closely mirrored the 'classical school' of management with a focus on *scientific management* processes (scope, time and cost). These processes were developed from the work of Smith, Taylor, Fayol and Gantt (Young and Young, 2012), who collectively helped evolve management into a distinct business function that required study and discipline.

Taylor applied scientific reasoning to work by showing that labour can be analysed and improved by focusing on its elementary parts. He applied his thinking to tasks found in steel mills, such as shovelling sand and lifting and moving parts. Before then, the only way to improve productivity was to demand harder and longer hours from workers (Weaver, 2007). Taylor's associate, Gantt, studied in great detail the order of operations in work. His studies of management focused on Navy ship construction during the First World War. His Gantt charts, complete with task bars and milestone markers, outline the sequence and duration of all tasks in a process. Gantt chart diagrams proved to be such a powerful analytical tool for managers that they remained virtually unchanged for nearly a hundred years. It wasn't until the early 1990s that link lines were added to these task bars depicting more precise dependencies between tasks (Geraldi and Lechler, 2012; Weaver, 2007).

Following the Second World War, the complexities of projects and a shrinking war-time labour supply demanded new organisational structures. These techniques quickly spread to other industries as business leaders sought new management strategies and tools to handle their growth in a quickly changing and competitive world.

Cleland and Gareis (2006) identified that it was in the 1950s that PM was formally recognised as a distinct contribution arising from the management discipline, with names and labels being given to various elements of the PM discipline (Bredillet, 2006). In the early 1960s, general system theories of science began to be applied to business interactions with the publication of *The Theory and Management of Systems* (Johnson, Kast and Rosenzweig, 1963). The contingency approach which was developed during this period assumes that managerial behaviour is dependent on a wide variety of elements and questions the use of universal management practices. It advocates using selected and appropriate traditional, behavioural and systems viewpoints independently or in combination to deal with various circumstances as they arise.

By the 1970s the focus of PM was spreading from its roots in scheduling and its origins in the defence and construction industries. The distinctive nature of PM as a specialist management discipline if not a profession also began to emerge. More recently the emphasis has shifted towards the 'soft skills' more closely aligned with the 'human relations' and 'human resources' schools of management theory including more focus on stakeholders, communications and leadership. Some academics and practitioners also started exploring how PM could be used in a broader enterprise or organisational context.

## Enterprise-Wide Approaches to Project Management (PM)

As the field of PM expanded, various methodologies were developed to formalise the way organisations managed their many projects. The popularity of 'methodologies' grew rapidly from the beginning of the 1970s into the 1980s. However, since the turn of the century, the focus seems to have shifted from organisations buying expensive 'methodologies' from commercial vendors towards adopting the use of maturity models (Weaver, 2007).

To support the improvement of maturity, enterprise-wide PM approaches were implemented, seeking to adopt a common, systematic, organisational-wide approach to PM in a multi-project context. In an effort to apply individual PM principles across the enterprise to standardise the management of projects, the focus has been on the implementation and management of standards, tools and templates; individual project manager competency assessment and development or project approvals and review mechanisms (Cooper, Edgett and Kleinschmidt, 1999; Artto, Martinsuo and Aalto, 2001). It is through the application of such quality management and quality control techniques that the organisation improves its overall PM maturity.

## Development of Multi-Project Management

Management of individual projects has a well-conceptualised body of knowledge with underpinning tools and techniques (Project Management Institute, 2008). When projects are aggregated into programmes and portfolios, however, the literature on how to manage a collection of projects or programmes is somewhat sparse, divergent and poorly integrated. Further developments in our understanding of projects and PM have occurred with the conceptualisation of programme management, portfolio management and enterprise-wide approaches to PM (Pelligrinelli et al., 2007; Morris and Jamieson, 2004). There remains some confusion, however, amongst both the academic and practitioner communities as to the meaning of these terms (Thiry, 2004), as portfolio management, programme management, enterprise PM and multi-project management have been used interchangeably in the literature (Killen, 2008; Buttrick, 2000; Center for Business Practices, 2005; Dye and Pennypacker, 2000; Milosevic and Srivannaboon, 2006; Morris and Jamieson, 2004). These terms have been used to describe an *environment* (Patanakul and Milosevic, 2005; Platje and Seidel, 1994). Others such as Gareis (2006) have instead examined the *social* (network of projects) or *temporal* (chain of projects) *relationships* between individual projects, for example.

In this multi-project context, individual project managers attempt to resource their project from a common pool of resources that exist within the organisation. Project team members perform work and consume financial resources and in turn (ideally) generate deliverables, implement solutions and achieve business outcomes. There have also been many other developments in PM theory.

## Examining Project Management (PM) Theory

Theory is a statement of concepts and their interrelationships that shows how and, or why a phenomenon occurs (Gioia and Pitre, 1990). Theory allows researchers to understand and predict outcomes of interest and also allows researchers to describe and explain a process or sequence of events (DiMaggio, 1995; Mohr, 1982) that is bounded by the theorist's assumptions (Bacharach, 1989). Brief and Dukerich (1991) suggest that theory acts as an educational device that can raise consciousness about a specific set of concepts. Finally, Kerlinger and Lee (2000) went so far as to describe theory as the basic aim of science.

Good theory is practical precisely because it advances knowledge in a scientific discipline, guides research towards crucial questions and enlightens the profession of management (Van de Ven, 1989).

Whetton (1989) suggests for a theory to be complete, it must contain four essential elements: It must contain the factors (variables, constructs, concepts) that should be logically considered as part of the explanation of the social or individual phenomena of interest; how these factors are related; it should identify the underlying psychological, economic, or social dynamics that justify the selection of these factors and any associated causal relationships; as well as propositions that exist which limit the theory or establish theoretical boundaries.

A major criticism of PM as a whole is that it suffers from a scanty theoretical basis and a lack of concepts (Koskela and Howell, 2002; Sauer and Reich, 2009; Shenhar, 2001; Turner, 1999), with most of the research literature being relatively young (Shenhar and Dvir, 2004). Others such as Packendorff (1995) suggest that the shortcomings of PM research and theory are that: research on PM is not sufficiently empirical and as result the research lacks credibility and acceptance in mainstream management literature. Packendorff (1995) also suggests that the view of 'projects' is quite myopic, with projects being viewed largely as tools which results in a limited diversity of theoretical perspectives. Lundin and Soderholm (1998) suggest that the focus of PM has been much too narrow which is perhaps a result of continued evolution of the field.

Attempting to overcome these identified criticisms, there have been a number of recent attempts to develop a universal theory or set of theories of PM (Kwak and Anbari, 2009) that can be applied to every project regardless of its size, shape, complexity or industry domain in which the project is delivered. However, no one has succeeded to date (Snider and Nissen, 2003). Others such as (Bridellet, 2006; Söderlund, 2004; Shenhar, 2001) believe that it is not possible to describe the complex actions undertaken and the broad scope of covering PM in a single, all-encompassing theory.

## Schools of Project Management (PM)

In his series of editorial articles in 2007 and 2008 in the *Project Management Journal*, Bredillet proposed the existence of nine schools of PM research, building on *Söderlund's* (2010) seven schools (see Table 2.1). These proposed PM typologies support the notion that there is no 'one best way' of understanding or managing project, and marks a significant conceptual departure from the roots of scientific management.

Each of these schools of PM seeks to explore and explain the field of PM from various ontological stances. Contingency theory suggests the search for the 'one best way' universal theory of PM may be inappropriate, for a number of reasons.

Firstly, given the fundamental differences between each unique project, and the industry domain in which they are managed, the scientific management tradition may not hold true. As such, there may not actually be a single and easily definable approach to PM. Secondly, the engineering tradition and the social science tradition are axiologically incompatible: one avoids uncertainty to achieve determinateness, while the other assumes uncertainty and indeterminateness. By exploring the world from different perspectives we can build a much richer picture which improves our understanding of the complex set of interactions occurring during the management of projects. Thirdly, the goals of the academic and practitioner audiences appear to be divergent and as such a divide has developed between the practical and the theoretical sides of the field of PM (Söderlund, 2004; Koskela and Howell, 2002; Morris, 2003). Whilst it is important that we continue to develop new underpinning theoretical perspectives, given the applied nature of PM, we should not lose sight of the need for relevance.

It is important to note that research in PM has broadened into new disciplines and domains, such as systems engineering, IT and strategic management, whilst in-depth research has developed new concepts in cost engineering scheduling or resource management. Bredillet (2006) offers some noticeable trends for the field of PM suggesting it is characterised by an abundance of initiatives, including: research; development of standards; and increasing use of PM methods and techniques. These trends will now be explored in more detail.

**Table 2.1    Schools of management (taken from Bredillet (2006) and Söderlund (2010))**

| Bredillet's Schools of Project Management | Söderlund's Schools of Project Management | Key Concepts | Examples of Current Research |
| --- | --- | --- | --- |
| Optimisation School | Optimisation School | Optimising the outcome of projects using mathematical techniques | Earned Value Management |
| Modelling School | | Use of hard and soft systems theory to model the project | Integration of hard systems and soft systems methodology |
| Governance School | Governance School | Govern the project and the relationship between project participants | Effectiveness of project offices Projects as temporary organisations Governance of projects |
| Behaviour School | Behaviour School | Manage the relationships between the people on the project | Virtual project teams Cross-cultural issues in projects Knowledge sharing |
| Success School | Factor School | Define success and failure and identify causes | Project success factors Stakeholder satisfaction |
| Decision School | Decision School | Information processing through the project lifecycle | Decision making at project start up Alignment of portfolios to strategy |
| Process School | | Find an appropriate path to the desired outcome | PM process improvement Project categorisation |
| Contingency School | Contingency School | Categorise the project type and apply appropriate systems | Methods for different project settings |
| Marketing School | Relationship School | Communicate with all stakeholders to obtain their support | Selling PM to senior executives Alignment of PM and senior executives perspectives Customer relationships management in projects |

# Trends in Project Management (PM) Research

Since the publication of the 'rethinking' PM agenda in 2006 there have been calls for a change of PM paradigm from the traditional linear, mechanistic, tools and techniques-based perspective. The *Rethinking Project Management Research Agenda* found that the PM body of research to be limited and developed a new framework complementing and extending this existing Body of Knowledge (Winter, Smith, Morris and Cicmil, 2006), consisting of five key themes.

The first research direction recognises the complexity of projects and that there are a number of ways to manage them, thereby leading to numerous models and theories. The second direction recognises the social nature of projects involving human interactions, multiple stakeholders and power relations. The third direction shifts the focuses to value creation in projects process thereby highlighting emergence, sense-making and multiple expectations and meanings (Winter, Smith, Morris and Cicmil, 2006; Sauer and Reich, 2009). The fourth direction concerning broader conceptualisations of projects acknowledges the multidisciplinary, emergent and negotiable concepts and approaches that can be pursued. The fifth direction involves a movement of practitioners from trained technicians to that of becoming reflective practitioners who can learn, adapt and apply theory effectively in their practice domains (Winter, Smith, Morris and Cicmil, 2006).

There have been numerous studies that have explored emerging PM trends or attempted to identify the future of PM or the next wave of thinking. As a result, some authors have suggested we have entered *PM 2.0* or the second order of PM. Others see that we are at the limits of our existing discipline and are about to jump to a new innovation curve. Each of these developments are following various lines of enquiry and exploring the PM *landscape* through a variety of lenses and in time may lead to a number of middle-range theories on different types of projects.

Undertaking an extensive literature review of academic papers published since 1960, Kloppenborg and Opfer (2002) observed a significant increase in literature on PM issues, with a strong focus on planning and control. Whilst Kloppenborg and Opfer (2002) identified many trends, the key items identified in their literature review were: a trend towards standardisation or process and tools; an increasing focus on project selection and prioritisation and; an increasing emphasis on formal PM training and certification.

Using expert questioning, Archibald (2003) identified a number of major PM trends, suggesting that not only will PM be applied in new application areas and disciplines, but also that the linking of strategic and PM will occur through project portfolio management practices. Archibald (2003) also suggests that PM will be expanded to include the realisation of project benefits.

Drawing on his extensive personal experience, Tanaka (2004) proposes numerous PM models that have developed of four generations and offers views on PM opportunities and challenges into the future. Tanaka suggests that the first generation classical PM model has evolved into the fourth generation versatile, user-friendly management method for all organisations.

In 2005, Crawford, Pollack and Englund (2005) examined the trends in PM research by analysing the keywords from academic papers published over the previous ten years in the *International Journal of Project Management* and the *Project Management Journal*, building upon seven previous studies of this type. When all eight studies are synthesised, Crawford et al. (2005) identified a number of clear trends. These trends include a reduced focus on quality management and interpersonal skills over time, suggesting that interest in these topics has peaked; an increased focus on project evaluation and improvement and strategic alignment. They also identified a consistent significance in the studies of Relationship Management, Resource Management, Time Management, Cost Management and Risk Management.

Bredillet (2006) also offers a number of predictions, suggesting a continuous interest in and focus on: information and optimisation techniques; financial, investment and economic aspects; and training and education. New possible areas of interest include: improving organisational maturity; organisational performance and metrics; change and the role of project teams as change agents; and the professionalisation of PM. Bredillet (2006) also indicates that '... project management is becoming more focused on implementation of organisation strategy'.

## Changing Our Research Paradigm

Given these developments in PM research and practice, it is important to also examine the need to explore new research methods and approaches. This shift in thinking and the associated change of the PM paradigm requires researchers to reconsider the type of research being pursued and the ontological and epistemological stances taken. Much of the research to date has been reductionist in nature, with some researchers exploring ever smaller aspects of the PM discipline. Whilst research into the use of particular methods and techniques are useful, the greatest impacts may possibly come from integrative research that explores macro-level concepts and applications in particular industries, contexts or the application of organisational-wide approaches. Or perhaps they will come through examining the world through multiple lenses.

## Building New Theories by Combining Lenses

PM is a rich context in which to develop theory. It is a broad subject with dimensions that are able to be examined from a variety of perspectives and observed through many lenses. As a multidisciplinary area of inquiry, organisational and management theory is said to rely heavily on borrowed concepts and theories (Whetten, Felin and King, 2009). These concepts and theories have been drawn extensively from other foundational disciplines, including biology, education, engineering, history, law, linguistics, mathematics, philosophy and politics (Ostwick, Fleming and Hanlon, 2011). There is a strong assertion that the majority of theories consumed in organisational and management theory are externally produced: that is, they are developed in other disciplines and adopted by organisational studies or management.

Theory development that builds on multiple lenses has an important role to play (Gioia and Pitre, 1990). Using multiple perspectives to examine organisations allows us to sustain a healthy critique on the work and practice of management (Currie, Knights and Starkey, 2010). Multiple lenses can also bridge silos with and across disciplines: by highlighting areas of overlap or complementarity, as well as identifying areas where new contributions can be made.

By using the combination of ideas or blends of theories, new and novel hypotheses can be developed and tested empirically. By using multiple lens, the resultant theories are rich with phenomena being able to be described using a number of theoretical approaches and can lead to their theoretical integration or resolution.

Many important pieces of breakthrough research in management and organisational studies have come from scholars who sat astride two or more academic disciplines. Porter's (1980; 1985; 1996) work in strategy resulted from his having combined insights from business policy and industrial organisation economics. Behavioural economics and behavioural finance are another case in point. By using cognitive and emotional actors to understand individual decisions, these new fields combine theoretical insights from both economics and psychology to advance our understanding of individuals and collectives (Rabin, 1998).

Given the extensive blending of concepts from various disciplines, various ontological approaches have been developed, providing a range of methods and techniques to support the development of theory using multiple lenses. Some authors, such as Cornelissen (2005), champion a process that focuses on points of similarity between two similar domains, whereas others, such as Alvesson and Karreman (2007), advocate the examination of differences between similar domains.

In an attempt to make sense of the development of theory by combining disciplines, Fauconnier and Turner (2002) developed the *Domains Interaction model*. This model draws from cognition theory in psychology and is based on the notion of conceptual blending and relies on the functions of comparison and correspondence between two reference disciplines to craft a new synthetic insight.

## Exploring New Perspectives

In addition to exploring emerging research themes, we must also change our epistemological or ontological stance and explore the world of PM from new perspectives. One such new approach is the examination of practice-based perspectives in PM.

Drawing on the *practice turn* (Bourdieu, 1977; Giddens, 1979) and the work of Jarzabkowski (2003; 2004) and Whittington (1996; 2002) on *strategy-as-practice*, Blomquist et al. (2010) have pursued a research theme examining *projects-as-practice*, establishing a research agenda for examining the actual work undertaken by project managers in projects.

Traditional system research has sought to identify best practice, guidelines and forecasting of relevant behaviour for practitioners. Some of its results are transferred into textbooks, guidelines, formalised norms and expectations, such as the various bodies of knowledge. Process studies are mostly concerned with processes defined by the structure, which results in a focus on projects as defined by these organisational structures. The critical perspective questions common project knowledge and explores more details of human behaviour and patterns of behaviour.

The *practice* field focuses on human actors and their actions and interactions and focused on *practitioners* (the people who do the work of projects), *practices* (the social, symbolic and material tools through which projects are done) and *praxis* (the flow of activity in which projects are accomplished) (Jarzabkowski and Spee, 2009). Therefore, a practice-based examination of PM requires the study of action, activities and actors within projects.

Blomquist et al. (2010) argue that any traditional PM topic can be made suitable for a project-as-practice research approach. They continue, suggesting that to do so it is important to focus on how things are being worked out in real life, how actions are designed, performed, and related to other actions, communities, institutions and the like.

## Conclusion

This chapter has provided a brief overview of the history and origins of PM as well as some of the recent developments in PM research. The intent of this chapter is not to be exhaustive, but instead, the chapter attempts to provide an overview of the range of perspectives being explored. The chapter also attempts to challenge the thinking of prospective researchers and students and suggests that there are many more PM perspectives than that offered by PMBoK or by the dominant scientific management perspective.

So, as a PM student or researcher, what aspect of PM piques your interest? Where will you make your contribution to the development of our knowledge and understanding of projects and the theory and practice of PM?

## Tips and Exercises

### TIPS FOR STUDENTS

* PM is no longer mechanistic and rational in nature but has expanded in its application to operate in dynamic and complex contexts.

- A paradigm shift is needed in PM and more attention needs to be paid to social dimensions and the organisational context.
- Project-based management research needs to explore new perspectives. These perspectives may come from other disciplines.

## TIPS FOR SUPERVISORS

- Direct the students to review several research articles and texts that examine or explore different schools of thought.
- Ask students to consider the notion of project success and to identify the metrics or measures used to determine whether a project was considered successful. Have the students examine large, high-profile publicly funded construction projects to determine how perception and politics can have an effect of the perception of whether a project was successful or not.
- Work with the student to examine a case study project and identify how the project would be examined from the perspective of each of Bredillet's *Schools of Project Management*.
- Probe students to consider why it is important to consider new perspectives in PM.
- Ask students to review the concept of 'projects as temporary organisations', and discuss how this fresh perspective makes us think differently about the discipline of PM.

## EXERCISES

1. Undertake a quick review to identify key concepts in another field or discipline. For example, in the field of ecology, a key concept is that of carrying capacity – this is a term that describes the volume of animals that can be sustained by a particular ecosystem. Examine how such concepts could be applied to the discipline of PM. For the example provided above, carrying capacity could be examined as a concept in portfolio resource management.
2. Consider the Schools of Project Management. Does each school lend itself to either a quantitative or a qualitative research method?
3. Read Blomquist et al.'s (2010) paper on projects-as-practice. How could the examination of the actual work undertaken by project managers in projects improve PM?
4. It is important to examine the differences in the way in which projects are seen, identified and described. Identify five different ways the word 'project' is used. Identify different ways projects are described or defined.

## References

Alvesson, M. and Karreman, D. (2007). Construcing mystery: Empirical matters in theory development. *Academy of Management Review*, 32(4), 1265–1281.

Archibald, R. (2003). State of the Art of Project Management: 2003. *Project Management Conference, Escuela Colombiana de Ingeriera*. Bogota, Columbia.

Artto, K.A., Martinsuo, M. and Aalto, T. (2001). *Project Portfolio Management*. Finland: PMA.

Bacharach, S. (1989). Organisational theories: Some criteria for evaluation. *Academy of Management Review*, 14(4), 496–515.

Blomquist, T., Hällgren, M., Nilsson, A. and Söderholm, A. (2010). Project-as-practice: In search of project management research that matters. *Project Management Journal*, 41(1), 5–16.

Bourdieu, P. (1977). *Outline of a Theory of Practice*. Cambridge, UK: Cambridge University Press.

Bridellet, C. (2006). 'The Future of Project Management: Mapping the Dynamics of Project Management Field in Action' in D. I. Cleland and R. Gareis, *Global Project Management Handbook: Planning, organizing, and controlling international projects* (2nd edition). New York, NY: McGraw Hill.

Brief, A. P. and Dukerich, J. M. (1991). Theory in organisational behaviour: Can it be useful? *Research in Organisational Behaviour,* 13, 327–352.

Buttrick, R. (2000). *The Interactive Project Workout* (2nd edition). London, UK: Pearson Education Limited.

Center for Business Practices. (2005). *Project Portfolio Management Maturity: A benchmark of current business practices.* (J. S. Pennypacker, ed.) Havertown: Center for Business Practices.

Cooper, R., Edgett, S. and Kleinschmidt, E. (1999). New product portfolio management: Practices and performance. *Journal of Product Innovation Management,* 16(4), 333–351.

Cornelissen, J. P. (2005). Beyond compare: Metaphors in organisation theory. *Academy of Management Review,* 30(4), 751–764.

Crawford, L., Pollack, J. and Englund, D. (2005). Uncovering the trends in project managemnet: Journal emphases over the last 10 years. *International Journal of Project Management,* 24(2), 175–184.

Currie, G., Knights, D. and Starkey, K. (2010). Introduction: A post critical reflection on business schools. *British Journal of Management,* 21(Supplement), S1–S5.

DiMaggio, P. (1995). Comments on 'What Theory is Not'. *Administrative Science Quarterly,* 40, 391–397.

Dye, L. D. and Pennypacker, J. S. (2000). Project Portfolio Management and Managing Multiple Projects: Two Sides of the Same Coin? *Proceedings of the Project Management Institute Annual Seminars & Symposium.* Houston, Texas: Project Management Institute.

Fauconnier, G. and Turner, M. (2002). *The Way We Think: Conceptual blending and the mind's hidden complexities.* New York, NY: Basic Books.

Gareis, R. (2006). 'Program Managment and Project Portfolio Management' in D. I. Cleland and R. Gareis (eds), *Global Project Management Handbook* (2nd edition). New York, NY: McGraw-Hill.

Geraldi, J. G. and Lechler, T. (2012). Gantt charts revisited: A critical analysis of its roots and implications to the management of projects today. *International Journal of Managing Projects in Business,* 5(4), 578–594.

Giddens, A. (1979). *Central Problems in Social Theory: Action, structure and contrdiction in social analysis.* London, UK: Macmillan.

Gioia, D. A. and Pitre, E. (1990). Multi-parradigm perspectives on theory building. *Academy of Management Review,* 15(4), 584–602.

Jarzabkowski, P. (2003). Strategic practices: An activity theory perspective on continuity and change. *Journal of Management Studies,* 40(1), 23–55.

Jarzabkowski, P. (2004). Strategy as practice: Recursiveness, adaptation, and practices-in-use. *Organisation Studies,* 25(4), 529–560.

Jarzabkowski, P. and Spee, A. (2009). Strategy-as-practice: A review and future directions for the field. *International Journal of Management Reviews,* 11(1), 69–95.

Johnson, R., Kast, F. and Rosenzweig, J. (1963). *The Theory and Management of Systems.* Michigan: McGraw Hill.

Kerlinger, F. N. and Lee, H. B. (2000). *Foundations of Behavioural Research.* California: Harcourt College Publishers.

Killen, C. P. (2008). Learning investments and organisational capabilities: Case studies on the development of project portfolio management capabilities. *International Journal of Managing Projects in Business,* 1(3), 334–351.

Kloppenborg, T. and Opfer, W. (2002). The current state of project management of research: Trends, interpretations and predictions. *Project Management Journal,* 33(2), 5–18.

Koskela, L. and Howell, G. (2002). The underlying theory of project management is obsolete. *PMI Research Conference.* Project Management Institute.

Kwak, Y. H. (2003). 'Brief History of Project Management' in Y. H. Kwak and F. Anbari (eds), *The Story of Managing Projects.* Westport: Quorum Books.

Kwak, Y. and Anbari, F. (2009). Analysing project management research: Perspectives from top management journals. *International Journal of Project Management,* 27(5), 435–446.

Lundin, R. A. and Soderholm, A. (1998). 'Managing the Black Boxes of the Project Environment' in J. Pinto (ed.), *The Handbook of Project Management*. San Francisco: Jossey-Bass.

Milosevic, D. Z. and Srivannaboon, S. (2006). A theoretical framework for aligning project managment with business strategy. *PMI Research Conference Proceedings*. Montreal: Project Management Institute.

Mohr, L. (1982). *Explaining Organisational Behaviour*. San Francisco: Jossey-Bass.

Morris, P. (1994). *The Management of Projects*. London, UK: Thomas Telford Services Ltd.

Morris, P. (2003). The irrelevance of project management as a professional discipline. *17th World Congress on Project Management*. Moscow, Russia.

Morris, P. and Jamieson, A. (2004). *Translating Corporate Strategy into Project Strategy: Realising corporate strategy through project management*. Newton Square: Project Management Institute.

Ostwick, C., Fleming, P. and Hanlon, G. (2011). From borrowing to blending: Rethinking the process of organisation theory building. *Academy of Management Review*, 36(2), 318–337.

Packendorff, J. (1995). Inquiring into the temport organisation: New directions for project management research. *Scandanavian Journal of Management*, 11(4), 319–334.

Patanakul, P. and Milosevic, D. (2005). Multiple-Project Managers: What competencies do you need? *Project Perspectives*, 28–33.

Pelligrinelli, S., Partington, D., Hemingway, C., Mohdzain, Z. and Shah, M. (2007). The importance of context in programme management: An empirical review of programme practices. *International Journal of Project Management*, 25(1), 41–55.

Platje, A. and Seidel, H. (1994). Project and portfolio planning cycle: Project-based managment for multiproject challange. *International Journal of Project Management*, 12(2), 100–106.

Porter, M. (1980). *Corporate Strategy: Techniques for analysing industries and competitors*. New York: Free Press.

Porter, M. (1985). *Competitive Advantage: Creating and sustaining superior performance*. New York: Free Press.

Porter, M. (1996). What is strategy. *Harvard Business Review*, (November–December), 61–78.

Project Management Institute. (2008). *A Guide to the Project Management Body of Knowledge* (4th edition). Newtown Square: Project Management Institute.

Rabin, M. (1998). Psychology and economics. *Journal of Economic Literature*, 36(1), 11–46.

Sargeant, R. (2010). *Creating Value in Project Management using PRINCE2*. Brisbane: Queensland University of Technology.

Sauer, C. and Reich, B. (2009). Rethinking IT project management: Evidence of a new mindset and its implications. *International Journal of Project Management*, 28(2), 182–193.

Shenhar, A. J. (2001). One size does not fit all projects: Exploring classical contingency domains. *Management Science*, 47, 394–414.

Shenhar, A. J. and Dvir, D. (2004). 'How Projects Differ, and What to Do About It' in P. W. Morris and J. K. Pinto (eds), *The Wiley Guide to Managing Projects*. New York, NY: John Wiley & Sons.

Snider, K. F. and Nissen, M. E. (2003). Beyond the body of knowledge: A knowledge-flow approach to project management theory and practice. *Project Management Journal*, 34(2), 4–12.

Snyder, J. R. and Kline, S. (1987). Modern project management: How did we get here – where do we go? *Project Management Journal*, 18(1), 28–29.

Söderlund, J. (2004). Building theories of project management: Past research, questions for the future. *International Journal of Project Management*, 22(3), 183–191.

Söderlund, J. (2010). Pluralism in project management: Navigating the crossroads of specialisations and fragmentation. *International Journal of Project Management*, 28(1), 1–24.

Tanaka, H. (2004). The changing landscape of project management. *4th International Project Management Workshop*. ESC Lille.

Thiry, M. (2004). 'Program Management: A Strategic Decision Management Process' in P. W. Morris and J. K. Pinto (eds), *The Wiley Guide to Managing Projects*. New York, NY: John Wiley & Sons, pp. 257–287.

Thomas, J. and Mullaly, M. (2008). *Researching the Value of Project Management*. Newton Square: Project Management Institute.

Turner, J. R. (1999). *The Handbook of Project-Based Management* (2nd edition). Maidenhead, UK: McGraw-Hill.

Urli B and Urli, D. (2000). Project management in North America: Stability of the concepts. *Project Management Journal,* 31(3), 33–43.

Van de Ven, A. (1989). Nothing is quite so practical as a good theory. *Academy of Management Review,* 14(4), 486–489.

Weaver, P. (2007). The origins of modern project management. *Fourth Annual PMI College of Scheduling Conference.* Vancouver: PMI.

Whetten, D. (1989). What constitutes of theoretical contribution. *Academy of Management Review,* 14(3), 490–495.

Whetten, D. A., Felin, T. and King, B. G. (2009). The practice of theory borrowing in organisational studies: Current issues and future directions. *Journal of Management,* 35(3), 537–563.

Whittington, R. (1996). Strategy-as-practice. *Long Range Planning,* 29(6), 731–735.

Whittington, R. (2002). Practice perspectives on strategy: Unifying and developing a field. *Academy of Management Proceedings,* C1–C6.

Winter, M., Smith, C., Morris, P. and Cicmil, S. (2006). Directions for future research in project management: The main findings of a UK government-funded research network. *International Journal of Project Management,* 24(8), 638–649.

Young, M. and Young, R. (2012). The rise and fall of project management: Are we witnessing the birth of a new discipline? *International Journal of Project, Program and Portfolio Management,* 3(1), 58–77.

# 3

# The Paradigm as a Steering Mechanism for New Research Endeavours

Thomas Biedenbach

*Researchers rarely state the philosophical assumptions despite their value for both the research process and advancing the research field. I would like to encourage students and researchers to explicitly utilise reflections about paradigms in their studies.*

The purpose of this chapter is to show the value of utilising paradigms and articulating the research philosophy to effectively direct a new research endeavour. The explicit utilisation of paradigms has various benefits: allowing a fundamental categorisation of the research field, incorporating challenging viewpoints (paradigmatic pluralism), offering new conceptual perspectives when taking a different ontological perspective, and gaining legitimacy outside the field of PM. Paradigms can serve as a powerful facilitator not only for directing research towards significant contributions that progress the research field, but also for guiding doctoral students through the research process.

At the end of this chapter, the reader can:

- describe the term *paradigm* and the philosophical assumptions concerning ontology, epistemology and axiology;
- recognise the dominating philosophies within PM research and its current paradigmatic trends;
- recognise the value of paradigms during the research process.

Keywords: Paradigm, ontology, epistemology, axiology, research process

When initiating a new research project, much reflection is required until a researcher has defined the purpose of the study. After having found a general area of interest, may it be following one's hunch or individual passion, the common starting point for identifying and specifying a new research topic is by conducting a thorough literature review in the particular research area. This procedure provides a solid overview of the research area and identifies theoretical gaps in previous research. Recent debates among researchers question the dominance of this approach for initialising new research areas (Sandberg and Alvesson, 2011).

Problematisation is highlighted as a complementary approach in order to identify and to challenge the inherent assumptions underlying existing theories (Alvesson and Sandberg, 2011).

By adopting such a perspective, researchers may formulate research questions, which are likely to result in a more intriguing and influential theory. Underlying this problematisation is the term *paradigm* and its assumptions. Paradigms can be defined as our basic belief system or worldview and thus direct the research epistemologically (that is, the nature and scope of knowledge), ontologically (that is, the nature of reality) and in selecting a suitable research method (Guba and Lincoln, 1994).

Nevertheless, for the analysis of the maturity of PM and its sub themes, review articles provide valuable insights. However, the philosophical assumptions are usually not a research focus in the field of PM. Previous reviews of PM research look into the underlying assumptions and theoretical debates (Kloppenberg and Opfer, 2002; Söderlund, 2004; Themistocleous and Waerne, 2000), methodologies (Smyth and Morris, 2007), and relationship to related disciplines within the scientific field of management (Kwak and Anbari, 2009). Biedenbach and Müller (2011) investigated philosophical stances in PM research by examining IRNOP conference papers over 15 years. The vast majority of researchers are silent about the philosophical underpinning of PM studies (Biedenbach and Müller, 2011). Researchers tend to follow the dominant practice, thus misinterpreting the relevance of paradigms, and might even feel discouraged from articulating the underlying paradigm of their research.

The purpose of this chapter is to show the value of utilising paradigms and articulating the research philosophy to effectively direct a new research endeavour. While the paradigm corresponds to the basic belief system of the researcher, the research philosophy holds important assumptions, which underline the research design (and resultant research strategy and research methods). The research philosophy is premised by the researcher's assumptions concerning how the world operates (that is, ontology), how acceptable knowledge is defined (that is, epistemology), and the role values play (that is, axiology). These perspectives have the power to direct and to steer the researcher through the research process. New doctoral students can benefit from these reflections and their careful application.

The identification of trends and shortcomings of PM research (Biedenbach and Müller, 2011) serves as a starting point to illustrate the benefits of paradigmatic considerations. This chapter calls for a more explicit utilisation of paradigms when setting up a new research project, in order to conduct research with a significant contribution for advancing the particular field of studies. Moreover, deviating from existing paradigms can open up new research areas such as seen, for example, in the emergence of critical perspectives of PM (Cicmil and Hodgson, 2006). Paradigms can also limit the research scope, determine the chosen methodology, influence the sequence of methodological steps and finally affect the degree of certainty in which the findings are communicated.

## Defining Paradigms and Research Philosophies

The term *paradigm* was initially proposed by the philosopher Kuhn (1962) in his seminal work 'The Structure of Scientific Revolutions'. The ambiguity of the term *paradigm* has been evident since its first appearance, with Masterman (1970) noting the application of a paradigm in 21 different senses. Masterman (1970) classified three different paradigm categories: (1) a *metaphysical paradigm* or *metaparadigm* that relates to wider beliefs such as a worldview, (2) a *sociological paradigm* that concerns a set of scientific habits and (3) a *construct paradigm* that can be seen as a concrete artefact or research vehicle for puzzle-solving. Despite its missing concreteness, the term *paradigm* continues to provoke debate among philosophers and has become a significant concept for scientific development in general.

Stepping aside from the philosophical debates, the paradigm offers facilitation benefits for developing and conducting research. For this reason a more comprehensive definition of the paradigm can be used by researchers. A research paradigm is the belief system 'that guides how research should be conducted, based on the people's philosophies and their assumptions about the world and the nature of knowledge' (Collis and Hussey, 2009: p. 11). A paradigm can be seen as basic beliefs directing researchers' actions in a net of epistemological, ontological and methodological premises (Guba, 1990). The paradigm thus frames the philosophical stance of the researcher and determines, to a large extent, the choices of how the research will be conducted. In this respect, Johnson, Onwuegbuzie and Turner (2007) use the term *paradigm* on a methodological level referring to quantitative, qualitative and mixed methods as possible research paradigms.

As visible in the initial debate among philosophers and different categorisations, the paradigm can be considered as a multi-dimensional term for aggregating various issues. Morgan (2007) points out that the paradigm is commonly used on four different hierarchical levels. On the first and broadest level, paradigms represent worldviews comprised of ways of experiencing and thinking about the world containing morals, values and aesthetics. On the second level, paradigms refer to epistemological stances such as positivism and interpretivism. Thus, it is a narrower belief system about the nature of knowledge affecting how research questions are asked and answered.

On the third level, paradigms denote shared beliefs within a research community of a certain field of specialisation. The paradigm represents the consensus about the most meaningful questions and the most suitable research approaches to answer these questions. An illustration of this is the Scandinavian School of Project Management, which emphasises projects as temporary organisations (Lundin and Söderholm, 1995), contingency perspectives (Engwall, 2003) and case study methodologies. On the fourth and most detailed level, paradigms are a particular model, an exemplar for how research is conducted in a certain field. A special perspective or model may be outstanding in its significance so that it acts as a paradigm.

Not only the paradigm term itself, but also contrasting worldviews on different paradigms have led to extensive debates in research communities. These debates were even referred to as paradigm wars occurring between qualitative and quantitative research communities due to their competing worldviews, fundamentally opposing beliefs and methodological issues (for example, Gage, 1989; Howe, 1988). The underlying incompatibility thesis asserts that methods with contradictory philosophical assumptions cannot be mixed in a study or set of studies (Howe, 1988). However, there is a growing number of researchers arguing for a less strict position by proposing that paradigms allow the combined use of opposing methods.

These advocates of mixed methods emphasise the benefits of combining qualitative and quantitative methods and oppose other views suggesting their epistemological inconsistency (for example, Morgan, 2007; Teddlie and Tashakkori, 2009). Epistemological paradigms such as pragmatism (Howe, 1988) and critical realism are examples where qualitative and quantitative methods can co-exist (Mingers, 2006). Based on the broadest view, paradigms contain philosophical assumptions concerning ontology (that is, nature of reality), epistemology (that is, relationship between researcher and researched) and axiology (that is, role of values) (Creswell, 2007).

*Ontology* concerns the question whether social entities have a reality independent of social actors, or whether they are social constructions of social actors through their actions and perceptions (Bryman and Bell, 2011). The ontology can be divided into two categories: First, objectivism that assumes the existence of one reality, which is external, objective and independent of the researcher and social actors (Collis and Hussey, 2009). Second, subjectivism that views reality as socially constructed, where actors engage in social interactions and social phenomena are in a constant state of change (Saunders, Lewis and Thornhill, 2012).

*Epistemology* underlines what is accepted as valid knowledge. Four epistemological stances can be distinguished from each other, which are positivism, realism, interpretivism and pragmatism.

Positivism relates to natural science traditions in which interrelationships between objects are studied and are unaffected by the research activities (Collis and Hussey, 2009). Realism assumes that objects exist independent of the human mind and also takes a natural science approach to the development of knowledge (Saunders et al., 2012).

Direct realism implies that with our senses we are capable of experiencing the world accurately, whereas critical realism denotes that instead of experiencing the world directly, we only experience images of the world (Saunders et al., 2012). Interpretivism sees the world as too complex to develop precise law-like generalisations alike in the natural sciences but sees it as necessity for the researcher to understand the differences between social actors (Saunders et al., 2012). Pragmatism recognises that there are many ways to conduct research and interpret the world and, thus, accepting different philosophical positions and multiple methods (Saunders et al., 2012).

*Axiology* concerns the judgment of values and what role the researcher's values play in the research process (Saunders et al., 2012). For example in a qualitative study, researchers recognise that the study is value-laden and actively position themselves in their study based on their values and possible biases (Creswell, 2007). Lincoln and Guba (2003) highlight that values affect the choices within the research process and that axiology containing ethics, aesthetics and religion is indeed a fundamental philosophical dimension of a paradigm. Table 3.1 concludes this section with an overview of the four main paradigms and their philosophical assumptions.

**Table 3.1    Four main philosophies compared by assumptions (adapted from Saunders et al., 2012)**

|  | Pragmatism | Positivism | Realism | Interpretivism |
|---|---|---|---|---|
| **Ontology –** Researcher's view on nature of reality | External, multiple, most appropriate view chosen for answering the research question. | External, objective and independent of social actors. | Objective, exists independent of human thought or knowledge about their existence (realism) but is interpreted through social conditions (critical realism). | Subjective, socially constructed, may alter, multiple. |
| **Epistemology –** Researcher's view on acceptable knowledge | Depending on research question, either or both, observable phenomena and subjective meanings can provide acceptable knowledge. | Only observable phenomena enable the production of facts and credible data. Focuses on causality and law-like generalisations. | Observable phenomena provide credible data and facts. Insufficient data means inaccuracies in sensations (realism) or phenomena create sensations which are open to misinterpretations (criticalrealism).Focuses on explanations within a context. | Subjective meanings and social phenomena. Focus on details of situation and its reality, subjective meanings motivating actions. |
| **Axiology –** Researcher's view on role of values in research | Large role of values in interpreting results. A researcher takes both an objective and subjective view. | Value-free research with the researcher being objective and independent of the data. | Value-laden research, because the researcher is biased concerning worldview, cultural experiences and background, which affect the research. | Value-bound and subjective. The researcher is part of what is researched and cannot be separated. |

## Paradigms in Project Management

In the field of PM, researchers rarely state in an explicit manner their philosophical foundations. In a review of published articles, Smyth and Morris (2007) found that 90 per cent of the studies are neither explicit in their philosophical statements nor are explicit enough in describing the choices of research methodology, which often makes it difficult to clearly categorise the research in its epistemological and paradigmatic context. These findings have been confirmed also concerning conference papers, where only a small number of authors have explicitly stated their philosophical stances (Biedenbach and Müller, 2011).

Overall, research in PM is dominated by a mechanistic worldview based on a positivist epistemology (Cooke-Davies, Cicmil, Crawford and Richardson, 2007; Smyth and Morris, 2007). Also Pollack (2007) has found that a hard view of PM based on positivistic thinking is the dominating paradigm, but he emphasises that there seems to be a trend towards a soft view associated with interpretivism. Therefore, despite the long mechanistic traditions of PM, the research field seems to become more diverse concerning paradigms and research topics.

The pluralism where researchers emphasise different ontological and epistemological stances is important for developing a research field. The current state of knowledge can be advanced by adding creativity, encouraging debates and enriching understanding by complementing or even contrasting viewpoints (Pellegrinelli, 2011; Söderlund, 2010). For the research field it is vital to incorporate contrasting viewpoints and to overcome the tendency of project research that to a large extent only re-emphasises the underlying assumptions of previous research (Hällgren, 2012).

A different ontology perspective of what we see as a project reality can be such a starting point to enhance knowledge. Linehan and Kavanagh (2006) contrast the dominating 'being' ontology (that is, objectivism) to a 'becoming' ontology (that is, subjectivism), which tends to represent better the daily project reality. They highlight that a becoming ontology focuses on activities, processes, construction of entities and sense-making, which are issues that fit into a dynamic and evolving project environment.

Not surprisingly, researchers recognise a need to shift from a being ontology towards a becoming ontology (Winter, Smith, Morris and Cicmil, 2006; Bredillet, 2010). In this respect, subjectivism with its differing assumptions offers a beneficial perspective. In addition, researchers can apply theoretical lenses from related research disciplines, which were previously inconsistent with an understanding of reality based on objectivism. Pellegrini (2011) gives an example by asserting that subjectivism can contribute to the enhancement of programme management by offering a valuable conceptual and practice-orientated perspective. From a subjectivist view, researchers would observe programme managers in their day-to-day activities in order to include the situational context in which programme management is shaped.

The findings of the review of IRNOP conference papers show a dominance of studies based on subjectivism and interpretivism (Biedenbach and Müller, 2011), which is in contrast to published research. For example, 66 per cent of the papers published in the *International Journal of Project Management* follow positivism (Smyth and Morris, 2007). Of course these findings need to be interpreted cautiously. Nevertheless, they indicate a trend towards a more balanced mix of research with positivist studies increasing in IRNOP conferences and interpretivism increasing within project management journals. While such pluralism is beneficial to gain legitimacy outside the field of PM, there is a need for methodological rigour (Oyegoke, 2011). However, an explicit statement of the philosophical underpinnings is essential for achieving consistency and high rigour within the methodology applied in the field of PM.

It is important to notice that there seems to be an increase in a mutual acceptance of positivism and interpretivism from their proponents. The reasons may have been partly due to the need to address complexity within PM (for example, Cooke-Davies et al., 2007; Williams,

1999) and the calls for paradigmatic pluralism (Pellegrinelli, 2011; Söderlund, 2010). A way to overcome the dualism has been found in the paradigms of pragmatism and critical realism, which are more tolerant (pragmatism) or comprise influences from the two opposing paradigms (critical realism).

First, pragmatism means that the exact position on a positivism/interpretivism continuum is determined by the research question, which directs the methodological choices in order to gain best knowledge from the research (Saunders et al., 2012). Within pragmatism, there is an unquestioned co-existence of positivism and interpretivism. Pellegrini (2011) calls for pragmatism in PM research, but at the same time points out the need to contribute not only to the research community, but also to provide guidance for practitioners.

Second, critical realism is philosophically a more complex position that incorporates the need to critically evaluate objects to gain an understanding of social phenomena (Sayer, 1992). Elements from both positivist and interpretivist paradigms are thus integrated within critical realism. For research in PM, critical realism means that topics can be investigated more comprehensively by applying mixed methods when conducting research. Depending on the dominating paradigm within an area of PM, mixed methods may complement or vastly enhance knowledge by providing a novel research perspective. The practical application of mixed methods can take the form of different designs conducted concurrently or sequentially, while applying quantitative and qualitative methods equally, or emphasising one of them (Johnson and Onwuegbuzie, 2004).

Concerning axiology in PM research, there is a clear lack of studies which explicitly address it. However, there are two observations that can be made regarding this issue. First, the trend towards soft paradigms in PM (Pollack, 2007) indicates that values of the researcher start to play a larger role when interpreting social project phenomena. Therefore, it can become more important for interpretivist researchers to show methodological rigour and to illustrate how their values have been fruitfully applied for the generation of knowledge.

Second, the research field of PM is intertwined with industry associations such as the Project Management Institute (PMI) and the International Project Management Association (IPMA). Practitioners meet researchers at the conferences and some senior researchers act as advisors for PMI and IPMA. However, these interrelations makes the role of values more complex, since the bodies of knowledge from the project associations are themselves driven by their idiosyncratic values while emphasising positivist perspectives (Smyth and Morris, 2007). Thus, there might be occasions where the values of a particular researcher and an industry association clash. In such cases, influences of the researcher might be limited. However, potential tensions can also be sources for a fruitful dialogue and the development of the field of PM.

## The Value of Paradigms in the Doctoral Research Process

The previous sections have shown that paradigmatic considerations are extremely valuable for progressing science and enhancing knowledge in the particular field of research. To summarise, the explicit utilisation of paradigms has various benefits: allowing a fundamental categorisation of the research field, incorporating challenging viewpoints (paradigmatic pluralism), offering new conceptual perspectives when taking a different ontological perspective, and gaining legitimacy outside the field of PM.

For new doctoral students, considerations about paradigms are highly beneficial already for directing and gearing their research process from the very beginning. Doctoral students should not avoid the examination of philosophical stances and should rather consider them already when searching for a suitable research topic. This consideration means becoming familiar with the terminology, identifying predominant philosophical stances within the research area of interest and within their research community, and reflecting upon how they will fit in with their individual way of perceiving reality and knowledge.

Throughout the research process, paradigmatic considerations can be valuably applied by doctoral students. Taking as an example the different steps of the research process suggested by Collis and Hussey (2009), this section illustrates the potential benefits of utilising paradigm considerations. The first step starts with systematically screening the literature and collecting potential research topics. The common objective in this step is to identify research gaps within theory, which require a deeper investigation. The action that is mostly neglected by doctoral students in this initial step of the research process is a review of the philosophical foundations of the potential research area. Already in the early beginning of the research project, doctoral students can identify additional gaps by analysing philosophical considerations and making contributions by adding a diverging philosophical perspective on a paradigm-dominated research area.

The second step continues with a literature review, which is conducted in more detail for defining the research questions. Doctoral students can benefit from having a clear philosophical standpoint, which can help them to phrase questions appropriately and to sequence potential sub-studies (for example, in a paper-based dissertation). Pragmatism or critical realism can open avenues for research following paradigmatic pluralism and emergent research process, whereas being bound to positivism or interpretivism might exclude many methodological choices.

The third step concerns the research design and the specification of the methodology. Doctoral students need to choose the methodology corresponding to their paradigmatic stance, so that the methodology is in line with their philosophical assumptions (Collis and Hussey, 2009). Since these steps are usually addressed during the evaluation of a research proposal, it is essential to pay attention to these issues in order to achieve coherence, to get ethical clearance, and to consider feasibility based on the required skills, experiences, resources, data access and so on (Saunders et al., 2012). In this respect, doctoral students can benefit from a clear paradigmatic foundation.

The fourth step relates to the data analysis, which again has to be in line with the researcher's paradigm. In this step, the focus can be on axiology, specifying to what extent the values of the doctoral student will be applied within the interpretation of data in consistency with the underlying philosophical foundation.

The final step leads to writing up and to finalising the research project. Doctoral students need to be clear and consistent in what type of knowledge has been generated and in what way it is communicated. Some questions that need to be addressed in this step include the following examples: Is this research generalisable? Are the results transferable to some areas? Did we gain a deeper understanding of a complex phenomenon? Paradigms can provide a direction in the final step of the research process and can be used for developing suggestions for future research, which can complement or even contrast the current state of research, or even limit future studies to more specific areas.

Following the recent trends in PhD education, more doctoral students are opting for writing dissertations including multiple papers compared to dissertations written as monographs. For a dissertation consisting of multiple papers, consideration and utilisation of knowledge about paradigms provide additional benefits in directing, refocusing and outlining the different papers. Positions that allow paradigmatic pluralism, add flexibility and prove to be valuable for addressing the emergent character of subsequent papers based on the previous results. In this respect, some key factors may emerge that require a deeper investigation within the same paradigm or from an opposing paradigm.

Critical realism is one example of a paradigm that can offer additional value for a dissertation consisting of multiple papers. In critical realism, a scientific endeavour can be seen without having a clear end, since a phenomenon tends to be explained in an ever-deepening level with the deeper level itself becoming a new phenomenon (Patomäki and Wight, 2000). Patomäki and

Wight (2000) describe this notion as a constant spiral of discovery and understanding, further discovery, modification and even more precise understanding. In this respect, critical realism enables the investigation of the research topic by doctoral students by gaining comprehensiveness and precision, while having methodological flexibility.

The author's own experience of completing a dissertation including multiple papers (Biedenbach, 2011) illustrates how critical realism and philosophical considerations can steer the emergent nature of a comprehensive investigation. A paradigmatic review of the research field conducted in one paper, which is included in the doctoral dissertation, guided the author in completing another paper and making a theoretical contribution while applying mixed methods. An interesting thought concerning the spiral of discovery and understanding is that paradigmatic pluralism may broaden the research for a moment, before it will be narrowed down in a coherent sequence of research findings that build on each other.

To conclude, paradigms can serve as powerful facilitators for directing research towards significant contributions that progress the research field. For doctoral students during their doctoral research process, paradigmatic considerations can be extremely valuable for specifying the research topic, stating relevant research questions, selecting an appropriate methodology, sequencing subsequent studies, conducting a comprehensive investigation and generating results of high impact for the current state of research and practice. Doctoral students should feel encouraged to early on familiarise themselves with the philosophical terminology and consider paradigms as a challenging but rewarding inspiration, which might unfold many valuable opportunities during the research process.

## Tips and Exercises

### TIPS FOR STUDENTS

- Become familiar with the philosophical terminology and participate in a course on philosophy of science early within your doctoral studies.
- Paradigms can restrain your research strategy or open up for applying mixed methods. Be aware of the implications and take a perspective that is appropriate for your research process concerning time constraints, personal background and local research community.
- Throughout the entire research process keep the philosophical foundation in mind when selecting the methodology, interpreting the results, outlining future research avenues and in general contributing to knowledge in the field.

### TIPS FOR SUPERVISORS

- Engage doctoral students in philosophical discussions early in the process and encourage them to use the paradigm as a facilitator.
- Introduce the philosophical foundation of the particular research environment (local community and the partner institutions) and their historical origin.
- Encourage pragmatic pluralism and support the possible emergent character of subsequent studies with access to a support network based on experts within this paradigm, methodology and analysis technique.

## EXERCISES

1. Describe the philosophical assumptions which will underlie your research. Explain how these assumptions will affect your research strategy and methodology.
2. Explain the meaning of paradigmatic pluralism. Describe two paradigms which enable paradigmatic pluralism.
3. Discuss the advantages of considering the paradigm in the early stage of the research process. Exemplify how you are intending to use paradigms for directing your research process.

# References

Alvesson, M. and Sandberg, J. (2011). Generating research questions through problematization. *The Academy of Management Review*, 36(2), 247–271.

Biedenbach, T. (2011). Capabilities for frequent innovation: Managing the early project phases in the pharmaceutical R&D process. Doctoral dissertation, Umeå School of Business and Economics, Umeå University.

Biedenbach, T. and Müller, R. (2011). Paradigms in project management research: Examples from 15 years of IRNOP conferences. *International Journal of Managing Projects in Business*, 4(1), 82–104.

Bredillet, C. N. (2010). Blowing hot and cold on project management. *Project Management Journal*, 41(3), 4–20.

Bryman, A. and Bell, E. (2011). *Business Research Methods*. New York, NY: Oxford University Press.

Cicmil, S. and Hodgson, D. E. (2006). New possibilities for project management theory: A critical engagement. *Project Management Journal*, 37(3), 111–122.

Collis, J. and Hussey, R. (2009). *Business Research: A practical guide for undergraduate and postgraduate students*. Basingstoke, UK: Palgrave Macmillan.

Cooke-Davies, T., Cicmil, S., Crawford, L. and Richardson, K. (2007). We're not in Kansas anymore Toto: Mapping the strategic landscape of complexity theory, and its relationship to project management. *Project Management Journal*, 38(2), 50–61.

Creswell, J. W. (2007). *Qualitative Inquiry and Research Design* (2nd edition). Thousand Oaks, CA: Sage.

Engwall, M. (2003). No project is an island: Linking projects to history and context. *Research Policy*, 32(5), 789–808.

Gage, N. L. (1989). The paradigm wars and their aftermath: A 'historical' sketch of research on teaching since 1989. *Educational Researcher*, 18(7), 4–10.

Guba, E. G. (1990). 'The Alternative Paradigm Dialog' in E. G. Guba (ed.), *The Paradigm Dialogue*. Newbury Park, CA: Sage, pp. 17–30.

Guba, E. G. and Lincoln, Y. S. (1994). 'Competing Paradigms in Qualitative Research' in N. K. Denzin and Y. S. Lincoln (eds), *Handbook of Qualitative Research*. London, UK: Sage, pp. 105–117.

Hällgren, M. (2012). The construction of research questions in project management. *International Journal of Project Management*, 30(7), 804–816.

Howe, K. R. (1988). Against the quantitative-qualitative incompatibility thesis or dogmas die hard. *Educational Researcher*, 17(8), 10–16.

Johnson, R. B. and Onwuegbuzie, A. J. (2004). Mixed methods research: A research paradigm whose time has come. *Educational Researcher*, 33(7), 14–26.

Johnson, R. B., Onwuegbuzie, A. J. and Turner, L. A. (2007). Toward a definition of mixed methods research. *Journal of Mixed Methods Research*, 1(2), 112–133.

Kloppenberg, T. and Opfer, W. A. (2002). The current state of project management research: Trends, interpretations and predictions. *Project Management Journal*, 33(2), 5–19.

Kuhn, T. S. (1962). *The Structure of Scientific Revolutions*. Chicago, IL: University of Chicago Press.

Kwak, Y. H. and Anbari, F. T. (2009). Analyzing project management research: Perspectives from top management journals. *International Journal of Project Management*, 27(5), 435–446.

Lincoln, Y. S. and Guba, E. G. (2003). 'Paradigmatic Controversies, Contradictions, and Emerging Confluences' in N. K. Denzin and Y. S. Lincoln (eds), *The Landscape of Qualitative Research* (2nd edition). Thousand Oaks, CA: Sage, pp. 253–291.

Linehan, C. and Kavanagh, D. (2006). 'From Project Ontologies to Communities of Virtue' in D. Hodgson and S. Cicmil (eds), *Making Projects Critical*. New York, NY: Palgrave, pp. 51–67.

Lundin, R. A. and Söderholm, A. (1995). A theory of the temporary organization. *Scandinavian Journal of Management*, 11(4), 437–455.

Masterman, M. (1970). 'The Nature of a Paradigm' in I. Lakatos and A. Musgrave (eds), *Criticism and the Growth of Knowledge*. Cambridge, UK: Cambridge University Press, pp. 59–90.

Mingers, J. (2006). A critique of statistical modeling in management science from a critical realist perspective: Its role within multimethodology. *Journal of the Operational Research Society*, 57(2), 202–219.

Morgan, D. L. (2007). Paradigms lost and pragmatism regained: Methodological implications of combining qualitative and quantitative methods. *Journal of Mixed Methods Research*, 1(1), 48–76.

Oyegoke, A. (2011). The constructive research approach in project management research. *International Journal of Managing Projects in Business*, 4(4), 573–595.

Patomäki, H. and Wight, C. (2000). After postpositivism? The promises of critical realism. *International Studies Quarterly*, 44(2), 213–237.

Pellegrinelli, S. (2011). What's in a name: Project or programme? *International Journal of Project Management*, 29(2), 232–240.

Pollack, J. (2007). The changing paradigms of project management. *International Journal of Project Management*, 25(3), 266–274.

Sandberg, J. and Alvesson, M. (2011). Ways of constructing research questions: Gap-spotting or problematization? *Organization*, 18(1), 23–44.

Saunders, M., Lewis, P. and Thornhill, A. (2012). *Research Methods for Business Students*. Harlow: Pearson.

Sayer, A. (1992). *Method in Social Science: A realist approach* (2nd edition). London, UK: Routledge.

Smyth, H. J. and Morris, P. W. G. (2007). An epistemological evaluation of research into projects and their management: Methodological issues. *International Journal of Project Management*, 25(4), 423–436.

Söderlund, J. (2004). Building theories of project management: Past research, questions for the future. *International Journal of Project Management*, 22(3), 183–191.

Söderlund, J. (2010). Pluralism in project management: Navigating the crossroads of specialization and fragmentation. *International Journal of Management Reviews*, 13(2), 153–176.

Teddlie, C. and Tashakkori, A. (2009). *Foundations of Mixed Methods Research*. Thousand Oaks, CA: Sage.

Themistocleous, G. and Waerne, S. H. (2000). Project management topic coverage in journals. *International Journal of Project Management*, 18(2), 7–11.

Williams, T. M. (1999). The need for new paradigms for complex projects. *International Journal of Project Management*, 17(5), 269–273.

Winter, M., Smith, C., Morris, P. and Cicmil, S. (2006). Directions for future research in project management: The main findings of a UK government-funded research network. *International Journal of Project Management*, 24(8), 638–649.

# 4

# Finding a Way in Broceliande Forest: The Magic Domain of Project Management Research

Christophe N. Bredillet

*I wanted to offer a chapter in order to suggest some assumption-challenging perspectives that contrast to the dominant paradigm supporting doctoral studies leading usually to nice research but with little impact to organisation life.*

This chapter examines the challenges PM research faces in order to meet the expectations of practice. The place of projects in global economy, the consequences of uncertainty and complexity of the environment, the failure of rationalist project approaches to deliver expected benefits, both with regards to Practice and Theory, lead us to consider a praxeological style of reasoning balancing both modernism and post (or pre)-modernism approaches and so-called kaleidoscopic and pluralistic perspectives. Building on the example of PM schools of thought, three main aspects for research are discussed (non- (or post) paradigmatic PM science; ontological argument about the existence of projects and their management; and the relationship Theory–Practice). An emancipatory methodology for praxeological inquiry is then suggested.

At the end of this chapter, the reader can:

* understand the need for thinking that goes beyond the rationalist 'box';
* move beyond the dichotomy between social and natural science approaches in suggesting a balanced praxeological style of reasoning;
* recognise the key tenets of reflexive praxeological inquiry.

Keywords: praxeology, style of reasoning, Aristotelian philosophy, schools of thought, paradigm, ontology, epistemology, Theory–Practice

## The Context of Project Management Research

For the past 60 years, organisations have increasingly been using projects and management of, by and for projects – below PM – to achieve their strategic objectives (Morris and Jamieson, 2004;

Morris and Geraldi, 2011; Geraldi and Teerikangas, 2011). PM makes an important and significant contribution to value creation globally. For instance, World Bank data[1] indicate that 22 per cent of the world's $48 trillion gross domestic product is gross capital formation.

However, the 'glocal' context in which projects are performed shows increasing volatility, uncertainty, complexity, and ambiguity ('VUCA') affecting organisations and the socio-economic environment, described as 'Chaordic' (Hock, 1995), within which they operate (Gareis, 2005). Two main dimensions are considered in research: uncertainty, and its two dimensions: volatility and ambiguity, and complexity.

Because action takes place over time, and because the future is unknowable, action is inherently uncertain (Aristotle, 1926, 1357a; Von Mises, 1949). Acts involve time, irreversibility, indetermination and contingence, uncertainty and therefore risk. Many authors (for example, recently Winch and Maytorena, 2011; Sanderson, 2012) refer to Knight (1921) (external environment, asymmetric information and related market perspective) (on Knight see, for example, Jarvis, 2010) and to Keynes (known unknowns: '... there is no scientific basis on which to form any calculable probability whatever. We simply do not know' (Keynes, 1937: pp. 113–114)) (on Keynes see, for example, Dow, 1995). Volatility, as rate and unpredictability of change in an environment over time which creates uncertainty about future conditions, and Ambiguity, as degree of uncertainty inherent in perceptions of the environmental state irrespective of its change over time, are therefore two dimensions of Uncertainty (Carson, Madhok and Wu, 2006: p. 1059).

Management situations (here both Practice and Research) are complex systems in the way they involve interdependence and connections between actors, 'objects' and the context. Drawing on Complexity Science, Andriani and McKelvey (2007, 2009), Boisot and McKelvey (2010) and McKelvey and Boisot (2009), and have demonstrated how the Gaussian (atomistic ontology) and the Paretian (connectionist ontology) worlds are linked through scalable free patterns and power law distributed phenomena rooted: (1) on adaptive tension between the internal variety of a system and the variety external solicitation; and (2) on connectivity and interdependency in social phenomena. In this context, systems are fluctuating between edge or order and edge of chaos of the Ashby Space. Drawing on Ashby's law of requisite variety (1958), the Ashby Space is defined by a vertical axis measuring the variety of external stimuli imposed on a system, and the horizontal axis measuring the variety of responses of the system. The gap to be filled between the two, in order for the system to preserve its integrity and survive, leads to the emergence of adaptive tension.

Thus, the uncertainty and complexity leads to an increased variety of stimuli from the organisational and socio-economic environment (Practice) to PM research (Theory), and to adaptive tension between the variety of stimuli and the variety of response provided by research (and conversely).

Developing efficient and effective response involves moving beyond the traditional dichotomy between modernism and postmodernism. Many have questioned the rationalist, positivist and quantitative tradition and paradigm supporting PM research and practice (Bredillet, 2010) and the lack of relevance to practice of the current conceptual base of PM, despite the sum of research, development of standards, best practices and the related development PM 'Bodies of Knowledge' (for example, Kreiner, 1995; Packendorff, 1995; Cicmil and Hodgson, 2006; Hodgson and Cicmil, 2007; Winter, Smith, Morris and Cicmil, 2006).

Borrowing from both Hodgson (2002) and Giddens (1993), we could say that 'those who expect a "social-scientific Newton" to revolutionize this young field "are not only waiting for a

---

[1]   From World Bank Indicators website: http://data.worldbank.org/indicator/NE.GDI.TOTL.ZS accessed on 31 March 2012.

train that will not arrive, but are in the wrong station altogether'" (Hodgson, 2002: p. 809; Giddens, 1993: p. 18).

This questioning mirror similar one made within Social Sciences (for example, Say, 1964; Koontz, 1980; Menger, 1985; Warry, 1992; Rothbard, 1997; Tsoukas and Cummings, 1997; Flyvbjerg, 2001; Boisot and McKelvey, 2010), calling for new thinking. In order to get outside the rationalist 'box', Toulmin (1990) suggest number of possible paths, summarising the thoughts of many authors:

> It can cling to the discredited research program of the purely theoretical (i.e. 'modern') philosophy, which will end up by driving it out of business: it can look for new and less exclusively theoretical ways of working, and develop the methods needed for a more practical ('post-modern') agenda; or it can return to its pre-17$^{th}$ century traditions, and try to recover the lost ('pre-modern') topics that were side-tracked by Descartes, but can be usefully taken up for the future. (Toulmin, 1990: p. 11)

Paradoxically and interestingly, in their quest for the so-called postmodernism, many authors build on 'pre-modern' philosophies such as the Aristotelian one (for example, MacIntyre, 1985; Tsoukas and Cummings, 1997; Flyvbjerg, 2001; Blomquist, Hällgren, Nilsson and Söderholm, 2010; Lalonde, Bourgault and Findeli, 2012). And authors such as Boisot and McKelvey (2010) suggest approaches to integrate the two philosophies.

As Hodgson and Cicmil (2007) note, the question to be considered should be, 'What do we do when we call something "a project"' rather than, 'What is a project?' (Hodgson and Cicmil, 2007: p. 432). The first question refers to 'action' – post(pre)-modernist perspective – although the second refers to 'discipline' – modernist perspective – meaning both 'body of knowledge and expertise underpinning the field' and 'a system of training and (self-)control' (Hodgson, 2002: p. 804). Interestingly the distinction made by the two questions enables the link between 'project' (situation[2] (Dewey, 1938)) and 'project management' (acting) to be clarified, and, in the coming development about the concept of project, the discussion will address both aspects in an Aristotelian perspective (Tsoukas and Cummings, 1997).

On the one hand, classifications of phenomena governed by a tradition of natural sciences, rationality, universality, objective reality and value-free decision making (Cicmil and Hodgson, 2006) exemplify the development of 'Standards' and 'Bodies of Knowledge'. On the other hand 'the organizational reality, which is often messy, ambiguous, fragmented and political in character' (Alvesson and Deetz, 2000: p. 60) leads to the quest of *Verstehen* – 'the intuitive quickness of enlightened understanding' (Schütz, 1964: p. 4). This can be related to the notion of relevance by feasibility (Le Moigne, 2007: p. 117), and *Ingenium* – 'an "intelligent" action, "Ingenium," this mental faculty which makes possible to connect in a fast, suitable and happy way the separate things' as stated by Le Moigne (2007: p. 118), quoting Vico (1708).

## Some Implications for Research

As said above, following Andriani and McKelvey (2007, 2009) and Boisot and McKelvey (2010), the PM field needs to be complex in order to respond, via adaptive tension, to the variety of stimuli. This is reflective of the outcomes of research studies that call for new and pluralistic perspectives for PM (for example, Williams, 2002; Söderlund, 2004; Maylor, 2006; Hodgson and Cicmil, 2006; Cooke-Davies, Cicmil, Crawford and Richardson, 2007; Leybourne, 2007). To quote Söderlund

---

2    Dewey (1938) specifies that a situation 'is not a single object or event or set of objects and events. For we never experience nor form judgments about objects and events in isolation, but only in connection with a contextual whole. This latter is what is called a "situation"' (Dewey, 1938: p. 66).

(2011: p. 153), it is not easy to handle the pluralism (Knudsen, 2003: p. 271) offered by the field and to navigate between specialisation and fragmentation.

> *In the absence of unambiguous foundational truth in the social sciences, the only sensible way forward can be conscious pluralism. (Pettigrew, 2001: p. S62)*

The development of middle-range theories (Merton, 1949), 'petits récits' (Lyotard, 1984) or middle-level theorising (Gell-Mann, 2002) – conventions or patterns in this work – is the privileged goal of such inquiry. The researcher needs to act (to do research) and to learn (from this research) and create some 'configuration of order', or patterns, in order to provide meaningful contribution while coping with the complexity of the domain. Pluralism involves recognising that past and concurrent events and situations contain a number of discrete fragments – patterns shaped by contingencies, not a collective and cumulative learning process (Foucault, 1966). Moving diachronically and synchronically from one period ('thought-cum-practice', one form of pattern) to another involves to 'twist the kaleidoscope' and create a new pattern (Tsoukas and Cummings, 1997: p. 663). The roots of these 'configurations of order', patterns, meta-structures and categories can be found, whatever the research method employed (quantitative, quantitative, mixed...), in what Le Moigne (2003) proposes: acting and learning in complex situations involves 'modelling to understand' that is, to do ingeniously.

As Piaget observed, 'intelligence organizes the world by organizing itself' (quoted in von Glaserfeld, 1984: p. 24). Following this reasoning, Tsoukas and Hatch (2001) recommend to use a narrative approach to the PM complex field that is to explore complex ways of thinking about PM field-as complex system, a 'second order complexity approach' where the observer, here the researcher, is part of the system (Tsoukas and Hatch, 2001: p. 979). Recognising patterns, meta-structures and categories and their key characteristics is of primary importance for the relevance of research and therefore to the scientific and practical contribution to field. Once again, there is no 'one best way' of structuring the field this, but rather a matter of *Verstehen* or *Ingenium*!

In this context, authors have shown the need to adopt alternative challenging assumptions stance (Alvesson and Sandberg, 2013) and styles of reasoning (Hacking, 2002a: p. 159–177) based on contextualised and situational perspectives including the social dimension and the practice and acting dimension (for example, Packendorff, 1995; Cicmil and Hodgson, 2006; Hodgson and Cicmil, 2007; Lalonde et al., 2012). I would like to offer the three following interrelated aspects for research:

- non- (or post-) paradigmatic PM science;
- ontological argument about the existence of projects and their management;
- Relationship Theory–Practice; and suggest a way towards a praxeological style of reasoning.

## The Non-Paradigmatic Nature of the Project Management Field

The question 'Has anyone found a paradigm out there?' has been raised (Bredillet, 2010: p. 6) and is particularly relevant with regards to pluralistic perspective.

Discussing paradigms in the Social Sciences, Dogan (2001) addresses the question: 'Is scientific progress in the social sciences achieved mostly by steady accretion or mostly by abrupt jumps?' He then summarises Kuhn's view point:

> *For Thomas Kuhn, who devised the concept 'paradigm,' there are no paradigmatic upheavals in the social sciences. For him the use of this term in these sciences is not justified. Three arguments can be advanced against its polysemic use or abuse. In contrast with the universal truth in the natural sciences, contextual*

*diversity and social change are two important parameters in all social sciences. In political science, sociology, and economics, progress is achieved by cumulative knowledge, by the adding of successive layers of sediments. The third argument is the pattern of mutual ignorance among great social scientists. In the social sciences, theoretical and methodological disagreements are beneficial to the advance of knowledge. (Dogan, 2001: p. 11023)*

Flyvbjerg (2001) suggests that social sciences should focus on what he describes a 'non-paradigmatic' phronetic social science (for example, Van de Ven and Johnson, 2006: p. 805). Schram (2004), commenting Flyvbjerg position, puts forward the use of 'post-paradigmatic' science – 'post' meaning carry on 'but differently' – emphasising 'the aspiration to move beyond a situation where such a hegemonic approach is imposed on the discipline' (Schram, 2004: p. 432–433).

## Ontological Argument about the Existence of Projects and Their Management

While acknowledging a pluralistic view of the project world, and somehow regardless of this view, we can state that as soon as we name a situation 'project' we create it. But naming alone ('say') is never enough and 'for a name to begin to do its creative work, it needs authority. One needs usage within institutions. Naming does its work only as a social history works itself out' (Hacking, 2002b: p. 8). Objects and subjects come into 'being' while 'becoming' (the notion of 'historical ontology' in Foucault, 1982: p. 66; Hacking, 2002c). The distinction made between the ontology of 'being', related to the traditional rationalist paradigm, and the ontology of 'becoming', related to projects, project situations as shaped by human actions in interactions and PM, is therefore clear. However, I consider that these two perspectives should not been seen as a dichotomy or incommensurable.

The reason is that actors, practices and their contexts are located in a physical world and involve, therefore, a certain degree of materiality. But in the meantime, the physical world is informed and transformed by the choice, deliberations, values and politics of actors (for example, 'experience-distant' and 'experience-near' concepts, Geertz, 1987; 's'O'bjectivism', Pouliot, 2007: p. 359; 'real' and 'preferable', Lalonde et al., 2012: p. 428). As Bourdieu explains, both perspectives and related forms of knowledge 'are equally indispensable to a science of the social world that cannot be reduced either to a social phenomenology or to a social physics' (Bourdieu, 1990: p. 25). Thus I propose an alternative style of reasoning embracing the continuum ontological perspective both to Parmenidean 'being' and Heraclitean 'becoming'. I have no intention to separate judgment, wisdom and deliberation from scientific method. I argue that, in project situations, knowledge creation and production have to integrate both classical scientific aspects and 'fuzzy' or symbolic aspects (Bredillet, 2004a, 2004b; Boisot and McKelvey, 2010).

## Beyond the Theory–Practice Gap

The links and the gaps between Practice and Theory(ies) and their relation to knowledge production and transfer, and to the rigour and relevance argument, is strongly anchored in the role dichotomy between scholars versus managers/workers.

'Scholarly work and managerial work differ, however, in the context, processes, and purposes of their practices' (Aram and Salipante, 2003: p. 1900; Van de Ven and Johnson, 2006: p. 806).

In order to challenge the dominant mechanistic-cum-rationalistic assumptions, some authors suggest an alternate such as historical-cum-comparative thinking (Tsoukas and Cummings, 1997: p. 673; Knorr-Cerina, 1981: p. 336),

> We argue that reconnecting organizational and management research with systems of thought other
> than those traditionally associated with the 'discipline', and adopting a 'kaleidoscopic' view of history, can
> enable researchers to think differently about key issues and inform future development. (Tsoukas and
> Cummings, 1997: p. 657)

The assumptions about the roles, behaviours and expectations of the people, as framed by the classical classes' dichotomy, involved in knowledge creation and transfer, is at the centre of the Theory–Practice relevance and rigour debate.

Kondrat (1992) claims:

> The roots of both science and practice are to be found in the everyday processes and achievements of
> human beings who seek to manage [techne] their world and to orient their action [praxis] in relation to
> others in that world. (Kondrat, 1992: p. 243)

While Van de Ven and Johnson (2006) stipulate:

> We agree with Hodgkinson et al. (2001) and Pettigrew (2001) that research needs to achieve the dual
> objectives of applied use and advancing fundamental understanding. (Van de Ven and Johnson, 2006:
> p. 803)

In order to address this burning question of rigour and relevance, some authors have pleaded for some kind of junction or integration between the 'scholars–experts–researchers' and the 'managers/workers–practitioners–participants' (for example, social science practitioner (Warry, 1992: p. 160); engaged scholars (Van de Ven and Johnson, 2006: p. 803); 's'O'bjectivim' style of reasoning (Pouliot, 2007: p. 360); 'practitioners in the context of project-as-praxis' (Blomquist et al., 2010: p. 13); practitioner–researcher (Jarvis, 1999), and researcher–practitioner (Lalonde et al. 2012: note 8; p. 429).

I suggest we need to go further in-depth to fully grasp the importance of moving to consider one single class of actors in project situations. Hacking (2002b), while reflecting about classifications posits that:

> The human and the social sciences do not differ from natural ones primarily because they deal in what
> are called social constructions, or because they require 'Verstehen' rather than explanation, prediction
> and control. They differ because there is a dynamical interaction between the classifications developed in
> the social sciences, and the individuals or behaviour classified. (Hacking, 2002b: p. 10)

He develops the idea of 'interactive classifications' (Hacking, 2002b) and 'looping effects' (Hacking, 1995) about 'how classification affect us and how we create new classes anew' (Hacking, 2002b: p. 12).

As consequence, moving from the two classes dichotomy 'scholars–experts–researchers' and the 'managers/workers–practitioners–participants' to one single class 'practitioners' – I should say 'praXitioner' – is all but neutral, with regards to a praxeological style of reasoning (Fleck, 1979; Hacking, 2002b: p. 3) and to go beyond the Theory–Practice gap.

## Conclusion: Towards a Praxeological Style of Reasoning

I argue that this move away from the current dichotomy may contribute to create new perspectives through new class and open up new ways to think and act in project situations. Warry (1992) offers an appropriate view, well aligned with the balanced praxeological style of reasoning I advocate and with regards to the mediating role of praxis and phronesis:

> Gadamer's observation that understanding and interpretation must be integrated into the 'moment' of application is critical (Gadamer, 1975: p. 273–274; see also Bernstein, 1985: p. 159). Praxis, as a particular form of activity, can serve as a focal point through which the discursive testing of theory is grounded through decision making and experience (Habermas, 1973: p. 20). Simply stated, praxis can serve as a common ground for those interested in basic and applied research by providing knowledge of the reality in which action, informed by theory takes place. (Warry, 1992: p. 156)

Praxis and phronesis, in their mediating role serve as focal point (Habermas, 1973: p. 20) between the logico-scientific and the narrative mode, and have been recognised as 'emancipatory' (Habermas, 1971: p. 314; Gadamer, 1975), and offering 'a way of reflecting on disjuncture between the formal rationality and the substantive rationality' (Kondrat, 1992: p. 253). PM authors such as Cicmil and Hodgson (quoting Balck, 1994: p. 2 in Cicmil and Hodgson, 2006: p. 13), Blomquist et al. (2010: p. 9) and Lalonde et al. (2012: p. 428) have acknowledged a similar view.

This mediating role is specially to be considered in praxeological inquiries of phase transition situations where effects are scalable (Boisoit and McKelvey, 2010: p. 422) located in complex regime area of the Ashby Space, between 'edge of order' and 'edge of chaos' (Nicolis and Prigogine, 1989), in the 'melting zone' (Kauffmann, 1993) and state of 'self-organized criticality' (Bak, 1996).

If I had to define in one word the essence of praxeological inquiry methodology, I would say 'serendipity'. As Merton conceptualised a then little-known term in 1945, serendipity is 'the discovery, by chance or sagacity, of valid results which were not sought for' (Merton, 1945: p. 469). Of course, praxeological inquiry can rest on some key features, as I suggest below. However, in doing so, I am not looking at being exhaustive, a vain endeavour which would ultimately contradict the inherent unlimited creative nature of human spirit.

Improvisation and bricolage are inherent to the process of research (Garfinkel, Lynch and Livingston, 1981; Latour, 1986, Knorr-Cetina and Amann, 1990; Boxenbaum and Rouleau, 2011). As noticed by Van de Ven and Johnson (2006), 'Both practitioners and scientists engage in what Levi-Strauss (1966) termed bricolage, improvising with a mixed bag of tools and tacit knowledge to adapt to the task at hand' (p. 806). Improvisation is related to how thoughts and response are developed in partly novel situations. Mentioning Ryle (1979: p. 125), Leybourne advises that 'the vast majority of things that happen [are] unprecedented, unpredictable, and never to be repeated,' and that 'the things we say and do ... cannot be completely pre-arranged' (Leybourne, 2010: p. 18). Bricolage refers to 'an assembly of readily available elements' (Boxenbaum and Rouleau, 2011: p. 278), 'to make do with those materials that area available'. (Leybourne, 2010: p. 18). As Leybourne rightly states, 'Bricolage can, of course, also occur in nonimprovisational contexts, and not all improvisation will involve bricolage' (Leybourne, 2010: p. 18). The praXitioner is a 'bricoleur' – a 'flexible and responsive' agent willing 'to deploy whatever research strategies, methods or empirical materials are at hand, to get the job done' (Denzin and Lincoln, 1994: p. 2). Boxenbaum and Rouleau (2011), discussing what they name 'epistemic script of bricolage', specify:

> The researcher acts as a handyperson who, rather than inventing a new theory or new paradigm, repairs or remodels existing theories by combining various theoretical concepts, ideas, and observations at his or her immediate disposal. Components are selected based on contextual factors, such as local constraints on knowledge production, practical value, and their potential for generating novel insights. (Boxenbaum and Rouleau, 2011: p. 281)

The diversity and variety of situations, and the very nature of human beings acting, involve a non-paradigmatic (other would say post-paradigmatic) perspective. There is no preferred methodology or methods supporting a praxeological inquiry; but rather a place for *ingenium*, intelligent action and moral reasoning. 'The substance of moral reasoning is an interpretation of traditional beliefs and commitments applied to concrete problems of the present' (McGee, 2001: p. 12). 'Phronesis gained from hermeneutical reflection has nothing to do with domination, but rather with willing subordination' (McGee, 2001: p. 13). Hermeneutics, in the sphere of the discourse, is not knowledge as domination, but knowledge as interpretations, including application, as a form of service of what is considered as 'good' and valid (Gadamer, 1975: p. 278 in McGee, 2001). Emancipation comes, therefore, from a praxeological inquiry resting on transformative and operative hermeneutics of the Book of the World.

Some tenets on the praxeological inquiry, the following 'guidelines' may be suggested. Of course, there is no 'one best way' in this matter but rather a matter of 'ingenium' and wisdom, and many authors (for example, Pascal and Bertram, 2012: p. 7), in particular some quoted in this work, propose some invaluable approaches.

Here are the four key points to be considered:

1. Addressing a big question or research problem embedded in the Real World (Flyvbjerg, 2004: p. 295; Van de Ven and Johnson, 2006: p. 810). The research problem and related question is based on specific empirical situation, practice and focuses on concrete phenomena (Czarniawska, 1993; Lalonde et al., 2012: p. 429);

2. Scoping of the research project as a collaborative and engaged acting and knowing community within a social site. Trust and adoption of a behaviour fostering emancipation, consciousness, active and positive praxis should be promoted. (Brown and Duguid, 1991; Van de Ven, 2000; Aram and Salipante, 2003; Schatzki, 2005: p. 473; Van de Ven and Johnson, 2006: p. 811; Blomquist et al., 2010: p. 13; Lalonde et al., 2012: p. 429);

3. Designing the research in order to enable a multiple perspective inquiry process. Bottom-up research, choose an appropriate duration, select methods to obtain empirical evidence, focus on values, power, 'little things', consider practices and discourses, study cases in context, do narrative... (Packendorff, 1995: p. 329; Czarniawska and Sevon, 1996; Flyvbjerg, 2004: p. 295; Chia and Holt, 2006: p. 644; Van de Ven and Johnson, 2006: p. 812–813; Whittington, 2006: p. 623–627; Pouliot, 2007: p. 368–374);

4. Enabling application, dissemination of the research findings and reflection (second and third level of learning, Bateson, 1973) about the roles of the participants, assumptions, models, theories and philosophical stance (Czarniawska and Sevon, 1996; Van de Ven, 2000; Aram and Salipante, 2003; Flyvbjerg, 2004: p. 290; Van de Ven and Johnson, 2006: p. 810, 814; Pouliot, 2007: p. 372; Lalonde et al., 2012: p. 429).

Praxeological inquiry shows important strengths. It clearly shows way to improve practice and who takes the responsibility. It supports collaborative acting and knowing, and makes transparent the ethical dimension, power games and values, and what should be done to improve a situation. Furthermore, because it is grounded in the real world, it is a credible and useful approach. The main weakness, according to the tenants of positivism and natural sciences, is the focus of the particular, on unique or extreme events. Moreover, it doesn't address causal relationships and doesn't lead to predictions or comparisons. Lastly, the apparent lack of rigour, in a world of statistical fallacy, may lead to some defiance from the decision-makers (Leguérinel, 2007: p. 17; Pascal and Bertram, 2012: p. 19) so deeply anchored in 'functional stupidity' (Alvesson and Spicer, 2012).

## Tips and Exercises

TIPS FOR STUDENTS

- This chapter is not for the faint-hearted. Paralleling Tsoukas and Cummings (1997: p. 655), I suggest focusing on an assumption challenging rather than gap-spotting view of research (Alvesson and Sandberg, 2013), and making sure to relate three key aspects, covering the ontological, epistemological and praxeological dimensions of the PM 'discipline' in action.
- Projects are ontologically 'becoming' realities shaped by human actions, not something 'being' given. However, this doesn't preclude to investigate 'general patterns' or dynamic configurations transcending specific situations.
- Research approaches should be appropriate for generating contributions that matter to both Theory and Practice with regards to what a 'project' is or to what do we do when we call a specific situation 'a project' and free themselves from any 'hegemonic' disciplinary paradigm.
- Special attention should be paid to reconciling rigour – relevance and Theory–Practice. Close relationship with the practice (and the practitioners) and becoming 'native' of the project situation (for example, action research) offer unique opportunities to move beyond the dichotomy scholars versus practitioners, and close the above-mentioned gaps.

TIPS FOR SUPERVISORS

- Direct students to read papers on philosophy of science and make them reflect on them in order to facilitate the praxis of Bateson's 'level 3 learning'. Encourage them to understand the art of transformational research (change the framework of contextualised learning and acting experience).
- Support students in clarifying their research particular contexts and situations, and link to relevant set of pluralistic rich perspectives. Suggest, for example, the value of narratives and rich case studies.
- Develop the sense of engaged scholarship, deliberation and arbitrage with regards to contextual and situational praxeological inquiry.

EXERCISES

1. There are more than 100 references in this chapter – more than any other in this book. Take some time right now to slowly review and consider each citation. How could they support your research?
2. Look up the following references and email your supervisor with an explanation of their meaning and relevance to your work (including why they might not be), Alvesson and Sandberg (2013), Hodgson (2002) and Leybourne (2007).
3. Create a small study group with colleagues and present your interpretations of issues in this chapter that are especially meaningful to you.

## References

Alvesson, M. and Deetz, S. (2000). *Doing Critical Management Research*. London, UK: Sage.

Alvesson, M. and Spicer, A. (2012). A stupidity-based theory of organizations. *Journal of Management Studies*, 49(7), 1194–1220.

Alvesson, M. and Sandberg, J. (2013). Has management studies lost its way? Ideas for more imaginative and innovative research. *Journal of Management Studies*, 30(1), 128–151.

Andriani, P. and McKelvey, B. (2007). Beyond Gaussian averages: Redirecting organization science toward extreme events and power laws. *Journal of International Business Studies*, 38(2), 1212–1230.

Andriani, P. and McKelvey, B. (2009). From Gaussian to Paretian thinking: Causes and implications of power laws in organizations. *Organization Science*, 20(6), 1053–1071.

Aram, J. D. and Salipante, P. F., Jr. (2003). Bridging scholarship in management: Epistemological reflections. *British Journal of Management*, 14(3), 189–205.

Aristotle (1926). *On Rhetoric. A theory of civic discourse*. J. H. Freese (ed.). Retrieved from http://www.perseus. tufts.edu/hopper/text?doc=Aristot.+Rh.+1.1.1&redirect=true). Accessed: 27/08/2014.

Ashby, W. (1958). Requisite variety and implications for control of complex systems. *Cybernetica*, 1(2), 83–99.

Bak, P. (1996). *How Nature Works: The science of self-organized criticality*. New York, NY: Copernicus.

Balck, H. (1994). 'Projects as Elements of a New Industrial Pattern: A Division of Project Management' in D.I. Cleland and R. Gareis (eds), *Global Project Management Handbook*. New York, NY: McGraw-Hill International Editions, pp. 2–11.

Bateson, G. (1973). *Steps to an Ecology of Mind*. St Albans, UK: Paladin Books.

Bernstein, R. J. (ed.) (1985). *Habermas and Modernity*. Cambridge, MA: MIT Press. BoK, Sissela.

Gadamer, H-G. (1975). *Truth and Method*. G. Barden and J. Cumming (trs). New York, NY: Seabury.

Blomquist, T., Hällgren, M., Nilsson, A. and Söderholm, A. (2010). Project-as-practice: In search of project management research that matters. *Project Management Journal*, 41(1), 5–16.

Boisot, M. and McKelvey, B. (2010). Integrating modernist and postmodernist perspectives on organizations: A complexity science bridge. *Academy of Management Review*, 35(3), 415–433.

Bourdieu, P. (1990). *The Logic of Practice*, R. Nice (tr). Stanford, CA: Stanford University Press.

Boxenbaum, E. and Rouleau, L. (2011). New knowledge products as bricolage: Metaphors and scripts in organizational theory. *Academy of Management Review*, 36(2), 272–296.

Bredillet, C. N. (2004a). Theories and research in project management: Critical review and return to the future. Unpublished doctoral thesis, Lille School of Management (ESC Lille), France.

Bredillet, C. N. (2004b). Beyond the positivist mirror: Towards a project management 'gnosis'. *Proceedings of IRNOP VI*, Turku, Finland.

Bredillet, C. N. (2010). Blowing hot and cold on project management. *Project Management Journal*, 41(3), 4–20.

Brown, J. S. and Duguid, P. (1991). Organizational learning and communities of practice: Toward a unified view of working, learning and innovation. *Organization Science*, 2(1), 40–57.

Carson, S. J., Madhok, A. and Wu, T. (2006). Uncertainty, opportunism, and governance: The effects of volatility and ambiguity on formal and relational contracting. *Academy of Management Journal*, 49(5), 1058–1077.

Chia, R. and Holt, R. (2006). Strategy as practical coping: A Heideggerian perspective. *Organization Studies*, 27(5), 635–655.

Cicmil, S. and Hodgson, D (2006). 'Making Projects Critical: An Introduction' in D. Hodgson and S. Cicmil (eds), *Making Projects Critical*, Management, Work and Organisations series. Basingstoke, UK, and New York, NY: Palgrave Macmillan, pp. 1–25.

Cooke-Davies, T., Cicmil, S., Crawford, L. and Richardson, K. (2007). We're not in Kansas anymore Toto: Mapping the strange landscape of complexity theory, and its relationship to project management. *Project Management Journal*, 8(2), 50–61.

Czarniawska, B. (1993). *The Three Dimensional Organization: A constructionist view*. Lund: Studentlitteratur.

Czarniawska, B. and Sevon, G. (eds) (1996). *Translating Organizational Change*. Berlin, Germany: De Gruyter.

Denzin, N. K. and Lincoln, Y. S. (1994). *Handbook of Qualitative Research*. Thousand Oaks, CA, and London, UK: Sage.

Dewey, J. (1938). *Logic. The Theory of Inquiry*. New York, NY: Henry Holt and Company.

Dogan, M. (2001). *Paradigms in the Social Sciences.* International Encyclopedia of the Social & Behavioral Sciences, pp. 11023–11027. Retrieved from http://dx.doi.org/10.1016/B0-08-043076-7/00782-8. Accessed: 27/08/2014.

Dow, S., 1995. 'Uncertainty about Uncertainty' in Dow, S. and Hillard, J. (eds), *Keynes, Knowledge and Uncertainty.* Aldershot, UK: Edward Elgar, pp. 117–127.

Fleck, L. (1979). *Genesis and Development of a Scientific Fact,* T. J. Trenn (ed.) and R. K. Merton (tr.). F. Bradley and T. J. Trenn, foreword by T. S. Kuhn. Chicago, IL: Chicago University Press.

Flyvbjerg, B. (2001). *Making Social Science Matter: Why social inquiry fails and how it can succeed again,* S. Sampson (tr.). Cambridge, UK: Cambridge University Press.

Flyvbjerg, B. (2004). Phronetic planning research: Theoretical and methodological reflections. *Planning Theory & Practices,* 5(3), 283–306.

Foucault, M. (1966). *The Order of Things: An archaeology of the humanities.* London, UK: Tavistock/Routledge.

Foucault, M. (1982). 'Afterword: The Subject and Power' in L. Dreyfus and P. Rabinow (eds), *Michel Foucault: Beyond structuralism and hermeneutics,* 2nd edition. Chicago, IL: The University of Chicago Press.

Gadamer, H-G. (1975). *Truth and Method,* G. Barden and J. Cumming (trs.). New York, NY: Seabury.

Gareis, R. (2005). *Happy Projects!* Vienna, Austria: Manz.

Garfinkel, H., Lynch, M. and Livingston, E. (1981). The work of a discovering science construed with materials from the optically discovered pulsar. *Philosophy of the Social Sciences,* 11(2), 131–158.

Geertz, C. (1987). 'From the Native's Point of View: On the Nature of Anthropological Understanding' in M.T. Gibbons (ed.), *Interpreting Politics.* London, UK: Blackwell.

Gell-Mann, M. (2002). 'What is Complexity?' in A. Q. Curzio and M. Fortis (eds), *Complexity and Industrial Clusters.* Heidelberg: Physica-Verlag, pp. 13–24.

Geraldi, J. and Teerikangas, S. (2011). From project management to managing by projects: Learning from the management of M&As. *Proceedings of the IRNOP 2011 Conference,* Montréal.

Giddens, A. (1993). *New Rules of Sociological Method.* Cambridge: Polity Press.

Habermas, J. (1971). *Knowledge and Human Interests,* J. J. Shapiro (tr.). Boston, MA: Beacon.

Habermas, J. (1973). *Theory and Practice,* J. Viertel (tr.). Boston, MA: Beacon Press.

Hacking, I. (1995). 'The Looping Effects of Human Kinds' in D. Sperber, D. Premack and A. Premack (eds), *Causal Cognition: An interdisciplinary approach.* Oxford, UK: Oxford University Press, pp. 351–383.

Hacking, I. (2002a). *Historical Ontology.* Cambridge, MA: Harvard University Press.

Hacking, I. (2002b). Inaugural Lecture: Chair of Philosophy and History of Scientific Concepts at the College de France, 16 January 2001. *Economy and Society,* 31(1), 1–14.

Hacking, I. (2002c). *Historical Ontology.* Cambridge, MA: Harvard University Press.

Hock, D. W. (1995). The chaordic organization: Out of control and into order. *World Business Academy Perspectives,* 9(1), 1–9.

Hodgkinson, G. P. (ed.). (2001). Facing the future: The nature and purpose of management research reassessed. *British Journal of Management,* 12(Special Issue), S1–S80.

Hodgson, D. (2002). Disciplining the professional: The case of project management. *Journal of Management Studies,* 39(6), 803–821.

Hodgson, D. and Cicmil, S. (2006). *Making Projects Critical.* Basingstoke, UK: Palgrave Macmillan.

Hodgson, D. and Cicmil, S. (2007). The politics of standards in modern management: Making 'the project' a reality. *Journal of Management Studies,* 44(3), 431–450.

Jarvis, P. (1999). *The Practitioner–Researcher: Developing theory from practice.* San Francisco, CA: Jossey-Bass.

Jarvis, D. S. L. (2010). Theorising risk and uncertainty in social enquiry – Exploring the contribution of Frank Knight. *History of Economics Review,* 52, 1–26.

Kauffman, S. A. (1993). *The Origins of Order.* New York, NY: Oxford University Press.

Keynes, J. M., 1937. The general theory of employment. *Quarterly Journal of Economics,* 51(2), 209–223.

Knight, F. H. (1921). *Risk, Uncertainty and Profit.* Boston, MA: Houghton Mifflin.

Knorr-Cerina, K. (1981). Social and scientific method or what do we make of the distinction between the natural and the social sciences? *Philosophy of the Social Sciences*, 11(3), 335–359.

Knorr-Cetina, K. and Amann, K. (1990). Image dissection in natural scientific inquiry. *Science, Technology & Human Values*, 15(3), 259–283.

Knudsen, K. (2003). 'Pluralism, Scientific Progress, and the Structure of Organization Theory' in H. Tsoukas and C. Knudsen (eds), *Oxford University Press Handbook on Organization Theory*. Oxford, UK: Oxford University Press, pp. 262–288.

Kondrat, M. E. (1992). Reclaiming the practical: Formal and substantive rationality in social work practice. *Social Service Review*, 66(2), 237–255.

Koontz, H. (1980). The management theory jungle revisited. *Academy of Management Review*, 5(2), 175–188.

Kreiner, C. (1995). In search of relevance: Project management in drifting environments. *Scandinavian Journal of Management*, 11(4), 335–346.

Kuhn, T. (1970). *The Structure of Scientific Revolutions*. Chicago, IL: University of Chicago Press.

Lalonde, P.-L., Bourgault, M. and Findeli, A. (2012). An empirical investigation of the project situation: PM practice as an inquiry process. *International Journal of Project Management*, 30(4), 418–431.

Latour, B. (1986). Visualization and cognition: Thinking with eyes and hands. *Knowledge and Society: Studies in the Sociology of Culture Past and Present*, 6(6), 1–40.

Leguérinel, L. (2007). *Enjeux et Limites des Théories Contemporaines de l'Action: de la Praxéologie à la Pragmatique*. Thèse de doctorat. Université Paris 8 – Vincennes-Saint Denis, U.F.R Arts, Philosophie et Esthétique.

Le Moigne, J.-L. (2003). *Le Constructivisme – Tome 3 modéliser pour comprendre (Constructivism: Volume 3 Modeling to Understand)*. Paris: Ed L'Harmattan, Coll. Ingenium.

Le Moigne, J.-L. (2007). Do the ethical aims of research and intervention in education and training not lead us to a 'new discourse on the study method of our time'? Conference Intelligence of Complexity, *Educational Sciences Journal*, 4, 115–126.

Levi-Strauss, C. (1966). 'The Science of the Concrete' in C. Levi-Strauss (ed.), *The Savage Mind*. Chicago, IL: University of Chicago Press, pp. 1–33.

Leybourne, S. A. (2007). The changing bias of project management research: A consideration of the literatures and an application of extant theory. *Project Management Journal*, 38(1), 61–73.

Leybourne, S. (2010). Project management and high-value superyacht projects: An improvisational and temporal perspective. *Project Management Journal*, 41(1), 17–27.

Lyotard, J-F. (1984). *The Postmodern Condition: A report on knowledge*. Manchester: Manchester University Press.

Maylor, H. (Guest ed.) (2006). Rethinking project management. *International Journal of Project Management* (Special Issue), 24(8), 635–637.

MacIntyre, A. (1985). *After Virtue*, 2nd edition. London, UK: Duckworth.

McGee, M. C. (1998). *Phronesis in the Gadamer versus Habermas Debates in Judgment Calls: Rhetoric, politics, and indeterminacy*. J. M. Sloop and J. P. McDaniel. Boulder, CO: Westview Press, pp. 13–41.

McKelvey, B. and Boisot, M. (2009). 'Redefining Strategic Foresight: "Fast" and "far" sight via complexity science' in L. Costanzo and B. MacKay (eds), *Handbook of Research on Strategy and Foresight*. Cheltenham, UK: Edward Elgar, pp. 15–47.

Menger, C. (1985). *Investigations into the Method of the Social Sciences with Special Reference to Economics*, L. Schneider (ed.), F. J. Nock (tr.). New York, NY: New York University Press.

Merton, R. K. (1945). Sociological theory. *American Journal of Sociology*, 50(6), 462–473.

Merton, R. K. (1949). *Social Theory and Social Structure*. New York, NY: Free Press.

Morris, P.W. G. and Jamieson, H.A. (2004). *Translating Corporate Strategy into Project Strategy: Achieving corporate strategy through project management*. Newtown Square, PA: Project Management Institute.

Morris, P.W.G, and Geraldi, J. (2011). Managing the institutional context for projects. *Proceedings of the IRNOP 2011 Conference*, Montréal.

Nicolis, G. and Prigogine, I. (1989). *Exploring Complexity: An introduction*. New York, NY: Freeman.

Packendorff, J. (1995). Inquiring into the temporary organization: New directions for project management research. *Scandinavian Journal of Management*, 11(4), 319–333.

Pascal, C. and Bertram, T. (2012). Praxeological research within a learning community: Developing evidence based practice. Center for Research in Early Childhood Learning Circle, *2nd BECERA Conference*, February 2012, Retrieved from http://www.slideshare.net/CREC_APT/praxeology-keynote-becera-2012. Accessed: 27/04/2012.

Pettigrew, A. M. (2001). Management research after modernism. *British Journal of Management*, 12(Special Issue), S61–S70.

Pouliot, V. (2007). 'S'o'bjectivism': Toward a constructivist methodology. *International Studies Quarterly*, 51(2), 359–384.

Rothbard, M. N. (1997). 'Praxeology as the Method of the Social Sciences' in M. Natanson (ed.), *Phenomenology and the Social Sciences*. Evanston, IL: Northwestern University Press, pp. 31–61.

Ryle, G. (1979). *On Thinking*. Oxford, UK: Basil Blackwell.

Sanderson, J. (2012). Risk, uncertainty and governance in megaprojects: A critical discussion of alternative explanations. *International Journal of Project Management*, 30(4), 432–443.

Say, J-B. (1964). *A Treatise on Political Economy*. C. C. Biddle, (tr.). New York, NY: Augustus Kelley.

Schatzki, T. R. (2005). The sites of organizations. *Organization Studies*, 26(3), 465–484.

Schram, S. F. (2004). Beyond paradigm: Resisting to the assimilation of phronetic social science. *Politics & Society*, 32(3), 417–433.

Schütz, A. (1964). *Collected Papers, vol. 2, Studies in Social Theory*, A. Brodersen (ed.). The Hague: Nijhoff.

Söderlund, J. (2004). Building theories of project management: Past research, questions for the future. *International Journal of Project Management*, 22(3), 183–191.

Söderlund, J. (2011). Pluralism in project management: Navigating the crossroads of specialization and fragmentation. *International Journal of Management Reviews*, 13(2), 153–176.

Toulmin, S. (1990). *Cosmopolis: The hidden agenda of modernity*. Chicago, IL: The University of Chicago Press.

Tsoukas, H. and Cummings, S. (1997). Marginalization and recovery: The emergence of Aristotelian themes in organization studies. *Organization Studies*, 18(4), 655–683.

Tsoukas, H. and Hatch M. J. (2001). Complex thinking, complex practice: The case for a narrative approach to organizational complexity. *Human Relations*, 54(8), 979–1013.

Van de Ven, A. H. (2000). 'Professional Science for a Professional School: Action Science and Normal Science' in M. Beer and N. Nohria (eds), *Breaking the Code of Change*. Boston, MA: Harvard Business School Press, pp. 393–413.

Van de Ven, A. H. and Johnson, P. E. (2006). Knowledge for theory and practice. *Academy of Management Review*, 31(4), 802–821.

Vico, G. B. (1708). *De nostri temporis studiorum ratione – La Méthode des études de notre temps* (The method of studies in our time). Presentation and translation by A. Pons, 1981 (text from 1708). Paris: Grasset.

Von Glaserfeld, E. (1984). 'An Introduction to Radical Constructivism' in P. Watzlawick (ed.), *The Invented Reality*. New York, NY: Norton.

Von Mises, L. (1949). *Human Action: A treatise on economics* (4th revised edition). San Francisco, CA: Fox & Wilkes.

Warry, W. (1992). The eleventh thesis: Applied anthropology as praxis. *Human Organization*, 51(2), 155–163.

Whittington, R. (2006). Completing the practice turn in strategy. *Organization Studies*, 27(5), 613–634.

Williams, T. (2002). *Modelling Complex Projects*. Chichester, UK: Wiley.

Winch, G.M. and Maytorena, E. (2011). 'Managing Risk and Uncertainty on Projects: A Cognitive Approach' in P. W. G. Morris, J. K. Pinto and J. Söderlund, J. (eds), *The Oxford Handbook of Project Management*. Oxford, UK: Oxford University Press, pp. 345–364.

Winter, M., Smith, C., Morris, P. W. G. and Cicmil, S. (2006). Directions for future research in project management: The main findings of a UK government funded research network. *International Journal of Project Management*, 24(8), 638–649.

# 5

# Ontology and Epistemology

Ole Jonny Klakegg

*As a researcher and reviewer I have found that many manuscripts and even accepted articles seem to be the result of 'self-evident' or unconscious choices of research strategy. I have struggled with this too.*

It is difficult to isolate the researcher from the research. Whatever the researcher believes or assumes about the world, and about research, will inevitably put colour and scent to his or her research activities and findings. This chapter identifies some of the most fundamental reasons for this. The basis for these effects is found in general theories of knowledge and in two specific areas of philosophy of science: ontology and epistemology. Having knowledge about these effects, and a language to discuss and describe them, is vital for a researcher that wants to be able to design a good research strategy.

At the end of this chapter, the reader can:

- understand assumptions about knowledge and reality which influence your choice of research questions and research approaches;
- appreciate that there is more than one way to achieve good research, and that diverse language is needed to discuss them. This is of particular importance in a PM context where researchers from many fields meet.

Keywords: research strategy, ontology, epistemology

## The Researcher and His/Her Positions

The researcher should be aware of his or her choices of position towards the following issues; the relation between theory and practice; research and knowledge; epistemology (theory of knowledge – what is true and what is not true); and ontology (how things really are). On deciding on a specific research strategy for his or her work, an assessment of the potential positions should be done and a set of choices has to follow as a consequence. These choices include deductive versus inductive approaches, positivist versus relativist or realist orientation in epistemology, objectivist versus constructivist orientation in ontology which in the end adds up to choosing the adequate qualitative, quantitative or combination of methods.

There are several traditions and schools on how the different positions in epistemology and ontology should be named and described. In the following, the main structure follows Bryman (2004). A complicating factor in understanding these concepts is that some sources are not clear about the differentiation between epistemology and ontology. Some authors and philosophers describe similar phenomena with different words. Others use the same words to describe different things. Be prepared to be confused when you enter this world for the first time.

Recent developments in literature indicate a growing awareness that there is a need for multi-disciplinary, multi-perspective, multi-method approaches in research. There are clear signs that the authors discussing these issues also stress the importance of methodological fit – choosing the appropriate research strategy to fit the situation and purpose of the research – and to make assumptions transparent and the chosen research strategy explicitly clear. This makes review and criticism easier, but also helps defend the research if the work is done well.

A researcher that is not aware of his/her own positions, or reckless in designing a research strategy, should not expect good results, and reviewers of scientific papers and articles have to look for signs of such methodological flaws. If these indications are found, the research should be rejected. The results cannot be trusted. If the results are OK, it will be by coincidence or pure luck. Only carefully designed research strategies considered on a basis of awareness about fundamental positions in philosophy of science will be expected to produce good results with a high degree of trustworthiness.


## Knowledge and Theory

The object of study in sciences is the world or nature (Gilje and Grimen, 1993: p. 17). The world is complex and studying it is difficult. Therefore, one unavoidable question comes up: How can you recognise good knowledge or good research? This is a part of the philosophy of science – where the object of study is science itself (ibid). The basic discussion of what knowledge and science is goes all the way back to the ancient Greek philosophers and maybe beyond. Aristotle explains different kinds of knowledge (Schram and Caterino, 2006: p. 8):

> Techné – know-how, craftsmanship.
> Episteme – abstract and universal knowledge.
> Phronesis – practical wisdom coming from intimate familiarity with contingencies and uncertainty embedded in complex social settings.

All these concepts of knowledge are necessary and useful, but as the description above indicates, not for the same purposes. Techné – craftsmanship; being good at what you do, having excellent practical skills. Episteme – abstract knowledge, analytical science, being theoretically strong. Phronesis – simply being excellent at what you do – as Flyvbjerg calls it, virtuoso expert (Flyvbjerg, 2001) or the art of judgement.

Two other words frequently used to characterise theories are normative and descriptive. Normative theories tell how things ought to be (Næss, 2004: p. 134), and descriptive theories telling how some part of reality is.

One interesting distinction is often made between theory and practice. Bryman and Bell (2006) refers to Gummeson (2000). He has studied the relationship between theory and practice in business and management research. One observation is that academic researchers and management consultants as groups of knowledge workers place different emphasis on theory and practice. 'Backed by bits and pieces of theory, the consultant contributes to practice, whereas the scholar contributes to theory supported by fragments of practice' (ibid: p. 9).

Bryman and Bell (2006: p. 5) found that their roles are fundamentally closely related and said Gummeson sees researchers and consultants as involved in addressing problems that concern management, thereby reinforcing the view that the value of both groups is determined by their ability to convince the business community that their findings are relevant and useful.

The relations between theory and research can be described as *deductive* (theory guides research) or *inductive* (theory follows from research). Induction means drawing universally valid conclusions about a whole population from a number of observations. Deduction means deriving logically valid conclusions from given premises – to derive knowledge of individual phenomena from universal laws (Næss, 2007).

According to Edmondson and McManus (2007: p. 1166) scholars have long advocated cycling between inductive theory–creation processes and deductive theory-testing strategies to produce and develop useful theory. Other modes of thought operation are *abduction* – when a particular phenomenon is interpreted from a general set of ideas or concepts, and *retroduction*; a reconstruction of the basic conditions for anything to be what it is. This means that one seeks to identify qualities beyond what is immediately given (Næss, 2007). As will be shown later, all these positions are both relevant for the definition of a robust position.

Except for mathematics and logics, sciences are regarded as *empirical* (based on experience, studying primarily phenomena perceived through our senses. Ideas must be subject to rigorous testing before they become knowledge. The word *empiricism* is used for this approach (Bryman, 2004: p. 7). In the beginning of science, nature was in focus. The origin of science was the effort to understand phenomenon's observed in nature

All the way into modern times the rational logic of nature science was considered the ideal research approach. This is called *rationalism*. Also social scientists oriented their disciplines towards this ideal (Schram and Caterino, 2006: p. 2) in their studies of human systems (as opposed to nature systems). This developed into *behavioralism* in political science, post Second World War. The ideal of the rational approach is accumulating knowledge by revealing the truth of nature, gradually adding new knowledge to the existing knowledge base. In political science, behaviouralism strived to develop predictive causal models to explain human behaviour.

# Epistemology

A core question in the philosophy of science is what is true and what is not true. The word used for this is *epistemology* (theory of knowledge). Epistemological discussions stem back to the Greek philosophers Plato, Socrates and Aristotle. A central discussion today is whether human activities should or should not be studied with the same kinds of approaches as nature (Bryman, 2004: p. 11). In this section we will look at three distinct directions in epistemology, as indicated in Figure 5.1.

Popper (1959) rejected classical empiricism and argued that scientific theories are abstract in nature. They can be tested only indirectly, by reference to their implications. He also held that scientific theory, and human knowledge generally, is irreducibly conjectural or hypothetical, and is generated by the creative imagination in order to solve problems that have arisen in specific historic–cultural settings.

Logically, no number of positive outcomes at the level of experimental testing can confirm a scientific theory, but a single counterexample is logically decisive: it shows the theory, from which the implication is derived, to be false. This asymmetry between verification and falsiability lies at the

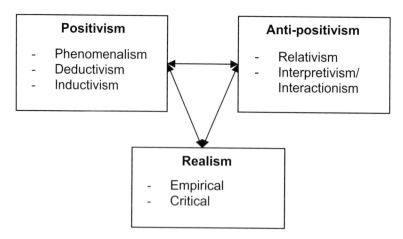

**Figure 5.1    Epistemological positions**

heart of his philosophy of science. Falsifiability was suggested by Popper as criterion of demarcation between what is and is not genuinely scientific: a theory should be considered scientific if and only if it is falsifiable. Popper coined the term *critical rationalism* to describe his philosophy.

Kuhn (1970: p. 22) proposed the concepts of 'normal science' as research that is solidly based on previous scientific work accepted as a basis for further research in a research community progressing steadily and incrementally for a period of time; and he viewed 'paradigms' – generally – as accepted scientific achievements which for a period of time work as models for problems and solutions within a community of researchers (ibid: p. 9). He argued that scientific crisis occurs when the paradigm does not give acceptable results anymore and that the necessary scientific revolution in the form of a shift in paradigm is a sign of progress.

Latour (1987) developed the methodological dictum that science and technology must be studied 'in action', or 'in the making'. Because scientific discoveries become esoteric and difficult to understand, it has to be studied where discoveries are actually made in practice. The concept of *black box* is introduced. A black box is a metaphor borrowed from cybernetics denoting a piece of machinery that 'runs by itself'. It functions only by giving it 'input' and 'output' data. Its inner complexity doesn't have to be known; one only needs to use it in his/her everyday activities.

*Positivism* is the name used for the direction based on phenomenalism (only the measurable facts count – truth which can be registered by our senses, in contrast to 'metaphysical speculations'), deductivism (theory generates hypothesis for testing), inductivism (gathering of facts makes basis for laws and thus knowledge), objectivity (science should, and presumably can, be conducted in a value-free way) and that there is a distinction between scientific statements and normative statements (Bryman, 2004: p. 11).

A statement is true knowledge if you can explain how to confirm the statement by data. Positivism is regarded as the natural science epistemology. The origin of the concept is attributed to August Comte in the early nineteenth century. The form described above is the 'modern' form established in the 1950s. In connection with positivism the term *reductionism* also occurs; the view that all complex systems can be understood by the interactions of its parts. Account of the complex system can be reduced to accounts of individual constituents (Inters, 2008). Reductionism is closely linked to *causality* which in turn says there is a directional relationship between one event (cause) and another event (effect) which is the consequence (result) of the first.

*Relativism* is based on the idea that the studied phenomenon is relative to, that is, dependent on, some other element or aspect. Humans can understand and evaluate beliefs and behaviours only in terms of their historical or cultural context.

Truth relativism is the doctrine that there are no absolute truths, that is, that truth is always relative to some particular frame of reference, such as a language or a culture. It is held that our own cognitive bias prevents us from observing something objectively with our own senses, and notational bias will apply to whatever we can allegedly measure. In addition, we have a culture bias – shared with other trusted observers – which cannot be eliminated. Relativism does not say that all points of view are equally valid. Absolutism in contrast argues there is but one true and correct view.

In sociology the position of the *interpretivism* or interactionism has a similar anti-positivist position. It promotes the idea that nothing in society is determined, and that people can break free of a label as individuals. The origin of this position seems to be Max Weber's social theories on rationalisation of religion and government (Weber, 1905). Weber described the concept of 'verstehen' that is supplemented with the hermeneutic–phenomenological tradition and symbolic interaction (Bryman, 2004: p. 13). Like relativism, the basic idea is that one has to respect the difference between people and the objects of the nature. This requires social scientists to grasp the social meaning of social action. The term *postmodernism* has been used about such approaches.

The third direction in epistemology is *realism*. Realism shares two assumptions with positivism according to Bryman (2004: p. 12): a belief that natural and social sciences can and should apply the same approach to the collection of data and explanation, and that there is an external reality to which scientists direct their attention (a reality separate from our description of it). According to Mir and Watson (2000: p. 944) the realist tradition may be traced back to the works of Kant, who posited the existence of an a priori reality which existed independently of our comprehension of it. There are two separate directions:

- Empirical realism (reality can be understood through the appropriate choice of method – this position is sometimes referred to as naïve realism).
- Critical realism (this direction recognises the reality of the natural order, and at the same time the events and discourses of social world – they acknowledge and accept our understanding of reality is provisional). For critical realists, even generative mechanisms that are not directly observable but admissible since their effects are observable.

*Critical realism* is a philosophical approach that defends the critical and emancipatory potential of rational (scientific and philosophical) enquiry against both positivist, broadly defined, and 'postmodern' challenges (relativism and interpretivism). Its approach emphasises the importance of distinguishing between epistemological and ontological questions.

## Research and real life

A core question in science is how things really are (above the question was how knowledge about things are – we now shift to the thing itself). This question is related to social sciences and is called *ontology*. Ontological discussions stem back to the Greek philosophers Plato ('being') and Aristotle ('methaphysics'). The core question today points to whether social entities (for example, organisations) can and should be considered objective entities with a reality external to social actors (people), or whether they should be considered social constructions built on the perceptions and actions of social actors (Bryman, 2004: p. 16). In this section we will look at these two distinct directions in ontology, as indicated in Figure 5.2.

One position is known as *objectivism*: This position asserts that social phenomena does have a meaning and existence independent of the people associated with it. An organisation is made up of structural elements like hierarchy, roles and responsibilities, rules and regulations. The degrees

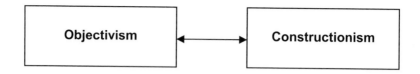

**Figure 5.2    Ontological positions**

to which these features are present vary, but thinking in these terms shows the use of objectivism and the assumption that the organisation does not only exist but is meaningful independent of other social entities. The organisation represents a social order and values to which individuals conform. Similarly one can look at culture and other social phenomena. An objectivist researcher will tend to 'speak truth to power' in the meeting with society (Lasswell, 1971; Wildawsky, 1979 as referred by Hawkesworth, 2006: p. 160).

The opposite position is called *constructionism* or constructivism: This position asserts that social phenomena and their meanings are continually being accomplished by social actors; they are produced by social interactions and in constant state of revision (Bryman, 2004: p. 16). In this perspective an organisation is more like a negotiated order constantly worked out by the individuals within the organisation. Similarly, culture can be seen as an emergent reality in constant construction and reconstruction. No set of cultural understandings can provide perfectly applicable solutions to any problem (Becker, 1982 referred by Bryman, 2004 p. 17). Most constructionists accept that this position cannot be pushed to the extreme, but a constructivist will tend to question whether there is a truth to be told in the meeting with society.

One important point about ontology is that the researcher's position here influences how research questions are formulated and how research methods are utilised. Research questions formulated from a position of objectivism (structuralism) will tend to emphasise formal dimensions of an organisation and beliefs and values of cultures. Research questions formulated from a constructionist position will emphasise the active participation of people in reality construction (Bryman, 2004 p. 19).

## Research Strategy

The issues described above are elements of research strategy. The chosen research strategy should mirror the researcher's position in the above questions. Some authors use the word methodology for this: 'A method is a tool or a technique that is used in the process of inquiry. In contrast, a methodology may be regarded as an 'intricate set of ontological and epistemological assumptions that a researcher brings to his or her work' (Prasad, 1997: p. 2). This author chooses to use the word research strategy in a similar meaning as Prasad expresses as methodology, as indicated in Figure 5.3.

Recent development within relevant PM research areas indicates a growing awareness that there is a need for multi-disciplinary, multi-perspective, multi-method approaches in research. There are clear signs that the authors discussing methodology issues also stress the importance of methodological fit – choosing the appropriate research strategy to fit the situation and purpose of the research – and to make assumptions transparent and the chosen research strategy explicitly clear. This makes review and criticism easier, but also helps defend the research if the work is done well.

Many researchers find a useful distinction between *quantitative* and *qualitative* methods, as indicated in Figure 5.3 (based on Table 1.1. in Bryman, 2004: p. 20, significantly extended). These methodological positions are typically a result of looking at research through a set of lenses. The

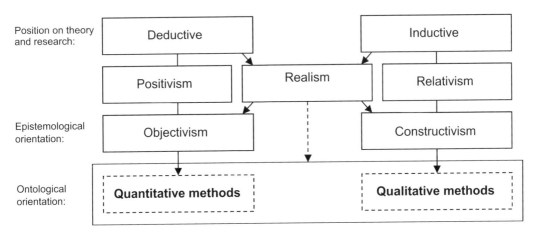

**Figure 5.3     Methodological positions as part of research strategy**

lens may be dominated by deductive, positivistic and objectivist positions on one hand – often leading to choice of quantitative methods for data collection and analysis. On the other hand, the lens may be dominated by inductive, relativistic and constructivist positions usually leading to a choice of qualitative methods for data collection and analysis. The sum of these choices is the chosen research strategy.

In research the question of which method to choose will always be important. As pointed out by many authors and obvious from the discussion above, there is no one method which is best in all situations. However, in practical life it is natural to prefer the methods you are familiar with. Bouchard (1976: p. 402) suggests the key to good research lies in asking the right question – and picking the most powerful method for answering that particular question. Consequently, if you want to stay with one research method, you need to be able to ask the right questions – the ones that benefit your favourite method.

The distinction between quantitative and qualitative methods is useful as a sorting criteria for categorising methods and tools. On the surface, the distinction implies that researchers employing quantitative methods use measurement, and those using qualitative methods do not. In Figure 5.3 it is obvious that the distinction goes deeper and has to do with the whole research strategy. The distinction, however, has been characterised by writers as everything from fundamental to simply false. Examples of critical authors are Layder (1993: p. 110), Flyvbjerg (2001: p. 49), Schram and Caterino (2006: p. 3).

Bryman (2004) talks about breaking down the quantitative/qualitative divide and combining quantitative and qualitative research. He also pointed out that we should be reluctant to drive a wedge between the two. Flyvbjerg said we should not think in terms of 'either–or' but in terms of 'both–and'. Schwartz-Shea (2006) discusses the plurality position and divides it into three scenarios (this author puts name on scenario 2):

1. 'Happy pluralism' where any approach contributes; rules, logic, signs and rationality is not criticised as such and 'all is good'.
2. 'Conscious pluralism' where judgments are made about the significance of the problems defined and researched by different research approaches.
3. 'Reflexivity' where researchers think more critically about the value of their research and how it will be used – not only in a pragmatic way but also in a political way that goes beyond 'both–and'. The researcher's role in socio-political–economic power structures is important.

The description of the pluralist position here makes it very clear that the first scenario is rather naïve. See also the parallel to empirical realism mentioned above. Researchers should be more critical about their work.

The conclusion to this chapter is that PM researchers should be very cautious in choosing their research methods and be aware of the consequences of different positions they inherently have to choose from when planning their research. Researchers may get away with not explicitly saying much about their position as long as they stay within an established tradition and a well-known research area. As soon as they approach the boundaries of their area they need to make some conscious and adequate choices. Being aware of your own positions on ontology and epistemology helps you make good choices and defend them.

PM is an example of a research field that is rather diverse with positivist, realist and interpretivist research communities. It can be argued that it is extra important and fruitful to be clear and explicit on the philosophical underpinning in this field.

## Tips and Exercises

### TIPS FOR STUDENTS

- The philosophy of science is a set of lenses that helps you focus on different sides of research strategy. Use it to become more aware of what sort of research fits your own individual orientation and strengths.
- Some of these concepts are abstract and may seem difficult. Discuss these issues with your fellow students to understand them better.
- Be aware that different literature may present and define the concepts differently, according to which research tradition the author represents. There is no guarantee that this author has the best possible description. Read more than one source.
- Think carefully through the terms used in this chapter to describe the fundamentals of a research strategy – it will help you in defending your research and in future reviews.

### TIPS FOR SUPERVISORS

- The philosophy of science includes different ways of thinking about knowledge and reality. It represents a language of its own, with many difficult and unusual terms. Some of them may seem confusing. Reading through the chapter will usually not be enough. A discussion in a group is advised.
- The theme in this chapter is abstract and more fundamental than practical. There are not many 'easy to use' practical tips and tricks presented here. This challenges the motivation of some readers. Focusing on the fundamental importance of these issues may help.

### EXERCISES

1. In daily life a person's level of skills may be described as for example 'beginner', 'intermediate' and 'expert'. How do these words relate to different kinds of knowledge? Tip: use the concepts described in the knowledge and theory section.
2. Discuss the concepts 'theory' and 'practice' from a research point of view. How do you think these concepts relate to quantitative and qualitative research methods?

3. Consider the case of a brand new field of science – one where practically no knowledge is established (you can choose one specific field, or discuss in general terms). If you were to do research in this field – what fundamental positions in epistemology could you then choose to base your research on? Give examples of research approaches you could use and how they relate to these positions. Where do you feel you personally, as a researcher, belong in this picture?

4. True or false? Consider this quote from Apple co-founder Steve Jobs (Thinkexist 2012): 'Your time is limited, so don't waste it living someone else's life. Don't be trapped by dogma – which is living with the results of other people's thinking. Don't let the noise of other's opinions drown out your own inner voice. And most important, have the courage to follow your heart and intuition. They somehow already know what you truly want to become. Everything else is secondary.' Discuss Jobs' contemplations in an ontological perspective and with the concepts presented in the ontology section.

5. Think through the connections between positions in ontology and epistemology and the choices of research approaches we generally tend to choose. Discuss with yourself, or in a small group, what this means for you. How does your positions and orientation influence your research? How can you tell – what are the signs?

# References

Bouchard, T. J. Jr. (1976). 'Field Research Methods: Interviewing, Questionnaires, Participant Observation, Systematic Observations, Unobtrusive Measures' in M. D. Dunnette (ed.) *Handbook of Industrial and Organizational Psychology*. Chicago, IL: Rand McNally, pp. 363–413.

Bryman, A. (2004). *Social Research Methods*. Second Edition. Oxford University Press.

Bryman, A. and Bell, E. (2006). *Business Research Methods*. Second Edition. Oxford University Press.

Edmondson, A. C. and McManus, S. E. (2007). Methodological fit in management field research. *Academy of Management Review*, 32(4), 1055–1179.

Flyvbjerg, B. (2001). *Making Social Science Matter: Why social inquiry fails and how it can succeed again*. Cambridge University Press.

Gilje, N. and Grimen, H. (1993). *Samfunnsvitenskapenes forutsetninger; Innføring i samfunnsvitenskapenes vitenskapsfilosofi*. [Social science' assumptions; Introduction to the science philosophy of social science]. Universitetsforlaget.

Gummeson, E. (2000). *Qualitative Methods in Management Research*. Second Edition. Sage Publications.

Hawkesworth, M. (2006). 'Contesting the Terrain: Flyvbjerg on Facts, Values, Knowledge, and Power' in Schram and Caterino (eds) *Making Political Science Matter; Debating Knowledge, Research and Method*. New York University Press, pp. 152–170.

Inters (2008). Interdisciplinary Encyclopedia of Religion and Science. Available at http://www.disf.org/en/default.asp. Accessed: 29 March 2008.

Kuhn, T. S. (1970). *The Structure of Scientific Revolutions* [Vitenskapelige revolusjoners struktur] Norwegian edition 1996. Spartacus Forlag AS.

Lasswell, H. (1971). *A Preview of Policy Science*. New York, NY: Elsevier.

Latour, B. (1987). *Science in Action*. Harvard University Press.

Layder, D. (1993). *New Strategies in Social Research: An introduction and guide*. Polity Press. Referred to in Bryman (2004).

Mir, R. and Watson, A. (2000). Strategic management and the philosophy of science: The case for a constructivist methodology. *Strategic Management Journal*, 21(9), 941–953.

Næss, P. (2004). Prediction, regressions and critical realism. *Journal of Critical Realism*, 2(2), 133–164.

Næss, P. (2007). *Critical Realism – A Fruitful Basis for Planning Research?* Lecture. Department of Development and Planning. University of Aalborg.

Popper, K. (1959). *The Logic of Scientific Discovery.* (First published as *Logik der Forschung* in 1934). Basic Books.

Prasad, P. (1997). 'Systems of Meaning: Ethnography as a Methodology for the Study of Information Technologies' in Lee and Degross (eds) *Qualitative Methods and Information Research.* Kluwer, pp. 1–33.

Schram, S. F. and Caterino, B. (eds) (2006). *Making Political Science Matter: Debating knowledge, research, and method.* New York University Press.

Schwartz-Shea, P. (2006). 'Conundrums in the Practice of Pluralism' in Schram and Caterino (eds) *Making Political Science Matter: Debating knowledge, research and method.* New York University Press.

Thinkexist (2012). Truth quotes. Available at http://thinkexist.com/quotations/truth/2.html. Accessed: 22 September 2012.

Weber, M. (1905). *Die protestantische Ethik und der Geist des Kapitalismus* (The Protestant Ethic and the Spirit of Capitalism), translated into Norwegian by Sverre Dahl, Pax Publishers, 1995.

# 6

# The Praxeology of Applied Research in Autoethnographical Research Settings: A Case Study of a Radical Learning Journey

Louis Klein and Christian A.P. Weiland

*The project management community has become a beacon in thriving towards an interdisciplinary praxeology of applied research. It is my personal goal to contribute to this community of practice and help expand the field. (LK)*

*Project management research has become more than the development and improvement of tools. By being able to bring reflections from my own field of work into this reader I hope to contribute to the further development. (CW)*

When your work becomes the object of your research project, an autoethnographic learning journey starts. Systematic reflection of the paradigmatic conditions and contexts of this situation will allow for continuous feedback and additional learning throughout the research. Research is a project and a process, which creates a specific self-referential learning loop in the case of PM research. The case study of the SEgroup will illustrate such a radical learning journey, its frames, milestones and flow leading to an understanding of the systemic contexts of co-creating praxeological research. In the end some learning can be derived for PM research, not only for autoethnographic research settings.

At the end of this chapter, the reader can:

*   illustrate the challenges of applied research especially for researchers in autoethnographic settings;
*   understand the dynamics of learning loops and multi-frame research settings;

- encourage the management of your research as a project and enabling to balance autoethnographical research settings.

Keywords: praxeology, paradigmatic reference, autoethnography, research processes, mental models, systems theory, narrative, critical theory, co-creation, context

## Embarking on an Auto-Ethnographical Learning Journey

When your work becomes the object of your research project, autoethnographic research settings come for a lot of researchers as a pragmatic necessity as well as the ultimate excitement of practically relevant research. Especially for PhD research projects, the utilisation of daily work as empirical data is highly attractive. Yet it comes at a price: autoethnographic research settings create immediate feedbacks and learning loops, which can develop their own dynamics. On the other hand, if properly framed, these dynamics can foster a lot of exciting insight and relevant learning for the research as well as for the field. Regarding PM research, another layer comes into play: writing an academic paper is itself a project. The subject of the research becomes at the same time the frame of reference and the method of implementation.

The development of the Systemic Excellence Group (SEgroup) as a think and do tank is chosen as an illustration of the dynamics and emergences of applied research in autoethnographic research settings. In 2001, SEgroup started to engage in organisational development and change projects. Since then, PM has evolved naturally as a third integrated discipline for both application and reflection. This learning over the years is here brought forward as the narrative of a radical learning journey.

The following chapter will present the momentary snapshot of this journey, what frames of references have developed over the years, how these frames have led to milestones in the journey towards a praxeology of applied research and how process thinking has developed from a milestone to a more permanent flow. Being part of a global stakeholder community, it will be presented how the interdisciplinary discourse and the journey have been gone beyond the organisational borders of SEgroup and examples for applied research in the area of PM will be presented. This reflection will also undergo a second-order reflection in form of lessons learnt: what is there to learn from this journey for a praxeology of applied research in autoethnographical research settings not only for PM, but for all fields of action research.

### FRAMES OF THE JOURNEY

Looking at any kind of substantial research, we expect a full account of the scientific frame of research, the methodological frame of research and a proper description of the field in which the research is taking place. Looking into the research of change projects we expect the same. In reference to the idea of the radical learning journey, there has been movement in these frames of reference and a process of development towards an adequate completion for the research endeavour. Looking for a praxeology of applied research, these frames go from the academic meta-level to more practical ones: from scientific over methodological frames to the disciplines of their work.

### SCIENTIFIC FRAMES OF REFERENCE

Stringing the frames from research to application equals going from the greatest to the smallest, from abstraction to concretisation. On the one end stand the scientific theory, to be understood as a well-substantiated explanatory framework that gains strength through its capability to explain diverse phenomena. A theory should therefore invite different methodologies to test themselves in this frame. Considering the case of SEgroup, we can separate between a foundation of cybernetics and systems theory and the evolutionary enrichment through further theories.

## THE SYSTEMIC FOUNDATIONS

Starting with scientific frames of reference, it was all cybernetics and systems theory in the beginning. Niklas Luhmann's theory of social systems (1984) can be marked as a founding stone of SEgroup research. This opens up a sociological perspective onto the dynamics of organisations and links into an epistemological tradition of constructivism, especially Watzlawick (Watzlawick, Bavelas, Jackson, and O'Hanlon, 1967) and Heinz von Foerster (1979). Management cybernetics in the tradition of Stafford Beer (1995) created a good counterbalance and served as a bridge into management sciences. Chaos theory (Gleick, 1998) and debating complexity, however, called for a critical systems perspective as it was brought forward by Jackson (1991) and Flood (1990). And although over the years new frames were added to the focus on cybernetics and systems theory they served reliably as a scientific centre for the group's research in change.

## ENRICHING SCIENTIFIC FRAMES

Exploring the conditions for the possibility of social systems to emerge and support their viability over time, an additional set of scientific frames came into the play. We are looking at discourse theory, critical theory, epistemology, and anthropology and ethnography.

- Discourse theory relating to the works of Foucault, Bourdieu and Derrida (cp. Wetherell, Yates, Taylor and Open University, 2001) allows for a thorough analysis of the worldview and the paradigmatic embedment as a specific context of a specific social system (cp. Klein and Weiland, forthcoming). This goes hand in hand with Berger and Luckmann's insights in the social construction of reality (1967). In a certain sense this links back to constructivism, yet discourse theory puts that into a broader context.
- Critical theory is often used synonymously with the Frankfurt School and its five leading protagonists: Macuse, Adorno, Horkheimer, Benjamin and Fromm (cp. Schirmacher, 2000). It is, however, not the general critical perspective on society as brought forward in the Frankfurt School which makes critical theory so valuable. Especially seen from a systems perspective, critical theory provides the ground to counterbalance the conservative tendency of the processes of emergence. Emergent systems are conservative by nature and, due to operational closure, it is difficult to generate a critical perspective from the inside. A counterbalance of this view can be provided by the perspective of the critical theory. The second generation of the Frankfurt School, especially Jürgen Habermas (1983) and even more so the recently brought forward theory of conventions (cp. Diaz-Bone, 2008), allow, based on critical theory, for a calculus of values. Especially in times when value-driven management is highly rated yet poorly operationalised, critical theory puts the debate back on its feet.
- Epistemology in the tradition of Ludwig Fleck (1986), Thomas Kuhn (1962) and Georgio Agamben (Agamben, D'Isanto and Attell, 2009) may have been put first in the list of additional scientific frames of reference, yet what makes them so valuable for the research is not only looking at the scientist's paradigm but much more at the ecology of paradigms that is used in the field to give rough answers to communities of practice (Klein, forthcoming). The intrigue that accompanys the

notion of ecology of paradigms is that, for example, managerial practices should not be thought of as being homogeneous. Different cultural means and different activities within a practice are heterogeneous and may relate to each other in ways which go all along the scale of ecological coexistence, from conflict and competition on the one side and symbiosis on the other side. This feeds the notion that the paradox in organisational practices is the rule and not the exception.

• Anthropology and ethnography are listed last but not least. Understanding cultures remains a difficult exercise if I only refer to the latter works of Trompenaars (Trompenaars and Hampden-Turner, 2004; Trompenaars and Woolliams, 2003; Trompenaars, 1994) and Hofstede (Hofstede, 1984; Hofstede, Hofstede and Minkov, 2010). The key to understanding cultures rather lies with the anthropological classics of Norbert Elias (1969, 1982), Bronislaw Malinowski (1923), Johan Huizinga (1939) and Marcel Mauss (1925). Likewise valuable are the ethnographic works of Harold Garfinkel (1984). Especially for the cultural dynamics of self-observation and self-description of social systems, anthropology and ethnography serve as a strong frame of reference.

## METHODOLOGICAL FRAMES OF REFERENCE

Methodology is the systematic analysis of the methods applied to different disciplines. It, typically, encompasses concepts such as paradigm, theoretical model and phases. On the methodological level we only want to highlight the schools of thought rather than going into the various details of research methodologies. These three schools of thought are multi-disciplinarity, design thinking, system dynamics and process thinking.

• Multi-disciplinarity has a long tradition based on trans-disciplinarity and interdisciplinarity. The notion of multi-disciplinarity as a co-creation of different disciplines overcoming systematically the limitation of the single disciplines and co-creating emergence in their interplay became a hallmark of our research practice. Multi-disciplinarity links into the tradition of holistic thinking and is very much reflected in the use of tools like lateral thinking (cp. De Bono, 1973) and mind mapping (cp. Buzan and Buzan, 1993).

• Design thinking was hyped in the last ten years. The methodological tradition however is much older and dates back to the works of Rowe (1987) and Buchanan (1992) in the late 1980s and early 1990s. Especially for fieldwork and action research, tools like rapid prototyping or micro-anthropology are very valuable.

• System dynamics link to the work of J. Forester, Peter Senge and Frederick Vester. Especially in reference to cybernetics and systems thinking as a scientific frame of reference, tools like causal loop diagrams or simulations (cp. Forrester, 1961; Senge, 2006) allow for a better understanding of the specific dynamics of specific social systems.

## DISCIPLINES OF THE FIELD

Disciplines, last but not least, are included here as the traditional descriptions of the relevant fields. For the research of the group it has been especially organisational development, change management and PM. Overall the reference to a professional discipline comes at the cost of drowning in oceans of handbooks and how-to literature. This makes it difficult to identify the major works and even more so the recent advances.

• Organisational development looks gratefully on a rich tradition of research and seminal work seeking to understand organisations. Development, learning and management shall be highlighted in three sub-categories which feed on a rich discourse driven by key figures like Edgar Schein (1980), Charles Handy (1993), W. Edward Deming (1982), Chris Argyris (1990) and Peter Senge (2006).

- Change management as a discipline is a mess. Building on the foundations of organisational development, change management proliferates into all kinds of idiosyncratic perspectives suggesting different recipes to manage change. So the focus is more on change processes such as those suggested by Kotter (1996) or tools like Appreciative Inquiry (cp. Cooperrider and Whitney, 2005) or Open Space (cp. Owen, 2008).
- PM on the contrary, seems to be refreshingly in order. The hallmark for PM as a discipline is the idea of hedging a body of knowledge, where the knowledge of the discipline comes together and is taken care of. Apart from that we see two large world organisations with the Project Management Institute (PMI) and the International Project Management Association (IPMA) that provide various platforms for the discipline to integrate and, last but not least, fairly successful academic journals – the *Project Management Journal* (PMJ) and the *International Journal of Project Management* (IJPM) can be seen as the chronicles of a well-managed profession.

## Milestones of the Journey

While the opening up of new theories, methodologies and disciplines have framed the journey and the milestones, what has actually happened in both the practice and the research reflects the milestone and how the frames come alive in praxeology. There have been a lot of these milestones on the learning journey of the SEgroup, which can be distinguished as methods and tools,

### METHODS

The operating model of SEgroup pursues the unity of research and service practices. Three innovative methods, understood as techniques to investigate certain phenomena, to illustrate the praxeology shall be presented: systemic inquiry, process facilitation and agile change PM.

- Systemic inquiry (Klein and Weiland, forthcoming; Klein, 2004, 2005) was SEgroup's first application where research and consulting came together in a very fruitful way. Already in the early days of SEgroup there had been applications of systemic inquiry in change management assignments to access the systemic readiness for change of the relevant social system exploring not only the status of a social system or an organisation but furthermore the realms of possibilities within that very system. There had been publications and revisions on systemic inquiry over the years and just recently a critical reflection, balancing and reinforcing the initial idea of facilitating organisational self-observation and self-description pointing at social systemic emergence which serves as a fermentation process in which the individual contribution does not have to be a factual statement to be a valuable input to the process. This is to say it is not really relevant if people lie in the course of a qualitative interview. The relevant information is in the pattern over all interviews.
- Process facilitation is a valuable self-description of change management processes which allowed referring to inner structure as in change design and change architecture and giving credits to moderation as the key balancing activity. Linking to group dynamics, process facilitation not only took into account the technical aspects of change but much more than that human dynamics as they occur in social systems and the psychology of change (Klein and Wong, 2010; Klein, 2012b).

The latest logical advancement can be rendered to the headline 'agile change project management'. Especially in order to meet the social complexity of change projects (Biesenthal and Klein, 2013; Klein, 2008, 2012a), agile PM offers valuable possibilities. This relates to the different requirements of organisations to described projects in their a classic, operational function – that is, for procurement processes – as well as describing projects in their procedural capacity to deal with complexity – for example in the logic of a continuous stakeholder management.

## TOOLS

On the level of the tools, a set of five can be described as being extraordinarily beneficial for the work of a think and do tank: The TPC-matrix, mind mapping, wallpaper reviews, rapid prototyping and visual thinking.

- The TPC-matrix is derived from the works of Noel Tichy (1983). In our work it had proven to be the key of levelling social complexity through distinguishing very different ideas of organisational activities: a technical perspective, a political perspective and a cultural perspective.
- Mind mapping has been without work since the very beginning. However, it was not before the middle of the last decade that we were able to work with mind maps on site. Today the work with mind maps goes without further notice.
- The wallpaper review as a tool was developed in the field of academic writing; however it sprang over to any kind of documentation and presentation done within the SEgroup. The idea of the wallpaper review is to stick a document or a presentation, paper by paper, slide by slide, chapter by chapter to the wall, allowing access to the structural balance and aesthetics within communication.
- Rapid prototyping, as we included it into the work of the SEgroup, was inspired less by design thinking and more derived from a systemic solution orientation in change management practices. It uses pragmatism as a process and project accelerator.
- The tools of visual thinking proved to be very beneficial on the research side. The graphical mapping of arguments and their arrangement is a quality enhancer. Only a clear line of arguments can survive the graphical challenge.

## FLOW OF THE JOURNEY

Process thinking is in some way a methodology in the making and has yet to reach the tradition of the other three. It has developed as from a milestone to a meta-flow of the learning journey – reflected upon with systemic theories. It has nevertheless become more than a method used in change management and organisational development (eq. Goldratt, 1999). Inspired by quality management, process thinking aims at a systematic and integrating approach to specific sets of activities (cp. Bauder and Weiland, 2013). Inspired by quality management, process thinking aims at a systematic and integrating approach to specific sets of activities. Here, four areas of process thinking shall be highlighted: PM processes, business management processes, process innovation and supervision.

## PROJECT MANAGEMENT PROCESSES

Integrating PM into consultant research activities seems to be a natural thing out of a PM perspective. Change, as well as research, usually comes in the form of a project. Those fields, however, consulting as well as research, developed with a tradition focused on individual excellence and seniority. Unless the activity landscape is segregated along the lines of PM, cooperation, co-creation and quality management turns out to be a burden to some. Viewed from another angle, it proved that even the integration of PM basics comes as an innovator for quality and results. Especially on the change management side of SEgroup, the focus on PM allows for teamwork where even junior professionals can substantially contribute to the project success.

Combining classic PM and agile PM in change projects seems to be the next level after integrating PM into SEgroup's change management and research. Once PM as such is established, agile PM can be integrated to meet especially the social complexity, the political and cultural aspects which usually dwell in the blind spot of scientific management.

## BUSINESS PROCESSES

The set up of business processes works into the same direction as the integration of PM. For SEgroup, over the years business processes proved to be performance enhancers – the books process, the white paper process and the self-initiated projects process.

- The books process describes the lifecycle of a change project, it starts with a white book looking at the stakeholder landscape and change readiness resulting in a so-called white book which serves as an input to the blue book which is the elaborated offer following the requirements of the Logical Framework (Logframe). Triggered by the actual assignment, the PM perspective of the Logframe switched over in the so-called orange book into an agile PM logic embedded in rigid project monitoring and controlling. The closure of a project results in the so-called black book. The black book sums up the lessons learned and the reflections of the change project, and prepares them for dissemination to the stakeholder community.
- The white paper process looks at SEgroups' research. The idea behind this process is the acceleration of academic work. The white paper process starts with a research note which is published on the SEgroup website. The research note reads like an extended abstract and serves as input for academic conferences and for white paper drafts. The white paper draft is a provisional academic paper which is targeted at conference proceedings. In the process of gathering two to three conference presentation feedbacks, the white paper draft is developed into a full-fleshed academic paper which is published as a white paper onto the SEgroup website until it is transferred into a peer-reviewed publication. In this case the white paper is taken from the SEgroup's website and substituted by an abstract at the actual academic presentation.
- The self-initiated project process is the latest entry in the SEgroup business process landscape. The standard format for commercial change management projects is the assignment. Consulting comes as a service. A business model is time for money. The various attempts to develop this change management as a service business model into a more entrepreneurial business model which is explicitly exposed to share risks could not be established so far. SEgroup's answer to that was to venture with its change expertise into the field of social entrepreneurship. In essence, the self-initiated project processes are very close to the books process. Only what is described as a white book in the books process becomes more prominent and follows a different inner logic. The major aspect in that is to distinguish between a concern, a pool of ideas and a project. The systemic perspective, is a loose coupling between the concern as the reason why for the project and the pool of ideas comprising, so to speak, the Lego blocks of a potential project and, finally, loosely coupled with the project as a specific configuration of a selection of ideas. In this logic, projects can fail even in an as early stage as failing to find

funding without damaging the pool of ideas or the actual concern. This approach gives the freedom to fail and to learn in a rapid manner, minimising the involved risks and maximising knowledge creation.

## PROCESS INNOVATION

Next to integrating PM and business processes, there are two characteristic process innovations to be identified along the learning journey of the SEgroup – first, the chain of exploring mapping trading and second, reflection in action.

The three-step of exploring, mapping, trading plays with the image of overseas trade in the times of Christopher Columbus. Exploration and discovery marks the first stage in a change project when we are looking at the stakeholder landscape and change readiness. Mapping visualises knowledge out of the first step and allows for broader communication. In the third step we can build on the mapping and identify possible routes and decide upon the course to steer. For change projects we look at the necessity of exploring social systems and the dynamics of organisations. A rigorous academic approach to research as a basis of any kind of exploration makes all the difference and allows for quality.

The idea of reflection in action has been around for a while longer. So here we are looking at a specific SEgroup interpretation, which links the idea of reflection and action not only to action research but to autoethnography and discourse analysis. Autoethnography shall not be too surprising for a think and do tank. Self-application is a question of integrity, discipline and rigour. It allows for critical perspective and prohibits a generic drift towards the identification with the role of the mere consultant or researcher. In a think and do tank you do not want to go native.

A discourse practice analysis shall be distinguished from discourse analysis by allowing to analyse the debate of managers about books they haven't read to reference their managerial practice. This is to appreciate the relevance of these discourses and acknowledge their dynamics.

## SUPERVISION

Supervision, last but not least, is included systematically in the operating model of the SEgroup as the dominant means of quality assurance. Supervision acknowledges that the person with their mental models, skills and experiences is the starting point for any meaningful practice. This ranks from the mandatory training in group dynamics over coaching and peer-to-peer evaluation to classical settings of inter-vision and supervision. Linking this to process thinking allows for systematically stabilising these practices without interfering with the actual content, which may touch upon privacy and shall be safeguarded to allow for personal development.

## Co-Creating the Journey

The journey of SEgroup has never been an isolated one. The principle of co-creation has gone beyond internal cooperation and led into the creation of a conscious self-reflection to be part of a global stakeholder community for creating an interdisciplinary body of knowledge for change in which PM plays a vital part.

## CO-CREATING QUALITY

We may call it a four-eyes-principle. In the field as well as in the reflection we realised that there was an immense quality leap going from one person to a team of at least two persons. The net benefit, however, of adding a third person to the team was more to do with distributing the work load than with actually gaining substantial benefits on the quality. For the white papers of the Group that sums up in the maxim to always have a co-author. From a systemic perspective, a set of two authors does not only allow for two perspectives on the first level of observation, it allows for an observation according to second order cybernetics and it allows for observing observations. So the position of the second observer does not only observe what is observed, more than that it allows observing how the observation is done. This leads us back to the importance of reflecting the mental models and frames of reference the research is based on.

## CO-CREATING THE DISCOURSE

At another level of co-creation, international research association or disciplinary practices come into the play. For the work of SEgroup, three fields have been exceptionally fruitful: PM, system sciences and critical narratives. Next to these, we were, over the years, lucky to participate in special single topic conferences.

## PROJECT MANAGEMENT

The international discourse on PM can be best observed at conferences and meetings of the PMI, the IPMA and especially with the International Centre for Complex Project Management (ICCPM) and the International Network on Organising by Projects (IRNOP). As already remarked, the hallmark of PM as a discipline is its dedication towards a body of knowledge. Evaluating and integrating new models, methods and instruments seemed to be an ongoing concern. Especially ICCPM and IRNOP push the limits and set a benchmark for a contemporary state of the art in PM research, which aims at integrating perspectives far beyond engineering and management. Although attending the single PMI or IPMA conference may be sobering regarding the expectations what take-away could be harvested, the interesting perspective is, like in a second order observation, the analysis of the PM discourse over the years. Different topics have a different life span. New ideas come and go. And others are actively ignored or marginalised before they finally make into the discourse or pearl off.

## SYSTEM SCIENCES

System sciences in contrast to PM appear fragmented. They are not really looking at a discipline with immediate professional application. For SEgroup, four platforms have proven to be very valuable: the annual meeting of the International Society of the Systems Sciences (ISSS), the tri-annual meeting of the World Organisation of Systems and Cybernetics, the bi-annual European Meeting for Cybernetics and Systems Research and, last but not least, the yearly meeting of the International Sociological Associations Research Committee 51 on Sociocybernetics. It is again the discourse pattern over the year which gives an orientation for SEgroup's own research, especially in the field of social complexity, and it occurs as a parallel to the PM discourse to see to which extent the self-description as a science seems to make it difficult to include the individual as a whole person into the focus of the research.

## CRITICAL NARRATIVE

Critical narratives as a discourse and field of research embark on the challenge of integrating the whole person into the systemic contacts of conversations and teams, the family, organisations and the entire society. The Standing Conference on Management and Organizational Inquiry (SCMOI) as well as the Forum for Critical Narrative Inquiry stand out as two highly reflective and critical platforms where, almost radical and painfully, the limits of the subjects are pushed further and further.

## TOPIC CONFERENCES

In contrast to the above-described three scientific discourses, topic conferences crystallise different perspectives to co-create upon a chosen subject. There are general symposia or forums like the St Gallen Symposium or the Tällberg Forum, which try to re-visit the global agenda year by year and facilitate an extraordinary exchange between theory and practice. Out of the more specific conferences, two on the subject of cross-cultural encounter were outstanding: Leadership and Management in a Changing World and Managing the Asian Century. Leadership and Management in a Changing World was a conference held in 2011 in Athens. The idea was to derive learning from the encounter of the philosophy of Aristotle and the teaching of Confucius. The result of the conference, however, was not so much a praise of the ancient philosophers as the sober insight that the individual experience of globalisation calls for rethinking philosophy. In 2013, Managing the Asian Century, held in Singapore, recommended that we let go of our mutual stereotypes concerning culture and philosophy. While Asia is importing cultural memes from the west at a rapid pace, the west seeks inspiration and salvation in Asian spirituality and philosophy.

And although all this discourse observation and conference participation may be not called co-creation in a direct sense, it very much facilitates the co-creation with the relevant context. And from SEgroup's perspective, the discourse contribution follows the process of exploring, mapping and trading, which allows for a strategic perspective beyond the immediate benefits of reflection and research.

## A Current Research Example: Cross-Cultural Complex Project Management (CCCPM)

In 2009, SEgroup launched together with the International Centre for Complex Project Management (ICCPM) a research project on cross-cultural complex project management (CCCPM). It was integrated into the research agenda of the ICCPM as research group number one on social and cultural complexity. In a multidisciplinary way, CCCPM currenlty combines 12 PhD projects, looking at PM from alternative perspectives. The idea is to enlarge the PM discourse and allow for a wider space in which the issue of complexity in PM can be enlightened and new models, methods and instruments for practitioners can be conceived. As an illustration, eight projects will be listed here:

- The first project is a discourse practice analysis looking at the discourse dynamics of complex PM. This is participative research comparing the mainstream PM discourse with expert opinions and the alternative discourse on agile PM.

- The second research project brings together Jungian psychology and PM and looks at the shadow of PM. This research is organised in the form of a personal learning journey, starting at the level of individual shadow work, climbing up the ladder to reflect not only organisational perspectives but also the implications for the PM discourse.
- The third research project is a case study that brings together research about social change and PM. Looking at social change projects in Brazilian favelas, the research explores to what extent PM is actually beneficial for facilitating social change.
- The fourth research project looks at the idea of crowd-sourcing PM. The question is pursued to what extent the management of a project can be crowd-sourced and distributed amongst several independent agents. The research is an autoethnographical study reflecting the international growth of a company for coaching services.
- The fifth research project switches over to the perspective of arts and looks at the context dependency of PM in the field of site-specific art projects. The assumption is that the specific context suggests a specific way of managing projects.
- Project six is another perspective on the arts and looks at the leadership of dance ensembles. The focus is on choreography as the orchestration of complexity throughout the different levels from the single dancer and the pair to the dynamic interplay within the ensemble on stage.
- Project example number seven looks at the culture of development projects and explores to what extent development projects in international aid contexts benefit from applying PM beyond reducing the Logframe to an accounting instrument.
- Last but not least, project number eight looks at culturally adapted and localised PM education and certification at the level of vocational training. This is a wider issue of context dependency. Next to the cultural aspect comes the challenge of the political balance of east and west, north and south, rich and poor. The project pursues the idea that PM as an approach can be linked to the cultural heritage of a region, a nation or a people beyond the established toolboxes, hence providing accessibility and balance for PM in vocational training at the full range from employability to micro-entrepreneurship.

The CCCPM research project illustrates that research leading the PM discourse does not necessarily have to be theoretical. On the contrary, the CCCPM project shows that multidisciplinarily and action research allow for break-through, to an extent which is hardly possible from within a disciplinary paradigm.

## Lessons Learned from the Journey

The learning journey of the SEgroup did not come to an end yet and it will not allow itself to retire. At the time of writing this short reflection on the praxeology of applied research, six lessons learned describe the essence for a praxeology of applied research so far: think and do, know thyself, mind the context, create your own meaning, co-create and be bold.

1. Think and do: The idea of a think and do tank reflects very much the possibilities of a praxeology of applied research. Reflective action research is not only quality assurance in the field, it allows observing an open and still accessible future. It is a research in a situation where the future is still meaningful in the sense of Niklas Luhmann (cp. 1984). It is a situation where there is still a warm and lively representation of options which will after the case be cold and pointless.
2. Know thyself: Know thyself is a starting point of any fruitful reflection. Knowing your mental models and your frames of reference allows evaluating implications against alternatives. And

this not only accounts for the research in a much broader way but accounts for praxis, too. In this sense: mind your thoughts for they create your world.

3. Mind the context: Mind the context as well. First, it is a matter of exploring, mapping and trading, second it is the appeal to curate it. In organisations we may want to rely on the extraordinary and outstanding researcher as the heroic individual. We have learned, however, that the quality of any research is with its context. Organising for applied research looks at structures and processes to support it and at agile research management leading even B-players to A-performance.

4. Innovate: Meaning-creation is the basis for innovation. Try not to be boxed in by fashionable school of thoughts or categories. If you personally can apply aspects from different scientific frames of reference, methodologies, disciplines, even stories for your own work, go for it. Innovation is rearranging and expanding the boxes, not just stacking them up.

5. Co-create: Co-creation may be a claim for interpersonal cooperation and for teaming up. Allow for second order observations, not only looking at the 'what' but also at the 'how' of the research and its quality. However, co-creation calls for co-creating with the context as well. Know the context of the discourse. This is not only what people have written about the subject, it is much more the applied discourse praxis analysis. As in a conference, it is not so much interesting what is presented, it is much more interesting to see the reception of the presentation and the conversation that points at the presentation.

6. Be bold: Be bold! Dare to challenge, dare to fail, dare to learn. Any research that does not dare to challenge the existing thinking and practices is pointless. It is all about new thinking and alternative practices. It's nice to be successful. It is nice to prove one's initial hypothesis. But this it is just reconfirming what you already know. Learning thrives on failure. And be aware also that learning has a technical, a political and a cultural perspective. The Ouroboros bites its tail and we may well start all over again.

## Tips and Exercises

### TIPS FOR STUDENTS

- Your research is first of all a project: managing your research as a project is the inevitable self-application of PM research.
- Mind the different frames of references in the research and the field: different academic discourses and different people in the field might use a different terminology for describing the same phenomena.
- Be co-creative: talk with others about your research project; it often helps if they are not experts in the field and thereby force you to express yourself in a different terminology.
- Remember your original concern, the 'why' of your research: there is always a different perspective, theory and methodology. Be aware that they are just frames that allow you to expand your own perspective but not a blueprint for your research.

### TIPS FOR SUPERVISORS

- In autoethnographical research, there is always a danger of getting caught in constant readjustment: help your students to balance quality adjustments and output focus.
- Allow the student to be a project manager and entrepreneur of his/her research by asking questions instead of giving answers.

- Co-create communication routine and quality gates: how often do you want to meet for feedback? At what stages of the research project is a meeting essential for the project's success?

## EXERCISES

1. Explore and visualise the different paradigmatic references framing your research. What are the scientific frames? What are the methodological frames? What discourses are describing the field?
2. Describe your research as a project according to the Logical Framework (Logframe).
3. Rapid-prototype your research in the form of an abstract and a graphic: what is the key message/spin?

## References

Agamben, G., D'Isanto, L. and Attell, K. (2009). *The Signature of All Things: On method*. New York, Cambridge, MA: Zone Books, distributed by the MIT Press.

Argyris, C. (1990). *Overcoming Organizational Defenses: Facilitating 'organizational learning*. Boston, MA: Allyn and Bacon.

Bauder, B. and Weiland, C. (2013). *Processing the Process: A Balanced Approach to Process Engineering* (White Paper). Berlin: SEgroup.

Beer, S. (1995). *Brain of the Firm* (2nd edition). Hoboken, NJ: Wiley.

Berger, P. L. and Luckmann, T. (1967). *The Social Construction of Reality: A treatise in the sociology of knowledge*. Garden City, NY: Doubleday.

Biesenthal, C. and Klein, L. (2013). *Towards a Praxeology of Resilient Project Management – A Conceptual Framework* (White Paper Draft). Berlin: SEgroup. Retrieved from http://www.segroup.de/library. Accessed: 20.08.2014.

Buchanan, R. (1992). Wicked problems in design thinking. *Design Issues*, 8(2), 5, doi:10.2307/1511637.

Buzan, T. and Buzan, B. (1993). *The Mind Map Book: How to use radiant thinking to maximize your brain's untapped potential*. New York, NY: Plume.

Cooperrider, D. L. and Whitney, D. K. (2005). *Appreciative Inquiry: A positive revolution in change*. San Francisco, CA: Berrett-Koehler. Retrieved from http://www.books24x7.com/marc.asp?bookid=11869. Accessed: 20.08.2014.

De Bono, E. (1973). *Lateral Thinking: Creativity step by step*. New York:, NY Harper & Row.

Deming, W. E. (1982). *Quality, Productivity, and Competitive Position*. Cambridge, MA: Massachusetts Institute of Technology, Center for Advanced Engineering Study.

Diaz-Bone, R. (2008). Économie des conventions – ein transdisziplinäres Fundament für die neue empirische Wirtschaftssoziologie (The Économie des Conventions – Transdisciplinary Discussions and Perspectives). Presented at the ahrestagung der Sektion Wirtschaftssoziologie der DGS, Berlin.

Elias, N. (1969). *The Civilizing Process, Vol. I. The history of manners* (Vols I–II, Vol. I). Oxford: Blackwell.

Elias, N. (1982). *The Civilizing Process, Vol II. State formation and civilization* (Vols I–II, Vol. II). Oxford: Blackwell.

Fleck, L. (1986). 'The Problem of Epistemology [1936]' in *Cognition and Fact*, Dordrecht: Springer Netherlands, pp. 79–112. Retrieved from http://link.springer.com/chapter/10.1007/978-94-009-4498-5_5. Accessed: 20.08.2014.

Flood, R. L. (1990). Liberating systems theory: Toward critical systems thinking. *Human Relations*, 43(1), 49–75, doi:10.1177/001872679004300104.

Forrester, J. W. (1961). *Industrial Dynamics*. Waltham: Pegasus Communications.

Garfinkel, H. (1984). *Studies in Ethnomethodology* (1. Auflage.). New York, NY: John Wiley & Sons.

Gleick, J. (1998). *Chaos. Making a New Science*. London, UK: Vintage.

Goldratt, E. M. (1999). *Theory of Constraints: What is this thing called and how should it be implemented?* Croton-on-Hudson, NY: North River Press.

Habermas, J. (1983). *Moralbewusstsein und kommunikatives Handeln* (Moral Consciousness and Communicative Action ). Frankfurt am Main: Suhrkamp.

Handy, C. B. (1993). *Understanding Organizations*. New York, NY: Oxford University Press.

Hofstede, G. H. (1984). *Culture's Consequences: International differences in work-related values*. Beverly Hills, CA: Sage Publications.

Hofstede, G., Hofstede, G. J. and Minkov, M. (2010). *Cultures and Organizations: Software of the mind; intercultural cooperation and its importance for survival*. New York, NY: McGraw-Hill.

Huizinga, J. (1939). *Homo ludens. Versuch einer Bestimmung des Spielelementes der Kultur. [Gebundene Ausgabe]* (Homo ludens. A Study of the Play-Element in Culture). Amsterdam: Pantheon.

Jackson, M. C. (1991). The origins and nature of critical systems thinking. *Systems Practice*, 4(2), 131–149, doi:10.1007/BF01068246.

Klein, L. (forthcoming). Thoughts on an ecology of paradigms – A socio-cybernetic perspective on social complexity. *Systems Research & Behavioral Science*.

Klein, L. (2004). Systemic inquiry. Theorie, methodologie und praxis (Systemic inquiry. Theory, methodology and practice). *Unternehmensberater*, 1, 22–24.

Klein, L. (2005). Systemic inquiry – Exploring organisations. *Kybernetes*, 34(3/4), 439–447.

Klein, L. (2008). Designing Social Complexity – Towards a Next Practice of Complex Project Management Based on a Comprehensive Theory of Social Systems (pp. 158–163). Presented at the 22nd IPMA World Congress 'Project Management to Eun,' Roma: IPMA. Retrieved from http://www.iccpm.com/sites/default/files/kcfinder/files/Mastering%20Complex%20Projects%20LKlein.pdf. Accessed: 20.08.2014.

Klein, L. (2012a). *Social Complexity in Project Management* (White Paper). Berlin: SEgroup. Retrieved from http://www.systemic-excellence-group.com/sites/default/files/klein_2012_scpm.pdf. Accessed: 20.08.2014.

Klein, L. (2012b). The three inevitabilities of human being. A conceptual hierarchy model approaching social complexity. *Kybernetes*, 41(7/8), 977–984.

Klein, L. and Weiland, C. (forthcoming). 'Critical Systemic Inquiry' in K. Molbjerg Jorgensen and C. Largacha-Martinez (eds), *Critical Narrative Inquiry – Ethics, sustainability and action*. Hauppauge: Nova Science Publisher.

Klein, L. and Wong, T. S. L. (2010). *Yin and Yang of Change – Systemic Efficacy in Change Management* (White Paper). Berlin: SEgroup.

Kotter, J. P. (1996). *Leading Change*. Harvard: Harvard Business School Press.

Kuhn, T. S. (1962). *The Structure of Scientific Revolutions*. Chicago, IL: University of Chicago Press.

Luhmann, N. (1984). *Soziale Systeme: Grundriß einer allgemeinen Theorie* (15th edition). Berlin: Suhrkamp Verlag.

Malinowski, B. (1923). 'The Problem of Meaning in Primitive Languages' in C.K. Ogden and I.A. Richards (eds),: *The Meaning of Meaning: A study of the influence of language upon thought and of the science of symbolism*. New York: Harvest/HBJ, pp. 451–510.

Mauss, M. (1925). *The Gift: Forms and functions of exchange in archaic societies*. Mansfield Centre, CT: Martino.

Owen, H. (2008). *Open Space Technology: A user's guide* (3rd revised edition). New York: McGraw-Hill Professional.

Rowe, P. G. (1987). *Design Thinking*. Cambridge, MA: MIT Press.

Schein, E. H. (1980). *Organizational Psychology*. Englewood Cliffs, NJ: Prentice-Hall.

Schirmacher, W. (2000). *German 20th-century Philosophy: The Frankfurt school*. New York: Continuum.

Senge, P. M. (2006). *The Fifth Discipline: The art and practice of the learning organization*. New York: Doubleday/Currency.

Tichy, N. M. (1983). *Managing Strategic Change. Technical, political, and cultural dynamics*. New York, NY: Wiley-Interscience.

Trompenaars, A. (1994). *Riding the Waves of Culture: Understanding diversity in global business*. Burr Ridge, IL: Irwin Professional Pub.

Trompenaars, A. and Hampden-Turner, C. (2004). *Managing People Across Cultures*. Oxford: Capstone.

Trompenaars, A. and Woolliams, P. (2003). *Business Across Cultures*. Chichester: Capstone. Retrieved from http://search.ebscohost.com/login.aspx?direct=true&scope=site&db=nlebk&db=nlabk&AN=105142. Accessed: 20.08.2014.

Von Foerster, H. (1979). *Cybernetics of Cybernetics*. Urbana: University of Illinois.

Watzlawick, P., Bavelas, J. B., Jackson, D. D. and O'Hanlon, W. H. (1967). *Pragmatics of Human Communication: A study of interactional patterns, pathologies, and paradoxes*. New York, NY: W.W. Norton & Co.

Wetherell, M., Yates, S., Taylor, S. and Open University. (2001). *Discourse Theory And Practice: A reader*. London, UK, and Thousand Oaks, CA: Sage.

# PART II
# FOCUSING YOUR
# RESEARCH EFFORT

Moving from foundational issues and setting the context of your research now demands of you the need to focus your research effort. This will require you to critically engage the literature, understand the parameters of your subject domain and construct question(s) that will ultimately drive your thesis. This is not an easy step but one that will serve you enormously throughout your career whether it is inside or outside the academy. You will develop your skills in sourcing, reviewing and critically analysing the literature and, in doing so, increase your ability to specify issues, develop arguments and articulate questions.

What does this step involve? The authors in this section offer perspectives, techniques and examples that will help you take these steps. The tips, questions and exercises will help you work through the challenges of navigating the literature and narrowing the parameters of your topic domain to reach the point of question design. Rather than interpret the authors, the following list offers brief summaries of how they do this taken from the abstracts of their chapters.

- Rogerio Lacerda and Leonardo and Sandra Ensslin examine the impact of the vision of success in projects and the methodological approaches to solving research problems in PM.
- Lehtiranta, Junnonen, Kärnä and Pekuri introduce the principles of constructive research to solve practical problems of PM while also producing an academically appreciated theoretical contribution.
- Hällgren examines the choosing and strategising of a strategy for your research contribution and framing it for a specified audience. Such choices are integrated and are crucial for your research and possibly academic career.
- Beverley and Derek Walker offer chapters that were specifically written as stages in the process of engaging the literature to explore research methods and determine a research question. Their perspectives are based on the successful supervision of dozens of master's and doctoral students and have been written here as lessons for your own efforts.
- Jonasson and Ingason focus on ethics – one of the most fundamental issues of research in PM or anywhere else. They introduce methods to heighten ethical awareness and encourage project researchers to develop their own approach to investigating project, programme and portfolio management realities.
- Tong and Thomson delve even further into the details of reviewing literature and provide an overview of the process and procedures to help shape your literature review.
- Nijhuis ends this section with a specific example of his use of a literature review based on the comparison of studies (PM competences in this case) that will show you how to use such a comparison as a resource in your own review.

# 7

# Research Methods and Success Meaning in Project Management

Rogério T.O. Lacerda, Leonardo Ensslin and Sandra Rolim Ensslin

*Our purpose in writing this chapter is to create a critical view in the researchers and to contribute to the robustness of the scientific results in the PM field.*

The practice and scientific progress in the field of knowledge in PM has been influenced by various worldviews. Each worldview carries assumptions thought to be the successful projects and it is part of the set of elements that makes the researchers adopt a certain methodological approach for their researches. In this context, this chapter examines the impact of the vision of success in projects and the process of choice of methodological approaches to solve research problems in PM. At the end of this chapter, you will understand how the decision-making process regarding the project success is differentiated based on the research approach and the respective role of the stakeholders or project sponsor.

At the end of this chapter, the reader can:

- analyse how the PM practices have been influenced by scientific paradigms;
- describe the relevance of the alignment between the methods and the concept adopt of the project success;
- examine the repercussions of the concept of project success adopted by the researcher in the methods that he/she uses in his/her research.

Keywords: methodological choices, project success, decision, research design

## Contextualisation

PM practitioners and researchers have developed practices for the corporate environment without having a broad theoretical understanding of the knowledge field (Williams, 2005). However, in the last years, the management scientists have demonstrated a growing interest in PM and published articles in good quality management periodicals, discussing the theory of PM. In this way, Shenhar and Dvir (2007) believe it is time to develop a new understanding of PM, because such an understanding will probably have an impact on practice and education in the discipline, and eventually influence the development of tools and processes.

Because the development of PM has been influenced by a hard approach (Williams, 2005), the traditional tool of PM tends to emphasise efficient, expert-led delivery, control against predetermined goals and an interest in underlying structure (Pollack, 2007). In contrast with this, the soft paradigm makes practical use of learning, participation, the facilitated exploration of projects, and typically demonstrates an interest in underlying social processes to manage the project to the success (Lacerda, Ensslin and Ensslin, 2011b).

Framing the success of a project with focus on stakeholders instead of pre-established requirements brings reflections against the classic iron triangle (Tukel and Rom, 2001). Some studies show that successful projects are influenced by several variables, including the management techniques used and types of projects (Coombs, McMeekin and Pybus, 1998; Dvir, Lipovetsky, Shenhar and Tishler, 1998; Lacerda et al., 2011b; Shenhar, Tishler, Dvir, Lipovetsky and Lechler, 2002).

This issue is relevant because the final result of the project is evaluated differently by different stakeholders, and the success criteria must reflect different points of view (Lipovetsky, Tishler, Dvir and Shenhar, 1997; Shenhar et al., 2002). If the project manager missed any point of view may conduct the project to fail. Thus, there are opportunities for research aiming to explain what success means and discuss the approaches to get a successful project (Lacerda et al., 2011b).

Some authors observe that the soft approach has positive impacts on management when technological uncertainty is high (De Meyer, Loch and Pich, 2002), the long-term consequences are diffuse, the project is liable to external factors, the project results in a change in the organisation or market, and the complexities of the project are high (Atkinson, Crawford and Ward, 2006). These conditions represent the complex and ambiguous world companies face on a daily basis in a more accurate way (Pich, Loch and Meyer, 2002). Model analysis should consider the context of possible use, to ensure the identification of appropriate approaches.

The projects need to be analysed individually and are broadly dependent on the internal and external context of the project (Lacerda et al., 2011b), since a successful approach or technique of PM in a specific environment may produce failure in another project or in different circumstances (Engwall, 2003).

Nevertheless, it is important to remember that hard interpretations of PM are not said to be either right or wrong (Lacerda et al., 2011b). The adequacy of an approach will depend fundamentally on the view of what it means to be successful in PM, and this choice will propagate in the research methods and the scientific results.

Therefore, it is necessary to analyse the approach more deeply in order to see how it has influenced the development of PM to date, as well as to question whether the approach is adequate for a discipline dealing with the dynamic reality nowadays, where the physical context interacts with the actors' values and preferences (Roy, 1996).

Having contextualised the research challenges of PM nowadays, there is a need to understand the means that science has to meet these challenges. These ways of dealing with such problems are approaches adopted by the researcher or professionals when finding solutions to organisational problems. Each approach carries with it a set of assumptions that affects the way that PM is understood, developed and implemented during the research process (Karlsson, 2008; Roy, 1993).

Thus, the approaches and their work assumptions are worldviews that act as filters in the eyes of researchers and professionals, making them see specific things and ignore others in the context in which they operate (Melão and Pidd, 2000).

For an understanding of these approaches, Roy (1993) categorises three ways to deal with problems in the decision-making process and these are treated in the following sections: (1) the path of realism, (2) the axiomatic path and (3) the method of constructivism.

## The Path of Realism

The path of realism is based on the assumption of the generation of knowledge from experiments that need to be determined objectively, that is, without the interference of human perception.

In light of this approach, the problem of a project is restricted to the physical pole, represented by some of the physical properties that are recognised by a group of researchers as representative of the reality in which the problem is present.

For the path of realism, the researchers' interaction with the world and the environment of the problem are not taken into account in the formulation of the problem. In this view, the data for model construction are sought in the physical world and the scientific knowledge developed. Thus, the roles of the researchers are the roles of those who choose the model to be used or observers. These are roles that divide the path of realism into two views: normative and descriptive.

## The Path of Normative Realism

The path of normative realism delegates to researchers the roles of selecting which theoretical model (mathematical or economic) will be used and, for the model chosen, collecting the data and determining the optimal solution to the problem modeled. This approach of normative realism assumes a decision-maker who wants to decide by rationality, that is, a decision-maker who operates according to principles that reason itself creates and that are consistent with reality as it is accepted by a rational being, devoid of emotions.

For this to occur, the representations and basis for understanding the problems are defined by mathematical models and/or previously developed economic models that make explicit the factors to be taken into account to reach project success.

In order for this approach to be valid, there is a need for recognition that: (1) the stakeholders of the projects are rational beings and (2) the stakeholders recognise that reality is adequately represented in the model. That is, in view of the normative realism approach, the models are universal and the information for the formulated model is sought in the physical context in question. The path of normative realism defines that the stakeholder *must* decide and deviations from the results of the models chosen are considered bad decisions.

## The Path of Descriptive Realism

Specifically, the method of descriptive realism is based on the search for relationships between (1) the decisions made by the practitioners in the past, (2) the available variables and (3) the results collected from the past. For this to be achieved, researchers assume the role of observers of the environment studied, where their main function is to discover which variables interfere with the results expected by the project sponsors or decision-makers.

Thus, the models do not pre-exist, but are deducted by means of the empirical studies of the past, that is, collecting data on a given context. Once deducted, the models are used by researchers to determine the value of the controllable variables that would have allowed the best result for the problem to be achieved in the past when the uncontrolled variables assumed certain behaviours.

The descriptive approach assumes that stakeholders:

- agree that the results of the past will be repeated in the future;

- agree the use of statistics (mean, median and mode) as the estimate to be used for the probability distribution of the variables considered;
- agree that the variables considered represent the project success sufficiently.

The determination of which variables are taken into account and the intensity of their interest is a function of the correlation of the data (variables) available with the desired results. These approaches do not bother to test the sufficiency of the variables to explain the phenomenon since they examine all the variables with available data. Thus, if there are important variables that have not previously been documented, they will be ignored.

Compared with the normative vision, the project sponsors continue to be rational beings, since the models are derived from the analysis of the correlations between the properties of the physical context and the desired results.

This understanding of descriptive and normative realism carries with it the recognition of a generic (universal and rational) decision-maker. This is one of the reasons why Roy (1993) makes no distinction between the descriptive and the normative approach, calling them generically realism. However, despite the widespread role of actors in the decision-making process, the descriptive approach *can* recognise the uniqueness of the context; then, for this approach, empirical studies *may* arise both *from the specific project* and *from similar projects*, while for the path of normative realism, the data collection is performed in a unique project.

Given the considerations of the previous sections, the path of realism can be characterised by recognising that:

- the stakeholders' perceptions about the project success are not taken into account;
- the models are universal while the normative data are necessarily unique to the context;
- the descriptive models may be universal or unique;
- the origin of the normative model stems from the economic or mathematical formulations made and adopted by the researcher as truth;
- the origin of the descriptive model arises from the correlations of the variables used in the past with the result desired by the project sponsors.

## The Axiomatic (Prescriptive) Path

The axiomatic method is also called the prescriptive approach and aims, from the discourse of the decision-maker or project sponsors, to identify deductive logic to identify the values and preferences of the stakeholders to build a model and therefore prescribe solutions that must be accepted by the stakeholders in the decision process.

In contrast to the path of realism, the prescriptive approach recognises that deductive logic should be used to construct a model showing the system of values and preferences of the project sponsor, from his/her perception (Montibeller, Belton, Ackermann and Ensslin, 2007).

The consequence of this approach creates another category of the decision context: contexts in which the decision-maker and his interpretation of project success is part of the process of identifying and measuring the variables to be taken into account in the model building for project success definition, in contrast to the path of realism, in which the stakeholders do not participate in the process of defining the variables used by the model.

For the prescriptive path, the key element to be considered for the evaluation of the project is the perception of the project sponsor about the physical context of the project. This perception of the decision-maker can evolve throughout the process, as a result of the learning that is the result of the feedback from his/her own speech.

Once built, the model is used by researchers (1) to represent the project success, from the perspective of the sponsors, (2) to highlight the strengths and weaknesses of the project, as perceived by the sponsors, and (3) to pursue actions to improve performance as perceived by the sponsors.

A particularity of the prescriptive approach is that the decision-maker should faithfully express his or her worldview through speeches and answers to questions that the project manager or experts formulate and through *feedback* to the decision-maker about the partial models built by the specialists, which are the result of previous interactions with the decision-maker. The role of the researchers is to instigate the decision-maker speech that allows the researchers (in the role of facilitator) to draw the criteria, the organisation and its measurement, ensuring that they are accepted by the project sponsors as representative of their values and preferences.

What characterises the prescriptive method is the recognition that the sponsors' perceptions about the context will define the variables and their importance in the project success definition. In the prescriptive model, understanding what is important in a given project is manifested by the sponsor in his/her speech at first. The speech is interpreted by the facilitator secondly. The continuation is represented in the model by the facilitator. Finally it is legitimised or denied by the project sponsor, who in the latter case restarts the speech. The process only ends with the complete legitimacy of the decision-maker.

The prescriptive path assumes that the project sponsor has sufficient understanding of the project to address the criteria and scales that represent his/her values and preferences for the project.

Thus, the origin of the prescriptive models stems from the deductions made from the sponsors' speech and the data to feed the models are necessarily unique to each project evaluated.

## The Path of Constructivism

The constructivist approach, like the prescriptive path, recognises that the project success definition must emerge from the discourse of the sponsors or decision-makers (Montibeller et al., 2007). The difference between the two ways is that the path of constructivism assumes that the project sponsors do not have sufficient understanding to explain the criteria associated with the preferences and values needed to define the project success (Bortoluzzi, Ensslin and Ensslin, 2010; Lacerda, Ensslin and Ensslin, 2011a).

The project sponsors want to be helped by the facilitator (researcher) to expand his/her knowledge along with the definition of project success. In the constructivism path, the researcher should make use of a process that first creates the conditions for the decision-maker to expand his understanding of values and preferences and how these may be represented in the model. In a second stage, this knowledge can be utilised in the model for the decision-maker to see the consequences of his/her decisions for the criteria associated with the values. In a third step, the constructed knowledge should enable the decision-maker to have a process to identify opportunities to improve the consequences of the impact of the context on his values and preferences.

This approach aims to generate knowledge in decision making during the construction of the model, so that the project sponsor can understand the consequences of the current situation and its evolution caused by the project for the strategic objectives. Thus, for the path of constructivism, the values and preferences of the project sponsor do not pre-exist in a stable form. The project sponsors' value system is explained in the course of project success definition, and from this process, the project sponsors' preferences are constructed and stabilised in a parallel and successive way (Dias and Tsoukiàs, 2003; Roy, 1993).

In addition to this recursive process of learning, according to the constructivist approach, the project definition success also involves other stakeholders who are in a larger context and who affect and are affected by the decisions under review.

Towards constructivism, the role of the researcher is to instigate further the decision-maker's speech for explicit information to enable the facilitator to assist him in building the criteria, the organisation and its measurement, and also to provide feedback to the decision-makers and actors involved in the evolution of the model (Keeney, 1996).

This activity allows the facilitator to understand the consequences of the decision-making context for the values and preferences, and so justify or revise the decision. In addition, the process gives the opportunity to all to participate in the process of constructing the model, favouring the expansion of understanding of the decision-maker with the perceptions of other stakeholders. However, the final decision on what the model will consist of and how it will be produced will be the responsibility of the project sponsor.

The inconsistencies of the decision-maker between his/her speech and what he/she realises about the model are not considered a problem, but are sources of discussion and the generation of knowledge about the context and his value system (Dias and Tsoukiàs, 2003).

With these considerations, it can be inferred that what characterises the method of constructivism is the recognition that:

1. the decision-maker's value system defines the variables and their importance in the project success definition;
2. the construction of knowledge of what is important in a given project is focused on the decision-maker;
3. the data to feed the models are necessarily unique to the project;
4. the origin of the constructivist model stems from deductions made from the decision-maker's speech, but also from the feedback process of the decision-maker in assessing the model during the process of model building.

## Conclusions

As shown in this chapter, each research approach carries with it a set of assumptions that should be accepted as truth by the researcher in order to align research objectives with scientific procedures adopted (Table 7.1 summarises).

The choice of methodological approach is closely linked with the scientific research objectives. Thus, researchers should pay attention to this alignment, as well as be explicit in their research reports, papers and the assumptions that were taken into account when selecting the methodological approach.

It is important to highlight that there is not a better approach than the other. However, there are research questions that are better suited to be answered by certain methodological approaches. Thus, the methodological framework and alignment between objectives and approaches of research are critical success factors in scientific research and these conditions must be explained in the body of the research report, thesis, dissertation or papers.

## Tips and Exercises

### TIPS FOR STUDENTS

• Be clear about the concept of the project success assumed in the report research. There is not a right or wrong concept of project success, but the omission of this issue could denote a weakness of the research.

**Table 7.1    Summary of approaches**

| Characteristics/ Approaches | Normative | Descriptive | Prescriptive | Constructivist |
|---|---|---|---|---|
| Participation of decision-maker | Little or none. | | Full participation of the decision-maker because the model contains what is important to monitor and improve from decision-maker perspective. | |
| Who legitimises the results? | The legitimating is out to the context in which decisions are made. | | The decision-maker legitimises and informs that the model contemplates what is important in the context. | |
| The results aim to help who? | The results consider the views that have been identified by the researcher as representative. Thus, the model is intended to be generic. | | The results represent the perception, values and preferences of the decision-maker, so it is recommended only for the decision-maker. | |
| The related decision process | Decision making (which project to choose?) | | Decision aiding (Build the project scope around the decision-maker's objectives) | |
| Role of the researcher | Select the appropriate model and use this model to find the optimal solution. | Describe how the decision-makers decided in practice and from there select and use practices of more successful results. | From the decision-maker's speech, build a model that eliminates inconsistencies and help the facilitator to find alternatives that best meet the criteria of the model. | Interact with the decision-maker to expand their understanding as well as to model the relationship of their values with the physical and social context to help the decision-maker understandhow to act on the context to achieve his values. |
| Typical methodological procedures | Math modelling, fuzzy logic, pre-existing models in the literature or business environment, international standards, so on. | Survey, simulation, Data Envelopment Analysis (DEA), variance analysis, ethnography, so on. | Unique case study, Multicriteria Decision Analysis (MCDA), Analytic Hierarchy Process (AHP), ELECTRE family (Elimination and Choice Expressing Reality), action research, so on. | Unique case study, action research, Soft System Methodology (SSM), MCDA Constructivist, so on. |
| Typical research questions | 'Which project must be executed (selected)?' | 'What factors explain the success of projects in general, from a historical basis?' | 'What are the criteria to be selected to explain the project success, from the perception of the sponsor?' | 'How to expand the understanding of the sponsor in order to identify the criteria associated with his objectives?' |
| Project success is… | … submit to sponsor the way he must manage the project in order to achieve maximum efficiency in use of resources. | … analyse data from past projects and identify the variables associated with the desired results, ensuring that future projects observing these aspects. | … capture what the sponsor desires and to propose project activities that meet these interests. | … to build in the sponsor the knowledge in order for him/her to understand the consequences of the project activities on his objectives. |

- Recognise that there is not a better methodological approach for any research. Consider the most suitable methodological design for *your* research when your focus is 'project success'.
- Examine your research questions and analyse if they are aligned with the research methods and the concept of project success that you are adopting. Express your position and be consistent with your worldview throughout the research.
- What is the relation about the success meaning and the choice of the research approach to deal with the PM challenges today?

## TIPS FOR SUPERVISORS

- Encourage students to express their opinions about what is project success. The supervisor's role is to create an environment in which the most varied opinions can be expressed.
- Compile the different worldviews of project success and link them with the methodological approaches presented in this chapter.
- Ensure that all students participate in the discussion. Do not let a worldview dominate the discussions, even if the supervisor is closely linked to some worldview.
- Be the facilitator of the learning process always presenting the pros and cons of each approach.

## EXERCISES

For better absorption of the concepts presented, as well as its practical usefulness for scientific research, below are some suggestions of exercises that can be conducted by the supervisor or teacher when their classes.

1. Ask students to carry out a framing of their own research into one of four approaches presented. To present the role to be played by the project sponsor (decision-maker) and the researcher. To present which vision of project success that the researcher is adopting. If you change the project sponsor, will the vision of project success be the same? Explain the concept of alignment between project success and the approach taken.
2. Ask students to bring papers that will be references of their research or well-cited articles from qualified journals that deal with PM practice. With each paper, consider
   - the execution of each paper with one of the approaches;
   - possible limitations of research that can be met by using another approach;
   - possible research questions for each approach presented in this chapter.
3. Ask students to list the techniques of PMBoK and discuss how each approach might have most influenced their development.
4. Explore what the critical skills, abilities and knowledge are that the researcher must develop in order to develop their research in each of the approaches.

## References

Atkinson, R., Crawford, L. and Ward, S. (2006). Fundamental uncertainties in projects and the scope of project management. *International Journal of Project Management*, 24(8), 687–698.

Bortoluzzi, S. C., Ensslin, S. R. and Ensslin, L. (2010). Avaliação de desempenho dos aspectos tangíveis e intangíveis da área de mercado: Estudo de caso em uma média empresa industrial. *Revista Brasileira de Gestão de Negócios (RBGN)*, 12(37), 425–446.

Coombs, R., McMeekin, A. and Pybus, R. (1998). Toward the development of benchmarking tools for R&D project management. *R&D Management,* 28(3), 175–186, doi:10.1111/1467-9310.00094.

De Meyer, A., Loch, C. H. and Pich, M. T. (2002). From variation to chaos. *MIT Sloan Management Review,* winter, pp. 60–67.

Dias, L. C. and Tsoukiàs, A. (2003). *On the constructive and other approaches in decision aiding.* Paper presented at the Proceedings of the 57th meeting of the EURO MCDA working group.

Dvir, D., Lipovetsky, S., Shenhar, A. and Tishler, A. (1998). In search of project classification: A non-universal approach to project success factors. *Research Policy,* 27(9), 915–935.

Engwall, M. (2003). No project is an island: Linking projects to history and context. *Research Policy,* 32(5), 789–808.

Karlsson, C. (2008). *Researching Operations Management.* Routledge.

Keeney, R. L. (1996). Value-focused thinking: Identifying decision opportunities and creating alternatives. *European Journal of Operational Research,* 92(3), 537–549.

Lacerda, R. T. O., Ensslin, L. and Ensslin, S. R. (2011a). A performance measurement framework in portfolio management: A constructivist case. *Management Decision,* 49(4), 1–15.

Lacerda, R. T. O., Ensslin, L. and Ensslin, S. R. (2011b). A performance measurement view of IT project management. *The International Journal of Productivity and Performance Management,* 60(2), 132–151.

Lipovetsky, S., Tishler, A., Dvir, D. and Shenhar, A. (1997). The relative importance of project success dimensions. *R&D Management,* 27(2), 97–106, doi:10.1111/1467-9310.00047.

Melão, N. and Pidd, M. (2000). A conceptual framework for understanding business processes and business process modelling. *Information Systems Journal,* 10(2), 105–129.

Montibeller, G., Belton, V., Ackermann, F. and Ensslin, L. (2007). Reasoning maps for decision aid: An integrated approach for problem-structuring and multi-criteria evaluation. *Journal of the Operational Research Society,* 59(5), 575–589.

Pich, M. T., Loch, C. H. and Meyer, A. D. (2002). On uncertainty, ambiguity, and complexity in project management. *Management Science,* 48(8), 1008.

Pollack, J. (2007). The changing paradigms of project management. *International Journal of Project Management,* 25(3), 266–274.

Roy, B. (1993). Decision science or decision-aid science? *European Journal of Operational Research,* 66(2), 184–203.

Roy, B. (1996). *Multicriteria Methodology for Decision Aiding.* Kluwer Academic Pub.

Shenhar, A. J. and Dvir, D. (2007). Project management research – the challenge and opportunity. *Project Management Journal,* 38(2), 93.

Shenhar, A. J., Tishler, A., Dvir, D., Lipovetsky, S. and Lechler, T. (2002). Refining the search for project success factors: A multivariate, typological approach. *R&D Management,* 32(2), 111–126, doi: doi:10.1111/1467-9310.00244.

Tukel, O. I. and Rom, W. O. (2001). An empirical investigation of project evaluation criteria. *International Journal of Operations & Production Management,* 21(3), 400.

Williams, T. (2005). Assessing and moving on from the dominant project management discourse in the light of project overruns. *IEEE Transactions on Engineering Management,* 52(4), 497–508.

# 8

# The Constructive Research Approach: Problem Solving for Complex Projects

Liisa Lehtiranta, Juha-Matti Junnonen, Sami Kärnä and Laura Pekuri

*We wrote this chapter on the constructive research approach because we have found it a motivating and productive choice for doctoral students who wish to solve practical problems while producing an academically appreciated theoretical contribution.*

The aim of constructive research is to solve practical problems while producing an academically appreciated theoretical contribution. The solutions, that is, constructs, can be processes, practices, tools or organisation charts. The research process involves the following: (1) selecting a practically relevant problem; (2) obtaining a comprehensive understanding of the study area; (3) designing one or more applicable solutions to the problem; (4) demonstrating the solution's feasibility; (5) linking the results back to the theory and demonstrating their practical contribution; and (6) examining the generalisability of the results. The purpose of this chapter is to introduce readers to the principles of the constructive research approach. In addition, a case study is presented to demonstrate how the constructive research process and the related methodological choices may be applied to solve a PM problem.

At the end of this chapter, the reader can:

* understand the principles of the constructive research approach;
* explain how the constructive research approach can be coupled with different research methods;
* demonstrate how the constructive research approach can be applied to PM process improvement.

Keywords: constructive research, case study, pragmatism, pluralism

This chapter will introduce a pragmatic, yet rigorous, methodological approach that enables the combination of practical problem solving and scientific theory contribution. Ideally, a real-world management problem is solved by implementing a novel construct, such as a management tool, technique, process, or organisation chart (Lukka, 2000). The dual aims of constructive research are achieved by combining existing theories with real-world problems (Figure 8.1). Therefore, the constructive research approach has significant potential to bridge (some of) the gap between academia and practice.

Kasanen et al. (1993) have advanced the use of the constructive research approach in management accounting research. A few examples of project-based operations research employ a constructive approach, such as Oyegoke's (2011) suggestion of a specialist task organisation procurement approach and Alsakini's (2012) design of models to manage the virtualisation of construction firms. This chapter aims to introduce an application of constructive research to design and test PM process improvement.

The case study illustrated in this chapter is based on a pressing issue in construction PM: the projects and project organisations are increasingly complex, but the traditional standard risk management processes are not fully adequate. A key to construction project risk management is fitting management structures into complex, collaboration-intensive construction project organisations. A need exists to complement the single-organisation risk management process with practices and techniques that utilise and support interdisciplinary expertise and collaboration in a complex construction project organisation. The illustrative example in this chapter comprises a real research project and demonstrates how the constructive research approach has been coupled with a set of research methods to design and test constructs for collaborative risk management.

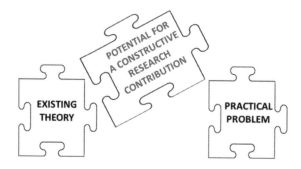

**Figure 8.1**    **Potential for a constructive research contribution**

## The Rationale of Constructive Research

### RESEARCH PHILOSOPHY

In its inherent assumptions, the constructive research approach leans on pragmatism (Lukka, 2000) for the core idea that the meaning of knowledge is determined by its practical consequences (Hammersley, 2004). Thus, constructive research is interested in problem resolutions, which could have an impact on the current state of affairs, that is, that knowledge should have instrumental value. In addition, the idea that the practical feasibility of a construct should be determined by a practical test comes down to pragmatist notions. Although the constructive research approach has emerged from practical needs and the requirements for applied research, there are also the philosophical premises underlying the approach that a researcher should consider.

The constructive research approach may be regarded as a form of case/field research parallel to ethnographic research, grounded theory, illustrative case research, theory testing case research, and action research (Lukka, 2000). Constructive research is distinct from action research, which is described in other chapters in this book, by two main differences. First, constructive research always focuses on the construct as an outcome, whereas action research may have other goals. Second, the researchers' interaction with practice and practitioners is (only) common in constructive research but obligatory in action research.

Kasanen et al. (1993) present the constructive research approach as a type of applied study that aims to produce new knowledge as a normative application. That is, the results of constructive research should express how one should act in a current situation to achieve a desired state. There is, thus, an assumption about the causality of things: to propose an action to fix a problematic situation, there is an assumption that the action will cause some anticipated effects. Without the assumption, presenting these types of technical norms would be illogical. It is this normative character and the pursuit of change in reality that differentiates constructive research from other case/field research types and especially from other less empirical and more basic types of research.

Constructive research should always begin by finding a practically relevant research problem (Kasanen et al., 1993). Common ways of devising these types of problems include being offered a problem by a company or identifying a practically relevant research gap from the literature (Labro and Tuomela, 2003). After finding a practical problem that also has research potential, researchers' actions should focus on solving the problem. Thus, the research process proceeds by obtaining a comprehensive understanding about the problem situation and the relevant theories that may contribute to constructing the solution.

It should be noted, however, that although solving a practical problem is at the centre of all constructive research, not all problem-solving activities should be called constructive research. Kasanen et al. (1993) introduce four elements that should always be included in constructive research, which are displayed in Figure 8.2. To fulfill the requirements of a dual audience, constructive research should be evaluated based on both practical and theoretical contributions.

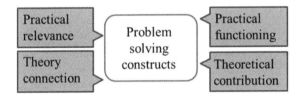

**Figure 8.2    Elements of constructive research (adapted from Kasanen et al., 1993)**

## Applicability to Project Management (PM) Research

Projects with complex organisations challenge researchers due to their complex networks of PM objectives, processes, cultures and tools. However, project complexity can be interpreted and operationalised in terms of differentiation and interdependencies, which, in turn, can be managed by coordination, communication, and control (Baccarini, 1996). Research in such contexts requires a comprehensive approach, enabling the researcher to immerse himself in the characteristics, challenges and opportunities in the collaborative interfaces from different viewpoints and with various complementary methods. The constructive research approach may help obtain such a comprehensive standpoint.

PM is based on the application of various skills and techniques to practical problems. This practicality is reflected in PM research, where every effort is made to develop PM skills and techniques or, in a broader sense, to make human-made artefacts or methods work more effectively (Dewey, 1984). Therefore, it is beneficial to regard pragmatic scientific philosophy as the basis for PM research. Indeed, the goal of PM research may be said to be effecting change and finding relationships within chains of events, instead of focusing only on formulating irrefutable theories that may never even be utilised due to the changing nature of the business environment.

This phenomenon also needs to be acknowledged when considering constructive research: the constructs are, essentially, the best available solutions relative to the dimensions of time and space (Kasanen et al., 1993).

Whereas constructive research is not the most common approach, this tack may significantly narrow the gap between academia and industry. However, operational modes and publication rights should be mutually agreed upon with the industry partners in the early phases of the applicable study.

## LOGICS OF REASONING

The two basic logics of reasoning are deductive and inductive logic. Deductive logic aims to apply general theories to a particular situation, whereas inductive logic proceeds from a particular situation to statements about the results' general applicability. However, neither of the basic logics fully describes constructive research, which employs both logic types. Therefore, constructive research can be regarded as following the abductive logic of reasoning, which involves a cyclical alternation between the inductive and deductive processes. This approach does not produce results that are as certain as those in purely deductive studies, or as probable as those in inductive studies in general, but are nonetheless plausible (Shank, 2008).

Two main cycles of reasoning logic can be identified in the constructive research process. The early stages of the constructive research process resemble deductive logic: from the vast amount of knowledge gained through pre-studies, a single construct is designed and then tested in the situation where the problem was initially identified. In the later stages, where the results' theoretical and practical contributions as well as their wider applicability are considered, the reasoning more closely follows inductive logic.

## Constructive Research Process

The core process, as presented by Kasanen et al. (1993) and Lukka (2000), guides the researcher from research problem selection, through construct design and testing and to the retrieval of practical and theoretical conclusions, as shown in Figure 8.3.

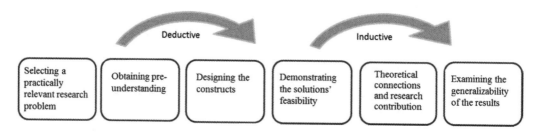

**Figure 8.3    The constructive research process (Kasanen et al., 1993)**

## METHODOLOGICAL CHOICES

Constructive research should be regarded as a research approach that provides a pragmatic goal-oriented umbrella for tailor-made research designs. The approach can be coupled with various methods, techniques and tools for scientific inquiry. In constructive research design, as in PM research in general (Dainty, 2008), a pluralistic approach is strongly recommended. Thus, the varying perspectives offered by several methods add their own unique value to the research, making it stronger than it otherwise would be (Figure 8.4).

The tailor-made methodologies can be used to analyse various sets of data with multiple methods. Commonly accepted research methods, such as interviews, can be used to gather quantitative evidence, qualitative evidence or both for analysing the constructs (Oyegoke, 2011). Several other chapters of this book can be used for more specific methodological guidance.

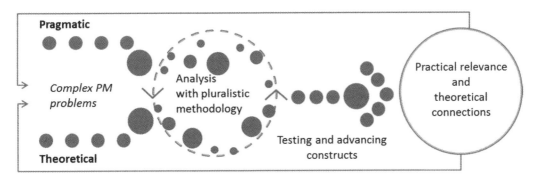

**Figure 8.4**    **Pluralistic research methodology as the 'engine' for anlaysing complex PM problems**

## EVALUATION OF CONSTRUCTIVE RESEARCH

A distinction should be made between the validity of constructive research and the validity of the construct, both of which are invoked in constructive science.

Construct validity is commonly connected to the functionality of the construct, that is, its ability to solve the organisational problem for which it was designed (Lukka, 2000; Oyegoke, 2011). A pilot case study is the preferred means to test and improve a construct (Oyegoke, 2011). While no universal process exists for validating constructs, Kasanen et al. (1993) propose a three-level market-based validation that suits PM research. The weak market test is based on the willingness (not demonstrated action) of a manager to apply the construct. The semi-strong market test is based on the rate of adoption of the construct as demonstrated by companies. The strong market test aims to analyse whether the business units applying the constructs systematically produce better results than those that are not (Kasanen et al., 1993).

However, constructive research involving a failed construct is not necessarily invalid research. The constructive piece of research as a whole can be validated if, and only if, (a) the construction exists and (b) variations in the functionality of the construction causally produce variations in the testing outcomes (Pekuri, 2013 following Borsboom, Mellenbergh and van Heerden, 2004). Whereas the existence of an applied construct is easy to show, the second condition is more challenging to satisfy in the case of a single pilot case project. Projects are unavoidably complex one-off endeavours where parallel tests or detached causal relationships are not feasible. However, the extremes of possible causal relationships can be outlined, and the researcher may evaluate and justify the construct application's success between these extremes. Lukka (2000) suggests applying the following general evaluation criteria of field research to constructive research: relevance of research topic, theoretical connections, clear and fruitful research design, credible study, theoretical contribution, and clear and economic reporting.

## A Constructive Research Design – Case Study

The case research design is based on a doctoral research project and focuses on the Finnish construction industry. The purpose of this example is to demonstrate conducting the constructive research process as guided by Kasanen et al. (1993). The methodological choices made during the process are examples of pluralistic scientific inquiry and should be rethought for each individual study.

The constructive research case sought to identify and test possible solutions for developing collaborative risk management in construction projects. Risk management is an increasingly timely topic in construction PM because complex project environments shape requirements for effective processes. Typical organisational structures in large construction projects can be described as multi-organisations: several firms working together for a fixed time period with partly shared goals. A key issue in determining the success of a multi-organisation is its ability to handle risk and learning (Cherns and Bryant, 1984). Risk management is acknowledged as one of the core competences in all types of projects in the global standard for project risk management (PMI, 2009).

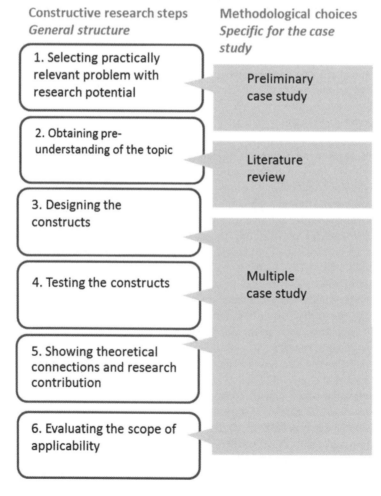

**Figure 8.5**    **Methodological choices in the case research project**

The need for dynamic, collaborative approaches in construction project risk management has increased tremendously. Still, the dominating theories, practices and tools for project risk management are focused on single-organisational contexts. In practice, risk management is generally performed intra-organisationally or as a partially collaborative application within contractual borders. The multi-organisational setting creates a challenging environment for inter-organisational (risk) knowledge management and learning. Thus, a need has arisen to explore processes and methods to enhance the collaborative, multi-organisational approaches to risk management in large Finnish construction management projects. All focal project participants' expertise should be utilised for risk identification and response, including that of the owner, project consultant, designers and contractors.

The constructive research steps are matched with suitable research methods and data so that the methodology reveals different angles of the research problem with a heterogeneous mix of complementary methods, as illustrated in Figure 8.5. Each research step is introduced in more detail in the following paragraphs.

## SELECTING A PRACTICALLY RELEVANT PROBLEM WITH RESEARCH POTENTIAL

Constructive research problems can generally be based on anecdotal evidence, practical experience or theoretical work (Oyegoke 2011). A suitable research problem should offer opportunities for both practical and theoretical contributions. Herein, a preliminary case study was conducted to deepen the understanding of the focal industry context, to define specific research problems, and to form the insight of a suitable theory base for further research. The case study was commenced as an iterative process between empirical interview data and alternative theory bases. Two schools of thought of PM theory were reviewed to identify their theoretical lenses and to observe which base would provide the most realistic view of the interview data:

> **Data:** The empirical data were collected through seven in-depth interviews encompassing all focal parties of the construction project: owners, project consultants, contractors and designers. The prerequisites and hindrances of efficient collaboration in construction projects were discussed in loosely structured theme interviews. One of the focal themes was the challenges and opportunities the multi-organisational working practice sets for project risk management. The interviews were tape recorded and ranged from 36 to 97 minutes. A learning diary enabled reflection on emerging concepts based on the interviews.
>
> **Analysis:** Large construction projects were found to be complex undertakings where the organisational issues represent more perceived risks than technical challenges. The interviewees reported problems related to knowledge management and a lack of structured processes and tools for risk management, which would utilise and support collaboration. Complexity thinking was found to be a better fit to the data than traditional PM theory because it addresses informal, as well as formal, connections and the dynamic nature of PM.
>
> **Conclusions:** The main learning from the preliminary case study was the fit of complexity thinking to the human-based challenges. This finding emphasises the lack of multi-organisational risk management processes and suitable tools and techniques for collaboration-dependent construction projects. The potential for addressing multi-organisational risk management solutions with a complexity-based approach will guide designing constructive research contributions that have practical relevance. The initial selection of the research problem is followed by forming the research question: which complexity-based processes, practices and tools (potential constructs) utilise and support collaborative risk management in collaboration intensive construction project organisations?

## OBTAINING PRE-UNDERSTANDING OF THE TOPIC

The second research step continues to expand the needed pre-understanding for the intended constructs. The pre-study, which is usually based on the literature, should provide the researcher with a thorough understanding of the research problem and its context (Oyegoke, 2011). The experiences of the researcher and participants will influence their understanding of the problem and the context. Herein, a systematic literature review was performed to learn the existing solutions to the stated research question:

> **Data:** The systematic literature review included research papers on multi-organisational project risk management published between 2000 and 2012 (inclusive) in four journals: *International Journal of Project Management* (IJPM), *Project Management Journal* (PMJ), *Journal of Construction Engineering and Management* (JCEM) and *IEEE Transactions on Software Engineering* (TSE). The journal selection covered the PM-focused journals listed in the 2011 JCR Social Sciences Edition complemented with two industry focuses that most prominently feature collaborative risk management applications, that is, construction and software development. JCEM and TSE were the only journals representing suitable scopes in the 2011 JCR Sciences Edition.
>
> **Analysis:** Information was extracted for analysis with regard to the multi-organisational risk perception and risk management approach addressed in each reference. Gaps were identified related to the scope of addressed risks, sharing of responsibilities and utilising collaborative working for risk management.
>
> **Conclusions:** Researchers and practitioners could adopt a wider perspective on risk and advanced risk management approaches as the scope for multi-organisational risk management research and applications. A holistic approach to risk management includes combining the dual perception of risks as both threats and opportunities with the dual role of multi-organisational collaboration as a risk source and a risk management resource. A dynamic approach to risk management involves a shared response, which is designed to be proactive, reactive, and aware.

## DESIGNING THE CONSTRUCTS

Constructs are suggested solutions to the selected research problem. The design phase is creative and heuristic by nature, but it may not be randomly imaginative. This phase needs to be firmly grounded in the actual problem and the knowledge gathered through the pre-understanding phases. Still, very few methodological means can be named to aid the innovation process (Lukka, 2000) or the means are case-specific. The innovation process is dependent on the innovators, which indispensably leaves a certain 'innovative leap' between the evidence and the results. The constructs can be co-created with the target company as a result of long-term research collaboration. Accordingly, the innovation process becomes a consultative iteration between the researcher and the practitioners to ensure the constructs' suitability for practice.

This research aimed at designing collaborative solutions for multi-organisational risk management. Ultimately, the constructs are the result of researchers' suggestions based on the pre-understanding phase, the target project's specific needs, the project organisation's key individuals' preferences and amendments in the application phase.

Based on the special problems that have been detected in multi-organisational construction projects that are related to the lack of suitable tools for collaboration-based risk management, there is a need for involving multiple participants in risk identification and response and a need for managing the risks related to the collaboration itself. The solutions for these challenges will need to address how the risk management processes are integrated as a part of collaborative relationships with the means of procurement and meeting practices. Furthermore, the risk–knowledge management issues within the multi-organisation need to be considered.

Three constructs are suggested to make improvements that correspond to the above needs. The constructs include:

1. Risk workshop – Construct 1 is a focus group application for project-specific risk identification and response planning. The purpose of the construct is the effective kick-off for risk management collaboration, which involves all focal participants.
2. Contractor risk integration – Construct 2 is a procurement and project planning process that integrates contractors as parts of the project risk management process. The purpose of the construct is to trigger contractors' risk awareness and self-management by sharing project-specific risk information in the procurement phase and by asking the contractors to develop contract-specific risk identification and response planning documents.
3. Performance feedback – Construct 3 is a methodology for identifying strengths and weaknesses in collaborative interfaces by collecting and responding to multidirectional performance feedback from the participants (Kärnä, 2009). The construct has two main purposes. First, it is meant to work as a powerful, structured quality risk identification system that utilises the project participants' observations. Second, this construct functions as a development system, as the participants receive useful feedback of their own performance as viewed through others' eyes.


## TESTING AND EVALUATING THE CONSTRUCTS

The objectives of the remaining research steps are to identify, test and evaluate the emerging best practices for interdisciplinary collaboration in construction project risk management. The feedback from this testing phase is crucial for the research results and may lead to changing the constructs. The target organisation's role is prominent in the testing phase. The organisation can influence the research work, for instance as an active developer of constructs, or suffer from resistance to change or lack of resources or interest.


## Case: A Commercial Centre

**Analysis:** Hypotheses were set for testing the three constructs in a commercial centre construction project as listed in Table 8.1. The case was analysed to recognise the benefits and shortcomings of the constructs and their implementation vis-à-vis the hypotheses.

The success of a construct can be evaluated by practical relevance, practical functioning, theory connection and theoretical contribution (Kasanen et al., 1993). To qualify as science, the research contributions need to be explicitly linked to prior theoretical knowledge (Lukka, 2000). This phase may be one of the most demanding phases of the constructive research process and one that distinguishes it from other forms of problem solving, such as consultancy. The means for theory connection usually emerges from the pre-understanding phases, where an emerging theory may already have started guiding the research. Finally, the theory's connection and justification is made explicit after the testing phase, during which the emerging theory may develop substantially.

Generalisability (the scope of applicability of the constructs), can be evaluated once the theory's connections and limitations are acknowledged. In these final steps of the research, the researcher needs to distance herself from the context and again take an academic, critical stance regarding the research process and its results.

**Table 8.1**     **Hypotheses and the bases for conclusions**

| Hypotheses | Rival Theory | Basis for Construct Validation and Improvement |
|---|---|---|
| Construct 1 Risk Workshop | | |
| H1. Risk workshop increases participants' understanding of the project and its risks | H0. Does not result in successful risk management | Project success in terms of budget, schedule, quality and client satisfaction |
| H2. Risk workshop facilitates the mobilisation of collective expertise to identify risks in multidisciplinary teams | | Researcher observations |
| H3. Risk workshop initiates interdisciplinary collaborative risk management | | 16 expert opinions on functionality and development needs |
| Construct 2 Contractor Integration | | |
| H4. Contractor integration improves trade contractors' understanding of project characteristics and risks | H0. Does not result in successful risk management | Project success in terms of budget, schedule, quality and client satisfaction |
| H5. Contractor integration promotes trade contractors' risk responsibility and risk communication | | Researcher observations. Eight participant opinions on functionality and development needs |
| Construct 3 Performance Feedback | | |
| H6. Multidirectional performance feedback facilitates the identification of strengths and weaknesses in multi-organisational project delivery | H0. Does not result in successful risk management | Performance feedback including 36 participants |
| H7. Multidirectional performance feedback facilitates the innovation of process improvements during the project | | Workshop report with identified performance strengths and weaknesses and performance improvement ideas |
| H8. Multidirectional performance feedback facilitates multi-organisational learning | | Researcher observations on functionality and development needs |

## Conclusions

The target organisation primarily functioned to enable further development of the constructs. The evidence indicated that the constructs were mainly positive enablers of risk awareness and communication. Lessons were learned on developing the methods in the future. The knowledge will be used to form suggestions for advancing project risk management processes to better utilise and support the needs and structures of multi-organisational construction projects, as envisioned in Figure 8.6. This will conclude the final requirement of constructive research as the creator of pragmatic theory contributions.

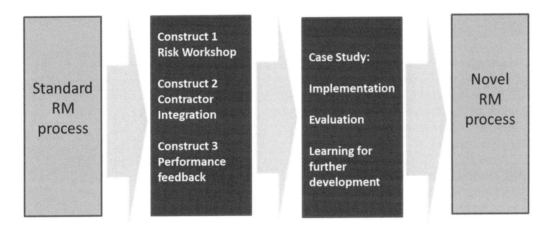

**Figure 8.6     Developing project risk management through constructive research**

# Tips and Questions

## TIPS FOR STUDENTS

- Balancing practical and academic demands is one of the key success factors in constructive research. It is also notable that the pluralistic approach might fit within one study or among several studies in a research programme. This characteristic also renders this approach suitable for an article-based dissertation.
- Case studies take time. Start the negotiations early in the process, and involve the project team in designing the constructs.
- If the time-scale or cost of a case study implementation is not feasible, consider a weak market test for construct validation. It can be conducted through, for example, interviews or surveys.

## TIPS FOR SUPERVISORS

- Ensure a sustainable and open relationship with the target company or project. The constructive research approach demands the time and dedication of the target organisation members, and the benefits for the target organisation must be explicit. Be clear about the nature of the research collaboration with the target company or project. Agree on the borders of publishable information and business secrets. The researcher must have access to research data through interviews, observation and/or document reviews.
- In addition to the practical aims, ensure that the result of the constructive research process has a clear theoretical connection and academic contribution. Ask students to conduct literature reviews on needed theoretical bases and to outline the potential for contribution.
- Constructive research is both ambitious and time consuming. Plan the research schedule and publication scheme ahead of time with the help of the constructive research steps.

## QUESTIONS

1. What similarities and differences are there between constructive research and consultancy?
2. What types of strategies would help overcome resistance to change in the target organisation?

3. What preparations would you need to make before approaching a case study project organisation?

# References

Alsakini, W. (2012). Two models for managing the virtualisation of construction management firms in the context of Finnish construction markets, Aalto University doctoral dissertation 108/2012, School of Engineering, Department of Civil and Structural Engineering, Espoo, Finland.

Baccarini, D. (1996). The concept of complexity – A review. *International Journal of Project Management*, 14(4), 201–204

Borsboom, D., Mellenbergh, G. J. and van Heerden, J. (2004). The concept of validity. *Psychological Review*, 11(4), 1061–1071.

Cherns, A. B. and Bryant, D. T. (1984). Studying the client's role in construction management. *Construction Management and Economics*, 2, 177–184.

Dainty, A. (2008). 'Methodological Pluralism in Construction Management Research' in Knight, A. and Ruddock, L. (eds) *Advanced Research Methods in the Built Environment*. West Sussex, UK: Blackwell Publishing, pp. 1–13.

Dewey, J. (1984). 'The Quest for Certainty' in Boydston, J. A. (ed.) *The Later Works of John Dewey, 1925–1953*, Volume 4. Carbondale, IL: Southern Illinois University Press.

Hammersley, M. (2004). 'Pragmatism' in Lewis-Beck, M. S., Bryman, A. and Liao, T. F. (eds) *The Sage Encyclopedia of Social Science Research Methods*. Retrieved from http://srmo.sagepub.com.pc124152.oulu.fi:8080/view/the-sage-encyclopedia-of-social-science-research-methods/SAGE.xml. Accessed: 25.3.2013.

Kärnä, S. (2009). Concepts and attributes of customer satisfaction in construction. Doctoral dissertation, TKK-R-DISS-2. Helsinki University of Technology.

Kasanen, E., Lukka, K. and Siitonen, A. (1993). The constructive approach in management accounting research. *Journal of Management Accounting Research*, 5(fall), 241–64.

Labro, E. and Tuomela, T-S. (2003). On bringing more action into management accounting research: process considerations based on two constructive case studies. *European Accounting Review*, 12(3), 409–442.

Lukka, K. (2000). 'The Key Issues of Applying the Constructive Approach to Field Research' in Reponen, T. (ed.) *Management Expertise for the New Millennium*. Turku, Finland: Publications of the Turku School of Economics and Business Administration, A-1.

Oyegoke, A. (2011) The constructive research approach in project management research. *International Journal of Managing Projects in Business*, 4(4), 573–595.

Pekuri, L. (2013) Perspectives on constructive research approach – In search of the basis for validation, Master's Thesis. Oulu Business School, University of Oulu, Finland.

Project Management Institute (PMI) (2009) *Practice Standard for Project Risk Management*. Newton Square, PA: Project Management Institute.

Shank, G. (2008). 'Abduction' in Given, LM. (ed.) *The Sage Encyclopedia of Qualitative Research Methods*. Thousand Oaks, CA: Sage Publications, Inc.

# 9

# Novel or Incremental Contributions: The Construction of Research Questions

Markus Hällgren

*I wrote this chapter because I was fascinated by the ignorance of novel approaches in project and temporary organisation research, and its consequences for aspiring academics.*

This chapter is about constructing the opportunities for an incremental or novel theoretical research contribution. This is a pertinent decision to any academic since it will have an impact not only on how a paper is positioned but also on the individual career. The chapter elaborates on the impact of choosing the contribution, and specifically on how to deliberately choose a strategy for the contribution, positioning and the importance of choosing the audience for the contribution, and how to frame the contribution for the previously specified audience. These issues are not isolated but often integrated with each other; nevertheless they are crucial for any research, and by extension academic career.

At the end of this chapter, the reader can:

- deliberately chose the research strategy and know about the difference and impact of choosing a novel or incremental contribution;
- understand how to chose your audience and 'pick your fight' with the right one;
- frame the contribution for the targeted audience so that they respond to it in a favourable way.

Keywords: theory construction, novel contribution, incremental contribution, assumptions

Research relies on the exploration of the uncertain, and thereby on the development of novel or incremental contributions to the scientific body on how things work. Recognising the differences between incremental and novel contributions are paramount following pressures from publishing in certain journals, its relevance for the academic profession and for promotions and recognitions (Alvesson, 2013). Moreover, for the aspiring academic's dissertation work, the issue is further accentuated with strong theory development giving way for applied sciences (Shalley, 2012). In practice, without awareness and a well-designed construction of the research question, even the most technically sound research design and execution is at significant loss.

This chapter is part of a long-standing debate on incremental or novel scientific discoveries (Alvesson and Sandberg, 2011; Alvesson and Sandberg, 2013; Barrett and Walsham, 2004; Bartunek, Rynes and Ireland, 2006; Davis, 1971; Ferris, Hochwarter and Buckley, 2012; Glynn and Raffaelli, 2010; Golden-Biddle and Locke, 1993; Johnson, 2003; Kuhn, 1962/1996; Locke and Golden-Biddle, 1997; Mathiassen, Chiasson and Germonprez, 2012; Nicolai and Seidl, 2010; Sandberg and Alvesson, 2011; Tadajewski and Hewer, 2011). Both modes of discovery are important, incremental contributions refines and tests existing knowledge (Tourish, 2011), and novel contributions carry promise of making significant scientific leaps (Alvesson and Sandberg, 2011).

There is however an identified one-sided focus on incremental contributions, posing a challenge in organisation theory in general (Locke and Golden-Biddle, 1997; Sandberg and Alvesson, 2011), and sub-areas such as marketing (Johnson, 2003), information systems (Mathiassen, Chiasson and Germonprez, 2012) and research on temporary organising and projects (Hällgren, 2012). The latter despite the acclaimed worry about the pre-paradigmatic state (Bredillet, 2010), scanty theoretical basis (Shenhar, 2001) and need to 'reclaim' (Blomquist et al., 2010) and 're-think' project research (Winter, Smith, Morris and Cicmil, 2006). The dominant strategy for handling the challenge is a call for stronger theorising and methodological rigour (for example, Donaldson, Qiu and Luo, 2013) but the culprit is arguably not the rigour, nor the theorising, but the way the research question is framed and constructed (Alvesson and Sandberg, 2013).

In the heart of any contribution lies the construction of the research question. To understand that construction is to understand what the scientific process will produce. While incremental and the novel mode of scientific discovery need to co-exist, the distribution between the two could be rebalanced. To do that there is a need to understand the specifics of each strategy. The purpose of this chapter is therefore to elaborate on the underlying arguments of the two modes of research question construction, and its consequences.

## Challenging Assumptions for Projects and Temporary Organising

Broadly speaking research on temporary ways of organising can be divided into research on temporary organisations and/or organising, and projects (Goodman and Goodman, 1972; Kenis, Janowicz-Panjaitan and Cambre, 2009; Lundin and Söderholm, 1995; Söderlund, 2011). The difference between temporary organisations and projects is that every project is by definition a temporary organisation, but not every temporary organisation is a project. For example, a construction project is assumed to end at a certain point in time and is therefore a temporary organisation. In contrast, the team that gathers to care for a patient is also assumed to end, but is hardly relying on project methodologies, nor seen as a project, but indeed as a temporary way of organising (Faraj and Xiao, 2006).

The common denominator is the assumption that the operations will end at a certain point in time. Beyond the contextual differences they also differ significantly in how they operate. This, and other assumptions (such as relying on teamwork), is important to recognise when constructing the argument for the research question and thus the theoretical contribution. Without awareness, long-held beliefs prevail despite becoming outdated. For example a focus on temporary organising instead of projects indicate less focus upon the organisation per se, and more of the events and constant flux of activities in a setting known to end (Tsoukas and Chia, 2002; Weick, 2012).

To discuss the construction of the theoretical contribution there is a need to briefly discuss what a theory is. Theory is 'an ordered set of assertions about a generic behavior or structure assumed to hold throughout a significantly broad range of specific instances' (Sutherland, 1975: p. 9, cited in Weick, 1989: p. 517). Developing a theory for temporary organising, or projects, is thus about identifying a generic behaviour or structure of that particular way of organising (see, for example, Andersen, 2006; Jugdev, 2004; Lundin and Söderholm, 1995; Peippo-Lavikka et al., 2011; Shenhar, 2001; Turner, 2006a, 2006b, 2006c, 2006d). While there is no consensus on whether there are such thing as 'project theory', nor what it might be, the state of the research have been continuously criticised, for example for being fragmented, lacking a sound theoretical bases, and lacking thought provoking ('interesting') novel research (Cicmil and Hodgson, 2006; Hällgren, 2012; Jacobsson and Söderholm, 2011; Packendorff, 1995; Shenhar, 2001; Söderlund, 2011; Söderlund and Maylor, 2012).

The debate on novel and incremental scientific discoveries and the obstacles thereof is all but new. A seminal piece is 'The Structure of Scientific Revolutions' (Kuhn, 1962/1996) that elaborates on the difficulties of making novel scientific contributions due to the lock-in effects of contemporary paradigms. Take, for example, Christopher Columbus, without his personal courage to challenge the paradigms it would probably have taken many more years to discover the Americas. A later contribution is Davis's (1971) paper that discusses what makes a paper interesting. Similar to Kuhn, Davis argues that the generic behaviour and/or structure of a theory relies on a series of assumptions about the same. To be perceived as novel some *but not all* of these assumptions should be challenged, for the purpose of getting recognised, accepted for journals by reviewers and editors and reviewers (Bedeian, 2003, 2004; Davis, 1971)

Articles in the four major North-American organisation theory outlets makes use of two major strategies for creating the opportunity of a contribution; structuring intertextual coherence and problematising the situation (Locke and Golden-Biddle, 1997). Both of these strategies were later identified as strategies for gap-spotting, and found to be reflected in both North American and European top journals (Sandberg and Alvesson, 2011). Similar patterns are repeated in marketing (Johnson, 2003), information systems (Mathiassen et al., 2012) and project research. In the latter Hällgren (2012) found that none of the 61 papers in the four major dedicated outlets, *International Journal of Project Management*, *Project Management Journal*, *International Journal of Managing Projects in Business*, and *International Journal of Project Organization and Management*, challenged the assumptions of project theorising. Although the approaches varied there was a clear focus upon practical implications, and less on theoretical development. A gap-spotting strategy constructs the opportunity for a theoretical contribution by the identification of a gap in the literature, and using this gap as an argument for why the particular work is important, and subsequently developing the research question from that. The dominant paradigm in both organisation theory and temporary organising/project research thus follow a gap-spotting strategy.

In contrast to gap-spotting, a problematising strategy 'try to disrupt the reproduction and continuation of an institutionalized line of reasoning. It means taking something that is commonly seen as good or natural, and turning it into something problematic. Specifically, problematization [...] aims to question the assumptions underlying existing theory in some significant ways.' (Sandberg and Alvesson, 2011: p. 32). That is, the theorising starts with the assumptions and the intent of the research is to challenge one or several of those, thus following the general idea of Davis (1971) and Bartunek et al. (2006). Note that a problematising construction of the research question seldom is exclusively problematising or incremental, but a blend of the two since research has to relate to previous work, at least to identify which assumptions that are worthwhile to challenge. The differences in how the opportunity for the contribution is constructed between the two strategies leads up to the choice of the mode of research question construction.

## Deliberatively Chose the Strategy

### GAP-SPOTTING CONSTRUCTION MODES

The modes for constructing a gap-spotting incremental contribution, and consequently the research question include:

- *Neglect spotting* that can be divided into the sub-themes of an overlooked-, under-researched-, or lack of empirical support area, and argues that previous theory have neglected parts or lack empirical evidence. For example, Simsarian Webber (2008, pp. 72,73) argues that 'blending service and client employees into a team is widely used by information technology service companies as well as other service providers' and there is a 'lack [of] empirical evidence of its proposed benefits for effectively building and sustaining client engagements.'
- *Empirical need or example spotting*, seen as the practical need to study a certain phenomena. Fox (2009: p. 537), explains that such questions are constructed to 'facilitate a change from ineffective generic methods for the communication of information to more effective designed information and communication'.
- *Application spotting* which complements existing theory. Ling and Tiong argue that previous studies 'are at the macro and strategic management levels and did not consider the challenges and problems that are faced at the project level [and they need to] investigate the challenges that were faced' (Ling and Tiong, 2008: p. 87).
- *Confusion spotting* where findings are not coherent and they, for example try 'explain these contradictory results' with empirical research (Zwikael and Unger-Aviram, 2010: p. 413).
- *Research overview* where an overview of the existing literature on a topic is provided. An example of this is Biedenbach and Müller (Biedenbach and Müller, 2011: p. 84) who built their question on the argument that 'underlying paradigms and philosophical foundations change slowly and possibly [go] unnoticed [and their overview is] needed and necessary for a better understanding of the past, present and possible future of research paradigms in project management' (see Hällgren, 2012; Sandberg and Alvesson, 2011 for details).

### PROBLEMATISING CONSTRUCTION MODES

Six basic types of assumptions can be challenged; in-house-, root metaphor-, paradigmatic-, ideological-, and field assumptions (Alvesson and Sandberg, 2011). One way to approach the task of challenging these assumptions and produce 'interesting' research is to consider the building blocks of academic texts, that is; Theory, Methodology and Context (Barley, 2006; Dubois and Gibbert, 2010; Ladik and Stewart, 2008). Together they are the basis for the opportunity of making a contribution, the analytical work and the subsequent results, in addition to being the representation of assumptions. Using theory, methodology and context as assumption challenging tools thus serves as 'a proxy for unlearning, for adaptation, for flexibility, in short, for many of the dramas that engage organizational scholars.' (Weick, 1996, pp. 301–302) First, theory.

*The theory* is naturally one of the major cornerstones in constructing new theories about a subject (Ferris, Hochwarter and Buckley, 2012: p. 94). With the help of the context (theoretical or empirical data) and methodology for gathering and analysing, assumptions may be revealed and new knowledge about the subject gained. Challenging assumptions through theory is therefore close to the problematising methodology, and focus on the assumptions of theoretical paradigms. Assumptions can be identified and challenged by identifying a domain in the literature, identify and articulate the assumptions, evaluate articulated assumptions, develop alternative assumptions, relate assumptions to audience and finally evaluate alternative assumptions. (see Alvesson and Sandberg, 2011). One example of a study that challenges the assumptions of project work is Hodgson (2002), arguing that projects serve as a tool for re-bureacratisation, instead of the de-bureaucratisation it is commonly assumed to be.

*The methodology* can also identify and challenge assumptions of a particular subject. There are fashions in terms of what methods to use (Bort and Kieser, 2011) and project research often includes case studies and surveys (Biedenbach and Müller, 2011; Smyth and Morris, 2007; Söderlund, 2011). By making use of less traditional methods, for example archival data, assumptions that are otherwise hidden might emerge because of a sensitivity to alternative issues. One example is Ezzamel's (2004) study of ancient Egypt and the construction of the pyramids through the use of documents dating back thousands of years. He showed, instead of assumed, that the oft-cited construction of the pyramids indeed followed accounting and organising systems that were similar to contemporary project practices.

*The context* is the third way to expose assumptions. One can distinguish between contributions *to* theory and contributions *of* theory. *Of theory* applies existing theory to a novel context. In contrast contributions *to theory* start with the context and create theory from that vantage point (Whetten, 2009). Both approaches may challenge the assumptions but *of theory* are closer to a gap-spotting construction since it often relies on the original assumptions. In contrast, *to theory* challenges assumptions by initially identifying the assumption in practice. Thus, one way to expose assumptions is to choose a particular context, for example through opportunity-based case selection. Here the case itself has properties that makes it possible to reveal assumptions of a subject, and challenge the same (Eisenhardt and Graebner, 2007: p. 27). Without opportunity-based selection of a context, the ability to identify rare circumstances is lost. See for example Weick's (1993) work on the Mann Gulch disaster. It is a rare disaster and a 'deviant case', that in contrast to confirming existing knowledge is exploratory (Seawright and Gerring, 2008: p. 297) allowing for the identification of the particularities of the contexts, which is frequently unrecognised (Denrell and Kovacs, 2008: p. 136).

In project research most interest is clustered around construction, information systems and education (accounting for more than 50 per cent of the research) (Crawford, Pollack and England, 2006; Kloppenborg and Opfer, 2002), and seem to hold for later work too (Söderlund, 2011). One way to approach the situation is therefore to heed the call for less traditional environments as contexts for temporary organising (Bredillet, 2010; Walker, 2011) to expose traditional assumptions.

## PICK YOUR FIGHT

Independently of whether one chooses a strategy that aims at an incremental or a novel contribution the choice relate to assumptions. An incremental strategy builds on previous assumptions without challenging them. This is gap-spotting research and is relatively safe because the contemporary practice and thought is maintained, and is thus perceived as less provoking and aligned with the social construction of contemporary thought. For example, it is widely held that authors published in A-level journals barely recognise the paper they first submitted because of the changes they do to adapt to the reviewers assumptions (Bedeian, 2003, 2004). For the individual academic a less risky strategy is therefore to rely on accepted assumptions to make an incremental contribution.

In contrast the search for an 'interesting' and novel contribution challenges assumptions and is a riskier strategy. Researchers should therefore not challenge all, but only a few of the assumptions, since they would not be taken seriously otherwise (Davis, 1971). Bartunek et al. (2006) makes similar findings, emphasising among other things that the findings should be counterintuitive, that a reviewer/reader should be challenged but still feel be able to take the contribution seriously.

Assuming that a paper is well-written and relies on a technical sound research design and execution, the choice of the contribution strategy influences the individual academic's career significantly. The choice influences the possibility of getting published (incremental are less controversial than novel), in what outlets (top-tier journals emphasise novel theoretical contributions, while lower-ranked journals would not get the same contributions), and the speed (a incremental contribution in a lower-ranked journal is faster than a novel contribution in a higher-ranked journal, so is probably also a novel contribution in a lower-ranked journal). Following how the opportunity for a contribution is constructed through the research question thus extends beyond the paper, including the possibility of getting hired, promoted and recognised by peers (Alvesson, 2013; Alvesson and Sandberg, 2011; Bartunek et al., 2006; Bedeian, 2003, 2004).

## FRAME THE CONTRIBUTION FOR A SPECIFIED AUDIENCE

Hitherto the chapter has focused on how to frame opportunities for contributions, and risks and advantages of a novel or incremental contribution. Finding the audience ties together previous discussion since regardless of whether one chooses a gap-spotting or problematising construction strategy, and thereby is cautious or bold, the assumptions that can be identified are tied to the audience one is addressing (Davis, 1971; Jacobsson and Söderholm, 2011). Put another way, the contribution is in the eye of the beholder.

Project research, for example, is highly fragmented but also quite coherent. It is fragmented in that there is an abundance of 'schools', 'themes', and 'theoretical interests' (Bredillet, 2007a, 2007b, 2007c; Bredillet, 2008a, 2008b, 2008c; Kwak and Anbari, 2009; Söderlund, 2002; Turner, 2006a, 2006b, 2006c, 2006d; Winter et al., 2006), and coherent in the sense that within these, the assumptions, the methods and the contexts are similar (Hällgren, 2012; Kloppenborg and Opfer, 2002; Söderlund, 2011) thus upholding the research paradigms of the sub-interests.

What is a 'taken for granted assumption' in one subject matter is therefore not necessarily so in another. Take, for example, a projects-as-practice approach where the dynamics and nitty-gritty details of everyday work are assumed to be pertinent to understand how temporary organising is accomplished. This can be compared to a traditional structural approach, or a more structural process approach for that matter. From a practice-based perspective inefficiencies in a project are seen as natural and unavoidable, but a consequence of bad management in the traditional approach, and a longitudinal phase-dependent outcome in a process view (Blomquist et al., 2010; Hällgren and Söderholm, 2011). If one wishes to communicate and make a contribution one has therefore to start with identifying the assumptions of that particular audience. If the audience are academics with a keen interest in temporary organisations for example, one possible avenue for incremental research is to examine the properties of the temporary organisation by adding a less investigated context, such as special forces to the plethora of studies; if one wants to make a novel contribution one possible avenue for research is to challenge the very basis of the temporary organisation; the assumed temporality.

## TOWARDS A DELIBERATE STRATEGY

This chapter has elaborated on two modes of research question construction, and their consqeuences in terms of deliberately choosing the strategy, picking the right fight and framing the contribution for a specified audience. Following pressures for journal publications for promotion and recognition and the journal's demand for novel contributions (Alvesson, 2013), a change from strong theory development giving way for applied sciences in doctoral sciences (Shalley, 2012) and a clear lack of assumption challenging research (Alvesson and Sandberg, 2011; Hällgren, 2012), any researcher should be aware of the consequences since they all influence the future of the individual and their academic contributions.

Without deliberately making a choice, research on temporary organising and projects are quite likely to stall since most efforts hitherto are incremental and thus hardly correspond to the call for reclaiming and rethinking project research. In this chapter three identified consequences of the choice for a contribution are summarised (see Table 9.1). The questions in the table apply slightly differently to the doctoral student and the supervisor. The questions are for the doctoral student to consider and apply and the supervisor to initiate a discussion and educate the doctoral student about. Ideally the doctoral student and the supervisor end up as the researcher both aspire to be.

**Table 9.1    Consequences and questions to consider**

| Consequence to Consider | Feature | Questions to Consider |
|---|---|---|
| Deliberately chose the research question construction strategy | Two modes of research opportunity construction with subsets of ways for framing the contribution, involving theory, method and context | What kind of construction strategy applies? What subset of construction mode is applicable? With what tool (theory, method, context) may the assumptions be revealed? |
| Pick your fight | Novel contributions are rare, highly recognisable but also risky. Incremental contributions are frequent, less recognisable and less risky | What is the potential of the research? What are the available resources (time, writing support)? Considering a future in academia? |
| Frame the contribution for a specified audience | Research is fragmented and consequently so are the assumptions that it relies on | To what audience is a piece of work communicating? What are the assumptions of that audience? What assumptions should be challenged, and which should be maintained? |

Consequences that should be considered are interlaced and should not be viewed in isolation. For example, choosing a construction strategy (for example, novel strategy) implies picking a fight with a particular audience (for example, what has become known as the 'Scandinavian School of Project Management') for whom the contribution needs to be framed (for example, the assumption of temporariness). This reflects the need for initiating, discussing and applying the consequences and questions such as those in the table. Making a novel and 'interesting' piece of work may lead to fame, a permanent position and publications in the best journals, *but* it is also a risky strategy, since an absolute majority of all contributions are incremental. Incremental contributions bring less attention to the individual, but it is also perceived as less controversial and thus a way to get published in decent journals. The questions that are brought up are thus relevant to senior faculty as well as graduate students, and an issue that should be discussed openly. There is however a significant difference. Senior faculty have often chosen an academic career and they may also have tenure, which give them the slack necessary to use wider and more exploratory search patterns without sacrificing future security. In contrast, a graduate student may not have chosen an academic career yet, they certainly do not have tenure and there is often a clear deadline for their efforts, contributing to search patterns that are exploitative and closer to previous efforts.

## Tips and Questions

### TIPS FOR STUDENTS

- Be aware of that most research is incremental. Part of it is that constructing the opportunity for a novel contribution is not easy and there are many obstacles, for example, getting published. Depending on how you approach these obstacles will most likely have consequences upon your future career. (See Prasad, 2013 for an interesting perspective and experience.)
- Ensure that you make a deliberate choice when you construct your opportunity for a contribution. There is significant value to both strategies, but they unfold in different ways.
- Novelty for the sake of novelty is not good. Therefore, make sure that you have a solid argument and listen and try your ideas with colleagues at the department and conferences. Sometimes, the assumptions are there for a reason.

### TIPS FOR SUPERVISORS

- The assumptions of a research field are essential to being able to identify both an incremental and a novel approach. Therefore, make sure to discuss these assumptions with the student.
- Ensure that you discuss how to construct the research question, and its implications on the chosen strategy with the student.
- Initially allow the student to stretch their mind and embrace their approach instead of immediately rejecting the same. Regardless of whether it challenges your own long-held assumptions. Remember how it was to be young. When you see that the argument is going nowhere, make sure to refocus the student without discouraging the same.

### QUESTIONS

1. Discuss the different theory construction strategies, and apply them to the specific research project.
2. Describe the difference in outcome if you change construction strategy. What creates the difference/lack of difference?
3. What are the central assumptions underlying your specific research project? Can or cannot the assumptions be challenged? Why/why not? If they can, how and on what grounds can the assumptions be challenged?
4. Who are the main stakeholders of the assumptions?

## References

Alvesson, M. (2013). Do we have something to say? From re-search to roi-search and back again. *Organization,* 20(1), 79–90.

Alvesson, M. and Sandberg, J. (2011). Generating research questions through problematization. *The Academy of Management Review*, 36(2), 247–271.

Alvesson, M. and Sandberg, J. (2013). Has management studies lost its way? Ideas for more imaginative and innovative research. *Journal of Management Studies*, 50(1), 128–152.

Andersen, E. S. (2006). Toward a project management theory for renewal projects. *Project Management Journal*, 37(4), 15.

Barley, S. R. (2006). When I write my masterpiece: Thoughts on what makes a paper interesting. *The Academy of Management Journal*, 49(1), 16–20.

Barrett, M. and Walsham, G. (2004). 'Making Contributions from Interpretive Case Studies: Examining Processes of Construction and Use' in Kaplan, K., Truez III, D. P., Wastell, D., Wood-Harper, T. A., DeGross, J. I. (eds). *Information Systems Research: Relevant theory and informed practice*. New York, NY: Springer.

Bartunek, J. M., Rynes, S. L. and Ireland, R. D. (2006). Academy of Management Journal Editors' Forum: What makes management research interesting, and why does it matter. *Academy of Management Journal*, 49(1), 9–15.

Bedeian, A. G. (2003). The manuscript review process. *Journal of Management Inquiry*, 12(4), 331.

Bedeian, A. G. (2004). Peer review and the social construction of knowledge in the management discipline. *Academy of Management Learning & Education*, 3(2), 198–216.

Biedenbach, T. and Müller, R. (2011). Paradigms in project management research: Examples from 15 years of IRNOP conferences. *International Journal of Managing Projects in Business*, 4(1), 82–104.

Blomquist, T., Hällgren, M., Nilsson, A. and Söderholm, A. (2010). Project as practice: Making project research matter. *Project Management Journal*, 41(1), 5–16.

Bort, S. and Kieser, A. (2011). Fashion in organization theory: An empirical analysis of the diffusion of theoretical concepts. *Organization Studies*, 32(5), 655–681, doi: 10.1177/0170840611405427.

Bredillet, C. (2007a). Exploring research in project management: Nine schools of project management research (Part 1). *Project Management Journal*, 38(2), 3–4.

Bredillet, C. N. (2007b). Exploring research in project management: Nine schools of project management research (Part 2). *Project Management Journal*, 38(3), 3–5

Bredillet, C. N. (2007c). Exploring research in project management: Nine schools of project management research (Part 3). *Project Management Journal*, 38(4), 2–4.

Bredillet, C. N. (2008a). Exploring research in project management: Nine schools of project management research (Part 4). *Project Management Journal*, 39(1), 2–6.

Bredillet, C. N. (2008b). Exploring research in project management: Nine schools of project management research (Part 5). *Project Management Journal*, 39(2), 2–4.

Bredillet, C. N. (2008c). Exploring research in project management: Nine schools of project management research (Part 6). *Project Management Journal*, 39(3), 2–5.

Bredillet, C. N. (2010). Blowing hot and cold on project management. *Project Management Journal*, 41(3), 4–20.

Cicmil, S. and Hodgson, D. (2006). 'Making Projects Critical: An Introduction' in S. Cicmil and D. Hodgson (eds), *Making Projects Critical*. New York, NY: Palgrave Macmillan.

Crawford, L., Pollack, J. and England, D. (2006). Uncovering the trends in project management: Journal emphases over the last 10 years. *International Journal of Project Management*, 24(2), 175–184.

Davis, M. S. (1971). That's interesting. *Philosophy of the Social Sciences*, 1(2), 309.

Denrell, J. and Kovacs, B. (2008). Selective sampling of empirical settings in organizational studies. *Administrative Science Quarterly*, 53(1), 109–144.

Donaldson, L., Qiu, J. and Luo, B. N. (2013). For rigour in organizational management theory research. *Journal of Management Studies*, 50(1), 153–172.

Dubois, A. and Gibbert, M. (2010). From complexity to transparency: Managing the interplay between theory, method and empirical phenomena in IMM case studies. *Industrial Marketing Management*, 39(1), 129–136.

Eisenhardt, K. M. and Graebner, M. E. (2007). Theory building from cases: Opportunities and challenges. *The Academy of Management Journal*, 50(1), 25–32.

Ezzamel, M. (2004). Work organization in the middle kingdom, Ancient Egypt. *Organization*, 11(4), 497–537.

Faraj, S. and Xiao, Y. (2006). Coordination in fast-response organizations. *Management Science*, 52(8), 1155–1169.

Ferris, G. R., Hochwarter, W. A. and Buckley, M. R. (2012). Theory in the organizational sciences: How will we know it when we see it? *Organizational Psychology Review*, 2(1), 94–106.

Fox, S. (2009). Information and communication design for multi-disciplinary multi-national projects. *International Journal of Managing Projects in Business*, 2(4), 536-560.

Glynn, M. A. and Raffaelli, R. (2010). Uncovering mechanisms of theory development in an academic field: Lessons from leadership research. *The Academy of Management Annals*, 4(1), 359–401.

Golden-Biddle, K. and Locke, K. (1993). Appealing work: An investigation of how ethnographic texts convince. *Organization Science*, 4(4), 595–616.

Goodman, L. P. and Goodman, R. A. (1972). Theater as temporary system. *California Management Review*, 15(2), 103–108.

Hällgren, M. (2012). The construction of research questions in project management. *International Journal of Project Management*, 3(7), 804–816.

Hällgren, M. and Söderholm, A. (2011). 'Projects-as-Practice: New Approach, New Insights' in J. Pinto, P. Morris and J. Söderlund (eds), *Handbook of Project Management*. Oxford: Oxford University Press.

Hodgson, D. (2002). Disciplining the professional: The case of project management. *Journal of Management Studies*, 39(6), 803–821.

Jacobsson, M. and Söderholm, A. (2011). Breaking out of the straightjacket of project research: In search of contribution. *International Journal of Managing Projects in Business*, 4(3), 378–388.

Johnson, M.S. (2003). Designating opponents in empirical research reports: The rhetoric of interestingness in consumer research. *Marketing Theory*, 3(4), 477.

Jugdev, K. (2004). Through the looking glass: Examining theory development in project management with the resource-based view lens. *Project Management Journal*, 35(3), 15–26.

Kenis, P., Janowicz-Panjaitan, M. and Cambre, B. (2009). *Temporary Organizations: Prevalence, logic and effectiveness.*: Cheltenham, UK: Edward Elgar Publishers.

Kloppenborg, T. J. and Opfer, W. A. (2002). 'Forty Years of Project Management Research: Trends, Interpretation, and Prediction' in D. P. Sleving, D. I. Cleland and J. K. Pinto (eds), *The Frontier of Project Mangement Research*. Newton Square, PA: PMI.

Kuhn, T. S. (1962/1996). *The Structure of Scientific Revolutions*. Chicago, IL: University of Chicago Press.

Kwak, Y. H. and Anbari, F. T. (2009). Analyzing project management research: Perspectives from top management journals. *International Journal of Project Management*, 27(5), 435–446.

Ladik, D. M. and Stewart, D. W. (2008). The contribution continuum. *Journal of the Academy of Marketing Science*, 36(2), 157–165.

Ling, F. Y. Y. and Tiong, J. H. (2008). Managing large commercial projects with a tight schedule in China: A case study. *International Journal of Project Organisation and Management*, 1(1), 86–104.

Locke, K. and Golden-Biddle, K. (1997). Constructing opportunities for contribution: Structuring intertextual coherence and 'problematizing' in organizational studies. *The Academy of Management Journal*, 40(5), 1023–1062.

Lundin, R. A and Söderholm, A. (1995). A theory of the temporary organization. *Scandinavian Journal of Management*, 11(4), 437–455.

Mathiassen, L., Chiasson, M. and Germonprez, M. (2012). Style composition in action research publication. *MIS Quarterly*, 36(2), 339–346.

Nicolai, Al. and Seidl, D. (2010). That's relevant! Different forms of practical relevance in management science. *Organization Studies*, 31(9–10), 1257–1285.

Packendorff, J. (1995). Inquiring into the temporary organization: New directions for project management research. *Scandinavian Journal of Management*, 11(4), 319–333.

Peippo-Lavikka, P., Walker, D., Artto, K., Gemunden, H. and Aaltonen, P. (2011). 'Towards A Project Theory: Theoretical Contents of Project Management in 9 Industry Sectors' in A. Gambardella and M. Zollo (eds) *11th EURAM Conference: Management Culture in the 21st Century*, Tallinn, Estonia, 1–4 June 2011, pp. 1–40.

Prasad, A. (2013). Playing the game and trying not to lose myself: A doctoral student's perspective on the institutional pressures for research output. *Organization*, 20(6), 936-948.

Sandberg, J. and Alvesson, M. (2011). Ways of constructing research questions: Gap-spotting or problematization? *Organization*, 18(1), 23.

Seawright, J. and Gerring, J. (2008). Case selection techniques in case study research. *Political Research Quarterly*, 61(2), 294–308.

Shalley, C. E. (2012). Writing good theory: Issues to consider. *Organizational Psychology Review*, 2(3), 258–264.

Shenhar, A. J. (2001). One size does not fit all projects: Exploring classical contingency domains. *Management Science*, 47(3), 394–414.

Simsarian Webber, S. (2008). Blending service provider/client project teams to achieve client trust: Implications for project team trust, cohesion, and performance. *Project Management Journal*, 39(2), 72–81.

Smyth, H. J. and Morris, P. W. G. (2007). An epistemological evaluation of research into projects and their management: Methodological issues. *International Journal of Project Management*, 25(4), 423–436.

Söderlund, J. (2002). On the development of project management research: Schools of thought and critique. *International Project Management Journal*, 6(1), 20–31.

Söderlund, J. (2011). Pluralism in project management: Navigating the crossroads of specialization and fragmentation. *International Journal of Management Reviews*, 13(2), 153–176.

Söderlund, J. and Maylor, H. (2012). Project management scholarship: Relevance, impact and five integrative challenges for business and management schools. *International Journal of Project Management*, 30(6), 686–696.

Tadajewski, M. and Hewer, P. (2011). Intellectual contributions and 'gap-spotting'. *Journal of Marketing Management*, 27(5–6), 449–457.

Tourish, D. (2011). Leading questions: Journal rankings, academic freedom and performativity: What is, or should be, the future of Leadership? *Leadership*, 7(3), 367–381.

Tsoukas, H. and Chia, R. (2002). On organizational becoming: Rethinking organizational change. *Organization Science*, 13(5), 567–582.

Turner, R. (2006a). Towards a theory of project management: The functions of project management. *International Journal of Project Management*, 24(3), 187.

Turner, R. (2006b). Towards a theory of project management: The nature of the functions of project management. *International Journal of Project Management*, 24(4), 277.

Turner, R. (2006c). Towards a theory of project management: The nature of the project governance and project management. *International Journal of Project Management*, 24(2), 93.

Turner, R. (2006d). Towards a theory of project management: The nature of the project. *International Journal of Project Management*, 24(1), 1.

Walker, D. (2011). Perceptions of project management in traditionally non-PM industry sectors. *International Journal of Managing Projects in Business*, 3(1).

Weick, K. E. (1989). Theory construction as disciplined imagination. *The Academy of Management Review*, 14(4), 516–531.

Weick, K. E. (1993). The collapse of sensemaking in organizations: The Mann Gulch disaster. *Administrative Science Quarterly*, 38(4), 628–652.

Weick, K. E. (1996). Drop your tools: An allegory for organizational studies. *Administrative Science Quarterly*, 41(2), 301–313.

Weick, K. E. (2012). *Making Sense of the Organization, Volume 2: The impermanent organization*. Chichester, UK: Wiley.

Whetten, D. A. (2009). An examination of the interface between context and theory Applied to the study of Chinese organizations. *Management and Organization Review*, 5(1), 29–55.

Winter, M., Smith, C., Morris, P. and Cicmil, S. (2006). Directions for future research in project management: The main findings of a UK government-funded research network. *International Journal of Project Management*, 24(8), 638.

Zwikael, O. and Unger-Aviram, E. (2010). HRM in project groups: The effect of project duration on team development effectiveness. *International Journal of Project Management*, 28(5), 413–421.

# 10

# Moving from Hunches to a Research Topic: Salient Literature and Research Methods

Beverley Lloyd-Walker and Derek Walker

*Mature candidates often lack confidence in explaining background literature to establish the foundation for their research. Identifying salient relevant literature and weaving in their experience and access to practitioners with deep contextual knowledge provides a critical advantage. We wrote this to help them shape and craft their research literature and methods plan.*

An extensive but targeted literature review is required to clarify the research topic, develop the research question and inform the decision related to research methods that will best facilitate answering the research question. An example is provided of an innovative approach taken by a doctoral candidate to demonstrate how candidates might choose a defendable research approach and methods and also to explore the fast-growing PM field in ways that have not been previously attempted. This chapter should be of value to mature PM practitioners engaged in study and scholarship.

At the end of this chapter, the reader can:

- develop a sound understanding of the link between the research topic questions and the relevant literature;
- justify their research approach, including the analysis of their data, and their contribution to theory and practice;
- achieve clarity in conceptualising the research problem and question and link these to the salient theory and a defendable and practical research approach;
- enhance open-mindedness to engage in formal and informal conversations and presentations to help a thesis topic from an initial hunch.

Keywords: literature search, ontology, epistemology, research topic

Candidates need to decide upon the salient literature they should consider, gain mastery of and refer to when justifying their research topic. This is an extremely important stage as it provides the foundation for all that follows. It reveals the current gap in knowledge and enables good decision making on the proposed research approach. It enables the decision to be based on clear evidence that alternative methods were considered and the most appropriate method for the investigation selected. The selected research approach may enable new knowledge to be generated by exploring the topic from a different perspective from that documented in the literature by others.

The objective of this chapter is to address the reality that aligning a research topic with the salient literature and a research method is difficult for many potential doctoral candidates and their supervisors. Potential candidates may experience frustration and doubts when attempting to make clear their research strategy for several reasons. Such strategies include:

- Though possibly fully aware that a doctorate makes an 'original contribution' they may not be clear on the theoretical and practice domain to which they are making a contribution. This poses a *relevance* and *scope* challenge.
- Candidates may lack confidence in their ability to explain the background literature and establish the foundation for their research base and points of departure in a manner that does not sound either trivial or overly complex. Identifying the salient literature and achieving a balance between being too broad or too narrow or between delving too deeply or too superficially may present challenges.
- New to the research-specific terminology, candidates may find demonstrating mastery of available research method choices and making an informed decision about how the most appropriate methods match their stated worldview, ontological, epistemological and axiological stance poses a challenge. Until the research problem can be clearly stated, the supervisor may also find guiding the candidate to a suitable research approach difficult. Candidates and their supervisors confront an issue of framing and effectively communicating their research methods strategy.

For a candidate with significant work experience in PM in particular, and for any supervisor advising that doctoral candidate, two sets of alignment need to occur:

- the research approach should be matched against that person's research resources; and
- their technical expertise, the professional network and their accumulated understanding of the research problem context should be aligned with the research investigation topic.

So how do you know what literature is salient, which research methods you should choose and how should you justify your choices?

Anchoring your research in relevant and salient literature clearly demonstrates your mastery of both foundational theory and how that theory has been developed to the contemporary period. Your academic contribution should clearly identify its place in the historical trajectory of developing broader or deeper understanding of the topic and how it can be appreciated and acknowledged. Sadly, it is far too easy to get bogged down and overcommitted to a broad range of literature resulting in the thesis literature review chapter taking on the appearance of an unfocused general textbook. Conversely, a short literature review chapter could appear narrow, shallow and ill-informed about recent relevant theoretical developments and how seminal work has been extended, challenged and contextualised over time. You need to balance demonstrating mastery over the evolution of knowledge about the topic with avoiding getting bogged down in ancillary literature.

Deciding upon the appropriate research method presents its own challenges. The research question, the ontological and epistemological positions must inform the research method. This is also influenced by the salient literature because any gaps found that are addressed by answering the research question may best be addressed through choosing a novel or particular research approach; one that has not been used to address the topic before.

Developing the research problem, objectives and question moves the research candidate towards undertaking meaningful research. However, several more facets of the research process need to be clarified in terms of the research method chosen to answer the research questions and meet the research objectives. These are:

- choosing the relevant literature to help you know what data is required and how to measure the data gathered; and
- deciding upon a research vehicle (the research method) that allows the researcher to develop a credible basis for undertaking research.

Your stated ontological and epistemological positions guide your decisions on what data will be measured, and how to measure it so that you make sense of the data. Part of your literature review is about exploring and justifying the basis for your research instrument that you will develop. You may be adopting a well-established instrument and research approach or adapting a previously established instrument and approach or you may decide to develop the instrument and approach from scratch. After gathering data (quantitative or qualitative) you will use various tools, techniques and approaches to make sense of it in order to explain your findings and develop models and other intellectual outcomes. Whatever the situation may be, you will use the literature to explain and justify your choices. We will now comment about this decision from both positivist and interpretivist perspectives.

Data that is used to provide the basis for making sense of a phenomenon under study can take many forms. Quantitative data is likely to be used when you take a positivist philosophical stance. You may be gathering numerical data about the number or quantity of X (whatever you are measuring) to arrive at statistical results. These data may help you to construct a 'reality' that these numbers represent in terms of models that can be used to explain or predict something about that phenomenon. The purpose, aim and framed research questions will determine the level of 'accuracy' required, the level of significance and the reliability statistics that determine the usefulness of any interpretation. These factors impact your measures, what you measure and how.

The decision on what you will measure is determined by you using an instrument that you design. Using a positivist perspective that values scientific methods means that the phenomenon *can* be measured and that there is a *correct* and *valid* way to measure it. The scope, scale and limitations of your research proposal will provide boundaries to help you gather sufficient but not excessive data. Insufficient data may compromise the results or restrict the statistical methods that can be employed and thus conclusions that might be drawn; too much may lead to confusion, prove expensive in both cost and time, and result in data that is redundant.

You may design, as part of your research method, a way to automatically mine data (such as collecting cost or time data) either by access to existing data or through an instrument such as a questionnaire. The choice of constructs in the survey instrument will be determined by the salient literature guiding you as to the most likely theory and helping you decide on what data to gather. For example, you may be studying project success factors in Russia. You may learn from the literature of well-validated (epistemologically sound) survey instruments for the UK or USA however you would need to test whether cultural or other, perhaps economic environment factors, may affect the study conclusions. It is the Russian context that may constitute your contribution to knowledge, because there are few if any studies readily available in the literature for Russian project success factors. You may need to find credible similar instruments and argue that these are validly used in measuring, for example, general management success. Alternatively, you may have to start from scratch, hypothesise factors/constructs and what should be the appropriate measures (granularity of accuracy) needed to design your research instrument, then trial it.

Having a clear ontological, epistemological and axiological stance is necessary if you are to defend your research approach and feel comfortable that your data will be useful in developing models that make sense of the phenomena being studied. Your decision about what you are going to measure and how to measure it will be determined by your stated philosophical position and your assessment of the salient literature. Quantitative studies generally provide models to test hypotheses, to predict or explain something about a phenomenon.

Qualitative data may also be linked to a positivist or constructivist philosophical stance. A quantitative study may need contextual qualitative data such as the characteristics of the country that will aid data interpretation. Descriptive data about participant survey demographics, details from the website of an organisation, a company profile or other case study descriptive forms of data and information may be required. Most qualitative data is used to construct and interpret 'reality' from gathered data. Because the data's purpose is to illuminate the phenomenon and for you to make sense of it, you will likely be taking an eclectic view of data sources and measures. This will still be governed and justified by your stated ontological, epistemological and axiological stance.

Qualitative studies, whether a case study, action research or ethnographic studies, will require their own types of data measured and results interpreted in a variety of ways. This could include a range of data: audio, visual from pictures or video images, or electronic/paper-based 'factual' data. Your aim may be to measure how people feel about an issue, to understand their emotions or opinions, or to learn of their perceptions such as their level of like/dislike or approval/disapproval in relation to a matter, using a Likert scale 1 = low to 5 = high. You may be recording accounts of significant events from participants, or constructing history from archival records or even from interpreting expressions on images. Whereas with positivist quantitative studies data are considered as 'proof' to be used to test hypotheses or to predict or explain, interpretive qualitative data are considered as a chain of evidence to support or not support a proposition that enables understanding about a phenomenon. Data is gathered until a point of saturation occurs where additional data does not substantially change the interpreted outcome. Significance is judged by epistemological standards that are stated as part of the ontological and axiomatic stance within the relevant and acknowledged paradigm.

The key is to understand how you can frame your hunch within the paradigm, ontology, epistemological and axiological stance that you choose to guide you in developing and executing the research plan. All else will fall into place, including determining what data is needed and how it can be measured and analysed using acceptable norms of the chosen paradigm.

## Choosing the Relevant Literature and Access Tools to Support the Research Project Hunch

Today the Internet makes it easier to locate relevant literature for your topic to fully understand the current situation, but it can also make it more confusing. There can be much information about your topic available from a range of sources and some of it may be contradictory, of questionable validity or incomplete. Knowing where to go to get the most appropriate and reliable information to firm up your research topic and provide the foundation for your research by clearly demonstrating the current knowledge gap is important. Your supervisor will be able to assist you here. By enrolling at your university or college you will be able to gain access, through their library, to refereed literature, government reports and theses from around the world.

Your library website will usually provide a special section for researchers, guiding you towards the type of literature required to support your research. Opinion, hearsay and unsubstantiated facts are not what you want here. By accessing the refereed literature you are provided with the assurance that you are reading only those items that have been assessed by two or usually three experts in the field. Yes, refereed journals do contain some non-refereed items: book reviews and editorial commentary for instance. However, most items are refereed articles usually providing results of research conducted.

A good way to commence your search is by accessing specific databases, such as EBSCO host or Emerald direct, or by using Google Scholar to search across a range of databases using keywords and specifying the date range from which you wish to view articles. By beginning broadly, covering literature on your topic in general, you can narrow your search down to your research setting. For instance, from leadership general (parent discipline), to leading teams you can move to project team leadership (immediate discipline) (Rao and Perry, 2003) and the industry in which you expect to conduct your research. In this way you have not moved into unrelated discipline areas, but you have helped to provide the background setting, position your research within the overarching field of research and specifically within the immediate field of research.

Locating the seminal works in the field may be a good place to start, but as you firm up your topic and concentrate on understanding the most recent research findings, you may wish to confine your research, within your immediate discipline, to the last five years. However there will be many articles from earlier times that will help to inform your decision making. Remember, this part of the literature review is being conducted so that you may arrive at a clear description of your research topic and establish its worth. It is from what you learn here, the gap in knowledge you identify and your identification of a point of departure from the more recent work in this topic area that you will generate your research question. Remember also that your future examiners are likely to be amongst the authors you locate during your research, largely within your immediate field of research.

Check your university's library website for easy access to all recent theses successfully completed at your university and ways of accessing those from universities around the world. Your research must meet the criterion of 'adding to the body of knowledge'. It is important that you learn about all recent research, not just that reported in the refereed literature for it may take recent doctoral students a few years to move their papers through the review process to publication in refereed journals. Importantly, these theses will contain a Methodology chapter that will explain the candidate's worldview and how they went about deciding their research methods, interpreting their data and reporting it.

Government and, at times industry, reports or professional association publications may also be valuable sources of information in honing your research topic and ensuring that your research will add to the body of knowledge. Once again, your university's library website is likely to provide excellent access to these publications. Books can also provide excellent information, especially those that are based on academic research results. Some examples of books on emerging areas of PM research may be helpful for you such as those that may alert you to new ways of looking at PM (Hodgson and Cicmil, 2006; Smith, 2007; Andersen, 2008; Winter and Szczepanek, 2009; Morris, Pinto and Söderlund, 2011) and framing your hunch in an established emergent or established theoretical context. Special issues of some PM journals (Hällgren and Lindahl, 2012; Söderlund and Geraldi, 2012) and seminal papers (Winter, Smith, Morris and Cicmil, 2006) may also be of value in helping you to better understand recent trends in PM research.

One recent example of a research book within the PM team behaviour field is Bredin and Söderlund's (2011) *Human Research Management in Project-Based Organizations*. Bredin and Söderlund reveal a new and large area for research. The use of teams across almost all organisations today means that most people now work in either a project-oriented organisation (where teams are formed to carry out a specific task, for instance, new product development, or a change program) or a project-based organisation (where the organisation's core business is conducted in project teams such as in construction and infrastructure companies). This change in the way that organisations structure work has opened up new areas requiring research within the broad PM profession. Likewise, in the emerging field of collaborative forms of project procurement, Doherty's (2008) *Heathrow's Terminal 5: History in the Making* and Walker and Rowlinson's (eds) (2008) *Procurement Systems: A Cross-Industry Project Management Perspective*, reveal new and different ways in which projects are being conducted around the world. These new ways of managing projects have created the need for new and different knowledge, skills and attributes for project managers. The type of literature cited above will both assist you to refine your research topic and ensure that you are choosing a topic that relates to the increased use of PM across industries and government and the changing forms that projects might now take. It can also open up new research method possibilities for your thesis.

The Internet in general, and even newspapers and magazines, may also help you to narrow your research focus, but it is important to remember that as you move to this broader range of sources the reliability and validity of information provided may not meet the standards expected in academe. Confirming your findings from these sources by referring back to the refereed literature, books written by researchers or government publications is required.

Overall, your aim here has been to learn all you can about the idea you began with, to understand the broader field, or parent discipline, within which it sits, and to trace through developments in the field to the present time. You commence with the background to your research, moving through the broader field and narrowing down to the research problem (Perry, 2011; Perry, 2012) that began with your hunch. This may involve commencing with seminal works in the field and finishing with literature, and theses, published in the last few years, even weeks, to ensure that you are truly identifying a current research gap; an area of need worthy of research.

## Deciding Upon the Appropriate Research Method

Having researched the literature you are now in a position to develop your research questions or, depending on the type of research you are now moving toward, research hypotheses. Working through the literature from parent to immediate discipline area literature gaps in the current knowledge, related to your area of research, will become apparent. You will now be in a position to develop, based on your literature review, a new and different theoretical framework upon which you can make decisions related to the design of your research. Now you know what you are researching, how it or fields closely related to it have been researched in the past. You might decide to pursue a topic previously researched, clearly identifying how your research methods will ensure a new and different approach is taken to the topic, or you might research a new topic using appropriate data-gathering techniques. Put simply, you now ask yourself: How have others previously researched in this field? How might I best research my topic? Based on the knowledge you have of how others have researched in related areas, you are now in a position to argue why you will or will not adopt the same methods to answer your research question.

You may choose to create a conceptual framework at this stage. A well-presented conceptual framework can make communicating your research topic to others easier. It acknowledges how the review of the literature has influenced your choice of topic and explains how issues within your area of research are connected to one another. It identifies the research variables and relationships between each of them. Though this may be presented using words alone, it is often presented in graphical form, better helping the reader to understand the topic. The conceptual framework clearly identifies the research problem and provides the setting from which the research questions can be presented. From the research questions – the problem that needs to be addressed and the questions that need to be asked to address it – the research methods that will best enable the questions to be answered can be selected. Research methods include all instruments used to collect data and explanation of how the data will be analysed. They include details of how each method will be used: the type of questions that might be asked, of whom they will be asked, and why.

You may have a personal preference for your research approach. Perhaps you believe that the positivist approach provides the most credible results, or maybe you prefer to understand more of the underlying reasons for a phenomenon and thus prefer the interpretivist approach. A range of writers in the research methodology area have begun to recommend that a mixed method approach be adopted in order to increase the number of perspectives on the phenomena under study they 'argue that mixed methods research is one of the three major "research paradigms" (quantitative research, qualitative research, and mixed methods research)' (for example, Easterby-Smith, Thorpe and Lowe, 1991: p. 112) and others in more recent years have called for mixed methods to be considered by researchers (Armitage, 2007; Johnson, Onwuegbuzie and Turner, 2007; Creswell, 2009; Tashakkori, 2009).

Illustrative of the philosophy behind this approach is the point made by Johnson et al. (2007: p. 113): 'We would position mixed research between the extremes Plato (quantitative research) and the Sophists (qualitative research), with mixed research attempting to respect fully the wisdom of both of these viewpoints while also seeking a workable middle solution for many (research) problems of interest. Today, the primary philosophy of mixed research is that of pragmatism. Mixed methods research (MMR) is, generally speaking, an approach to knowledge (theory and practice) that attempts to consider multiple viewpoints, perspectives, positions, and standpoints (always including the standpoints of qualitative and quantitative research).' Thus, if your hunch requires a mixed methods approach, it can be justified.

The approach you select and the methods that you use within it, will depend on the research question to be answered, but will be influenced by your personal preference. The research methods may also be chosen in order to address a research topic from a different perspective to those used by others in order to provide new and different information on the topic. Alternatively, the research methods may be chosen in order to answer a research topic not previously researched in order to close a gap in the knowledge. To demonstrate how this is done, we provide two examples of how successful candidates, both experienced PM professionals, worked through from hunch to graduation.

## Case Study – Dr Alejandro Arroyo (2009)

The assets that Alejandro brought were his intimate knowledge of and access to the case study businesses, their leaders and staff and this was considered more important than any potential bias or restrictive perspectives he might hold. He acknowledged these potential biases and took stringent measures to minimise them. Figure 10.1 illustrates his chosen salient literature and research approach and the link between literature, ontology and research methods.

This thesis was about making sense of the impact of economic forces and competitive advantage that triggered a set of business transformations. It also involved investigating how the studied firms translated strategy and in many instances survival and sustainable business strategies. The translation of strategy into managing projects to deliver the strategy involved changes in leadership style, knowledge sharing and collaboration from the approach the research companies had adopted prior to joining the Atlantic Corridor entity. These general contextual areas framed his

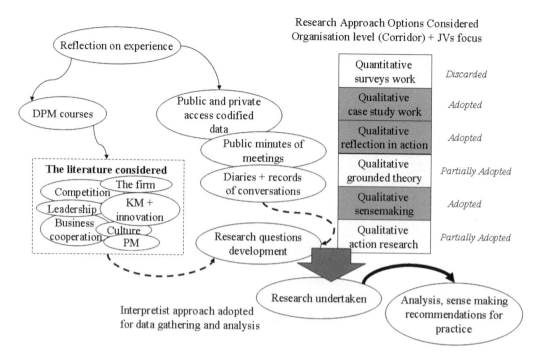

**Figure 10.1    Research approach of Alejandro Arroyo (Arroyo, 2009: p. 10)**

choice of literature. Alejandro had to make sense of what triggered behavioural and organisational structure changes and how strategy was developed and implemented.

The nature of his study led him to write a context chapter explaining the history of the formation of the Mercosur, the resulting Atlantic Corridor initiative in response to global changes in the logistics business and of its formation, and his own role in the study as a participant researcher. In many cases such a chapter can clearly frame the context of the thesis topic. He reviewed the bodies of knowledge indicated in the above figure so that he could identify various theories of knowledge creation, sharing and use together with theories of leadership that enable this, and how culture at the national and organisational level affected knowledge management and leadership. All this was framed from a PM perspective and in terms of the PM of business transformation and change management.

Alejandro used a case study combination using data gathered from personal and company files, notes and documentation, publicly accessible information supported by his reflection on practice. He conducted numerous interviews with a range of Corridor participants. Originally he intended combining a set of case studies with a quantitative study but upon reflection on the research questions and his epistemological and axiological stance there did not seem any justification to do so. Survey data would not have provided the needed depth of understanding and so he considered this of little benefit and value to his study. He used grounded theory and sense making from his case study data, reflection and interview data to answer his research questions.

The thesis topic research objective was defined and questions were then developed from seeking to understand Corridor project objectives that led to its conceptualisation as a strategic community of practice (CoP). Alejando's stated research objective was: 'The aim of this study is to establish how a huge geographical region along with a growing number of players can re-engineer its business methods to encourage intra-regional cooperation by focusing on an efficient knowledge management while exercising a different leadership style to that normally adopted in the region' (Arroyo, 2009: p. 5). For his supporting research questions of the thesis, it may be accessed from: http://researchbank.rmit.edu.au/view/rmit:7891. His thesis provides a benchmark for readers of this chapter to review and think about how it could have been even clearer and better targeted to the identified research question, stated paradigm and appropriate research method. This case study demonstrates how Alejandro's role and position in his work role led him to frame this research problem, with his choice guided by what was possible: this was a key determinant.

## Tips and Exercises

### TIPS FOR STUDENTS

- The candidate's aim is to choose salient literature to frame the chosen research topic by investigating salient seminal and contemporary literature, in order to identify gaps in context, scope or through apparent paradoxes with observed practice.
- Identified gaps help to refine research questions, hypotheses or propositions and to identify constructs and how they may be measured, and whether the literature offers instruments that might be adopted or adapted.
- Be careful to choose the most powerful, strongly supported and validated and authoritative literature to inform your research – think of yourself as a barrister presenting evidence at a trial to skilfully select the most effective to communicate the basis of their argument.

### TIPS FOR SUPERVISORS

- Any literature accessed should offer suggestions about research approach options and a range of ontological, epistemological and axiological stances for the candidate to consider. Apart from flushing out the candidate's potential contribution through their hunch, a rigorous literature review can help candidates to better explain and justify their contribution.
- Be open-minded and engage in dialogue to help the candidate frame their thesis approach from their initial hunch and to effectively embed their own reflections and expertise into the thesis in an authoritative way.
- If the above is undertaken then the thesis topic will be interesting and both candidate and supervisor will learn much from each other and that the thesis will be most likely an engaging and intriguing work for examiners to also learn from.

### EXERCISES

1. Outline the literature themes that you feel would be salient to your proposed research topic. Identify your current impression of what gaps exist that your hunch may shed light on and how you may develop a research proposal to fill the gaps you choose to fill.
2. Identify from the literature which key authors are likely to provide guidance on your research approach and how you might develop data-gathering instruments and approaches.
3. Discuss and present in a table the options that you have considered for gathering and analysing data and indicate how these relate to your stated ontological, epistemological and axiological stance.

4. Download one or more doctoral theses. Examine each thesis to assess how effectively the candidate has addressed their explanation and justification of their research design and literature review. You will realise that numerous theses that have been passed and are successful do not always explain very well to you what you may now perceive to be 'best research practice' as presented in this chapter and other chapters of this book.

# References

Andersen, E. S. (2008). *Rethinking Project Management – An organisational perspective*. Harlow, UK: Pearson Education Limited.

Armitage, A. (2007). *Mutual Research Designs: Redefining Mixed Methods Research Design*. British Educational Research Association Annual Conference, University of London, Institute of Education, p. 10.

Arroyo, A. C. (2009). The Role of the Atlantic Corridor Project as a Form of Strategic Community of Practice in Facilitating Business Transformations in Latin America. Doctorate, *School of Property, Construction and Project Management*, Melbourne: RMIT University.

Bredin, K. and Söderlund, J. (2011a). The HR quadriad: A framework for the analysis of HRM in project-based organizations. *International Journal of Human Resource Management, 22*(10), 2202–2221.

Bredin, K. and Söderlund, J. (2011b). *Human Resource Management in Project-based Organizations: The HR quadriad framework*. Basingstoke, UK: Palgrave Macmillan.

Creswell, J. W. (2009). *Research Design: Qualitative, quantitative, and mixed methods approaches*. Thousand Oaks, CA: Sage Publications.

Doherty, S. (2008). *Heathrow's T5 History in the Making*. Chichester: John Wiley & Sons Ltd.

Easterby-Smith, M., Thorpe, R. and Lowe, A. (1991). *Management Research: An introduction*. London, UK: Sage.

Hällgren, M. and Lindahl, M. (2012). How do you do? On situating old project sites through practice-based studies. *International Journal of Managing Projects in Business, 5*(3): 335–344.

Hodgson, D. and Cicmil, S. (2006). *Making Projects Critical*. Basingstoke, UK: Palgrave Macmillan.

Johnson, R. B., Onwuegbuzie, A. J. and Turner, L. A. (2007). Toward a definition of mixed methods research. *Journal of Mixed Methods Research, 1*(2), 112–133.

Morris, P. W. G., Pinto, J. K. and Söderlund, J. (eds) (2011). *The Oxford Handbook of Project Management*. Series The Oxford Handbook of Project Management. Oxford: Oxford University Press.

Perry, C. (2011). A structured approach to the journey of doctoral research. *International Journal of Organisational Behaviour, 6*(1), 1–12.

Perry, C. (2012). A Structured Approach for Presenting Theses: Notes for Students and Their Supervisors.

Rao, S. and Perry, C. (2003). Convergent interviewing to build theory in under-researched areas: Principles and an example investigation of Internet usage in inter-firm relationships. *Qualitative Market Research: An International Journal, 6*(4), 236–247.

Smith, C. (2007). *Making Sense of Project Realities: Theory, practice and the pursuit of performance*. Aldershot, UK: Gower Publishing.

Söderlund, J. and Geraldi, J. G. (2012). Classics in project management: Revisiting the past, creating the future. *International Journal of Managing Projects in Business, 5*(4), 559–577.

Tashakkori, A. (2009). Are we there yet?: The state of the mixed methods community. *Journal of Mixed Methods Research, 3*(4), 287–291.

Walker, D. H. T. and Rowlinson, S. (eds) (2008). *Procurement Systems – A Cross Industry Project Management Perspective*. Series Procurement Systems – A Cross Industry Project Management Perspective. Abingdon, Oxon: Taylor & Francis.

Winter, M., Smith, C., Morris, P. W. G. and Cicmil, S. (2006). Directions for future research in project management: The main findings of a UK government-funded research network. *International Journal of Project Management, 24*(8), 638–649.

Winter, M. and Szczepanek, T. (2009). *Images of Projects*. Farnham, UK: Gower Publishing.

# 11

# Moving from 'Hunches' to an Interesting Research Topic: Defining the Research Topic

Derek Walker and Beverley Lloyd-Walker

*Most mature experienced PM practitioners that consider a doctorate have an enduring but fuzzily expressed hunch for an interesting and valuable dissertation topic. We wrote this to help potential candidates and their supervisors develop a robust doctoral project.*

The scope and range of potential PM research topics and approaches that might be taken to conduct that research has increased greatly since the turn of this century. This provides the potential doctoral candidate with opportunities, but perhaps also greater challenges in working from idea to research question. This chapter provides guidance on foundational requirements for sound decision making about framing a research question and objectives that lead to valuable research that in turn contributes to a body of knowledge. Many of these lessons apply to honours and master's candidates (both research and coursework with a minor thesis) and other students undertaking assignments that requires theory to be compared to practice.

At the end of this chapter, the reader can:

- develop a level of comfort about their ability to use their experience to identify a research topic and develop it into a research question;
- achieve clarity in conceptualising the research problem and question then link these to the salient theory and a defendable and practical research approach;
- enhance their open-mindedness to engage in formal and informal conversations and presentations to help develop a thesis topic from an initial hunch.

Keywords: research topic, problem definition, research objectives, value proposition

This chapter is intended to illuminate the process that all doctoral candidates, but especially mature doctoral candidates with PM experience, face when developing a research topic. Many, in our experience, have a vague 'gut-feeling' for a topic that is highly tacit, implicit, embedded in their praxis but generally poorly expressed when first discussed with a potential supervisor. Part of the supervisor's skill is to help the candidate to bring all these emotions and ideas 'onto the table' so that its essence can: be distilled and an interesting perspective developed that has potential to add to the body of knowledge; be rigorous enough to be a doctorate; identify and bridge a knowledge gap; and be of sufficient interest to sustain both the candidate and supervisor along a journey that usually lasts for over half a decade!

We aim to help guide mature experienced doctoral candidates to be more confident and assertive in translating their hunch for a good topic idea into something that provides special and insightful material for their thesis. It should help them reflect on what is special about their hunch so that they do not allow themselves to abandon what may well be great ideas or to be cajoled into taking on a 'second or third best' safe topic that leaves them feeling that they missed a rare opportunity to explore their hunch.

The research problem set for this chapter is that moving from a hunch to an interesting topic can be difficult for many potential doctoral candidates. This chapter has as its focus candidates who are mature industry practitioners and also it provides guidance for their potential supervisors. Candidates may experience frustration and fear in making clear their research idea for several reasons (see Table 11.1).

**Table 11.1    Topic/idea definition issues of concern and reasons for them**

| Issue | Reasons |
| --- | --- |
| 1. Originality | Though fully aware that a doctorate makes an 'original contribution' the contribution to be made is vague and difficult to make explicit. The candidate is not sure that their 'good topic' is original enough. |
| 2. Balance and clear expression of the topic | They may lack confidence in their ability to explain the problem, question and how they will resolve the research topic in a way that does not sound trivial or overly complex. |
| 3. Thesis strategy framing | Potential supervisors may experience difficulty understanding the complexity of a yet to be well-described problem or context. The value of the research idea may be underestimated and the potential supervisor may be unable to help the prospective candidate make explicit complex contextual undercurrents that identify the problem as doctoral study material. |

Deciding on an interesting topic is your first step in planning your research and this links to deciding upon an appropriate methodology and related research methods that are informed by the relevant literature. The research question, the ontological and epistemological positions and the salient literature will inform the research approach.

There are other considerations for both the experienced doctoral candidate and their supervisor. The research approach should be matched against the candidate's research resources, technical expertise, professional network and accumulated understanding of the research problem context. To ignore these assets deprives academia of a thesis that provides a near-unique perspective originating from a hunch about an apparently intriguing paradox. The question is, how can this hunch become a topic that will be worth an investment of several years in the project?

## The Project Management (PM) Research Context

The PM research context now offers researchers interesting research topics, disciplinary contexts, perspectives and recognised research methods that are considered 'worthy of a doctorate'. This was not the case until the late 1990s. At the turn of the new century a series of PM research initiatives challenged the status quo in a productive and fruitful way. A range of influential papers and research initiatives followed (Winter, Smith, Cooke-Davies and Cicmil, 2006; Winter, Smith, Morris and Cicmil, 2006) the rethinking PM network in the UK, funded by the Engineering and Physical Sciences Research Council (EPSRC) Network from 2004–2006 (Winter and Smith, 2006). Another important related research network, the Making Projects Critical group formed resulting in a book (Hodgson and Cicmil, 2006) revealing the 'lived reality' of PM for its various actors and positioning PM research in the social sciences arena. Two main forums for PM research were the PMI research conference meetings, with a strong North American/UK following, and the mainly Nordic-influenced International Research Network on Organizing by Projects (IRNOP) founded in 1993. Both forums have researchers from all over the world building upon PM seminal work (for example, by Lundin and Söderholm (1995); Packendorff (1995)). Morris (2002) called for PM and strategy to be researched and for broader perspectives to be considered (Crawford, Morris, Thomas and Winter, 2006) considerably widening the potential topics for PM research. Readers interested in the history of PM scholarship should refer to Morris (2010; 2011), Lenfle and Loch (2010), and the *International Journal of Managing Projects in Business* special issue edited by Söderlund and Geraldi (2012). PM scholarship is an evolving field of study with practitioner hunches influencing research ranging from technical to human aspects and support available for supervision and examination.

## Choosing and Planning Your Research Topic

### ACKNOWLEDGING YOUR WORLDVIEW

The discussion of the PM research context highlights the changed ways that PM is viewed and investigated. The highly positivist view of the world as best being understood through indisputable 'facts and figures' has been supplemented by a series of social and behavioural science perspectives that have a completely different view of what is 'real' and what constitutes 'truth'.

This change in PM research makes it necessary for us to now be clear about what we believe to be true, how we judge the validity and veracity of evidence, what we value and how we see the world. PM research covers a broad range of topics. A research project that focuses on mathematical algorithms for planning projects or for assessing and managing risk cannot be perceived to be any less or more valuable or valid than research that investigates the sources and application of power within a project management office (PMO) or how it 'feels' to be a blind person working in a project team. These are all valid vehicles for advancing PM theory and practice.

We need to understand the worldview of other PM scholars and practitioners and help them understand our view if we want to engage in serious and meaningful exchanges. We need a common baseline to understand each other's terms and language.

Discussion of paradigms in PM research is covered earlier in the book and it is useful to see the concept *paradigm* in terms of being a worldview: a lens through which to perceive the research problem and what evidence can be accepted as valid to study that problem. This helps us to work out what is necessary to dispel doubts, and to gather important evidence to justify an interpretation of 'truth'. The term paradigm as embodying systems of ideas and beliefs is a good way to describe a *worldview* but it leaves gaps in precision. Slicing and dicing the term into its components of ontology, epistemology and axiology can add some precision but can also add confusion.

It is necessary for doctoral candidates to address precision when stating their worldview and that of participants to the work. In a mixed-methods approach, a significant part of the study may be targeted at a need for 'hard facts' while another complementary part could drill down to explain these 'facts' in human terms using assessment of elusive concepts such as feelings, fear, motivation, loyalty or revenge. Without stating the worldview elements needed to study and understand the mixed method components, a candidate is in danger of sounding unconvincing and confused. Hence it is important to explain and justify the ontological, epistemological and axiological positions so that scope and limitations can be acknowledged. When a thesis is examined it is examined against the holistic paradigm that is stated as being adopted.

## DEFINING THE RESEARCH PROBLEM MAKING THE TACIT EXPLICIT

We can now start focusing upon hunches as a threshold source of interesting and intriguing scholarship. Experienced PM practitioners and thesis supervisors often have hunches that require discussion, exploration and transformation to become well-identified research problems and questions. Candidates with work experience possess a powerful source of knowledge about what does or does not work and the context in which this knowledge is sustained. Extending the work of Dreyfus (2004), and Dreyfus and Dreyfus (2005), Cicmil's thesis (2003) identified stages of people's PM competence. Cicmil (2006: p. 35) presents a table 'Expertise, competence and knowledge in PM mapped against Dreyfus' (2004) model of adult learning' that provides useful insights into how competent, proficient and expert virtuoso practitioners with substantial PM experience use feelings and knowledge of context to formulate responses to problems and challenges. Often these people have a great deal of valuable tacit knowledge that when reflected upon and tested can be made both explicit and highly contextually explained and thus make a genuine and real contribution to theory and practice.

Davis states in his seminal paper (1971: p. 309) that, 'A theorist is considered great, not because his theories are true, but because they are interesting. Those who carefully and exhaustively verify trivial theories are soon forgotten; whereas those who cursorily and expediently verify interesting theories are long remembered.' His 'elements' provide tips for prospective candidates (Table 11.2).

**Table 11.2    Davis' elements of interest: tips for candidates**

| | |
|---|---|
| Apparent paradoxes … | Those assumed to be unorganised or chaotic may have some structure (or vice versa), or indeed what was thought to be stable may in some circumstances be highly unstable. |
| Unitary/separable | What was assumed to be generally unitary may be shown to be separable so that a single phenomenon is really an assortment of linked phenomena, or what was thought to be singular can in fact be abstracted. |
| Contradictory | Findings reported may be contrary to the prevailing wisdom. |
| Novelty | Using a new approach (research method) to studying a topic. |

Davis points out that the 'taken-for-granted' world contains theoretical assumptions and contextual assumptions. Thus a gut feeling about what may or may not work can be studied from existing theory that is set in a specific context that invalidates the assumed contextual settings. This opens up enormous potential for research to lead researchers well beyond their theoretical comfort zone.

'Interesting' studies could research the 'lived reality' of project organisations and how teams interact or a narrower and more focused area exploring how time scheduling or budget plans evolved based on analysis of a series of documented plans through various project stages as reported in project control meetings. Studies of specific under-represented sectors, for example PM, as a way of managing complex medical surgery could also be categorised 'interesting'. Research that is viewed as unitary/separable could look at how teams in a project form perspectives about what the aims and vision of the project are and how these perspectives guide them.

Challenging the basis for competition, for example research into project alliances (Bresnen, 2007; Lahdenperä, 2009; Brady, Maylor and Johnson, 2011; Walker and Lloyd-Walker, 2011), or a challenge to the prevailing wisdom about how PM evolved, for example the intriguing research on PM memes undertaken by Whitty (2005), could be categorised as 'contradictory'.

An example of novelty when selecting research methods is demonstrated by a study undertaken into how project teams interacted on stages of the enlargement of the Panama Canal (Smits and van Marrewijk, 2012). An ethnographic research method was used to understand PM relationships and culture. This is rare and novel because it is about a mega-project in Panama, a part of the world from which PM research has rarely been reported. Using this unfamiliar approach to PM research creates interest and reveals new and different PM insights. When considering how to develop a research topic 'hunch' it is worth thinking about the topic's value proposition to a range of audiences that will eventually read outputs from the work. See Table 11.3 for considerations based on audience/readership.

Most candidates (and some supervisors) fail to appreciate the fact that the above readership actually learns from the work if it is truly 'interesting', novel and engaging. We have learned much from being examiners, supervisors and co-authors with our doctoral candidates. Our colleagues that are exposed to progress seminars, formal and informal discussions also learn from our candidates. An interesting 'hunch' developed into a suitable topic provides us all with an engine of creativity and a valued learning experience. Table 11.4 identifies helpful questions for topic identification.

These questions should help you start a process of mapping the 'hunch' in terms of dilemmas, quandaries, inconsistencies between theory and practice, changes in context and ways in which the word 'something' in your vague description of a hunch can be substituted into more specific terms, which may, with discussion and reflection, be substituted for that original vague description.

When you have identified your 'hunch' as a specific problem and potential way to resolve that issue, as illustrated in Table 11.5, you are ready to state the purpose of the research.

## OPERATIONALISING THE RESEARCH PROBLEM INTO EXPLICIT RESEARCH QUESTIONS OR PROPOSITIONS

Creswell (2009, Chapter 7) recommends that candidates frame a broad central research question that asks for exploration of the central phenomenon identified in the research problem. The question should be consistent with your adopted worldview so that you may pose, for example, a 'how many?' question which needs a positivist and predominantly quantitative worldview, or you may ask a 'why' or 'how to' question which is likely to need a constructivist worldview using

**Table 11.3    Tips on considering the value proposition when exploring hunches**

| Who are Your Audience/ Readers? | What are Their Possible Motivators | Tips |
|---|---|---|
| Examiners | The thesis must demonstrate critical understanding and mastery of the topic's theory and knowledge base; demonstrate an authoritative ability to argue using an appropriate research framework and to be able to present convincing evidence to support the work; produce a new contribution to theory and in PM, practice; and be publishable in part (Australian Quality Framework, 2011). | From a purely selfish perspective, candidates should remember that examiners are the prime stakeholder–readers. If they are not convinced that the topic is worthy then the thesis is unlikely to pass examination. Examiners are chosen for their expertise in methodology and subject matter content. This does NOT mean that they are expert in the specific research method adopted or that they are as knowledgeable about the topic as the candidate. This has advantages because an interesting research methods approach is welcomed if it fits the stated research problem and questions. Examiners LEARN from examining a thesis. Also, if the candidate's perspective is novel and contextually rich then this is another learning opportunity about the nuance of the topic. |
| The university | All universities have a reputation to consider. The number of doctoral successes matter, as does its reputation for being 'cutting edge'. Publications and their number and quality are also highly valued. | Cutting-edge research provides the engine for scholarly achievement. In PM, this usually translates to advancing the PM discipline through new tools, techniques but also practices and better understanding of PM practice. |
| Supervisors | A supervisor's reputation is partially maintained through doctoral theses supervised and publications. Supervisors also learn from their candidates and this provides them with an opportunity to see PM through another point of view. | An interesting and novel topic usually generates more publication possibilities. Enhancing practice through better understanding the PM context provides learning opportunities for supervisors. This is particularly true for candidates with extensive practical experience. |
| Other scholars | Students, researchers and teachers are interested in and learn from new perspectives. The 'further research' part of a thesis poses new directions and departure points for others to follow. | Interesting 'hunches' often highlight a paradox that is intriguing and combines several incomplete theories. Not only does the thesis provide answers or new findings but highlights further research directions beyond the thesis scope that trigger more research. |
| Practitioners | Some, but only a few, practitioners (unless they are work colleagues) will be interested in the thesis itself but they will be interested in extracts as papers, presentations and commercialised tools. | The main value that practitioners gain from a thesis is indirect. They gain from the researcher interaction that makes them think about and explain their complex problems. They gain from ancillary products such as publications and presentations. |
| The candidate – tips on considering the value proposition when exploring hunches | Explaining to others is the most effective way to ensure you best understand the topic. | Most value from the work is gained by the candidate's personal growth in knowledge and confidence. This should not be underestimated. |

**Table 11.4    Questions to help clarify and shape a hunch into an interesting topic**

| Questioning Level of Interest | Main Points to be Clarified |
| --- | --- |
| What paradox does this hunch expose? | Identify the theoretical 'rules' or 'guidelines' that seem to be challenged or exposed as being deficient/incomplete. |
| To what literature and theory does this topic seem to most closely relate? | Conceptually map the theories in some Venn-type diagram to identify overlaps and potential gaps. Identify the main points of departure from what is published. |
| Have the assumptions about the problem 'hunch' I identified revealed poorly articulated or understood influences? | Map and identify assumptions in terms of geographical, economic, political or cultural factors so that you can specifically explain how your hunch is either set in a context that is well known or where the presented context is novel or poorly understood. |
| Is this hunch likely to be new and potentially ground breaking? | Maybe your hunch is not new, but the context (as you see it) or some other aspect provides you with rare insights that give your topic a sense of being leading edge. |
| Can I usefully test my hunch from an alternative paradigm or methodological approach? | Investigate the paradigm that has dominated the way that similar studies that address your 'hunch' and the research approach. You may propose your study to take an alternative approach to that previously used in the salient literature either from a paradigm or research methods approach to make your contribution. |
| Can I sustain interest in this topic for at least three to four years? Do I want to publish on this topic for several years afterwards? | Identify YOUR motivation for working with this hunch. Map out how resolving the quandary/learning from the research process will be of benefit to your career and identify what doors you believe it may open and how the research process may satisfy your curiosity. |

**Table 11.5    Research topic purpose statement**

| Statement Elements | Dimensions to be Described |
| --- | --- |
| What precisely is the problem? | A brief narrative of the problem and how it raises dilemmas, issues and calls for action. Think about key words that would be used to index this problem in the final written thesis summary. |
| How will studying this problem using my hunch impact PM theory and/or practice; how will it make a contribution? | Its impact on how your topic challenges or supports prevailing assumptions by: providing a new and valuable ontological or organisational level perspective; and/or developing new ways of measuring and assessing evidence. |
| Why is it important to address this problem? | Justification of your position in terms of why the topic is interesting and capable of delivering benefit to PM theory and practice and what useful new contribution it offers. If the topic hunch was sufficiently intriguing to grip your imagination for many years then there must be something special about it and your perspective of it. You need to explain its importance to others who may be grappling with the same problem but as yet have not recognised it. |
| Why do I think I am equipped to tackle the research into this problem? | Clarification of the skills, expertise, knowledge assets and network of useful contacts that you can draw upon. This will provide insights into the credibility of your resources to tackle this topic. |
| What limitations and qualifications do I feel should be stated up-front to better understand the scope of the proposed work? | Clarify how you limit the scope of the hunch, its boundaries and constraints and its potential for further future work. |

qualitative research approaches. He recommends one or two central questions, followed by no more than five to seven sub-questions. This is because you need to be aware of scope and time/resource limitations, because as a doctoral candidate you are on your own, solving a problem and need to acknowledge the limits to your work.

Developing the research problem, objectives and question allows the researcher to move towards undertaking meaningful research. However, several more facets of the research process need to be clarified. These are: deciding what and how to measure, choosing the relevant literature to know what to, and how to, measure data, and deciding upon a research method that allows the researcher to develop a credible basis for undertaking research.

Your stated ontological and epistemological positions provide you with guidance about what to measure and how to measure. The aim of this chapter section is to help you move from a hunch to developing an interesting research topic. The key, as stressed above, is to understand how to frame your hunch within your choice of paradigm. All else will fall into place, including determining the data needed and how it might be gathered, measured and analysed.

**Table 11.6    Questions to understand 'the Corridor' project objectives**

| | |
|---|---|
| 1. | What are the variables granting the Corridor project the ability to generate trust to facilitate knowledge transfer among stakeholders? |
| 2. | How do Corridor stakeholders share vital internal information and join forces to face extra-regional threats? |
| 3. | Why do Corridor stakeholders show their current attitudes and motivations towards committing themselves with partnerships, alliances and joint ventures? |
| 4. | How does culture play a role in easing or impeding the development of the Corridor vision throughout the region? |
| 5. | What factors hold a more relative influence on stakeholders to allow vertical or horizontal integration to occur? |
| 6. | What is the degree of awareness among stakeholders with respect to sustainable development and its future relevance over the region? |

## Example of a Successful Candidate Choosing a Research Topic

The above section provided a useful guide for potential doctoral candidates. This section's purpose is to provide some examples. Each doctoral candidate's experience is unique as is each supervisor's, so each person will have different experiential and theoretical resources to draw upon. We will now outline a case study of a thesis topic hunch development to a successful thesis to illustrate how a 'hunch' was developed into a successful doctoral thesis. We will then provide a synthesis of lessons learned from our experience.

## CASE STUDY – DR ALEJANDRO ARROYO (2009)

Alejandro Arroyo was (and is) chief executive officer of a logistics consultancy based in Buenos Aires with offices across Latin America and in Canada. He first made contact for information about courses offered in triple bottom line (3BL) issues at the University of Tasmania. Alejandro was interested in professional development and a better understanding of 3BL to service his clients in Bolivia and Brazil who were engaged in oil and gas development in the Camisea Basin. While in Australia, he came to talk to Derek and this resulted in a six-year doctoral journey. The discussion that took place provides a useful example.

Initially Alejandro was unsure whether what he was doing in his practice was PM or logistics or something entirely different. At the meeting in Melbourne, that lasted several hours, it became clear that Alejandro's company carried out its work as projects as defined by Gareis (1989) through the Atlantic Corridor organisation (Arroyo, 2009; Arroyo and Walker, 2009). Two potential research topics emerged; one about 3BL in Camisea Basin projects and the other about the way that the Atlantic Corridor emerged as a form of Community of Practice (CoP) (Wenger and Snyder, 2000) in which interested parties shared knowledge about problems and issues they faced (mainly logistical but later about a range of supply chain integration issues and collaboration forms).

The former topic theme presented potential ethical issues in terms of undertaking research and the latter was 'safer' but had excellent potential. Both involved Alejandro as an active participant in the research with deep contextual knowledge and phenomenal access to a range of organisational participants from the top of the organisation to its 'coal face'. Clearly, this research opportunity was exciting for both potential candidate and supervisor. Both parties had sufficient business, project and life experience to be able to collaboratively explore, risk assess and refine the thesis topic over an extended time. The Doctor of Project Management (DPM) at RMIT University in Melbourne, Australia required a front-end coursework component of advanced postgraduate study, research methods and pilot studies to test the viability of the thesis topic. During the two years of part-time remote online study, a continuous dialogue took place between the student and supervisor about the thesis topic (the thesis forms 67 per cent of the doctoral effort), to refine his 'hunch' to become a research topic. Figure 11.1 illustrates how they mapped together the important characteristics that underpinned Alejandro's hunch and how it could be operationalised into research propositions and questions.

The identified project problem statement revolved around an interesting contextual development. The formation of the South American form of the European Union (EU), together with global expansion leading to fierce competition in international shipping and logistics, had forced logistics companies in South America to rethink and adapt their business models. The thesis problem statement was framed as follows:

> *The aim of this study is to establish how a huge geographical region along with a growing number of players can re-engineer its business methods to encourage intra-regional cooperation by focusing on an efficient knowledge management while exercising a different leadership style to that normally adopted in the region. (Arroyo, 2009: p. 5)*

The thesis topic research question was then developed from seeking to understand the following Corridor project objectives that led to its conceptualisation as a strategic CoP (Table 11.6).

This case study demonstrates how Alejandro's role and his work role led him to frame this research problem, the choice being guided by what was possible – a key determinant. The 3BL research topic hunch could have been fruitful but, after discussion and reflection, access to data

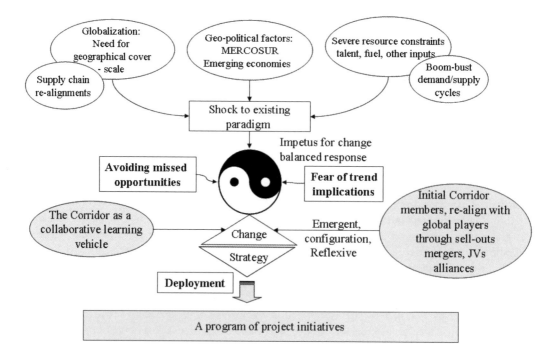

**Figure 11.1**   **The operationalisation of Alejandro's thesis topic (Source: Arroyo, 2009: p. 44)**

and ethical considerations ruled it out. Such considerations are common. Alejandro's thesis can be downloaded from http://researchbank.rmit.edu.au/view/rmit:7891.

## Tips and Exercises

### TIPS FOR STUDENTS

- No 'hunch' that an experienced person expresses is too trivial or shallow to not be worth further consideration and exploration.
- Clarity of the research problem leads to a clear research question and an understanding of the relevant and salient literature that will inform the thesis so that a practical and workable research method can be developed. Developing this clarity usually takes time and considerable effort; it can be very hard work with much thought, often with little initial documentation of the effort. This evolves across the research project process with periods of questioning, challenge and reassessment. Those candidates that do not develop this level of clarity are in danger of feeling lost and being lost.
- Stating the ontological, epistemological and axiological stance is important; it helps keep the candidate safely within a defined and defensible paradigm. A confident candidate with a sound hunch and a proposed research approach can progress to develop innovative research instruments and approaches that will make the research project interesting whilst perhaps also providing a methodological contribution.
- If the candidate and supervisor produce conference and journal papers as the thesis proceeds, their shared knowledge is refined and opportunities for ideas to be contested further help clarify the thesis purpose, conduct and outputs.

## TIPS FOR SUPERVISORS

- Potential supervisors need to be open-minded to accept the validity of numerous paradigms and to be able to steer conversations to help the candidate to work within their favoured ontological stance. It is the candidate that frames the research problem based on their experience and so they naturally have a worldview that shapes their perception of the hunch and research problem. The supervisor may suggest alternative paradigms for the candidate to consider, even if only so the candidate might justify their own worldview.
- Supervisor suggestions should be contestable; they should not force the candidate to accept any or all of the supervisor's suggestions. While it is useful to confront the candidate with ideas that take them outside their comfort zone to stretch their intellect, it should be remembered that the candidate 'owns' the topic. They need to be able to live with it for three to four years. This requires high levels of affective (want to) commitment by both candidate and supervisor.
- The level of joint learning and knowledge transfer between candidate and supervisor cannot be understated. Both parties gain from each other and from the struggle they are engaged in. Often the candidate has deep contextual knowledge of the subject matter that complements the theoretical knowledge of the supervisor. However, once candidates are solidly engaged in the literature review it is common that they end up leading their supervisors by concentrating effort on current literature and discovering new ideas and evidence.

## EXERCISES

1. Use Tables 11.3 and 11.4 as frameworks to discuss and describe your 'hunch'. Transcribe your explanation and play around with mapping it so that you can begin to develop a research purpose, problem, hypothesis or propositions, acknowledging your worldview and assumptions through your description of your ontological, epistemological and axiological position. State your justification of your choice of topic and your rationale using these tables as guides.
2. With these same tables, use Venn diagrams and tables of value propositions against stakeholders for the hunch potential benefits – use mind maps or play with words that emerge to keep substituting something more concrete and specific for more vague and general words. Keep refining the problem until you feel that you have a reasonably workable description of the research problem.
3. Download one or more doctoral theses and examine them using the tables of this chapter to assess how effectively the candidate has addressed their explanation and justification of their topic. You could then search databases such as Google Scholar or your university's library databases of academic publications to see the type of contribution the thesis has made so far in academic terms. You might then reflect on the impact on practice you believe may be made by the thesis in the future.

## References and Further Reading

Arroyo, A. C. (2009). The Role of the Atlantic Corridor Project as a Form of Strategic Community of Practice in Facilitating Business Transformations in Latin America. Doctorate, *School of Property, Construction and Project Management*. Melbourne: RMIT University.

Arroyo, A. C. and Walker, D. H. T. (2009). *A Latin American Strategic Organisational Transformation Project Management Experience: The Motivation to Transform Business*. European Academy of Management EURAM: Renaissance & Renewal in Management Studies, Liverpool, May 11–14, C. Bredillet and C. Middler, p. 20.

Australian Quality Framework (2011). Australian Qualifications Framework. Canberra: Australian Quality Framework Council, 110.

Brady, T., Maylor, H. and Johnson, M. (2011). *Complex Government Procurement, Paradoxes and the Intelligent Client.* EURAM 2011, Management Culture in the 21st Century, Tallinn, Estonia, June 1–4, M. Martinsuo, H. G. Gemünden and M. Huemann, European Academy of Management, p. 30.

Bresnen, M. (2007). Deconstructing partnering in project-based organisation: Seven pillars, seven paradoxes and seven deadly sins. *International Journal of Project Management,* 25(4), 365–374.

Cicmil, S. (2003). From Instrumental Rationality to Practical Wisdom. PhD. Leicester: Simon de Montfort.

Cicmil, S. (2006). Understanding project management practice through interpretative and critical research perspectives. *Project Management Journal,* 37(2), 27–37.

Crawford, L., Morris, P., Thomas, J. and Winter, M. (2006). Practitioner development: From trained technicians to reflective practitioners. *International Journal of Project Management,* 24(8), 722–733.

Creswell, J. W. (2009). *Research Design: Qualitative, Quantitative, and Mixed Methods Approaches.* Thousand Oaks, CA: Sage Publications.

Davis, M. S. (1971). That's interesting! Towards a phenomenology of sociology and a sociology of phenomenology *Philosophy of the Social Sciences,* 1(2), 309–344.

Dreyfus, H. L. and Dreyfus, S. E. (2005). Expertise in real world contexts. *Organization Studies,* 26(5), 779–792.

Dreyfus, S. E. (2004). The five-stage model of adult skill acquisition. *Bulletin of Science Technology and Society,* 24(3), 177–181.

Gareis, R. (1989). 'Management by projects': The management approach for the future. *International Journal of Project Management,* 7(4), 243–249.

Hodgson, D. and Cicmil, S. (2006). *Making Projects Critical.* Basingstoke, UK: Palgrave Macmillan.

Lahdenperä, P. (2009). Project Alliance – The Competitive Single Target-Cost Approach. Espoo, VTT, 79.

Lenfle, S. and Loch, C. (2010). Lost roots: How project management came to emphasize control over flexibility and novelty. *California Management Review,* 53(1), 32–55.

Lundin, R. A. and Söderholm, A. (1995). A theory of the temporary organization. *Scandinavian Journal of Management,* 11(4), 437–455.

Morris, P. W. G. (2002). 'Research Trends in the 1990s: The Need to Focus on the Business Benefit of Project Management' in D. P. Sleven, D. I. Cleland and J. K. Pinto, *The Frontiers of Project Management.* Newtown Square, Pennsylvania: Project Management Institute, pp. 31–56.

Morris, P. W. G. (2010). Research and the future of project management. *International Journal of Managing Projects in Business,* 3(1), 139–146.

Morris, P. W. G. (2011). 'A Brief History of Project Management' in P. W. G. Morris, J. K. Pinto and J. Söderlund (eds) *The Oxford Handbook of Project Management.* Oxford: Oxford University Press, pp. 15–36.

Packendorff, J. (1995). Inquiring into the temporary organization: New directions for project management research. *Scandinavian Journal of Management,* 11(4), 319–333.

Smits, K. and van Marrewijk, A. (2012). Chaperoning: Practices of collaboration in the Panama Canal expansion program. *International Journal of Managing Projects in Business,* 5(3), 440–456.

Söderlund, J. and Geraldi, J. G. (2012). Classics in project management: Revisiting the past, creating the future. *International Journal of Managing Projects in Business,* 5(4), 559–577.

Walker, D. H. T. and Lloyd-Walker, B. M. (2011). Profiling Professional Excellence in Alliance Management Summary Study Report. Sydney: Alliancing Association of Australasia, 36.

Wenger, E. C. and Snyder, W. M. (2000). Communities of practice: The organizational frontier. *Harvard Business Review,* 78(1), 139–145.

Whitty, S. J. (2005). A memetic paradigm of project management. *International Journal of Project Management,* 23(8), 575–583.

Winter, M. and Smith, C. (2006). EPSRC Network 2004–2006 Rethinking Project Management Final Report, Final report. Manchester: EPSRC, 15.

Winter, M., Smith, C., Cooke-Davies, T. and Cicmil, S. (2006). The importance of 'process' in rethinking project management: The story of a UK Government-funded research network. *International Journal of Project Management,* 24(8), 650–662.

Winter, M., Smith, C., Morris, P. W. G. and Cicmil, S. (2006). Directions for future research in project management: The main findings of a UK government-funded research network. *International Journal of Project Management,* 24(8), 638–649.

# 12

# Ethical Considerations in Project Management Research

Haukur Ingi Jonasson and Helgi Thor Ingason

*Good PM research should examine both the given research topic and deeply consider all the ethical implications of the research project. Critical questions must be asked that reflect ethically on the research principle, processes and outcome. We believe that such an inquiry throughout the lifecycle of the research project will better guarantee good work, a more satisfying experience and a more sustainable contribution. We write the chapter to guide PM researchers and their advisors in doing so.*

All project researchers should, if they want to be taken seriously, carry out their research in both a methodologically and ethically sound manner. Among the questions a project researcher needs to answer are: How does one choose, plan, execute and complete a research project? How does one identify the ethical risks at stake and avoid the pitfalls that might befall the researcher, the research team, the research organisation, society and even future generations? This chapter shows how such questions can be approached by taking a look at project management research through four methodological dimensions: the subjective/qualitative dimension, the subjective/quantitative dimension, the objective/qualitative dimension and the objective/quantitative dimension. In each dimension, typical ethical considerations for that dimension are discussed. Five classical ethical approaches are also introduced that should help project researchers to identify ethical risks and make morally sound decisions. The method demands ethical thinking, urges ethical awareness and encourages project researchers to develop their own approach to investigating project, programme and portfolio management realities.

At the end of this chapter the reader can:

* understand how project management research can methodologically be conducted from four different, however interrelated, perspectives;
* identify ethical risks by critically reflecting on the project management research project through the lens of five ethical approaches;
* conduct his or her own project management research in an ethically sound fashion.

Keywords: qualitative, quantitative, subjective, objective, virtue, utility, duty, rights, ethics

Project management research can be fun and stimulating. Having the privilege to dedicate both time and effort to gaining new knowledge and introducing fresh ideas in the field of PM is both exciting and satisfying. Project management research will refer here to the systematic investigation of *project realities*, that is, to any aspect of a project, project portfolio or programme. Project researchers do their research for a variety of reasons. It might be their job; they might be students; they might have a thirst for knowledge; or they might need to understand some project realities, either as project owners, project managers, project evaluators or as a controlling agents. Whatever the reason, their research must, if it is to be valid and sound, stand up to the rigours of scientific and academic methodologies as well as to moral values and ethical standards.

This chapter will, discuss some of the fundamentals of project management research ethics by breaking the discussion up into four interrelated dimensions. These may all have their own special ethical blind-spots which the project researcher has to be aware of, and which need to be dealt with.

## Formal and Informal Ethical Obligations

Most project management research, especially if it is research conducted within the academia and intended for scientific publication, must conform to formal ethical guidelines defined by universities, research committees and governments. This includes, for instance, the need for the informed consent of participants and approval of the research by appropriate research committees. However, it will be claimed here, all serious project management research, regardless of the obligation imposed by formal authorities (or the lack of such authorities), should be conducted in a morally sound manner. This entails that researchers should be able to justify, at any time and to anyone, *what* they are doing, *why* they are doing it, and *how* they are doing it. Project management research therefore requires the ability to think critically in ethical terms, where researchers think about the quality of their moral reasoning and its implications for their research.

## The Integrated Research Model (IRM) and Project Realities

Before further explaining how to apply project management research ethics, let us explain our four-dimensional *Integrated Research Model* (IRM) (see Figure 12.1).

To explain the IRM let us begin by saying that anything which can be studied will essentially fall into either of two categories: subjective (left of the vertical line) and objective (right of the vertical line). *Subjective project realities* are all the *intangible* aspects of projects, such as values, attitudes, emotions, thoughts, ideas, opinions, theoretical abstractions, aesthetics, worldviews, intangible cultural manifestations, politics, and so forth. *Objective project realities* are the more *tangible* aspects of projects that the researcher can look at and measure. Examples of these are processes, data, products, facilities, machines, vehicles, building materials and natural resources.

These two basic types of project realities that project management research tries to grasp, call for two essentially different research methods; and different methods impose different ethical considerations. Separating subjective and objective project realities is mainly pragmatic, since many project researchers look at both subjective and objective aspects simultaneously within the same research. Such a mixed approach requires the researcher to take a holistic view in addition to looking at the different project realities separately.

But there is more to our picture, as subjective and objective project realities can each be investigated both with *qualitative* (above the horizontal line) and *quantitative* (below the horizontal line) research methods.

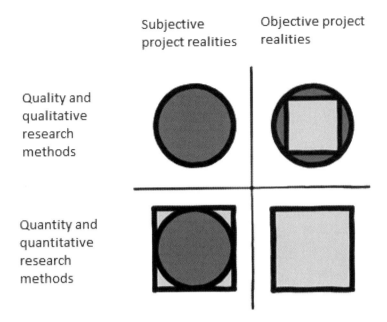

**Figure 12.1    The Integrated Research Model (IRM) explaining different dimensions of project management research (2011)**

*Qualitative project management research* is any high-level enquiry conducted to find, and interpret, data that can be collected or laid out *without quantifying it*. This can be achieved either by focusing on something that is *subjectively* held (for instance, feelings within the project team) or the intangible qualities of something that is *objectively present* (for instance, the effect of a bridge on social mobility). In either case, the researcher is looking at the qualities – the uniqueness and specific attributes – of something that is either subjective or objective. The data can, for instance, take the form of stories, written accounts, transcripts, aesthetical reasoning, quality measures or evidence of functionality. Qualitative methods are used to gain an in-depth understanding of a specific phenomenon and their aim is to understand if it is authentic, functional, right, useful, beautiful and so on, without relying on numerical data.

*Quantitative project management research* is any high-level enquiry into project realities that seeks to establish knowledge by translating reality into measurable units expressed in numbers. It comes in handy, for instance, when collecting information from a large number of respondents or outputs from machines. Quantitative data can be processed and analysed with statistical tools.

All of the above is summarised in the IRM, which provides a holistic view of project realities and how they relate to project management research. The four dimensions of project management research, as illustrated by the IRM, can each give rise to specific ethical concerns. When conducting ethical analysis, the PM researcher needs to consider these context-specific dimensions, as well as looking at the 'big picture' using the five classical ethical approaches that we will now introduce.

## The Integrated Research Model (IRM) and Project Research Ethics

When it comes to ethical considerations in project management research, each dimension of the IRM has its special attributes. However, we suggest all project management research projects should also be analysed from five predominant ethical perspectives. These are: (1) *Virtue-based ethics*, where the rationale for action is derived from considering the effect on the project researcher's *character* (Aristotle, 1999); (2) *Utility-based ethics*, where the rationale for action is based on the *consequences* for all affected in the long run (users, team, society, and so on) (based on Mill, 1863); (3) *Duty-based ethics*, where the rationale for action is defined as the *imperative* to act in accordance with the rule that you would want all morally conscious project researchers to follow under similar circumstances (based on Kant, 1785); (4) *Rights-based ethics*, where the rights of people – and perhaps increasingly, of animals and nature – are based on a definition which should be the same for all (based on Locke, 1988; Hobbes, 1994); and finally, (5) *Care-based ethics*, which demands that project management research is conducted with care and compassion towards all involved (based on Gilligan, 1982). In short, project researchers should look to virtue, utility, duty, rights and care in all their conduct. The various ethical approaches can suggest different – and even conflicting – results. In such cases, one must illuminate the ethical issues at hand from all different perspectives and based on that reflection make the best moral decision (see further discussion in Jonasson and Ingason, 2013). We will now look at some of the specific ethical considerations that tend to surface in each of the dimensions of the IRM.

## THE SUBJECTIVE AND QUALITATIVE DIMENSION – HUMANITIES

The *subjective and qualitative dimension* of the IRM is, generally speaking, the world of the humanities, introspection and theoretical speculation; and at a higher academic level, critical theory, postmodern studies, feminist and gender studies. Qualitative studies are conducted by collecting descriptive data about the subject. These can be in-depth interviews, transcripts, verbal statements, or the researcher's description of what he or she has observed. The methods can be *structured*, where the activities and behaviour are accounted for in a comprehensive way; or they can be *non-structured*, where the researcher is basically working with whatever material he or she has at hand. The different methods used to conduct qualitative research all have their ethical 'grey areas'. An example could be the attempt to understand the subjective internal processes of people, which can only be accessed if the researcher communicates trust to the participants. Ethically, when the researcher is trying to grasp data about subjective project realities, participants need to feel safe, protected from exposure and participating with informed consent.

Naturally, an exhaustive list of ethical considerations cannot be provided here, but it is essential to consider the following: obtaining the informed consent of participants (or a very sound justification for not obtaining it); safeguarding against an inappropriate level of enquiry into personal matters; safeguarding against bias in interpreting the data; installing protective measures to safeguard employees against being fired for participating in research; asking effective, non-leading, questions; not drawing general conclusions from a single case; and applying critical thinking in all research analysis and interpretation. Many of these points are of course not particular to qualitative studies of subjective project realities, but the (frequently) close contact with participants and inherent intangibility of the subject matter require the researcher to be very conscious of these ethical issues when conducting such study.

Further, since researchers are trying to put their finger on a subjective reality, they need to think about the ethical implications of their own impact on the participants. Researchers sometimes use *participatory observation*, where they join their subjects and get to know them by working with them. This is done with or without the subjects' knowledge. In the latter case, the ethical question arises as to whether it ethical for the researcher to operate as an undercover agent within the team. The researcher has an ethical obligation to be aware of phenomena such as *suggestions* (planting ideas in people's minds), *psychological transference* (the influencing impact of the researcher on the subject) and *counter-transference* (the influencing impact of the participant on the researcher). One example of such phenomena coming into play is the Hawthorne Study (Roethlisberger and Dickson, 1964).

It revealed the Hawthorne effect, which is when people change their behaviour once they feel they are being observed. Another study, the Milgram experiments, revealed how far ordinary people are capable of going in harming others if urged to do so by an authoritative figure playing the role of a scientist (Milgram, 1963). Both studies point towards ethical considerations sparked by the subjects' conscious or unconscious will to 'please' the researcher.

## THE SUBJECTIVE AND QUANTITATIVE DIMENSION – SOCIAL SCIENCES

The subjective and quantitative dimension proposes a different way to study subjective project realities. In simplified terms, this is the world of the social sciences. Instead of using qualitative measures, it suggests applying quantitative measures. Here researchers try to understand the subjective reality of people's opinions, feelings and attitudes by using quantitative research tools, such as surveys and questionnaires. The aim is to neutralise the researcher's biases and reveal truths through statistical pathways. However, as in the other three dimensions, personal biases can surface when selecting references for literature review, in choosing questions and methods and through interpretation of data. Quantifying subjective realities through collective surveys can also, if interpreted universally, undermine the ability to see the particular.

Finally, the researcher has the ethical duty to use research methods that follow best practice in conducting surveys and questionnaires. This means checking the validity and reliability beforehand and guaranteeing that what should be measured really gets measured in a sound and consistent way, because not all that can be counted counts. Sometimes PM researchers, due to their technical background, try to quantify and measure with numbers realities that would be better studied with qualitative methods. Such an effort might not only yield irrelevant results, but would neither be meaningful nor appropriate to the extent that it only feeds ignorance within the field. The method used may be statistically valid, but one ought nevertheless to ask: Is this truly meaningful? Good research ethics in this dimension requires answering this question honestly.

## THE OBJECTIVE AND QUALITATIVE DIMENSION – APPLIED SCIENCES

The objective and qualitative dimension studies tangible project realities through qualitative methods, so in this case the researcher has something tangible to look at. This is the world of the applied sciences, such as engineering, medicine and architecture, where researchers look at objective, tangible factors through qualitative lenses. They look at objective things – usually constructed artefacts and project outcomes – in terms of functions, utility, structure, application, optimisation and alignment. They study something that is objectively in front of them and try to see if it works, if it fits, if it is effective or efficient.

Ethical considerations in this dimension can take various forms. The researcher's desire to find practical applications – to build an artefact, a tool, a machine, a construct or a method – can create biases and consequently raise ethical issues. Monetary rewards can tempt researchers to 'prove' that an item works when it really does not. Artifacts, objects, methods or products might serve some needs, but do so in a very unsustainable manner. The ethical obligation here would be to neutralise such biases by committing to truthfully revealing the actual utility, function or applicability of what is being tested, often through trial and error. The issues might crystallise in the following questions: Can you be sure that the defined qualities of the artefact, tool, machine, construct or method have not been compromised? Does the research model truly grasp the qualitative reality that it is supposed to grasp? Is the interpretation accurate? If there are financial rewards involved, how do they influence the results?

## THE OBJECTIVE AND QUANTITATIVE DIMENSION – NATURAL SCIENCES

Researchers in the *objective and quantitative dimension* aim to discover hard facts by solely applying the quantitative measures of natural sciences. They look at things that can be measured, counted, weighed, tracked and mapped. In this dimension, ethical issues concern, for instance, finding appropriate measurements and defining well what to count and measure in order to get valid results. This also means counting well what can be counted and measuring well what is to be measured. The natural sciences demand that all subjectivity is laid aside. Objectivity is, however, neither easily achieved nor overly common, but safeguarding objectivity in research is an ethical concern. Even though objectivity is fundamentally the 'name of the game' in all research in all of the IRM dimensions, it is in this dimension where it becomes most obvious. The ethical obligation is to gain reliable data, interpret it accurately and truthfully point out anything which might affect that accuracy.

## Mixed Project Management Research Strategies

So far, the different research dimensions have been split up to illustrate the possible different ethical concerns arising in each dimension. However, as said before, PM researchers often use mixed research strategies to grasp project realities. This means that they use methods from some or all of the dimensions. When that is the case, the researcher must keep in mind the specific ethical considerations for each dimension, while also thinking about the ethical implications for the project as a whole. One example of mixed strategies could be a project with the scope of designing a new airplane. First the researcher carries out an in-depth interview with five people who travel a lot (subjective, qualitative). Based on these interviews, a survey with a Likert Scale is prepared and sent out to a large group of users, who are asked about their opinions and needs (subjective, quantitative). Then a prototype of the airplane is designed and built and its quality is tested by test pilots (objective, qualitative); finally, all along the way the hard facts are counted and measured (objective, quantitative). When using mixed project management research strategies one would reflect upon the ethical issues at stake from all of the perspectives that are introduced in this chapter.

## Practical Implications

In project management research, regardless of the research method, researchers should use ethical reflection to identify issues that could have moral implications. One way to identify morally-charged areas is to ask: Are there competing values at stake? If so, what are they? This often highlights ethical issues that might require the researcher's particular attention. Regardless of the project management research dimension(s) the research falls under, ethical reflection is best concluded by considering the project as a whole from the five moral perspectives that the following questions are based on:

- **Virtue-based perspective:** How can I guarantee that my research will enable me in the future to face myself in the mirror and say: 'I did my research in a virtuous way, it was a job well done. I feel content as it is a manifestation of a good character'?
- **Duty-based perspective:** How can I guarantee that my research is conducted in accordance with rules that I could will to become universal morally sound principles?
- **Utility-based perspective:** How can I guarantee that my research is conducted in such a way that it will create more happiness for more people in the long run?

- **Rights-based ethical perspective:** How can I guarantee that the rights of all interested parties are protected?
- **Care-based ethical perspective:** How can I guarantee that all involved are treated with care and compassion?

The practical implication of what has been described above is that it can (1) support project researchers in carrying out higher quality research; (2) enable them to have more satisfying research experiences; and (3) help them to avoid moral risks and hazards in designing, planning, executing and reporting their project research.

## Tips and Questions

### TIPS FOR STUDENTS

- Check whether there are formal ethical guidelines that apply to your research, defined by for example by your university, research community or government – study them and follow them.
- Critically answer the following questions – note that some of your answers could form a part of your research paper.
  - Why you are doing your research?
  - Who will benefit from your research?
  - Who stands to financially gain from your research?
  - Whom will your research affect? How will it affect them?
  - Will your research benefit yourself? If so, how will the research benefit you?
  - If working within an organisation (association, business, university, or institute) how will your research impact your organisation?
  - How could your research affect society?
  - How could your research affect future generations?
  - What other obligations do you have, or what roles do you play, that might have an impact on your research?
  - If your research can have an impact on people, how will you protect the rights of those people?
  - If your research can have an impact on animals, how will you respect their rights?
  - If your research has an impact in nature, how will you guarantee that it will be conducted in a sustainable manner?
  - How will your research be an expression of care and compassion?

### TIPS FOR SUPERVISORS

- Ask the student to write up an analysis of possible ethical risks they might encounter.
- Encourage the student to focus on the analysis as well as how ethical risks might be addressed. Exercise in ethical evaluation is best gained through thinking about and explaining why something could be problematic, or carefully justifying why it isn't.
- You, as supervisor, can use the following questions to make the student ethically reflect upon the research project:
  - In what way might your research compromise your well-being?
  - Could the research project compromise the integrity of your organisation? If yes, how so? If no, why not?

- How might the research project compromise the well-being of people in society? If yes, how so? If no, why not?
- Could the research project compromise the well-being of future generations? If yes, how so? If no, why not?
- Could your research project challenge the collective reputation of project researchers? If yes, how so? If no, why not?
- Could your research project compromise the reputation of your organisation within the international research community? If yes, how so? If no, why not?
- What duties do you owe as a project researcher, and to whom? Why are these duties owed?
- How do your duties to your fellow researchers differ from the duties you owe to participants in your research?
- What harm and damage can your research cause? To what and to whom? (Do especially consider minorities and people who are vulnerable).

## QUESTIONS

1. What have you done to safeguard the rights of participants in your research? What rights may be affected?
2. How might your research project undermine the rights of the project team?
3. Could your research project affect the rights of future generations? If yes, how so? If no, why not?
4. How will you support other members of your project team?

# References

Aristotle (1999). *Nicomachean Ethics* [350 BCE]. Terence Irwin (trans.) (2nd edition). Indianapolis: Hackett Publishing.

Gilligan, C. (1982). *In a Different Voice*. Cambridge, MA: Harvard University Press.

Hobbes, T. (1994). *Leviathan* [1651]. E. Curley (ed.). Chicago, IL: Hackett Publishing Company.

Jonasson, H. I. and Ingason, H. T. (2013). *Project Ethics*. Farnham, UK: Gower Publishing.

Kant, I. (1985). *Grounding for the Metaphysics of Morals* [1785], James W. Ellington (trans.). Indianapolis: Hackett Publishing Company.

Locke, J. (1988). *Two Treatises of Government* [1690], Peter Laslett (ed.). Cambridge, UK: Cambridge University Press.

Milgram, S. (1963) Behavioral study of obedience. *Journal of Abnormal and Social Psychology*, 67, 371–378.

Mill, J. S. (1969). 'Utilitarianism [1863]' in *J.S. Mill: Collected Works*, vol. 10, J. M. Robson (ed.). Toronto, ON: University of Toronto University Press.

Roethlisberger, F. J. and Dickson, W. J. (1964). *Management and the Worker: An account of a research program conducted by the Western Electric Company, Hawthorne Works, Chicago*. Cambridge, MA: Harvard University Press.

Sigurðarson, S. F. (2009). Critical success factors in project management: An ethical perspective. Available at http://skemman.is/handle/1946/3020. Accessed: 9 June 2009.

# Further Reading

Anand, P. (1993). *Foundations of Rational Choice Under Risk*. Oxford, UK: Oxford University Press.

APM Publishing (2000). *Body of Knowledge* (4th edition). High Wycombe, UK: Association for Project Management.

APM Publishing (2004). *Project Risk Analysis and Management Guide* (2nd edition). High Wycombe, UK: Association for Project Management.

Atkinson, R. (1999). Project management: Cost, time and quality, two best guesses and a phenomenon, its time to accept other success criteria. *International Journal of Project Management*, 6, 337–342.

Baggini, J. and Fosl, P. S. (2007). *The Ethics Toolkit*. Malden, MA: Blackwell 30 Publishing.

Baker, B. N., Murphy, D. C. and Fisher, D. (1988). *Factors Affecting Project Success: Project Management Handbook* (2nd edition). New York, NY: Van Nostrand Reinhold Co.

Belassi, W. and Tukel, O. I. (1996). A new framework for determining critical/success failure factors in projects. *International Journal of Project Management*, 14(3), 141–152.

Bentham, J. (1948). *Introduction to the Principle of Morals and Legislation* [1789]. Oxford, UK: Basil Blackwell.

BSI (2010). British Standards Institute. BS6079-3:2010 Project Management – 1 Guide to the Management of Business Related Project Risk.

Bryde, D. J. (2005). Methods for managing different perspectives of project success. *British Journal of Management*, 16, 119–131.

Cicero. (2001). *On Obligations* [44 BCE]. P. G. Walsh (ed.). Oxford, UK: Oxford University Press.

Cooke-Davies, T. (2002). The 'real' success factors in projects. *International Journal of Project Management*, 20, 185–190.

De Wit, A. (1988). Measurement of project success. *International Journal of Project Management*, 6(3), 164–170.

Flyvbjerg, B. (2001). *Making Social Science Matter: Why social inquiry fails and how it can succeed again*. Cambridge, UK: Cambridge University Press.

Freeman, M. and Beale, P. (1992). Measuring project success. *Project Management Journal*, 23(1), 8–18.

Geertz, C. (2001). Empowering Aristotle. *Science*, 293, 461–469.

Harman, G. (1999). Rosalind Hursthouse, On Virtue Ethics. Available at www.princeton.edu/~harman/Papers/Hursthouse.pdf. Accessed: 10 January 2012.

Helgadóttir, H. (2007). The ethical dimension of project management. *International Journal of Project Management*, 26, 743–748.

Hughes, G. J. (2001). *Aristotle on Ethics*. London, UK: Routledge.

ICB Competence Baseline. (2006). Version 3, IPMA International Project Management Association.

Jonasson, H. I. and Ingason, H. T. (2011). *Leiðtogafærni* ('Leadership skills'). Reykjavik: Forlagid Publishing.

Kreps, D. M. (1988). *Notes on the Theory of Choice*. Boulder, CO: Westview Press.

Lim, C. S. and Mohamed, M. Z. (1999). Criteria of project success: An exploratory re-examination. *International Journal of Project Management*, 17(4), 243–248.

Liu, A. M. M. and Walker, A. (1998). Evaluation of project outcomes. *Construction Management and Economics*, 16, 209–219.

Loo, R. (2002). Tackling ethical dilemmas in project management using vignettes. *International Journal of Project Management*, 20, 489–495.

MacIntyre, A. (1985). *After Virtue: A Study in Moral Theory*. London, UK: Duckworth.

Meredith, J. and Mantel, S. (2003). *Project Management: A managerial approach* (5th edition). New York, NY: John Wiley & Sons.

Nicoló, E. (1996). Fundamentals of the total ethical-risk analysis method (TERA method) with a study of crucial problems in managing distributed multimedia. *International Journal of Project Management*, 14, 153–162.

Olson, R. G. (1967). 'Deontological Ethics' in *The Encyclopaedia of Philosophy*, P. Edwards (ed.). London, UK: Collier Macmillan, pp. 49–62.

Pinto, J. K. and Slevin, D. P. (1988b). Critical success factors across the project life cycle. *Project Management Journal*, 19(3), 67–75.

Plous, S. (1993). *The Psychology of Judgement and Decision-Making*. New York, NY: McGraw-Hill.

PMI (2004). *A Guide to the Project Management Body of Knowledge* (PMBOK Guide) (3rd edition). Newton Square, PA: PMI Publications.

PMI (n.d). Project Management Institute Code of Ethics and Professional Conduct. Available at http://www.pmi.org/PDF/AP_PMICodeofEthics.pdf. Accessed: 1 October 2013.

Reidenbach, R. E. and Robin, D. P. (1990). Toward the development of a multidimensional scale for improving evaluations of business ethics. *Journal of Business Ethics*, 9, 639–653.

Rorty, A. O. (ed.) (1980). *Essays on Aristotle's Ethics*. Berkeley, CA: University of California Press.

Shenhar, A. J. and Dvir, D. (2007). Project management research: The challenge and opportunity. *Project Management Journal*, 38(2), 93–100.

Singer, P. (ed.) (1990). *A Companion to Ethics*. Oxford, UK: Basil Blackwell.

Sorabji, R. (1973/74). Aristotle on the role of intellect in virtue. *Proceedings of the Aristotelian Society*, 74, 107–129.

Turner, J. R. and Müller, R. J. (2005). The project leader's leadership style as a success factor on projects: A review. *Project Management Journal*, 36(2), 49–61.

Westerveld, E. (2003). The project excellence model: Linking success criteria and critical success factors. *International Journal of Project Management*, 21, 411–418.

Wiggins, D. (1975–76). Deliberation and practical reason. *Proceedings of the Aristotelian Society*, 76, 29–51.

# 13

# Developing a Critical Literature Review for Project Management Research

Michael Tong and Craig Thomson

*This chapter aims to provide an accessible reference for supervisors to direct postgraduate students when initiating a critical literature review as part of their dissertations.*

The literature review is an essential step in any research project, but its function and significance is often poorly understood or taken for granted. This chapter explores the notion that a literature review provides a much more significant role in shaping and evolving the future direction of a research project by establishing an understanding and critical appraisal of the background context of your research. The aim here is to provide an overview of the process and procedures to help shape the literature review as well as providing guidance to key techniques supported by examples.

At the end of this chapter, the reader can:

- understand the role that a critical literature review plays within your research;
- view the literature review as a systematic process;
- be able to utilise techniques relevant for specific stages of your review process.

Keywords: criticality, systematic literature review, mapping and search techniques

## Defining a Literature Review and its Role in Project Management Research

For a researcher to deliver an effective literature review, it is necessary to have a clear understanding of what is meant by this in the academic context. The literature has an important function to help provide background and context to the research, establishing the research problem and the gap which you aim to fill through the consideration of previous work. Whilst many students often grasp this, students often struggle to view a literature review as a critical assessment of the body of knowledge from which to establish themes and concepts to be addressed within the research.

There is no one way to present or conduct a literature review, but it is clear that there exists a shared set of principles which an effective review should reflect. Fink (1998: p. 3) defined a literature review as being 'a systematic, explicit and reproducible method for identifying, evaluating and interpreting the existing body of recorded work produced by researchers, scholars and practitioners'. Some key principles emerge from this definition worthy of exploration.

'*Systematic, explicit and reproducible method*' suggests that a review needs to be planned and to have an established process which the researcher should follow. A literature review is a method in its own right, and needs to be implemented in a traceable, transparent manner with a logical process behind it which can be revisited or replicated by others.

'*Identifying, evaluating and interpreting*' suggests that relevant literature sources need to be identified and sourced first, prior to evaluating its relevance and meaning, with its implications interpreted within the review for the context of the research. Taking each of these steps in sequence is important as from this they can develop the understanding of the theoretical foundation and debates surrounding the research, and from which to establish the research scope and questions from an informed standpoint.

'*Recorded work produced by researchers, scholars and practitioners*' suggests that literature can exist from a variety of different sources, but that it needs to be held predominantly in the public domain. Researchers need to be aware of the implications of using different sources of literature whether it is academic, policy, practice or media based, and to ensure their position and standpoints are understood. Levy and Ellis (2006) draw attention to the need to ensure that the literature is published and the importance of ensuring this reflects suitable quality in order to establish the foundations of the research.

Hart (1998: p. 1) defined the literature review as 'the use of ideas in the literature to justify the particular approach to the topic, the selection of methods, and demonstration that this research contributes something new'. This definition highlights strongly the role of the review in justifying the selection of the topic, identifying the scope and rationale, or in selecting an appropriate methodology. Furthermore, it forces you to justify your contribution and novelty in relation to the established body of knowledge.

In order to position the research and to communicate its contribution to the body of knowledge there are two functions that the literature review should provide that ultimately lead to the scope of the research project (see Figure 13.1).

*The first* relates to its ability to communicate to the reader the background and context of the research, the foundations from which it is built, prior to addressing specific issues relating to your research (Shaw, 1995). Most literature reviews achieve this by outlining broad issues at the start, identifying those which overlap and then focusing on specific research relevant to your study area. Figure 13.1 reflects this narrowing of scope and increase in focus during the review process.

*The second* relates to the researcher's ability to critically appraise the literature. This is a skill which students need but often find difficult to move beyond a descriptive standpoint in their narrative of the existing body of knowledge. Critical evaluation is essential if the research is to question or challenge the status quo, identify its own research position or gap, and respond to contemporary problems.

## PROJECT MANAGEMENT IS MULTIDISCIPLINARY

Understanding the research traditions of the discipline is important. Many disciplines occupy tight parameters around which the literature is thematically centred and similar in its research traditions

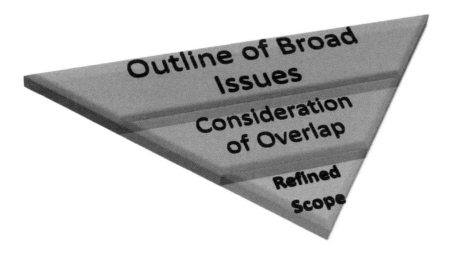

**Figure 13.1    Narrowing the scope of the literature review**

often revolving around literature from a small group of academics. PM as a discipline is broad, covering different themes such as planning, organising, securing, managing, leading and controlling resources within a fixed timeframe; each with its own established literature. PM research may also require consideration of the dynamics of the project team with theoretical roots often founded in the social sciences. It must be emphasised that the basis of PM research often owes its roots to theories pioneered in other disciplines, and researchers need to engage with these theories and to build on them.

PM research is mainly conducted with consideration to a specific sector and a need exists to ensure that this context is reflected in the literature review. For example, construction, aerospace or the automotive industries have very different industrial contexts, as do other sectors such as retail, finance and the public sector. Each sector will have its own established literature, explaining why projects may be approached differently in that sector and an awareness of this required in the literature review. If they are focused on one sector, an awareness of the specific literature is required, but awareness of related developments in other sectors may also be important.

An example of this can be provided by a student conducting research into managing innovation in construction projects. The student will need to draw on literature from:

- a variety of disciplines relating to specific themes involving managing innovation within construction projects such as process management, leadership, culture and teamwork;
- general management relating to innovation management (drawing on established theoretical models developed for a general audience);
- PM focusing on innovation management within projects;
- construction management (exploring the context and need for innovation within this sector).

## A NEED TO REFLECT A PRACTICE-BASED AUDIENCE

PM research often necessitates consideration of practice-based problems and opportunities for development, and its output needs to be accessible to practitioners in order to ensure relevance and provide impact. Therefore, when engaging with complex theories or philosophical discussions, a narrative is required that is understandable to practitioners as well as academic audiences.

Indeed PM research students may also be practitioners whether they are returning to studies after a period in industry or studying part time and the review plays an important role in forming the bridge between theory and practice.

## NEITHER PURELY SCIENCE, ENGINEERING NOR A SOCIAL SCIENCE

It can be difficult to classify PM research in terms of whether it is a science, engineering or a social science in terms of its research traditions. The training and assumptions which scientists or engineers share will be different from those with roots in the social sciences. However, PM research can often find itself required to consider engineering problems and human resource issues within the same research project. When bridging different research traditions it is important that the researcher writes and shares their ideas in a way that does not alienate unintentionally part of the readership by making their work inaccessible through the use of specific language associated with one of these traditions without contextualising it for the rest of the audience. It is acceptable to have our own research preferences, but it is important that a narrative is found which can satisfy both traditions whilst at the same time engaging with the state of the art and promoting contemporary thinking.

## What is a Critical Review?

Management research, unlike some academic disciplines, makes use of a wide range of literature. It is important, therefore, to be aware of what constitutes a critical literature review and its purpose. A well-constructed review will provide the foundation for your research and its main purpose is to help you develop a good understanding of previous research and current trends. The precise purpose of the review is dependent on the approach you are intending to take. Research using a *deductive approach* will use the literature to identify theories and ideas that will be tested with data. On the other hand, research using an *inductive approach* will aim to develop theories from data that is subsequently related to the literature. This approach still requires a competent knowledge of the subject area.

Given the fact that we all have different knowledge and experience, adopting a critical frame of mind that maintains a little scepticism is appropriate. Wallace and Wray (2011) suggest that in reading an academic article, we might keep in our mind these sceptical provisos:

- The authors mean to be honest, but may have been misled by the evidence into saying something that I consider to be untrue.
- The authors mean to be logical, but may have developed a line of reasoning that contains a flaw.
- The authors mean to be impartial but may have incorporated into the account some assumptions that I don't share.
- The authors mean to tell me something new, but may not have taken into account other information that I possess.

The majority of novice critical readers may initially struggle to interpret an author's signals, and to develop an appropriate response. This usually ends up going too far towards extremes; either uncritical acceptance or overcritical rejection of purported claims. Given that published materials do vary substantially in terms of rigour, the necessity for a healthy amount of scepticism is both challenging and desirable.

Mingers (2000: pp. 225–226) argues that there are four aspects of a critical approach that should be fostered:

- Critique of rhetoric: to evaluate a problem with effective use of language, using your skills of making reasoned judgments and arguing effectively.
- Critique of tradition: questioning the conventional wisdom, with justification.
- Critique of authority: questioning the dominant view in the literature.
- Critique of objectivity: acknowledging that the knowledge and information being discussed are not value free.

Being critical is about adopting a sceptical stance and be willing to question what you read. This requires you to constantly consider and justify your own critical stance. It requires you to have gained topic-based background knowledge, understanding, the ability to reflect upon and to analyse the literature and, based on this, to make reasoned judgments that are argued effectively. Being critical is increasingly being seen as a requirement of academic study; the extract below from 'Skills for all Master's programmes', subject benchmark statement from the Master's Awards in Business and Management, Quality Assurance Agency for Higher Education (UK) states:

> Critical thinking and creativity: managing creative processes in self and others; organising thoughts, analysis, synthesis, critical appraisal. This includes the capability to identify assumptions, evaluate statements in terms of evidence, detect false logic or reasoning, identify implicit values, define terms adequately and generalise appropriately. (https://www.qaa.ac.uk/academicinfrastructure/benchmark/masters/MBAintro.asp)

O'Leary (2004: pp. 82–83) uses an interesting analogy of a dinner party to explain criticality:

> Imagine you are at a dinner party with prominent researchers in your area. You are just another guest, an equal, not someone in a disparate power position. You are conducting research in the same area, you pretty much know the field, and are able to engage in interesting and relevant conversation. Through the course of the night, you hear of research that you find interesting, exciting, and inspiring. But other studies seem old hat, premised on assumptions that you don't believe hold water, or lacking credibility due to some really questionable methods. The most interesting part of the night, however, was the conversation you had with other researchers that had you learning, arguing, and developing your own ideas simultaneously … The engagement in the work of others has conspired to develop your ideas in a way that would have never happened in isolation. The good dinner party conversationalist is neither hypercritical nor sycophantic. Rather, the consummate dinner party conversationalist is an individual who engages, learns, debates, argues, contributes, and even evolves his or her own ideas. And this is exactly what needs to happen in order for you to develop and write a good literature review.

## DEDUCTION AND INDUCTION

For most research projects it is often theory that drives research questions. Both deductive and inductive research comprises of elements of each rather than the exclusive use of a pure version of either. In most situations, theory can be depicted as something that precedes research (as in quantitative research) or as something that emerges out of it (as in qualitative research).

You will need to be clear at an early stage about the way in which theory will be applied to the subsequent design of your study. You have to make a choice of whether to choose the deductive approach, in which you develop an existing theory and test hypotheses, or opt for the inductive approach whereby a theory is developed based on the analyses of data collected.

## DEDUCTION: THEORY TESTING

Deduction involves rigorous and controlled testing of theory, often providing accurate explanation and prediction of natural phenomena. It is often associated with scientific research and positivism. The principal goal is to test a hypothesis from the theory through falsification. By doing so, the hypothesis can then be expressed in specific terms (where conditions are controlled) to propose a relationship between two or more variables. The hypothesis can then be confirmed or falsified from subsequent findings, leading to the modification (if any) of the theory (Robson, 2011).

The main characteristics associated with deduction include ascertaining causal relationships between variables, testing of hypotheses through accurate controls and striving for replication that ensures reliability by adopting a structured methodology. In addition, researcher independence and objectivity are important, as well as the reduction of the problem to the simplest elements that will allow the 'facts' to be measured quantitatively. Finally, deduction allows findings to be generalised through inferences on the wider population and the approach is illustrated in Figure 13.2.

| Theory | Hypothesis | Data Collection | Findings | Hypothesis testing | Revise Theory |

**Figure 13.2    The deductive approach**

## INDUCTION: THEORY BUILDING

Induction emerged from the development of the social sciences during the twentieth century as a direct critique to the dominant deductive approach associated with the natural sciences. The criticism of deduction lay with the unproblematic nature in which cause–effect links are made between variables without understanding the way in which humans interpreted their social world. Developing this understanding is where the strength of induction lies.

An inductive approach involves collecting data at the outset to establish what is happening and to better understand the nature of the problem by asking questions about the phenomenon of interest. Once data is collected, it needs to be categorised into meaningful categories from which a theory may be developed. This approach creates a more flexible structure that allows for alternative explanations of the phenomenon to be considered, and the approach is illustrated in Figure 13.3.

**Figure 13.3    The induction approach**

## SO WHY IS THE CHOICE OF RESEARCH APPROACH IMPORTANT?

Easterby-Smith, Thorpe and Lowe (2002) suggest three reasons as to why the choice of approach is important. First, it enables you to take a better informed decision about your research design. Second, it helps you to think about the associated research strategies that will and will not work for you. Third, knowledge of the different research traditions enables you to adapt your research design to cater for constraints, such as limited access to data or a lack of prior knowledge of the subject.

## Combining and Choosing Research Approaches

It would appear that there are rigid divisions between deduction and induction which is misleading as it is both feasible and often advantageous to do so. Topics with a wealth of literature will be suited to deduction; whereas newer topics with little existing literature may be better off with adopting an inductive approach. Deductive research can be quicker to complete, whereas inductive research usually takes longer as ideas and themes usually emerges gradually. In terms of risk, deduction can be argued to be lower-risk although there is always the risk of non-return of questionnaires. Induction, on the other hand, runs the risk of not generating useful data patterns and theory.

Although there are many reasons for combining approaches, the novice researcher may not have the time, resources and expertise to effectively combine them. The advice would be to go for one, unless you are confident in your ability to do both or it is beneficial towards answering your research question. The choice should also be based on the research problem you want to address and the skills you have, not on what tasks you want to avoid. Common examples of poor reasons for choosing an approach include a dislike of statistical analyses for choosing an inductive approach and a dislike for writing in choosing a deductive approach. Table 13.1 provides a guide for choosing between the different approaches. Each item should be considered carefully before making the final decision. They are not arranged in the order of importance.

Table 13.1    Choosing a research approach

| Use This Approach if: | Quantitative (Deductive) | Qualitative (Inductive) |
| --- | --- | --- |
| 1. You believe that: | There is an objective reality that can be measured | There are multiple possible realities constructed by different individuals |
| 2. Your audience is: | Familiar with/supportive of quantitative studies | Familiar with/supportive of qualitative studies |
| 3. Your research question is: | Confirmatory, predictive | Exploratory, interpretive |
| 4. Your available literature is: | Relatively large | Limited |
| 5. Your research focus: | Covers a lot of breadth | Involves in-depth study |
| 6. Your time available is: | Relatively short | Relatively long |
| 7. Your ability/desire to work with people: | Medium to low | High |
| 8. Your desire to structure is: | High | Low |
| 9. You have skills in the area(s) of: | Deductive reasoning and statistics | Inductive reasoning and attention to detail |
| 10. Your writing skills are strong in the area of: | Technical, scientific writing | Literary, narrative writing |

Source: Leedy and Ormrod, 2005: p. 106

## Process and Procedures Shaping a Literature Review

It is apparent that those new to research find the literature review a daunting element of the process. Seen by many as not exciting and potentially onerous, daunted by the sheer volume and variety of sources available, unclear about how to find and then manage it, unsure how to relate to inconsistencies between established authors, difficulty managing time, and generally feeling that they lack the knowledge base to make informed judgments about the direction of travel. Part of the problem stems from a failure to recognise that the review needs to be viewed as a managed process which is systematic and supports different stages of the research with a range of techniques.

The literature review process can be represented as an upward spiral (Figure 13.4). The initial stage involves defining the parameters of your research aim and objectives. After generating initial keywords and conducting a preliminary search, parameters may be refined and further searches will be undertaken, whilst still focusing on the research aim and objectives. As the process develops, subsequent searches will become more precise in terms of relevance. At the same time, the research aim and objectives will be further refined in light of the review.

## Preliminary Literature Review

Those new to research often view the literature review as merely representing the second or third chapter of a dissertation or thesis, occurring after the research is designed. This ignores its contribution to shaping the initial idea and in establishing the credibility of the research question

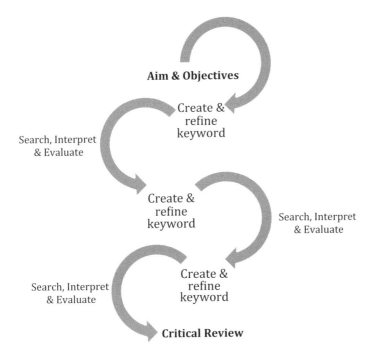

**Figure 13.4    The literature review process**

posed. Saunders, Lewis and Thornhill (2007) suggest that a preliminary search of the literature is essential to aid the generation of ideas, develop an understanding of where the research sits in relation to the body of knowledge and establish research questions that are relevant and add value. Initially ad hoc and unstructured by nature, this search enables the themes to evolve and allows issues, questions and key words to emerge as greater understanding is established. Understanding what has and hasn't already been researched is important when establishing the scope for a research project, and helps ensure that it is original and worthwhile by eradicating duplication. The initial stages need to be supported by an awareness of existing literature in order to inspire, inform, educate and enlighten; thus aiding creativity in idea generation and in shaping the direction of the project from an informed position. Exploring how your ideas relate to those of others is important, as it strengthens the credibility of your own and also helps raise important questions. In the early stages of the research this helps establish the rational for your research and begins to place it in context of the state of the art, with the review of literature being written up to support the initial proposal or even inform the background/ rational section of the introduction of the dissertation.

   **Technique**: *Concept and thematic mapping* is a common technique used to during the initial stages of the research to help establish key words and to explore the linkages between emerging themes. This can be used as the starting point of the literature search but can then be used to capture ideas which emerge from it to support the creativity required during research design (see Figure 13.6).

## Establishing Research Themes and Systematic Literature Reviews

Following the design of the research, the literature review adopts a more structured and methodical function supporting the exploration of the main themes of the research. Any research project will span a number of thematic issues, with the review reflecting these by identifying the key authors and related theoretical discussions in order to demonstrate that the background understanding has been established. The review of these themes contributes by helping the researcher establish a narrative around each theme, aiding them to make connections between these in order to contribute to the future development of the project. A systematic literature review ensures that researchers do not miss key authors or concepts related to these themes, and therefore provides creditability. New themes can emerge, and through a better understanding of the body of knowledge it is possible that the intended narrative within the research may evolve. However, it is important to point out that exploring themes around which the research (and therefore the literature review) is shaped needs to be controlled. It can be tempting to explore the individual themes fully, but in order to control the scope the focus needs to be placed around the intersection of the theme with the other themes and the rational of the research (illustrated thematic intersection Figure 13.5).

A number of search techniques are available to help establish the key sources around keywords for themes or sub-themes, or focused searches around particular authors or references whether it be backwards (historical look at references cited) or forwards (following at influence of publication by following future citations).

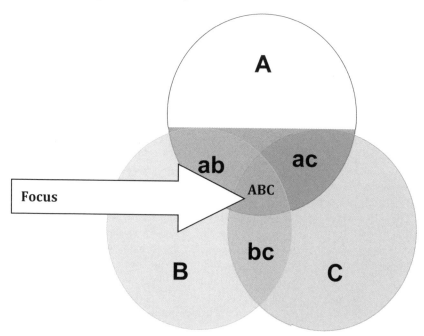

**Figure 13.5    Controlling scope and ensuring relevance**

Source: Levy and Ellis, 2006

## CLASSIFICATION OF LITERATURE SOURCES

If the literature review is to provide creditability to the research, it is important that the quality of the sources which form the review are ensured. Levy and Ellis (2006) argue that sources should be published, and this means available in the public domain. However, the means of publication can vary around three general categories of literature with implications of these sources relating to the level of detail, extent of scientific rigour and the length of time it takes to publish.

These three general categories of literature are: primary, secondary and tertiary. Literature sources can be classified as:

1. Primary sources – these sources provide first-hand accounts of investigation:
   - journal articles/theses;
   - conference proceedings;
   - reports (technical or research group)/occasional papers (by research units);
   - government publications;
   - standards (BSI);
   - catalogues, specifications, directories;
   - trade journals and newspapers.
2. Secondary sources – this provides summaries of information gathered from primary sources:
   - monographs;
   - review series (annals);
   - review papers in primary journals;
   - subject abstracts;
   - indexes of publications.
3. Tertiary sources – this provides an overview on a subject or of a field:
   - textbooks;
   - handbooks;
   - guides to specific literatures;
   - subject bibliographies;
   - general bibliographies;
   - encyclopaedias.

## Awareness of Your Own Disciplines Key Sources

PM is a discipline with a set of academic journals which tackle the latest thinking and research related to the general development of the discipline. A need exists to explore publications by the relevant professional bodies such as International Project Management Association (IPMA) and Project Management Institute (PMI) as these reflect the direction of travel for practice proposed by these bodies to their members. Two key international journals that are closely linked to these professional bodies which influence the direction of the state of the art are:

- *International Journal of Project Management*
- *Project Management Journal*

However, there is a need to ensure that if the research focuses on a specific sector that the review addresses the established journals of that sector. For example, PM issues within construction and the built environment will be addressed in journals such as *Construction Management and Economics; Engineering, Construction, Architecture and Management* but also in specific journals focused on PM in this sector such as *Journal of Building Project and Asset Management*.

## Searching the Internet: Main Databases

- *Compendex on Engineering Village.* Over five million summaries of engineering journal articles and conference proceedings. Some links to full-text.

- *Emerald* manages a portfolio of over 280 journals, more than 2,000 books and book series volumes, as well as an extensive range of online products and services.
- *ISI Web of Knowledge/Web of Science*. Citation database of references from scholarly journals. When you find an article you can link to others on the same subject, even ones published later.
- *ProQuest.* Articles from business, management, engineering and social science journals as well as newspapers.
- *Science Direct*. Full text of some 1,500 key scientific journals. Subjects include engineering, technology, power and environmental science.
- *Google Scholar*. Although not a database, it provides a simple way to broadly search for scholarly literature across many disciplines and sources.

## Search Techniques

For a systematic literature review, a variety of techniques need to be followed to ensure that key themes and sub-themes are fully explored, and the state of the art is established and made available for review. Internet search engines facilitate increasingly both basic and specialised searches around these; however there are also search techniques designed to ensure key authors and seminal literature are accessed known as backward and forward searches and again Internet search engines facilitate this.

### KEYWORD SEARCH

Using keywords to structure your search whether it be themes, sub-themes, combination of themes, phrases and so on. A trail is provided using a range of search mechanisms such as Internet searches, and the specified main databases.

### BACKWARD SEARCHES

Taking references or authors from a previous search (that is, pulling the references from the references and following them). Search engines provide links to and within the reference lists of academic references to make this easier. Seeing who other researchers are referring to gives the review an understanding of the foundations of the theory.

### FORWARD SEARCHES

An alternative approach is to look at those who have citied a particular article (facilitated by Internet search engines like Google Scholar) in a bid to assess its influence on the research community and to identify contemporary research.

## Mapping Techniques

### CONCEPT AND RESEARCH QUESTION MAP

An aid to help researchers establish the key concepts and research questions can be through a mapping technique that takes the form of a flow map. The researcher, as they conduct the review of literature, can establish concepts and develop the map by answering emerging questions. This helps establish where the gaps exist within the research as well as aiding the evolution of the project. Figure 13.6 overleaf demonstrates how such a map can be used to explore the concepts and questions emerging from an article.

## CONCEPT AND THEMATIC MAPPING

An alternative mapping technique which is more fluid by nature and related strongly to mind mapping methods is used to help researchers identify concepts and themes and to then establish their interconnections and relationships with each other. Concept maps can be used in the preliminary stages of the research to help establish the thematic coverage and design. Figure 13.7 on p. 161 illustrates the principles of this technique.

## CITATION MAP

Understanding who the key authors are within the literature review is important, and a key technique is the citation map. Charting the key authors within the themes emerging within the literature review is important to visually see the development of the research and aids in establishing the state of the art. In addition, it can be used to identify overlaps when authors make connections with the themes. Essentially this technique helps provide a visual aid to help with the writing of the review. Figure 13.8 on p. 168 illustrates a citation map.

# Systematic Reviews

Tranfield, Denyer and Smart (2003: p. 207) highlighted the need for an evidence-informed approach to the review of literature because the body of knowledge that we encounter has become 'increasingly fragmented and transdisciplinary as well as being interdependent from advancements in the social sciences' due to the pace of knowledge production in the discipline and profession of management. With origins from medical science and healthcare, systematic reviews adopt a replicable, scientific and transparent process that provides an audit trail.

An excellent example of the use of a systematic review is provided by Geraldi, Maylor and Williams (2011) in their study of complexities of projects. They used two databases as a starting point of the search: Web of Science and Scopus. The sources obtained were used in combination to provide a wider view of the subject area. The keywords used were 'complexity' OR 'complex' AND 'PM'. The time span of the search was from 1996 to June 2010 due to the fact that the first journal article in these databases to meet these keyword criteria was published in 1996. The two key project management journals used were: *International Journal of Project Management* (IJPM) and *Project Management Journal* (PMJ).

The sample selection process involved six steps:

1. Identification of publications – predominantly a detailed scan of PMJ and IJPM.
2. Focus on academic papers – citation information, abstract and keywords of all papers were downloaded to a referencing software.
3. Focus on PM and on complexity (or complex) – based on an analysis of the abstracts of the articles, the sample was refined to publications explicitly related to 'PM' AND complexity, OR 'complexity of projects'.

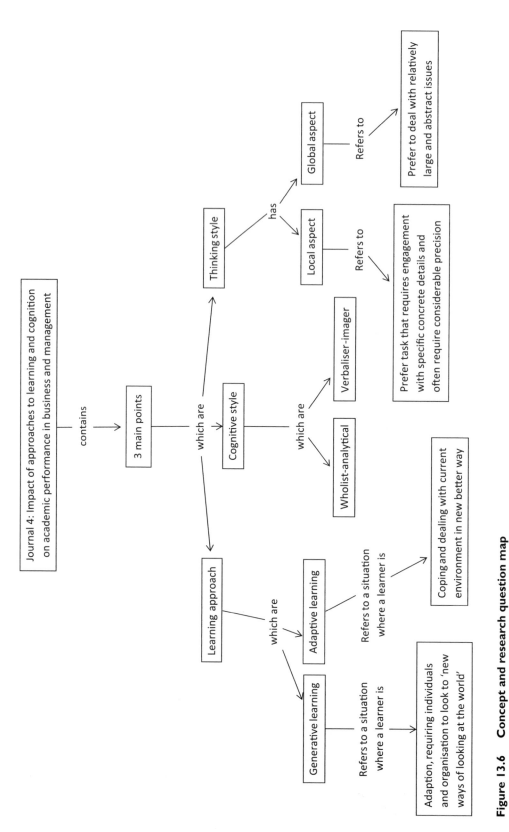

**Figure 13.6   Concept and research question map**

Source: Thomson and Munns, 2010

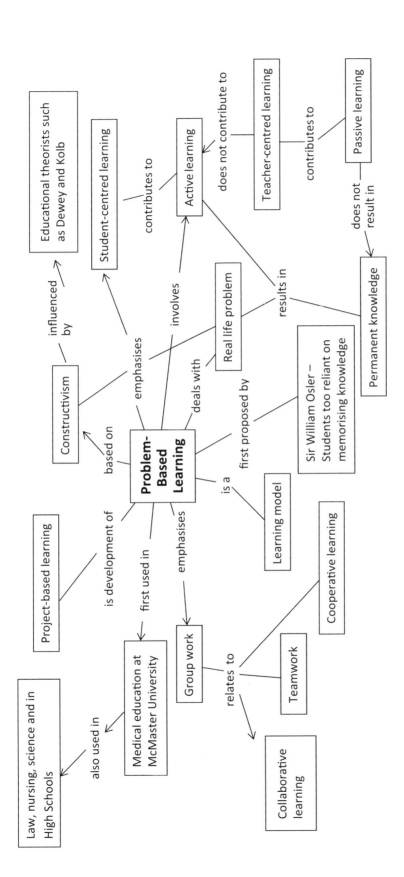

**Figure 13.7   Concept and thematic map (adapted from Alias and Suradi, 2008)**

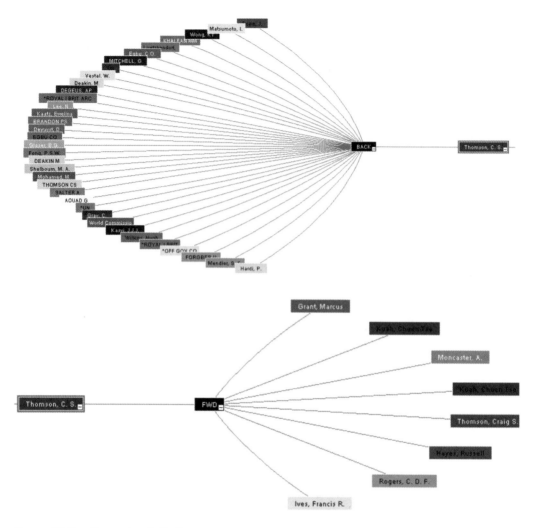

**Figure 13.8    Example of citation map**

Source: Thomson et al., 2009

4.  Checking completeness – the references of the resulting articles were examined for further relevant publications to minimise the chances of not considering relevant studies, especially books, which were not in the search engines.
5.  Focus on 'complexity of projects' – the papers selected were from both 'complexity in projects' and 'complexity of projects' streams.
6.  Final filter – this identified the articles that provided a framework or explicit definition of complexities, reducing the sample to 25 publications.

Analysis of the publications followed a further five steps. In the first three, they identified a framework of five types of complexity that emerged from previous works. The last two steps explored suitable indicators for each of these complexities.

## Plagiarism

Many inexperienced researchers faced with an overwhelming volume of literature and complex arguments presented within this, may be tempted to lift text from these texts and use this directly within the literature review. There is nothing wrong with citing ideas or concepts from established research as long as it is effectively referenced using the appropriate reference. Direct text from other sources can be taken as quotes and should be cited through the same referencing conventions. However, text which is not your own (that is, lifted directly or paraphrased without acknowledging its source) and is not referenced will be regarded as plagiarism.

## Endpoint – Knowing When to Quit

So how do you know when the review is complete? According to Leedy and Ormrod (2005), the answer, in theory, might be 'never'. As long as there are people continuing to do research in the topic, there will always be additional information that may be of use to you. However, practically speaking, the review has to be conducted within a finite amount of time in order for the rest of the research process to take place. They suggest looking for repetitive patterns in the materials collected and when you get a feeling of déjà vu or when you no longer encounter new viewpoints then it may be good time to stop.

## Learning Aids: Conference Paper

To help dissertation students develop their literature review for their research project, the MSc programme in International Project Management at Glasgow Caledonian University asks students to develop a conference paper (of eight pages) around which they explore the aim and objectives for their research project, and review the state of the art relating to the key thematic areas. This exercise helps students in the early stages of their dissertation to clarify their thinking, and to use the preliminary literature search and review to actively evolve the research aim and objectives. Since implementing this initiative, the programme has observed an increased level of familiarity amongst students around the themes of their research, an ability to evolve the direction of the projects themselves and to adopt a proactive and informed stance towards their research.

## Tips and Exercises

TIPS FOR STUDENTS

- A literature review should never be just a list.
- Need to focus on the relationships between the authors and their views.
- Need to establish themes from what they are saying.
- Tell the story in your own words.
- Where can you add value to the story?
- Don't let other authors tell your story for you, draw on them but what do you think?
- Without your own narrative it can look incoherent, lack logic and lack an overall argument.

## TIPS FOR SUPERVISORS

- Be sure to direct your students to the school's policies and documents concerning plagiarism. This should include any information on the software that reviews assignments and other submissions.
- If you or a colleague prefers visual explanations, encourage your students to submit updates using one or more of the techniques used in this chapter (for example). This practice can significantly and positively affect your communication and information flow with your students and will develop their skills for thesis completion.
- Consider sharing the literature reviews from your thesis (or other supervisors). These documents can be a great source of inspiration as well as impress upon your candidate your expectations.

## EXERCISES

1. PM is multidisciplinary and students can undertake research from a number of different backgrounds. To help establish your focus, try and identify literature from the following categories: general PM; your discipline; and outside your discipline but relating to your area of research.
2. Consider how critical you are in your standpoint to the literature within the review. Did you merely restate what the literature was telling you, or to what extent did you display criticality in the review? Things to consider may include: theoretical debates; research gaps; linkage between your discipline and solutions offered by general PM literature or other sectors.
3. Examine whether your research preference is deductive or inductive. Is this preference influenced by your discipline? Consider how this choice will influence your literature review, and establish the implications for your research.
4. Have you considered your literature review as a process? Examine your approach and relate this to the process outlined in Figure 13.4.
5. How did you manage the scope of your research? By using Figure 13.5, try to scope the literature that you have collected into similar categories and identify areas of overlap.
6. Have you explored any mapping techniques to help guide the thematic coverage and development of your review?
7. Select a mapping technique and try to apply it to a recent paper that you have downloaded.

## References

Alias, M. and Suradi, Z. (2008). *Concept mapping: A tool for creating a literature review. Concept mapping: Connecting educators.* The Second International Conference on Concept Mapping. Tallinn and Helsinki.

Easterby-Smith, M., Thorpe, R. and Lowe, A. (2002). *Management Research: An introduction* (2nd edition). London, UK: Sage Publications.

Fink, A. (1998). *Conducting Research Literature Reviews: From paper to the Internet.* Thousand Oaks, CA: Sage.

Geraldi, J., Maylor, H. and Williams, T. (2011). Now, let's make it really complex (complicated): A systematic review of the complexities of projects. *International Journal of Operations & Production Management*, 31(9), 966–990.

Hart, C. (1998). *Doing a Literature Review: Releasing the social science research imagination.* London, UK: Sage Publications.

Leedy, P. D. and Ormrod, J. E. (2005). *Practical Research: Planning and design* (8th edition). Upper Saddle River, NJ: Prentice Hall.

Levy, Y. and Ellis, T. J. (2006). A systems approach to conduct an effective literature review in support of information systems research. *Informing Science Journal*, 9, 181–212.

Mingers, J. (2000). What is it to be critical? Teaching a critical approach to management undergraduates. *Management Learning*, 31(2), 219–237.

O'Leary, Z. (2004). *The Essential Guide to Doing Research*. London: Sage Publications.

Robson, C. (2011). *Real World Research: A resource for users of social research methods in applied settings* (3rd edition). Chichester: Wiley.

Saunders, M., Lewis, P. and Thornhill, A. (2007). *Research Methods for Business Students* (4th edition). London, UK: Prentice Hall.

Shaw, J. (1995). A schema approach to the formal literature review in engineering theses. *System*, 23(3), 325–335.

Thomson, C. S., El-Haram, M. A. and Hardcastle, C. (2009). Managing knowledge of urban sustainability assessment, *Proceedings of Institute of Civil Engineering, Engineering Sustainability*, 162, ES1, Thomas Telford, pp. 35–43.

Thomson, C. S. and Munns, A. K. (2010). Managing the implementation of component innovation within construction projects. In: Egbu, C. (ed.) *Proceedings of 26th Annual ARCOM Conference*, 6–8 September 2010, Leeds, UK, Association of Researchers in Construction Management, pp. 1121–1130.

Tranfield, D., Denyer, D. and Smart, P. (2003). Towards a methodology for developing evidence-informed management knowledge by means of systematic review. *British Journal of Management*, 14(3), 207–22.

Wallace, M. and Wray, A. (2011). *Critical Reading and Writing for Post Graduates* (2nd edition). London: Sage Publications Ltd.

# 14

# Critical Engagement of Previous Research

Steven Nijhuis

*I wrote this chapter because I was surprised to find that previous work was used in so many different ways. I translated this surprise into a discussion paper.*

There are several recent studies in competences in PM. Almost all used different sources for definitions for competence, used an own list of competences to research and chose their own route in getting responses for their research. Serving as examples, these studies show how to use (re)sources in research.

At the end of this chapter, the reader can:

*   identify the use of (re)sources in individual studies;
*   improve in using previously published literature on specific topics;
*   understand the compilation of lists of subjects for surveys for unique respondent groups.

Keywords: source usage, definitions, competences, previous research

## Introduction to Competences for Project Management

Higher education for several professions, such as Information and Communication Technology (ICT), Engineering, and Construction teach their students PM for various reasons (Car, Pripuzic and Belani, 2010; Divjak and Kukec, 2008; Fernández, Cabal, Balsera and Huerta, 2010; Lebcir, Wells and Bond, 2008; McDonald, 2001; Mengel, 2008; Nooriafsha and Todhunter, 2004; Reif and Mitri, 2005; Rennie and White, 2002; Rooij, 2009; Stoyan, 2008). Crawford, Morris, Thomas and Winter (2006) state: 'Project management is offered as a significant component in a range of undergraduate and postgraduate academic qualifications, including construction, engineering and IT,' which is in line with the desire to make the higher education studies more relevant to daily work practice (Pant and Baroudi, 2008). Martin (2000) claims that PM is an important element of both management and engineering education. Chipulu, Ojiako, Asleigh and Maguire (2011) postulate that the curriculum design should be coherent.

For a paper about literature research into evidence-based competences to incorporate in curricula in higher education that prepare students for PM (Nijhuis, 2012), several studies that used a holistic view of PM were combined to create a top ten of important PM competences. These studies are used as examples to stipulate the use of (re)sources.

For the paper only studies that used a survey among professionals were incorporated. An important selection criterion was if the study allowed a differentiation in importance between the competences. A total of nine different studies were incorporated into the construct of competences needed to incorporate into a curriculum, with only one published in a scientific journal (Table 14.1).

**Table 14.1  Authors of recent competence studies**

| Author (year) | Title | Place of Publication |
|---|---|---|
| Golob, M. P. (2002). | Implementing PM competencies in the workplace. | Phd, Capella University |
| Bauer, B. J. (2005). | A success paradigm for project managers in the aerospace industry. | Phd, Capella University |
| Crawford, L. (2005). | Senior management perceptions of PM competence. | *International Journal of Project Management*, 23(1) |
| Krahn, J. (2005). | Project leadership: An empirical investigation. | Phd, University of Calgary |
| Rodriguez, A. (2005). | Critical factors in hiring, promoting and designing job descriptions for strategic project managers. | Phd, Capella University |
| Valencia, V. V. (2007). | A project manager's personal attributes as predictors for success. | MSc, Air Force Institute of Technology, Ohio |
| Everts, P. (2008). | Analysis of current and desired PM competences in the building industry (translated). | Master, TU Delft |
| McHenry, R. L. (2008). | Understanding the project manager competencies in a diversified PM community using a PM competency value grid. | Phd, Capella University |
| Arras People and Thorpe, J. (2010). | PM benchmark report 2010. | Published on Internet |

## Using Previous Definitions, the Definition of Competence

Throughout the years what is meant with 'competence' has changed. As noted by Crawford (2005): Competence was once a simple term, with dictionary definitions such as 'power, ability or capacity (to do, for a task etc.)' and 'due qualification or capacity, adequacy or sufficiency' to do a task. However, as Robotham and Jubb (1996) state, 'the concept of competence' has developed 'different meanings, and it remains one of the most diffuse terms in the organizational and occupational literature.' According to Heywood Gonczi and Hager (1992), competence can be inferred from attributes, which include knowledge, skills and experience, personality traits, attitudes and behaviours (attribute-based inference of competence).

As recognised by Crawford, it is very important to observe the definition of what you are researching. All studies supplied a definition for the term competence, except Valencia (2007) who does not use the term competence, but studies a subset: personal attributes. They all refer to other research or publications for their definition.

Golob (2002) refers to the AIPM standard: 'the concept of competency focuses on what is expected of an employee in the workplace and embodies the ability to transfer and apply skills and knowledge to new situations and environments. Competency examples ... beliefs and values (Australian Institute of Project Management, 1996)'. Krahn (2005) refers to Nordhaug's (1998) perspective: 'skills and knowledge used by workers in the workplace ... the approach that appears to have been used by most studies of project manager competence.' Bauer (2005) refers to yet another one: 'An underlying characteristic of an individual that is causally related to criterion referenced effective and/or superior performance in a job or situation (McClelland, 1998)'.

In the same year, Rodriguez (2005) chooses yet another: 'This term refers to the knowledge, skill, ability or characteristic associated with high performance in the workplace. A few definitions of a competency include motives, beliefs, and values (Mirabile, 1997)'.

McHenry (2008) cites from the studies by Krahn, Golob, Bauer and Rodriguez, but still chooses another definition: 'An underlying characteristic of an individual that is causally related to criterion referenced effective and/or superior performance in a job or situation (Bauer, 2005). Critical skill or personality characteristic required to complete an activity or project or required for a certain position (Ward, 2000).'

Everts (2008) cites Crawford's description from the introduction and two others Meredith (1995) and Spencer and Spencer (1993) and chooses: 'According to Van Doorn and Van der Veen (2008), competences are ultimately one of knowledge, skills and traits' (translated).

The study of Arras People is not meant to be scientifically scrutinised, but still uses a definition of competence: The OGC definition is 'Competencies are the ability to use knowledge, understanding, practical and thinking skills to perform effectively to the standards required in employment. They are identified and demonstrated through sets of behaviours that encompass the skills, knowledge, abilities and personal attributes that are critical to successful role accomplishment.'

Looking at the scientific contributions it appears confusing. Crawford builds an elaborate model to incorporate all definitions. Ultimately there are three types of competence: input, personal and output. Input comprises of knowledge and skills, personal is about the core personality characteristics and output is about one's demonstrated performance (Crawford, 2005). McHenry and Arras People add the notion of criticality to the competences. When studying competences, criticality could be important to use. It could separate the 'nice to have' competences from the 'essential' ones. An example is the most important skill in the study of McHenry for hiring project managers: basic computer skills. This is an important skill, but would it be considered critical for a project manager? Most probably not.

The definition that is used should fit the intended use. If a researcher is looking for ways to separate a normal project manager from an outstanding, it would be good to use output competences, like PM success (IPMA, 2006) or stakeholder management (www.globalpmstandards.org, October 2007). On the other hand, if a researcher is looking for ways to develop training courses for project managers, input competences would be better suited like knowledge of PM tools and techniques and/or negotiating skills. Personality characteristics would be interesting for research aimed at job selection or career advisory. A good example would be decisive or trustworthiness.

The discussion above shows that the definition of terms used in research is not to be taken lightly. Building upon previous research looks easy as soon as you find the first one to quote, but becomes difficult if you find more that are (slightly) conflicting. Do not opt for an easy way out, editors and professors are likely to know about these conflicts and will confront (or reject) work that avoids it.

## Compiling a List of Competences to Research

As described previously, all researchers examined in a holistic way – not focusing on one specific aspect – what are important project competences. Although the reasons for this research differ, they all needed a list of competences as the basis for their research. In this part we look at how these researchers came to their respective lists.

Golob (2002) states: 'A literature review, internet search and discussions with academic and business professional project managers revealed no evidence of a validated survey instrument that ranked project management competencies ... Therefore a survey instrument was developed using the major themes from a literature review.' While Crawford argues in 2005: 'Two widely accepted project management standards, the Guide to the Project Management Body of Knowledge and the Australian National Competency Standards for Project Management were selected as a basis for testing.' In an earlier part of her article, Crawford explains that there is 'no research reported that ... performance against standards', which explains the choice for standards.

In that same year, Krahn (2005) quotes numerous researchers who have written about PM competences and concludes that there is little agreement among them and 'A Delphi Study was used in Phase I because the researcher sought some degree of consensus on the many skills and competencies that have been suggested as critical for a project manager to be successful'.

Bauer (2005) chooses a different route and uses a list 'developed in collaboration with the mentor, committee members, subject matter experts, and members of the focus group'.

Rodriguez (2005) decides to use the top ten found by Golob (2002) and 'the existing survey instrument was modified based on major themes found in the literature on project management competencies'.

Valencia (2007) uses the same approach, albeit on a different author: Pettersen's (1991) framework is used here as a basic guide to summarise these attributes because the process used to develop it was incredibly comprehensive (that is, he synthesised approximately 60 publications qualitatively). Petterson identified 21 traits and suggested that they could be grouped into five distinct categories, namely, problem solving, administration, supervision and team management, interpersonal relationships, and other personal qualities. Through this review, these categories were supplemented with three additional areas titled knowledge, experience and external factors.

McHenry (2008) uses validated instruments from previous authors: Recently completed dissertations (Bauer, 2005; Golob, 2002; Krahn, 2005; Rodriquez, 2005) containing their validated survey instruments were reviewed. In addition, there were various lists and questionnaires concerning project manager competencies and skills from PM authors (Baker and Baker, 1998; Kerzner, 2003; Lewis, 2000; Lewis, 2003; Portny, 2001) used as a basis for the initial pilot research survey instrument. Which is essentially the same as Everts' (2008) approach, who combines (translated) 'several previously published lists and added a few competences that did not appear in these lists but notwithstanding appear to be very important for project managers in construction, that is intelligence, discipline and integrity'.

Arras People (2010) consider the respondent and 'examined a number of competence models and created a short list of competencies which we believe are applicable to PPM practitioners and asked our respondents to indicate the top 3 competencies which they believe make them effective in their role. In order to avoid unnecessary complication for the purpose of this question we grouped methods, tools and domain knowledge into a single choice "Technical"'.

The Australian Institute of Project Management (AIPM) has published PM competency standards since the early 1990s (Australian Institute of Project Management, 2010). The PMBoK (PMI, 2008) and its previous versions focus mainly on processes instead of on competences. But a competency standard is not the same as a validated instrument. And most standards do not have a strong foundation in research (Crawford, 2004). Most authors recognise that just putting together a list of competences for a survey is not scientifically sound and seek ways to improve this. Not all report this process. Some use a giant to stand on: Valencia and Rodriguez take a previous instrument and add just a little extra. Others use multiple giants like McHenry, Everts and Arras People. This gives them more freedom for design of an instrument but also puts strain on the validation of their choices.

## Target Audience, Approach and Effect

In the third part we look at how the researchers approached their potential respondents. All want to do a quantitative research in order to rank the competences in order of importance.

Golob (2002) noted that a validated survey instrument that ranked PM competences was not available. So he constructed his own. He asked symposium attendees at the PMI's Annual Seminars & Symposium to fill out his survey. He received 193 respondents, 80 per cent of them project managers or managers of project managers.

Crawford (2005) does not explain how, but asked supervisors/senior management in three countries and in four application areas to rate project personnel on four dimensions. A total of 176 surveys were returned. Krahn (2005) used recommended experts for her first round, focus groups in the second round and a survey among the network (including rounds one and two) who were asked to forward it. A total of 99 respondents returned the survey of the last round, 60 per cent of them without prior involvement in the research.

Bauer (2005) collected a sample of managers currently employed with one (!) strategic business unit of a Fortune 100 aerospace corporation. Leads for survey participants were obtained through the Human Resources department of the corporation involved in the survey. Rodriguez (2005) approached the potential respondents through the PMI website after permission of PMI headquarters. A total of 500 responded.

Valencia (2007) asked two specific groups to participate in this study. First 76 project managers were invited to complete a questionnaire that assessed (the) seven personal attributes identified in the PM literature as important to project managers. Of these, 38 were willing and 25 provided usable data. The supervisors of these project managers were then asked to complete an appraisal of the project managers performance (seven of the nine asked agreed).

Everts (2008) interviewed experts and followed with an online survey, which was spread through members of the professional network of the members of the committee and participating businesses. A total of 129 project managers responded. McHenry (2008) got a lesser response. Only 53 members of Centre for Business Practices responded on his direct email requesting to fill in an electronic survey, which is in great contrast to the response to the electronic survey by Arras People (2010). They report a thousand respondents of 'project management professionals, some of whom have previously made contact with Arras People and were invited personally by email. In addition web and printed media campaigns were also used to attract PM professionals from all walks of life who have had no previous contact'.

Table 14.2 provides an overview of the contacting method, the number of respondents and the distribution over the main response groups.

**Table 14.2**  **Method of approaching, responding to and distribution of respondents**

| Author | Approach | Responses | Distribution over Functions |
|---|---|---|---|
| Golob | Giving survey in person | 193 | 43 per cent project mgr, 37 per cent mgr of project mgrs, 17 per cent consultant and/or trainer |
| Crawford | Unknown | 176 | 100 per cent mgr of project mgr |
| Krahn | Email snowball | 99 | 50 per cent project mgr, 25 per cent sponsors, 24 per cent team members |
| Bauer | Email through HR dept | 149 | 42 per cent project mgr, 17 per cent mgr of project mgrs |
| Rodriguez | PMI website | 500 | 41 per cent project mgr, 16 per cent director/ portfolio mgr |
| Valencia | Unknown | 25 / 9 | 100 per cent project mgr/ 100 per cent mgr of project mgr |
| Everts | Email snowball | 129 | 100 per cent project mgr |
| McHenry | Email direct to members | 53 | 49 per cent project mgr, 34 per cent portfolio mgr |
| Arras People | Email, web, printed media | 1000 | 88 per cent project mgr, programme mgr or change mgr, 12 per cent project support |

Looking at the number of responses, it can be concluded that it helps to have the support of an organisation, but it is not a one-stop solution. Only McHenry looks at the approach of the other researchers and chooses a new instrument (online survey instead of paper). McHenry speculates about the low response rate but does not come to a definitive conclusion. Valencia's survey is not having a high response number, but this research matches the actual project managers' capabilities to the perception of the manager of the project manager.

The number of desired responses varies according to the function of your research. When publishing a benchmark report (Arras People and Thorpe, 2010), less than 200 would not be considered good, when researching project managers attributes in one company (Bauer, 2005), 149 could be considered impressive.

## Tips and Exercises

TIPS FOR STUDENTS

- Be sure to provide strong argumentation for any change in the basis for research. Has a qualitative study argued that something is missing?
- Make sure that you have an expert review of your instrument to fill any gaps.
- If you quote a source where the basis is not definitive and needs to be changed, the approach Krahn (2005) used is quite suitable.


TIPS FOR SUPERVISORS

Consider the following topics in reflective sessions with your students:

- Look at the number of respondents, the distribution over functions of the respondents and the title of the publication (see Table 14.1), Which publication gives you the most confidence that the data gathering is in line with the intended purpose?
- For this discussion topic, there is no need to read more than described above. McHenry and Everts are the only two to have used previous researchers' material that are discussed in this topic, but still favour another choice than previously made. What would be a good argument for their choice? What would be a good counter-argument?


EXERCISES

1. There are studies about PM competences that offer a holistic view of PM and rank the competences but are published before 2000. What would be a good reason for not incorporating them?
   a) referencing to a published source that criteria for PM success has changed in recent years and therefore only recent publications are used;
   b) referencing to the number of quotations of the unused sources, claiming they were not referenced enough;
   c) showing that their results did not match with the ones incorporated, so it would make your meta-analysis too difficult.

A is the correct answer, B and C can never be a valid reason for not incorporating research.

4. What would be the best option if you wanted to research needed competences for PM in general?
   a) have a questionnaire filled in at a scientific congress about PM;
   b) have a questionnaire filled in by participants on a website for project managers;
   c) have a questionnaire filled in by human resource specialists in project-oriented firms.

B is the best option, but hardly a good one. Questions remain about the quality of the respondents and their representation from different subject domains. C would miss out all project managers in other firms and self-employed project managers. The scientific congress will only give you project managers that are interested in research, which is not a good representation of general PM.

# References

Arras People and Thorpe, J. (2010). *Project management benchmark report 2010,* Available at www.arraspeople. co.uk. Accessed: June 2010.

Australian Institute of Project Management. (1996). *AIPM professional competency standards for project management.*

Australian Institute of Project Management. (2010). *AIPM professional competency standards for project management* (Version 1.12).

Baker, S. and Baker, K. (1998). *The Complete Idiot's Guide to Project Management.* New York, NY: Alpha Books.

Bauer, B. J. (2005). A success paradigm for project managers in the aerospace industry. (Phd, Capella University).

Car, Z., Pripuzic, K. and Belani, H. (2010). Teaching project management to graduate students of electrical engineering and computing. *TTEM- Technics Technologies Education Management,* 5(1), 73–81.

Chipulu, M., Ojiako, U., Ashleigh, M. and Maguire, S. (2011). An analysis of interrelationships between project management and student-experience constructs. *Project Management Journal,* 42(3), 91–101.

Crawford, L. (2004). 'Global Project Management Body of Knowledge and Standards' in P. W. G. Morris and J. A. Pinto (eds), *The Wiley Guide to Managing Projects.* Hoboken, NJ: Wiley, pp. 1150–1196.

Crawford, L. (2005). Senior management perceptions of project management competence. *International Journal of Project Management,* 23(1), 7–16.

Crawford, L., Morris, P., Thomas, J. and Winter, M. (2006). Practitioner development: From trained technicians to reflective practitioners. *International Journal of Project Management,* 24(8), 722–733.

Divjak, B. and Kukec, S. K. (2008). Teaching methods for international R&D project management. *International Journal of Project Management,* 26(3), 251–257.

Everts, P. (2008). Een analyse van de huidige en gewenste projectmanagementcompetenties in de bouwsector. (Master, TU Delft) (www.pauleverts.nl). Available at http://www.pauleverts.nl/resultaten/. Accessed: October 2008.

Fernández, J., Manuel Mesa, Cabal, V. Á., Balsera, J. V. and Huerta, G. M. (2010). Application of PBL methodology to the teaching of engineering project management. *Journal of Professional Issues in Engineering Education & Practice,* 136(2), 58–63.

Golob, M. P. (2002). Implementing project management competencies in the workplace. (Phd, Capella University). Retrieved from Proquest database.

Heywood, L., Gonczi, A. and Hager, P. (1992). *A Guide to Development of Competency Standards for Professions.* Canberra: A.G.P.S. Australia. Department of Employment, Education, and Training.

IPMA (2006). In Caupin G., Knoepfel H., Koch G., Pannenbäcker K., Pérez-Polo F. and Seabury C. (eds), *ICB – IPMA Competence Baseline Version 3.0* (ICB Version 3.0, June 2006 edition) International Project Management Association.

Kerzner, H. (2003). *Project Management Workbook: To accompany project management: A systems approach to planning, scheduling, and controlling* (8th edition). Hoboken, NJ: Wiley.

Krahn, J. (2005). Project leadership: An empirical investigation. (Phd, University of Calgary).

Lebcir, R. M., Wells, H. and Bond, A. (2008). Factors affecting academic performance of international students in project management courses: A case study from a British post-92 university. *International Journal of Project Management,* 26(3), 268–274.

Lewis, J. P. (2000). *The Project Manager's Desk Reference: A comprehensive guide to project planning, scheduling, evaluation, and systems.* New York, NY: McGraw-Hill.

Lewis, J. P. (2003). *Project Leadership.* New York, NY: McGraw-Hill.

Martin, A. (2000). A simulation engine for custom project management education. *International Journal of Project Management,* 18(3), 201–213.

McClelland, D. C. (1998). Identifying competencies with behavioral-event interviews. *Psychological Science,* 9(5), 331–339.

McDonald, J. (2001). Why is software project management difficult? And what that implies for teaching software project management. *Computer Science Education,* 11(1), 55.

McHenry, R. L. (2008). Understanding the project manager competencies in a diversified project management community using a project management competency value grid. (Phd, Capella University).

Mengel, T. (2008). Outcome-based project management education for emerging leaders – A case study of teaching and learning project management. *International Journal of Project Management,* 26(3), 275–285.

Meredith, J. R. and Mantel, Sa. J. (1995). *Project Management: A managerial approach.* New York, NY: Wiley.

Mirabile, R. J. (1997). Everything you wanted to know about competency modeling. *Training & Development,* 51(8), 73.

Nijhuis, S. A. (2012). Learning for project management in a higher education curriculum. *Project Management Institute Research and Education Conference 2012,* Limerick, Ireland.

Nooriafsha, M. and Todhunter, B. (2004). Designing a web enhanced multimedia learning environment (WEMLE) for project management. *Journal of Interactive Learning Research,* 15(1), 33–41.

Nordhaug, O. (1998). Competence specificities in organizations. *International Studies of Management & Organization,* 28(1), 8–29.

Pant, I. and Baroudi, B. (2008). Project management education: The human skills imperative. *International Journal of Project Management,* 26(2), 124–128.

Pettersen, N. (1991). *Selecting Project Managers: An integrated list of predictors.* Drexel Hill, PA: Project Management Institute.

PMI. (2008). *A Guide to the Project Management Body of Knowledge (PMBOK guide) Fourth edition.* Drexel Hill, PA: Project Management Institute.

Portny, S. E. (2001). *Project Management for Dummies.* Foster City, CA: IDG Books Worldwide.

Reif, H. L. and Mitri, M. (2005). How university professors teach project management for information systems. *Communications of the ACM,* 48(8), 134–136.

Rennie, K. and White, M. (2002). Learning environments for project management using the internet as a medium. *South African Journal of Information Management,* 4(3).

Robotham, D. and Jubb, R. (1996). Competences: Measuring the unmeasurable. *Management Development Review,* 9(5), 25.

Rodriguez, A. (2005). Critical factors in hiring, promoting and designing job descriptions for strategic project managers. (Phd, Capella University).

Rooij, S. W. V. (2009). Scaffolding project-based learning with the project management body of knowledge (PMBOK®). *Computers & Education,* 52(1), 210–219.

Spencer, L. M. and Spencer, S. M. (1993). *Competence at Work: Models for superior performance.* New York, NY: Wiley.

Stoyan, R. (2008). 'PM for all™' – Intensive small group teaching in leadership and PM, for many students at low cost. *International Journal of Project Management,* 26(3), 297–303.

Valencia, V. V. (2007). A project manager's personal attributes as predictors for success (MSc, Air Force Institute of Technology, Ohio).

van Doorn, N. and van der Veen, R. (2008). *Competenties van PMrs: De 'HBG PMnt BOK',* Unpublished manuscript.

Ward, J. L. (2000). *Project Management Terms: A working glossary.* Arlington, VA: ESI International.

www.globalpmstandards.org. (October 2007). GAPPS project manager standards; A framework for performance based competency standards for global level 1 and 2 project managers. Available at fromhttp://globalpmstandards.org/_mgxroot/page_pm_standards_downloads.html. Accessed: 19 October 2011.

# PART III
# SPECIFIC DATA COLLECTION AND ANALYSIS TECHNIQUES

Moving from the identification of a research question to the determination of suitable research methods is the focus of this section.

I will be the first to admit that this collection is not exhaustive, but it is offered from the perspective of PM research as a social science. As a statement of the current and emerging choices of leading PM researchers is worthy of its own examination (but won't occur here).

Again, the rationale for each method is offered by the authors themselves.

- Shepherd places the use of interviews to address the social nature of project, programme and portfolio management. His chapter addresses the range and selection of interview methods in project-related studies and provides an overview of techniques.
- Reich discusses two ways that theory plays into case studies (as an input or output) and how you can choose the right approach for your topic. Her contribution is complemented by other chapters that also offer commentary on the use of case studies but with specific examples.
- Sankaran and Dick examine the use of action-oriented methods, specifically address the criticism of such methods and offer practical guidance on the use of such methods in PM research. The chapter also includes several exercises to help you and your supervisor in their use.
- Nogeste uses the specific use of dual-action action research in the context of a doctoral candidacy in PM. You and your supervisors will see a model of using this technique to both conduct PM research and solve a real-life problem.
- Wells and Smyth argue that a flexible, iterative and 'agile' approach to the selection and use of research methods best supports the reality you might encounter in conducting PM research. They focus on the use of single and multiple case studies.
- Nugapitiya, Boydell and Healy describe the use of autoethnography with a specific case of an incident in Australia. Embedded in this advocacy is their attempt to empower you – as a PM practitioner – to rely on and trust your own experiences to design and implement of advanced research.
- Owen, Algeo and Conner focus on the fundamental need of any PM researcher – the accessing of research sites. They offer multiple examples and discuss their approach in gaining such access, associated risks and the lessons learned from their experiences.

# 15

# Interview Methods for Project Management Research

Miles Shepherd

*Interviewing is the most frequently used data-gathering technique in PM research and it is often done very badly. I wanted to share some of my pragmatic experience and some academic perspectives on this critical method.*

In recent years, the social nature of project, programme and portfolio management has become widely recognised. Researchers are beginning to recognise, too, that the similarities of project management to the social sciences requires alternative approaches for research and greater use has been made of qualitative and mixed mode research. Interviews have long been a favourite means of gathering qualitative data and many project management-based studies have relied on this approach. This chapter addresses the range and selection of interview methods for research in project-related studies and provides an overview of techniques. Despite its more frequent use, interviewing is not an uncontested approach to gathering research data. Criticisms of the approach are reviewed and aspects of data quality are examined. The planning and preparation of an interview are set out including special situations involving various types of respondent.

After reading this chapter, the reader should be able to:

- identify when qualitative interview strategies are appropriate for your research study;
- design an interview plan;
- analyse and resolve data quality issues;
- assess the skills and logistical requirements needed to successfully implement an interview strategy.

Keywords: interview, justification of strategy, practicalities

## Introduction

This chapter addresses the use of qualitative interviews as a data-gathering approach for investigating issues in project, portfolio and programme management. The use of interviews in research has grown rapidly in recent years and is seen by many as a straightforward and effective method of gaining insight into real life situations: as Kvale and Brinkmann (2009) say, 'If you want to know how people understand their world and their lives, why not ask them.' Such a conversational approach is attractive: it involves little cost, is something that most people are familiar with through their everyday experience and does not require technical equipment (Denscombe, 2010). However, effective interviewing requires careful preparation, attention to logistic factors and no little skill.

Interviewing is ubiquitous and can be seen daily, in the media, particularly on television, newspapers, magazines and radio as well as in specialist publications. While all of these examples are what Khan and Cannell (1957) call 'a purposeful discussion between two or more people', most of them are not research interviews which generally require careful planning, detailed preparation, a sensitivity to the complex interaction between interviewer and respondent and are usually recorded in some way. In contrast, a conversation is frequently unplanned, relaxed, informal and almost never recorded.

## Underlying Assumptions

As already stated, there are significant practical differences between a conversation and a research interview. Denscombe (2010) builds on a considerable literature on interviewing to highlight the underlying assumptions which differentiate an interview from a conversation:

- *Consent.* Respondents makes themselves available for a discussion intended to produce material to be used for research purposes.
- *Attribution.* The interview is 'on the record' and 'for the record'.
- *Direction.* The agenda for the interview is set by the interviewer.

These assumptions have implications for research ethics and style of interview that will be addressed later in the chapter.

## Types of Interview

It can be seen that there are various forms of interview which may be classified in a number of ways such as style of delivery, medium for communication and plurality. Interviews may be conducted with one respondent at a time or with groups: face to face, by telephone or by using a computer. Interviews can be highly formalised with fixed questions delivered in a set sequence or can be more open-ended, relaxed and informal. Many researchers classify interviews according to the degree of structure of the questioning (for example, Saunders, Lewis and Thornhill, 2007, Denscombe, 2010) while others highlight the depth of the interview (Bryman and Bell, 2007). One way of categorising interviews is shown in Figure 15.1.

Standardised interviews or, as they are also known, structured interviews are essentially interviewer administered questionnaires, designed to gather data which, according to Saunders et al. (2007) may be subjected to quantitative analysis. The design of this type of interview follows a similar pattern to that used to develop a questionnaire and is delivered using questions with fixed wording and usually in a set order. The objective is to gather data in sufficient quantity and of a specific type that can be analysed using statistical techniques. By contrast, non-standard or qualitative interviews are designed to understand particular aspects of a situation and expect to explore situations as they arise in the interview.

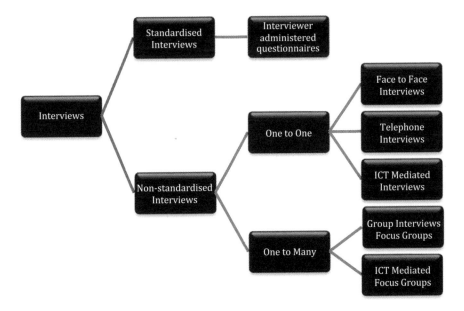

**Figure 15.1    Interview typology (after Saunders et al. 2007)**

Non-standardised interviews are sometimes referred to as qualitative research interviews (King, 1994) and take two forms; semi structured and unstructured interviews. For a semi-structured interview, the interviewer has a number of themes supported by open-ended questions. How the questions are posed and their sequence of delivery may be varied from interview to interview, depending on how the respondent reacts and which aspects of the replies are of significance to the Interviewer. The intention is to gather information that links to the research question and so the way the interview is conducted depends on the interaction between the respondent and the interviewer. Additional questions may be framed according to the progress of the interview or between interviews.

Unstructured interviews are the least formal of all research interviews. They are sometimes referred to as in-depth interviews as they allow the interviewer to explore more general areas in greater depth. Powney and Watts (1987) characterise in-depth interviews according to the manner in which the interview is conducted:

- Informant interviews are characterised by allowing the respondent's perceptions of the situation to guide the direction taken. These are also called non-directive interviews since the respondent is not directed to the next question by the interviewer. Such interviews are intended to allow the respondent to talk freely about the area of interest.
- Respondent interviews, by contrast, are guided by the agenda set by the interviewer. The respondent answers questions put by the interviewer who usually has some form of prompt list to help keep the interview flowing or encourage the respondent to add detail to areas of interest. The prompt list also ensures that all areas of interest are covered in the interview.

Both standardised and non-standardised interviews require specific skills. The design of standardised interviews is essentially the same as the design of survey questionnaires whereas the design and delivery of non-structured interviews allow much greater flexibility. This chapter addresses only the design, skills and techniques needed for qualitative, non-standardised interviews.

## Qualitative Research Interviews

This type of interview has grown in popularity among researchers since it is particularly suitable for situations where the meaning of a particular phenomenon to the participants is the focus of the study (King, 1994 cited in Robson, 2011: p. 271). Other situations where qualitative research interviews are appropriate include:

- the study of processes in a social unit – this allows study of individual perceptions in the project team or groups of stakeholders;
- understanding the development of a new phenomenon from historical accounts of participants – this approach is often used in the construction of case studies or the investigation of a particular project outcome;
- the initial investigation of a situation which will be studied later using quantitative methods – such as establishing the range of possible relationships within a leadership style;
- the follow up of a quantitative study, especially where issues have emerged that need clarification.

In terms of project-related research, interviews may be used either on their own, as the primary data-gathering instrument, or as part of a mixed-method approach. Interviews are seen as being particularly well suited to gathering data for the construction of case studies (see also Chapter 19), for piloting stages of broader studies and for exploring the lived experience of practice. Situations where it is necessary to understand phenomena offer opportunities to employ interviews.

## Interviews and the Research Cycle

Although there are many views of the research cycle, a simple example begins by establishing the conceptual framework for the enquiry and ends with reporting. For example, Kvale and Brinkmann (2009) illustrate a seven stage cycle: At each of these stages there are specific issues relevant to interview-based research:

1. conceptual framework, where the purpose of the study is clarified;
2. design the study, which is where the procedures and techniques of the project are formalised;
3. gather data, which consists of the actual interviews and activities cover preparation, logistics, the interview and data recording;
4. data preparation is the stage where the information gathered is transformed into data;
5. analysis of the data where the researcher reviews the data seeking answers to the research questions;
6. verification demonstrates that the data gathered from the interviews is both valid and reliable;
7. reporting goes beyond the simple writing up of the findings from the analysis and is intended to present a compelling case for the results and there are some ethical issues specific to an interview-based study.

## Conceptual Framework

The nature of the research design needs to be closely linked to purpose of the research since this purpose dictates the type of study to be carried out. The traditional purposes of research result in three types of study – exploratory, descriptive and explanatory. For an exploratory study, where the aim is to discover 'what is happening: to seek new insights' (Robson, 2002: p. 59), unstructured interviews are likely to be best suited to the nature of the research because the approach requires a less directive style in order to obtain a wide-ranging view of the issue in question. This approach may also be used effectively in the early stages of a research project where it is well suited to the identification of the main themes which can then be explored using other research methods. Respondent interviews should work well in this type of situation. Although semi-structured interviews are also used, this form is better suited to explanatory research situations where the aim is to identify causal relations. These relations may have been identified in a descriptive study, particularly where structured interviews have been used. Researchers will need to consider the intended outcome of the study in deciding whether an interview strategy is appropriate or not. Factors to consider include:

- the nature of knowledge involved – knowledge collection or construction;
- sensitivity of the subject matter – where the nature of the research requires attention to emotional of other considerations;
- privileged nature of the data required – who has the information needed and how accessible they might be.

## Study Design

Having determined, and recorded, the nature of the study and the epistemic stance to be adopted, the more detailed work of designing the data-gathering instrument can be undertaken. The first part of the design is determining the research questions and then, to plan the data-gathering instrument in detail. For the interview-based study, there are two key aspects to be determined: what information is needed to answer the research questions and who can provide that data.

Interviewing is best suited to studies where opinions, emotions and experiences are relevant. These aspects are likely to need exploration in depth and rich data recorded. The style of questioning should be considered at this point so that the nature of interviews, semi-structured or informal, may be decided. Whichever approach is used, a list of issues to be investigated must be prepared.

Who can provide the data requires careful thought. It is of limited value to randomly select individuals to interview since there is no guarantee they have the knowledge necessary to provide useful data. Most interviewers will have limited time at their disposal and so cannot interview large numbers of respondents thus some care in the choice of individuals to interview will be needed. Much depends on the intention of the study, thus where the intention is to produce results that can be generalised, a more or less representative cross-section of the potential population should be selected. On the other hand, in case study work or where the intention is to study a specific situation, then key players only are likely to be interviewed. Denscombe (2010: p. 181) notes that there are no hard and fast rules for selection or indeed how many interviews are needed. Bryman and Bell (2007: p. 497) illustrate approaches to limiting numbers of interviews but stress that any limitation needs to consider the purpose of the research and the limits indirectly imposed by the research questions addressed and will need to be fully justified when reporting.

Project managers are usually very busy people and so may not have time to allow a long interview. Similarly, a very eminent respondent on a high-profile project may be difficult to access and may also pose additional methodological issues when it comes to the actual interview. Interviewing so-called 'elites' brings into play a number of issues such as control of the agenda, comprehension of responses and reaction to probes for detailed information.

Outcomes of the design stage include:

- interview schedule – some form of timetable for the actual interviews. Aim is to estimate time needed and overall duration of the data-gathering stage – note two levels are needed to cover individual interviews and overall schedule;
- list of topics to be covered – ideas for what needs to be discussed with respondents, usually in terms of themes;
- list of potential respondents.

## Data Gathering

The logistics of interviewing are similar to those of other data-gathering approaches. Perhaps the most significant aspect is time and its management since interviewing usually takes far longer than expected. Time must be spent in planning and preparation, conducting the interview and then transcribing it. All these are necessary activities but how long to spend on the various components will need to be linked to the implications for the outcome of the study. Factors to consider include:

- how many respondents need to be interviewed;
- how long it will take to gather data from each respondent;
- time respondents are prepared to make available;
- interviewer travelling time;
- time required for transcription.

Other logistic factors may be summarised as follows:

- Gaining access – physical as well as organisational access, early warning and timings (negotiate, especially where elites or very busy people are involved).
- Social aspects – dress code, demonstration of level of knowledge (interviewer credibility).
- Location for interview – 'on site', difficult to ensure adequate isolation from workplace distractions but often convenient for the respondent or 'off site', which allows the interviewer more control, offers some privacy and should be suitably quiet.
- Equipment needed – minimum, will include means for recording the interview. Wherever possible, use a portable recorder but make sure that it works! Test before use at every interview, that it is working at intervals during the interview and finally after the interview. Ensure adequate power supply (mains preferably but if batteries are used, always carry a spare set).
- Set of items – usually questions but for less structured interviews, may be thematic notes to act as a prompt during the interview and to ensure all topics covered. Likely to include a proposed sequence for the interview, prompt list for the interviewer and probe list to remind the interviewer of means to make the interview flow.
- Suggestions for probes – device to encourage a respondent to go into more depth. Considerable skill is needed to employ these effectively – note TV interviewers. Includes verbal queues such as 'Anything more?...' or 'Could you expand on that?' and 'What are your personal views on that?' Non-verbal prompts include short periods of silence and an enquiring glance (See Zeisel, 2006: pp. 230–243 for more on probes).

There are no hard and fast rules for the sequencing of interviews but one commonly used approach identified by Robson (2011: p. 284) is as follows:

*Checklist for Introductions*
1. *Introductions:* The interviewer introduces herself, explains the purpose of the interview and how it fits into the overall research plan. It is also useful to remind the respondent about the ethical aspects of the interview such as confidentiality and anonymity: and request permission to record the interview either by taking notes or using recording equipment. It is useful to have a checklist or script for this part of the interview. The following is a typical approach:
   - formal introduction using name and affiliation;
   - outline selection process;
   - ethical assurances on confidentiality and anonymity;
   - stress that there are no right or wrong answers;
   - explain that the respondent may interrupt, ask for clarification, criticise the line of questioning or terminate the interview at any point;
   - tell the respondent something about yourself such as background, interests, and so on;
   - ask permission to record the interview, either by taking notes or digitally.
2. *Warm Up:* Establish a rapport with the respondent by using simple non-threatening questions, usually starting with demographic information. This ensures essential data is captured and allows both the interviewer and the respondent to settle down.
3. *Main body of the interview:* This covers the key questioning of the respondent. Generally, some form of interview schedule is used to remind the interviewer of the intended sequence of the interview, the main points to be covered and some key questions. Many interviewers also make use of prompts – in semi-structured interviews these remind the interviewer of some key questions and possible variations but it is usually important that the interviewer is guided in the conduct of this part of the interview by the responses of the respondent.
4. *Cool off:* At the end of the interview, this phase allows both the interviewer and respondent to relax. Robson also notes this is a useful way to reduce any tension that may have built up during the interview.
5. *Closure:* Every interview should be formally closed and the respondent thanked for their assistance, cooperation and time. Be prepared for what many interviewers call the 'hand on the door' syndrome where the respondent comes out with interesting and useful material when the recording device is switched off or the notebook closed. There are several ways of dealing with this, usually by restarting the interview and recording the new information but as Robson (2011: p. 284) says, you must be prepared for the situation and note how you dealt with it.

There are many different ways to ask a question. Observation of professional interviewers on TV will quickly illustrate some of these approaches. Kvale and Brinkmann (2009) listed nine types of question:

1. Introductory – 'Can you tell me about…?' or, 'What happened in the event you described…?'; the respondent is encouraged to provide rich descriptions of their experience.
2. Follow-up – often these are non-verbal sounds of encouragement such as 'Mmm…' and are designed to encourage the respondent to say more about the topic.

3. Probes – 'Can you say more about that…?'; the interviewer is probing for more information but is not setting out the dimensions to be explored.
4. Specifying – this is a variation on the probing question where the interviewer is more focused on a particular aspect such as 'What did you actually do when…?'
5. Direct – often used later in an interview where the interviewer needs to indicate the dimension to be explored. Questions are of the form 'When you mention …, do you mean…?'
6. Indirect – uses projective questions such as, 'What do you think other team members feel…?' to explore either other people's views or that of the respondent which has not been clearly stated. Care is needed when interpreting response to this type of question.
7. Structuring – where the interviewer wishes to close one theme and move onto another, or to break into a long and possibly irrelevant response by politely interjecting, 'I would like to introduce another topic now…'
8. Silence – a period of silence can be used to encourage the respondent to continue or to allow thoughts to be surfaced.
9. Interpreting – considerable variation is possible using this approach which seeks to clarify a response by rephrasing the reply, for example, 'Then you mean…' or some form of more direct question to ensure that the information is understood by the interviewer in the way it was meant by the respondent.

In practice, interviewers should use a variety of question types, mainly to ensure that appropriate responses have been elicited and that these have been understood correctly. A variety of question types also encourages the respondent to speak more freely as well as making the experience less of an inquisition and more like an informed discussion. Similarly, sensitivity in asking the questions encourages trust to develop between the participants. On the other hand, there are a number of questions to avoid:

- Long questions – the respondent is likely to forget the full question and the result is likely to be a partial answer.
- Multiple-part questions – again the respondent is likely to give a partial answer. Where a comparison is needed, it is best to break the question down into shorter parts and build up the response needed, for example, 'What do you feel about the way project knowledge is shared compared with five years ago?' should be broken down into three questions, one about current feelings, a second to recall feelings in the past and the final part to compare the two.
- Jargon – avoid jargon especially if it is likely to be unfamiliar to the respondent. Spell out acronyms and abbreviations to avoid any misunderstandings.
- Leading questions – it is usually straightforward to rephrase leading questions so that they are neutral but the skill lies in realising that leading questions are being used.
- Biased questions – while this may be an obvious aspect to avoid, it is sometimes easier to write neutral questions rather than asking them in an interview setting. This is where degree of scripting is helpful. Beware also of exhibiting bias in the way responses are received so that the interviewer seeks to avoid identifying with the views of the respondent.

Interviewing is not always an easy discussion. Despite your best efforts, you may encounter difficulty interviewing some respondents. Some situations and possible approaches to resolving them are shown in Table 15.1.

**Table 15.1    Potential problems and solutions**

| Problem | Suggestion |
| --- | --- |
| Respondent only provides monosyllabic answers. | Identify cause:<br>Time limitations and worries over anonymity can be minimised by careful interview opening (see Box 1). If opening has been done carefully, try rephrasing the question in a more open-ended manner. Use probes such as long pauses to indicate that more is expected. |
| Repeated long and digressive responses. | Some digression must be tolerated to allow full understanding, the interviewer must control how much can be accepted. Considerable care is needed in dealing with such situations to avoid giving offence. Use structuring or interpreting questions to return the respondent to an earlier and relevant response. |
| Respondent begins interviewing the interviewer. | While this may suggest that a rapport has been established, regaining control is important. Stress that their views are what is needed and that if they wish to raise questions, leave them till later. |
| Respondent is proud of status and criticises interviewer. | This is a very difficult situation and needs patience in order to remain respectful. Stay calm and avoid an argument. Establish your own credibility in the introduction by demonstrating your own knowledge of the topic, respondent and the organisation. |
| Respondent becomes noticeably upset during the interview. | Allow the respondent time to answer and ensure you do nothing to indicate that you need to move on or feel impatient.<br>Where the respondent is distressed, explain that the question does not need to be answered and move on to another question. Once the emotions have settled, it may be possible to return to the point but be careful to rephrase the question. |

## Data Preparation

The purpose of data preparation is to turn the information gathered into a form that can be analysed for research purposes. For interview data, this process entails the transcription of data from aural to written form. Whether the initial data consists of field notes or recordings the process is the same and consists of two stages: the conversion process and the coding process.

The conversion process is usually thought to be a simple task of typing up the utterances captured either in field notes or on a recording device. It is unwise to rely entirely on recording devices so field notes should always be made contemporaneously with the interview so that context and initial ideas are captured. Field notes also support the recorded interview where they may be used to capture context or other body language or use of irony. Field notes present a number of problems that the interviewer needs to understand and resolve:

- Speed of writing. Respondents usually speak faster than the interviewer can write and often some speech is missed or incorrectly recorded. Similarly, field notes need to be legible and speed often means writing is difficult to decipher later.

- Loss of context. Matters of tone of voice and body language are notoriously difficult to capture.
- Respondent review. Where the respondent is invited to review the outcome of the interview, their view of the 'transcript' differs markedly from the transcript.
- Transcriber. Who carries out the conversion process can affect the quality of the outcome. Good secretarial support often results in fast, accurate transcription of the words. Some of the context may be lost but field notes can be used to reduce the effect this might have. Kvale and Brinkmann (2009: p. 180) note that there are advantages to the interviewer doing the transcription as ideas for coding themes can be seen early and lessons on interview technique can also be identified.
- Transcription style. Transcripts may be verbatim records of the interview where every word and pause, repetition or interjection is included or semi-edited to remove such material. There are no rules to help decide which model or combination of approaches to use but whichever is adopted, a justification and explanation must be included in the dissertation. Where a third party is to do the transcription, it is important that a written instruction on method is provided to the transcriber and included in the dissertation.
- Where techniques such as Conversation Analysis are to be used, specialist transcription methods will be needed (see Table 15.2 for annotation symbols).

**Table 15.2    Annotation symbols**

| Symbol | Meaning |
| --- | --- |
| [ ] | Square brackets mark the start and end of overlapping speech. Position them in alignment where the overlap occurs. |
| ↑    ↓ | Vertical arrows precede marked pitch movement, over and above normal rhythms of speech. They are for marked, audibly significant shifts – and even then, the other symbols (full stops, commas, question marks) mop up most of that. Like with all these symbols, the aim is to capture interactionally significant features, hearable as such to an ordinary listener – especially deviations from a common sense notion of 'neutral' which admittedly has not been well defined. |
| → | Side arrows are not transcription features, but draw analytic attention to particular lines of text. Usually positioned to the left of the line. |
| Underlining | Signals vocal emphasis; the extent of underlining within individual words locates emphasis, but also indicates how heavy it is. |
| CAPITALS | Mark speech that is obviously louder than surrounding speech (often occurs when speakers are hearably competing for the floor, raised volume rather than doing contrastive emphasis). |
| °↑I know it° | 'Degree' signs enclose obviously quieter speech (that is, noticably produced – as quieter, not just someone distant). |
| that's r*ight. | Asterisks precede a 'squeaky' vocal delivery. |
| (0.4) | Numbers in round brackets measure pauses in seconds (in this case, four-tenths of a second). Place on new line if not assigned to a speaker. |
| (.) | A micropause, able to hear but too short to measure. |
| ((text)) | Additional comments from the transcriber, for example, context or intonation. |
| she wa::nted | Colons show degrees of elongation of the prior sound; the more colons, the more elongation. I use one per syllable length. |
| hhh | Aspiration (out-breaths); proportionally as for colons. |

| Symbol | Meaning |
| --- | --- |
| .hhh | Inspiration (in-breaths); proportionally as for colons. |
| Yeh, | 'Continuation' marker, speaker has not finished; marked by fall_/rise or weak rising intonation, as when enunciating lists. |
| Y'know? | Question marks signal stronger, 'questioning' intonation, irrespective of grammar. |
| Yeh. | Periods (full stops) mark falling, stopping intonation ('final contour'), irrespective of grammar, and not necessarily followed by a pause. |
| bu-u- | Hyphens mark a cut-off of the preceding sound. |
| >he said< | 'Greater than' and 'lesser than' signs enclose speeded-up talk. Sometimes used the other way round for slower talk. |
| solid. =<br>We had | 'Equals' signs mark the immediate 'latching' of successive talk, whether of one or more speakers, with no interval. |
| heh heh | Voiced laughter. Can have other symbols added, such as underlining, pitch movement, extra aspiration, and so on. |
| sto(h)p i(h)t | Laughter within speech is signalled by h's in round brackets. |
| uh um | How to spell 'er' and 'erm' the Jefferson way. (Can be added to, and so on.) |

Whichever approach has been adopted, it must be noted that the major problem is loss of context. Loss of aspects such as non-verbal cues, tone and use of irony are difficult to capture. Ethical issues related to reliability and validity of transcripts must also be taken into account. Kvale and Brinkmann (2009: pp. 183–187) draw attention to factors affecting transcription issues such as precision versus accuracy, syntactical aspects such as punctuation and different constructions of validity, particularly noting that the issue to be addressed is, 'What is a useful transcription for my research purposes?'

The transcript can then be prepared for analysis. Rapley (2011: p. 277) uses labels in preparation for analysis. These labels enable easy identification and retrieval of items of note and should be used consistently (see Table 15.3). This approach reinforces the need to review transcripts as the research proceeds and to modify interview approaches where themes are seen to emerge. Rapley also reinforces Kvale and Brinkmann's advice to reflect on what is being done – and to record decisions and reasons for approaches and changes. Both emphasise the iterative nature of review and reflection in interview research.

**Table 15.3     Labelling interview data**

| Labelling interview data |
| --- |
| • label key, essential striking, odd interesting things; |
| • label similar items with same label; |
| • labels can be drawn from ideas emerging from the close, detailed reading of the data as well as from the literature; |
| • with each application of a new label, check prior labelling to ensure consistency. |
| After Rapley (2011) |

## Data Analysis

As common with all qualitative methods, there are particular issues relating to analysis of interview data. The main issue is one of sheer volume. Interview transcripts are often long so it does not take many interviews to produce as much as 1,000 pages of transcription. So the question of how to analyse this volume of data is frequently asked. Kvale and Brinkmann (2009: p. 191) note that the question needs to be addressed in the design stage so that the researcher seeks to structure the interviews in such a way that they can be analysed in a coherent and meaningful way.

Kvale and Brinkmann (2009: pp. 195–196) identify six steps in analysis of interviews, the first three take place during the interview itself. The first two steps, where the respondent describes matters of interest to the interviewer and then discovers new relationships, involve little interpretation or analysis. The interviewer carries out some interpretation and condensation takes place as the third step. The fourth step is the transcription and may include coding for computer analysis. Their fifth step involves possible re-interview where clarification is needed after initial analysis of the transcript. The final stage is one where the 'continuum of description and interpretation' is extended to include action. Kvale and Brinkmann also note that interview analysis has various modes depending on the approach to be adopted (see Table 15.4 below).

**Table 15.4    Modes of analysis**

| Analytical Focus | Mode of Analysis | Description |
| --- | --- | --- |
| Meaning | Coding | Labelling approach often a key part of grounded theory and also used in content analysis and computer-assisted analysis (see Gibbs, 2004). Labels can be predefined so that the interview results in well targeted questioning. |
| | Condensation | Under this approach, meanings expressed by the respondent are converted into shorter reformulations using natural units which are then assigned a central theme in the form of a sentence or phrase. |
| | Interpretation | Often used in analysis of poetry or films and psychoanalytic situations. This approach attempts to identify what is not stated directly from the structures and relations of meaning not explicitly stated in the interview. |
| Language | Linguistic analysis | This addresses the characteristic uses of language, especially grammar and linguistic forms. Attention to form can assist the interviewer to formulate more precise questions. |
| | Conversation analysis | This investigates the structure and process of linguistic interaction in the interview and is intended to increase intersubjective understanding. This approach emerged from ethnomethodology and implies a pragmatic theory of language. Some analysts believe that this form of analysis is inappropriate in an interview situation as the talk is too formal. Other criticism is made of the lack of depth of the process. |
| | Narrative analysis | Focuses on the interview as a story and examines the meaning and linguistic form of the text. See Labov (1972, 2001) for a standard framework narrative analysis. |
| | Discourse analysis | Focuses on how truth effects are created within discourses that are neither true nor false. Based on work by Foucault (for example, 1972). This form of analysis examines how language is used to create, maintain and destroy social bonds, taking a postmodern view of the world as socially and linguistically constructed. |

| Analytical Focus | Mode of Analysis | Description |
|---|---|---|
| | Deconstruction | Based on Derrida's conception of deconstruction as a combination of destruction and construction, this form of analysis involves deconstructing one understanding of the text thus opening another understanding. According to Kvale and Brinkmann (2009: p. 230), the focus is not on what the person means but on the 'what the concept says'. |
| General | Bricolage | Traditionally, bricolage is something assembled using tools that are to hand, irrespective of whether these tools are used as intended or designed. This form of analysis makes use of mixed technical discourses, moving freely between different techniques and concepts (Kvale and Brinkmann, 2009: p. 233). This is a common form of analysis and calls upon many of the conceptual frameworks outlined by Rapley (2011: pp. 274–276). |
| | Theoretical Reading | Under this approach, a theoretically informed reading of the interviews is used. Key passages of the text are interpreted from different theoretical positions. This approach requires a strong knowledge of the available theories underpinning the phenomenon under investigation. |

# Reporting

Presentation of results and analysis from qualitative studies present a number of challenges as noted by Denscombe (2010: p. 320) and others. Some of these issues are the subject of common errors in reporting but for studies based on interview data, there are two major issues:

- editorial and ethical decisions on whether or not to include direct quotes from the interviews;
- provision of contextual data to enable judgments on validity, reliability and persuasiveness of the argument.

Representation of qualitative data involves an element of 'rhetoric' and so the credibility of the research owes something to the ability of the researcher to present a persuasive account, conveying a sense of authority and authenticity. Denscombe (2010: p. 320) notes that reporting of qualitative research is usually more of a 'retrospective *account* rather than a literal depiction' (emphasis in original). The report should:

- identify key issues accurately;
- be easily understood by the reader;
- follow some logical sequence that provides a suitable account of the results.

For reasons of space, all the assembled interview data cannot be presented so it will be necessary to be selective in what is reported: thus the writer effectively acts as an editor, opening criticism concerning objectivity. As the reader does not have access to all the data, they have no way of knowing whether the selection was a fair reflection of the data or not. Furthermore, any extract used is taken out of its context so its significance is diminished. However, the evidence presented does not need prove a point. Instead, it *illustrates* the point being made (Denscombe, 2010: p. 295

emphasis added). Furthermore, recognising the retrospective account aspect in the report and setting the context should counter any criticisms.

## Ethical Aspects

All the normal ethical requirements apply to interviews but there are some aspects that need greater attention than other forms of research. Interviewing is a highly personal activity and the need to probe and examine attitudes, knowledge and understanding brings the interviewer and the respondent very close to each other. A bond of trust is needed to make best use of what should be authentic data and to gain unique insight into research issues. This means that trust must not be betrayed, consent must be clearly and demonstrably informed and respondents must be offered the opportunity to withdraw at any point in the research process. Risk to respondents must also be considered, particularly during the reporting stage, since the consequences of interviews can be severe if anonymity is breached.

Researchers usually need some form of authority to carry out interviews and it is prudent to develop interview protocols that enshrine specific ethical considerations appropriate for the research strategy employed. It may also be necessary to obtain clearance from Ethics Committees so careful attention to professional and departmental expectations will be essential. In interview situations, it is particularly important to ensure that you operate within the law and that in your dealings with practitioners you are open, honest and do not use deception. Protocols should be constructed to demonstrate such an approach.

## Challenges to Interviewing

In common with nearly all qualitative techniques, the use of interviews as a research instrument is contested. Some ontological stances automatically exclude any form of qualitative research strategy and even those that allow qualitative or mixed method designs may reject interviews (see also Chapters 6 and 7). These general objections are addressed by many of the standard textbooks on research methods (for example, Bryman and Bell, 2007; Robson, 2011 and Denscombe, 2010). There are, however, specific challenges to the efficacy of interviews based on validity and reliability. These objections should be managed at the design stage. Then during detailed planning and execution, following normal good practice and recording reasons for methodological decisions should ensure that other researchers can see that reputable procedures and reasonable deductions have been made.

Demonstrating reliability can be difficult to achieve since it is almost impossible to show that other researchers would obtain similar data (Easterby Smith, Thorpe and Jackson, 2012) and would make similar deductions. However, findings from interview-based research may not be designed to be repeatable since they reflect reality at the time of the interview and may change over time, for example, after further reflection by the respondent (Marshall and Rossman, 1999). Saunders et al. (2011) explain that the issues involved may be complex and dynamic hence the use of non-standardised interviewing allows the necessary exploration of issues to overcome the problem. Marshall and Rossman (1999) stress the need for good field notes to support such an approach.

Another criticism of interviewing is that it can lack objectivity. The effect of the interviewer on the respondent can introduce biases that are difficult both to identify and to counter. Careful discussion of steps taken to minimise such effects will need to be included in the method justification and possibly also in the writing up of the analysis. In particular, steps to avoid criticism over leading the respondent in the development of the narrative are essential or results may be compromised. While some leading of the interview may be necessary or the interview will not cover all topics needed, the way this is done needs careful management. One way to do this is to include notes in the Prompt List that show specific aspects to be covered and possible lead-in questions. Similarly, reliability of the transcript may also be open to accusations of bias since interpretation can be highly subjective. Again, use of a transcription protocol can be useful as a counter to this type of accusation.

There are also epistemic objections to the use of interviews. Many of these objections are addressed in detail in Gubrium, Holstein, Marvasti and McKinney (2012) and there is an extensive literature on the weaknesses of interviewing as a data-gathering instrument. In outline, most of these objections concern reliability. Whether the responses recorded actually reflect the situation of interest depends on the epistemic stance adopted and, for many researchers, it is unlikely that the data that emerges from an interview represents reality: what people say they do is often at variance with what they actually do. For others, the interview is jointly constructed by the interviewer and the respondent so that interviews are an interpretative practice conditioned by location, how the dialogue is expressed and, according to Holstein and Gubrium, (2004), to whom it is said. These objections can in part be overcome by the use of careful pre-testing of interview schedules and interviewer training in the use of multiple ratings for coding of responses to open-ended questions (Silverman, 2011: p. 365).

The potential for bias in interviews is not confined to the interviewer as respondents may also introduce bias through slanted or partial responses. Generally, this can be avoided by checking the transcript with the respondent to make sure that no errors or misunderstandings have been included. It is also useful to corroborate the interview data using other sources. For this reason, many interviewers seek to identify themes across the interviews and look for consistency in multiple interviews.

Interviewing is an attractive method for gathering data and is particularly appropriate where influential players are the respondent community. These people are selected because they are presumed to be knowledgeable about the topic of interest and are prepared to speak 'on the record'. They are generally expert in their field and their testimony carries with it a high degree of credibility (Denscombe, 2010: p. 189).

The key to effective interviewing is closely linked to the selection and development of the research question. Once this has been decided, the ontological approach to data needs can be assessed and the data-gathering instrument designed. In this case, it is interview-based and detailed work on themes, prompts and logistics can be planned in detail, taking into account ethical considerations. The effective interviewer also needs to pay particular attention to interview logistics as well as the technique of interviewing.

Interviewing remains a contested approach but one that is used extensively in the social sciences. The main issues revolve around reliability and validity. Careful preparatory work and good writing up and reporting can be used to overcome many of the potential criticisms. In the end, it should be noted that interviewing is a practical skill. Technique is not learned from reading, it can only be learned from practice but careful planning and preparation makes the difficult job of obtaining effective research data from interviews less difficult.

## Tips and Questions

TIPS FOR STUDENTS

- Plan – interviews are time consuming!
- Identify coding process early – preferably before starting to interview.

- Make sure you have done your 'homework' on the organisational setting and Respondent background before you interview anyone.
- Do not start interviewing until you have sorted out your precise research question.

## TIPS FOR SUPERVISORS:

- Watch out for quantitative analysis of quantitative data.
- Early review of interview sample selection will help ensure that appropriate data sources are selected.
- Challenge coding process to ensure appropriate data presentation is achieved.

## QUESTIONS

1. Explain how qualitative research interviews differ from conversations and why does this matter?
2. Qualitative interviews are sometimes said to unscientific. Account for this view and outline how such objections can be overcome.
3. Why are qualitative interviews particularly suitable for project related research?

# References

Bryman, A. and Bell, E. (2007). *Business Research Methods*. Oxford, UK: Oxford University Press.

Denscombe (2010). *The Good Research Guide for Small Scale Social Research Projects*, 4th edition. Maidenhead, UK: Open University Press and McGraw Hill.

Easterby Smith, M., Thorpe, R. and Jackson, P. (2002). *Management Research*, 4th edition. Thousand Oaks, CA: Sage.

Foucault, M. (1972). *The Archaeology of Knowledge*. London: Routledge.

Gibbs, G. (2007). *Analyzing Qualitative Data*. London: Sage.

Gubrium, J. F., Holstein, J. A., Marvasti, A. B. and McKinney K. D. (eds) (2012). *Handbook of Interview Research*. Thousand Oaks, CA: Sage.

Holstein, J. A. and Gubrium, J. F. (1995). *The Active Interview*. Thousand Oaks, CA: Sage.

Jefferson, G. (1985). An exercise in the transcription and analysis of laughter. In Van Dijk, T. (ed.) Qualitative interviews in psychology. *Handbook of Discourse Analysis*, Volume 3. London: Academic Press.

Kahn, R. L and Cannell, C. F. (1957). *The Dynamics of Interviewing; Theory, technique, and cases*. Oxford, UK: John Wiley & Sons

King, N. (1994). The qualitative research interview. In Cassell, C. and Symon, G. (eds) *Qualitative Methods in Organisational Research*. London: Sage.

Kvale, S. and Brinkmann, S. (2009). *Interviewing: Learning the craft of qualitative research interviewing*, 2nd edition. Thousand Oaks, CA: Sage.

Labov, W. (1972). *Language in the Inner City*. Philadelphia, PA: University of Pennsylvania Press.

Labov, W. (2001). *Uncovering the event structure of a narrative*. Paper presented at the Georgetown University Round table, Washington DC. Retrieved 12 May 2013 from www://http.ling.upenn.edu/~wlabov/uesn.pdf.

Marshall, C. and Rossman, G. B. (1999). *Designing Qualitative Research*, 3rd edition. Thousand Oaks, CA: Sage.

Potter, J. and Hepburn, A. (2008). Qualitative interviews in psychology: Problems and possibilities. *Qualitative Research in Psychology*, 2(4), 281–307

Powney, J. and Watts, M. (1987). *Interviewing in Educational Research*. London: Routledge.

Rapley, T. (2011). 'Some pragmatics of data analysis' in Silverman, D. (ed.) *Qualitative Research,* 3rd edition. London: Sage.

Robson, C. (2002). *Real World Research,* 2nd edition. Chichester, UK: Wiley.

Robson, C. (2011). *Real World Research,* 3rd edition. Chichester, UK: Wiley.

Saunders, M., Lewis, P. and Thornhill, A. (2007). *Research Methods for Business Students,* 4th edition. Harlow: Pearson Education Ltd.

Silverman, D. (ed.) (2011). *Qualitative Research,* 3rd edition. London: Sage.

Stephens, N. (2007) Collecting data from elites and ultra elites: telephone and face-to-face interviews with macroeconomists. *Qualitative Research,* 7(2), 203–216.

Ziesel, J. (2006). *Inquiry by Design: Environment/behaviour/neuroscience in architecture, interiors, landscape and planning.* New York: Norton.

# 16

# Considering Case Studies in Project Management

Blaize Reich

*This chapter aims to help the reader produce good case study research in order to raise the probability of high quality publications and thereby to accelerate our knowledge of important issues and phenomena.*

This chapter will help you understand what a case study is and why and when you might choose this methodology when doing research. It discusses the two ways that theory plays into case studies – that is, it is an input or an output – and how to choose the right approach for your topic. It then examines two basic case research designs – single and multiple cases – and gives pointers on how to select good sites to explore your research questions.

At the end of this chapter, the reader can:

- recognise when to use the case study approach;
- understand the role of theory in case study research;
- understand some important decisions in selecting sites for a study of one or more cases.

Keywords: case study, literal replication, theoretical replication

## What is Case Study Research?

There are several other chapters in this reference text which talk about aspects of case research, so we'll limit the discussion in this section to some overview comments that will help you to choose between different research methods. The term 'case study' is a rather loose one, connoting both the unit of analysis (a 'case') and the richness of the data collection plan (case data is usually richer than survey or experimental data, but often less rich than ethnographic data). In this chapter, we'll use the term 'case' to mean the unit of analysis, and leave a discussion of data richness for later. As this is a text for researchers interested in PM, a case might be a project, a programme, a stage of a project or some variation on these themes.

In general, case study research will gather more data than some other research designs (for example, survey, experiment) and will use the data to understand the complexities in a 'case'. It may also gather data over a longer period of time, but this is not a required part of a case study. The steps in case study research are the same as for any other type – defining the question, creating the sample and data-gathering protocols, gathering the data, analysing the data and writing up the findings. Case study research often includes iterations between these steps. For example, you might test the data-gathering protocols with a pilot study and then revise them before going forward. However, the main steps are fairly straightforward.

Note: There are many resources which give guidelines for case study research design. Yin (2009) is probably the best used and cited source and a student of case studies needs to read and understand the principles in this seminal work. This short chapter has been designed to complement, not to replace Yin.

## Why do Case Study Research?

Case study research is very useful when you have a research question that may not have a set of clearly anticipated answers. For example, if I want to know what percentage of companies have project management offices (PMOs), I can survey a sample of the population and then extrapolate from the data. Question is answered. If I want to know how PMOs are structured, I can ask in a survey for respondents to tick off the possible answers or maybe even give me some 'free form' data input on the survey format. Question answered, assuming I can interpret the free form data and put it into a useful format. If I want to understand how a PMO has evolved, I need to talk to several people in a company, create a timeline and understand critical decisions and triggers. To answer this question, I need richer data and a longer timeline, therefore a case study is appropriate.

It is often said that case studies are 'exploratory' and therefore only good to be used at the beginning of the research into a phenomenon like agile PM. I disagree, although case studies can be useful at this point in the research arc. They can also be useful when there are pockets in a well-researched topic which we don't understand. Saying that a research question is 'exploratory' and therefore should be done through case study method isn't a short cut to start a data-gathering step without understanding what is already known about the topic. We'll talk more about this in the section on Research Design.

Case study research is useful for building theory or testing existing theory. For example, one might want to understand what factors are associated with successful completion of public private partnerships. By gathering data using a case study approach, participants can tell the researcher what they view as the most important elements and why. By aggregating these data over several cases, the researcher might be able to identify two or three dominant causal paths. On the other hand, if there is a theory that predicts a certain type of control should be used when the project has certain characteristics, one might use cases in new contexts to explore the boundaries of this theory.

Before going further, I'd like to state my bias about the purpose of research in general, and about case studies as a research method. Although I am generally curious about how projects are conducted, the bottom line for me is to understand how to advance the practice of PM. In other words I am interested in understanding the factors which might predict success in PM. This approach probably comes from the 20 years I spent as an IT practitioner, consultant and project manager, where one is constantly trying to achieve certain outcomes. The result of this perspective is that I always ask 'so what?' when someone pitches an idea to me. And I also look for a dependent variable, regardless of the study type. Case studies for me are opportunities to understand why and how certain outcomes (that is, dependent variables) happen.

## Role of Theory

In this section, I'll outline three approaches to answer the question: what is the role of theory in case studies? As said earlier, theory can be an input or an output. It's important that you decide what your approach will be and structure the study accordingly. Among others, Eisenhardt (1989, 2007) has written important articles on how to build theory from case studies. Dubé and Paré (2003) have provided guidelines on how to do a positivist case study.

If very little is known about your topic area or if you want to take a new approach to exploring a research question, then doing a multiple case study might be useful. You will design the sample to be very representative of a certain population, ask many questions and leave lots of opportunities for participants to provide unstructured input. Your analysis will consist of looking for themes in the data and proposing a theory from it.

If there are several studies that relate to your research question, but no strong theory on the topic, then you might construct a model which incorporates what the literature suggests. You can also add elements that may not be reported but that you theoretically argue should be examined. The data-gathering protocol (that describes who the participants are, what questions you ask) then is organised around the model, with opportunities for open-ended discussion and observation to discover new elements. The data analysis will then 'test' the model, adding in the new elements, to propose an overarching theory.

If there is a specific theory relating to your research question and your research domain (for example, projects), then the case study approach might not be appropriate. Perhaps you should do a more focused study to examine certain aspects of the theory. However, if the theory was created for a different domain (for example, a traditional organisation rather than a project organisation), then a case study approach might be used to test the applicability of this theory in a project domain. If this is the situation, then some upfront thinking about the differences between traditional and project organisations might suggest some additional variables to add to the model so that you don't just use the elements in the original theory. Your analysis will then confirm or refute the theory or suggest a new theoretical model.

Research is trying to describe, explain and ultimately to predict reality, whether you believe it to be socially constructed or absolute. You have to decide where on the continuum your research falls, and design your study appropriately. Making this decision comes after a careful examination of the existing research in your own and surrounding domains. For example, if you are interested in understanding something about search and rescue projects, you might consider that they are urgent, involve loss of life and are often unique situations. Therefore you might look for insights in the literature examining other high-velocity projects such as product recall projects or military operations projects. In this way, you learn from previous research and carry on the tradition of building on it.

At this point in your research, you are ready to be clear about the 'contribution' that your study will make to existing knowledge. The clearer you can be about your purpose, the easier it will be to craft a research design that will fulfill it. I suggest that when you can articulate your contribution, you write a half-page memo, laying out several elements:

What the importance of your topic area is (who cares about it and why?)

> Example. Approximately 9 per cent of IT projects are abandoned before implementation. Representing $X billion of investment that is wasted. Understanding how this loss can be reduced will have a positive effect on the national economy.

What is generally known about it (highlights of existing research).

> Example. Research shows that lack of executive support and scope control impact the completion rate of IT projects.

What you want to understand (your 'question').

> Example. Abandonment is a natural occurrence if projects are considered using a population economics lens, in which different projects vie for resources within a firm. My question is, 'Can population economics theory explain project abandonment or are within-project factors more influential?'

What the benefit will be (to research, to practice) after your study.

Example. *A new theoretical lens will be widen the perspectives available to PM researchers and may also be useful to project portfolio management theory. Findings may also influence senior management, who might redouble PM competence or let projects fight for their survival, based on the findings from this study.*

This memo is then your 'pitch'. Discuss it with your supervisor, your trusted peers (you don't want anyone scooping your great ideas) or some reflective practitioners. Get their input, trying not to be defensive. Incorporate their good ideas. If the response you get is generally enthusiastic, go further. If the response is tepid or negative, consider changing topics unless you are very, very wedded to this idea. Any research project (especially a dissertation) represents at least a five-year investment of your time and sweat equity. Be sure you are committed to it and also that there will be interest in it when it is finished so you have a chance to publish it. That's our end game.

In the previous paragraph, I revealed another bias of mine. I believe that research needs to develop new knowledge, not just result in a PhD or MSc or another paper that isn't cited. So I'll be expecting that you are willing to extend yourself, push the boundaries of what we know, and be the world leader in some small corner of your topic. A PhD is partly about learning the craft of research (so whatever you do, you do well) but more importantly it's also your first big opportunity to make a difference and add to our understanding about the world. Don't duck the challenge.

## Case Study Research Design

There are several decisions that need to be made in this step. In this chapter I am not trying to be exhaustive, but rather to cover the most important elements of research design. Assuming that you have read the salient literature, selected a theoretical approach and clarified your potential contribution, the next step is to determine how many and what kind of cases to investigate.

Let's assume that your unit of analysis is a certain type of project, an enterprise software (ES) implementation. You know that these IT-enabled business projects have several important characteristics – they may take over a year to complete, they involve multiple organisations (for example, consultants, vendors and the client), and they rely on business readiness as well as good technology. ESs have been around for many years and so you can't investigate them in general, since there are many studies that have already covered this ground. Perhaps you want to find out if the second or third ES project in an organisation are more successful and less costly – in other words, if there is a 'learning effect' around ES implementations. And further, if there is a learning effect, how can organisations institutionalise this. You study the literature on ES implementations, on learning organisations and consider potential industry effects (that is, the vendors are more knowledgeable over time). You develop a model to guide your investigation. How many cases do you need?

## Single Case Studies

You can do a single case study, if some conditions are in place, including the following:

- a reason why this particular case is worth studying;
- access to many people in the case, including people who may not be with the company anymore;

- access to many documents at the case site, including internal and external, private and public documents.

The first condition is the most important one for a single case study. If there is not a compelling reason why a reader (I am assuming that you will write an article or two about this case) will be interested in this case, don't pursue it. The chances of getting it published are slim. You need an exemplar case – for example a company that has won many awards for IT implementation and has implemented a number of ESs over the years. Or conversely, an organisation that has several ES failures in its history (potentially interesting but very difficult to access). Hanging your study on one case is risky; you may or may not find what you are looking for. So pick an outlier – an organisation that gives you the maximum chance to be successful.

The second and third conditions are secondary considerations, but are also very important. If you are only going to study one organisation, you need the freedom to look at it from many angles – at different times, from different role perspectives, from people who were positively and negatively affected by the history at play. You need to get approval from the site to explore widely.

## Multiple Case Studies

This topic is where you can really use help from regular guidebooks, such as Yin (2009). I'll give you a brief overview. You do a multiple case study when the value of having several units to examine outweighs the cost of collecting the data ... how's that for an economist's view of research?

You might consider a 'theoretical replication'. In this case all of the cases share some key characteristics (for example, they all are complex ES projects and all delivered on time, on budget), but you are not sure what or how several factors contributed to these outcomes. For example, for my first research project, I was interested in what factors influenced competitive advantage. I developed a sample of ten first-movers – companies that had created the first instance of a customer-facing IT product in their industry in Canada. I then gathered data (through multiple interviews and document collection) about factors that the literature predicted would influence this outcome. Analysis of the data showed that six of the factors were present in most of the cases. This finding was used to start developing theory about obtaining competitive advantage using IT (Reich and Huff, 1991).

Alternatively, you might use a 'literal replication strategy' if you don't know what outcomes to expect, but you are interested in looking at a specific factor or two. For example, let's say you are interested in how team size and cultural diversity affects engagement levels within a team. You might develop a sample with 12 (or eight or four) project cases – three that are small and diverse, three that are large and diverse, three that are small and homogeneous and three that are large and homogeneous. This is a little like designing an experiment, although we are not going to do any manipulation. The trick here is that you need to hold all other important variables constant. For example, you should probably stick to a single kind of project (for example, all marketing projects) in a single country (to hold country level influences constant). You might be able to source all the cases within a single company; there are pros and cons of this approach. On the positive side, you have held company level influence to a minimum. On the negative side, there may be organisational learning over time that you have to account for and need to select a company that is a good performer overall. There is not much appetite to take 'how to' lessons from a poor performer.

When I did my PhD, I again did a multiple case study. In this case I was interested in learning about factors that influenced alignment of business and IT strategies (Reich and Benbasat, 2000). I held as much constant as possible – all cases were insurance company strategic business units, all but one sold either individual or group insurance in Canada. I got my PhD and learned a lot in the process, but I probably should have thrown the one investment business unit out since IT was less salient to it than to the other units. What I learned from this is to be especially cautious when selecting case sites – if you are trying to create new knowledge you must be ruthless about putting together a great sample. It can be very difficult to do this – my colleague took more than ten months to get approval to study certain international joint ventures. In the end, her research was very compelling and highly cited.

Other chapters in this reference text will help you gain entry to a research site and analyse the data when you have gathered it. On this latter point, Miles, Huberman and Soldaña (2013) have produced a new version of the seminal text on qualitative data analysis and presentation.

I know from first-hand experience that case research is time consuming and difficult work. However, it is fascinating to piece together the stories about important decisions and outcomes in a project context. The rich data that you collect from case sites helps deepen your understanding of organisational reality and helps you grow both as a researcher and educator.

## Tips and Exercises

### TIPS FOR STUDENTS:

- Case studies are difficult to successfully execute since you need to obtain access to the right organisations, to conduct interviews with many different types of people and to have patience during an often long data analysis process. They look easy, but are not.
- After you have done the first interview or the first day of interviews, make notes about what was interesting, what you didn't expect, what you think you did well and poorly, and how you might change your methods or questions for the next day. Make this reflection a regular practice and check with your mentors if you are having trouble. This will help you improve as you continue and give you the chance to gather some really interesting data.
- Read some exemplar case studies before embarking on your own. This will give you a sense of what is required to be first class and will help you have the patience to stick to your research design goals even if they are difficult to achieve.

### TIPS FOR SUPERVISORS:

- Case studies are well suited for students that are comfortable with ambiguity and multiple explanations for the same data. If your student tends to interpret data very literally, case studies might be very frustrating for both of you.
- Try to match the level of analysis (for example, project, team, individual) with the level of analysis that the student has experienced in professional work or school work. For example, if the student has only ever been a junior person on a team, expecting him/her to interview the project sponsor might be too big of a stretch.
- Help your student analyse the data early in the data collection process so that corrections can be made in the protocol if necessary. Have the first interviews transcribed and then ask the student to develop some ideas from them relating to the research questions. You will then be able to guide the student's interviewing techniques so that interesting results are possible.

EXERCISES

1.  You have access to a very large organisation with several product divisions, each creating a different kind of software product (for example, accounting, marketing, mobile apps). Within the divisions, there are multiple project teams which use traditional, agile or hybrid methods to develop their products. Develop three case-based research designs based on the data from this organisation using the concepts in this chapter.

2.  Using another methodology (for example, survey research), design another research project based on the data from the organisation in question 1. What questions can you answer with a survey that you cannot access with case research?

3.  Many companies are investing in social media. You are interested in the ways in which they organise these initiatives and if there is a project methodology that works better than others. How would you design a research study to examine this topic? Tip: if you haven't thought about a dependent variable, think again.

# References

Dubé, L. and Paré, G. (2003). Rigor in Information Systems Positivist Case Research: Current practices, trends and recommendations. *MIS Quarterly*, 27(4), 597–636.

Eisenhardt, K. M. (1989). Building Theories from Case Study Research. *The Academy of Management Review*, 14(4), 532–550.

Eisenhardt, K. M. (2007). Theory Building from Cases: Opportunities and Challenges. *Academy of Management Journal*, 50(1), 25–32.

Miles M. B., Huberman, A. M. and Soldaña, J. (2013). *Qualitative Data Analysis: A methods sourcebook*, 3rd edition. Sage Publications.

Reich, B. H. and Benbasat, I. (2000) Factors that Influence the Social Dimension of Alignment between Business and Information Technology Objectives. *MIS Quarterly*, 24(1), 81–111.

Reich, B. H. and Huff, S. (1991). Customer-Oriented Strategic Systems. *Journal of Strategic Information Systems*, 1(1), 29–37.

Yin, R. K. (2009). *Case Study Research: Design and methods*, 4th edition. Sage Publications Inc.

# 17

# Linking Theory and Practice in Using Action-Oriented Methods

Shankar Sankaran and Bob Dick

*We felt that there is a great opportunity for PM researchers to use dialectical approaches such as action research, action learning and action science to link theory and practice.*

The aim of this chapter to provide doctoral students a practical way to use action-oriented methods – action research, action learning and action science – to carry out research in and about projects while making a theoretical contribution to the field. After briefly explaining each of these methods the chapter discusses ways in which these methods can be combined to provide synergy. The chapter discusses some common data collection strategies used with these methods, also pointing out that other methods of data collection are welcome if the research project requires such data. Action research is often criticised for not being scientific and therefore a discussion on how it can be made rigorous and valid at both data collection and data analysis stages is discussed. Action researchers often do not write up their research using the conventions used in conventional quantitative and qualitative research theses or dissertations. A section is therefore devoted to discussing how to write up action research in novel ways. The chapter includes several reflective exercises to guide the reader (student or researcher) as well as some tips for supervisors of action research projects.

At the end of this chapter, the reader can:

* understand the basics of action-oriented methods and how they can be used in a research project;
* justify adequately why action-oriented methods are applicable to your research project;
* establish a model/process to carry out your research applying action-oriented methods.

Keywords: action research, action learning, action science, dialectical approaches

## Characteristics of Action-Oriented Methodologies

Action research is not a single method or methodology but refers to a variety of approaches that involve working collaboratively with people facing a concern that needs some deliberate action to address it. Such collaboration creates buy-in for implementing the change that accompanies the action. The people who are working together with the action researcher are treated as co-researchers rather than informants. Action research is a cyclical process alternating between action and reflection upon the action to initiate further action converging towards improving the situation of concern.

For more information about various types of action research approaches, refer to the The SAGE handbook of action research (Reason and Bradbury, 2008). In this chapter, we will discuss an action research process that has been found useful in management and organisational research and is used in PM research.

## Action Research

There are several definitions of action research in the literature. This chapter will discuss a few of these to tease out the common characteristics of action-oriented approaches.

The Handbook of action research defines action research as:

> a participatory, democratic process concerned with developing practical knowing in the pursuit of worthwhile human purposes, grounded in a participatory worldview which we believe is emerging at this historical moment. It seeks to bring together action and reflection, theory and practice, in participation with others, in the pursuit of practical solutions of pressing concern to people and more generally the flourishing of individual persons and their communities. (Reason and Bradbury: p. 4)

This definition covers a wide variety of approaches under the umbrella of action research. From a PM research point of view, the key features of importance are:

- it is participatory and democratic as well as grounded in a participatory worldview;
- ilt brings together action and reflection;
- it values practical solutions or knowledge that addresses a concern or concern(s);
- it brings together theory and practice;
- it helps individuals, groups and communities.

For the purposes of this chapter we will use a simpler and more practical definition of action research:

> Action research is a flexible spiral process that allows action (change, improvement) and research (understanding, knowledge) to be achieved at the same time. The understanding allows more informed change and at the same time is informed by that change. People affected by the change are usually involved in the action research. This allows the understanding to be widely shared and the change to be pursued with commitment. (Dick, 2001: p 1) See Figure 17.1.

There are similarities between the two definitions. From the latter definition, we can add a few more points about action research.

- it often involves a change or changes to improve the situation;
- action and research happen at the same time;
- people affected by the change are involved in the research that builds commitment;
- the process is not linear but happens in a spiral (improvements happen in a cycle).

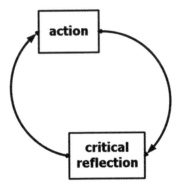

**Figure 17.1    Action research process (Dick, 2001: p. 21)**

While most action research is participatory there may be occasions in which participation could be limited (for example, an organisation in which action research is being conducted does not provide time for participation).This would then relegate the people involved in the research to an informant's role.While action research often happens in cycles, the cycles may not exactly take place as planned and a certain overlap between cycles can be experienced in practice. However, it is good not to skip the reflection phase and resist the temptation to jump into action as managers often do.

## Entry and Contracting

You could be engaged in action research as an external researcher (that is, helping to address a problem that you are not affected by) or as an internal researcher (that is, addressing a problem which affects you as well). In both cases gaining entry and establishing a contract for the research is important.

As part of the entry and contracting process, it is advisable to identify key stakeholders who are affected by the problem at the start. You would have learnt about stakeholder management applied to projects.You can apply some of these techniques that you have learnt to identify also to your research. Chapter 21 in this book has dealt with negotiating research sites and access which can provide good ideas about this phase of your research for you to consider.

The stakeholders in an action research situation could be clients (with whom you have contracted to do your research), direct or primary stakeholders who would be affected by your research in some way as well as indirect or secondary stakeholders who have a stake in your research but may not be directly affected by it. As action research involves change and understanding, you may like to separate the stakeholders as supporters and information providers. Your relationship with them is likely to differ based on which group they fall into.

Once you have identified your stakeholders it will be useful to set some time aside to build the appropriate relationship with them prior to contracting. You should continue to build the relationship as you engage in the research activities. As action research is often carried out to take action or achieve outcomes it is good to negotiate the goals of your engagement with the stakeholders as well as your respective roles.This is necessary to build and sustain commitment.

In order to set goals, it may be necessary to conduct some initial investigation with the client and direct stakeholders. This may take the form of interviews or group discussions. This is the stage at which the level of participation can be ascertained and negotiated.This engagement also has the benefit of building relationships for the future. Interviewing each stakeholder provides in-depth information on his or her needs and fears. You should also endeavour to have group discussions to understand group dynamics, which could be important.

With stakeholders who are not directly involved but have an impact on your research you could ask them to appoint representative(s) with whom you can engage. It is best to persuade the representative to be actively involved rather than speak for the group of stakeholders they represent when you engage with them.

Action research works best when the research project involves changing a situation with the participants as co-researchers and includes a reflective process as opposed to other approaches that attempt to link theory and practice.

Let us now look at two other action-oriented strategies that were mentioned in the abstract of this chapter.

## Action Learning

Action learning can often be combined with action research when an action research project requires carrying our several embedded projects. These projects also contribute the required data for the research. Later in this chapter we will suggest a model to set up a doctoral research programme where the two can be combined fruitfully.

McGill and Brockbank (2004) define action learning as a 'continuous process of learning and reflection that happens with the support of a group or "set" of colleagues, working on real issues, with the intention of getting things done. The voluntary participants in the group or "set" learn with and from each other and take forward an important issue with the support of the other members of the set' (p. 11).

As the originator of action learning, Reg Revans, who was a physicist, uses the term 'set' and also an equation $L = P + Q$ while describing action learning. In the formula L is learning, P is programmed instruction (for example, courses that you attend) and Q is questioning insight (Revans, 1982). Revans strongly suggests that P is often inadequate to address today's problems as it is based on yesterday's knowledge. He believes that insightful questioning by peers contributes to 90 per cent of learning that occurs during action learning.

To carry out an action learning project you need to work on a problem of mutual concern for a 'set' (normally recommended to be between five to eight members) supported by a 'set adviser' or facilitator. The set advisor's role is to help the set follow the action learning process. He/she may have a directive role at the start, becoming less involved as the set gains experience with the process and leave the set if it becomes self-managing.

The action learning set is expected to meet at regular intervals to address problem(s) of the members of the set. For example, if your action learning project is aimed at reducing quality issues in a project, the set would work to find the best way to address this immediately. It will also reflect on why the problem occurred in the first place and recommend processes that would prevent them from occurring in the future.

In an action learning set meeting, there could be one or more 'clients' or 'problem owners' who take responsibility to act on the problem. Sometimes a 'sponsor' is also present during the set meetings. The sponsor is usually someone who has the power or influence to clear obstacles in the path of the 'problem owner'. This is similar to the role we expect of a project sponsor. In an action learning intervention, in which one of the authors was involved, the sponsor was the CEO of the organisation. He was also interested in developing managers to take on senior positions in his organisation through what they learnt through action learning.

When an action learning set meets, usually one or more of the 'problem owners' would explain his/her problem. The other members of the set will ask questions to assist the 'problem owner' to probe his/her problem further. The set members would be asked to avoid asking questions that could provide a solution. Questions in an action learning meeting would be open probing questions to help the problem owner dig deeper. This is often compared to 'peeling an onion'. Sometimes the set members will also deliberately ask challenging questions, when they observe that the 'problem owner' is not thinking deeply enough, in an effort to get the 'problem owner' to reflect and move towards a solution. Towards the end of a set meeting, 'problem owners' will be asked to commit to actions they will undertake before the set meets next. They will also be expected to report on actions in between set meetings.

## Action Science

Action science can be used as part of an action research project or on its own to study one's own practice. This could be useful for a project manager or project team member to improve their effectiveness. Action science is a useful strategy for what is known as 'first-person action research as an inquiring approach to his or her own life' (Reason and Bradbury, 2008: p. 6). Action science became prominent by the work carried out by Chris Argyris (Argyris and Schön, 1974, Argyris, Putnam and Smith, 1985). These researchers' aim in developing action science was to find ways to improve professional effectiveness.

Raelin (1999: p. 116) sums up action science by stating that 'people can improve their interpersonal organisational effectiveness by exploring the hidden beliefs that drive their actions'.

According to the website explaining action science (http://www.actionscience.com/actinq. htm#theory), learning through action science takes place 'when individuals in groups detect and correct gaps between descriptive claims and practical outcomes'. While there is no prescribed process to carry out action science, similar to action learning, there are some basic concepts and tools that can be useful in practising it. The first is to distinguish between 'espoused theory' and 'theory-in-practice'.

Espoused theories are theories that we often think we adopt whereas theory-in-practice are theories that we actually use when faced with a situation involving taking action. Often we are unaware of the difference between our espoused theory and our theory-in-practice. One of the reasons why managers exhibit this incongruence between the two theories is because they are under some threat or embarrassment. We also have governing values that often guide our behaviour. In a recent class that one of the authors taught, the students exhibited defensive behaviour during a negotiation game even after being taught collaborative strategies on negotiating.

Another useful concept in action science is the modelling of theories-in-use. Model 1 theory results in very rational behaviour, focusing on winning and goal achievement and being a 'hero' hiding negative feelings. This could result in mistrust, defensiveness and cause single-loop learning. Single-loop learning forces us maintain the status quo and take actions in line with our Model 1 governing variables.

When we put Model 2 theory in practice, we are open to information, believe in freedom of choice and commit ourselves to the choices we make. This results in reducing our defensiveness, increasing collaboration and offering a high degree of freedom of choice among other benefits. It also facilitates double-loop learning where we question our goals to accept changing of our governing variables. This would lead to effective problem solving and decision making.

One of the tools useful in action science is the use of a two-column analysis or often called the 'left- and right-hand columns'. To experiment with such an analysis divide a sheet of paper into two columns to write on. On the right-hand column record your observations during a conversation or your interaction with a group (or write it up as a recollection). On the left-hand column record your own thoughts about what is *really* happening.

Have a look at 'Two Column Analysis' in (Dick and Dalmau 1999: p.61-68) for more information about this tool.

## Combining Action-Oriented Methods

While action research, action learning and action science exhibit similarities they are different in some ways. Table 17.1 shows some of the differences if you want to learn more about their philosophical basis and beliefs. Chapter 5 in the book discusses epistemology and ontology that would be good to refer to when you review Table 17.1. You should take precautions to have the philosophical basis in mind when you apply them together.

Table 17.1    **Philosophical basis of action research, action learning and action science (adapted from Raelin, 1999: pp. 120–121)**

| Characteristic | Action Research | Action Learning | Action Science |
|---|---|---|---|
| Philosophical basis | Gestalt psychology, pragmatism, democracy | Learning from experience, action research, and other eclectic views | Lewinian action research, Dewey's theory of inquiry |
| Epistemology | Knowing through doing and applying discoveries | Problem solving and also problem framing | Reflecting-in-action, making explicit tacit theories-in-use |
| Methodology | Interactive cycles of problem defining, data collection, taking action or implementing a solution, followed by further testing | Cycles of framing, action, reflection, concluding, and reframing | Reflection on there-and-then and here-and-now reasoning, with an emphasis on online interactions |

## Vignette – Combining Action-Oriented Approaches in Project Management

Sam was a senior manager of a centre managing global projects in a Japanese multinational company when he enrolled in a PhD programme. An opportunity to do his research came up when his organisation faced a severe problem that required investigation and action. He decided to use action research as it promised to deliver both management and research outcomes. He wanted to convince his management to use action research to implement change in the way work was being allocated and executed in projects. He was unsure if the management would support using a research methodology. He then learnt about action learning and found that the process had similarities to action research. He also observed that action learning was similar to the *kaizen* or continuous improvement programmes adopted by the company. So he decided to use action learning principles with a group of managers who were involved in changing the way project work was carried out by the firm.

The reflections from the meetings he had with the action learning set, formed with his managers, became the source of data for his action research project. During the change process, Sam wondered if his managers were actually interested in action learning and not just following his instructions, which reflected the company culture. So he used the left- and right-hand column tool borrowed from action science to examine his use of power during the action learning meetings. This helped him to observe his own model of theory-in-use and the governing values he was using. By reflecting on the outputs of the left- and right-hand column entries he was able to improve the way he managed people. Sam was thus able to use action learning to achieve management outcomes, action research to achieve research outcomes and action science to achieve personal outcomes in his research.

## Data Collection Strategies

There are no set data collection methods that you have to use in an action research project. The methods that you use should fit the type of data you want to collect. Action research generally uses qualitative methods. Therefore methods used in qualitative research such as interviews, observations and focus groups are often used during data collection. It is also not unusual to use quantitative methods if they become necessary.

## Vignette: Systems Analyst Using Action Research

Shirley was a systems analyst who wanted to use action research to improve the way knowledge was used by her organisation. The company had several electronic knowledge-sharing systems in place but employees were found not to use them. She decided to conduct a survey to analyse how information and knowledge was used by employees who were geographically spread out. After analysing the survey using statistical analysis, she found some issues that the employees faced in sharing knowledge via the company's intranet. She then proposed and carried out key projects using an action research approach (in collaboration with key stakeholders) that improved knowledge collection, processing and dissemination in her organisation. Perry and Zuber-Skerritt (1992: p. 204) proposed a model to conduct postgraduate research using action research that has been found useful by several students. One of the authors of this chapter who was investigating management development in his organisation using action research used the model shown in Figure 17.2 adapted from the Perry and Zuber-Skerritt model. In this model the doctoral research process is considered to be the thesis action research cycle. As part of the 'act' phase of the thesis action research, the researcher set up core action learning projects that acted as the source of data for research. The writing of the thesis was also set up as a thesis writing cycle that is informed by the reflections from the thesis action research cycle.

While action researchers can use a variety of research methods, we will point out a few that could be particularly useful in action research projects.

## Convergent Interviewing

In a convergent interview, you will have to establish rapport with the informants, just as you would in a normal interview, to make them feel comfortable before introducing yourself and explaining the purpose of the interview. You will also inform who will have access to the information.

You then ask an opening question to get the informant talking. The question should be quite general to elicit a variety of information. As an example you may say,

> *I want to know more about the project you are working on right now. I would like to know what you like about working on this project. Is there something you do not like while working on this project?*

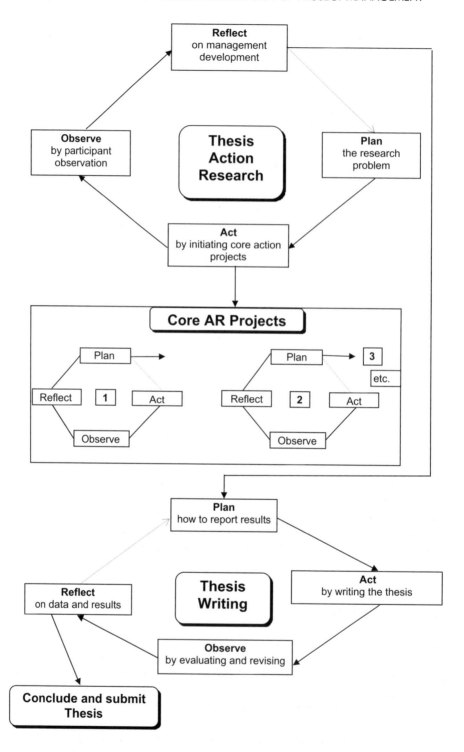

**Figure 17.2    Action research model for a doctoral programme**

Source: Perry & Zuber-Skerrit (1992: p. 204)

Get the informant talking for about 30 to 45 minutes and encourage them to talk by affirmations, paraphrasing and seeking more information when they are unclear or drifting. It is important to pay complete attention through active listening.

Towards the end of the interview, you will probe further. The questions that you use for probes should be prepared in advance. They may also be questions that have been prompted by earlier interviews you have conducted. At the end of the interview, it is good to ask the informant to summarise key points they have mentioned.

If it is possible, it is good to pair up with someone else to carry out convergent interviews and share the interviews. Discuss your summaries with each other after you have conducted one interview each. Sampling is very important if you want to increase the rigour of your action research. To ensure a diverse sample try to interview people who you expect to have quite opposing views on the topic. We will discuss why this is important when we discuss rigour in action research later.

- Have a look at *Questions for critical reflection* by Bob Dick [Online]. Available at http://www.aral. com.au/resources/iview.html

## Rich Pictures

Rich pictures, often associated with soft systems methodology, are a way to elicit information about multiple perspectives that stakeholders may have about a problem being investigated.

Rich pictures (situation summaries) are used to depict complicated situations. They are an attempt to encapsulate the real situation through a no-holds-barred, cartoon representation of all the ideas covered already – layout, connections, relationships, influences, cause-and-effect, and so on. One way to use 'rich pictures' in an action research project is to divide your stakeholders into groups (initially into similar groups, for example, same department of an organisation) and ask them to draw a rich picture of a problem of concern. Then ask the different groups to walk around to hear an explanation about the issues uncovered by the rich picture. This will help them to appreciate the different views about the situation.

A good book to refer to about the use of soft systems thinking is by Checkland and Poulter (2006) entitled *Learning for action: A short definitive account of soft systems methodology and its use for practitioners, teachers and students.*

## Rigour in Action Research

Action research is often conducted as qualitative research within an interpretivist paradigm. Therefore, action researchers tend to use techniques recommended to increase validity in qualitative research. A commonly used technique is one suggested by Guba and Lincoln (1985, 1994) to ensure trustworthiness and authenticity. Trustworthiness was proposed as an equivalent to ensuring validity and reliability in quantitative research. This could be achieved by establishing credibility (internal validity), transferability (external validity), dependability (reliability) and confirmability (objectivity). Authenticity, which was added later by Lincoln and Guba (1994) was expected to address political implications from the research. Bryman (2007: p. 414) explains authenticity by elaborating as follows:

- Fairness – Does the research represent different viewpoints of the members in the research setting fairly?

- Ontological authenticity – Does it promote better understanding?
- Educative authenticity – Does it allow multiple perspectives to be understood?
- Catalytic authenticity – Does it motivate members who are participating to engage in action to facilitate change?
- Tactical authenticity – Has it empowered members to take action?

Triangulation is another way of improving validity in qualitative research. One way of achieving triangulation, a metaphor borrowed from navigation, is to use different methods to collect data. Other forms of triangulation include investigator triangulation (recall we suggested pairing up on convergent interviews), theoretical triangulation (use of alternate theoretical stance to interpret data) and data triangulation (collecting data from different sources).

When action research is carried out properly, it has several built-in characteristics that can improve rigour – participation that allows collection of richer data; being action-oriented allowing plans to be tested soon after and its responsive and emergent nature. Shorter action cycles also help to increase rigour.

## Data Analysis

The analysis of data in action research will usually match the type of data collected. For example, if you use interviews to collect data you could use content analysis or grounded theory techniques using coding and memos to develop themes.

The main data analysis in action research occurs during the critical reflection phase of an action research cycle. Dick (1999b) suggests a way to use multiple data sets to analyse data collected in an action research. Figure 17.3 summarises the process.

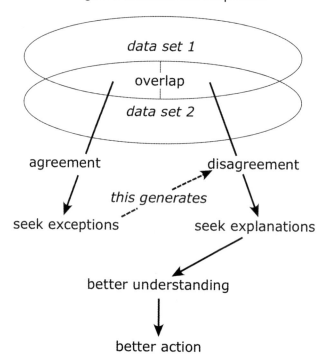

**Figure 17.3    Analysing data sets in action research**

The basic process is the continuous comparison of data you collect from subsequent interventions and analysing agreements and disagreements between the data sets. If there is agreement look to seek exceptions that can occur and if you find disagreements seek explanations. This could lead to a better understanding and better action in the next cycle.

Silverman (2006) also suggests the use of constant comparison and looking at deviant data (cases or data sets) as a means of increasing the credibility of qualitative research. These can be used in action research to confirm and/or disconfirm findings to increase the rigour.

## Writing Up

Action research theses are often written up in creative and innovative ways without following the conventions suggested for traditional doctoral research theses/dissertations.

The authors have encountered a number of ways in which action research theses have been written up while supervising or examining doctoral theses. Often action research theses are written up in the first person as the researcher is deeply involved in the research with the participants (Sankaran 1999). The literature review in action research continues through the research as more literature becomes relevant as the research is carried out. Often the literature is also used as a means of triangulation. Some researchers also write a chapter for each cycle of action research, where the data collected is described, analysed and discussed, instead of having separate data collection, analysis and discussion chapters. It is also common to find a chapter describing the personal learning of the researcher. Often pictures are embedded in the chapters to visually show what went on during the research.

Marshall (2008: pp. 688–693) recommends the following practices in writing about action research:

- accept and seek to express what is rather than what should be;
- employ disciplines and respect emergence;
- invoke the writer in you and your own direct voice, whatever shape it takes;
- create resonant processes and conditions for writing;
- defend emergent form, claim authority;
- value the imaginal and metaphorical guides to form.

## Tips and Exercises

### TIPS FOR STUDENTS

- Read a paper by Kath Fisher and Renata Phelps (2006) titled 'Recipe or performing art? Considering challenging conventions for writing action research theses'.
- Do a search on the web about search conference or download the paper http://www. elementsuk.com/libraryofarticles/searchconference.pdf. Search for other methods that you might use to bring people together. Do a search on 'large group intervention' if you are unfamiliar. Or have a look at *The change handbook: The definitive resource on today's best methods for engaging whole systems* by Peggy Holman (2012) or *Large group interventions: Engaging the whole system for rapid change* by Barbara Bunker and Billie Alban (1997).
- Think about some questions you may ask in an action learning set meeting. How will they be different to the questions you usually ask at your meetings? Check out the website http://www. actionlearningassociates.co.uk/resources/vanbriefing.php to look at some typical questions to

ask. Have a look at *Action learning for managers* by Mike Pedler (2008) or *The action learning handbook* by Ian McGill and Anne Brockbank (2004). You can also find some resources at the International Foundation of Action Learning site http://ifal.org.uk/.

- Read the book titled *The Reflective Practitioner: How Professionals Think in Action* by Donald Schön (Schön 1983) and differentiate between 'reflection-in-action' (pages 49 to 69) and 'reflection-on-action' (pages 276 to 278)

## TIPS FOR SUPERVISORS

- Action research often does not require a considerable amount of time for upfront reading to find gaps in the literature. A literature review is often required in many universities to confirm candidature. Finding a balance between how much of the literature needs to be reviewed upfront and how much should be read and used during the research needs to be considered.
- Action researchers need to be sceptical about what they find and continuously attempt to disconfirm what they find to increase rigour. So it is good to pose questions to your students when they get excited about what they find.
- You should encourage your students to analyse data as they go rather than pile it up to analyse at the end. This also encourages critical reflection.
- Critical reflection is important. You should encourage your students to develop skills of reflection. Encouraging them to keep a journal or diary and reflect on their own actions during the research could help. Have a look at *Questions for critical reflection* by Bob Dick [Online]. Available at http://www.aral.com.au/resources/reflques.html. Encourage your students to think about how they will write up action research. You should, however, caution them about how much latitude examiners may allow.
- Encourage your students to enrol in a course teaching action research where they will have an opportunity to engage with other students. An open-learning programme called AREOL (action research and evaluation online) facilitated by Bob Dick is offered twice a year. See http://www.aral.com.au/areol/areolind.html.

## EXERCISES

1. Make a list of all the techniques you have read or experienced in conducting an analysis of stakeholders. Do a quick reflection of successful and not so successful engagement with stakeholders. What did you learn from them?

2. At this time, you may also want to think about the types and quality of participation in your engagement. You would have to try and work towards a deep engagement with direct stakeholders (unless circumstances do not allow this). Sometimes, if you have a very large group to deal with, you may have to develop strategies to work with them in small groups periodically. A large group intervention process that can be used to achieve this is a 'search conference'. Search conferences are also recommended in an action research process by Greenwood and Levin (2006).

3. Set up a conversation with someone you are trying to persuade to take some action that is difficult for them. On the right-hand column write down what you said while on the left-hand column write down what you were thinking when you said something. Compare the two after the conversation. What differences did you find? What was your theory-in-use? What governing variable guided your conversation? For more information about action science have a look at http://www.actionscience.com/actinq.htm#theory. Read also *Values*

*in action: Applying the ideas of Argyris and Schön*, by Bob Dick and Tim Dalmau (1999). Take a look at some tools that can help to analyse mental models in Chapter 33 of the *Fifth discipline fieldbook: Strategies and tools for building a learning organisation* by Peter Senge and Associates (1994).

4. Think of a topic you want to conduct a convergent interview about in your own organisation. It would be good if you can find a controversial topic that people are passionate about. Think of an opening question as well as some probe questions you would ask. How will you ensure that you will get a diverse sample?

5. Consider how you will remember the key points from a convergent interview without recording the interview or taking notes as one of the authors of this chapter does. See http://www.mindtools.com/memory.html to develop some techniques for this. This will help you focus better on the interview without being distracted.

# References

Argyris, C., Putnam, R. and Smith, D. (1985). *Action Science: Concepts, methods, and skills for research and intervention*, San Francisco, CA: Jossey-Bass.

Argyris, C. and Schön, D. A. (1974). *Theory in Practice: Increasing professional effectiveness*, San Francisco, CA: Jossey Bass.

Bryman, A. and Bell, E. (2007). *Business Research Methods*, 2nd edition, Oxford: Oxford University Press.

Bunker, B. B. and Alban, B. T. (1997). *Large Group Interventions: Engaging the whole system for rapid change*, San Francisco, CA: Jossey Bass.

Checkland, P. and Poulter J. (2006). *Learning For Action: A short definitive account of soft systems methodology and its use for practitioners, teachers and students*, Chichester: John Wiley.

Dick, B. (1999). *Qualitative Action Research: Improving the rigour and economy* [Online]. Available at http://www.uq.net.au/action_research/arp/rigour2.html. Accessed: 24 August 2014.

Dick, B. (2001). Action research: Action *and* research, in S. Sankaran, B. Dick, R. Passfield and P. Swepson, *Effective Change Management Using Action Learning and Action research: Concepts, frameworks, processes and applications*, Lismore, Australia: Southern Cross University Press, pp. 21–27.

Dick, B. and Dalmau, T. (1999). *Values in Action: Applying the ideas of Argyris and Schön*, Brisbane, Australia: Interchange.

Fisher, K. and Phelps, R. (2006). Recipe or performing art?: Challenging conventions for writing action research theses. *Action Research*, 4(2): 143–164.

Greenwood, D. J. and Levin, M. (2006). *Introduction to Action Research: Social research for social change*, 2nd edition. Thousand Oaks, CA: Sage.

Guba, E. G. and Lincoln, Y. S. (1985). *Naturalistic Inquiry*, Thousand Oaks, CA: Sage.

Guba, E. G. and Lincoln, Y. S. (1994). Competing paradigms in qualitative research, in N. K. Denzin and Y. S. Lincoln (eds) *Handbook of Qualitative Research*. Thousand Oaks, CA: Sage, pp. 105–117.

Holman, P. (2012. *The Change Handbook: The definitive resource on today's methods for engaging whole systems*, 2nd edition. San Francisco, CA: Berrett Koehler.

Marshall, J. (2008). Finding form in writing for action research, in P. Reason and H. Bradbury (Eds) *The SAGE Handbook of Action Research*, 2nd edition. London: Sage: pp. 682–694.

McGill, I. and Brockbank, A. (2004). *The Action Learning Handbook: Powerful techniques for education, professional development and training*. London: Routledge-Farmer.

Pedler, M. (2008). *Action Learning for Managers*. Aldershot, UK: Gower.

Perry, C. and Zuber-Skerritt, O. (1992). Action research in graduate management research programs. *Higher Education*, 23(2): 195–208.

Raelin, J. (1999). Preface, *Management Learning*, 30(2): 115–126.

Reason, P. and Bradbury, H. (2008). Introduction, in P. Reason and H. Bradbury (eds) *The SAGE Handbook of Action Research*, 2nd edition. London: Sage, pp. 1–10.

Reason, P. and Bradbury, H. (eds) (2008). *The SAGE Handbook of Action Research*, 2nd edition. London: Sage.

Revans, R. (1982). *The Origins and Growth of Action Learning*. Bromley, Kent: Chartwell-Bratt.

Sankaran S. (1999). An action research study of management learning: Developing local engineering managers of a Japanese multinational company in Singapore. PhD Thesis. Adelaide: University of South Australia.

Schön, D. (1983). *The Reflective Practitioner: How professionals think in action*, New York: Basic Books.

Senge, P. M., Kleiner, A., Roberts, C., Ross, R. B. and Smith, B. J. (1994). *The Fifth Discipline Handbook: Strategies and tools for building a learning organization*, London: Nicholas Brealey.

Silverman, D. (2006). *Interpreting Qualitative Data*, 3rd edition. London: Sage.

# 18

# Dual Cycle Action Research: A Doctor of Project Management (DPM) Research Case Study

Kersti Nogeste

*As a PM practitioner, the option of using a dual cycle action research model which combines practice and research inspired me to undertake and complete a doctoral level research study.*

The research study described in this chapter provides postgraduate PM student researchers and their academic supervisors with an example of how a dual cycle action research model comprising the interlinked cycles of problem solving and research can be used to both conduct PM research and solve a real-life PM problem situation. The dual cycle action research model offers dual appeal to student researchers and their academic supervisors because it enables the student researcher to advance the practice of PM by applying a research methodology which is both practically relevant and academically rigorous.

At the end of this chapter, the reader should be able to:

- demonstrate how action research is incorporated in a research strategy;
- define their role as a researcher conducting action research;
- plan the use of a dual cycle action research model which concurrently addresses a real-life PM problem situation and a PM research interest.

Keywords: Action research, meta-methodology, researcher role, exploratory action research

Drawing on the 'Rethinking project management' network work dating from 2006 (Cicmil, Williams, Thomas and Hodgson, 2006), Walker et al. (2008) called for PM research to address the concept of 'outcomes' at two levels. Firstly, for PM researchers to undertake research which leads to practical outcomes and secondly, for these outcomes themselves to assist 'the PM profession in general to better deliver value (outcomes) rather than just products or services' (Walker et al., 2008: p. 171). The research study described in this chapter, which led to the researcher being awarded a doctoral research degree, addresses both of these calls for outcome focused research – delivering practical research outcomes focused on project outcomes.

The chapter is structured as follows. First, the research idea and question are explained, followed by a description of the research strategy, including the choice of a dual cycle action research model that addresses problem solving and research in parallel. The remainder of the chapter describes how the dual cycle action research model was applied to a series of five case study projects, followed by discussion and conclusions that provide useful insights for postgraduate PM student researchers and their academic supervisors.

## The Research Idea and Question

The doctoral-level PM research study described in this chapter was prompted by a preliminary coursework study that identified two key points. Firstly, that the delivery (or even acknowledgement) of intangible project outcomes was considered a 'point of difference' between good and better project managers (and projects) and secondly, that intangible project outcomes could be directly related to tangible project outputs, despite the absence of a known clear method for doing so. This led to the research idea of *how to improve the way in which project stakeholders define and align intangible project outcomes, with tangible project outputs*.

A further detailed literature review identified that intangibles are of increasing strategic importance to organisations, so it could be expected that the importance of intangibles would cascade from an organisation's strategy through to its operations and projects, in terms of both outcomes and outputs. Therefore, the delivery of an organisation's strategy and the benefits expected of intangibles would be partially dependent upon project stakeholders identifying, prioritising and defining intangible project outcomes and their associated tangible project outputs. The literature review identified that no such method existed; prompting the research question, 'How to improve the way in which project stakeholders define and align intangible project outcomes with tangible project outputs?'

Figure 18.1 illustrates the context and focus of the research idea, research question and corresponding research study (Nogeste, 2006: pp. 133–134).

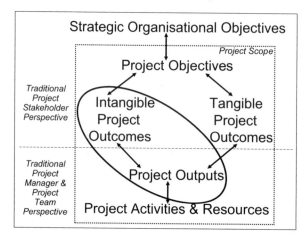

**Figure 18.1**    The context and focus of the research idea, research question and corresponding research study (Nogeste, 2006)

## The Research Strategy

The research strategy framework designed to address the research question of, 'How to improve the way in which project stakeholders define and align intangible project outcomes with tangible project outputs' is illustrated in Figure 18.2. The strategy defined in a top-down manner comprises the realist paradigm, a combination of inductive and deductive reasoning and an action research meta-methodology combined with case study research and grounded theory to collect data via individual and group meetings, group workshops and reference documentation.

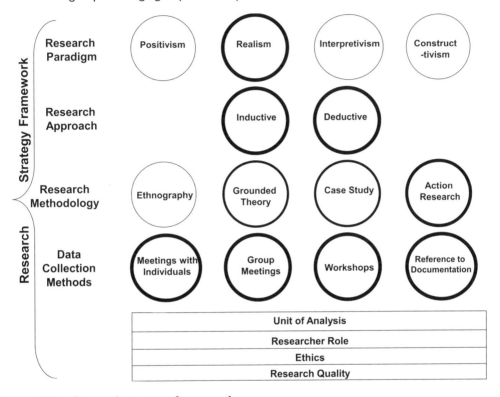

**Figure 18.2   Research strategy framework**

METHODOLOGY

Having considered the qualitative methodologies of ethnography, grounded theory, case study research and action research, the researcher determined that action research was the most suitable methodology for the research study that would focus on a small number of cases, with elements of grounded theory applied in initial exploratory cases. With the inclusion of cases and grounded theory in the larger context of action research, action research could be considered to be the 'meta-methodology' (Dick, 2002b).

UNIT OF ANALYSIS

Based on the definition of a unit of analysis comprising a valid sample of 'people, behaviours, events or processes' (Marshall and Rossman cited in Rocco, 2003), each action research cycle would involve a research client's workplace project, therefore the corresponding unit of analysis would comprise a diverse group of project stakeholders preselected by each research client.

## RESEARCHER ROLE

Based on the typology illustrated by Figure 18.3, it was planned that the researcher would start as an Observer as Participant during the initial exploratory action research cycles, changing to become a Participant as Observer during the major action research cycles.

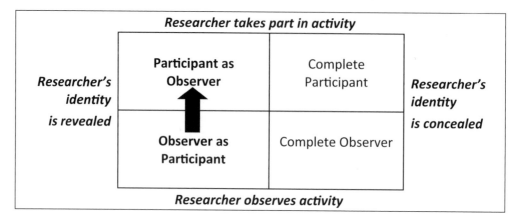

**Figure 18.3    Typology of participant observer researcher roles (Saunders, 2003)**

The change in the balance of participation/observation during the course of a research study is considered acceptable because participant observers could assume a number of roles within the context of case study research, depending on the level of research validity, participation and observation (Yin, 1994).

## ETHICS

Ethical considerations were governed by

- the research design proposal being approved by the RMIT University Human Research Ethics Committee;
- Prescribed Consent Forms being completed and signed by each research participant; defining the 'authentic relationship' between the action researcher and research participant (Coughlan and Coghlan, 2002);
- the original signed paper copies of the consent forms being held on file by the researcher.

## Research Quality

The quality of the proposed research strategy was confirmed by

- conducting a literature review of research quality;

- defining quality requirements based on the literature review (for example, research validity, reliability, rigour and workability);
- assessing the quality of the proposed research strategy according to the defined quality requirements.

## Action Research Methodology

A key characteristic of an action research methodology is that it comprises a series of successive research cycles, which when connected become a spiral (Saunders, 2003: p. 95). With each cycle in turn comprising planning, action and reflection (Dick, 2002a: p. 163). The results of the researcher's reflections in one cycle may result in the planning stage of the following cycle actually being one of replanning; to ensure alignment between the most recent (reflective) learning and the next actions to be taken (Saunders, 2003: p. 94).

Single cycle models are provided by a number of authors, including Dick (2002a: p. 2), McNiff and Whitehead (2000, 2002) and Kemmis and McTaggart (1988: p. 11) who depict the single combined action research cycle as illustrated in Figure 18.4.

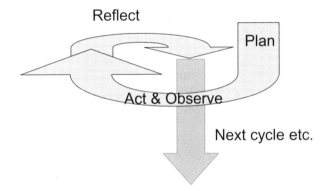

**Figure 18.4    Action research spiral (adapted from Kemmis and McTaggart, 1998: p. 11)**

Single cycle/spiral representations of action research cycles rely on the researcher 'remembering' to maintain a dual focus on research and action. A challenge which can be addressed by dual cycle action research models which provide improved rigour (McKay and Marshall, 2001: p. 57), and 'a ready reminder that reflection and learning are essential aspects of action research' (McKay and Marshall, 2001: p. 57).

Dual cycle models are provided by a number of authors, including Rowley (2003: pp. 133–134), Locke (2001: p. 14), Zuber-Skerritt and Perry (2002) and McKay and Marshall who describe action research comprising the dual cycles of problem solving interest and responsibilities (action/practice) and research interest and responsibilities (research/theory) (McKay and Marshall, 2001: p. 46 and p. 50).

The dual cycles provided by McKay and Marshall can be represented both graphically and in table-text form as per Figure 18.5 and Table 18.1.

Of the available action research models, the researcher elected to base their research on McKay and Marshall's dual cycle model because it was considered to provide an effective and efficient framework.

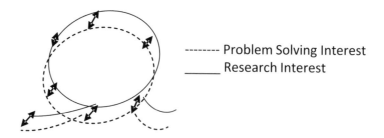

------- Problem Solving Interest
_____ Research Interest

**Figure 18.5**  **Action research viewed as a dual cycle process (adapted from McKay and Marshall, 2001: p. 52)**

**Table 18.1**  **The problem solving interest and research interest in action research (adapted from McKay and Marshall, 2001: pp. 50–51)**

| Step | The Problem Solving Cycle | The Research Interest Cycle |
|------|---------------------------|-----------------------------|
| 1 | Problem identification | Research themes/interests/questions |
| 2 | Reconnaissance/fact finding about problem context stakeholders and so on | Reconnaissance/fact finding in relevant literature |
| 3 | Plan the problem solving activity | Plan and design the research project to answer research questions, hypotheses and so on |
| 4 | Define the action steps | |
| 5 | Implement the action steps | |
| 6 | Reflect upon the problem solving efficacy of the actions | Reflect upon the efficacy of the intervention in terms of research interests |
| 7a | Amend the plan if further change is required and return to step 4 | Amend the plan and design further explanation and research as required and return to step 4 |
| 7b | Exit, if outcomes are satisfactory | Exit, if questions are satisfactorily resolved |

## The Action Research Cycles

The research study described in this chapter comprises a series of five action research cycles as depicted in Figure 18.6. The first two cycles are exploratory action research cycles and the latter three, major action research cycles, which is consistent with a doctoral-level action research project needing to 'progress through at least two or three major action research cycles to make a distinctive contribution to knowledge' (Zuber-Skerritt and Perry, 2002).

In practice, each of the problem solving projects was independent from the others, with exploratory action research cycles 1 and 2 running concurrently to some extent, as did major action research cycles 1, 2 and 3.

## The Exploratory Action Research Cycles

The decision for the initial action research cycle/s to comprise exploratory cases was based on the apparent lack of literature linking intangible project outcomes to tangible outputs combined with the open-ended research question; an approach which is consistent with advice provided by

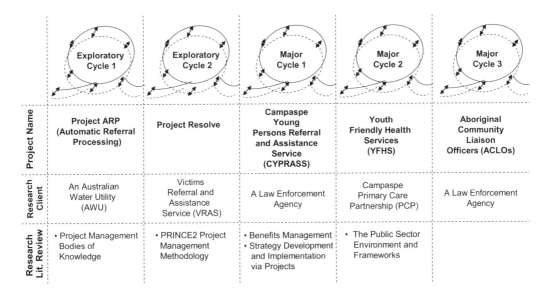

| | Exploratory Cycle 1 | Exploratory Cycle 2 | Major Cycle 1 | Major Cycle 2 | Major Cycle 3 |
|---|---|---|---|---|---|
| **Project Name** | Project ARP (Automatic Referral Processing) | Project Resolve | Campaspe Young Persons Referral and Assistance Service (CYPRASS) | Youth Friendly Health Services (YFHS) | Aboriginal Community Liaison Officers (ACLOs) |
| **Research Client** | An Australian Water Utility (AWU) | Victims Referral and Assistance Service (VRAS) | A Law Enforcement Agency | Campaspe Primary Care Partnership (PCP) | A Law Enforcement Agency |
| **Research Lit. Review** | • Project Management Bodies of Knowledge | • PRINCE2 Project Management Methodology | • Benefits Management • Strategy Development and Implementation via Projects | • The Public Sector Environment and Frameworks | |

Figure 18.6    Overview of action research cycles

a number of authors including Cavana (2001), Saunders (2003), Robson (as quoted in Saunders, 2003) and Sekaran (as cited in Walker, 2002).

The first two exploratory action research cycles comprised the problem solving projects of Project ARP at an Australian Water Utility (AWU) and Project Resolve at the Victorian state government Victims Referral and Assistance Service (VRAS) in Australia; both IT projects for which tangibles and intangibles are interdependent, with 'everything around the technology – everything needed to make the technology do what it is supposed to do – is intangible' (Low and Kalafut, 2002). Exploratory action research cycles 1 and 2 were conducted near concurrently.

For both exploratory action research cycles, at Step 1 the researcher, along with the respective AWU and VRAS project manager, identified the problem interest as being the identification and definition of project intangible outcomes and their associated tangible outputs, with the aim of applying key related learnings to future projects. The research interest was defined by the research question.

For both exploratory action research cycles, Step 2 reconnaissance of the problem comprised the researcher meeting with the respective AWU and VRAS project manager to discuss their real-life project and also reading a combination of publicly available information and commercial in confidence project specific documentation. Step 2 reconnaissance of the research interest comprised the researcher conducting a further literature review of the mention of the terms 'intangible' and 'outcome' in the PRINCE2 PM methodology and the Association for Project Management (APM) and Project Management Institute (PMI) PM bodies of knowledge.

For both exploratory action research cycles, Steps 3 and 4 of the problem solving cycle were similar, starting with the respective AWU and VRAS project manager gaining agreement from a small number of project stakeholders to participate in the research study. For exploratory action research cycle 1 (AWU), the researcher scheduled meetings with individual stakeholders and for exploratory action research cycle 2 (VRAS), the researcher scheduled meetings with groups of like project stakeholders and team members.

For both exploratory action research cycles, Steps 3 and 4 of the research interest cycle comprised the researcher defining the interview format, form of data collection and reporting format. With the format of the interview and data collection being based on the categories of intangibles defined by the UK Government Future and Innovation Unit (Future and Innovation Unit, 2001) that is, leadership, communication, culture/values, innovation, relationship, learning, processes, reputation and trust.

For both exploratory action research cycles, Step 5 was implemented as planned, with the following exceptions.

- the interview/meeting format had to be changed because it did not fit with the way stakeholders defined intangible project outcomes;
- it took far longer than expected to document the interview/meeting results in a format that would support the problem solving activity cycle.

For both exploratory action research cycles, in Step 6 when reflecting on the problem solving cycle, the respective AWU and VRAS project manager considered the problem of identifying and defining expected intangible project outcomes and their associated tangible outputs as having been partially satisfied, in that the intangible outcomes were identified and defined, however the process for doing so took too long to be of practical use during project planning/review. Similarly in Step 6, when reflecting on the research interest, the researcher considered the research interest to have been partially satisfied. Project stakeholders were indeed able to define expected intangible project outcomes and their associated tangible outputs. However the process used to do so took too long to be of practical use during project planning/review.

Therefore, due to the near concurrent timing of exploratory action research cycles 1 and 2, Step 7 – Amend Plan or Exit for both exploratory action research cycles was combined with the result being the decision to revise the action steps used to identify and define expected intangible project outcomes. So, as per the action research steps in Table 18.1, the researcher returned to Step 4 to revise the action steps to become the following for major action research cycle 1:

1. Identify project stakeholders.
2. Schedule and conduct introductory meeting with project stakeholders.
3. Conduct stakeholder workshop.
4. Identify and prioritise intangible project outcomes (using the categories of intangibles defined by the UK Government Future and Innovation Unit (Future and Innovation Unit, 2001) as a checklist).
5. Define priority intangible project outcomes using an Outcome Profile™ template comprising the following sections:
   - outcome title
   - outcome identifier
   - short description
   - benefit description
   - presentation format
   - associated tangible outputs
   - dependencies.
6. Document Outcome Profiles™ which are then used as the basis for preparing a summary table cross-referencing intangible project outcomes to tangible project outputs.
7. Review tangible project outputs.

## The Major Action Research Cycles

Major action research cycles 1, 2 and 3 comprised the problem solving projects of the Campaspe Young Persons Referral and Support Scheme (CYPRASS) project, the Youth Health Services (YFHS) project and the Aboriginal Community Liaison Officers (ACLOs) Feasibility Study.

These three problem solving projects were similar, all being pro-active, preventative, multi-agency, public sector-driven community service projects with a focus on crime prevention (the CYPRASS project and ACLOs Feasibility Study) or health promotion (the YFHS project).

All three major action research cycles were conducted by following the steps listed in Table 18.1, as follows.

## Major Action Research Cycle 1 – The Campaspe Young Persons Referral and Support Scheme (CYPRASS) Project

### THE PROJECT ORGANISATION

The Project Organisation for major action research cycle 1 was a law enforcement agency which included a Community and Cultural Division ('the Division') responsible for delivering a large number and a wide variety of community law enforcement projects and programmes which were expected to deliver key intangible outcomes including improved relationships, communications and leadership. The Divisional Commander nominated the CYPRASS project as a problem solving project.

As a condition of participating in the research study, the law enforcement agency required anonymity in all publications subsequent to the researcher's doctoral thesis (Nogeste, 2006).

### THE PROBLEM SOLVING PROJECT

The core of the CYPRASS project was a referral process initiated by law enforcement agency representatives working in the Shire of Campaspe, when a young person came to their attention. With the permission of the young person and/or their guardian, the law enforcement agency representative completed a standard Referral Form identifying the young person's 'at risk' profile. Based on this profile, the law enforcement agency representative referred the young person to a local agency capable of helping them address their 'at risk' factors. Within seven days of receiving the referral, the local agency provided the young person with the appropriate services (CYPRASS Management Committee, 2003).

The CYPRASS project was governed by a Management Committee comprising representatives from the Division, the Shire of Campaspe, government and non-government social welfare and legal aid agencies, local schools, employment brokers and community projects.

### APPLYING THE DUAL ACTION RESEACH CYCLE

*Step 1 – Identify the problem and research interest*

In this step the problem was identified as:

*   identify and define CYPRASS project intangible outcomes so that the delivery of these outcomes can be integrated into project delivery;

and the research interest was identified by the research question, as

*   how to improve the way in which project stakeholders define and align intangible project outcomes with tangible project outputs?

## Step 2 – Reconnaissance

Reconnaissance for the problem solving cycle comprised a combination of meetings with law enforcement agency staff and the reading of relevant state government and law enforcement agency reports and documents.

Reconnaissance for the research interest cycle comprised broadening the literature review to include the topics of benefits management, benefits realisation, strategy development and strategy implementation via projects.

## Steps 3 and 4 – Plan and define the action steps

The problem solving cycle comprised the revised action steps arising from exploratory action research cycles 1 and 2.

Based on the broadened literature review, the planning of the research interest cycle resulted in the following revised version of the Outcome Profile™ template:

- outcome description
- outcome owner
- expected benefits
- expected beneficiary/ies
- assessment: quantitative and qualitative
- roles and responsibilities
- tangible outputs
- dependencies
- risk assessment
- financial summary.

## Step 5 – Implementation

The action steps for the combined cycles were implemented as expected, with the following exceptions:

- during the stakeholder workshop, when using the Outcome Profile™ template to define intangible project outcomes, the stakeholders decided to omit the definition of financial summaries;
- the project stakeholders chose to depict the priority intangible outcomes as a CYPRASS 'cypress tree' as depicted in Figure 18.7.

## Step 6 – Reflection

When reflecting on the results of the problem solving cycle, the CYPRASS Management Committee considered the problem to have been solved – intangible CYPRASS project outcomes and related tangible project outputs were identified, prioritised and documented, with the summary research report handed to the CYPRASS Project Officer for implementation.

When reflecting on the research interest cycle, the researcher considered the research question, 'How to improve the way in which project stakeholders define and align intangible project

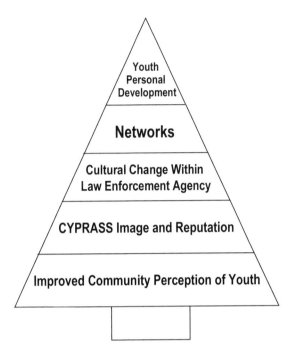

**Figure 18.7    Major action research cycle 1: The CYPRASS project – 'Cypress Tree' depicting intangible outcomes in order of priority**

outcomes with tangible project outputs?' to have been addressed by the approach implemented in major action research cycle 1.

*Step 7 – Amend plan or exit*

The action steps had solved both the problem and addressed the research interest. So, neither the problem solving nor research interest cycle were amended.

The same action steps were repeated for both major action research cycles 2 and 3, generating very similar problem solving and research interest results to those generated by major action research cycle 1. Therefore at Step 7 – Amend Plan or Exit of major action research cycle 3, the researcher and their academic supervisor agreed that the completion of major action research cycle 3 signalled the exit point from the series of action research cycles. This decision was based on the combination of major action research cycles 1, 2 and 3 having satisfied the following predetermined conditions of action research which served as Exit Criteria:

- the extent to which an additional cycle will contribute to understanding (Shaw, 1999: p. 63);
- the researcher having reached a point of 'theoretical saturation' (Eisenhardt, 1989: p. 545) with diminishing levels of return expected from any additional action research cycles;
- the researcher's results considered to be replicable since 'two or more cases are shown to support the same theory' (Yin, 1994: p. 31); and
- the 'useability' of action research results to find solutions to real problems (Levin and Greenwood, 2001: p. 107).

## DISCUSSION

During the course of the five action research cycles, the method for identifying and defining intangible outcomes evolved from individual and small groups of project stakeholders identifying and defining intangible project outcomes during structured interviews and meetings, through to a three-part approach comprising the key elements of the:

1. Outcome Profile™ template;
2. Workshop-based step-wise process for project stakeholders to use the Outcome Profile™ template to collaboratively define and align intangible project outcomes with tangible project outputs;
3. Summary cross-reference table that mapped intangible project outcomes to corresponding tangible outputs.

Exploratory action research cycles 1 and 2 resulted in the problem solving and the research interest being only partially addressed. As a consequence, the first two exploratory action research cycles resulted in the combined research interest and problem solving action steps being revised prior to the start of major action research cycle 1.

Major action research cycles 1, 2 and 3 resulted in both the problem solving and research interest being successfully addressed, with the researcher and their academic supervisor agreeing that the completion of major action research cycle 3 signalled the exit point from the series of action research cycles because the research satisfied predetermined action research research conditions.

In terms of the action research methodology, key limitations of the research study include:

- the limited sample of problem solving projects – comprising five public sector projects of similar complexity and pace conducted by Australian state government departments and agencies from late 2002 through to late 2003;
- the researcher being the sole facilitator and scribe for all action research cycle interviews, meetings and workshops.

In addition, it is worth noting that the research study described in this chapter was conducted in 2002 and 2003 based on the dual cycle action research model described in McKay and Marshall's journal article from 2001 which includes a recommendation for their model to be adopted in both the thinking and practice of action research (McKay and Marshall, 2001: p. 52). However, subsequent to this, in their jointly authored book chapter from 2007, McKay and Marshall describe their dual cycle action research model as a conceptual model only and not a performance model, stressing that it is not a model 'of how to proceed with an action research study'.

Nevertheless, as has been demonstrated by this action research research study based on McKay and Marshall's journal article from 2001, an adaptation of their dual cycle action research model did indeed serve as a sound practical framework for this action research study.

Other evidence in support of the researcher's successful practical application of McKay and Marshall's dual cycle action research model is provided by the researcher being granted a doctoral research degree on the basis of the research study, publishing related journal articles and presenting related conference papers, along with the research study being cited as a good example of collaboration between academic research and industry (Walker et al., 2008: pp. 178–179).

# Conclusions

The principal purpose of this chapter was to provide postgraduate PM student researchers and their academic supervisors with an example of how a dual cycle action research model could be used to both conduct postgraduate PM research and solve a real-life PM problem situation.

By combining 'scholarly theorising and practitioners' narratives', the dual cycle action research model also helps postgraduate PM student researchers to address the call for an increased focus on the actuality of projects by 'combining scholarly theorising and practitioners' narratives' (Cicmil et al., 2006: p. 677) that 'explain the richness of what actually occurs in project environments' (Cicmil et al., 2006: p. 684) and contribute to the 'co-production of knowledge' (Cicmil et al., 2006: p. 677). Therefore, it can be expected that the dual cycle action research model which combines practice and research may be of particular interest to current or prospective postgraduate PM student researchers who are questioning if PM research is sufficiently relevant to their practice. Of a complementary nature, the dual action research cycle model offers academic supervisors with a potential means of attracting practitioners to undertake post graduate PM research.

# Tips and Exercises

## TIPS FOR STUDENTS

- Review and reconfirm the practical and academic value of your research idea/question/proposal with both experienced PM practitioners and academics.
- When discussing your planned action research study with potential research clients, ensure that they understand that the action research cycle that you will conduct with their assistance may generate interim results which will need to be further refined via successive action research cycles.
- When planning an action research research study, ensure that the research study Exit Criteria are clearly defined and understood, so that the results of each action research cycle can be checked against the Criteria to determine the exit point from the action research cycles.

## TIPS FOR SUPERVISORS

- When reviewing a student researcher's planned action research study, ensure that they clearly demonstrate an understanding of the combined problem solving and research goals and that multiple action research cycles will be required to achieve these combined goals.
- When reviewing a student researcher's planned action research study, seriously consider exploratory action research cycles as a means of progressing the design of the problem solving/ research interest cycle/s.
- When reviewing a student researcher's planned action research cycle, assess if and how, the existing literature review needs to be enhanced to address the cycle.

## EXERCISES

1. Use a diagram to illustrate your research strategy, including the research paradigm/s, approach/es, methodology/ies and data collection methods that you considered, highlighting those that you have chosen to employ.

2. Review your researcher role. Are you a research participant or observer? Does your role change over time, or remain the same? Make sure you can justify why your role changes over time, or remains the same.

## References

Cavana, R. Y. (2001). *Applied Business Research: Qualitative and quantitative methods*. Milton, Queensland: John Wiley and Sons Australia Ltd.

Cicmil, S., Williams, T., Thomas, J. and Hodgson, D. (2006). Rethinking Project Management: Researching the actuality of projects. *International Journal of Project Management*, 24(8), 675–686.

Coughlan, P. and Coghlan, D. (2002). Action research for Operations Management. *International Journal of Operations and Production Management*, 22(2), 220–240.

CYPRASS Management Committee. (2003). CYPRASS Newsletter October 2003. Echuca, Victoria, Australia: CYPRASS Management Committee.

Dick, B. (2002a). Action research: Action and research. Retrieved: 19 February 2005, from http://www.scu.edu.au/schools/gcm/ar/arp/aandr.html>.

Dick, B. (2002b). Postgraduate programs using action research. *The Learning Organization*, 9(4), 159–170.

Eisenhardt, K. (1989). Building theories from case study research. *Academy of Management Review*, 14(4), 532–550.

Future and Innovation Unit. (2001). *Creating Value From Your Intangible Assets*. London, UK: Department of Trade and Industry (UK), p. 38.

Kemmis, S. and McTaggart, R. (1988). *The Action Research Planner*, 3rd edition. Victoria, Australia: Deakin University Press.

Levin, M. and Greenwood, D. (2001). Pragmatic Action Research and the Struggle to Transform Universities into Learning Communities. In P. Reason and H. Bradbury (eds), *Handbook of Action Research, Participative Inquiry and Practice*. Thousand Oaks, CA: Sage Publications, pp. 103–113.

Locke, K. D. (2001). *Grounded Theory in Management Research*. London, UK: Sage Publications Ltd.

Low, J. and Kalafut, P. C. (2002). *Invisible Advantage – How intangibles are driving business performance*. Cambridge, MA: Perseus Publishing.

McKay, J. and Marshall, P. (2001). The dual imperatives of action research. *Information Technology and People*, 14(1), 46–59.

McKay, J. and Marshall, P. (2007). Driven by two masters, serving both. In N. Kock (ed.), *Information Systems Action Research: An applied view of emerging concepts and methods*. New York: Springer, pp. 131–158.

McNiff, J. and Whitehead, J. (2000). *Action Research in Organisations*. London, UK: Routledge.

McNiff, J. and Whitehead, J. (2002). *Action Research: Principles and practice*, 2nd edition. London, UK: Routledge Falmer.

Nogeste, K. 2006) *Development of a Method to Improve the Definition and Alignment of Intangible Project Outcomes with Tangible Project Outputs*. (Doctor of Project Management Professional Doctorate), RMIT University, Melbourne, Australia.

Rocco, T. S. (2003.) Shaping the future: Writing up the method on qualitative studies. *Human Resource Development Quarterly*, 14(3), 343–349.

Rowley, J. (2003). Action research: An approach to student work based learning. *Education + Training*, 45(3), 131–138.

Saunders, M. (2003). *Research Methods for Business Students*, 3rd edition. Harlow, UK: Pearson Education Limited.

Shaw, E. (1999). A guide to the qualitative research process: Evidence from a small firm study. *Qualitative Market Research: An International Journal*, 2(2), 59–70.

Walker, D. H. T. (2002). Undertaking research – Guidance Notes 1. Melbourne, Australia: RMIT University.

Walker, D. H. T., Anbari, F. T., Bredillet, C., Söderlund, J., Cicmil, S. and Thomas, J. (2008). Collaborative academic/practitioner research in project management. *International Journal of Managing Projects in Business,* 1(2), 168–192.

Yin, R. K. (1994). *Case Study Research: Design and methods,* 2nd edition. Thousand Oaks, CA: Sage Publications Inc.

Zuber-Skerritt, O. and Perry, C. (2002). Action research within organisations and university thesis writing. *The Learning Organization,* 9(4), 171–179.

# 19

# An Agile Approach to the Real Experience of Developing Research Methodology and Methods

Hany Wells and Hedley Smyth

*Research is frequently retrofitted to a post-rationalised methodology and methods chapter, choosing from an established menu. We wanted to write a chapter that more closely informed how research is conducted in practice.*

Researchers commence their work with a research topic and a preliminary idea about how they will conduct the fieldwork. This may have been developed in a proposal, for example for doctoral study. In addressing research methodology and methods for conducting the fieldwork and write-up, post-rationalisation is conducted to fit the work to an acceptable structure and content. The extent of post-rationalisation will depend on the research methodologies employed. This chapter addresses the problems using an interpretative methodology, an inductive approach, case studies and units of analysis. We argue a flexible, iterative and agile approach accords with reality.

At the end of this chapter, the reader can:

- highlight the challenge of interpretative research methodology, particularly using an inductive approach;
- develop relevant methods from the research methodology and apply these to research;
- recognise the iterative and agile activity in conducting research as reflective practice.

Keywords: agile, case studies, inductive approach, interpretative methodology, iterative method, qualitative data, sense-making

How research work is conducted and written follows different approaches. Research methodology and methods are usually written to convey a logical structure and sequence. The reality is frequently 'messy' in practice. A loose structure and content are initially formed and detail added subsequently, typically after the fieldwork has been conducted. This is most often the case for qualitative research. The reality therefore is frequently iterative and more akin to an 'agile' non-linear approach.

Selecting an appropriate research approach is critical to any investigation. The beliefs about the phenomena and the nature of their existence (ontology) alongside the criteria for constructing knowledge (epistemology) and methods employed are fundamental to the analysis, discussion and final outcomes. Yet, researchers find selecting the approach challenging. Many doctoral students, for example, end up focusing upon the mundane issues in detail and skate over many difficult issues, for example procedures how data should be collected rather than what is actually being investigated.

We believe there are at least three reasons for these difficulties. First, there is no unified theory of the management of projects (Smyth and Morris, 2007), therefore the examination of a phenomenon in PM without theoretical underpinning is a challenge. Second, PM is always located in a context (for example, Fitzgerald, Russo and Stolterman, 2002) hence the selected research methodology has to enable the study to address the contextual aspects of PM. Third, the complexity of business and PM environments pose problems for establishing research parameters.

## Towards an Interpretive Methodology

In PM, how do we know what we know through research? This is what we call epistemology, in other words the science of knowledge. In PM, what is its nature? The essence of what being studied is what we call ontology. Epistemology and ontology are two key building blocks for developing a research methodology or strategy. Research methods are the tactical tools and techniques of implementation.

Selecting the appropriate research philosophy is a key starting point for any research. The three philosophies that have played important parts in business and management research are: Positivism, Interpretivism and Realism (Saunders, Lewis and Thornhill, 2003), each having different ontological and methodological implications for issues such as observation and examination, identifying patterns and causality, generality of findings, and claims about the outcomes.

Positivism was dominant in social science from the 1930s through to the 1960s; its core argument being that the social world exists through what is knowable to research, and that its properties can be measured through observation (Gray, 2009). Positivists imply that 'the researcher is working with an observable social reality and that the end product of such research can be the derivation of laws or law-like generalisations, similar to those produced by the physical and natural scientists' (Remenyi et al., 2002: p. 32). Positivism is dominant in much PM research and informs the PMI approach and implicitly PRINCE2 (Smyth and Morris, 2007). The perceived value of such research is based upon using independent observations to generate facts. Yet facts are challengeable:

> ... facts have evaluative implications. They comprise, or are wielded as, reasons for or against particular points of view, which they accordingly buttress or discredit. ..In common with all sciences, statistical results, while not morally evaluative, evaluate theories, and the acceptance of those theories (as well as the associated practices). (Krige, 1979: p. 55)

Realism is based on reality existing independently of human thoughts and beliefs. This is sometimes considered inappropriate for business and management, where people and management socially construct a lot of what is around them according to how they think and act (Smyth and Morris, 2007).

Interpretivism holds the view that observation cannot be pure in the sense of altogether excluding the interests and values of individuals. This supports an effective approach for understanding perceptions. Investigations must employ empathic understanding of those studied. The basic assumptions of interpretivism are:

- phenomena can be analysed as issues;
- data is collected by participants and observers, all of whom have varying degrees of involvement;
- truth cannot be determined in any absolute way;
- the purpose of enquiry is to gain sufficient understanding as to anticipate possible future outcomes;
- there is no need to apply theories; understanding is both theory-from-action and theory-in-action (cf. Jankowicz, 2005).

Interpretivism allows for understanding of social processes, involving getting inside the world of those generating it (Rosen, 1991). This includes context and subjectivity and the understanding of perceptions. The interpretive epistemology strongly advocates that the complexity of the world should not be entirely reduced to a series of law-like generalisations. It may be used to find general patterns or particular issues of significance. This can start by being informed by previously generated theory or can start with the emphasis upon context and what is happening on the ground – a deductive versus inductive approach.

The deductive approach emphasises the scientific principle of moving from theory to data for verification, often with a significant need for collection of quantitative data to justify verification. On the other hand, an inductive approach starts with the empirical data and relies upon a close understanding of the research context with the collection of quantitative or qualitative data. Qualitative data sources have proved more popular over the last decades. The aim is to derive explanatory patterns and identify particular events of causal significance. We will now expand on the inductive approach.

## Inductive Research Approach

Induction is the process of collecting empirical information from the field first. Then patterns and particular events or outcomes of importance are identified. The patterns and events may be analysed for content, but can also be used as a basis for tracing causes. Identifying causes can provide the building blocks for concept generation or theory development. An inductive approach relies upon a close understanding of the research context. Qualitative methods are useful for more intensive investigation that quantitative examination and are frequently adopted to explore context. Semi-structured interviews are often selected as one source of data. This raises the issue of observation in relation to interpretation for inductive methods, a factor frequently overlooked in recent times. What is being observed?

Observation is via actor perceptions, which provide an indirect form of data collection about events, but are themselves events for observation that can be interpreted. Thus, their interpretation of events from indirect sources and via the interviews, as well as the interpretations of the researcher are being used. What sorts of levels of interpretation are in play for such research? Table 19.1 has been devised to address this point. It proposes seven possible levels and stages, each stage of interpretation potentially enriching interviewee and interviewer understanding. The totality of experience gives the interviewee a rich depth of understanding and allows selectivity of the significant issues to be drawn out (akin to edited highlights). Post-rationalisation can be enhancing too. Interpretation can also act to dilute or distort interviewee perceptions.

**Table 19.1    Levels and stages of interpretation**

| Levels of Interpretation | Agent | Stage of Interpretation |
|---|---|---|
| 1. | Interviewee in their field of operation | Interviewee interprets the event (including processes) as it occurs – a sense-making activity |
| 2. | Interviewee in their field of operation | Interviewee with other actors moderate their interpretation – an iterative sense-making activity |
| 3. | Interviewee in their field of operation | A degree of post-rationalisation as a result of subsequent events, also moderated by social and other contextual factors |
| 4. | Interviewee as informant | Recall moderation in context of interview – interpretative selectivity |
| 5. | Interviewee as informant | Responsiveness to the researcher's agenda and selectivity as to what the actor perceives the researcher wants to hear |
| 6. | Researcher as data collector | Selectivity of information according to values and research context in note-taking or post-transcription of the interview |
| 7. | Researcher as analyst | Researcher interprets the event as perceived – a sense-making activity |

This may be further disrupted by the application of software for analysis. Software tends to be applied as if it is independent and objective, even in research acknowledged as value-laden. For example, the logic of NVivo contains a further selectiveness and thus a 'hidden' filter of unintended interpretation. Keyword and phrase selection do not account for the content and meaning in transcripts and exclude other language that conveys messages and meaning of significance. A more evaluative approach is needed for using such tools.

For those contesting value-laden research and interpretivism, these levels and stages do not facilitate rich data analysis but provide good reasons for avoiding an interpretive approach. For those embracing the approach it provides an excellent reflection of the social construction of reality. Further, the interpretations involved down to level 5 will inform the actions of the actors and thus is significant in that it informs future action. This is pertinent for the approach and can be critical in action research. However, levels 6 and 7 provide caution about the claims researchers make about their findings, especially where theory building is an outcome, for example where induction is used to build theory, such as in the application of grounded theory. In sum, there is flexibility about how researchers proceed, recognising that rigid plans can be too constraining or have to be changed and post-rationalised. However, there is also a need to have a precise method structured around certain protocols to guide research. One option is to follow agile principles.

## Towards an Agile Research Approach

Agile is an approach that is closely linked with rapid application, development and prototyping, where the primary focus is on producing effective results, through responding to change promptly with the minimum interruption to the work process. As an approach or method that was first formed for IT/information systems development, it is now finding its way into many aspects of work delivery and management.

> Agile is focused on responding to change rather than following a plan. (Cobb, 2011: p. 46)

> Instead of thinking of rigidly defined methodologies with fixed characteristics, we need to recognize that any methodology can and should be customized and tailored to fit the situation at hand. (Cobb, 2011: pp. 46–47)

The linear conception where every step is prescribed does not align with research conduct. In practice, a flexible and iterative approach is needed as the quotes transposed from agile PM above help illustrate. A prescribed method at a general level helps identification of the intended sources from which to gather the relevant data and helps to focus upon the problems that may be faced. In facing the problems, reflective practice leads to refinement of the method. An inductive approach leaves more room for manoeuvre and refinement as the research proceeds. Deductive and reductive approaches leave little or no formal room. The researcher is constantly adjusting the research objectives with the research process as well as the findings.

## Case Studies

Case studies are a commonly used inductive research method. They are exploratory in the sense of giving room for manoeuvre in defining methods, being open-ended concerning the type of findings that may emerge, as well as being used in areas where there are few theories (Collis and Hussey, 2003). They can be used for sensitivity to context (Yin, 2003). They are used for examination as they can be rich in data and suitable for in-depth analysis. A case study 'involves an empirical investigation of a particular contemporary phenomenon within its real life context using multiple sources of evidence' (Robson, 2002: p. 178). It is widely employed for deductive and inductive analysis (Cavaye, 1996). Case study methods answer intensive and in-depth 'why' and 'how' questions, focusing upon understanding the dynamics present within single settings. Eisenhardt (1989) recommends a range of a single case study up to 10 cases, or multiple settings of 30 cases have been proposed (Pagell and Lepine, 2002) for comparative analysis. Yin (2003) identifies the following characteristics of case study research:

- aims to understand phenomena within a particular context;
- sets open-ended questions;
- uses multiple methods for collecting data, which may be qualitative and quantitative.

There can be confusion between the cases and the unit of analysis. They can be but need not be synonymous. The unit must be comparable, for example in order to apply compare and contrast techniques, but the case may define the parameters of the study rather than be the unit of analysis, for example examining temporary project teams as the cases may have decision-making meetings as the unit of analysis, so it would not matter if the projects vary highly providing the decision making is reasonably comparable.

Cavaye (1996) identifies a range of benefits of case study analysis:

- capturing of 'reality' and detail by studying a phenomenon in context;
- enabling the study of a large number of variables and different features of a phenomenon;

- developing and refining concepts for further study, which sometimes, we add, can form iterations within as well as between studies;
- making use of the multiple case study method allows the researcher to examine and relate the differences in context to stable and constant features, processes and outcomes.

There are also limitations to a case study approach, including the inability to generalise, sifting and filtering other causal factors or independent factors that constrain confidence about the general and particular issues of import in the case, and, where causality is being sought, establishing the causal direction, although these issues also occur in quantitative analysis where recognition of such problems are overlooked or are assumed away.

## Conducting a Multiple Case Study

The purpose at this point is to illustrate some of the issues raised through a research example. The research investigated the application of 'PM methodologies', strictly speaking 'methods' in practitioner terms, on IT projects. Selecting the case studies as part of the inductive research approach needed understanding how to design the methods at a general level, although the detailed methods emerged iteratively during the conduct of the fieldwork and analysis. The initial write-up was presented as if the research had been determined step-by-step in advance. The reality of reflective research practice gave rise to sense-making at a fine grain of method detailing (cf. Weick, 1995). Iterative tailoring to context and refining the details step-by-step were akin to an agile approach to research practice.

A comparative case study approach of four sources was applied: one being PRINCE2 reflecting the significant attention given by the UK government and emulated elsewhere – and three others being organisationally embedded. The PM methodologies that were investigated in their organisations were extensive in nature and had been in existence longer, so organisational embeddedness was appropriate, but the unit of analysis remained the four PM methodologies, the others being Waterfall, an in-house Gated-based approach and an Agile PM methodologies approach. As the unit of analysis was the PM methodologies, varied organisational settings were beneficial in order to show contextual variance and examine commonalities despite varied contexts (Wells, 2011). The organisational settings were multiple for PRINCE2, an IT/Systems Integrator in the software sector, an Information Provider to the finance sector, and a Telecommunications business. Some of the main features the case study approach was able to articulate are summarised in Table 19.2.

A combination of four cases were used – archive searching, interviews, documentation and observation, but participant observation and physical artefacts being excluded. The interviews of informants were drawn from different roles to solicit a variety of viewpoints and actor interpretations, covering senior managers, consultants and directors, heads of best practices and project management methodologies, senior project managers, product managers, project leaders, team members and systems engineers (Wells, 2011). There has been a recent and growing trend, especially in doctoral studies, to describe in detail the process and protocols for conducting data collection and analysis, particularly around interviews as a source. There is nothing wrong with this, yet it is an easier option than, say, expounding upon the methodological underpinnings, extensive versus intensive research, what is being observed, causality, values in research, the type of interpretation, many of which are underplayed or neglected.

There are issues in data analysis connected with values and interpretation that are not always made apparent. The researcher viewpoint may become apparent, but how that influenced

**Table 19.2    Summary features of selected cases**

|  | Case 1 | Case 2 | Case 3 | Case 4 |  |
| --- | --- | --- | --- | --- | --- |
| Discipline | Varied<br>Public and Private | IT/Systems<br>Integrator | Information Provider<br>to the Finance<br>Sector | Telecommunications | Research Context |
| Organisation<br>Size | Varied | Large | Large | Large |  |
| Project Range | 6 months – 50,000<br>Complex – £50m | Wide range from<br>£50k to multimillion | £100k to £40m | £30k to multimillion |  |
| Project Types | IT design and<br>development | IT design and<br>development | Systems design and<br>implementation | IT and product design<br>and development |  |
| Number of<br>Employees | Varied | 40,000 in 39<br>countries | 16,800 in 94<br>countries | 106,200 in 106<br>countries |  |
| Client /<br>Customer | Internal and<br>External | External | Internal | External and Internal |  |
| Contractual<br>Forces | Varied | Strong<br>contractual bindings<br>External clients | Weak<br>contractual bindings<br>Internal client | Mixed – Strong with<br>external client and<br>weak with internal<br>users |  |
| Project<br>Managers'<br>Level of<br>Competencies | Senior Project<br>Managers | Mixed | Mixed | Mixed |  |

interpretation is not always clear. Collis and Hussey (2003) cite the challenge of data reduction posed in qualitative analysis. Data reduction is informed by values and shapes interpretation. This does not quite align with that claim that reduction is 'a form of analysis that sharpens, sorts, focuses, discard and reorganise data in such a way that "final" conclusions can be drawn and verified' (Miles and Huberman, 1994: p. 11). The protocol might be verifiable, but is the interpretation explicit? The role of interpretation in data reduction is less where patterns are being identified, for example using a 'pattern coding' procedure, whether as content or inductively linked to causal explanation (cf. Thomas, 2006). However, many researchers also look for single and irregular events as significant that nudge outcomes or are shocks to the system. Some researchers only seek the particular. Which events are selected as important shapes interpretation.

In the PM methodologies research case example above, the first step towards analysis was the creation of raw data categories, based on content (Thomas, 2003) and in the light of research questions informed by the literature review (cf. Eisenhardt, 1989). The research questions had provided an informed 'springboard' to prompt responses that prompted interviewee responses and follow-up questions as well as leading to inductively generating patterns. Patterns emerged from close rereading of transcribed text to gain detailed familiarity and understanding of the data (Eisenhardt, 1989; Miles and Huberman, 1994). Text was organised primarily under research questions and classified using a colour coding system to identify patterns within each case and across the cases. The analysis yielded some unexpected findings.

Whilst unexpected findings provide no guarantee, they do provide reassurance regarding the degree of interpretation applied. A loose or reasonably open-ended degree of interpretation is necessary, especially for an inductive approach. A tight or rigid form tends to determine the outcomes and thus can exclude findings that are non-conforming to the belief and value system of the researcher. Loose interpretation is part of the agile approach to interpretative research.

## Summary and Conclusions

This chapter addressed some key issues in conducting research from both a conceptual and an applied perspective. Particular focus was given to an interpretative methodology, an inductive and case study set of methods. Three specific goals were for this chapter and a summative response is provided below:

1. Highlighting the challenge of interpretative research methodology, particularly using an inductive approach – seven levels of interpretation have been set out which demand attentive rigour for interpretative analysis as well as providing riches of data understanding.
2. Developing relevant methods from the research methodology and applying these to research – rigour of interpretation requires a careful and evaluative selection of means for interpretation, especially when using software applications that might lead to considerable yet unintended distortions.
3. Recognising the iterative and agile activity in conducting research as reflective practice – precise research plans are disruptive on many occasions during the research process so a more open-ended approach supported by a flexible method can prove useful as long as the method is sufficiently precise in the protocols used.

A prime argument has been that research is 'messy' in practice and the post-rationalised write-up that implies a detailed chronology is typically misleading. Post-rationalisation is used to justify the actual process of undertaking research, which departs from the plan. A flexible, iterative and agile approach accords with reality and was illustrated through a research project. A further conclusion was that detailed procedures have a role but should not be developed at the expense of important issues of methodology and method, for example, what is being observed and how that is interpreted which this chapter has begun to redress. Some consideration was also given to more detailed issues, such as the selection of case studies, units of analysis and how data is handled for analysis.

We recommend on the one hand researchers continue to take a reasonably light touch to issues of methodology and methods to avoid their studies being overwhelmed by the demands of methodology and methods, especially concerning the more procedural issues. On the other hand, methodology and methods need to be taken seriously. Methodology in particular is frequently given short shrift and addressed in uncritical ways. In sum, a rebalancing is needed.

## Tips and Exercises

### TIPS FOR STUDENTS

- An inductive approach leaves more room for manoeuvre to refine and develop the detail method as the research work progresses. A pilot study formally recognises the need in all research. Make sure you are also aware of the informal refinements!
- As part of good reflective research practice, be aware of the interpretation being used. Describe the research process as it happened and relate back to the logic. Make interpretation explicit!
- Do not over-determine inductive research design. Loose fit for identification of data, including unexpected findings. Loose fit in analysis to avoid temptation to only see what you expect to find!

### TIPS FOR SUPERVISORS

- Encourage students to accurately reflect how they conducted the research.

- Ask them to keep a reflective journal as to how the research was conducted, particularly the changes in topic, theoretical approach, choice of methods, collection of data and analysis.
- Provide guidance on how the actual conduct of the research can be written up in terms of methodology and methods to avoid post-rationalisation and the recasting of events to fit a prescribed formula.

## EXERCISES

1. Imagine you are starting a research journal, anticipate what kind of divergences from the research plan can be anticipated in practice at three levels: methodology development, data collection and data analysis?
2. In applying an inductive approach how do you know when you have collected enough data at the end of the fieldwork prior to the analysis, and how do you know when the analysis is complete? Is making sense of the data sufficient or concepts/theory generation necessary in order to complete the analysis?
3. Assuming data has been collected, how would you apply the seven levels of interpretation presented in the chapter to your analysis and in the write-up?

## References

Cavaye, A. L. M. (1996.) Case study research: A multi-faceted research approach for IS. *Information Systems Journal,* 6(3), 227–242.

Cobb, C. G. (2011). *Making Sense of Agile Project Management: Balancing control and agility.* Hoboken, NJ: John Wiley and Sons.

Collis, J. and Hussey, R. (2003). *Business Research: A practical guide for undergraduate and postgraduate students,* 2nd edition. New York: Palgrave Macmillan.

Eisenhardt, K. M. (1989). Building theories from case study research. *Academy of Management Review,* 14(4), 532–550.

Fitzgerald, B. Russo, N. L. and Stolterman, E. (2002). *Information Systems Development: Method-in-action.* New York: McGraw Hill.

Gray, D. E. (2009). *Doing Research in the Real World,* 2nd edition. London: Sage Publications.

Jankowicz, A. D. (2005). *Business Research Projects,* 4th edition. London: Thomson London.

Krige, J. (1979). *What's so great about facts? Demystifying Social Statistics,* J. Irvine, I. Miles and J. Evans (eds), London: Pluto.

Miles, M. B. and Huberman, A. M. (1994). *Qualitative Data Analysis,* 2nd edition. Thousand Oaks, CA: Sage.

Pagell, M. and LePine, J. A. (2002). Multiple case studies of team effectiveness in manufacturing organisations, *Journal of Operations Management,* 20(5), 619–639.

Remenyi, D., Williams, B., Money, A. and Swartz, E. (2002). *Doing Research in Business and Management: An introduction to process and method.* London: Sage Publications.

Robson, C. (2002). *Real World Research,* 2nd edition. Oxford, UK: Blackwell.

Rosen, M. (1991). Coming to terms with the field: Understanding and doing organisational ethnography. *Journal of Management Studies,* 28(1), 1–24.

Saunders, M., Lewis, P. and Thornhill, A. (2003). *A Research Method for Business Students,* 3rd edition. Harlow: Prentice Hall.

Smyth, H. J. and Morris, P. W. G. (2007). An epistemological evaluation of research into projects and their management: Methodological issues. *International Journal of Project Management,* 25(4), 423–436.

Thomas, R. (2006). A general inductive approach for analysing qualitative evaluation data. *American Journal of Evaluation*, 27(2), 237–246.

Weick K. E. (1995). *Sensemaking in Organizations*. Thousand Oaks, CA: Sage Publications.

Wells H. (2011). An exploratory investigation into the contribution of project management methodologies to the successful management of IT/IS projects in practice. PhD Thesis. University College London.

Yin, R. K. (2003). *Case Study Research: Design and methods*, 3rd edition. Thousand Oaks, CA: Sage.

# 20

# Giving Voice to the Project Management Practitioner

Mano Nugapitiya, Spike Boydell and Patrick Healy

*In this chapter we share our insights and an interesting story from a project that pushed the limits of PM research by using a controversial research approach. We hope that other researchers and supervisors too will be inspired to look beyond the current boundaries.*

This chapter demonstrates how we can give a voice to the PM practitioner through a synthesis of case study research and autoethnography. We achieve this by providing a vocabulary that draws on the concepts of social psychology and philosophy, in particular the Chicago School of Sociology and the Continental Philosophers in phenomenology, to help articulate our description of PM practice. This allows us to explore and interrogate the 'lived experience' of the PM practitioner and the social processes that dominate real projects.

At the end of this chapter, the reader can:

* realise that their own lived experiences as a project manager provides a wealth of research data;
* undertake interpretive research and respond to the inherent issues of validity, generalisation, and bias, in interpretivist research;
* incorporate pre-existing case studies within your research;
* engage autoethnography as a research methodology.

Keywords: autoethnography, case study, lived experience, interpretive research

This chapter does come with a caveat. As an emergent and serious research tool, autoethnography provides a cathartic journey that forces you to be deeply introspective and to interrogate not only your past triumphs but also your own frailties in projects that may have been less than optimal.

Have you ever wondered how you can use your 10, 20, or maybe even 30 or more years of professional experience as a practising project manager within an academic research context? Or perhaps you have just been involved in a handful of projects and need to make some sense out of them. This chapter is about finding your voice as a project manager, about understanding the meaning in what you do and how you interact with others, and about how you can use yourself as both the subject and the object of your research. We hope that this chapter will help you to reflect on your past projects, find meaning in them and discover useful lessons that you and others can apply in future projects by taking an autoethnographic approach to analysing rich case studies.

## Researching the 'Truth' of Project Management through Lived Experience

Self-reflection is one thing, but finding an appropriate lexicon to help you articulate your lived experience to a wider audience requires an engagement with theories and philosophies that often lie beyond the guidance afforded by the PM body of knowledge. Such an approach allows us to gain access to truth in a way that is not accessible through the application of the scientific method (Gadamer, 1993). The research approach we offer does not prove anything in the sense of having absolute certainty. Rather, it demonstrates how a set of ideas developed in a sphere outside PM can be useful in both describing and understanding PM practice.

This research approach was inspired by a question posed by Söderlund (2004: p. 190) who asks, 'What do project managers really do (and why)?' This provides a timely rejoinder to calls from academia for *a better understanding of project actuality*. Our response was to explore the practice of PM by examining the 'lived experience' of project managers. To achieve this we recognised that we had to move beyond the positivist and scientific tradition, and immerse ourselves in the interpretive approach, so that we could use the context of a real-world project to understand the actual thoughts, feelings and actions of a project manager. Such a methodology allows us to understand how the project manager interacts with and responds intersubjectively to others. The importance of such a method will be quickly apparent to many established project managers who may bring a wealth of lived professional experience to their research journey and are looking for a way to utilise that extraordinary dataset rather than attempting to use a new project as a focus of their academic research.

By drawing on the internal personal experience of the practitioner we can build theory that is grounded on contemporary PM practice.

One of the opportunities that is created through the development of research in a relatively new academic discipline like PM, is the ability to engage emergent and contemporary research methods that would be more difficult to apply (or gain acceptance) within established scientific fields. Drawing on Corley and Gioia (2011) we make the point that for theory to be relevant to practice it must be tested and extended through application on real projects. Each project is different. It is practically impossible to meet the 'scientific method' criterion of repeatability because each project is different; there are different participants in each project who interact differently through their respective intersubjectivity with other members of the team, the client, the end-user and other stakeholders.

Our approach is unconventional and may contrast with other research methods that have been explored in this book. Our unconventional approach was intentional as it allowed us to deliberately explore a number of gaps that we had identified in other approaches to exploring the experience of PM. Drawing on Creswell (2007: p. 16), the adoption of a particular research approach and methodology has to evolve from researchers' philosophical and theoretical stance. A central feature of this process involves consideration of issues such as: how reality is viewed (ontology); how the researcher comes to know what he or she knows (epistemology); the role of values influencing the research (axiology); and the vocabulary of the research (rhetoric). What we introduce is a move from the PM conceptual base that emphasises a current paradigm of hard reality, and instead offer an alternative view that is based upon people's understandings, interpretation and feelings. As Creswell identifies (2007: p. 37), a qualitative approach is more appropriate when studying research problems that inquire into the meaning individuals and groups ascribe to social or human problems.

## Taking an Interpretivist Approach

To explore the social processes in PM practice, what we refer to as the 'lived experience' of the project manager, we engage with concepts and vocabulary largely drawn from the Chicago School of Sociology (predominantly the work of Mead, Cooley, Blumer and Goffman) and Continental Philosophy (predominantly the work of Husserl and Schutz in phenomenology). A critical review of this sociological and philosophical literature affords a rigorous theoretical basis to the research, engaging seven concepts that provide a lens through which a case study can be interrogated autoethnographically. We elaborate on each of these seven concepts below:

1. The role of the self, self concept and the generalised other.

    There is a complex interaction between the 'self' (comprising the 'I' and the 'me'), 'the generalised other' and the 'self concept'. From your perspective as a project manager, this concept investigates the complex internal thought process comprising the PM practitioner's imagination of what others expect of him or her; how the PM practitioner perceives themself; and what the PM practitioner believes others think of them. Drawing from Nugapitiya, Healy and Boydell (2011), such thoughts usually remain internalised and personal, so it is only the PM practitioner who will have access to them. Both Mead (1934) and Cooley (1922) explain that such thoughts are constructed and reconstructed from social experiences and activity. In this complex process, the self-interaction (the process of talking to one's self) becomes a powerful means for the reconstruction of the 'self concept'. The process is ongoing both consciously and during the subconscious hours of sleep. Construction and reconstruction of the 'self-concept' is an iterative and ongoing social process that inevitably changes through interaction with others and engagement in new experiences.

2. The conversation of gestures.

    Everyday gestures such as hand movements, facial expressions, posture/body language and vocalisation facilitate meaningful interaction (or reaction) between humans. We often react to our perceived meaning of these gestures, rather than the actual gesture itself. The PM arena is no different. Whilst there is a potential cultural aspect to this dependent on the variables of society, religion and gender, the concept of gestures set out here purely relates to the ideas arising from Mead (1934). When the gesture has the same meaning for both the actor making the gesture and the respondent, then the two parties understand each other.

3. Taking the 'Role of the Other'.

    A project manager is expected to be a facilitator, integrator, decision-maker, inter-personnel relationship manager, negotiator, mentor, and crisis manager, all in the one person. The discipline also engages in projects that embrace relationship contracting such as partnering and forming alliances. In fulfilling these various roles, and interacting with many others, the project manager is expected to 'step into the other's shoes' and to see issues from multiple perspectives. This 'stepping into the other's shoes' is essentially what Mead (1934) means by his concept of role taking. It is through this process of role taking, as well as interpreting the meaning of the other's 'gestures', that the actor will adjust his or her 'self-concept'. In order to interpret the other's ideas, perspectives, behaviours and feelings, the project manager needs to be aware that there is a natural process of role taking of the other. As a consequence of taking the role of the other, there are processes occurring that are also internal to the project manager.

4. Meanings.

    Potential meanings are everywhere, and everything has multiple potential meaning. An event such as the Olympic Games is full of potential meaning: it signifies tradition, bringing together nations regardless of their status and differences to compete on the sports field, whilst providing a vehicle for large-scale development and expectations for economic payback and recognition. Meanings are only understood when a person has grasped the significance (arising from the positive or negative value, or impact, or consequence for that person) of something. People construct, break down, reconstruct and negotiate meanings through their interpretation of social interaction. Face-to-face interactions are a powerful and effective means for constructing and negotiating meanings. Meanings are grasped more from both what was said and what might have been left unspoken. We react based on our experience and our guiding ideals (such as honesty, independence). Mere observation of another's outward behaviour, expression or gestures can rarely provide an understanding of their 'subjective' meanings. Meanings inform social order, rationality, reality and things that people accept as holding society together in terms of conflict or cooperation. Put in the context of PM, tools and techniques (such as project start-up, progressive elaboration, work breakdown structures, configuration management, scope development or scope change) are developed by human interaction between the various participants, as they give meaning to their experiences (Nugapitiya, Healy and Boydell, 2009).

5. Intersubjectivity.

Intersubjectivity between humans is a dynamic concept that takes place at different intensities and at different times, sometimes temporarily retreating and then returning (Hui, 2003). The term is difficult to pin down but we could broadly regard 'intersubjectivity' as the issue of whether or not mutual understanding is possible. It is also role based, grounded on where 'my' intersubjective relationship with another is formed by the role the other plays in society, whether as a parent, employer, colleague, soul mate, lover, wife or child. The traditional literature on 'intersubjectivity' points towards five simple contributing factors:

- human 'consciousness' stemming largely from Husserl's (1950/1995, 1965, 1981, 1997) work;
- the human desire for recognition from Sartre's (1943/2003; Jean-Paul Sartre, 1948) work;
- other body's disclosure as discussed by Merleau-Ponty (1953/1988, 1992);
- the concept of 'mutual understanding' or reciprocity as discussed by Husserl (op. cit.) and several others; and
- empathy, widely discussed by Husserl (op. cit.), Scheler and Stikkers (1980) and Bakhtin and Holquist (1990).

Intersubjectivity implies that, as well as being single human units, individuals may also be a component of a larger unit as a pair, threesome or a wider group.

6. Human interaction as a stage play.

Human interaction as a stage play (initially assumed based on an individual human taking the role of the 'actor') can be extended to a stage play involving a 'group of actors' performing as a team. The individual actors, whilst performing to each 'other', will also perform as a group act to a wider audience. Their group act will be based on a common set of meanings. A well-choreographed performance requires 'intersubjectivity' between the individual actors. They should be acutely aware of their role in the team, not wanting to miss a 'step'.

7. Impression management.

Humans have a natural desire for recognition. We desire to be desired and desire to desire others (Yar, 2001). We desire to be recognised, according to a certain set of perceptions and understandings or image of self, as a human being. Accordingly, in a PM situation, the natural tendency is to control the impression others have of us in line with our desired goals or agenda. This impression of who and what we are, is defined by how we do what we do. This is dependent on our impression management of any particular situation.

## Incorporating Your Pre-Existing Case Studies

To provide context for what follows, we are going to draw on one particular PM experience. It is provided as just one example of many so that readers can gain an insight into this particular research method. The experience we will relate to is grounded in the Alpine Way Reconstruction in Thredbo, New South Wales, Australia, following the 1997 landslide that resulted in 18 fatalities when the embankment holding up the road known as the Alpine Way collapsed, taking with it two large multilevel ski lodges. Drawing on the day-to-day interactions and experiences of the project manager involved in this particular case study, we looked to define a vocabulary and develop a set of concepts to explore the question, 'Can the lived experience of the project manager be described in a meaningful way, and if so, how?'

Where possible, in utilising a case study approach, it is useful to select a 'classic' case study (Dyer (Jr), Wilkins and Eisenhardt, 1991) as the platform for data analysis and testing the veracity of the sociological concepts identified by the literature. Our choice of the Alpine Way Reconstruction offered a unique case study, and one where the technology was uncertain. This allowed greater visibility of the social processes. The project manager went to Thredbo assuming that the project would involve a straightforward engineering solution to reconstruct the Alpine Way. However, as is typical in many projects, on arriving in Thredbo the project manager was confronted with the reality and complexity of the task at hand, and the role expanded to engage in the broader mission of contributing to the restoration of the confidence of the Thredbo people. Curiously, perhaps, at the conclusion of its first stage of work, the project was awarded an Engineering Excellence award by the Institution of Engineers, Australia. This was largely supported and promoted by the external stakeholders, who on other projects would be largely ignored. By virtue of its circumstances, the Thredbo case study is a valuable, powerful and engaging case study that illuminates the practice of PM and, in this case, unique social processes.

Lessons that other researchers can learn from this sample case study include:

- it represents a real project and the data is naturally occurring;
- the project was a challenging and award-winning project representing what some would construe as good PM practice; and
- the case study and the 18 key events that we examined actually took place; they are real, not abstract or hypothetical. To address the valid concern of the authenticity of the researcher's recollection, the researcher's PM superior confirmed that the key events took place. Newspaper articles and reports from the time also validated the data.

## Autoethnography

Where our approach differs from a conventional case study is that the data was interrogated autoethnographically by the PM practitioner. The term autoethnography was coined to describe a genre of autobiography (Brodkey, 1996). It is both a way of writing and a research methodology that insists on forging a connection between personal identity and cultural forces. It looks beyond what facts and generalisations offer toward meaning, understanding and social criticism (Ellis and Bochner, 2000).

Autoethnography is an emergent method in social research that has developed out of the tradition of qualitative research using autobiographical data as both a direct and an indirect source (Hesse-Biber and Levy, 2006). More precisely, autoethnography is located at an intersection between autobiography and ethnography, where the informant's own voice rewrites and reclaims authority from the genre of participant–observer methodology (Chiu, 2004). By offering a new way of pursuing social knowledge (Wall, 2006: p .4) an autoethnographic text develops from the researchers embodied position. Indeed, permitting the researcher to share his or her interpretation and personal experience as a research participant is what 'enhances the study for the reader' (Smith, 2005: p. 4), and what makes it such a relevant tool in socialising the learning experience from other practitioners projects.

Good autoethnography has to be emotionally engaging. It should strive to use a relational language and style that creates a purposeful dialogue with the reader (Spry, 2006), by opening a door onto the intimacies of your particular world. In so doing, it should encourage the reader to reflect on his or her own experiences, thoughts and emotions (Sparkes, 1996: p. 467).

There is no one particular way to undertake autoethnography (Mischenko, 2005). It is a process whereby 'the researcher chooses to make explicit use of their own positionality, involvements and experiences as an integral part of ethnographic research' (Butz and Besio, 2004: p. 353). There is a developing body of literature on the use and application of autoethnography that has expanded significantly over the last decade. If, as a PM researcher, you decide to utilise this particular methodology, you are encouraged to run a Google Scholar search for 'autoethnography' so that you can engage with the most recent research published in this emerging field.

## Defending an Emergent Approach

Despite giant leaps in the acceptance of qualitative research over the last 20 years, those of us who engage emergent approaches such as autoethnography are unfortunately still expected to respond to the inherent issues of validity, generalisation, and bias, in interpretivist research. As Denzin and Lincoln (2000) highlight, even well-established qualitative research methods are continually called upon to defend their research as valid science. From a conventional scientific perspective methods that 'connect with real people, their lives, and their issues' are disparaged as being soft and fluffy (Wall, 2006: p. 2). Fortunately, there is acceptance in PM research that the traditional 'positivist/functionalist' methods of conventional science often fall short of adequately capturing the 'organisational realties' of PM. We contend that the actualities of the lived experience of the project manager can be better understood through interpretative accounts.

## Tips and Questions

### TIPS FOR STUDENTS

- 'Define' the language: The topics under examination in qualitative research are often malleable and go to issues at the border of what is linguistically describable. Meaning, understanding and inter-subjectivity are examples of concepts that can be difficult to tie down. Many of the terms may not be fully defined, but they need teasing out to be used in the research. Humans regularly talk about things they cannot define – for example, define 'human', but a lack of a satisfactory definition of this term has been no barrier to discussing and researching the human condition. Tying down the definitions will continue in parallel with the research.
- Keep narrowing the topic: This requires choosing what to discard. Research by its nature keeps opening out possibilities, which need to be carefully sifted. Controlling the language is one way of making the choices explicit.

- Think through the issue of 'truth', and what you might expect to establish, by developing an explicit statement or description of what you regard as 'sufficient' evidence. Practice defending this statement.

## TIPS FOR SUPERVISORS

- Maintain a clear oversight of the distinction between the 'autobiographical' and the 'objective', and push for honest and confronting statements of the personal experience being mined.
- Question the definitions and push for clarity or agreed 'fuzziness' in the language. Be on the lookout for a tendency to assume a meaning is explicit in the mind of the researcher, when that meaning is not shared.
- Discuss the issue of 'truth' with the researcher and contribute to the definition of sufficient evidence.

## EXERCISES

1. How would you address a concern from positivist scientists that the data is limited and has not been collected in a controlled research setting?

   *Readers should be mindful that other participants in the same project would have a different lived experience. Such a perspective is valid, for as Goffman (1974: p. 10) suggests the experience of opposing supporters at a football game can be somewhat different, contingent on the score at the final whistle. Hopefully the research approach that we have outlined can provide a helpful vocabulary and framework for other PM researchers to explore their own lived experience.*

2. How do you feel about being an actor participant (the subject and object) of your research?

   *Our view is that by interrogating a case study autoethnographically, through a robust theoretical lens, a PM researcher can position themselves centrally as an active participant with findings grounded on the inside knowledge of what actually went on from their own perspective, resulting in a richer source of data that reduces the distance between the researched and the researcher.*

3. How will you counter researcher 'bias'?

   *We share Silverman's (2005) perspective that it is the concept of 'truth' that should concern researchers, rather than questions of 'bias' or 'validity'. Researchers need to convince themselves and their audience that their findings are genuinely based on the critical investigation of all their data and not reliant on a few chosen examples.*

# References

Bakhtin, M. M. and Holquist, M. (1990). *The Dialogic Imagination: Four essays*. Austin, TX: University of Texas Press.

Brodkey, L. (1996). Writing Permitted in Designated Areas Only. In H. Giroux and R. Simon (eds), *Pedagogy and Cultural Practice* (Vol. 4). Minneapolis, MN: University of Minnesota Press.

Butz, D. and Besio, K. (2004). The Value of Autoethnography for Field Research in Transcultural Settings. *The Professional Geographer,* 56(3), 350–360.

Chiu, J. (2004). I Salute the Spirit of My Communities. *College Literature,* 31(3), 43–70.

Cooley, C. H. (1922). *Human Nature and the Social Order.* New York: Charles Scribner's Sons.

Corley, K. G. and Gioia, D. A. (2011). Building Theory About Theory Building: What Constitutes a Theoretical Contribution? Academy of Management. *The Academy of Management Review,* 36(1), 12–32.

Creswell, J. W. (2007). *Qualitative Inquiry & Research Design: Choosing among five approaches* (2nd edition). Thousand Oaks, CA: Sage Publications.

Denzin, N. K. and Lincoln, Y. S. (2000). Introduction: The Discipline and Practice of Qualitative Research. In N. K. Denzin and Y. S. Lincoln (eds), *Handbook of Qualitative Research* (pp. 1–28). Thousand Oaks, CA: Sage Publications.

Dyer (Jr), W. G., Wilkins, A. L. and Eisenhardt, K. M. (1991). Better Stories, Not Better Constructs, to Generate Better Theory: A Rejoinder to Eisenhardt; Better Stories and Better Constructs: The Case for Rigor and Comparative Logic. *The Academy of Management Review,* 16(3), 613–619.

Ellis, C. and Bochner, A. P. (2000). Autoethnography, Personal Narrative, Reflexology: Researcher as Subject. In N. K. Denzin and Y. S. Lincoln (eds), *Handbook of Qualitative Research,* 2nd edition. Thousand Oaks, CA: Sage Publications, pp. 733–768.

Gadamer, H.-G. (1993). *Truth and Method,* 2nd rev. edition. London: Sheed and Ward.

Goffman, E. (1974). *Frame Analysis.* New York: Harper Colophon.

Hesse-Biber, S. N. and Levy, P. (2006). Emergent Methods in Social Research Within and Across Disciplines. In S. N. Hesse-Biber and P. Levy (eds), *Emergent Methods in Social Research.* Thousand Oaks, CA: Sage Publications.

Hui, D. (2003, 15–18 July 2003). *Managing Intersubjectivity in the Context of a Museum Learning Environment.* Paper presented at the 10th International Literacy and Education Research Network Conference on Learning, University of London.

Husserl, E. (1950/1995). *Cartesian Mediations* (D. Cairns, tr.). Dordrecht, The Netherlands: Kluwer Academic Publisher.

Husserl, E. (1965). *Phenomenology and the Crisis of Philosophy* (L. Quentin, tr.). New York: Harper & Row.

Husserl, E. (1981). Pure Phenomenology, Its Method and Its Field of Investigation Inaugural Lecture at Freiburg im Breisgau, 1917 (R. W. Jordan, Trans.). In P. McCormick and F. A. Elliston (eds), *Husserl: Shorter Works.* Notre Dame, Indiana: University of Notre Dame Press.

Husserl, E. (1997). *Psychological and Transcendental Phenomenology and the Confrontation with Heidegger (1931–1931)* (T. Sheehan and R. E. Palmer, trs.). Dordrecht: Kluwer Academic Publishers.

Mead, G. W. (1934). *Mind, Self and Society.* Chicago, IL: The University of Chicago Press.

Merleau-Ponty, M. (1953/1988). *In Praise of Philosophy and Other Essays* (J. Wild, J. Edie and J. O'Neill, trs.). Evanstone, IL: Northwestern University Press.

Merleau-Ponty, M. (1992). *Texts and Dialogues* (e. a. Michael B. Smith, trs.). New Jersey: Humanities Press.

Mischenko, J. (2005). Exhausting Management Work: Conflicting Identities. *Journal of Health Organization and Management,* 19(3), 204–218.

Nugapitiya, M., Healy, P. L. and Boydell, S. (2009), 'Engaging "Meaning" in the Analysis of the Project Start-Up Workshop', Presented at IRNOP IX International Research Network on Organizing by Projects, Berlin, Germany, October 2009, Jonas, D. and Meskendahl, S. (eds), International Research Network on Organizing by Projects, Berlin, Germany, pp. 1–25.

Nugapitiya, M., Healy, P. L. and Boydell, S. (2011), 'The Self Aware Project Manager', Presented at the 10th conference of the International Research Network for Organizing by Projects. Conference theme 'The Expanding Domain of Project Research', Montreal, Canada, June 2011, Hobbs, B. (ed.), IRNOP/University of Quebec at Montreal, Montreal, Canada, pp. 1–29.

Sartre, J.-P. (1943/2003). *Being and Nothingness* (H. Barnes, tr.). London: Routledge Classics.

Sartre, J.-P. (1948). *Existentialism and Humanism* (P. Mairet, tr.). London: A. Methven and Co.

Scheler, M. and Stikkers, K. W. (1980). Problems of a sociology of knowledge. Retrieved from http://www.lib.uts.edu.au/sso/goto.php?url=http://www.aspresolver.com/aspresolver.asp?SOTH;S10021301. Accessed: October 2012.

Silverman, D. (2005). *Doing Qualitative Research – A practical handbook* (2nd edition). London: SAGE Publications.

Smith, C. (2005). Epistomological Intimacy – A move to autoethnography. *International Journal of Qualitative Methods,* 4(2), 1–7.

Söderlund, J. (2004). Building Theories of Project Management: Past Research, Questions for the Future. *International Journal of Project Management,* 22(3), 183–191.

Sparkes, A. C. (1996). The Fatal Flaw: A Narrative of the Body-Self. *Qualitative Inquiry,* 2(4), 463–494.

Spry, T. (2006). Performance Autoethnography. In S. N. Hesse-Biber and P. Leavy (eds), *Emergent Methods in Social Research.* Thousand Oaks, CA: Sage Publications.

Wall, S. (2006). An Autoethnography on Learning about Autoethnography. *International Journal of Qualitative Methods,* 5(2), 1–12.

Yar, M. (2001). Recognition and the Politics of Human(e) Desire. *Theory, Culture & Society,* 18(2–3), 57–76.

# 21

# Enter or Not – How to Gain and Sustain Access to Research Sites

Jill Owen, Chivonne Algeo and James Connor

*We wrote this chapter because we want to share the lessons learned via our experiences and problems negotiating access to and managing our research in diverse data collection sites.*

Identifying, gaining access to and negotiating a relationship with your research site/participants is crucial. This chapter provides advice on how to select your research site, start negotiations with them and manage your ongoing relationship. We outline a range of strategies to select and set up your research site, including utilising networks, social media and professional bodies. We then explore key questions of ethics approval, anonymity and identification of the site and people, data ownership, publishing permissions and legal agreements. We outline communication and risk strategies, and mitigation strategies that can be employed to ensure the research relationship is productive for both parties. There cannot be research without participants and this chapter gives you the knowledge to negotiate successful research relationships.

At the end of this chapter, the reader can:

* identify, access and undertake PM research with external parties, drawing on real case studies;
* select a research site, participants and open negotiations so that you gain the access that you require, including advice on developing and utilising research networks;
* discuss the risks and opportunities presented by different types of research engagement; and
* understand the importance of site access and ideas on how to negotiate formal research agreements with third parties and/or informal agreements with collaborators.

Keywords: research site selection; negotiating site access; project management fieldwork

Gaining access to appropriate research sites for empirical work is critical for research success. This is an area that proves difficult for all researchers, and rarely do we realise that our method of research will also be determined by the type of organisation researched and the agreement struck with them. While in approaching an organisation we have to have a method in mind (for example, action research), you must always allow for the modification of approach based on both the identified requirements of the site and on your imperatives as a researcher. Finding a promising site and starting the negotiations presents problems and even when a research site is identified and agreement is reached in principle there are often failures in terms of negotiating contracts, site/personnel access, agreeing to what data can be accessed (including how it is accessed), and what can be published. This chapter draws on three researchers' experiences in obtaining access to research sites using formal and informal networks, with a catalogue of the lessons learned.

Granovetter (1973) coined the term, 'the strength of weak ties' to explain how you can gain access to social groups that are beyond your immediate ties of friends, family and colleagues. The research sites we provide as case studies, using formal and informal networks to gain access, arose because of the presence of the researchers in academic and professional networks. This only occurred because we had done the work to establish ourselves in the community, via research and practitioner engagement. This can be difficult for new researchers, especially if they cannot draw on previous work and/or professional networks.

Drawing on the common themes of formal and informal networks we explore the lessons learned through an analysis of the case study sites and approaches, including negotiating with individuals and organisations. We discuss: site identification; negotiating research deliverables; contract negotiation; types of funding; identification of the research 'champion'; implementation; close out; publication of results; ongoing development of the relationship/network, and finally, what to do when negotiations fail.

The chapter is structured to present the chapter goals followed by our experiences. We conclude with a discussion of the lessons learned of how research sites were accessed using formal and informal networks.

The two sites discussed below were major change programmes, one in the Australian Department of Defence and the second in an Australian Federal Government Agency. The programmes were complex, multi-year programmes designed to fundamentally change how business was conducted.

## Site One: Defence

### SET UP

One of the authors was invited to give a keynote speech on organisational change to a Command (akin to a group/division) within the Australian Defence Force. This Command was embarking on a major change programme that incorporated process and IT change, amalgamation of buildings and services, and construction of new facilities, changing the way that they had conducted business over the last 40 years. The programme was flagged as a key driver of savings for the Australian Government within the Defence portfolio. Amazed at the audacity of the change programme, we asked what academic input they had into the process. Not surprisingly the answer was none. We seized on and offered our services as academic researchers who would be able to offer a very different perspective on the programme's progress in comparison to the consultants and permanent staff.

### DOING

It was a simple question that began a year-long process that ultimately failed to achieve any research engagement. Given the scale of the change programme we proposed an ongoing action research engagement across the life of the programme plus one year. Initially five academics were involved in the proposal, covering a range of methodologies and expertise in data analysis, which decreased to three academics as time progressed. We achieved initial agreement from the Command to proceed with the negotiation of a multi-year, seven dollar figure research agreement. Much of this initial agreement was based on the trust built by one of the academic team with the key research sponsor within the Command.

## RISKS

With acceptance of the costings and research proposal, the lawyers for the University and Command became involved. It was at this point that the discussions became protracted and difficult. As academic researchers it is fundamental that we maintain our independence and carry out, analyse and publish research with freedom (while following the best practices of our disciplines). Our negotiations included the clause that the University would hold the rights to all the data generated and that we could publish all of our research, after anonymising, without the Command being able to veto what we wrote. The maintenance of research integrity was crucial to the team but created an enormous problem for the lawyers. Even with the intervention of the research sponsor, on behalf of the Commander of the unit, the Defence lawyers were never comfortable allowing us the freedom and control to publish the data. Our use of the data was obviously a major risk for the organisation. The legal wrangling continued for a year and we also had continuing problems with how the research was going to be funded by Defence – they saw the arrangement as a procurement-based contract with specified deliverables, rather than a research contract.

They withdrew their interest after 15 months of work from the research team and a significant investment from the University in terms of legal and grant administration support.

## LESSONS LEARNED

- The adage that you learn more from a loss than a win also holds in the realm of research. The different approaches to funding and access can materially affect your ability to get sign off. Don't assume that the potential participants understand the research process versus consultant work – explain how and why research is different. The knowledge gleaned from the failed attempt stood us well for the next opportunity. We recycled much of the research ideas and experiences with lawyers and research contracts into the next potential site. Our knowledge from the failed process allowed us to circumvent and/or assure the next partner on the issue of confidentiality, while also providing us with the freedom to research and publish the results.

## Site Two: Government Agency

### SET UP

We were approached by a Federal Government Agency, via a contracted Programme Manager who knew of our research reputation via our involvement in the Project Management Institute (PMI), specifically the worldwide academic and professional reputation of one of the researchers. There was a professional relationship between one researcher and the Programme Manager via PMI. They initially conducted a Post Implementation Review (PIR) of Tranche One of a major IT heavy change programme.

## DOING

We offered the Agency the option of commercial consultant rates for our time or the option of 'free' work if we owned the data and could publish any material with no right of organisational veto. As part of the initial agreement we secured a promise to discuss a two-year ongoing research relationship with the Agency and Programme Manager. After successfully conducting and reporting our PIR for Tranche One, the Agency agreed to the two-year option. This is the classic 'foot-in-the-door' sales technique and it allowed us to 'prove' the value of the research with limited risk to both sides.

## RISKS

Reflecting on the risks involved in long research agreements, you need a strong sponsor in the organisation who shares the vision and is willing to accept the risk. The risks of research need to be clearly communicated to the host organisation and sponsor, in terms they understand as research is very different from consultancy work.

## LESSONS LEARNED

- Constant communication is essential with the people in the potential research site.
- Failure must be considered a learning experience and you can take the knowledge of what got you close, then why it failed, into the next research site.
- The resources you build can also be recycled, such as research proposals, contracts, and explanations of process which can and should be reused for multiple sites.
- You will need legal advice for any formal contract. Take advantage of the expertise in your university legal office as they will have done this many times before.
- You can start small, get the early 'wins' and show the sponsor that you can deliver value to them and undertake rigorous research.

## Examples of Informal and Formal Site Negotiations

### CONTEXT

One of the researchers has conducted case study research using two sites, one as exploratory and the second as in-depth sites. These two sites researched the role of Knowledge-Based Practices (KBPs) in the effective management and delivery of Information Systems Development (ISD) Projects.

## 2 Site: Engineering Consulting Organisation; and Outsource Provider in a Government Department

### SET UP

The first case study was negotiated at the beginning of the research with access to this site being gained due to the researcher's networks. An associate of the researcher had met a representative from this organisation at a conference and they had continued to network and exchange communication on a topic in which they had a shared interest, namely Knowledge Management Systems. The researcher had an industry background that enabled her to understand the context of the work carried out in the organisation. The researcher developed a research proposal and presentation and met with people within the organisation outlining the proposed area of research. The organisation was enthusiastic and supported the researcher in conducting her research within the organisation. Several projects were considered as targets for the research. A complex innovative project that was a component of an inter-organisational (alliance) project was decided on as it could be accessed within the organisation. Access was gained without signing a Memorandum of Understanding and instead used a Non-Disclosure Agreement (NDA).

For the second case study the researcher used her extensive professional and personal networks to assess potential sites. After two meetings with a target organisation they agreed to the research proposal. Different client sites and the organisation itself were explored as potential sites. A number of the projects were discounted due to political and geographical reasons. The research site was ultimately chosen due to the complex nature of the project and the fact that key project team members were part of the researcher's professional network. The site involved the researcher researching the implementation of software into a major Australian Federal Government Department.

## DOING

Stakeholder management was key in ensuring that the research site participants were aware of what was happening and that their collaborative research needs were met. The researcher met with the stakeholders at key points that were agreed to prior to the research commencing. This allowed the research to be managed as a project, which was a comfortable and understandable way of communicating with staff. Other tools, such as status reports, were tabled and any emerging issues or risks identified. In one case people did not understand why they were being interviewed, even though an explanatory statement had been supplied. After consultation between the researcher and the project manager the process was changed by the project manager following up on this, to ensure that the participants understood the collaborative research and why the research was being undertaken.

At the completion of each phase of the study the researcher wrote a technical report for the organisations and presented research findings to interested parties within the organisations. Not only did this allow each organisation to obtain an independent report on particular aspects of project management within their organisation (the quid-pro-quo for access) but the presentation was also used as a validation exercise for the research. In both cases there has been an ongoing relationship with both research sites to ratify that the published research reflects their view of factual accuracy and does not identify the organisations involved.

## RISKS

Both of the successful research sites still had risks associated with them, in particular change in engagement over time. As access became more difficult, alternative ways to obtain data had to be found or we risked not being able to complete the research. In the case of the project management consulting firm that specialised in implementing enterprise software, when formal access to one of their consulting sites was proving difficult, the risk was mitigated via a modification of the access to site (fewer interviews, partially redacted data). Other data sources supplemented the research and helped make up for the reduced access, in this case the researcher's network was consulted for views and experiences based on the public data.

As with any project, one of the risks is that during the research the stakeholders change their interests or feel that it is no longer of importance to the organisation. The key to managing this risk is to manage the stakeholders, communicate with them and ensure that their needs are addressed as part of the research. As their interests change, if it is possible you need to ensure that these emerging interests are incorporated.

## Informal and Formal Site Negotiation: Action Research Context

### CONTEXT

The action research methodology was selected by the researcher as the basis to investigate how project managers exchange knowledge while delivering projects. Action research involves collecting data in a social setting through cycles of interventions, each requiring planned reflection (Cardno and Piggot-Irvine, 1996: p. 20). This cyclical approach provides the researcher scope to adjust the process while 'intervening' in the research site and addressing any emergent requirements. Unlike other more detached research methodologies, action research relies on the interpretation of data through an iterative and yet structured method that marries the researchers' experiences with what they are observing to develop and test a theory or hypothesis. The research sites for this investigation were located in Australia and included large private and public sector organisations, with the participants selected for their experience in managing projects.

### SET UP

The research framework was formally structured through a review of the literature which indicated that a valid unit for analysis was to involve five project managers in the research. The decision to limit the participants to five was based on the seminal research conducted by Kotter (1999a, 1999b) into 'What Leaders Really Do' and 'What Effective General Managers Really Do'.

The research focused on observations and interventions in the workplace of the selected participants. Initially eight project managers were selected to participate in the research, which allowed for the risk of redundancy. Two project managers left the research as they did not have senior management support to continue with their involvement. This was due to changes in their organisations which resulted in the research not being considered an essential business activity.

The participants were selected from the researcher's informal network of project managers to represent a range of industries and project types. This network was established over many years of engaging with the participants, initially in professional and subsequently in academic settings, with some participants already established in the researcher's social network. Several of the participants were initially not known to the researcher, as their managers, who were known to the researcher, recommended them for the research. This represented a 'snowball' approach where the initial contact is not the primary source in the research. This 'cold' start required the researcher to dedicate time to establish a level of trust with these unknown participants. Trust was initially established through the recognition of the relationship that the researcher had with the actor's colleague/manager.

The participants all had a minimum of five years' PM experience and were employed full time as a project manager in Australia. The industry sectors that the participants were selected from were deliberately diverse so that the research captured how knowledge may be exchanged with a minimal effect of industry-specific behaviours. This was important so that generalisations could not be made based on assumed industry specific behaviours, for example construction project managers will all behave in a predictably similar manner. The research sites were representative of the IT, engineering, financial services and public infrastructure sectors.

## DOING

To secure the participants agreement, a formal letter of consent outlining both their and the researcher's obligations, and the confidentiality of the data collected, was provided to the actor. Once formal approval was gained from the manager and the individual actor the research began. The first intervention required the researcher to coordinate a one-hour meeting with each actor in their place of work. The first meeting was conducted, due to the actor's schedule, in a restaurant, which proved challenging from a noise and distraction perspective. The remaining interventions with all the participants were conducted in the workplace and at the researcher's university. This required the researcher to maintain ongoing contact with the participants either through phone calls, emails or in actual face-to-face interventions.

## RISKS

The potential for some of the participants to leave the research was mitigated through initiating the research with more project managers than the five required. This risk occurred with the departure of two participants due to lack of senior management support. The data that was generated from the interviews with these participants was kept, although not used in the final analysis, as they did not participate in all three interventions.

Loss of data through inappropriate or inadequate storage of the interview transcripts and notes can occur, requiring formal processes to be planned and implemented. This provides ease of retrieval and confidentiality, and in some cases the return of proprietary or personal documents 'borrowed' by the researcher for analysis.

Respect for the confidential nature of the data gathered by the researcher, especially when asked to disclose findings to colleagues or managers that work with the actor, can create an ethical dilemma. It is therefore imperative for the researcher to negotiate at the very beginning what information can and cannot be shared with third parties, even management. This can be managed through maintaining a level of formal 'distance' at the research site and avoid being seen as part of the participants project team, or the workplace in general.

## LESSONS LEARNED

- To provide a different perspective of what the actor is disclosing, and with their knowledge but not their participation, interview one of their colleagues who is involved in the work that you are researching.
- The researcher needs to keep notes of not only the specific research data, but also relevant personal information to assist in continuing meaningful conversations at subsequent meetings which fosters a level of trust.
- Prepare a robust plan for your research, with in-built mitigation strategies for the identified risks, and then test the plan with trusted colleagues who will provide constructive feedback. Always have a contingency if participants or organisations change priorities and drop out of the research.

- Develop a level of trust with your participants through informal conversations to identify shared areas of knowledge or experiences. Also arrange where possible to provide your participants with third-party endorsements of your capabilities.
- Your professional and in some cases your personal networks will prove to be highly valuable when sourcing participants. Establish an equal relationship where all parties gain from the research and are appropriately recognised.
- When the research has finished and the results are published, the relationships that you have developed with your participants may need to be formally closed. Alternatively, the relationships may continue through networks, or informally if friendships have developed.

## Conclusion

While we justifiably make much of the research methodology and its rigor that you will use in your research, it is pointless without site access. Establishing a research location and the access you have will partly determine the methodologies employed. If you lack a professional history or a solid research network then draw on colleagues' networks and establish yourself via them. Engage in the practitioner organisations and use social media to get your presence noticed. Once you have established a reputation, or used the leverage/support of others, begin managing the research like you would a project.

Constant communication with the gatekeepers at the potential site is crucial, in particular around issues of ethics, anonymity and access to/control of the data you collect. Plan for the input of lawyers on both sides to ensure that the research agreement meets the needs of all the parties – in particular have the data ownership and process of pre-publishing approval clear and agreed to. Once you are on-site, communication and risk mitigation are still key. Communicating why you are there and what you are doing and finding is crucial to keeping trust and access open. Mitigate the risks of withdrawal from the research or change in circumstances as best you can. Finally, like the 'campsite rule', leave a research site and the participants better off than how you found them so that they will say yes to further research.

## Tips and Questions

### TIPS FOR STUDENTS

- Assess and manage the risks associated with relying on other organisations and people for your research data.
- Have a back-up plan (or two) and accept that research evolves and requires flexibility while adhering to the research objectives.
- Be up front with research contracts, ethics and the question of data ownership with the research participants and maintain communication throughout the research with these key stakeholders.
- A good, successful relationship can be an ongoing one for further research or employment, a bad engagement severely damages your reputation and closes that site for research for all.

### TIPS FOR SUPERVISORS

- Manage the expectations of the student in regards to the difficulty of access and how permissions can change.

- Assess the risks involved in access and advise appropriately.
- Utilise your own networks to assist the student gain access.

## QUESTIONS

These deceptively simple questions may assist in breaking down your research approach when negotiating access to the site and to engage the participants:

1. What is a key way of gaining access to empirical data?
2. What role do networks play in gaining access to research sites?
3. What lessons learned can you take from one research site to the next?
4. What is the role of communication in gaining access to and managing research sites?
5. How do you manage change in participants, their organisations, and research sites?

# References

Cardno, C. and Piggot-Irvine, E. (1996). Incorporating action research in school senior management training. *International Journal of Educational Management*, 10(5), 19–24.

Granovetter, M. (1973). The strength of weak ties. *American Journal of Sociology*, 78(6), 1360–1380.

Kotter, J. P. (1999a). What effective general managers really do. *Harvard Business Review*, March–April, 145–159.

Kotter, J .P. (1999b). *What Leaders Really Do*. Boston: Harvard Business School Press.

# Suggested Reading

Brydon-Miller, M. and Greenwood, D. (2006). A re-examination of the relationship between action research and human subjects review processes. *Action Research*, 4(1), 117–128.

Checkland, P. and Holwell, S. (1998). Action research: Its nature and validity. *Systemic Practice and Action Research*, 11(1), 9–21.

Dick, B. (2004). Action research literature. *Action Research*, 2(4), 425–444.

Edmondson, A. C. and McManus, S. E. (2007). Methodological fit in management field research. *Academy of Management Review*, 32(4), 1155–1179.

Feldman, M. S. and Orlikowski, W. J. (2011). Theorizing practice and practicing theory. *Organization Science*, 22, 1240–1253.

Kemmis, S. (2009). Action research as a practice-based practice. *Educational Action Research*, 17(3), 463–474.

Punch, K. F. (2005). *Introduction to Social Research: Quantitative and qualitative approaches*. London: Sage Publications.

Scandura, T. A. and Williams, E. A. (2000). Research methodology in management: Current practices, trends, and implications for future research. *Academy of Management Journal*, 43(6), 1248–1264.

# PART IV
# EXAMPLES OF MIXED METHODS STRATEGIES

Selecting chapters for this section was one of the most difficult decisions in editing this book. As you've seen (or will see), many chapters in other sections illustrate the use of mixed method strategies and could have been included here. The difference was (in my opinion) that those other chapters emphasised methodological choices in designing a research strategy while these show the application of mixed methods with a specific examples.

- Cameron and Sankaran provide a broad view of mixed methods research (MMR) for doctoral students. They discuss it in the context of competing paradigms, design options, typologies and notation systems.
- Thomas and George dive deeper into the value of mixed methods with specific comparisons between it and qualitative and quantitative methods. They present guidance on designing a strategy based on their recent experience with a large PM research initiative as an example.
- George and Thomas examine the management of research in large collaborative teams – a truly compelling example that many emergent researchers will likely experience as virtual teamwork increases. They offer insight to the relationship between team structure, mixed method design and the resulting complexities of data collection and analysis.
- Bosch-Rekveldt describes her application of mixed methods for researching Dutch-based engineering projects (based on her own doctoral work). Her study was based on a unique combination of exploratory case studies, a quantitative survey, explanatory case studies and an evaluative survey.
- The importance of sequencing in multimethod research is examined based on my own research that focused on the PM capability associated with the management of e-Learning projects within Canadian universities.
- The last chapter by Li Yongkui, Yang Qing and He Qinghua, is quite interesting as it examines a mixed methods strategy in a mega-consruction setting (in China) while also being an adaptation of a conceptual model from an altogether different organisational setting. It will, hopefully, challenge (perhaps even inspire) readers of this book to re-examine the (re-)use of their own models in unanticipated settings.

# 22

# Mixed Methods Research in Project Management

Roslyn Cameron and Shankar Sankaran

*The inspiration behind this chapter derives from a passion for mixed methods research (MMR) and many years of teaching and providing capacity building in mixed methods to novice and experienced researchers alike. Other management fields have started adopting mixed methods in their research. PM needs to keep up, as we naturally think qualitatively and quantitatively to solve problems we encounter in projects.*

The aim of this chapter is to provide doctoral students with a broad-brush view of mixed methods research (MMR) and to place MMR historically and paradigmatically against the paradigm wars of the 1970s. This will provide an historical context for MMR's growing popularity and utility across many disciplines and fields of inquiry. The chapter defines MMR and provides a discussion on the paradigmatic stances, designs, typologies and notation systems of MMR. It reviews MMR prevalence studies and the purposes for utilising a MMR study before advising on the reporting of MMR studies. The chapter includes tips for supervisors and researchers/students and exercises to assist those new to MMR in a practical and applied sense.

At the end of this chapter, the reader can:

- define MMR and the associated mixed methods notation system;
- recognise the need for those utilising MMR to position themselves paradigmatically and explicitly articulating the rationale for using MMR designs;
- apply the good reporting of a mixed methods research (GRAMMS) framework when reporting an MMR study.

Keywords: mixed methods; paradigms, typologies, GRAMMS

MMR has been lauded as the third methodological movement, and several authorities, texts and journals have emerged as leading the movement's increasingly popular growth from within education, the social and behavioural sciences and health, medicine and nursing, to a much wider audience and discipline fields. In business and management fields, the use of MMR is growing and has been researched through several prevalence studies (Bazeley, 2008; Bryman, 2008; Cameron, 2010, 2011; Currall and Towler, 2003; Molina-Azorin, 2008, 2009; Molina-Azorin and Cameron, 2010).

The definitions of MMR will be explored before tracing the MMR movement's history and evolution. The paradigmatic stances taken in MMR will be presented before discussing MMR design typologies and associated notation systems. This will be followed by reference to MMR prevalence studies across business and management disciplines before discussing rationales and purposes for MMR. Case studies demonstrating how MMR is being utilised in the field of PM will then be presented.

Defining MMR becomes critical to establishing what we are discussing, and this is no simple matter. The definitions of MMR have evolved as the movement has, and now more than ever, the problematic issue of definitions needs to be addressed. As De Lisle (2011) noted, 'The complexity and diversity of mixed methods approaches means that definition and typology have become critical to good practice' (p. 92).

## Definitions of Mixed Methods Research (MMR)

There are several definitions of MMR and as the field of MMR has developed and evolved, these definitions have multiplied, leading Johnson, Onwuegbuzie and Turner (2007) to undertake a detailed analysis of MMR definitions. Creswell (2011) claimed that the 'changing and expanding definitions of mixed methods research' (p. 270) is one of 11 current controversies and questions raised in respect to MMR. He cited definitions that have made an impact and signify the different stages in the development of MMR. Some of these definitions have been listed in Table 22.1.

**Table 22.1    Significant definitions of MMR (1989–2007)**

---

Greene, Caracelli and Graham (1989: p. 256)

'In this study, we defined mixed method designs as those that include at least one quantitative method (designed to collect numbers) and one qualitative method (designed to collect words), where neither type of method is inherently linked to any particular inquiry paradigm.'

Tashakkori and Teddlie (1998: p. ix)

'…the combination of 'qualitative and quantitative approaches in the methodology of a study'.

Tashakkori and Teddlie (2003: p. x).

'…mixed methods research has evolved to the point where it is a separate methodological orientation with its own worldview, vocabulary and techniques'.

Creswell and Plano Clark (2007: p. 5)

'Mixed methods research is a research design with philosophical assumptions as well as methods of inquiry. As a methodology, it involves philosophical assumptions that guide the direction of the collection and analysis and the mixture of qualitative and quantitative approaches in many phases of the research process. As a method, it focuses on collecting, analysing and mixing both quantitative and qualitative data in a single study or series of studies. Its central premise is that the use of quantitative and qualitative approaches, in combination, provides a better understanding of research problems than either approach alone'.

Johnson, Onwuegbuzie and Turner (2007: p. 123)

'Mixed methods research is the type of research in which a researcher or team of researchers combines elements of qualitative and quantitative research approaches (e.g. use of qualitative and quantitative viewpoints, data collection, analysis, inference techniques) for the purposes of breadth and depth of understanding and corroboration'.

---

# The History and Evolution of Mixed Methods Research (MMR) as a 'Third Methodological Movement'

Tashakkori and Teddlie (2003) referred to the emergence of MMR as the third methodological movement: 'The mixed methods movement is a 'quiet' revolution in that its orientation has been to resolve conflicts between qualitative and quantitative inquiry' (p. 697). The movement gained momentum in the 1980s as a distinct methodological force.

The formal emergence of MMR has been mapped by Johnson and Gray (2010), who claimed that after 1935, 'the social and behavioural sciences became increasingly dominated by QUAN approach because it seemed to have the most promising future. The post-1935 period also was a time of increasing disciplinary crystallis ation instead of disciplinary integration of earlier times' (p. 87). Then, in 1966, the concept of triangulation emerged and was developed by Jick (1979) and Denzin (1978). From the mid-1980s and into the late 1990s, MMR concepts and practices were developed, especially in the field of programme evaluation. According to Johnson and Gray (2010), 'During the emergence of MM as a third methodological paradigm ... MM has struggled somewhat to develop a corresponding philosophical pragmatism' (p. 87). The relationship between pragmatism and MMR will be addressed later in the chapter.

Creswell and Plano Clark (2007) also mapped the emergence of MMR across four overlapping periods as follows:

- formative period: began in the 1950s to 1980s;
- paradigm debate period: 1970s to 1980s;
- procedural developments: 1980s to 2000; and
- advocacy as a separate design period: 2000 to present.

They saw the mixed methods movement as currently entering a stage of increasing interest across multiple disciplines, as exemplified by publication of mixed methods studies, mixed methods texts and journals, funding opportunities and special interest groups.

# Paradigmatic Stances in Mixed Methods Research (MMR)

Teddlie and Tashakkori (2003) viewed the utility of MMR as being based on how it:

- answers research questions that other methodologies cannot;
- provides better (stronger) inferences;
- provides the opportunity for presenting a greater diversity of divergent views.

Despite the advances in mixed methods theoretical and methodological foundations over the last ten years, however, several controversies remain.

It is important for those utilising MMR to be cognisant of the common criticisms that are made of mixed methods so that these can be addressed and considered when designing and implementing a mixed methods study. Tashakkori and Teddlie (2010) identified the most frequently mentioned critiques of MMR as follows: the costs of conducting MMR; unrealistic expectations regarding a researcher's competence in both qualitative and quantitative methodology; the complexity of putting together teams to carry out MMR; and the impossibility of examining issues from different perspectives/worldviews or what is referred to as the *incompatibility thesis*. The authors had earlier listed six controversial areas or unresolved issues in relation to MMR as follows:

1.  The nomenclature and basic definitions used in MMR.
2.  The utility of MMR (why we do it).
3.  The paradigmatic foundations for MMR.
4.  Design issues in MMR.
5.  Issues in drawing inferences in MMR.
6.  The logistics of conducting MMR (Tashakkori and Teddlie, 2003: p. 672).

This section of the chapter will present the paradigmatic stances taken in relation to MMR. Many within the MMR community have made strong links between MMR and pragmatism, which has also been a source of criticism for the movement. Biesta (2010) presented seven different levels at which ideas about mixing methods, at what levels mixing methods is relatively unproblematic and at what levels issues become more serious, as follows:

*   Level 1: Data (unproblematic to have both text and numbers in same research).
*   Level 2: Methods (unproblematic to have data collection methods that generate numbers and text in the same research).
*   Level 3: Design (issues with having interventionist and non-interventionalist designs in one study).
*   Level 4: Epistemology (problematic: which epistemological set of ideas is most appropriate to account for knowledge generated through a mixed methods study?).
*   Level 5: Ontology (problematic: is it possible to combine different assumptions about reality in the same research?).
*   Level 6: Purposes of research (issues with combining research which seeks to explain and research which seeks to understand).
*   Level 7: Practical roles of research (unproblematic to have research oriented toward both technical and cultural role) (p. 100).

The levels at which issues arise are at Level 3, when interventionist and non-interventionist design are used in one study, and at Level 6, when research is trying to combine research that is seeking to explain and seeking to understand. The more serious and complex issues arise at Level 4 and Level 5. Those wishing to utilise MMR need to be aware of these issues and to address them when explaining the methodological choices they are making.

For many researchers, mixing methods and approaches presents important philosophical and paradigmatic dilemmas. In 2003, Teddlie and Tashakkori presented the six philosophical stances taken in relation to research and in particular MMR as follows: the a-paradigmatic stance; the incompatibility thesis; the complementary thesis; the single paradigm thesis; the dialectic thesis; and the multiple paradigm thesis. Researchers wishing to use MMR can position themselves using this framework of paradigmatic stances (see Table 22.2).

Modell (2010) chose an approach to mixed methods that stimulates inter-paradigmatic dialogue through the use of meta-triangulation:

> The basic idea of meta-triangulation is to mobilize multiple paradigms in examining a particular social phenomenon and at least initially preserve their integrity (rather than modifying and integrating them) whilst remaining aware of the potential transition zones between them. Differences and similarities in research findings may then be systematically analyzed at the levels of ontology, epistemology and methodology. For instance, a particular accounting issue may be examined with the aid of both quantitative and qualitative methods informed by theories and philosophical assumptions associated with the 'mainstream' and the 'alternative' paradigm, respectively, using a team of researchers affiliated with both paradigms. This might reveal whether research findings converge or diverge as a result of methodological artifacts or due to more fundamental similarities and differences in philosophical

**Table 22.2    Paradigmatic stances in MMR (Teddlie and Tashakkori, 2003)**

| Stance | Description |
|---|---|
| A-paradigmatic stance: | *Methods and paradigms are independent of each other* |
| Incompatibility thesis: | *MMR is impossible (purists)* |
| Complementary thesis: | *Mixed methods possible BUT must be kept separate to ensure strengths of each paradigm (situationalists)* |
| Single paradigm thesis: | *A single paradigm should serve the foundation of mixed methods* |
| Dialectic thesis: | *Mixed methods engages in multiple sets of paradigms and their assumptions. All paradigms are valuable but are only partial worldviews. Reject the selection of one paradigm over another* |
| Multiple paradigm thesis: | *Multiple paradigms may serve MMR. The difference between this and dialectic is the need to choose one type of paradigm for a particular study over another* |

*assumptions. Such research may also be extended by paying explicit attention to the positions adopted by various researchers as a result of differences in their backgrounds, such as research training, institutional affiliations and paradigmatic commitments. (p. 127)*

A favoured approach to paradigmatic positioning in MMR is to align with pragmatism or a dialectic approach. According to Molina-Azorin and Cameron (2010), 'Pragmatism advances multiple pluralistic approaches to knowing, using "what works", a focus on the research questions as important with all types of methods to follow to answer the questions, and a rejection of a forced choice between postpositivism and constructivism. Thus, a major tenet of pragmatism is that quantitative and qualitative methods are compatible' (p. 97). The development of MMR as a third methodological movement has also seen the evolution of an array of MMR design typologies. This chapter will present two of these.

## Mixed Methods Research (MMR) Design Typologies and Notation Systems

As De Lisle (2011) stated, 'Typologies are classification schemes used to describe various mixed methods designs, and are important to good practice because they include implicit rules, procedures, and criteria for mixing. Currently, there are several typologies in the literature' (p. 93). One of the earliest MMR typologies developed was by Morgan (1998). Figure 22.1 provides a visual depiction of the four complementary MMR designs Morgan (1998) developed for health research, as follows: qualitative preliminary, quantitative preliminary, qualitative follow-up and quantitative follow-up. You will also notice that this was the beginning of an MMR notation system where qualitative research is noted by either QUAL or qual depending on whether the qualitative data is more dominant or has greater priority and Quantitative data is noted by QUAN or quan. Arrows (→) denote sequential data collection and plus sign (+) denotes concurrent or simultaneous data collection. This notation system was first developed by Morse (1991, 2003) and has been further developed by Morse and Neihaus (2009) and Cameron (2012).

Another set of MMR designs has been developed by Creswell, Plano Clark, Gutmann and Hanson (2003). A summary of these designs is provided in Table 22.3 and indicates whether the designs is sequential, concurrent or nested, at what stage the qualitative and quantitative elements of the research are integrated and which has priority.

| Qualitative Preliminary | Quantitative Preliminary |
|---|---|
| Qual → QUAN | Quan → QUAL |
| Qualitative Follow-up | Quantitative Follow-up |
| QUAN → qual | QUAL → quan |

**Figure 22.1   Complementary MMR designs (Morgan, 1998)**

**Table 22.3   MMR designs (Creswell et al., 2003)**

| Creswell et al. (2003) | Stage of Integration | Implementation | Priority/Status |
|---|---|---|---|
| Sequential designs Sequential explanatory | Interpretation | QUAN→qual | Usually QUAN, can be QUAL or qual |
| Sequential exploratory | Interpretation | QUAL→quan | Usually QUAL, can be QUAN or equal |
| Sequential transformative | Interpretation | QUAL→QUAN QUAN→QUAL | Either dominant or both equal |
| Concurrent designs Triangulation | Interpretation or analysis | QUAL+QUAN | Equal |
| Nested | Analysis | Qual within QUAN Quan within QUAL | Either dominant |
| Transformative | Usually, analysis, can be interpretation | QUAL+QUAN | Either dominant or both equal |

There are many more MMR design typologies and those wishing to use MMR need to find the designs that best suit their research purposes.

## Prevalence Studies of Mixed Methods Research (MMR)

Prevalence studies of the use of MMR in disciplines are studies which analyse the prevalence of mixed methods studies within a discipline through samples of published research, usually in academic outlets such as journals and conferences proceedings (Alise and Teddlie, 2010). Cameron and Molina-Azorin (2011) undertook a synthesis of the MMR prevalence studies undertaken in several disciplines in management and business. These disciplines included marketing, international business, strategic management, organisational behaviour, operations management and entrepreneurship. Table 22.4 is a summary of the synthesis undertaken by these two authors. All of the studies aimed to discover the extent and current role of qualitative, quantitative and

**Table 22.4**     **Summary of empirical papers aligned with discipline fields (adapted from Cameron and Molina-Azorin, 2011)**

| Discipline | Quant | Qual | Mixed | Total |
|---|---|---|---|---|
| Marketing | 553 | 78 | 105 | **736** |
| 3 Journals 1993–2002 | (75%) | (11%) | (14%) | (100%) |
| Hanson and Grimmer (2005) | | | | (31%) |
| International business | 269 | 57 | 68 | **394** |
| 4 Journals 2000–2003 | (68%) | (15%) | (17%) | (100%) |
| Hurmerinta-Peltomaki and Nummela | | | | (17%) |
| (2006) | | | | |
| Strategic management | 441 | 30 | 99 | **570** |
| 1 Journal 1997–2006 | (78%) | (5%) | (17%) | (100%) |
| Molina-Azorin (2009) | | | | (24%) |
| Organisational behaviour | 197 | 17 | 17 | **231** |
| 1 Journal 2003–2008 | (85%) | (7.5%) | (7.5%) | (100%) |
| Molina-Azorin and Lopez-Fernandez | | | | (10%) |
| (2009) | | | | |
| Operations management | 146 | 23 | 18 | **187** |
| 1 Journal 2003–2007 | (78%) | (12%) | (10%) | (100%) |
| Molina-Azorin (2008) | | | | (8%) |
| Entrepreneurship | 178 | 37 | 20 | **235** |
| 2 Journals 2003–2007 | (76%) | (16%) | (8%) | (100%) |
| Molina-Azorin (2008) | | | | (10%) |
| **Total** | **1,784** | **242** | **327** | **2,353** |
| | (76%) | (10%) | (14%) | (100%) |

mixed methods in these business and management fields through a process of content analysis of empirical studies published in academic journals. After taking the conceptual articles out of the analysis, the following summary table was presented on the empirical papers (qualitative, quantitative or MMR).

Cameron and Molina-Azorin (2011) identified disciplines where the prevalence of mixed methods was minimal (organisational behaviour and entrepreneurship) and where it was more prevalent than qualitative research (strategic management, marketing and international business). The authors concluded that:

> Quantitative methods (76%) overwhelmingly dominates the methodological choice of the empirical articles reported in the journal samples across the fields reported. Nonetheless, mixed method studies represent 14% of empirical articles followed by qualitative studies at 10%. If the framework for acceptance levels devised by Creswell and Plano Clark (2007) is applied it would seem, for the business and management fields covered in this synthesis of mixed methods prevalence rates studies, there exists at the least, minimal signs of acceptance of mixed methods. (Cameron and Molina-Azorin, 2011: p. 267)

These studies are now four to ten years old, and current prevalence rates may have increased as MMR has become more widely known and legitimated through the development of the MMR conceptual and foundational knowledge base. The following section of the chapter looks specifically at the utility of MMR within PM research.

## Purposes and Rationales for Using Mixed Methods Research (MMR)

The following papers were selected from three key PM journals as examples of how mixed methods has been applied in PM. The journals are *Project Management Journal* (PMJ), *International Journal of Project Management* (IJPM) and *IEEE Transactions on Engineering Management* (IEEE TM).

### 1. MILOSEVIC AND PATANAKUL, 2005 (PMJ): 'STANDARDIZED PROJECT MANAGEMENT MAY INCREASE DEVELOPMENT PROJECT SUCCESS'

Although this paper did not specifically state that it was MMR, an analysis of the paper showed this to be a good example of MMR in project management. Instead, the authors called it a three-step approach (Figure 1: p. 184) and confirmed that it combined qualitative and quantitative methods. The research problem they tried to address was as follows:

> What are the major factors in SPM [Standardised Project Management] efforts on the OPM [Organizational Project Management] level? And what SPM factors on the OPM level are of interest because they may impact project success? (p. 182)

The first step used a case study methodology to develop SPM constructs for hypothesis testing through a quantitative study. This was followed by case interviews of a qualitative nature. Thus, the sequence was qual-QUAN-qual.

Step 1 included semi-structured interviews with 12 project managers and a review of SPM-related documents and observations. The data were analysed using content analysis and cross-case analysis to develop sharper construct definitions.

The data from Step 1 were used to develop seven hypotheses and a questionnaire. A sample of 55 participants from development projects in high-velocity industries – computer/software and electronics – were surveyed. The data collected were analysed using two bivariate analysis methods and one multivariate method.

In Step 3, multiple follow-up interviews were conducted in the five companies included in the sample. Five individuals were interviewed.

The discussion used results from both the quantitative and qualitative analysis. While the quantitative results seemed to indicate a mediocre level of project managementstandardisation, which was surprising, the interviews offered an explanation for these results. Herein lies the advantage of using mixed methods, as using only one method might not have given the valid results. Finally, the researchers compared their findings with industry practices, which helped to throw additional light on their research.

The major contribution of this study was the identification of critical factors at OPM level and the finding that companies standardised PM only to a certain level to maintain flexibility.

### 2. LEE-KELLY, 2006 (IJPM): 'LOCUS OF CONTROL AND ATTITUDES TO WORKING IN VIRTUAL TEAMS'

The researcher wanted to 'examine the influence of individual workers' general control expectancies on their attitudes towards distributed working' (p. 236). The purpose was to understand how workers in multi-location and multicultural project teams make sense of their environment beyond operational issues by looking at psychological and emotional drivers. The sequence was QUAN-qual. The authors did not explicitly refer to this as an MMR study.

The research was declared as two-staged. In the first stage, a survey of professional workers in defence projects tested the 'locus of control' on the perception of team members concerning role conflict and job satisfaction. This was followed by using a case study of IT professionals. In-depth interviews were used as the qualitative study method.

The survey used a *t*-test on locus of control and managerial position. The interviews were coded using NVivo qualitative analysis software. The qualitative study was used to elaborate on the results of the survey conducted in the first step. This is a good use of the two methods in sequence. The discussion employed the results of both the quantitative and qualitative study to derive conclusions that were useful for practice.

## 3. CHAI AND XIN, 2006 (IEEE TM): 'THE APPLICATION OF NEW PRODUCT DEVELOPMENT TOOLS IN INDUSTRY: THE CASE OF SINGAPORE'

The study investigated the diffusion and adoption of new product development tools in industry in Singapore. The authors did not specifically state that this was a mixed methods study.

The study used a case study and survey. The case study along with a literature review was used to generate hypotheses to be tested by a survey. The purpose of using two steps was to render the findings 'much richer' and add 'grounded understanding' (p. 344). These are generally good reasons for an MM approach.

The case study was carried out using semi-structured interviews of both practitioners and academics. There were some differences in opinions between the academics and practitioners, but there was broad agreement that benchmarking was commonly used.

Analysis of the interviews resulted in differentiating between tool-related factors and organisation-related factors. Both descriptive statistics and regression analysis were used to analyse the quantitative data. The discussion was mainly based on the quantitative study. This is an example of one good use of MM, starting with one method to initiate another method.

When we analysed project management journals for the prevalence of MM studies, we found that PM research is not keeping pace with the increased use of MM in management journals. The papers also do not seem to explicitly declare the studies as MM, but use other names to describe MMR. Despite this, they are good examples of the use of MM, as the three papers from the key PM journals demonstrate.

## Reporting Mixed Methods Research (MMR)

O'Cathain, Murphy and Nicholl (2008) undertook an analysis of mixed methods studies in the health services research published between 1994 and 2004. The aim of this study was to assess the quality of these mixed methods studies. The authors took note that there had been very little done on developing quality criteria for assessing mixed methods studies and did not wish to develop these as a result of their study. What they did produce was a set of quality questions to assess these MMR studies.

The study found that the main quality issue was a 'lack of transparency of the mixed methods aspects of the studies and the individual components. The qualitative components were more likely to be poorly described than the quantitative ones' (O'Cathain et al., 2008: pp. 96–97). In terms of integrating the qualitative and quantitative data, there were few if any attempts to do so as there was a 'tendency for researchers to keep the qualitative and quantitative components separate rather than attempt to integrate data or findings in reports or publications' (O'Cathain et al., 2008: p. 97).

The study offered the good reporting of a mixed methods study (GRAMMS) framework, which assists and encourages quality reporting of MMR. This six-item guidance framework includes prompts about the 'success of the study, the mixed methods design, the individual qualitative and quantitative components, the integration between methods and the inferences drawn from completed studies' (O'Cathain et al., 2008: p. 92). GRAMMS includes the following set of quality guidelines (O'Cathain et al., 2008):

1. describe the justification for using a mixed methods approach to the research question;
2. describe the design in terms of the purpose, priority and sequence of methods;
3. describe each method in terms of sampling, data collection and analysis;
4. describe where integration has occurred, how it has occurred and who has participated in it;
5. describe any limitation of one method associated with the presence of the other method; and
6. describe any insights gained from mixing or integrating methods.

It is highly recommended that those wishing to employ MMR designs reflexively use the GRAMMS when designing, conducting and reporting MMR.


## Tips and Exercises

### TIPS FOR STUDENTS

- The research methodology selected should match the research question(s) being asked. So you have to provide a convincing rationale to select MMR. See Chapter 30 of *The Sage Handbook of Mixed methods in Social and Behavioural Research* (Tashakkori and Teddlie, 2010) on how to write good MMR proposals. See also Chapter 8 in Creswell and Plano Clark (2007).
- The guidelines provided in this chapter on how to set up MMR should be carefully considered while coming up with an appropriate research design.
- You have to consider the integration of qualitative and quantitative integrations right from the start rather than as an afterthought.
- Writing up a mixed methods theses or dissertation can be challenging, as it may seem like writing two theses. Careful consideration of writing up the thesis or report up front could help in managing the task.
- MMR would need specific skills. Refer to Creswell and Plano Clark (2007), Chapter 9. There is also *The Sage Handbook of Mixed and Multimethod Research* being published by Oxford University Press (in press), which may have useful tips.


### TIPS FOR SUPERVISORS

- MMR requires both quantitative and qualitative data collection and analysis skills. The student needs to be taught both before venturing to take up mixed methods. Working in different paradigms may pose challenges to researchers. You have to ensure that they do not mix them up while carrying out their research.
- Writing up a MMR thesis or dissertation could be a challenge. Therefore, the chapters of the thesis, dissertation or report would have to be matched to the type of mixed methods design being adopted.

- Encourage your students to enrol in courses that would teach quantitative, qualitative and mixed methods such as the graduate certificate taught online at the University of Nebraska (http://online.unl.edu/Graduate/Programs/Mixed-Methods-Certificate.aspx).

## EXERCISES

1. Apply an MMR design to a particular PM research problem and position yourself paradigmatically. After you have done this, justify your methodological choice by arguing why an MMR study would better answer your research questions as opposed to a mono-method (QUAN or QUAL) or a multimethod (QUAN or QUAL) study.
2. Once you have undertaken exercise 1, follow this by choosing an appropriate MMR design and provide a diagram of the design which includes the key MMR notation system flow diagrams and MMR notation system (see Creswell and Plano Clark, 2007 or Creswell et al., 2003 as a good starting point for ideas on MMR designs).
3. After undertaking exercises 1 and 2, use the GRAMMS guidelines to justify your methodological choices. Use the first three guideline points from GRAMMS:
   - describe the justification for using a mixed methods approach to the research question;
   - describe the design in terms of the purpose, priority and sequence of methods; and
   - describe each method in terms of sampling, data collection and analysis.

## References

Alise, M. A. and Teddlie, C. (2010). A continuation of the paradigm wars? Prevalence rates methodological approaches across the social/behavioural sciences. *Journal of Mixed Methods Research*, 4(2), 103–126.

Bazeley, P. (2008). Mixed methods in management research. In R. Holt and R. Thorpe (eds), *Dictionary of Qualitative Management Research*. London: Sage, pp. 133–136.

Biesta, G. (2010). Pragmatism and the philosophical foundations of mixed methods research. In A. Tashakkori and C. Teddlie (eds), *Handbook of Mixed Methods in Social and Behavioral Research*, 2nd edition. Thousand Oaks, CA: Sage, pp. 95–118.

Bryman, A. (2008). Why do researchers integrate/combine/mesh/blend/mix/merge/fuse quantitative and qualitative research? In M. Bergman (ed.), *Advances in Mixed Methods Research*. Thousand Oaks, CA: Sage, pp. 87–100.

Cameron, R. (2010). A study of the use of mixed methods in management and organisational research journals: Justification and design. *Academy of World Business, Marketing & Management Development 2010 Conference*, 12–15 July, 2010, Oulu, Finland.

Cameron, R. (2011). Mixed methods in business and management: A call to the 'first generation'. *Journal of Management and Organisation*, 17(2), 245–267.

Cameron, R. (2012). Applying the newly developed Extended Mixed Methods Research (MMR) Notation System. *British Academy of Management 2012 Conference*, 11–13 September, Cardiff, Wales.

Cameron, R. and Molina-Azorin, J. (2011). The acceptance of mixed methods in business and management. *International Journal of Organizational Analysis*, 19(3), 256–271.

Chai, K-H. and Xin, Y. (2006). The application of new product development tools in industry: The case of Singapore, *IEEE Transactions on Engineering Management*, 53(4), 435–554.

Creswell, J. W. (2011) Controversies in mixed methods research. In N. K. Denzin and Y. S. Lincoln (eds), the *Sage Handbook of Qualitative Research*, 2nd edition. Thousand Oaks, CA: Sage, pp. 269–284.

Creswell, J. W. and Plano Clark, V. L. (2007). *Designing and Conducting Mixed Methods Research*. Thousand Oaks, CA: Sage.

Creswell, J. W. and Plano Clark, V. (2011). *Designing and Conducting Mixed Methods Research*. Thousand Oaks, CA: Sage.

Creswell, J. W., Plano Clark, V. L., Gutmann, M. L. and Hanson, W. E. (2003). Advanced mixed methods research designs. In A. Tashakkori and C. Teddlie (eds), *Handbook of Mixed Methods in Social and Behavioral Research*. Thousand Oaks, CA: Sage, pp. 209–240.

Currall, S. C. and Towler, A. J. (2003). Research methods in management and organizational research: Toward integration of qualitative and quantitative techniques. In A. Tashakkori and C. Teddlie (eds), *Handbook of Mixed Methods in Social and Behavioral Research*. Thousand Oaks, CA: Sage, pp. 513–526.

De Lisle, J. (2011). The benefits and challenges of mixing methods and methodologies: Lessons learnt from implementing qualitatively led mixed methods research designs in Trinidad and Tobago. *Caribbean Curriculum*, 18, 87–120.

Denzin, N. K. (1978). *The Research Act: A theoretical introduction to sociological methods*. New York: McGraw-Hill.

Greene, J., Caracelli, V. and Graham, W. D. (1989). Toward a conceptual framework for mixed-method evaluation designs. *Educational Evaluation and Policy Analysis*, 11(3), 255–274.

Hanson, D. and Grimmer, M. (2005). The mix of qualitative and quantitative research in major marketing journals. *European Journal of Marketing*, 41(1/2), 58–70.

Hurmerinta-Peltomaki, L. and Nummela, N. (2006). Mixed methods in international business research: A value-added perspective. *Management International Review*, 46(4), 439–459.

Jick, T. D. (1979). Mixing qualitative and quantitative methods: Triangulation in action. *Administrative Science Quarterly*, 24, 602–611.

Johnson, B. and Gray, R. (2010). A history of philosophical and theoretical issues for mixed methods research. In A. Tashakkori and C. Teddlie (eds), *Handbook of Mixed Methods in Social and Behavioral Research*. Thousand Oaks, CA: Sage, pp. 69–94.

Johnson, R. B., Onwuegbuzie, A. and Turner, I. (2007). Toward a definition of mixed methods research. *Journal of Mixed Methods Research*, 1, 112–133.

Lee-Kelley, L. (2006). Locus of control and attitudes to working in virtual teams. *International Journal of Project Management*, 24(3), 234–243.

Milosevic, D. and Patanakul, P. (2005). Standardized project management may increase development project success. *International Journal of Project Management*, 23(3), 181–192.

Modell, S. (2010). Bridging the paradigm, divide in management accounting research: The role of mixed methods approaches. *Management Accounting Research*, 21, 124–129.

Molina-Azorin, J. F. (2007). Mixed methods in strategy research: Applications and implications in the resource-based view. *Research Methodology in Strategic Management*, 4, 37–73.

Molina-Azorin, J. F. (2008, July). *Mixed methods research in business management: A comparison of the use of mixed methods in three specific areas*. Paper presented at the 4th Mixed Methods Conference, Cambridge, UK.

Molina-Azorin, J. F. (2009). Understanding how mixed methods research is undertaken within a specific research community: The case of business studies. *International Journal of Multiple Research Approaches*, 3(1), 47–57.

Molina-Azorin, J. and Cameron, R. (2010). The application of mixed methods in organisational research: A literature review. *Electronic Journal of Business Research Methods*, 8(2), 95–105.

Molina-Azorin, J. F. and López-Fernández, O. (2009, July). *Mixed methods research in behavioural sciences: A comparison of mixed methods studies in two specific fields*. Paper presented at the 4th Mixed Methods Conference, Harrogate, UK.

Morgan, D. (1998). Practical strategies for combining qualitative and quantitative methods: Applications to health research. *Qualitative Health Research*, 8(3), 362–376.

Morse, J. (1991). Approaches to qualitative-quantitative methodological triangulation. *Nursing Research*, 20(2), 120–123.

Morse, J. (2003). Principles of mixed and multi-method research design. In A. Tashakkori and C. Teddlie (eds), *Handbook of Mixed Methods in Social and Behavioral Research*. Thousand Oaks, CA: Sage, pp. 189–208.

Morse, J. and Neihaus, L. (2009). *Mixed Method Design: Principles and procedures*. Walnut Creek, CA: Left Coast Press.

O'Cathain, A., Murphy, E. and Nicholl, J. (2008). The quality of mixed methods studies in health services research. *Journal of Health Services Research and Policy*, 13(2), 92–98.

Tashakkori, A. and Teddlie, C. (1998). *Mixed Methodology Combining Qualitative and Quantitative Approaches*. Thousand Oaks, CA: Sage.

Tashakkori, A. and Teddlie, C. (eds). (2003). *Handbook of Mixed Methods in Social and Behavioral Research*. Thousand Oaks, CA: Sage.

Tashakkori, A. and Teddlie, C. (eds). (2010). *Handbook of Mixed Methods in Social and Behavioral Research*, 2nd edition. Thousand Oaks, CA: Sage.

Teddlie, C. and Tashakkori, A. (2003). Major issues and controversies in the use of mixed methods in the social and behavioural sciences. In A. Tashakkori and C. Teddlie (eds), *Handbook of Mixed Methods in Social and Behavioral Research*. Thousand Oaks, CA: Sage, pp. 3–50.

Teddlie, C. and Tashakkori, A. (2010). Overview of contemporary issues in mixed methods research. In A. Tashakkori and C. Teddlie (eds), *Handbook of Mixed Methods in Social and Behavioral Research*, 2nd edition. Thousand Oaks, CA: Sage, pp. 1–44.

# 23

# The Value of
# Mixed Methods

Janice Thomas and Stella George

*PM research raises many questions where the basic science and theories have not yet been developed. Mixed methods studies allow researchers to both develop and test theory. Researchers often conduct qualitative studies to develop theories based in the experience of managing projects and then larger sample size quantitative studies to generalise these theories. Sometimes quantitative survey research generates unexpected theories that need to be explained through qualitative study. This chapter presents guidance on how to design a mixed methods research (MMR) approach and explores an example of how this is done in practice.*

At the end of this chapter, the reader can:

*   understand what is meant by MMR, when it can be applied and explanation of same;
*   design a MMR study in project;
*   identify some of the likely challenges and potential mitigation strategies available to a research when undertaking a mixed methods approach.

Keywords: mixed methods, qualitative research, quantitative research, research design

## Introduction to Mixed Methods Research (MMR)

MMR is becoming more common in many disciplines as research questions become more complex (a definition is offered below). As we come to ask more sophisticated questions about PM, we too find a greater need to mix research design elements of both a qualitative and quantitative nature, where neither approach individually would adequately address the research question. Mixed methods studies take into account culture and context as well as measurement. These research designs are tricky as all research methods employed must be used intentionally and systematically to the highest level of competence (Cresswell and Plano Clark, 2011).

> *Mixed methods research is, generally speaking, an approach to knowledge (theory and practice) that attempts to consider multiple viewpoints, perspectives, positions and standpoints (always including the standpoints of qualitative and quantitative research. (Johnson, Onwuegbuzie and Turner, 2007: p. 113)*

Many of the challenges associated with mixed methods approaches arise from the necessary bridging of what some might consider incommensurable differences in ontology and epistemology (as discussed in detail in Part one of the book). Mixed methods requires a hybrid ontology that allows us to explore situations that are clearly social in nature while attempting to come up with reliable means of measuring or quantifying at least some aspects of the phenomenon. Similarly the epistemological position of mixed methods varies between the logical empiricism of attempting to observe empirical facts tempered by the knowledge that many managerial phenomenon are constructed through constructions of meanings by the social actors embedded in the phenomenon.

## When No Other Method Will Do

Social science typically involves (1) deductive approaches using quantitative research methods, or (2) inductive approaches using qualitative methods. However, contributions can also be made when (3) quantitative methods have laid the ground for inductive theory building or (4) qualitative methods are used in deductive theory testing (Bitektine, 2008). Increasing the number of methods used in any one study clearly increases the complexity of the research design. However, there are many research situations where a mixed method is the only real option for addressing the research question.

Specifically, a mixed method approach is used when:

- the study is requires a range of perspectives and requires critical multiplism to make valuable contributions to our understanding of complex phenomenon (Johnson et al., 2007);
- previous qualitative and quantitative research has only partly addressed the research question or may have produced contradictory results;
- capture of relevant, reliable and honest data can only be achieved by using a range of data collection methods;
- different methods are needed to increase the richness of measurements across different dimensions (Bryman, 2007) increasing the usefulness of the findings (Johnson et al., 2007);
- various philosophical perspectives on the research question result in conflicting perspectives of a phenomena. The implications of philosophical assumptions are more likely raised through conflicting data (Srnka and Koeszegi, 2007).

Mixed method approaches are particularly valued for their capacity to triangulate both data and method (Jack and Raturi, 2006). Multiple methods allow the researcher to use one method 'as a validation process that ensures that the explained variances are the result of the underlying phenomenon or trait and not the method' (Johnson et al., 2007: p. 113). By extending generalisability of the theory to those aspects of the social phenomena that are not amenable to quantification, theory testing using qualitative methods can reduce the need for 'leaps of faith' when translating quantitative results to other less-measurable aspects of social process (Bitektine, 2008).

## Not Without a Downside

Clearly a mixed methods design is a valuable approach to developing deep rich understandings of a phenomenon and testing their generalisability. However, the flexibility and potential of a mixed method approach does not mean that it should be used in all circumstances because its benefits do not come without relatively large practical issues. For these reasons mixed method approaches are recognised as difficult to complete successfully.

Some of the more common disadvantages of mixed method research (MMR) are:

- MMR projects require skill in multiple methods which can be difficult to find as very few individuals have experience in both quantitative and qualitative methods (Bryman, 2007). This is the primary reason why this approach is not often suggested for thesis research.
- Mixed methods studies require more effort on the part of the researcher than single method studies. Multimethod studies consume more time and resources as there is necessary duplication of effort in conducting multiple analsyes in order to facilitate triangulation.
- Integration of data from both methods is difficult, and there are few good examples of integrative results (Bryman, 2007). Different analysis can yield apparently contradictory results that require further investigation to explain or may nullify your research.
- The audience of the results of the project may prefer one type of data over another (Bryman, 2007) and the nature of the data means that one set is more interesting than the other to some researchers (Bryman, 2007).
- Using both qualitative and quantitative methods simultaneously to answer a research question can be controversial. Some believe that the assumptions underlying differing methodologies are inherently opposed, and cannot be meaningfully combined.
- It may be hard to publish results from a mixed method study as certain fields require data presentation within limited formats.

The additional cost to the researcher and difficulties in conducting and publishing this research serves as a caution to all researchers contemplating such a study and makes it critical that we only pursue this option when the benefits outweigh the costs. Thus, it is very important to carefully construct your research question before deciding on your methodological approach.

## How to Mix Methods

Mixed methods approaches are often used in combination, by alternating between methods – typically using qualitative research for theory generation and quantitative methods for theory testing. A grounded theory approach as described predominantly in Eisenhardt's grounded theory work is commonly used. This approach designs research to observe 'phenomena with multiple methods to ground the theory development process in different versions of an existing reality' (Jack and Raturi, 2006: p. 356). Theory is created by 'observing patterns within systematically collected empirical data' (Eisenhardt and Graebner, 2007: p. 30) by 'recursively iterating between (and thus constantly comparing) theory and data during analysis, and theoretically sampling cases…' (Eisenhardt and Graebner, 2007: p. 30). In a mixed methods study the iteration and theory building is strengthened by comparative analysis between quantitative and qualitative findings to create strong and detailed theory.

Cresswell (2006) however states there are three ways to mix methods (see Figures 23.1, 23.2 and 23.3).

- First, what could be called a two solitudes approach, whereby both quantitative and qualitative studies feed the results but they are done separately. The first approach is multidisciplinary where two (or more) different studies are completed independently and the results are combined after the fact. This can be a very time-effective way of completing a project as there is no dependency between the qualitative and quantitative studies

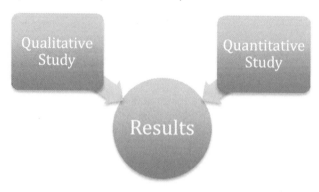

**Figure 23.1    Two solitudes of mixed methods**

- A sequential approach can be used, where qualitative analysis feeds quantitative analysis (or vice versa) to produces results. This approach also allows each methodology to be completed separately but the results of the first study (either quantitative or qualitative) informs the second study (either qualitative or quantitative). This approach is interdisciplinary in nature as the researchers need to work together at the planning and handoff points. This approach also allows you to maintain more separation between the types of studies and the underlying ontological and epistemological assumptions.

**Figure 23.2    Sequential use of mixed methods**

- Third, an integrated approach where both quantitative and qualitative analysis are conducted simultaneously and interact with each other in producing the final results. The third approach is highly interdisciplinary, or even trans-disciplinary, where all data collection occurs at the same time for the different analytical methods, usually through a common set of instruments. This approach to mixed methods is much more complex to design as it requires more coordination and integration between studies and more flexibility in ontological and epistemological positions. The synthesis of these trans-disciplinary approaches adds both value and costs to this form of mixed methods study.

**Figure 23.3     Integrated use of mixed methods**

## Structuring a Mixed Methods Project

Where research is not theory-driven but is about understanding a particular phenomenon, the research question drives the most appropriate methods for the study. A mixed method study only becomes appropriate when the questions being asked cannot be answered effectively by the use of a single method. There is no rigid formula for designing a mixed methods study, but the following checklist should provide some guidance in designing a mixed method project (Table 23.1). You can read in more detail on this topic in Cresswell and Plano Clark (2011) and Teddie and Tashakkori (2009).

Judging the quality of mixed methods studies entails looking at the way the study design addresses the following issues:

- How much consideration is given to the credibility, reliability and validity of the data? Credible data is data that is relevant to the study and also believable, convincing, probable and trustworthy.
- Reliability relates to whether the data is suitable (captured in an appropriate way, and in sufficient quantity) and recorded in a way that it is fit to be relied upon during analysis.
- Validity refers to a clear repeatable process that another researcher could recover (ideally replicate) the study and achieve comparable results (Checkland and Holwell, 1998). Meeting these requirements influences the empirical methods available to you.
- Is triangulation used to increase credibility, reliability and validity? Mixed methods approaches provide the ability to investigate the same question from a number of perspectives. Analysing data from these different perspectives allows us to build a stronger case for or against the research hypotheses. What is an interesting result from one perspective can be explained with a different perspective applied to the same or related data. This triangulation of data from a variety of sources is an integral part of ensuring that the data collected is reliable and credible.
- How generalisable are the results (in positivist quantitative studies)? Generalisability refers to the ability of the research to make claims based on the study to populations outside the original study. Generalisability usually has methodological implications in terms of sample size and nature of the measures and instruments used.
- How transferable are the results (usually a question asked of qualitative studies)? Transferability is often used as a measure of the usefulness and the degree to which the findings could apply to situations outside the original study. Highly detailed descriptions of the research site and methods allows the reader to identify how the situation is the same or different

**Table 23.1     Checklist for designing mixed method projects**

| Steps | Considerations |
|---|---|
| Step 1 – What are you interested in exploring? What is the high-level research question? | Consider the study's intent and its foundation. What is your philosophical and theoretical perspective and foundation for this area of study? Create a short title that identifies the topic, participants and site of study. Let it reflect the big question you are trying to answer. |
| Step 2 – What questions do you need to answer, to answer this overarching question? | Subdivide the main research question into concepts and identify what questions you need to answer about each of these concepts in order to answer the high-level research question. What small number of concepts are you interested in? How might they be related? If you can draw a conceptual diagram incorporating these concepts and relationships, it will help you visualise and explain the rest of your study. |
| Step 3 – What data do you need to answer these questions? | For each concept and question identified, what data would you ideally need to answer it? If it is unlikely you can get this ideal information, what proxies might be available? What measures exist in the literature for assessing these concepts? How will you ensure credible, reliable and valid results? How will you build triangulation into your data collection? |
| Step 4 – What are the appropriate methods for analysing this data? | Given this ideal data set, what types of analysis will be most helpful to make sense of the data and the relationships amongst the data items and concepts? Using a mixed method design, be clear how the methods will collaborate, combine or integrate to address the research questions. How will the data satisfy the needs of the different philosophical/discipline perspectives and support the larger sense-making process? Write a research purpose statement. Include the study aim, design, purpose of each method used, rationale for mixing methods. How will you ensure that the data collection and analysis methods selected allow for generalisabilty and transferability? Create tools, instruments and a procedure to use them. Mixed methods studies may be either fixed (methods are predetermined) or emergent (cyclical design during process of the research). Conduct a pilot study to be sure all instruments and the data they collect are adequate for answering the research questions. You may need to revise your instruments following the pilot. Is it possible to answer the research questions as defined with the instruments created and the data you are able to collect? This is the go–no go stage before data collection begins. Do you have the resources you need (time, finances, skills, access to data)? Create a strategy for conducting the study. Make sure all key stakeholders (your committee) buys into and signs off on your strategy. |
| Step 5 – Collect and analyse the data. | Now that you have built a strategy and a plan for conducting the mixed methods study, the fun begins. Use the instruments you created and tested to collect the data. If you have more than one researcher conducting any of the data collection activities make sure that you are both applying the instrument or coding structure in a similar way. Coding data independently then reviewing the results and clarifying any ambiguity is an important step to take before collecting all the data. Remember to pay attention to all the issues of rigour and effective methodological steps for each method (as discussed in other chapters). |
| Step 6 – Draw conclusions, report and share findings. | Keep asking yourself, 'What is the data telling me? And how do I know that?' Use comparative analysis within and between cases and modes of analysis to help you identify the most important findings. Once all the analysis is complete it is important to make sure that the findings from all of the methods are thoroughly explored. For team-based studies, a workshop approach may be appropriate. For single research studies, it is valuable to get as many different perspectives (practical, disciplinary) on your work as possible before finalising your conclusions. Here is where a strong and diversely skilled thesis committee is important but do not forget to rely on your student colleagues as well. Writing up mixed methods work can be challenging because of the complexity of explaining all the data, methods and analytical approaches within the constraints of a publishable paper or thesis. Remember to focus on one concept or research question at a time. Many drafts will be required. Submitting to conferences may be a way to help with both dissemination and getting enough feedback to help you prepare the paper for publication. |

from their own. In comparing the specifics of the research situation with one in which they are familiar, the reader may be able to infer that the results would be the same or similar in their own situation. Transferable studies have strong face validity, in that they resonate with knowledgeable readers.

- How appropriate are the methods of analysis to the data collected and the questions asked? The selection of empirical methods should include consideration as to how data is collected. Will the collection method influence the number, quality and veracity of replies? Could some replies omit more compromising information? How could a change in method avoid potential problems? The sources of data sought (numbers of responses required, range of participants on same question(s)) will also practically influence the methods chosen (surveys, interviews – paper, online, phone, in person, documents, observations and so on) as will the attempt to create multiple measures of key concepts.

Having reviewed the guidance available to us on how to conduct mixed methods studies, and some of the quality indicators, let us turn now to an example and see how this guidance played out against reality of our project.

## Example Case – A Mixed Method Project Framework

The Researching the Value of Project Management initiative (Value project) was a large-scale interdisciplinary (and sometimes trans-disciplinary) research project partially funded by PMI between 2005 and 2008. The project involved 48 researchers from 14 countries working in 18 teams to develop 65 detailed case studies. The research essentially needed to be a longitudinal study executed in a short timeframe across a wide geography.

The case study is a large, some may say mega, research project and some of you as students may be wondering about its relevance to planning your own research. While you may only run into a few of these issues on a smaller mixed methods study, our case provides the opportunity to examine all of the complexity associated with mixed methods studies and how we dealt with them. Having examined all of our challenges, we hope you can think about what you are most likely to face and how you will deal with these challenges in planning your own study.

### STEP 1 – WHAT ARE YOU INTERESTED IN EXPLORING? WHAT IS THE HIGH-LEVEL RESEARCH QUESTION?

The overarching question of interest was given to us through the request for proposal process. The professional association wanted to know what value PM delivers to organisations. Specifically they wanted to quantify that value.

A long-standing and tricky problem known to be important to the organisation, the research essentially needed to be a longitudinal study executed in a short timeframe. All previous studies had failed to answer the question because no baseline data exists. It was known that some of the relevant measures are intangible and often seen as non-credible; isolating answers from overall context and the results of other changes in an open system is difficult to achieve.

This research was based on a set of assumptions that drove us to particular choices about how best to conduct the study:

- there is no one right way to measure value or PM outside of an organisational context;
- both value and PM are multidimensional constructs and, therefore, a variety of disciplines across the management spectrum have contributions to make in answering these questions;

- the data to answer these questions is not easily available in most organisations.

Based on a pragmatic approach to the ontological and epistemological choices made in the design of the research and the belief that multi-paradigm inquiry is not only possible but is necessary to 'offer insights into the characteristic contradictions and tensions embodied in contemporary organisation' (Reed, 1985: p. 201), a mixed methods approach was identified from the outset as the best way to answer the question.

Recognising at the same time the difficulties associated with mixed methods studies we felt we had two major advantages to make this project possible. First, one of the co-leads was well trained and experienced in using both qualitative and quantitative methods. Second, the size and nature of the multidisciplinary team ensured that we had the expertise in various methodologies to manage a complex cross-method study.

## STEP 2 – WHAT QUESTIONS DO YOU NEED TO ANSWER TO ANSWER THIS OVERARCHING QUESTION?

The overarching question includes three concepts: PM; value; and Organisation. Related questions include:

- What is PM in organisations? Is PM a measurable thing?
- Is it different in different organisations/contexts? What organisational context differences effect the value of PM?
- What is value? Value to whom? From what perspective? How is value categorised? Measured?

The common conceptual model originated in the early literature reviews conducted by the principal investigators in preparation for proposing on this study and is illustrated opposite (Figure 23.4).

The conceptual model allowed team members from all disciplines a touchstone to return to throughout the project to stay focused on the questions we were trying to answer.

## STEP 3 – WHAT DATA DO YOU NEED TO ANSWER THESE QUESTIONS?

Deciding how to use a mixed methods approach will be to some extent driven by your data sources. Three influences should be considered when determining your approach. The first is consideration to which data that would both be relevant to the research question and available for collection. The second is to the methods and instruments used to access and collect this data as this will impact its reliability and veracity. The final factor will be the method of analysis to be applied to this data in order to make sense of it and hopefully answer your research question.

Our approach to answer these questions was to get all these experts in a room for three days to work our way through the three questions and what data we would need to answer these questions from different disciplinary approaches. The discussion was long (three days), and sometimes heated (conflicting epistemological and ontological positions). However, this first workshop set the tone for the type of flexibility and cooperation that would be needed to complete the project. The lesson is to deal with the big, hairy questions of how you will satisfy people coming at your research from different perspectives early rather than late and then keep all the players focused on the research questions.

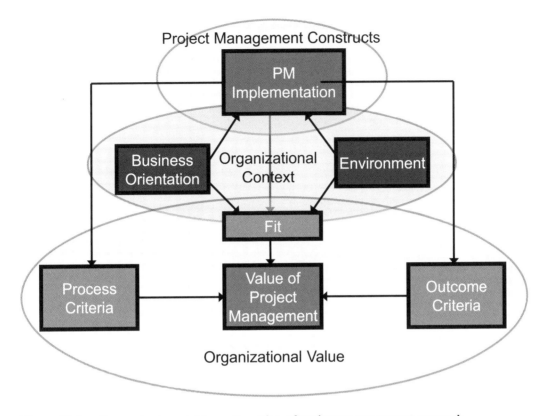

**Figure 23.4    Conceptual model from the value of project management research**

## STEP 4: WHAT ARE THE APPROPRIATE METHODS FOR COLLECTING THIS DATA?

There were at least three levels of data (individual, group, organisational) required to answer our questions. Our project investigated value at the organisation level and multiple case study approach was deemed appropriate. The professional society sponsoring this research wanted generalisable data, so a multiple case study approach was necessary –preferably with enough cases to allow for some statistical analysis of data at the organisational level. Case study methodology is often the foundation of mixed methodology studies. Data for each case study would come from:

- interview – to access perceptions and feelings as well as facts;
- individual surveys, for example, 'Do you use this tool?';
- organisational surveys, for example, 'So you provide these types of training?';
- document review – to assess formalised actions;
- observation – to assess culture and actual actions, situational choices.

Ensuring reliability, credibility and validity of our results was important. Approaches used included: researchers were trained in common data capture instruments and tools; stakeholder and advisory group assessment of process of data capture and analysis calculations and assumptions; multiple forms of evidence sought and triangulation in analysis at every opportunity; conservative (understatement) use of valuation and benefits; cautious and critical treatment of unsubstantiated outliers.

## Instrument Development and Testing

Based on the data requirements and methods discussion defined in the workshop, instruments for data collection were created by a small team employing the help of method experts. Once the complete instrument package was completed (including five different interview templates, an organisational survey, five different online survey scripts, a document review strategy, and a form for collecting information on practices documented, talked about and actually done in each organisation) that then went out to the entire team for feedback.

A pilot phase (of five cases) was used to test the reviewed instruments to determine data blind spots. The pilot cases were reviewed with the entire research team (at a workshop) in order to test the ability of the research instruments to collect the data we needed to answer the research questions and evaluate our ability to answer our research questions with the data we would be able to collect. We used this point of review – reality check – as a decision stage gate for the project. In our case there were some serious limitations in our ability to collect data on quantitative costs associated with PM implementations and some difficulty in estimating quantitative benefits. We believed that what could be accomplished would be valuable but the decision was the project sponsor's to make. They decided we should continue with the revised scope of delivery. Carrying out this type of review is very important in order to fall back to what is doable and realign stakeholder expectations as early in the process as possible.

Figure 23.5 illustrates the six types of data instruments developed for this study and the magnitude of the data collection undertaken. Data management is an issue for any research project. For a mixed method study, the magnitude of types of data as well as data elements makes this an even more serious consideration. We built a database that contained all quantitative and qualitative data referenced by case number in order to be able to manage the electronic and paper data.

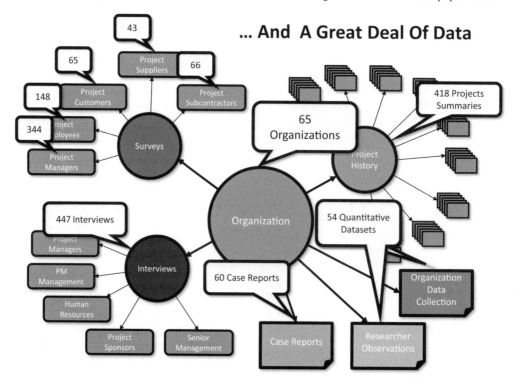

**Figure 23.5    Illustration of the complexity of data collected in a mixed methods study**

*Project design strategy*

We chose to start 'from qualitative material and transform it into numerical data to be used in further quantitative analysis aimed at deriving generalisable results' (Srnka and Koeszegi, 2007: p. 33) as well as separately collecting quantitative data. Both qualitative and quantitative data was analysed separately *and* jointly in a combination of the sequential and combined approaches to mixed methods studies in order to provide an overall picture of the value phenomenon. Adopting this generalisation approach to MMR design allows us to conduct discovery-oriented research that provides significant research insights while also allowing us to derive generalisable results from largely qualitative data (Srnka and Koeszegi, 2007).

Given the complexity of the research question and the multidisciplinary team, Phase I was designed to answer two questions: Can we figure out a way to answer these questions that would satisfy a multidisciplinary stakeholder group? Is the design developed do-able? Phase I included conceptual and methodological design of the project and testing of this design through pilot case data collection and analysis. Phase I completed with the stage gate decision discussed above.

Phase 2 involved an exploratory, theory development stage based on collection of multiple case studies and was to conclude with a large-scale survey-based stage to test the theories developed. However, as part of the stage gate decision, the original proposal of testing the developed theory with a large sample size (>200 organisations) was postponed in order to meet sponsor deadlines. Theories generated from the case study analysis were tested against the quantitative date collected to date. Further theory testing was left for future researchers.

The lesson here is that it is very easy to be overly optimistic in planning a mixed methods study as it is easy to underestimate the added complexity of dealing with two or more different types of analysis. Make sure you use good PM techniques and build off ramps and decision points into your project strategy that your committee and sponsors agree to. Having agreement early in your project on how these decisions will be made and by whom will save a lot of grief later on.

## STEP 5: DATA COLLECTION AND ANALYSIS OF THE DATA

The primary method for this study was comparative mixed methods, detailed cases on a large scale. Each team (16 in total) completed a cross-case analysis of the cases they collected. It was critical for each team to follow the project design to ensure the data would be comparative.

In addition, a qualitative and quantitative team worked across the whole data set, sometimes in isolation (content analyses, discursive analysis to identify trends in value perceptions and to analyse the consistency of perceptions across organisations and quantitative: descriptive statistics, to correlation and regression) and in the later stages in collaboration. The lesson for a smaller stage study is likely that you need to devote time to each type of analysis separately before you try to synthesise the results into a coherent whole. Make sure you know what the qualitative and quantitative findings are independently before trying to make sense of the whole story.

## STEP 6 – DRAW CONCLUSIONS, REPORT AND SHARE FINDINGS

*Building theories*

In our example case, the content and the process for accomplishing the project was planned as part of the methodological choice. '… methodological choices started to drive specific methods' (Thomas and Mullaly, 2008, p 55). The research did not follow a structured grounded theory approach, such as those set out in the work of Glaser and Strauss (1967); Glaser (1992); Strauss and Corbin (1998) but followed Eisenhardt's lead and 'engage(d) in systematic data collection and theory development processes that are reported with transparent description … of cross case comparison techniques. The key here is to convey the rigor, creativity, and open-mindedness of the research processes while sidestepping confusion and philosophical pitfalls' (Eisenhardt and Graebner, 2007). 'Standard data was collected from each participating organisation by every case team. In addition, each researcher collected any additional data they deemed necessary to explore the value phenomenon from their own unique disciplinary/theoretical perspective. Cross-case comparison using both qualitative and quantitative methods formed the foundation for both theory generation and theory testing' Thomas and Mullaly (2008: p. 55).

## Drawing Conclusions and Getting Published

The final workshop of our project was dedicated to joint sense-making based on the results of the individual case study analysis, the comparative case analysis by each research team, and the cross-case qualitative and quantitative analysis. In this way we used triangulation of both data and method to draw conclusions across all the work done.

So far this study has resulted in one book, several book chapters, many conference papers, a special edition of a journal, and more than 15 published papers. That said, meeting the page limitations and framing papers for publication in organisation theory journals has proven as difficult as the guidance suggests. It is difficult after completing a study of this magnitude to pick out very small insights to focus on for publication when the richness of the data available begs for greater description. Pick you target audience wisely and be prepared to put in the work to tailor your message.

## Conclusions

Adopting a mixed methods approach adds a level of complexity to all elements of research design. However, there are some research questions in PM that require this level of inquiry. If yours is one of these, make sure you build a strong supervisory team with the skills needed to guide you through the use of multiple methods or a research team that can provide these skill sets. From our experience, mixed methods are a challenging approach to take but worth it in terms of the sophistication and detailed understanding that they generate.

## Tips and Questions

### TIPS FOR STUDENTS

- Further information on MMR design can be gained from the references provided. In particular a fuller introduction to MMR can be found Creswell and Plano Clark (2011) *Designing and conducting mixed methods research*. Thousand Oaks, CA: Sage Publications, Inc. A great overview presentation of Cresswell's work can be found in the online presentation http://prezi.com/qsksml6l-_vi/introduction-to-mixed-methods-research.
- Another useful source is Teddie, C. and Yahakkori, A (2009) *Foundations of Mixed Methods*. Thousand Oaks, CA: Sage Publications. If you are interested in exploring the methods used in the Value Project in more detail, please see Thomas and Mullaly (2008).

## TIPS FOR SUPERVISORS

- Students adopting a mixed methods approach are tricky to supervise as expertise in both quantitative and qualitative methods are required on the committee. This can often cause dissension on the committee itself over what constitutes appropriate analysis to answer research questions. The student will require more sophisticated people skills to manage the committee through the process.
- Research questions need to be defined in ways that make it clear what types of data and analysis is required to answer them. Often defining research questions such that different methods are used to answer each question makes it easier to address the issues in Tip 1 as different committee members can focus on different questions.
- Make sure that your student understands both the benefits and costs of MMR, and that the research they want to undertake truly requires a more complex mixed methods approach.

## QUESTIONS

1. When are you most likely to adopt a mixed methods approach?
2. What are the three greatest challenges to conducting MMR and how can you deal with them?
3. How do you deal with the epistemological challenges presented by adoption of a mixed methods approach?

# References

Bitekine, A. (2008). Prospective Case Study Design: Qualitative Method for Deductive Theory Testing. *Organizational Research Methods*, 11, 160.

Bryman, A. (2007). Barriers to Integrating Quantitative and Qualitative Research. *Journal of Mixed Methods Research* 1, 8–22.

Checkland, P. and Holwell, S. (1998). *Information, Systems and Information Systems: Making sense of the field*. New York: Wiley and Sons.

Cresswell, J. (2006). *Qualitative Inquiry and Research Design: Choosing among five approaches*. Thousand Oaks, CA: Sage Publications.

Creswell, J. W and Plano Clark, V. (2011). *Designing and Conducting Mixed Methods Research*. Thousand Oaks, CA: Sage Publications.

Eisenhardt, K. M. and and Graebner, M. E. (2007). Theory Building from Cases: Opportunities and Challenges. *Academy of Management Journal*, 50(1), 25–32.

Glaser, B. (1992). *Basics of Branded Theory Analysis*. Mill Valley, CA: Sociology Press.

Glaser, B. and Strauss, A. (1967). *The Discovery of Grounded Theory. Strategies for Qualitative Research*. London: Weidenfield & Nicolson.

Jack, E. I. and Raturi, A. S. (2006). Lessons Learned from Methodological Triangulation in Management Research. *Management Research News*, 29(6), 345–357.

Johnson, R. B., Onwuegbuzie, A. J. and Turner, L. A. (2007). Toward a Definition of Mixed Methods Research. *Journal of Mixed Methods Research*, 1(2), 112–133.

Reed, M. (1985). *Redirections in Organizational Analysis*. London: Tavistock.

Srnka, K. J. and Koeszegi, S. T. (2007). From Words to Numbers: How to Transform Qualitative Data into Meaningful Quantitative Results. *Schmalenback Business Review*, 59(1), 29–57.

Strauss, A. and Corbin, J. (1998). *Basics of Qualitative Research. Techniques and Procedures for Developing Grounded Theory*, 2nd Edition. Thousand Oaks, CA: Sage Publications.

Teddie, C. and Yahakkori, A. (2008). *Foundations of Mixed Methods.* Thousand Oaks, CA: Sage Publications.
Thomas, J. and Mullally, M. (2008). *Researching the Value of Project Management.* Newmarket, PA: PMI.

## Suggested Reading

Flood, R. L. and Romm, N. (1997). *Critical Systems Theory – Current Research and Practice.* New York: Plenum Press.
Lewis, M.W. and Keleman, M. L. (2002). Mulriparadigm Inquiry: Exploring Organizational Pluralism and Paradox. *Human Relations,* 55(2), 251–275.
Siggelkow, N. (2007). Persuasion with Cases. *Academy of Management Journal,* 50(1), 20–24.

# 24

# Managing Research in Large Collaborative Teams

Stella George and Janice Thomas

*At a time when collaborative research is becoming a requirement for large granting bodies, and research programmes in universities must generate internationally valid results, knowing how larger-scale collaborative projects function is important to the soon to be post-doc. It is our aim in sharing our experiences that we will help newer researchers select and operate within such projects with quality and effectiveness.*

The use of large collaborative teams of researchers is necessary to address complex research questions. The challenge in this type of research includes the process of managing large teams across the globe as much as the methods employed in data capture and analysis. Understanding the relationship between team structure, methods used, and the resultant complex data and its analysis is key to the success of such projects. This chapter introduces what we know about managing large-scale, collaborative research teams through a discussion of our experiences with the 'Researching the Value of Project Management' project.

At the end of this chapter, the reader can:

- understand why and when research using large-scale teams is necessary and when it is not;
- be aware that the challenge of large team collaborative research comprises not simply of the intellectual challenge posed in the research question but in the challenge of how to manage these complex projects;
- understand strategies to mitigate risk and to build success in the management of large collaborative team research by focusing on three interwoven factors of people, process and governance.

Keywords: collaborative research; large research teams; research management

## Introduction

Large-scale collaborative research is highly complex. At the same time, it is also essential in many research areas to advance knowledge and create a research community around key research topics. Interdisciplinary and collaborative research is generally considered to be an important approach to tackling complex research questions (Glied, Bakken, Formicola, Gebbie, and Larson, 2007). This is a particularly important approach with respect to gaining insight into multidisciplinary and international fields of management (Shore and Cross, 2005) such as PM. In our field, there are few large-scale collaborative research projects to draw from (The Rethinking Project Management Project 2004–2006 (Winter, Smith, Morris and Cicmil, 2006), NETLIPSE 2005–2008 (Hertogh, Baker, Staal-Ong and Westerveld, 2008), The Value Project 2004–2008 (Thomas and Mullally, 2008), GAPPS which is ongoing (http://www.globalpmstandards.org)) and little defined theory about how interdisciplinary and collaborative research projects should be effectively managed.

In this chapter, we consider what collaborative and interdisciplinary research is by defining common terms and summarising the academic literature about it. We consider why and how we do interdisciplinary research. Process, people and governance are all important factors in successful large-scale interdisciplinary research. The main practical challenges of this research approach are illustrated using our case example, The Value Project (Thomas and Mullaly 2008). We explore the relationship between the researchers as individuals, the processes devised for managing the project and the governance challenges.

## Collaborative and Interdisciplinary Research Definitions

Collaboration, defined as working jointly with others especially in an intellectual endeavour, is often used in academic research to drive a new research agenda or move research forward (Reich and Reich, 2006; Teagarden et al., 1995). Through an ongoing, active and integrated working relationship, members of a broadly-based team of researchers can offer different perspectives on complex research questions. Such research questions often require long-term funding.

In collaborative work everyone involved must bring something of value to the project. Resources brought to the table can include: academic knowledge about the research question, a discipline, particular methods; cultural context; geographical location; access to data; access to equipment; expertise in use of equipment; and, additionally in all cases, their time, allowing for parallelism of work.

## Modes of Collaborative Research

Collaborative research typically happens in one of three ways as illustrated in Figure 24.1.

- Multidisciplinary
  A multidisciplinary approach *integrates the results* of separate perspectives on a single problem. The individual researchers involved work within their own methodologies and practices only.
- Interdisciplinary
  An interdisciplinary approach requires researchers from two or more disciplines to *pool and modify methods and approaches from different disciplines to achieve something new*. The joint methodology is thought to provide new insights via negotiated overlap of expertise.
- Trans-disciplinary
  A trans-disciplinary approach aims for holistic integration across disciplines. Trans-disciplinary research includes *integration of the methodology, implementation, and results*. It may address contemporary issues often requiring integration of views from not just academic but other areas, such as: business leaders, politicians, policy makers. The trans-disciplinary approach requires those using it to have a real understanding and motivation of why they wish to work in this way and requires a management structure of its own to operate successfully.

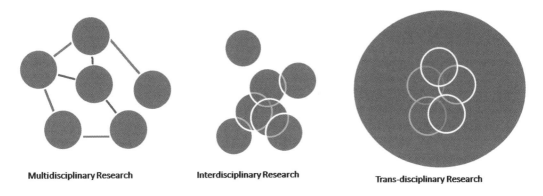

Multidisciplinary Research    Interdisciplinary Research    Trans-disciplinary Research

**Figure 24.1    Three modes of collaborative research**

The difficulty of managing research increases as you move from multidisciplinary through interdisciplinary to trans-disciplinary research. At the multidisciplinary level coordination is key, by the time you get to trans-disciplinary research, you need to be able to build an effective single cross-disciplinary team. Some would argue that trans-disciplinary research is not epistemologically possible because of the incommensurability of some disciplines. We leave this philosophical discussion for another venue and concentrate on the practical challenges of managing such work.

## Drivers and Enablers of Collaborative Team Research

Global economic changes have had an impact on research funding opportunities. Many national/federal and multinational, research-funding agencies have begun to encourage this collaborative, and particularly interdisciplinary, research (Glied et al., 2007). National funding agencies (such as Canada's Natural Science and Engineering Research Council (NSERC), Social Sciences and Humanities Research Council (SSHRC), US National Research Councils, EU 7th Research Framework Programme) share similar perspectives on encouraging research collaboration.

Many Centres of Excellence (CoE) have been funded to promote an interdisciplinary and collaborative research model whether it be by collaboration between academics of similar disciplines, between academics of different disciplines, or international teams. CoEs are seen as a mechanism to build research community to develop a research agenda to strengthen the prominence of a research area, improve the quality of research and offer educational experience to motivated doctoral candidates. The justification for CoEs is to facilitate multidirectional flow of research knowledge and to financially and cooperatively partner over the longer term with industry and community where it is appropriate. However, the personal, financial and environmental costs of travel to COEs is becoming prohibitive.

Development and increased availability of more immediate and interactive virtual and mobile technologies and the acceptance of time shifted, globally distributed, working patterns is enabling a new type of collaborative research. As it becomes more acceptable to work together at a distance, it becomes easier to link individuals interested in a specific phenomenon like PM, situated in various institutions around the world, into effective teams to address complex research questions. This approach also allows practitioners from sites that do not have physical CoEs to more easily participate in research.

Ultimately the decision to embark on collaborative research is driven by the nature of the research question. Researchers must assess if the *intellectual challenge* of the research requires a collaborative approach. Collaboration across disciplines is required when the research:

- question is complex (Glied et al., 2007) and previous studies have failed to answer it (Thomas and Mullaly, 2008). Research questions that seek answers to complex issues require multiple academic perspectives. These perspectives are needed to address what comprises the problem and for analysis and interpretation of the data captured. This may include mixed method analysis, mixed question analysis or a holistic approach involving many disciplines.
- demands specific expertise in more than a consulting capacity (O'Connor, Rice, Peters and Veryzer, 2003; Reich and Reich, 2006). Expertise can be in both the methods employed in gathering and interpreting data common across the whole of the social science disciplines, as well as expertise specific to the context of challenges in the study, including:
  - cultural or international knowledge (Collin, 2001; Tsui, Nifadkar and Ou, 2007; Shore and Cross, 2005); and
  - understanding of needs of funding agencies asking for interdisciplinary and collaborative work and the ability to meet them.
- requires multiple external data sources for triangulation (Jack and Raturi, 2006). In this case the geographic location and ability of the researcher to connect and access data is vital to the study. Researchers' knowledge of the data and combined understanding of the data will be key in producing meaningful results for the research overall.

All of these pragmatic (access to funding and or nature of the research question) and philosophic (based in a belief in the need for holistic approaches) reasons put increasing pressure on researchers to work collaboratively. While there are many intellectual, financial and philosophical reasons for choosing to carry out collaborative research, this chapter is concerned with what happens once this approach is selected. Specifically, what do we know about the practicalities of managing the performance of this type of research?

## What Does the Literature Say about Managing Collaborative Research?

The research literature on the management of collaborative research addresses three important factors:

- how people work together;
- the way they work and what they do as a process; and
- the rules that they follow, the project's governance.

Figure 24.2 provides our summary of the academic thought about the relationship between these three aspects of large-scale collaborative research projects and what influences each factor.

Few models in the literature provide guidance on how to set up a collaborative research projects. One such study is from 1985 (Cummings, Mohrman, Mohrman and Ledford, 1985). In this model, the success of collaborative research stems from (1) research relationships, both at content and relational levels; (2) researcher roles; and (3) researcher skills. Cummings, Mohrman, Mohrman, and Ledford focused on the relational aspects of the research process and the need

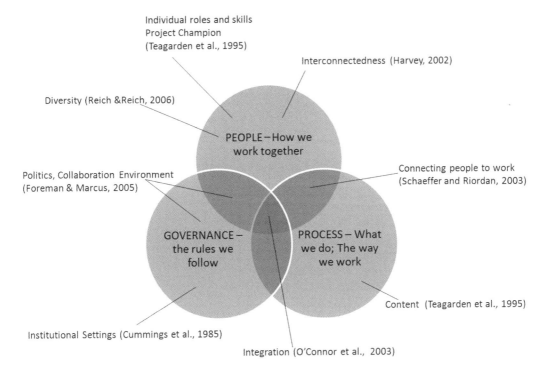

**Figure 24.2    Synthesising the research on managing collaborative research projects**

to establish an institutional setting that supported the research. They proposed a three-stage management model:

1. Identify individuals and organisations to be involved (for example, Project Champion, Team Composition and Diversity).
2. Bring these individuals and organisations together to agree on the need for and conventions of whether collaborative research was desirable (for example, Motivation, Research Design).
3. Organise to deliver by establishing the structures and mechanism for the collaborative system to function (for example, interactions: Level of Effort, Level of Knowledge/Skills, Coordination and Control Mechanisms and outputs: Reliable and Valid Data, Accurate Interpretation).

    Teagarden and her team (1995) revisited the Cummings et al. (1985) model in designing their own large-scale human resources management project. They extended the original model by adding a stage that considers:

4. Analysis and interpretation of the research – the *intellectual challenge*.

Subsequent research further extends this model to facilitate understanding of the management of collaborative research teams to include: paying attention to key external variables that impact this open system (that is, stakeholders, the impact of formal governance within the model and environmental pressures) (Foreman and Marcus, 2005; Thomas, George and Cicmil, 2010) and the dissemination of the results is a vital part of completing the project (O'Connor et al., 2003; Foreman and Marcus, 2005; Reich and Reich, 2006). The extended management model for collaborative research is depicted in Figure 24.3.

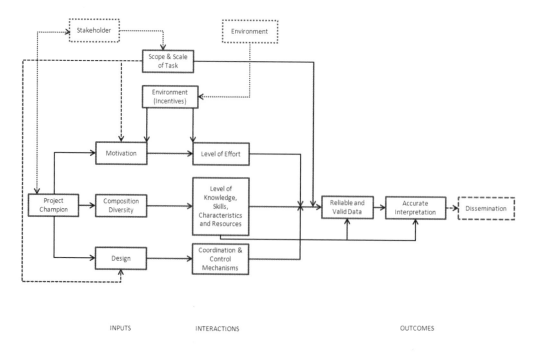

INPUTS                    INTERACTIONS                                    OUTCOMES

**Figure 24.3    Extended management model (elaborated from Cummings et al.,1985; Teagarden et al., 1995 cited in Thomas, George and Cicmil (2010)**

None of the elements (that is, inputs interactions or outcomes) really occur with the simple dependencies described in a boxes and arrows model. Nonetheless Figure 24.3 highlights the complexity in managing a successful collaborative team research project and some of the considerations important for collaborative research project success.

Critical success factors for collaborative research projects are complex. Harvey, Pettigrew and Ferlie (2002) concluded that high-achieving, high-impact research groups share a common set of characteristics including: strong leadership; skill at finding, motivating and retaining talent; strategies of related diversification; strong linkages between theory and practice; and network connectedness.They emphasised that 'collaborative working is intimately connected to networking; it represents ultimately a networking of resources: social, intellectual and infrastructural' (p. 769). The nature of human interactions, the composition and diversity aspect of a collaborative project, including leadership and network connectedness, should not be underestimated (Harvey et al., 2002). Creating the opportunity to be connected is fundamental to developing collaboration and paving the way for insights and moving the research forward.

The next section relates these theories to the real life management of a large-scale collaborative research project of this type.

## The Reality of Large Team Collaborative Research – Case Context

The Researching the Value of Project Management initiative (the Value Project) was a large scale interdisciplinary (and sometimes trans-disciplinary) research project partially funded by The Project Management Institute (PMI) between 2004 and 2008.The project involved 48 researchers from 14 countries working in 18 teams to develop 65 detailed case studies. It addressed a long-standing and tricky problem that was known to be important to PMI. The research essentially needed to be a longitudinal study executed in a short timeframe. All previous studies had failed to answer the question to the satisfaction of all stakeholders. It was known that some of the relevant measures are intangible and often seen as non-credible; isolating answers from overall context and the results of other changes in an open system is difficult to achieve.

Although this project was a very large research project, it covers many aspects of research PM that are relevant to contexts of research in large teams that doctoral students may soon be working in, such as: a suite of research within a CoE, those projects aligned with one supervisory academic (that is, those most likely to spawn PhD and post-doctoral research); post-doctorate research work is often carried out in this way. While you may not be managing a project of this type in the near future, it is highly likely that you may be working in one. Understanding the collaborative direction of one of these projects in more detail will help you assess how to interact effectively in collaborative research and what to consider when becoming involved in collaborative research projects.

A large team collaborative project has three main areas of risk:

1.  Are the goals of the project achievable? In our case, value had never been satisfactorily studied so this project would need to address why not.
2.  Can we get a large team of academics with diverse interests to work together? The disciplines have multiple approaches and associated conflicts and incommensurability even when considering the same research questions.
3.  Are the PM issues surmountable? Management issues ranged from the level of Principal Investigator's/Researcher's authority over participants; to scheduling unpredictability; change of the team and the sponsors needs; to managing multiple research project timelines to business world expectations.

Large-scale collaborative research requires a great deal of interplay between the researchers (personality, responsibility to the project), the project structure (including the environment), project governance (either externally imposed, or generated to deal with people and with processes with the project, the institution or external funding agency), and the research being done (including issues of research design such as research questions, data collection and data itself). The design decisions explicitly related to adopting a mixed methods approach are discussed in Chapters 22 and 23 The challenges and decisions associated with managing people, processes and governance on the Value Project are explored here.

## Designing Research around People

People challenges include getting the right people involved (for example, team diversity, level of knowledge/skill, motivation and so on), teambuilding efforts (for example, building trust and relationships, developing open communications, gaining buy-in and commitment and so on) and figuring out how to work at a distance. Proactively managing people issues was an important approach in managing for success in the Value Project. Serious time and effort needs to be devoted to consciously creating the project team; establishing sponsor relationships and developing appropriate collaborative an leadership.

Specific research design decisions we made include:

*   Select the right team.
    A prolonged and personal recruitment process was used to create the project team. We enlisted a strong multidisciplinary team from around the world that encompassed many disciplines, from both practical and academic research, with cultural experience. We sought to enlist researchers with research experience that addressed potential problems of earlier

research. The ultimate decision about including individuals in the team, however, was based on personality and the desire of individuals to work together as a team.

- Consciously create your project team.

People are a key asset for collaborative research and must be accommodated to ensure that everyone on the team must have something to contribute (for example, their personal or research history, geography, theory, methods, or simply time and hard work). Personalities must be handled – choose people you want to work with and 'know' everyone invited to participate, what they bring positively and negatively.

- Make the work as fun, stimulating and intellectually challenging as possible.

Attempt to inconvenience everyone equally. Good enough scheduling, home and office comforts and support made the difference between meeting and working. Eat your crow while it is young and tender. Do not let conflict fester. Be proactive about surfacing and dealing with disagreements.

- Create effective collaborative and interdisciplinary discussion and integration.

The research intentionally set out to be both interdisciplinary and collaborative. It was set up to accommodate the disciplines and allow integration to occur. Researchers who collected rigorous, solid data from the case organisations were included in the final data set. This included broad industry and geographic participation, enabling comparability of results across organisations and providing adequate data sets to develop statistically significant and convincing results. We recognised the potential conflict associated with this approach and built processes to encourage discussion and integration.

- Develop internal commitment to idea and work.

Developing the commitment of each individual researcher to the idea of the project and the work required to complete it was fundamentally important. Researchers who self-selected to be part of the process within contractual boundaries (contracts were put in place after definition of the project strategy) were more likely to complete their assignments. This self-selection process was an important step in creating overall commitment to the project.

- Establish effective sponsor relationships.

There can be many different types of sponsors – ranging from academic institutions through to professional association board and membership – on collaborative research projects. Each sponsor must share the project's common goal. When this does not happen, goals and plans must be changed to accommodate sponsors needs. Recognising the need for collaboration within a very broad base is crucial.

- Facilitate working at a distance.

The only way to complete this project was for research teams to work at a distance. Whilst this helped in maintaining research independence, it did require activities to be put in place to maintain the core team focus, consistency, connection and momentum. Bringing the whole team together at key stages of the project was essential and budgeted for. It was anticipated that over the course of nearly four years, some team changes would be necessary, as people may need to leave, absent themselves or join the team. Integrating new members into a large distance-based team required time investment from the core team. Building rapport and relationships over years with only rare occasions to come together meant that processes have to be developed for building relationships at a distance.

- Develop collaborative and integrative leadership.

Collaborative research work is NOT natural or intuitive to academics used to working in a disciplinary setting. That means the leader must meet the team where they currently are. You can't get to trans-disciplinary research if you team doesn't have the capability. The type of leadership needed is different in multi, inter and trans-disciplinary research. Leaders must manage the team and the possibilities available, not the ones they would like to have.

Working at a distance requires active leadership. Leaders cannot rely on the team to check in, they must follow up regularly. Hard decisions will need to be made. Interventions of all kinds will be necessary. Personal engagement is the glue that holds the team together while it is apart. The leader has to be able to work at a trans-disciplinary level even if the team cannot. Leading this type of team is a form of jazz that evolves and emerges within some guidelines. You must be able to facilitate the good sometimes at the expense of the perfect.

## DESIGNING RESEARCH PROCESS

The research process on the Value Project was consciously designed to fulfill four requirements.

1. Work was structured in order to generate a shared big picture understanding of the project including involving all researchers in the design of research questions, methods, and instruments such that individual researchers developed commitment and buy-in to the research.
2. Processes enabled consistent data capture to allow for cross-comparison.
3. Tools and instruments were jointly reviewed and automated to increase accessibility.
4. Processes were designed to enable and require individuals to complete the work in the time available.

Specific processes were designed to address advice identified in earlier research on large-scale collaborative teams. Ultimately the goal was to create a transparent process to coordinate activities between process between sponsors, researchers and research managers to facilitate: clearer communication; reduced misunderstandings; ease of knowledge transfer; effective governance; efficient administration; and parallel working.

## USE WORKSHOPS TO COMPLETE WORK AND BUILD RELATIONSHIPS

Strategic decision making (for example, research question formation, pilot testing, instrument validation and analysis) in workshops is critical to keeping to schedule and preventing some teams jumping ahead. Sharing ideas, defining research, getting a common understanding of project language and goals, opening minds, building optimism can all be accomplished in face-to-face workshops.

## ENHANCE COMMITMENT THROUGH A PROPOSAL PROCESS

Formalised 'competition' for funding and team leadership serves two main functions: (1) ensuring data is coming from a suitable range of sources and geographies – this can be vital in ensuring the data is capable of answering the research questions. And (2) opportunity for individual researchers to help shape the vision of the project helps build ownership of the project in the broader team. The vision is shared with the project champion, stakeholders and the full team.

## USE STAGE GATE CONTROLS

In a highly structured project, a common stage gate process allows teams to work independently towards common deadlines and goals. The major management challenge around stage gating is actually having processes to deal with projects that are not meeting requirements. Some team's inability to meet their commitments will impact the potential success of the project. Having a plan for how to deal with delinquent researchers is required. Processes for freezing the dataset at critical points, providing assistance, troubleshooting and ultimately dropping some researchers from the project will be critical to meet project timescales.

## Designing Research Project Governance

The organisational structure of the project provided a structure for governance purposes and decision making for the project overall; however, the majority of the work was expected to occur as a complex adaptive system within this relatively flat structure. This governance structure followed the organising principles of community described by Adler, Kwon and Hecksher (2008) as well as O'Connor et al.'s (2003) stricture that the relationships among the team are fundamentally important to the ultimate success of the project.

Well-established governance processes are required to ease the time required for administrative tasks to take place. The governance model should be designed to smooth the coordination and control challenges between major stakeholders (in our case, External Funder, University, Researchers, Researchers' Universities) and integrate some people and process issues.

The management of this project was influenced by this variety of governance systems in terms of having to manage the governance requirements of academic institutions, research projects and a funding professional organisation including:

* different financial systems and controls, fund management, expenses, invoicing, payment;
* funder reporting and stakeholder involvement – unusually for a research project, stakeholder participation in project meetings was requested then mandated;
* contract management was to make explicit the accountability of the researchers:
  - contractual and fixed deadlines;
  - disparate university processes;
  - confidentiality arrangements;
  - ethical approvals.

## Use of Contracts and Clear Definitions of Roles and Responsibility

These governance processes both protect researcher autonomy and reinforce responsibility. Researchers can be contracted to follow the project's research design, timescale and use the instruments agreed on and validated by the whole team. These processes are also important in collating consistent, relevant and reproducible data and expectation management, they will require strong leadership.

## Autonomy Facilitates Buy-In

Giving a research team as much autonomy as possible within the constraints of the project definition helps create buy-in. Autonomy around how researcher's own research collection teams are staffed and operated and the ability to develop parallel streams of research allow researchers to 'own' data they collect – this creates longevity in the study data allowing researchers to further their own research and publishing agenda.

## Reinforce Boundary Spanning

Collaboration is required outside the boundaries of the research team. Institutional services, that is, management of finance, ethics and reporting around your project, often operate complicated policies and procedures that you will be required to follow and are also vital to project success – it is worth cultivating good relationships in these areas. Make sure the whole research team does likewise at their own institutions. Even with good will, remember it takes way longer than you think to set up a contract or get expenses paid or hire research assistance.

Returning to the literature summary provided earlier, we highlight extensions in knowledge in the areas of researcher responsibility, leadership, accountability, attitudes, and approaches to scope change are also helpful. The contributions based on our understanding of managing collaborative research teams are illustrated in Figure 24.4.

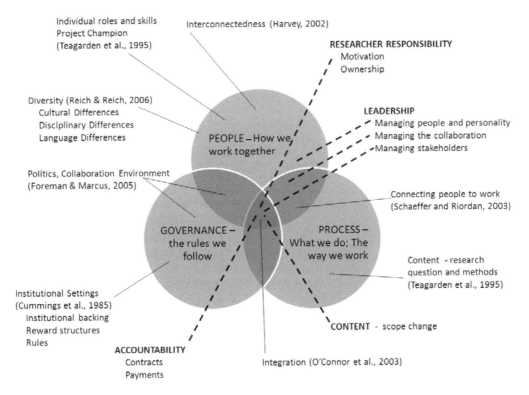

**Figure 24.4    Elaboration on practice on collaborative research from the academic literature**

## Final Comments

The success of large collaborative team research is dependent on the awareness and management of the interwoven nature of the people, process and governance over and above the content issues of research questions and methodology. Working in, and leading, this type of project is a difficult and stimulating experience that yields manifold benefits in answering tough questions.

So what advice do we have for co-coordinating collaborative research projects? Our primary recommendation is to rule out becoming too prescriptive. Maintaining focus on the people, process and governance whilst being informed by the elements of the extended Cummings model will provide good oversight and direction.

We hope that sharing our experience helps you understand ways in which your work can fit into larger collaborations and build effective collaborative work experiences in the future. We wish you well on your adventure.

## Tips and Questions

### TIPS FOR STUDENTS AND SUPERVISORS

- Ensure there is need for involvement in or development of a large-scale project – this approach can be time consuming and expensive to implement and must involve the right people to be successful.
- Check that data consistency, relevancy and reliability exists – once a large-scale research project is underway it is akin to a supertanker, very slow to change direction or even come to a halt, there can be no tweaks to the data capture once it has started, everyone needs to know up front that they are doing the right thing.
- Stage gate controls can be effectively used to ensure the progression, purpose, direction and timing of the project.
- Identify where the results can be published before data collection starts – develop an understanding of the journals in each of the interdisciplinary fields and be prepared to create a submission for each, tailoring the format and structure and content to building the relevance of the project's findings to that audience.

### QUESTIONS

1. What are the characteristics of research questions that benefit from collaborative research approaches?
    - Intellectual challenge – questions that require multiple academic perspectives on understanding how to investigate the problem and on understanding the data. Mixed method analysis, mixed question analysis require such a holistic approach.
    - Social science, context specific challenges, funding agencies asking for interdisciplinary and collaborative work.
2. What are the benefits and enablers of doing research collaboratively?
    Benefits:
    - Data from around the world, stop data source burn out, multiple perspectives, co-authors.
    Enablers:
    - Virtual technologies improve distance working, quick real -time communications, acceptance of decentralised research approaches, mixed methods and collaborative research.
3. What are the biggest risks in large team collaborative research projects? How will you mitigate them?
    Risks:
    - Failure to recognise the importance of managing the team interactions (people and process) and developing a solid governance structure.

Mitigation techniques:
- address potential problems of earlier research within the design and clearly using stage gates to determine at key points whether the project should continue;
- situate the phenomenon of PM within the organisation;
- develop common, credible and defensible measures of costs and benefits;
- collect rigorous, solid data from organisations;
- include broad industry and geographic participation;
- enable comparability of results across organisations;
- provide statistically significant and convincing results;
- enlist a strong multidisciplinary team: from around the world; encompassing many disciplines; both practical and academic research;
- leverage researcher expertise and familiarity with cultural perspective to build effective working relationships with case organisations;
- use parallelisation to meet the project timescale;
- provide access to organisations in a wide number of geographical locations using multiple research sites;
- provide concrete and timely deliverables back to the funding professional organisation.
4. Which measures can be put in place to address relevance, reliability, and validity of results in large collaborative projects?
- Team participation in making key methodological decisions. Standard data collection methods. Clear instructions for all data instruments. Pilot projects to test data instruments are collecting data that can address the research question and hypotheses, and serve as training for whole team.

# References

Adler, P. S., Kwon S.-W. and Heckscher, C. (2008). Professional work: The emergence of collaborative community. *Organization Science*, 19(2), 359–376.

Collin, A. (2001). Multidisciplinary, interdisciplinary, and transdisciplinary collaboration: Implications for vocational psychology. *International Journal for Educational and Vocational Guidance*, 9(2), 101–110.

Cummings, T. G., Mohrman, S. A., Mohrman, A. M. and Ledford, G. E. (1985). Organization design for the future: A collaborative approach. In E. E. Lawler, A. M. Mohrman, S. A. Morhman, G. E. Ledford, T. G. Cummings and Associates (eds), *Doing Research that is Useful for Theory and Practice*. San Francisco, CA: Jossey-Bass, pp. 275–305.

Foreman, J. and Marcus, M. L. (2005). Research on collaboration, business communication, and technology: Reflections on an interdisciplinary academic collaboration. *Journal of Business Communication*, 42(1), 78–102.

Glied, S., Bakken, S., Formicola, A., Gebbie, K. and Larson, E. L. (2007). Institutional challenges of interdisciplinary research centers. *Journal of Research Administration*, 38(2).

Harvey, J., Pettigrew, A. andd Ferlie, E. (2002). The determinants of research group performance: Towards mode 2? *The Journal of Management Studies*, 39(6), 747.

Hertogh, M., Baker, S., Staal-Ong, P. L., and Westerveld, E. (2008) *NETLIPSE. Managing Large Infrastructure Projects: Research on best practices and lessons learnt in large infrastructure projects in Europe*. Netherlands: Osbourne BV.

Jack, E. P. and Raturi, A. S.(2006) Lessons learned from methodological triangulation in management research. *Management Research News*, 29(6), 345–357.

O'Connor, G. C., Rice, M. P., Peters, L. and Veryzer, R. W. (2003). Managing interdisciplinary, longitudinal research teams: Extending grounded theory-building methodologies. *Organization Science*, 14(4), 353–373.

Reich, S. M. and Reich, J. A. (2006). Cultural competence in interdisciplinary collaborations: A method for respecting diversity in research partnerships. *American Journal of Community Psychology*, 38(1–2), 51–62.

Shore, B. and Cross, B. J. (2005). Exploring the role of national culture in the management of large-scale international science projects *International Journal of Project Management*, 23(1), 55–64.

Teagarden, M. B., von Glinow, M., Bowen, D. E., Frayne, C. A., Nason, S., Huo, Y. P., Milliman, J., Arias, M. E., Butler, M. C., Geringer, J. M., Kim, N. H., Scullion, H., Lowe,K. B. and Drost, E.A. (1995) Toward a theory of Comparative Management Research:An ideographic case study of the best international human resources management project. *Academy of Management Journal*, 38(5) 1261–1287.

Thomas, J., George, S. and Cicmil, S. (2011) Building Knowledge about the Management of Large-Scale Research Projects:The Value of a Good Case. Presented at IRNOP 2010 in Montreal.

Thomas, J. and Mullaly, M. (2008) *Researching the Value of Project Management*. Newmarket, PA: PMI.

Tsui, A., Nifadkar, S. S. and Ou, A. Y. (2007). Cross-national, cross-cultural organizational behavior research: Advances, gaps, and recommendations. *Journal of Management*, 33(3), 426–478.

Winter, M., Smith, C., Morris, P. W. G. and Cicmil, S. (2006) Directions for future research in project management: The main findings of a UK government funded research network. *International Journal of Project Management*, 24(8), 638–649.

## Suggested Reading

Ibbs, C.W. and Reginato, J. M. (2002). *Quantifying the Value of Project Management*. Newtown Square, PA: Project Management Institute.

Lee, Y. S. (1998). University-industry collaboration on technology transfer: Views from the ivory tower. *Policy Studies Journal*, 26(1), 69.

Nason, S.W. and Pillutla, M. M. (1998) Towards a model of international research teams. *Journal of Managerial Psychology*, 13(3/4), 156.

# 25

# Applying Mixed Methods for Researching Project Management in Engineering Projects

Marian Bosch-Rekveldt

*I hope this book stimulates the development of PM research. I'd like to share the knowledge and experience gained during my journey towards successfully obtaining my PhD degree in PM (2011).*

This chapter provides an illustrative example of PM research in engineering projects in the Dutch process industry. The study focused on identifying potential causes of complexity in projects and how the early project phase could be adapted to these complexities. The research was performed with companies of the NAP network.[1] The study was structured in four phases and comprised of exploratory case studies, a quantitative survey, explanatory case studies and an evaluative survey. By combining qualitative and quantitative work, this study is an example of successfully applying a mixed methods approach in PM research in engineering projects. Rather than presenting the content-results of the study, this chapter focuses on the research approach followed.

At the end of this chapter, the reader can:

- understand the differences between exploratory and explanatory case studies and how these could complement each other;
- understand the added value of applying a mixed methods research approach in PM research;
- be able to set up such a mixed methods research approach using multiple research instruments for your own domain.

Keywords: mixed methods, large engineering projects, project complexity, front-end development

---

1    NAP is a competence network bringing together companies from the entire value chain in the Dutch process industry.

## Research Background and Objectives

Research always should have some *raison d'etre*. For undertaking this research we found the motivation in the fact that project failure (in terms of cost overrun and time delays) is still common practice, also for large engineering projects (Flyvbjerg, Bruzelius and Rothengatter, 2003; Hall, 1981; Morris and Hough, 1987; Sauser, Reilly and Shenhar, 2009; Thamhain and Wilemon, 1986).

Literature suggests that one of the reasons for such project failure would be the increasing complexity of projects or an underestimation of the project complexity (Neleman, 2006; Williams, 2002, 2005). Literature also highlights the particular importance of the early project phases (the front-end phases) for improving project performance (Artto, Lehtonen and Saranen, 2001; Flyvbjerg, et al., 2003; Morris, 1994; Morris et al., 2006). A third observation from literature is a trend towards context-specific PM, which calls for applying a contingency approach to PM (Engwall, 2003; Howell, Windahl and Seidel, 2010; Sauser et al., 2009; Shenhar, 2001; Smyth and Morris, 2007; Williams, 2005).

Based on these observations, we defined our threefold research objective. The first objective was to investigate what project complexity actually comprises and how it influences project performance. The second objective was to investigate how front-end activities could be adapted to the project's complexity and how this influences project performance. The third objective was to investigate the relations between these variables (project complexity, front-end activities and project performance).

These objectives were summarised in the following main research question: *How could the front-end phase be adapted to the project's complexity in order to improve project performance?*

To tackle a complex problem like this, it is wise to limit the scope. Therefore in this study we focused on the process industry in the Netherlands. How could current projects in the process industry be characterised in very general terms? Such projects typically have a technological component, leading to technological as well as commercial risks. They have certain impact on the environment, either because it is a greenfield location (new facility, not so common) or because it is a brownfield location (extension or modification of existing facility, very common). A lot of parties are involved, including (sub) contractors, (local) communities and Non-Governmental Organisations (NGOs). Projects differ largely in size and content, ranging for example from several thousand euro (small maintenance project) to over one billion euro (major unique investment project). And last but not least, projects are performed by multidisciplinary project teams.

These very diverse project characteristics, together with the earlier mentioned poor track record that also holds for this sector (IPA, 2011), suggested an interesting playing field for research into managing project complexity. More specifically, this research was focused on technologically complex engineering projects in the process industry, undertaken in dynamic environments with multiple stakeholders, with a budget between approximately one to 500 million euro. The selected budget range was chosen because the projects under consideration should have some serious 'content' (hence the lower range value was set to one million euro), but not be overly unique (hence upper range value was set to 500 million euro). The owner's perspective was taken as a starting point, but in later stages of the research the contractor's perspective was also included.

The research was performed within the NAP network, which brings together companies from the entire value chain in the Dutch process industry, including engineering agencies and the academic community (NAP, 2009). It consists of about 100 member organisations. For the different stages of the research, different selections of companies were included. The interest of the NAP network in (improving) the front-end phase of projects was evident from earlier publications (de Groen et al., 2003; Oosterhuis, Pang, Oostwegel and de Kleijn, 2008), which made them very well-suited for participation in our research.

# Research in Social Science

## POSITIVISM VERSUS CONSTRUCTIVISM

Before we can introduce our research design, we need to introduce some theory on research in social science in more general terms. Research in the field of PM often has a positivist character (Smyth and Morris, 2007; Williams, 2005), for example, it is assumed that there is one reality that can be described by laws with causal relationships, observed by an objective observer (Braster, 2000). Positivism attempts to control the context by isolating the phenomenon under study. Also the systemic view on PM has a positivist character. However, particularly the interaction of the project (management) with its environment is important since we aimed to study adapting the PM to the project complexity. Therefore a pure positivist approach was not sufficient in the current research: inclusion of the environment would ask for a more constructivist approach (Pellegrinelli, 2011).

In constructivism (or interpretivism), there can be more views of reality, without underlying causal relationships, and the context is inseparably connected with the phenomenon under study (Braster, 2000). Whereas in positivism events are explained based on linear thinking in one view of reality (Smyth and Morris, 2007), in constructivism understanding by in-depth analysis of the different realities prevails. An example of a constructivist approach is found in the equifinality view expressed in the contingency theory (Donaldson, 2001). An equifinality view means there is no unique solution but there are more ways in which improvement can be achieved.

To investigate the management of complex projects, a pure positivist research approach would limit the directions for resolving the complex management problem beforehand. On the other hand: a positivist approach might also provide a starting point to handle complex problems; for example by providing a model, method or a tool. This then should not be considered as the end-point, but the starting point for solving the complex problem at hand by including more constructivist principles. Such 'mixed' approaches are suggested more often (Blaikie, 2009; Tashakkori and Teddlie, 1998). Hence the current research aimed to use a constructivist approach in which positivist aspects were embedded.

## INDUCTIVE VERSUS DEDUCTIVE REASONING

In a research approach, two main methods of logic can be distinguished: deductive and inductive reasoning. These are described in the well-known 'Wheel of Science' (Wallace, 1971), as shown in Figure 25.1. In a deductive approach the starting point is a theoretical basis. From the theory, the hypotheses are derived that are checked by observations. This can lead to confirmation or non-confirmation of the original or new theories. In an inductive approach, the starting point is the observation. From specific observations, patterns are searched for and preliminary hypotheses are formulated, leading to the development of new theory. Eisenhardt, for example, successfully shows how an inductive approach can lead to new theory building (Eisenhardt, 1989).

In the Wheel of Science, phases of inductive and deductive research are naturally following each other. For example, when there is no theory available, one starts with observations, which via empirical generalisations can lead to new theory (induction). From this newly developed theory, hypotheses are formulated which are then tested by, again, observations (deduction). Although there is no single, unified theory on PM, different disciplines in PM do have a firm theoretical basis from which hypotheses can be formulated. Subsequently, these hypotheses are tested based on observations, which is at the deductive side of the deductive/inductive spectrum.

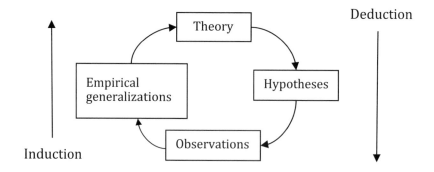

**Figure 25.1    Wheel of Science (adapted from Wallace, 1971)**

Often, positivism and deductive reasoning are associated with the hard paradigm of PM and interpretivism and inductive reasoning with the soft paradigm of PM (Pollack, 2007). In the hard paradigm, PM practices 'tend to emphasise efficient, expert-led delivery, control against predetermined goals and an interest in underlying structure' (Pollack, 2007: p. 267). In the soft paradigm, practices 'emphasize learning, participation, the facilitated exploration of projects, and typically demonstrate an interest in underlying social process' (Pollack, 2007: p. 267). The Wheel of Science nicely connects the hard and soft paradigms.

## RESEARCH APPROACH AND INSTRUMENTS

Dependent on the research approach, multiple research instruments can be used within one research project, such as experiments, surveys and/or case studies (Braster, 2000). In PM research, an experiment could have the form of a simulation or a game. Professionals could be asked to participate in such a simulation or a game to study how they would behave in a simulated project environment. Surveys could provide global information on large numbers of projects, whereas in-depth information, post-project or even longitudinally, could be obtained by case studies.

Different types of case studies can be distinguished, such as exploratory, descriptive and explanatory (Yin, 2003). In an exploratory case study, the focus is on exploration, whereas this is on description and explanation (causality) in case of a descriptive or explanatory case study, respectively. Explorative case studies are often done in initial phases of the research in a certain area, having the most inductive character of the different types of case studies. Case studies would be useful in both deductive and inductive approaches, as 'the case study is useful for both generating and testing of hypotheses but is not limited to these research activities alone' (Flyvbjerg, 2011: p. 306).

Often interviews are part of a case study or a survey study. Interviews can have a structured or an unstructured character (and all steps in-between). In unstructured interviews there is no standard questionnaire but questions arise during the interview, giving the possibility to elaborate on the answers of the respondent. In structured interviews, there is a strict protocol or questionnaire to be followed. Where case studies more often use the unstructured or semi-structured interviews, surveys more often use structured interviews. The use of different research instruments and sources of information within one research is called 'triangulation' (Tashakkori and Teddlie, 1998), which use adds to the validity of the overall research.

## UNDERLYING CONCEPTUAL MODEL OF THE CURRENT RESEARCH

The basic underlying conceptual model of this research consisted of three building blocks: project complexity and front-end development activities as the independent variables and project performance as the dependent variable.

Where did the arrows in Figure 25.2 stem from? Based on both literature and some exploratory work, we assumed that performing front-end activities positively contributes to project performance (…that's what you do PM for…) in this high-level conceptual model. Putting significant effort in the front-end development phase is often recommended as a vital part of PM, with a high influence on the final project result (Bakker, 2008; de Groen, et al., 2003; Flyvbjerg et al., 2003; Morris, 1994; Morris et al., 2006; Oosterhuis et al., 2008; van der Weijde, 2008). Therefore we assumed that front-end activities have this (direct) relationship with project performance. Project performance was hypothesised to be negatively influenced by project complexity (Flyvbjerg et al., 2003; Hall, 1981; Morris and Hough, 1987; Neleman, 2006; Williams, 2002, 2005). Hence, we assumed that project complexity has a (direct) negative relationship with project performance.

Next to these two direct relations; a third moderated relation was hypothesised: the front-end development phase of a project should be adapted or fitted to the specific project complexity and a fit between these would positively contribute to project performance. This was based on literature that suggests the application of contingency theory to PM (Engwall, 2003; Shenhar and Dvir, 1996; Smyth and Morris, 2007). Here project complexity would act as the moderator: based on the project complexity, the front-end activities should be adapted.

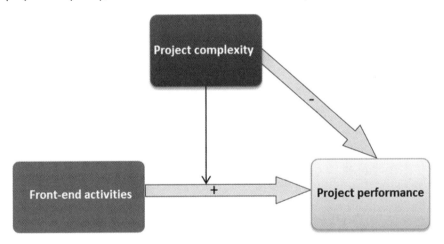

**Figure 25.2    Model project complexity/front-end activities/project performance**

The fact that the starting point of this PhD research was a model suggests that this research was at the deductive side of the deductive/inductive spectrum (see Figure 25.1). The model, however, is just a high-level one and these main variables first needed further operationalisation and hence exploration of the field, which is at the inductive side of the spectrum. Therefore this research started with an exploratory character (induction) and progressed towards more evaluative phases (deduction), as is detailed below.

## EXPLORATORY CASE STUDIES (PHASE I)

In Phase I, the concept of project complexity was explored and a model representation of project complexity was developed. Also, relevant front-end activities were explored. Although from literature there were some starting points on modelling project complexity (Dombkins, 2008; Geraldi, 2008; Hass, 2007; Williams, 2002) in-depth investigations towards real projects were not yet reported. To gather in-depth information on activities in the front-end development phase and the factors determining and influencing project complexity *an exploratory case study approach* was chosen. In a limited number of exploratory case studies (six cases), semi-structured interviews were held with project team members (three per project) and written materials (official reports, project archives) were investigated. To prepare for the case study, all building blocks from Figure 25.2 before were explored by means of a literature review. The exploratory case study was performed in one company, an active member of the NAP network, with a very structured PM approach. By choosing different projects from one company – all projects were executed based on the same PM process –variations in the standard front-end activities applied in a project were limited.

For the exploratory case studies, a multiple-cases embedded design (Yin, 2002) was used, in which each case represents a completed project. The embedded design refers to the different dimensions to be analysed within one case: project complexity, the activities in the front-end development phase and the project performance. The multiplicity refers to the inclusion of a number of projects opposed to inclusion of a single project. The inclusion of multiple cases in an embedded design is assumed to give a broader view on the dimensions under consideration (Yin, 2002). Per case, semi-structured interviews were held with multiple people involved in the project. The information obtained from the case studies was used for development of the project complexity framework and for defining the relevant front-end development activities to deal with project complexity. In the development of these frameworks, the empirical findings were confronted with literature findings.

## QUANTITATIVE SURVEY (PHASE II)

Phase II was focused on finding the potential relationships between the building blocks in Figure 25.2 before. Relations between project complexity, the activities in the front-end development phase and the project performance were investigated. To obtain sufficient data to draw statistically relevant conclusions from, *a survey study* was done amongst a large number of completed projects in the Dutch process industry. The survey was distributed via the NAP network and 67 responses from more than 25 companies were received.

The survey study was used to investigate and quantify potential relationships between project complexity, PM (for example, front-end activities) and project performance, hence to further develop and operationalise the conceptual model of Figure 25.2 before. Also the newly developed complexity framework was evaluated in detail. The research in this phase was quantitatively-oriented and, together with Phase I, followed an exploratory mixed methods approach (Blaikie, 2009; Tashakkori and Teddlie, 1998): the qualitative part (Phase I), is followed by a quantitative part (Phase II).

## EXPLANATORY CASE STUDIES (PHASE III)

Phase III consisted of in-depth case studies. After the exploration of several relations between project complexity, front-end activities and project performance in Phase II, Phase III of the research investigated in what way certain front-end activities contributed to project performance.

Four cases were selected from the survey sample of the second phase. To explore the different perspectives of owners and contractors, an additional owner project was added as a fifth case (also from a NAP company). Again a multiple cases embedded design (Yin, 2002) was chosen. Based on the quantitative outcomes of the second phase, this case study investigated more deeply in what way specific front-end activities contributed to the project performance. Actually this phase focused on the assumed direct relation between front-end activities and project performance in Phase III had a more explanatory character and was qualitatively-oriented.

Phase II and III together are again an example of mixed methods approach, but now it is explanatory rather than exploratory (Blaikie, 2009; Tashakkori and Teddlie, 1998). Some of the quantitative findings of Phase II are further explained by means of the qualitative in-depth case studies in Phase III.

## EVALUATIVE SURVEY (PHASE IV)

Phase IV was a *validation survey*, in which it was investigated to what extent the different aspects of complexity indeed contribute to project complexity and how the newly developed framework to grasp project complexity (Phase I and II) could help in improving project performance in future projects. The questions in this survey were not project-specific but sector-specific to enable generalisation of the results outside the specific companies involved. The survey was sent to two owner companies and two contractor companies, all of which are participating in the NAP network. In total 64 completed responses were received. The research in this concluding phase was partly quantitative and partly qualitative. Quantitative, as to what extent each of the elements of the complexity framework indeed would contribute to project complexity and qualitative in how the framework could help in improving project performance.

## Summary of the Research

A summary of these four phases, the methods used, the main content and main results is provided in Table 25.1 (the data collection within the NAP network is presented in Figure 25.3.)

Across the different phases, the Wheel of Science was followed several times. The case study in the first phase started with observations, which were generalised and confronted with theory, resulting in a framework to characterise project complexity. The second phase evaluated the complexity framework and explored relations between complexity, front-end activities and project performance. Again results were confronted with literature findings. Based on the results of the second phase, the Wheel of Science was followed again in the third and the fourth phase. In the third phase the Phase II results were deepened by means of qualitative in-depth interviews and in the fourth phase the developed complexity framework was validated. To strengthen the results, links with literature were established where possible.

The constructivist character of the research consisted of the appreciation of different perceptions and dimensions of project complexity. The constructivist character of this research was also reflected in including broader discussions on the use of the models developed and the mere fact that projects were investigated with particular attention for their context. Overall, extensive use was made of triangulation (Yin, 2002): triangulation in the sense of data sources, triangulation in the sense of involving participants with different roles in projects, and triangulation in the sense of using multiple methods.

**Table 25.1    Overview of the research**

| Main method, sample | Content | Main result |
|---|---|---|
| **PHASE I**<br><br>CASE STUDIES<br><br>ONE COMPANY | • What is project complexity?<br>• How can we characterize project complexity?<br>• What are the relevant front-end activities to deal with project complexity? | Framework to characterize project complexity<br><br>Relevant front-end activities |
| **PHASE II**<br><br>SURVEY<br><br>DUTCH PROCESS INDUSTRY | • How does project complexity influence project performance?<br>• What are the relevant front-end activities to deal with project complexity?<br>• How can contingency theory be used to fit the front-end phase to project complexity?<br>• How could a framework to grasp project complexity be used to improve project performance? | Relations between complexity, FED and performance<br><br>Indications for foreseen use of the complexity framework |
| **PHASE III**<br><br>CASE STUDIES<br><br>MULTIPLE COMPANIES (≥25) | • In what way do certain front-end activities contribute to better project performance? | Recommendations on application of value improving practices |
| **PHASE IV**<br><br>SURVEY<br><br>FOUR COMPANIES | • How could a framework to grasp project complexity be used to improve project performance? | Improved framework to characterize project complexity and its foreseen use |

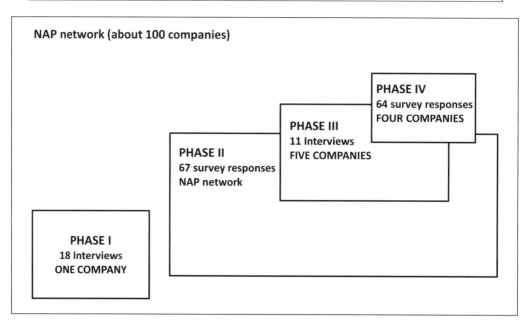

**Figure 25.3    Data collection within the NAP Network – overview of responses**

# Conclusions

What can we conclude from our study? For an elaborated 'content' answer to this question, please refer to the complete study (Bosch-Rekveldt, 2011). Please remember we couldn't have drawn those conclusions without extensively applying a mixed methods approach. Let us focus on the methodological part here.

The current research aimed to follow a constructivist approach in which positivist elements were embedded, in other words, applying qualitative methods as well as quantitative methods. What did this mixed methods approach bring us?

In Phase I, we explored the field to develop our model (qualitative approach). This model was tested in Phase II, by identifying *which* relations could be found between the building blocks, and Phase III aimed at investigating *how* certain front-end activities were contributing to project performance (explanatory question, qualitative approach). Phase IV, finally, aimed at evaluating the concepts developed (both quantitative and qualitative). Overall, different methods were applied; with specific aims but also to overall strengthen the results. By applying mixed methods in our study, a rich set of results has been gathered.

# Tips and Questions

## TIPS FOR STUDENTS

- Your first step always should be to define the goal of your research. What kind of knowledge are you looking for? In-depth or just scratching the surface? These considerations will guide your decisions for using a typical order and mix of research methods.
- Take into account that involving companies in your research takes a lot of time. Time for preparation to get their commitment, time for their actual participation and time for feeding back the results to them, as a specific target audience. But it's more than worth it!

## TIPS FOR SUPERVISORS

- Be careful not to overload your PhD candidate by unlimitedly mixing research methods. One of the external members of my PhD committee told me my PhD work could have been split into two or more separate PhD theses. My daily supervisor could have warned me…!
- The richness of in-depth case study results should not be undervalued compared to 'hard' quantitative results, just scratching the surface.
- If the possibility exists for multiple theses, explore them as soon as possible. Narrowing of the research scope will be incredibly helpful – in fact, necessary – to the student!

## QUESTIONS

1. What is the strength of applying the Wheel of Science?
2. What is the difference between a positivist approach and a constructivist approach?
3. How can you link the concept of 'triangulation' to the use of mixed research methods?
4. What would be an adequate research design for your own research, in terms of methods/ tools, and which order of application would you consider based on this chapter?

# References

Artto, K. A., Lehtonen, J. and Saranen, J. (2001). Managing projects front-end: Incorporating a strategic early view to project management with simulation. *International Journal of Project Management*, 19(5), 255–264.

Bakker, H. L. M. (2008). *Management of Projects: A People Process (inaugural adress)*. Delft: Delft University of Technology.

Blaikie, N. (2009). *Designing Social Research*, 2nd edition. Cambridge: Polity Press.

Bosch-Rekveldt, M. G. C. (2011). *Managing Project Complexity. A study into adapting early project phases to improve project performance in large engineering projects*. PhD, Delft University of Technology, Delft. (ISBN 978-94-91005-00-8)

Braster, J. F. A. (2000). *De Kern van Casestudy's*. Assen: Van Gorcum.

de Groen, T., Dhillon, J., Kerkhoven, H., Janssen, J. and Bout, J. (2003). *2x2: A Guide for Key Decision Makers in the Process Industry*. Nijkerk: NAP.

Dombkins, D. H. (2008). Project categorisation framework (PCAT) – System for the categorisation of projects, version 2.0, March 2008.

Donaldson, L. (2001). *The Contingency Theory of Organizations*. Thousand Oaks, CA: Sage publications.

Eisenhardt, K. M. (1989). Building theories from case-study research. *Academy of Management Review*, 14(4), 532–550.

Engwall, M. (2003). No project is an island: Linking projects to history and context. *Research Policy*, 32(5), 789–808.

Flyvbjerg, B. (2011). Case study. In N. K. Denzin and Y. S. Lincoln (eds), *The Sage Handbook of Qualitative Research*, 4th edition.. Thouand Oaks, CA: Sage, pp. 301–316.

Flyvbjerg, B., Bruzelius, N. and Rothengatter, W. (2003). *Megaprojects and Risk. An anatomy of ambition*. Cambridge: Cambridge University Press.

Geraldi, J. G. (2008). Patterns of complexity: The thermometer of complexity. *Project Perspectives 2008*, XXIX, 4–9.

Hall, P. G. (1981). *Great Planning Disasters*. London: Weidenfeld and Nicholson.

Hass, K. (2007). Introducing the project complexity model – A new approach to diagnosing and managing projects (part 1 of 2). *PM World Today*, IX(VII), 1–8.

Howell, D., Windahl, C. and Seidel, R. (2010). A project contingency framework based on uncertainty and its consequences. *International Journal of Project Management*, 28(3), 256–264.

IPA. (2011). Industry Benchmarking Consortium 2011: IPA.

Morris, P. W. G. (1994). *The Management of Projects*. London: Thomas Telford.

Morris, P. W. G., Crawford, L., Hodgson, D., Shepherd, M. M. and Thomas, J. (2006). Exploring the role of formal bodies of knowledge in defining a profession – The case of project management. *International Journal of Project Management*, 24(8), 710–721.

Morris, P. W. G. and Hough, G. H. (1987). *The Anatomy of Major Projects: A Study of the Reality of Project Management*. Chichester, UK: John Wiley.

NAP (Producer). (2009). NAP network. www.napnetwerk.nl. Retrieved from www.napnetwerk.nl. Accessed: October 2013.

Neleman, J. (2006). Shell gaat diep. *FEM Business*, 9(4), 30–34.

Oosterhuis, E. J., Pang, Y., Oostwegel, E. and de Kleijn, J. P. (2008). *Front-End Loading Strategy: A strategy to Achieve 2x2 Goals*. Nijkerk: NAP.

Pellegrinelli, S. (2011). What's in a name: Project or programme? *International Journal of Project Management*, 29(2), 232–240.

Pollack, J. (2007). The changing paradigms of project management. *International Journal of Project Management*, 25(3), 266–274.

Sauser, B. J., Reilly, R. R. and Shenhar, A. J. (2009). Why projects fail? How contingency theory can provide new insights – A comparative analysis of NASA's Mars Climate Orbiter loss. *International Journal of Project Management*, 27(7), 665–679.

Shenhar, A. J. (2001). One size does not fit all projects: Exploring classical contingency domains. *Management Science*, 47(3), 394–414.

Shenhar, A. J. and Dvir, D. (1996). Toward a typological theory of project management. *Research Policy*, 25(4), 607–632.

Smyth, H. J. and Morris, P. W. G. (2007). An epistemological evaluation of research into projects and their management: Methodological issues. *International Journal of Project Management*, 25(4), 423–436.

Tashakkori, A. and Teddlie, C. (1998). *Mixed Methodology: Combining Qualitative and Quantitative Approaches*. London: Sage Publications.

Thamhain, H. J. and Wilemon, D. L. (1986). Criteria for controlling projects according to plan. *Project Management Journal*, 17(2), 75–81.

van der Weijde, G. (2008). *Front-end loading in the oil and gas industry: Towards a fit front-end development phase*. MSc, Delft University of Technology, Delft.

Wallace, W. L. (1971). *The Logic of Science in Sociology*. New York: Aldine De Gruyter.

Williams, T. M. (2002). *Modelling Complex Projects*. London: John Wiley & Sons.

Williams, T. M. (2005). Assessing and moving on from the dominant project management discourse in the light of project overruns. *Ieee Transactions on Engineering Management*, 52(4), 497–508.

Yin, R. K. (2002). *Case Study Research: Design and Methods*, 3rd edition, Vol. 5. London: Sage Publications.

Yin, R. K. (2003). *Applications of Case Study Research*, 2nd edition, Vol. 34. London: Sage Publications.

# 26

# Importance of Sequencing in Mixed Methods Research Design

Beverly Pasian

*My doctoral research examined the conceptual and modular limitations of project management maturity (PMM) and associated models. This required a unique multimethod research design that demanded the analysis of the content of different model collections and a case study (both qualitative exercises) to explore the extent to which the resulting factors were present (or not). This chapter examines this strategy, designed to answer the research question: can non-process factors contribute to the maturity of a PM capability responsible for an undefined project?*

At the end of this chapter, the reader can:

*   appreciate the importance of sequencing in a PM inquiry;
*   be guided towards appropriate literature relevant to multi- and mixed methods theory;
*   understand the specifics of theoretical sampling in a mixed methods strategy.

Keywords: multimethod, project management maturity, e-Learning, universities, Canada

## Using a Multimethod Research Design

Thomas and Mullaly (2008) presented a new form of methodological strategies in the PM community: one that robustly used multiple methods to address research questions. The purpose of this next section is to demonstrate the application of such a 'multimethod' design in the study of project management maturity (PMM).

This research relied heavily on the research designs espoused by Datta (1997), Mingers (2001), Morse (2003), and Esteves and Pastor (2004). The first two offer the philosophical underpinnings justifying a pluralist approach to method design (Mingers, 2001, Datta, 1997), while Morse and Esteves offer more detailed perspectives on how such a design can be implemented (Esteves and Pastor, 2004; Morse, 2003). All advocate the use of multimethod design, with Datta (1997), in particular, commenting on the value of multimethod evaluations using case studies, which is of special relevance here.

The initial step of the research began with an analysis of existing maturity models (from various domains, both from within and outside of PM), where insight was possible concerning the expectations, definitions and understanding of 'maturity' in those fields. While valuable to the specific organisation or industry in question, such definitions provided a fresh perspective concerning the realities of others as they try to understand how their capabilities may or may not be mature. It is these other organisations – a university in this research – that can offer a different conceptual perspective on 'maturity' based on the practices they measure. These different worlds can generate different information, and different methods can be used to acquire it (Mingers, 2001).

Designing a research study with multiple stages that proceeds through a number of steps to reflect multiple interpretations is a logical approach. Morse advocates this approach on the basis of three key design principles for multimethod inquiries (2003):

- identify the theoretical drive of the research project;
- develop overt awareness of the dominance of each project; and
- respect methodological integrity.

## Identifying the Theoretical Drive of the Research Problem

The use of the term 'drive' is an essential characterisation of Morse's (2003) focus on research orientation. By using 'drive' to describe the theoretical dimension of the research activity, she is allowing for the inclusion of a 'minor component' (for example, a deductive element to an inductive programme and the reverse scenario). To be 'dominant' or offer a 'priority decision' (Morgan, 1998) suggests the need for a more flexible orientation of the Morse approach.

For this research, adopting a theoretical drive was appropriate for the nuanced connotations it suggests. While Morse (2003) seems to constrain the scope of 'drive' to inclusivity, the inductive or deductive influence on these phases is more textured than that. Reviewing the details and particular elements of (literally dozens of) maturity models is a drive characterised as much by a sense of discovery as destination. The journey through this literature is not quite a stroll down a wandering path, but nor does it have a straight trajectory.

This research follows an inductive drive initiated by the literature review and followed by a textual analysis of various industry, organisational and PMM models. Selections were chosen partly based on their representation of the project types associated with Types-2,-3 and -4 in Turner and Cochrane's typology (Turner and Cochrane, 1993). The drive shifted metaphorical gears once the initial conceptual framework (Figure 26.1) was created, and the case study was launched, where data was gathered that was specific to each site's PM capability. Through this, the veracity of this model was tested.

## Develop Overt Awareness of the Dominance of Each Research Project

The inductive drive travelled through two 'projects' using two qualitative data collection methods – document analysis and case study. Morse (2003) identifies four combinations of multimethod designs to support an inductive drive: QUAL→qual; QUAL→qual; QUAL→quan; QUAL→quan.

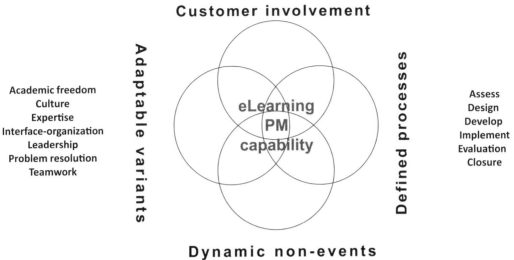

**Figure 26.1    Conceptual model (Pasian, 2011)**

Data collection and analysis within this research required a variation on the sequencing models identified and those identified by Sankaran et al. (2012). To satisfy the demands of this research, the following variation was designed (Figure 26.2).

The initial project used grounded theory techniques in the analysis of maturity models. Ultimately, this produced a conceptual framework for application in designated field sites. The content of the preliminary qualitative analysis was a distillation of elements from the selected maturity models. This enabled the creation of a conceptual framework for use in exploring the PM environment (as selected in the case study). The model itself did not generate sufficient data to adequately answer the primary research question and, for this reason, the first 'project' was the subsidiary investigation within this research design.

---

qual → QUAL    Indicating a sequential program where a qualitative project is followed by a second (more dominant) qualitative project.

---

**Figure 26.2    New sequence for multimethod design (Pasian, 2011)**

The dominance of the second project was intensified by its direct relationship to and support of the interpretivist paradigm that guided this research. At the core of this inquiry, an answer to the research question could not be found in the conceptual framework being used, or the maturity models that provide the basis for its development. Only by entering the world of a unique project environment (with an e-Learning project representing a Type-3 project) could true insight be found – through engagement with and analysis of the occupants of that world. The respondents can explain their views (or 'multiple realities') and also interpret them through the lens of my conceptual framework. In either case, the reality upon which theory is generated must occur on the constructed reality or interpretations of site participants, thus making the second project qualitative in nature.

## Respect Methodological Integrity

Maintaining the integrity of each chosen method is the last of Morse's trio of multimethod design principles. To this end, methods are used in each phase to independently collect data, but are sequenced in a way that secures the dominance of the relevant project (Morse, 2003). As identified above, in this research the dominant project is the case study launched after the completion of the document analysis. Figure 26.3 summarises the methods for each project.

In managing a multimethod design, data are not combined but rather concluded (at the end of each project) to answer a particular question (Morse, 2003). In this research, the following questions were the focus:

- Project #1 focused on the data found in the selected maturity model collections and asks: What processes (including sub-processes, practices and other properties) are used to measure maturity in a capability responsible for undefined projects or initiatives?
- Project #2 introduced these data (now in the form of a conceptual framework) to case sites. The goal in this project was to interpret the data provided against the conceptual framework. The question answered in this project was: What factors (processes, practices, properties) of a PM capability responsible for the management of an undefined project (for example, e-Learning) can contribute to its maturity?

| Project | Drive | Dominance | Research method used | | | | | |
|---|---|---|---|---|---|---|---|
| | | | Lit review | Document analysis | Grounded theory techniques | Pilot study | Case study (Interviews, Archived records, Direct observation, Field notes) |
| 1 | Inductive | qual | ✓ | ✓ | ✓ | | |
| 2 | Inductive | QUAL | | | ✓ | ✓ | ✓ |

**Figure 26.3    Summary of methods (Pasian, 2011)**

## Implementing the Multimethod Design

As described above, the multimethod design followed an inductive path and included two primary projects. The elements of which are described in detail below.

## Project 1: Document Analysis

Given the central role of maturity models in this research, an in-depth analysis of the text of these documents and records was necessary to fully explore the range of maturity model designs, lexicon and strategies. The initial search examined the compatibility of representative types with existing definitions of PMM and a second, more extensive review of models examined the text of the models themselves. This examination helped to:

- illustrate how these project types measure maturity;
- provide specific examples of the practices, processes and levels used to define and measure maturity in that specific project environment.

Document analysis is a key method of qualitative analysis, and one used in the production of reliable evidence about a large sample (Silverman, 2005). While often embedded in one method or another (for example, case study, interviewing), it is an approach that can provide data without the direct or indirect involvement of participants. The type of document can range dramatically, along with the purpose and advantages associated with its use. They can be examined with the aim of selecting facts from the material in question (Caulley, 1983). The documents can be categorised at a macro level as public or private, primary or secondary, and can come in myriad forms.

Definitions include those offered by Caulley (1983) who defines 'documents' as: written source of historical information, oral testimony, artefacts, pictorial survivals, archeological remains, and official/state papers such as treaties, laws, grants and deeds.

Bryman (2004) identifies several categories of documents, two of which were used for this research: official documents derived from private sources, and official documents derived from the state. Within this project, these types are almost entirely related to the description of maturity models, including examples of use or commentary on same. Based on the findings of the literature review, it was expected that private sector companies, government agencies and higher education institutions (universities) are the main sources for such documents.

Lincoln and Guba (1985) distinguish between two related terms – document and record – that were relevant for this inquiry. 'Document' is used to denote any written or recorded material (other than a record) that was not prepared specifically in response to a request from the inquirer (such as a set of interview notes). Examples of 'documents' include letters, diaries, speeches and case studies. 'Records' are any written or recorded statement prepared by or for an individual for the purpose of attesting to an event or providing an accounting. Examples include airline schedules, tax forms, government directories, birth certificates and audit reports.

The comparative value of the definitions hinges on this distinctive treatment of 'records.' Examining maturity models (in and outside of PM) from this perspective, one can see the distinction between documents and records. The former encompasses the models themselves, while the latter (records) are separate insofar as they were prepared for an individual person, organisation or other entity as a result of processes being evaluated (that is, audited) for their maturity.

Using the definitions of document and record as the basis for collecting, sorting and analysing material for Project #1 (the model analysis), a more specific typology is further offered below (Table 26.1).

**Table 26.1    Document and record typology**

|  | Type | Examples |
| --- | --- | --- |
| Documents | Industry/Specialised Maturity Models from across various industries, organisations and knowledge domains. (A full listing is available in the references.) | Maturity grids, Hybrids and Likert-type questionnaires, CMM-style models (Fraser, Moultrie and Gregory, 2002). |
|  | Descriptive collateral that describe model functioning, use or application. (This material differs from 'records'.) | Instructions, illustrations, templates or other material describing the model or its use (Marshall, 2006). |
| Records | Maturity audit (where a maturity assessment was prepared as a result of using a specific maturity model). | Report to model user (Marshall, 2005). |

# Project #2: Exploratory Case Study

## A PILOT CASE

A preparatory step towards the exploratory case study was the pilot case: a study that can help refine the concepts to be explored, intended content to be collected in the exploratory case study and the procedures to be followed (Yin, 1989). The selection criteria identified by Yin – convenience, access and geographic proximity (1989) – are relevant for this inquiry. The site was in the same city as the Alpha and Beta sites, accessible (through relationships with faculty and staff) and proximate to the other universities.

The pilot case contributed to the conceptual development by building on the properties emergent from the maturity model analysis and relevant literature from e-Learning research. It is, as Yin advocates (1989), 'broad and less focused' than the ultimate collection instrument (the conceptual framework) to be used in the case study sites. Specific issues for exploration included project team roles, description of PM processes and customer involvement.

## THE PRIMARY SITES

The nature of the research question revolved around the nature of a PM function as it manages an undefined project type – specifically an e-Learning project.

Broadly defined, e-Learning is the use of Internet technologies to create and deliver a rich learning environment that includes a broad array of instruction and information resources and solutions, the goal of which is to enhance individual and organisational performance (Rosenberg, 2006; Colvin Clark and Mayer, 2003).

The objective of e-Learning projects is to use technology-enabled resources to support the teaching and learning strategy of the host institution through the delivery of innovative instructional content. The challenge, however, lies in the interpretation of this broad goal at more operational levels where instructional designers and subject matter experts (SMEs) must identify project goals for their individual programmes, courses, subjects or units. 'E-Learning must be contextualised for individuals and enable the presentation and consideration of multiple perspectives' (Rossett, 2002).

Bullen and Janes (2007) describe three course categories that are consistent with the e-Learning projects managed at the sites explored in this research:

- e-Learning as distance education, referring to courses that are delivered entirely, or almost entirely, on the Internet.
- e-Learning as electronically mediated learning, including any teaching or learning that is mediated by technology (for example, learning objects that simulate concepts used as part of regular on-campus teaching). It is not necessarily distance education.
- e-Learning as facilitated transactions software, including software that is used to organise and manage teaching (such as learning management systems).

For the purposes of this research, e-Learning projects were being used as examples of Type-3 projects within the Turner and Cochrane typology. As such, their methods were considered highly defined, while their goals were not. Maintaining flexibility or open-endedness is a critical component in facilitating the teaching and learning experiences of end-users (both students and SMEs) where each will bring to their use of the course their own inclinations, behaviours and preferences. Such a 'notoriously difficult' (Turner and Cochrane, 1993) dimension demands flexibility within the project as it is being designed and, most critically, implemented. These projects must leave room for spontaneous, unplanned use that is supportive of stated learning objectives but expansive in potential use.

For this inquiry, the use of Yin's third category of case study design was used (1989) where the three primary conditions are: the type of research question posed; the extent of control an investigator has over actual behavioral events (I had none); and, the degree of focus on contemporary as opposed to historical events.

The focus on a contemporary situation is determined through a narrowing of the type of industry, organisation and project type that could be considered for case study. To accomplish this, the questions and answers in Table 26.2 served as the basis for site selection:

**Table 26.2    Delimitation table for case study selection**

| Delimiting Question | Indicator | Detail and/or Example |
|---|---|---|
| What types of organisations manage Type-3 projects? | Multiple | Colleges and universities |
| What sectors apply? | Public sector | Higher education |
| What project type is managed here? | Type-3 | e-Learning |
| Evidence of PM capability or techniques? | Yes | Published theory in multiple journals* |

* Relevant journals include (but are not limited to): *Journal of Distance Education, Australian Journal of Educational Technology, Educational Technology, The Internet and Higher Education*, and *Studies in Higher Education*.

Three sites were chosen that satisfied these criteria: each a university (situated in Canada) that used a demonstrable PM function (or techniques) in the design, development and implementation of e-Learning projects. In keeping with the parameters of the team profile, the unit of analysis for this inquiry was the individual project team (see Table 26.3).

## Theoretical Sampling in Multimethod Design

Bryman (1988) argues that, when choosing a theoretical sample, 'the issue should be couched in terms of the generalisability of cases to theoretical propositions rather than to populations or

**Table 26.3      Typical team roles for e-Learning projects**

| Role | Description |
| --- | --- |
| Course developer | A practitioner/expert in multimedia design, incorporating content through various digital media in a coherent and, generally, interactive fashion. |
| Instructional designer/Project manager | An expert in the science (study) of instruction. |
| Sponsor | The senior academic or administrative officer responsible for approval of project, including academic release, financials and content. |
| Subject-matter expert | An academic with recognised expertise in one or more areas. Responsible for content development in an e-Learning project. |
| Unit/Department head | A manager specifically responsible for IT services and application development, responsible for either a specific unit or centralised function. |

universes.' Silverman (2005) supports this position by identifying one of the features of theoretical sampling as 'choosing cases in terms of theory.' Mason (1996) further supports this position by explaining that 'theoretical sampling means selecting groups or categories to study on the basis of their relevance to you research questions ... and the explanation or account which you are developing.'

Examining case study selection within a multimethod setting has received little attention. To this end, this approach partially relied on the work of Datta (1997) who argues that better evaluations for results [will occur] if the following conditions are met:

> Selection of methods is parsimonious and appropriate to the [research] questions [see Figure 26.3] ... [The] key issue being the decision of what case study type and sequencing meets the needs.

Due care is used in anticipating threats to the integrity of the multimethod design, data collection, analysis and reporting. To address real or anticipated threats, a case study protocol was prepared.

Expectations are realistic concerning the value-added of case studies (and every other method in the overall design). Having and achieving realistic expectations is a dimension of the research process itself – one akin to solving a puzzle. And, like any puzzle, seeing the entire picture within a multimethod research design comes one piece at a time (Morse, 2003). Data associated with the case study, while highly influential, are of limited value. As Mingers (2001) emphasises: 'Different methods generate information about different aspects of the world ... It is desirable and feasible to combine together different methods to gain richer and more reliable research results.'

## SEMI-STRUCTURED INTERVIEWS

Semi-structured interviews are a key source of evidence within a case study, allowing the reporting of events to be the result of interpretation by directly involved subjects (Yin, 1989). By using interviews, the researcher can reach areas of reality that would otherwise remain inaccessible – such as people's subjective experiences and attitudes.

To address the themes of this inquiry, a careful and thoughtful unearthing of the circumstances surrounding the management of e-Learning projects was necessary. Because this inquiry touched on themes of procedural reliability, manageability and predictability, it was critical to understand not just whether a process existed but why and how it was received and used. It was expected that, by asking a project manager – or, more likely in this case, an instructional designer – to confirm the use of certain processes related to the management of projects, a perfunctory response would have been received. Asking why, on the other hand, would allow the interview subject to interpret and reveal the circumstances and conditions of its use.

## INTERVIEW SUBJECTS

Determination of appropriate interview subjects was the result of the purposeful selection of subject-matter experts and staff within the university setting responsible for various PM processes associated with e-Learning projects. Individuals were selected because of their roles in managing these projects.

Although job descriptions and titles differed slightly between institutions, key PM roles were chosen for interviews based on demonstrated relevance to e-Learning projects: course developer, instructional designer, project sponsor, SME (that is, specialised faculty), and unit/department head.

## DIRECT OBSERVATION

The researcher was an onlooker or observer in this inquiry, primarily collecting data through the methods identified in this section. Different site visits lent themselves to different types of observation: informal site visits to allow the researcher to conduct interviews and generally observe the offices of the PM unit or office. More formal observation will occur should the site have a testing period where the e-Learning project was being developed and evaluated. The researcher will observe these activities and conduct interviews with obliging participants. Other evidence sources in the case study included field notes, physical artefacts and archived records.

# Data Analysis

Data analysis occurred for both the document analysis and case study both using grounded theory techniques. The three basic elements of theory building through grounded theory are concepts, categories and propositions (Corbin and Strauss, 1990). Concepts as the basic units of analysis as they come from the conceptualisation of data, not the actual data per se, that theory is developed.

While categories are higher in level and more abstract that the concepts they represent, they are generated through the same analytical process of making comparisons to highlight similarities and differences that is used to produce lower level concepts. Categories are the 'cornerstones' of developing theory, they provide the means by which the theory can be integrated.

## PROJECT #1: DOCUMENT ANALYSIS

NVivo (version 8.0) software was used to analyse and code the content of PMM models and others from various industries and organisations. As Richards (1999) explains, categorising is a way to 'think up' from the data to greater generality. Two nodal types are used to categorise data: free nodes (in the document analysis of Project #1) and tree nodes (for the case study of Project #2). The former was advantageous in analysing the maturity models to facilitate its unorganised text and facilitate emergent ideas while the latter allowed for hierarchical order around growing concepts (1999). The generated properties were listed (in descending order) based on frequency of sources and references, with categories generated from the non-PM models. See Tables 26.4 and 26.5 for partial listings.

**Table 26.4**    **Results from open coding analysis of PMM models**

| Item | Sources | # of References |
| --- | --- | --- |
| Management | 23 | 42 |
| Organisation | 17 | 28 |
| Process management | 15 | 23 |
| Process, tool development | 13 | 22 |
| Awareness | 11 | 20 |
| Business case and benefits | 14 | 19 |
| Project specifications | 6 | 17 |

**Table: 26.5**    **Results from open coding analysis of models outside of PM**

| Item | Sources | # of References |
| --- | --- | --- |
| Culture | 17 | 62 |
| Customer | 11 | 61 |
| Organisational and management policies | 19 | 52 |
| Leaders, champions (individual roles) | 19 | 38 |
| Interface with host organisation | 19 | 36 |

## PROJECT #2: CASE STUDIES

Analysing data collected from the case sites involved a combination of several steps, beginning with interviews using the conceptual framework. The resulting data was coded multiple times (again, using the NVivo application) and a provisional list of codes generated based on emergent relationships identified from the coding.

Building case-ordered meta-matrices (Miles and Huberman, 1994) using the codes generated from the open coding allowed the detailed data to be allocated (based on team roles) across the sites for an illustration of a partial meta-matrix (see Figure 26.4 for a partial listing).

| | | Sponsor | Manager | Instructional designer | Department Head | Subject-matter expert | Course developer |
|---|---|---|---|---|---|---|---|
| **Dynamic non-events** | **Motivation** | | "Developing plan is easy…getting them to use it is hard." [O] | Team members (from a union) perceived with lesser skills affect motivations of others. [E] | Union regulations affect pay scales - affects motivation [E] There's motivation but not urgency. [O] | Motivation comes from team seeing project in development [P] Project success: more funding. [E] | The development team in different union: fewer opportunities [PT] |
| | **Commitment** | Evidence of lack of commitment can be found in union mentality, inactive participation [O] | Personal connection is needed by PMO, particularly when organizational units are dispersed. [E] | Comes from team (especially SMEs, designers) seeing project in development. [P] ID commitment to pc must be "inside and out." (Absence has project implications.) [E] Commitment stems from institutional values [P] | Unit management can commit resources after recognition of a problem [PR] Commitment to understanding the environment can be higher [O] | Work with designers reinforces SME commitment [E] | |

**Figure 26.4**    **Partial table using case matrix method (taken from Pasian DPM thesis)**

## PARTIAL RESULTS

Given the focus of this chapter on the methodological approach to this research, only partial results were provided in this chapter. Macro-level themes from these matrices identified variations to the conceptual framework. A revised conceptual framework that reflected each site's variations was included at the end of their individual analysis. A comparison between the sites was the final step of the analysis, resulting in a revised conceptual framework (see Figure 26.5).

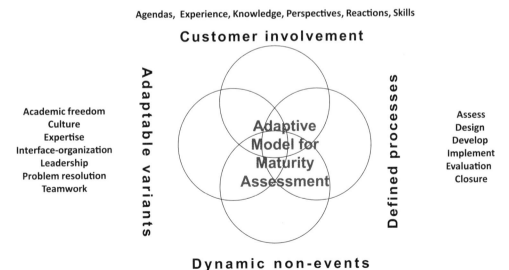

Agendas, Experience, Knowledge, Perspectives, Reactions, Skills

**Customer involvement**

Academic freedom
Culture
Expertise
Interface-organization
Leadership
Problem resolution
Teamwork

**Adaptable variants**

**Adaptive Model for Maturity Assessment**

**Defined processes**

Assess
Design
Develop
Implement
Evaluation
Closure

**Dynamic non-events**

Acceptance, Attitude, Commitment, Loyalty, Motivation, Trust

**Figure 26.5**    **Revised conceptual model (Pasian, 2011)**

## Implications for Methodology

Multimethod research is a relatively new design strategy. Unlike its 'mixed method' counterpart, it relies on two or more methods from either a quantitative or qualitative framework. Users of multimethod designs are given similar choices but existing strategies are limited – neither Burke Johnson and Onwuegbuzie (2004) nor Morse (2003) indicate the possibility of a sequential qualitative strategy where the second stage is more dominant than the first. This inquiry demonstrated the value, indeed the necessity, of this strategy because the first qualitative method is necessary but insufficient in providing sufficient data to satisfactorily answer the research questions.

Future researchers can use this strategy as a framework for similarly challenging inquiries where a partnership exists between multiple methods that are mutually reinforcing but unable to provide sufficient data independently.

This methodology also has broader implications for its possible use in other post-secondary institutions (certainly in the Canadian higher education community), other organisational types, industries and project types. All could consider this methodology to investigate the sophistication of their own PM capabilities.

## Tips and Exercises

### TIPS FOR STUDENTS

- Take the time to familiarise yourself with the multi- and mixed-methods literature. It is an important methodological paradigm in PM.
- Pilot cases can be a key step in multi- and mixed-methods designs, especially those that rely on a qualitative strategy.
- Be creative in selecting methods for a multi- and mixed-methods strategy. Shy away from the use of interviews and case study (not that there's anything wrong with them!).

### TIPS FOR SUPERVISORS

- Brainstorm with your student(s) to choose methods that might broaden their research strategy.
- Take the time to familiarise yourself with the multi- and mixed-methods literature. You'll be in a better position to advise your students.
- Speak with your colleagues (other supervisors) regarding their familiarity with multi- and mixed methods. This will broaden the resources available to all research students.

### EXERCISES

1. Look up the definitions of multi- and mixed-method design. Compose an email and send to your supervisors and other student colleagues.
2. Choose a data source that only relies on and/or generates documents. Categorise them either the document typology in this chapter or Bryman (2004).
3. Search the Journal of Mixed Methods. Choose an article related to PM or a PM inquiry. Discuss with other students.

# References

Bryman, A. (1988). *Quantity and Quality in Social Research.* London: Unwin Hyman.

Bryman, A. (2004) *Social Research Methods.* Oxford: Oxford University Press.

Bullen, M. and Janes, D. P. (2007). *Making the Transition to e-Learning: Strategies and issues.* Hershey, PA: The Idea Group, Inc.

Burke Johnson, R. and Onwuegbuzie, A. J. (2004). Mixed methods research: A research paradigm whose time has come. *Educational Research,* 33(7), 14–26.

Caulley, D. N. (1983). Document analysis in program evaluation. *Evaluation and Program Evaluation,* 6(1), 19–29.

Colvin Clark, R. and Mayer, R. E. (2003). *E-Learning and the Science of Instruction.* San Francisco, CA: Pfeiffer.

Corbin, J. and Strauss, A. (1990). Grounded theory research: Procedures, canons, and evaluative criteria. *Qualitative Sociology,* 13, 3–21.

Datta, L. (1997). Multimethod Evaluations: Using case studies together with other methods. In: Chelimsky, E. and Shadish, W. R. (eds) *Evaluation for the 21st Century: A handbook.* Thousand Oaks, CA: Sage Publications.

Esteves, J. and Pastor, J. (2004). Using a multimethod approach to research enterprise systems implementations. *Electronic Journal of Business Research Methods,* 2, 69–82.

Fraser, P., Moultrie, J. and Gregory, M. (2002). The use of maturity models/grids as a tool in assessing product development capability. *International Journal of Quality and Reliability Management,* 1, 244–249.

Lincoln, Y. S. and Guba, E. G. (1985). *Naturalistic Inquiry.* Beverly Hills, CA: Sage Publications.

Marshall, S. (2005). *eLearning Maturity Model: Capability Determination.* Example Determination of New Zealand Tertiary Institution eLearning Capability: An application of an eLearning Maturity Model – Report to the New Zealand Ministry of Education. Victoria, New Zealand: University of Wellington.

Marshall, S. (2006). *e-Learning Maturity Model: Capability Determination Workbook* (Version 2.0) [Online]. Victoria, New Zealand: University of Wellington. Available: http://www.utdc.vuw.ac.nz/research/emm/, accessed 15 September 2008.

Mason, J. (1996). *Qualitative Researching.* London: Sage Publications.

Miles, M. B. and Huberman, A. M. (1994). *Qualitative Data Analysis: An expanded sourcebook.* Thousand Oaks, CA: Sage Publications.

Mingers, J. (2001). Combining IS Research Methods: Towards a pluralist methodology. *Information Systems Research,* 12, 240–259.

Morgan, D. L. (1998). Practical strategies for combining qualitative and quantitative methods: Applications to health research. *Qualitative Health Research,* 8, 362–367.

Morse, J. M. (2003). Principles of Mixed Methods and Multimethod Research Design. In: Tashakkori, A. and Teddlie, C. (eds) *Handbook of Mixed Methods in Social and Behavioral Research.* Thousand Oaks, CA: Sage Publications.

Pasian, B. (2011). Project management maturity: An analysis of existing and emergent factors. Doctoral thesis, University of Technology (Sydney), Faculty: Design, Architecture and Building.

Richards, L. (1999). *Using NVivo in Qualitative Research.* Melbourne, AUS: Qualitative Solutions and Research Pty. Ltd.

Rosenberg, M. J. (2006). *Beyond E-Learning: Approaches and Technologies to enhance organizational knowledge, learning, and performance.* San Francisco, CA: Pfeiffer.

Rossett, A. (2002). *The ASTD E-Learning Handbook.* New York, NY: McGraw-Hill.

Sankaran, S., Cameron, R. and Scales, J. (2012). The utility and quality of mixed methods in Project Management Research'. EURAM 12th Annual Conference 2012, Erasmus University, Rotterdam, June.

Silverman, D. (2005). *Doing Qualitative Research: A practical handbook.* Los Angeles, CA: Sage Publications.

Thomas, J. and Mullaly, M. (2008). *Researching the Value of Project Management.* Newtown Square, PA: Project Management Institute.

Turner, J. R. and Cochrane, R. A. (1993). Goals-and-methods matrix: Coping with projects and/or methods of achieving them. *International Journal of Project Management*, 11, 93–102.

Yin, R. K. (1989). *Case Study Research: Design and methods*. Newbury Park: Sage Publications.

# 27

# An Empirical Research Method Strategy for Construction Consulting Services Projects

Li Yongkui (李永奎), Yang Qing (杨青) and He Qinghua (何清华)

*The application of project management maturity (PMM) principles in a Construction Consulting Services (CSS) project will not only benefit the performance of the consulting team but also facilitate the implementation of construction project itself.*

Based on the PMM contributing factors study for e-Learning projects, this chapter will reveal the process of transferring the research findings from one context to another. Empirical studies were carried out in this research with interviews identifying the CSS process and Delphi questionnaires exploring the significance of 4-dimensions, 19-factors and 122 metrics. Then reliability and validity test and the Analytic Hierarchy Process (AHP) were adopted for the data analysis. Results demonstrate that non-process factors including customer involvement, organisational variants and member performance play an important role in CSS-PMM.

At the end of this chapter the reader can:

* understand how a research strategy was adapted from one context to another;
* appreciate how cultural dimensions can affect the design implementation of a research strategy for Construction Project Management Maturity (CPMM);
* understand the unique and challenging elements of a mixed methods strategy in researching PMM.

## Introduction

The successful application of project management maturity models (PMMM) has been investigated in multiple fields (Wendler, 2012) including construction engineering, but CPMM was not well developed when we considered the situation in other industries, especially in the Petrochemical and Defence industries (Cooke-Davies and Arzymanow, 2003). The study of CPMM in China has a history of ten years which is relatively short when compared to more than 30 years of development of PMM. A review of CPMM literature has shown concentration on the owners' and the contractors' maturity while the maturity research on construction consultancy (including design, cost, supervision, tender invitation agent, PM services unit and so on) is relatively rare. What's more, there is a research gap for the study of CCS PMM. To fill this gap, the relevant research was conducted through international collaboration.

This international collaborative research was carried out by the research group from Utrecht University of Applied Sciences (Netherlands) and Tongji University in Shanghai, China. The core object of this research is to establish a PMM model for a CCS project in the construction industry context of China. The collaboration was based on the analysis of existing and emergent contributing factors to PMM identified through doctoral work (Pasian, 2011).

In this chapter, we focus on four research questions that reflected the main problems the research groups faced and the methods they have taken to establish a rigorous and solid PMM model for CCS projects.

- How to transfer the contributing factors (associated with e-Learning projects to CCS projects?
- How to develop metrics for each contributing factors?
- How to use the Delphi approach to help explore the significance of factors and their metrics?
- How to deal with the data from the interview and the questionnaires?

The factors identified through the doctoral thesis were associated with the management of e-Learning projects where the examination of the associated PM capability showed that multiple non-process factors contributed to the reliable management of these projects. This analysis revealed that the current view of PMMM – which were based on the control of management processes to show the maturity of the capability – was insufficient. The results were incorporated in a 4-node PMM conceptual framework (CF) that is shown in Figure 27.1.

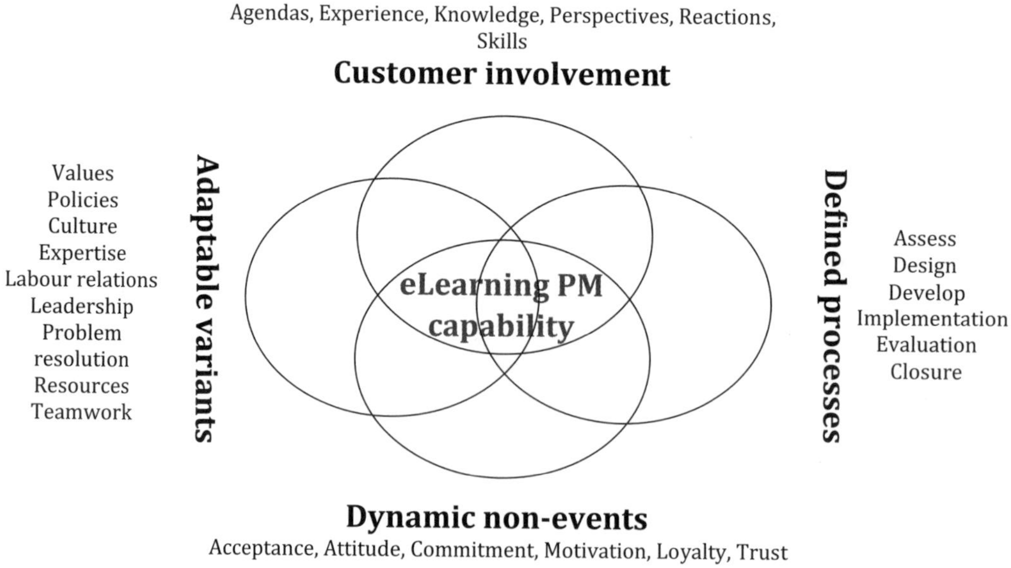

Figure 27.1    4-node PMM model (Pasian, 2012)

## CHOOSING A COLLABORATIVE RESEARCH APPROACH

In the construction industry, PMMM seldom consider the influence of non-process factors, as traditional construction PM keeps a tight grip on processes to reach the schedule, cost and quality objectives. Considering non-process factors was of interest and led to the inclusion of the 4-node CF in our research of CCS PMMM. When the 4-node CF was applied from higher education to the construction industry, adaptive changes were necessary. A review of the literature revealed that little previous research could support such an adaptation. In the absence of such support, it was necessary to interview practitioners.

## Seeking for Support in Literature

Organisational culture gives identity to an organisation and its importance in construction organisation (see Cheung, Wong and Wu (2011) study). Construction professionals working for developers, consultants and contractors were invited to assess the appropriateness of artefacts of organisational culture in construction. Seven factors were the focus: 'team orientation' and 'coordination and integration' second the factor 'teamwork' in CF strongly. Similar evidences in the construction engineering field were found for most of the factors such as agendas, perspective, culture, leadership, policies, problem resolution, resources, commitment, motivation, trust, loyalty and attitude.

Here two problems arise:

1. From the literature, it was seen that some factors could not be applied to the construction industry and new contributing factors emerged. Changes were unavoidable. The final result was that five factors were eliminated, one new factor was identified and three factors were combined to one.
   - Elimination: Acceptance, Reaction, Value, Labour Relations and Expertise.
   - Addition: Communication.
   - Combination: Knowledge, Experience and Skills were combined into one factor named Capability.

   'Labour Relations' was eliminated as a factor and is an example of how the context-specificity of the construction industry required such a change.

   Despite the government's active legislation to protect workers, labour rights still remain widely ignored and poorly enforced in China. Chinese labour legislation stipulates workers' individual rights regarding contracts, wages and so on, but it fails to provide them with collective rights, namely the rights to organise, to strike and to bargain collectively in a meaningful sense (Chen and Feng, 2007). Lee, Ching, Kwan and Friedman (2009) and Shen and Liu (2008) pointed out that labour unions in China are always weak and toothless separately in their studies of labour movement and labour protection policy. In the original framework, 'labour relationship' referred to the influence labour unions had on the team members associated with the project. Because labour unions have a limited impact in China, this factor was eliminated.

2. Sufficient documentary support regarding how the CCS process is divided or influenced was not found, so the decision was made to go for interviews for more information.

## Using Interviews in the Face of Inadequate Documentary Support

To determine which factors and metrics have influence on the process of CCS, interviews were conducted with eight related experts (coded as experts one to eight). There were multiple key points for designing the interviews:

- A thorough consideration before the interview, including the objective wished to reach, the questions asked and the people interviewed is indispensable.
- The purpose of this interview: Get opinions on the phase division of the CCS projects and key objects or successful standards in each phase.
- People you choose: When choosing experts involved in the interview, several criteria apply (Bryman, 1996). For this research, the criteria are displayed as follows:
  - have extensive experience in CCS;
  - have been directly involved in the practice of CCS;
  - deeply understand or are doing research on the whole process of CCS projects.
- Eight experts were invited, 60 per cent of which had more than ten years' work experience in CCS projects. What's more, 85 per cent of the experts had devoted more than ten years to construction engineering field practice.
- Some small but vital details:
  - check the voice recorder before every interview just in case. The time of experts is always precious and you are not allowed another chance;
  - inform the expert of theme of the research before the interview. It is preferable to outline the format of the interview and the estimated amount of time it will take;
  - control the time as you promised. If necessary, guide them to concentrate on the theme.

## Developing Metrics for Each Contributing Factor

The initial idea behind the CCS PMMM was to use a model that could guide the practitioners to evaluate and improve their performance in CCS (it was not a conceptual model), the initial model for CSS PMM is shown in Figure 27.2. This made the specific metrics for each factor imperative.

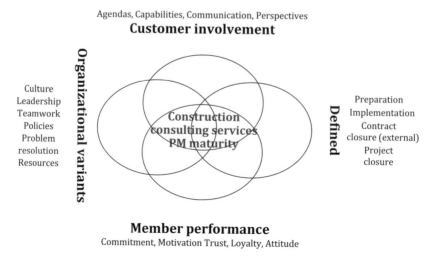

Figure 27.2    The initial model for CSS PMM

## LITERATURE-SUPPORTED METRICS FOR NON-PROCESS FACTORS

One hundred and three metrics were recognised as non-process factors, which were all extracted from previous research findings. 'Agenda' which is shown in Table 27.1 is used here as an example.

Coding is requisite when the number of metrics is around 100. A six-number coding was applied ('000000'). The first two digits represent the four dimensions (01 – customer involvement; 02 – organisational variants; 03 – member performance; 04 – defined process); the middle two digits represent the factors coded in sequence; while the last two digits represent the metrics coded in sequence as well.

**Table 27.1  Metrics associated with 'Agenda'**

| Factors | Metrics | Support Resources |
|---|---|---|
| 010100 Agenda (Definition: the extent the consulting team meets the owners' needs) | 010101 Construction project should be completed on time. (O)P | Al-Momani, 2000 |
| | 010102 Construction project should be carried out within budget. (O)P | |
| | 010103 Construction project quality should conform to the requirements of contracts. (O)P | |
| | 010104 Construction project planning is carried out correctly. (O)P | |
| | 010105 There are few rework and deficiencies during construction. (O)P | |
| | 010106 There should be a good relationship with trust between the customer and the consulting team. (O)S | |
| | 010107 The consulting team should ensure adequate comprehension of customer demands in order to meet them. (O)S | Yu, Shen, Kelly and Hunter, 2007 |

Note: The code in '()'refers to the subject who will answer the question when CCS project maturity evaluation is executed. Here 'O' represents the owner while 'C' represents project consulting team. The code outside '()'refers to the content the metric measures. If the merits and demerits of the construction project are measured, the code 'P' will be given; if the performance of CCS project itself is measured, the code'S' will be given. In addition, the quality of the construction project partly reflects the quality of CCS.

## DETERMINING METRICS FOR 'PROCESS FACTORS' USING THE LITERATURE AND INTERVIEWS

With the example of the factor 'CCS project closure phase', the way to figure out these metrics is shown in Table 27.2.

**Table 27.2   Metrics of CSS project closure phase**

| Factors | Metrics | Support Resources |
| --- | --- | --- |
| 040400<br>CCS project closure phase<br>(internal) | 040401 The consulting project has earned the profit as expected. C(S) | Expert 4, 5, 7;<br>Simon, Schoeman and Sohal, 2010 |
| | 040402 The consulting team should draw lessons or experiences from the past project in time. C(S) | Expert 1, 3, 5, 7;<br>Thomas and Chow, 2004;<br>Li, 2001 |
| | 040403 The consulting team should conduct knowledge management to produce related reports or generalisations beneficial to the development of the enterprise. C(S) | Expert 2, 5, 7, 8;<br>Yin, 2010 |
| | 040404 The consulting team should evaluate the continuous improvement of team members, the influence on customers and business impact in the future. C(S) | Expert 2;<br>Li, 2001 |
| | 040405 Appropriate customer maintenances should be carried out after the project. C(S) | Expert 3, 4, 6;<br>Simon, Schoeman and Sohal, 2010 |

## Using the Delphi Approach to Help Explore the Significance of Factors and Their Metrics

The Delphi method is a highly formalised method of communication that is designed to extract the maximum amount of unbiased information from a panel of experts (Chan et al., 2001). Panel members remain unknown to one another and respond to a series of questionnaires. The iterative nature of the procedure generates new information for panelists in each round, enabling them to modify their assessments and project them beyond their own subjective opinions.

Two rounds of Delphi questionnaires were implemented: one is for generating the significance of all the contributing factors; the other is quite similar, but for the significance of key metrics and four dimensions. In total, four questionnaires were used twice for each round (there were two rounds) of the Delphi Survey. They are simply called Questionnaire 1 (Q1), Questionnaire 2 (Q2), Questionnaire 3 (Q3) and Questionnaire 4 (Q4) in the time sequence.

A five-point Likert scale was adapted for the questionnaires (with 'one to five' indicating the increasing importance of factors/metrics/dimensions). Part of Q1 has been shown in Table 27.3. After gathering the data from Q1, the mean score for each factor was calculated and put in Q2 as references for experts to see if they needed to revise their initial grading.

The same logic appeared in Q3 and Q4, but for the metrics and four dimensions. What's more, experts would be asked one more question when they were grading: 'please choose the key metrics for each factor'. It helped to eliminate the repeatable or unnecessary metrics and control the number.

In Q1 and Q2, the precise explanation of all the factors is indispensable. If several experts pre-test your questionnaires the results you will received will be greatly improved. Their advice on any unreasonableness and ambiguity in the questionnaire will improve the quality – the bold font in Table 27.3 is a good example. It emphasises that the factor 'capability' does not simply refer to

**Table 27.3    Illustrative example of the Delphi questionnaire**

| Customer Involvement | Significance | | | | |
|---|---|---|---|---|---|
| Agenda: the extent the consulting team meets the owners' needs. | 1 | 2 | 3 | 4 | 5 |
| Capability: the owners' judgment on the knowledge, experience and skills of the consulting team. | 1 | 2 | 3 | 4 | 5 |
| Communication: the conveyance and feedback concerning thoughts, emotion and information between the owner and the consulting team. | 1 | 2 | 3 | 4 | 5 |
| Perspectives: a coherent belief of the owner in the construction project. | 1 | 2 | 3 | 4 | 5 |

the consulting team itself but the importance of the owner's judgment (justifying the inclusion of the factor in the dimension 'Customer Involvement').

In Q3 and Q4, the length of the questionnaires became a concern. In order to retain the respondents' attention, 122 metrics had to be organised into good typography. Finally, the length was successfully reduced to three pages. On the other hand, The questionnaire should make it easy for the respondent to answer. For instance, especially in electronic questionnaires, the tick symbol '✓' was needed for those experts unskilled in using MS Word.

## Reconciling Data from Interviews and the Questionnaires

Data analysis and discussion will reveal the answers to the research questions. Now the essential difference between the qualitative data from the interviews and the quantitative data from the questionnaires has to be distinguished.

*Qualitative data*
The procedure for handling the qualitative data is as follows:

1. Type up the transcripts from the interview recordings.
2. Code these transcripts by experts, interview questions, phases and probable metrics identified by experts and some keywords recognised by frequency analysis. Coding is an iterative process according to new findings or analytical roadmaps until satisfied results are captured.

NVivo is a useful qualitative analysis software enabling easy organization and analysing of unstructured information. With the unstructured interview materials imported and analysed into Nvivo, the clear phases of the CCS project emerged. The defined processes are: CCS project preparation, implementation, contract closure (external) and project closure (internal). The metrics for the project closure phase were displayed in Table 27.2 where you can clearly see which experts were in favour of each metric.

## QUANTITATIVE DATA

One way to think of reliability is that a person should get the same score on a questionnaire if they complete it at two different points in time (test–retest reliability). Cronbach's alpha is most commonly used when you have multiple Likert questions in a survey/questionnaire that form a scale and you wish to determine if the scale is reliable. So Cronbach's alpha was selected for testing the data reliability of Q1–4. A value above 0.7 is an acceptable value for Cronbach's alpha and values substantially lower indicate an unreliable scale (Field, 2006). Table 27.4 shows the high reliability of Q1–2.

**Table 27.4    The reliability test of Q1 and Q2**

| Reliability | Q1 | Q2 |
|---|---|---|
| Cronbach's alpha | 0.808 | 0.849 |
| Results | $\geq$0.70, high reliability | $\geq$0.70, high reliability |

Validity is an integrated evaluative judgment of the degree to which empirical evidence and theoretical rationales support the adequacy and appropriateness of interpretations and actions based on test scores or other modes of assessment (Messick, 1990). Grading the significance of identified dimensions/factors/metrics by experts belongs to multi-sample correlative data analysis that requires Kendall's coefficient of concordance W test to evaluate its validity. Kendall $w^a$ was calculated by SPSS and results are displayed in Table 27.5. The data of both Q1 and Q2 reached the criterion of high validity, and the higher Chi square value of Q2 compared to Q1 tells the increased validity, indicating that two rounds of the Delphi questionnaire enhanced the consistency of the experts' opinion. That is the core of the Delphi approach.

**Table 27.5    The validity test of Q1 and Q2**

| Validity | N | Kendall $w^a$ | Chi square | f | Significance | Critical value |
|---|---|---|---|---|---|---|
| Q1 | 22 | 0.339 | 134.075 | 18 | 0.000 | |
| Q2 | 21 | 0.482 | 182.046 | 18 | 0.000 | |
| Results | Chi square of Q1(2) > Critical Value with freedom 21(20) under 99.5 per cent confidence level, so the experts has reached the consistency on the 19 factors. The validity is high. | | | | | |

## ANALYTIC HIERARCHY PROCESS (AHP) METHODS

The AHP is a theory of relative measurement of intangible criteria. With this approach to relative measurement, a scale of priorities is derived from pair-wise comparison measurements (Saaty, 2005). In the AHP, paired comparisons are made with judgments using numerical values taken from the absolute fundamental scale which was derived from the five-point Likert scale questionnaires in this research.

The AHP is useful for making multi-criteria decisions involving benefits, opportunities, costs and risks. Here it was used to capture the significance of each factor/metric/dimension. Regarding the AHP algorithm, there are quite a lot of books and articles explaining it in detail (Saaty, 1988, 1990, 2008) so no further description will be added here. In addition, a simple but helpful software called Yaahp can assist you when you carry out AHP calculation.

## THE ESTABLISHMENT OF CONSTRUCTION CONSULTING SERVICES PROJECT MANAGEMENT MATURITY MODELS (CSS PMMM)

With the significance of all the dimensions/factors/metrics, the quantitative model of CCSPMM was set up with four hierarchies that are, respectively, CSS PMM, 4-dimensions level, 19-factors level and 70 key metrics level. This is shown in Figure 27.3.

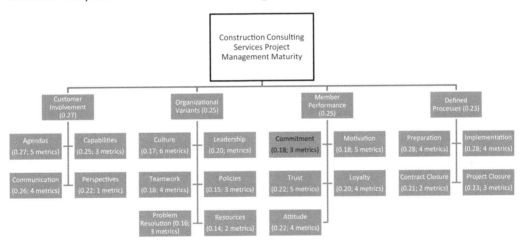

**Figure 27.3    The quantitative model of the CSS PMM**

In contrast to the traditional theories focus and practical experience, the research findings indicate that customer involvement was put in the first place in bright comparison with the lowest importance of defined process. And organisation and members also play a vital role in mature management of CSS projects.

For the customer involvement dimension, customers' judgment of the consulting team's capacity is no longer the primary problem; the mature handing of agendas and communication are the key points. Moreover, the proper perspectives of the customer do assist CCS projects.

For the organisational variants, leadership has the greatest influence on the performance, and this was pointed out in the opinions of the experts. Teamwork and the culture within the consulting team are the main recessive driving force for improvement. Next comes the issue of problem resolving. Relatively speaking, policies and resources do not require that much attention.

For members, their positive attitude and an atmosphere of trust are essential. Loyalty indicates the members' satisfaction is pivotal to organizational stability. Comparably, commitment and motivation are not crucial factors.

For the defined process, the equal importance of preparation and implementation has to be emphasised. This indicates that the time of just laying importance on the project implementation has passed. Comparatively, the project closure, in which lots of project summary and assessment are needed, transcends the significance of standard process in the contract closure phase.

After the analysis of dimensions and factors, a similar task was accomplished for the metrics. As 70 key metrics were too many to assess, just the metrics used for customer involvement were selected as an example of the analysis.

- For agendas, schedule is still the core issue for customers.
- Rapid response to emergencies demonstrates more impact than the consulting team's professional skills and relevant experience.
- The recording and preservation of official documents are crucial when communication between customers and the consulting team is going on because official documents, which can be evidence for claiming indemnity, have force of law in the construction industry. An open and honest information exchange atmosphere and timely communication also play a vital role. Another interesting finding is that timeliness shows more benefits than adequate sharing of information does.
- Customers prefer to make their own decisions by work value rather than simply by the project cost or schedule.

## Final Comments

The mature management of CCS projects is not only dependent on the tight control of processes but also strongly affected by non-process factors, including customer involvement, organisational variants and member performance, that have even more influence on CSS-PMM than processes. It is a tough journey to go through the transformation from e-Learning to CCS, interviews for CCS processes, Delphi Questionnaires for significance, a great deal of data analytical work both in quality and quantity, and the process of continuing to learn and digest new methods. The establishment of the CSS-PMM Model is the main outcome that can direct practitioners to evaluate and improve the performance and maturity of CCS projects continuously. The research process means more to the researchers involved than the outcomes, and hopefully these procedures and experiences will give you inspiration and guidance for your future research.

## Tips and Questions

### TIPS FOR STUDENTS

- Check the initial research goal regularly to make sure you are on the right path. When people throw themselves into literature and research materials, constantly emerging new ideas may cause them to digress from the right subject.
- The time you spend designing your research in draft form is always worth it, especially when it comes to the interviews and questionnaires. Good design is the foundation for getting credible data.

- Reliability and validity verification is the prerequisite for data usage, but please choose the statistical test method cautiously according to the data type. Single or multi sample, correlative or uncorrelated and nominal or interval scale really matters because they are appropriate for different statistical tests.
- SPSS, the most common statistics software, will aid you in avoiding tedious calculation but never choosing the correct statistical approach, and the same applies to Yaaph. You have to be concerned of the tiny differences among similar statistical approaches. For instance, there are many kinds of nonparametric tests, but their range of application is quite different and sometimes it is hard to distinguish. While you feel confused in choosing among statistical approaches, previous similar researches or a good statistical book will work for you.

## TIPS FOR SUPERVISORS

- Ensure your research theme and scope are clearly defined and express.
- Comparison with similar researches will lead you to a comprehensive understanding of your theme.
- For the empirical study, combining the qualitative and quantitative analysis is a good choice for more abundant information contained in qualitative data and more credible and solid data in quantitative research.
- Expressly understanding the statistical or mathematical methods you plan to use in your research will assist you in your data preparation and even the research design. What's more, it will offer you a reasonable expectation of your research findings.
- Have a good record of your research process, especially for the processes that take a long time. It not only helps you organise the materials in your publication but also does you a great favour when you encounter irrational mistakes/problems preventing your research from progressing.
- Be serious when choosing experts. Here are several criteria for selection:
  - experts have extensive work experience in your research context;
  - experts have a sound knowledge and understanding of what you are studying;
  - experts have current, recent or direct involvement in issues related to your research subject;.
- Eliminate the ambiguity and vagueness of your questionnaire – a pre-test will be quite beneficial.
- Control the length of your questionnaire in order to keep your respondents patient.
- Provide your respondents with convenience as much as possible.

## QUESTIONS

1. How to transfer the research findings from one context into another?
2. Literature reviews in the target context/domain are indispensable in order to search for supporting evidences for transformation probability. When not enough literatures are found, interviews and questionnaires can be helpful.
3. What are the differences in dealing with qualitative and quantitative data?
4. Coding, generalising, refining the core ideas or points in collected materials and seeking for some common cognition or regularity approved by these materials are the main methods applied in qualitative data. For quantitative data, many statistical or mathematical methods can be selected for the specific object. According to the experience of this research, a reliability and validity test is always the first step in guaranteeing the data credibility when you are handling quantitative data.

5. What is a Delphi questionnaire? Explain the key points in adopting it.
6. 'Delphi' is a structured communication technique with a panel of experts remaining unknown to one another. The experts are required to answer questions in two or more rounds. After each round, the experts will be provided with an anonymous summary of the experts' forecasts from the previous round as well as the reasons they provided for their judgments. Thus, experts are encouraged to revise their earlier answers in light of the replies of other members of their panel until they reach the consistency required.

# References

Al-Momani, A. H. (2000). Examining service quality within construction processes. *Technovation*, 11(20), 643–651.

Bryman, A. (1996). *Quantity and Quality in Social Research*. London: Routledge.

Chan, A. P. C., Yung, E. H. K., Lam, P. T. I., Tam, C. M. and Cheung, S. O. (2001). Application of Delphi method in selection of procurement systems for construction projects. *Construction Management and Economics*, 19(7), 699–718.

Chen, F. (2007). Individual rights and collective rights: Labor's predicament in China. *Communist and Post-Communist Studies*, 40(1), 59–79.

Cheung, S. O., Wong, P. S. P. and Wu, A. W. Y. (2011). Towards an organizational culture framework in construction. *International Journal of Project Management*, 29(1), 33–44.

Cooke-Davis, T. J. and Arzymanow, A. (2003). The maturity of project management in different industries: An investigation into variations between project management models. *International Journal of Project Management*, 21(6), 471–478.

Field, A. (2006). http://www.statisticshell.com/docs/reliability.pdf. Accessed: 15 October 2012.

Lee, C. K. and Friedman, E. (2009). The labor movement. *Journal of Democracy*, 20(3), 21–24.

Li, X. L. (2001). The procedures and evaluating methods of consulting management. Thesis for master degree, Sichuan University (in Chinese).

Messick, S. (1990). Validity of test interpretation and use. http://files.eric.ed.gov/fulltext/ED395031.pdf Accessed: 20 October 2012.

Pasian, B. (2011). Project management maturity: An analysis of existing and emergent factors. Doctoral thesis, University of Technology (Sydney).

Saaty, T. L. (1988). *What is the Analytic Hierarchy Process?* Heidelberg, Germany: Springer.

Saaty, T. L. (1990). How to make a decision: The analytic hierarchy process. *European Journal of Operational Research*, 48(1), 9–26.

Saaty, T. L. (2005). *Analytic Hierarchy Process. Encyclopedia of Biostatistics*. New York: Wiley and Sons, Ltd.

Saaty, T. L. (2008). Decision making with the analytic hierarchy process. *International Journal of Services Sciences*, 1(1), 83–98.

Shen, T. N. and Liu Q,. (2008). On Workers Protection Policy in China Service Economy Boost. Wireless Communications, Networking and Mobile Computing, 2008. WiCOM '08. 4th International Conference on IEEE, 2008.

Simon, A., Schoeman, P. and Sohal, A. S. (2010). Prioritised best practices in a ratified consulting services maturity model for ERP consulting. *Journal of Enterprise Information Management*, 23(1), 100–124.

Thomas Ng, S. and Chow, L-K. (2004). Framework for Evaluating the Performance of Engineering Consultants. *Journal of Professional Issues in Engineering Education and Practice*, 130(4), 280–288.

Wendler, R. (2012). The maturity of maturity model research: A systematic mapping study. *Information and Software Technology*, 54(12), 1317–1339.

Yang, Q., Pasian, B., Li, D. Y. and Li, Y. K. (2013). Review on Project Management Maturity in Construction Management Field. *Journal of Engineering Management*. 27(6), 65–70 (in Chinese).

Yin,T. (2011).The application of knowledge management in engineering consulting projects.Thesis for master degree, Ocean University of China (in Chinese).

Yu,A. T. W., Shen Q. P., Kelly, J. and Hunter, K. (2007). An empirical study of the variables affecting construction project briefing/architectural programming. *International Journal of Project Management*, 2(25), 198–212.

# PART V
# UNIQUE ENVIRONMENTS FOR PROJECT MANAGEMENT RESEARCH

Submissions received in response to the call for chapters were diverse and, as editor, I had a choice to make – support the diversity … or not. It wasn't a difficult choice to make. As I explained earlier, this book represents a collection of voices and it's my job as editor to give them a forum. This section is such for unique researchers who have worked in places and on projects that you will not typically find in other books on research methods. It is my hope that their uniqueness will both inform and inspire existing and emergent researchers.

- Staal-Org and Westerveld focus on three large infrastructure projects as part of NETLIPSE (the Network for the Management and Organisation of Large Infrastructure Projects in Europe). Theirs was a pioneering research effort and one included here to share the lessons of managing a multi-stakeholder project.
- Brookes, Hickey, Littau, Locatelli and Oliomogbe discuss key issues of conducting research in a mega-project environment – chief among these are the inductive and deductive considerations in a multi- and cross-case analysis. The chapter concludes with a detailed discussion of their MEGAPROJECT investigation.
- Earnest and Dickie examine the challenges of conducting empirical research of PM in the complex and unsettled environment of a war-torn country. They offer a much-deserved light on these challenges in their examination of Kosovo.
- Monteilh clearly demonstrates that advanced knowledge of organisational structures and culture will challenge the skills of any research student and supervisor. He focuses on oil and gas exploration in the Middle East to illustrate his points.

# 28

# A Practical Research Method: The NETLIPSE Case Study

Pau Lian Staal-Ong and Eddy Westerveld

*Research methodology is often regarded as a theme that should interest scientists only. While in my view choosing a proper methodology is extremely practical: when used correctly, it can greatly enhance the usefulness of both scientific studies and consultancy projects. This chapter was written to illustrate this viewpoint.*

In this chapter the NETLIPSE research is presented as a case study of a successful practical research approach. The research was carried out in 2006–2008, was sponsored by the European Commission (EC) and involved many organisations. The research consisted of a qualitative approach to finding best practices and lessons learnt in the management and organisation of Large Infrastructure Projects (LIPs) (transport) in Europe, the ultimate goal being to gather information that could help improve the PM and organisation of these projects in the future.

At the end of this chapter, the reader can:

- understand the practical research approach carried out in the NETLIPSE research case to identify best practices and lessons learnt;
- understand how using a qualitative triangulation approach helped provide scientific sound results;
- understand how stakeholder involvement in the research resulted in a broad acceptance of research results.

Keywords: practical, qualitative triangulation research, action research, best practices and lessons learnt, infrastructure project success

## Introduction to the Challenges of Large Infrastructure Projects (LIPs)

To meet rising and changing demands for interregional and international mobility, LIPs are being developed in Europe. In 2003, the EC reported that there was a need for enormous investments in infrastructure, especially in the countries that had recently joined or would soon join the EU. The EU needs to be able to deploy LIPs more effectively and in order to do so needed a tool that will help them to monitor and evaluate (both ex ante and ex post) these projects. In 2005 the EC reported that a €600 billion investment was required to complete and modernise the trans-European network. In the coming years the EC will be investing heavily in LIPs. So why are they so often delayed?

It appears that LIPs in Europe share similar characteristics. The projects are not only large scale and complex, but also have a major impact on their environment. The period of inception until realisation often covers decades; new technologies and legislation are developed and introduced in the project; the projects have immense budgets, often billions of euros; and many stakeholders are involved. It is no wonder then that the scope of a LIP changes through time. All these characteristics present the project's management with diverse challenges often resulting in time or cost overruns.

A large percentage of LIPs in Europe that have cost and time overruns seem to face or have faced similar problems. Due to their scale and complexity, these projects are often unique at the national level. There is often no other project within the country with which comparison can be made. In addition, the European LIPs do not have a forum where experience and knowledge about management and organisation can be shared; where their management, as well as key stakeholders, can learn and benefit from each other's experiences. In fact it seems that many projects spend time and effort in researching and developing tools and systems that have already been developed elsewhere.

The question is – why do project teams not know what other LIPs are doing and have done? Do they just not want to learn from others, due to time and money pressures? In order to improve the completion of the trans-European network of infrastructure projects the EU, as well as national policymakers, need to be able to deploy LIPs more effectively. Learning from the experiences and successes of others can help in reaching this goal.

## NETLIPSE: An Introduction

In 2006, a consortium consisting of eight organisations received EC financing from the Framework Programme 6 (FP6) to carry out a two-year research into success factors of LIPs. The NETLIPSE project focused on setting up an interactive and continuous network for LIPs in Europe for the dissemination of experience and knowledge on the successful management and organisational aspects of these projects. The core of the NETLIPSE project was the research of 15 LIPs that were reviewed to identify best practices to be disseminated to other projects. For key stakeholders such as national and European policymakers, the compilation of best practices lead to the development of an Infrastructure Project Assessment Tool (IPAT®) that can be used for more effective deployment and realisation of projects.

In short, the NETLIPSE project focused on four objectives:

1.  setting up a continuous and interactive knowledge network (that is still running to date, see www.netlipse.eu);
2.  gathering information on best practices and lessons learnt in the management and organisation of 15 LIPs in Europe;
3.  disseminating the knowledge gathered and promoting the research results;
4.  translating the best practices into an evaluation and monitoring tool (IPAT) that will allow for the quick and effective implementation of new policies.

# Characteristics of the NETLIPSE Research

Defining elements of the NETLIPSE research were:

- the research period was limited: the research had to be carried out within a 2-year period in order to fulfil the EC subsidy requirements;
- the research target group consisted of 15 LIPs that were geographically spread throughout Europe;
- there was no research method available to allow for the goals we had: a research approach needed to be developed in order to be able to gather and compare results;
- in order to obtain financing, the research approach and (interpretation) of results needed to be scientifically sound.

# Research Approach

In the NETLIPSE research approach, three elements had to be organised:

1. *How*: the research approach and methodology.
2. *What*: the topics researched.
3. *Who*: organisation of the research.

## 1. THE RESEARCH APPROACH AND METHODOLOGY

A consortium of eight organisations[1] from five countries was formed to carry out the NETLIPSE research. The organisations represented four public bodies, two research institutes and two private organisations. These organisations have a long history of large involvement in LIPs in their respective countries, either as sponsor, project delivery organisation or researcher and were responsible for designing and carrying out the research and fulfilling the NETLIPSE goals.

Members of the consortium took part in several roles in order to complete the research (Figure 28.1). The consortium consisted of:

- Executive Board: the 'internal' client for the research project responsible for approving phase results and deliverables;
- Technical Verification Board: responsible for maintaining the scientific level of the project;
- PM: responsible for carrying out all operational work;
- Knowledge Teams: responsible for carrying out the research.

An Advisory Board consisted of representatives from associated organisations was responsible for advising the Executive Board about the research approach and dissemination of results.

To gain knowledge on the management of LIPs, we chose to adopt the viewpoint of 'methodological pluralism' (Volberda, 1997). This means that the methodology is specifically tailored to answer this question and no universal methodology has been applied. The research can be classified as being on the border line between the field of public administration and

---

1    The NETLIPSE Consortium consisted of: Department for Transport (UK), Ministry of Infrastructure and the Environment (NL), National Laboratory for Civil Engineering (PT), Road and Bridge Research Institute (PL), Swiss Federal Institute of Technology (CH), Erasmus University (NL), KPC (CH), AT Osborne B.V. (NL).

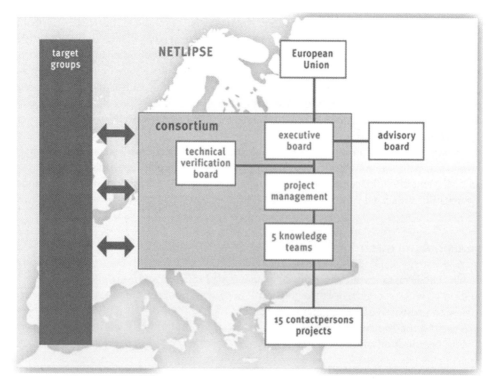

**Figure 28.1    Organisation of the NETLIPSE research (Hertogh, Baker, Staal-Ong and Westerveld, 2008)**

management science because the central objects of study are the 'project delivery organisations' and 'stakeholders' that are concerned with the implementation of LIPs. In addition to studying these entities we have described and analysed the implementation processes of LIPs. In this we study the management of LIPs, in which we defined management as:

> Management is 'every form of result oriented influencing'. (De Leeuw, 1993: p. 113)

Research in management science has some specific characteristics (Biemans and Van der Meer-Kooistra, 1994). These characteristics place specific demands on the chosen research strategy. These characteristics are:

- considering actual empirical objects (in our case the project delivery organisation and other stakeholders within the stakeholder network in a LIP);
- isolating the studied object from its context is impossible (also found in Van Aken, 1996);
- examination of the studied objects can only take place in its actual context.

This brings us to another important characteristic of our research. The research is done by researchers, consultants and managers within LIPs. This is a specific case of action research: the researcher is an important part of the studied subject. Action research is an iterative inquiry process that balances problem solving actions implemented in a collaborative context with data-driven collaborative analysis or research to understand underlying causes enabling future predictions about personal and organisational change (Reason and Bradbury, 2001). This means that action research is a process by which change and understanding can be pursued at the same time. It is usually described as cyclic, with action and critical reflection taking place in turn. The reflection is used to review the previous action and plan the next one. In our case this means that many of the concepts developed were discussed and tested with other practitioners and academics in the field of LIPs. Based on these discussions, concepts were changed, conclusions were altered and the research set-up sharpened. Action research challenges 'traditional social science', by moving beyond reflective knowledge created by outside experts (see Torbert, 2001). The traditional research can be typified as being focused on 'Reflection' instead of 'Action'.

The aim of this study was both practical and scientific. It has the goal to develop 'substantive theory' (Glaser, 1967). This theory will need to be helpful in solving practical dilemmas in the management of LIPs. The theory will contain heuristics, best practices and lessons learnt, to be used by stakeholders in the field of LIPs – based on the collection of empirical data.

In the NETLIPSE research, comparative case studies (Van der Zwaan, 1999) combined with some of the principles of grounded theory were used as the primary research strategy. In the research design of the NETLIPSE study an approach focusing on depth instead of breadth was chosen and a qualitative focus was predominantly applied (see Verschuren and Doorewaard, 2000). However this does not mean that quantitative techniques were not used to collect and analyse data.

The dominant term we used to judge the quality of this research is 'usefulness' (de Leeuw, 1993). To enhance the usefulness of findings, the following methods were used: triangulation, sensitising and analytic concepts, intersubjectivity, client-based research, measures of improving reliability (chain of evidence, case study protocol) and measures of improving validity (pattern matching and explanation building).

For this research a case study protocol was used to provide structure. This protocol contained the conceptual model and the research design. The conceptual model contains the theoretical framework used to collect and analyse the case study data. In order to answer our primary research question, 15 LIPs were studied.

## THE TOPICS RESEARCHED

The first step the Consortium carried out in designing the research approach was defining a conceptual modal (Figure 28.2). The NETLIPSE conceptual modal links:

- the organisational and managerial factors (project success factors) within the project delivery organisations;
- the project results (critical success criteria); and
- the context of the project.

Many PM approaches define the main criteria of success for projects to be the golden triangle of time, finances and required quality. We felt the issue of project success in LIPs to be broader than this. Often other criteria are identified and these criteria can vary during the course of a project. In short, project success could be defined as the satisfaction of all stakeholders. Therefore we introduced the 'context' of a project to broaden up the perspective of success. The context, especially changes in context such as changes in government or new safety regulations, can strongly influence both the results and organisation of a project.

There are no internationally accepted and standardised set of key performance indicators that allow for the quantitative and objective measurement of projects' success. The characteristics of

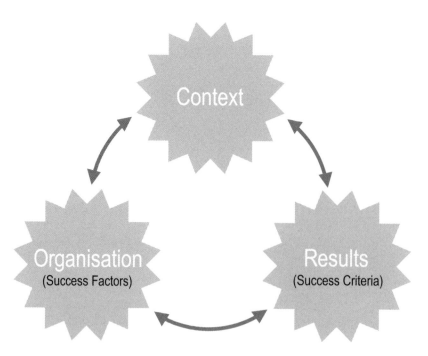

**Figure 28.2    NETLIPSE conceptual model (Hertogh, Baker, Staal-Ong and Westerveld, 2008)**

LIPs is their complexity and uncertainty meaning that the alignment of project costs at completion with initial cost estimates or meeting anticipated project deadlines are not reliable indicators of an outstanding PM performance. Project success may be a coincidence rather than the result of the application of best practices.

The conceptual model designed was the basis of our research approach. Next step was designing the Knowledge Protocol – the document (including the questionnaire) governing what the research would focus on and how the research was to be carried out to ensure a uniform research approach of all projects. In NETLIPSE we incorporated a dual focus in the knowledge protocol. Not only did we focus on the management capabilities of the project delivery organisation but we also researched the historical development of the project in its context.

On the basis of our experience with the realisation of complex projects and available PM approaches (for example, PRINCE 2) and quality management models (Project Excellence Model®, European Foundation for Quality Management (EFQM), ISO 9001:2003, IPMA Project Excellence Model), eight major themes were decided on as being the decisive factors in the realisation of LIPs (Westerveld, 2003). These themes were:

1.  objectives and scope;
2.  stakeholders;
3.  financial management;
4.  organisation and management processes;
5.  risks (threats and opportunities);
6.  contracting;
7.  legal consents;
8.  knowledge management and technology.

Each theme was divided into subthemes (31 in total) which were approached in a qualitative and quantitative manner.

> *Qualitative*: The qualitative part of the research consisted of ten to twenty predefined main questions per theme, and three more general questions consisting of open questions allowing for room for discussing interesting results in terms of problems (challenges), solutions and success factors.
>
> *Quantitative*: The quantitative part of the research consisted of four to eight specific multiple-choice questions per subtheme, allowing for the comparison of results.

The next step was defining the research group. Referring back to the characteristics of the NETLIPSE project, the research group comprised of 15 LIPs that responded in time to our invitation to join the NETLIPSE research project. The research group needed to be a well-balanced group representing the transport modalities part of the EC Trans European Network programme: road, rail and waterways. In total there were seven road, seven rail and one waterway projects researched in seven different European countries.

The research groups of the project are summarised in Table 28.1.

As you can tell from the table, the research group is a varied group. Not only were projects at different states of realisation, but also national, political, legal and cultural peculiarities had a substantial impact on how a project was being planned, approved, financed, managed and realised. Some projects were completed years before the research was carried out (Øresund), others were

**Table 28.1    The NETLIPSE research group (Hertogh et al., 2008)**

| Project Name | Country | Modality | Length | Budget (m.) (year/price level) | Planning and Construction Period |
|---|---|---|---|---|---|
| Betuweroute | Netherlands | Rail | 160 km | € 3.861 ('07/'95) | 1989–2007 |
| Bratislava Ring Road | Slovak Republic | Road | 12 km | € 242 ('07/'07) | 1972–2007 |
| Gotthard Base Tunnel | Switzerland | Rail | 57 km | € 5.900 ('06/'98) | 1992–2017 |
| HSL–Zuid | Netherlands | Rail | 125 km | € 5.282 ('08/'95) | 1987–2008 |
| Lezíria Bridge | Portugal | Road | 12 km | € 243 ('07/'05) | 2001–2007 |
| Lisbo–Porto | Portugal | Rail | 305 km | € 4.700 ('05/'05) | 1999–2015 |
| Lötschberg Base Tunnel | Switzerland | Rail | 35 km | € 2.676 ('06/'06) | 1992–2007 |
| Maaswerken | Netherlands | Water | 222 km | € 1.211 ('07/'07) | 1997–2022 |
| Motorway A2 | Poland | Road | 194 km | € 638 ('04/'00) | 1994–2004 |
| Motorway A4 | Poland | Road | 61 km | € 125 ('10/'05) | 1994–2001 |
| Motorway E18 | Finland | Road | 51 km | € 638 ('05/'04) | 1990–2008 |
| Nürnberg–Ingolstadt | Germany | Rail | 89 km | € 3.551 ('07/'07) | 1991–2006 |
| Øresund | Denmark | Road | 16 km | € 1.990 ('00/'90) | 1990–2000 |
| Unterinntalbahn | Switzerland | Rail | 40 km | € 1.933 ('05/'05) | 1995–2012 |
| West Coast Main Line | United Kingdom | Rail | 650 km | € 10.342 ('08/'06) | 1996–2008 |

in the planning phase (Lisboa–Porto High Speed Line). In some countries there is a presidential or parliamentary democratic system in place, whereas in other countries many important financial decisions are subject to a national plebiscite (Switzerland).

Beforehand, we expected that these substantial differences would make it difficult to compare the 15 projects and the knowledge gained from the site visits. This was not the case. The research results proved that many lessons learned and best practices are independent of the specific national framework conditions, context and cultural habits. As a result, the best practices and lessons learned that were gathered during the research were deemed to be of general relevance in defining project success (Staal-Ong and Westerveld, 2008; Staal-Ong 2009).

## RESULTS

The most important conclusion of the research is that effective management of LIPs needs a hybrid approach combining control and interaction (Figure 28.3).

In LIPs a fine balance should be found between the need for control and constructive interaction between stakeholders. Strong control helps to prevent purpose and scope creep. Constructive interaction can help projects to accept new, and often external, changes or delivery methodologies. These changes might potentially improve the project outputs, reduce costs or speed up the project delivery. Depending on the strategy (see Table 28.2) a different perspective on control and interaction approaches can be recognised.

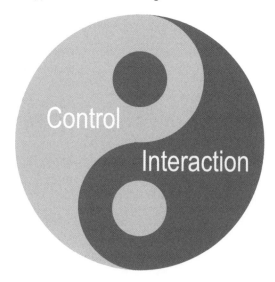

**Figure 28.3    Combining control and interaction (Hertogh and Westerveld, 2009)**

## ORGANISATION OF THE RESEARCH

The NETLIPSE consortium formed four regional Knowledge Teams ('research teams') that were responsible for gathering and analysing information: Knowledge Team North and West Europe, Knowledge Team Alps, Knowledge Team Central and East Europe and Knowledge Team South Europe. The Knowledge Teams consisted of practical and scientific professionals in the field of infrastructure PM and were coordinated by a General Knowledge Team, responsible for identifying

**Table 28.2     Views on control and interaction (Hertogh and Westerveld, 2009)**

| Strategy | Control | Interaction |
|---|---|---|
| 1. Problem | Unambiguous and fixed. | Ambiguous perceptions. |
| 2. Goal | Fixed, determines direction and course. | Goal is related to actors and is likely to change. Fixed goals block creativity. |
| 3. Management focus | Optimising content (schedule, costs, quality). | Satisfying needs. |
| 4. Structure | Unravelling makes sub-solutions possible. | Broadening and linking of needs leads to new opportunities. |
| 5. Information | Objective, robust and analysable. | Subjective, actor related and negotiable. |
| 6. Schedule | Linear. Start with agreements on the content. | Iterative. Start with process agreements. |
| 7. Relationship | Hierarchy, formal. | Network, informal. |
| 8. Complexity | Threat. | Opportunity. |

and finding projects to be researched, developing the project knowledge archive, developing the method for collecting and analysing the information gathered and carrying out the analysis.

The research carried out by the Knowledge Teams consisted of:

1. Desk study: information gathering and analysing relevant documents and writing them up in a Background Document consisting of project facts and figures, a stakeholder analysis and the project history (completed before the Site Visit).
2. Site Visits: interviews with key players of the projects on the basis of the Knowledge Protocol (this includes senior management of client and sponsor organisations and representatives from user and other stakeholder organisations).
3. Writing up the Case Study Reports.

The Knowledge Teams consisted of at least:

- one person with local knowledge (important for the context aspect and also to be able to read documents in local languages);
- one project person from the NETLIPSE network (important for the technical and PM knowledge);
- a lead assessor.

In total, 29 people were involved in the research teams and 142 project stakeholders were interviewed.

The Case Study Reports were sent to the Project Managers for verification an on the basis of all the Case Study Reports, the General Knowledge Team carried out the Comparative Case Analysis and wrote up the results in a book *Managing Large Infrastructure Project: Research on Best Practices and Lessons Learnt in Large Infrastructure Projects in Europe* (Hertogh et al., 2008).

During the research, the project progress was monitored and results discussed in four network meetings, published in bi-annual newsletters and on the website www.netlipse.eu. At the final network meeting in 2008, a peer group review of research approach and results took place. A panel of eight scientific and practical specialists in the field of infrastructure projects and PM as well as the EU TEN Coordinator verified the quality of the research methodology and research results presented.

In summary, the NETLIPSE research approach resulted in several important success factors:

- the conceptual model;
- the organisation of the research;
- the Knowledge Protocol;
- the Case Study Reports (research results including desk research results as described in the Background Documents);
- the Benchmark Report.

## Conclusion

The NETLIPSE research was organised and carried out by a combination of LIP stakeholders, comprising of client, project delivery and research organisations. This combination led to a practical and scientifically verified research project that delivered results that are still being discussed and developed on today. The collaboration was so successful that the NETLIPSE network, no longer subsidised by the EC, is now a knowledge network sponsored by various European government organisations. The network continues to strive on PM knowledge improvement and dissemination and implementing the IPAT.

## Tips and Exercises

### TIPS FOR STUDENTS

- Preparing a background document on the basis of available project documentation before carrying out the interviews as a desk study exercise, helped prepare the interview teams greatly, by understanding the context and development of the project to be researched.
- A visit to the Internet – 'googling' the project – before the research started, also helped find information on external views on the project as well as issues that might not have been provided by the project team members.
- In order to be able to compare the project's scope and results it is necessary to take into account budgets allocated in price levels.

### TIPS FOR SUPERVISORS

- One of the most important success factors in carrying out this international research is having all research teams include a team member with local knowledge to help understand and translate the context and cultural aspects of a specific project. (And to be able to read and translate relevant project documents!)
- In addition, including project managers in the knowledge teams helped create an informal atmosphere during the interviews as these had more the character of a peer review – with ensuing in-depth discussions – than an audit.

- The aspect of the research that most time was spent on was writing up the Case Study Reports and getting them accepted by the project organisations.

## EXERCISES

1. Considering the research approach taken in this practical research project: how could the outcomes of the research translate to new practical research approaches?
2. The hybrid control and interaction approach to successfully managing a LIP does not seem to be unique to only these types of complex projects. Explain how this approach could be translated to other PM fields.
3. Explain how action research – as a process by which change and understanding can be pursued at the same time – can be implemented by researchers more effectively in research theory.

## References

Aken, J. E., van, (1994). De bedrijfskunde als ontwerpwetenschap; de regulatieve en reflectieve cyclus. *Bedrijfskunde*, 66(1), 16–26.

Biemans, W. G., and van der Meer-Kooistra, J. (1994). Case research voor bedrijfskundig onderzoek 1. *Bedrijfskunde*, 66(1), 51–56

Glaser B. G. and Strauss, A. L. (1967). *The Discovery of Grounded Theory.* Chicago, IL: Aldine.

Hertogh, M., Baker, S., Staal-Ong, P.L. and Westerveld, E. (2008). *Managing Large Infrastructure Projects: Research on Best Practices and Lessons Learnt in Large Infrastructure Projects in Europe.* Baarn: AT Osborne B.V.

Hertogh, M. and Westerveld, E. (2009). *Playing with Complexity: Management and Organisation of Large Infrastructure Projects.* Baarn: AT Osborne, pp. 28–54.

Leeuw, A. J. C de, (1993). *Bedrijfskundige Methodologie, Management van Onderzoek.* Assen: Van Gorcum.

Reason, P. and Bradbury, H. (2001). *Handbook of Action Research.* London: Sage Publications.

Staal-Ong, P. L. (2009). Best Practices in Stakeholder Management in European Large Infrastructure Projects. Helsinki IPMA World Congress Paper (Seminar 15: Successful Megaprojects?).

Staal-Ong, P. L. and Westerveld, E. (2008). NETLIPSE: Best Practices and Lessons Learnt on the Management and Organisation of Large Infrastructure Projects in Europe. Rome: IPMA World Congress Paper (Stream S3: Project Management for Large Infrastructures and Industrial Plants).

Torbert, W. (1991). *The Power of Balance: Transforming Self, Society, and Scientific Inquiry.* London: Sage Publications.

Verschuren, P. J. M. and Doorewaard, H. (2000). *Het Ontwerpen van een Onderzoek,* 3rd edition. Utrecht: Lemma B.V., Chapter 2.

Volberda, H. W. (1997). Op zoek naar een gedisciplineerde methodologie: Een synthetische benadering in management en organisatie, M&O. *Tijdschrift voor Management en Organisatie*, 51, 65–91.

Westerveld, E. (2003). The Project Excellence Model®: Linking success criteria and critical success factors. *International Journal of Project Management*, 21(6), 411–418.

Zwaan, A.H. van der, (1999). Van geval tot geval; ontvouwen of beproeven? Over onderbenutting van gevalstudies, in: M. J. van Riemsdijk, *Dilemmas in de Bedrijfskundige Wetenschap.* Assen: Van Gorcum.

# 29

# Using Multi-Case Approaches in Project Management Research: The Megaproject Experience

Naomi Brookes, Robert Hickey, Paul Littau, Giorgio Locatelli and Gloria Oliomogbe

*We wrote this chapter because we feel that multi-case research has an invaluable role to play in developing robust and useful new PM theory especially in the context of large complex projects such as megaprojects.*

This chapter discusses the usefulness of a multi-case approach in PM research. It highlights the benefits multi-case research can bring in terms of extendibility and more robust theory. It presents popular approaches to multi-case research and focuses on the role of inductive and deductive case analysis within these processes. It raises some of the pragmatic issues, especially the resource needs, which researchers can encounter when adopting this type of approach. It concludes by presenting a case of its own, the MEGAPROJECT research investigation. This exemplifies the chapter's learning and allows the reader to compare the issues found in this case with his or her own experience.

At the end of this chapter, the reader can:

- appreciate the role that multi-case research can play in overcoming some of the drawbacks of single-case research;
- describe the differences between inductive and deductive pattern-spotting in multi-case research;
- use the experience of a large multi-case multidisciplinary investigation to help you to design your own multi-case protocol.

Keywords: multi-case research, inductive and deductive pattern-spotting, megaprojects

## Introduction

PM research questions are predominately open with, arguably, the questions of paramount importance being... How and why do projects behave as they do? This is closely followed in managerial perspectives with the question, 'How do we make projects perform better?' The propensity to ask open research questions is extant in much of the project research literature.

Case methods have a long association with research investigations seeking to answer this type of open research question (Yin, 2003). This is reflected in the widespread adoption of case approaches in PM research (for example, Nitithamyong and Skibniewski, 2011; Koners and Goffin, 2007). However case approaches are still perceived as problematic by some because of their perceived lack of rigour and extendability of findings. One approach to overcoming these criticisms is the use of multi-case research. This chapter aims to review multi-case methods in the context of PM research and to demonstrate their ability to overcome these and therefore offer a great potential for PM research.

This chapter begins by reviewing case approaches, commencing with single-case research and the associated problems. It then examines multi-case research and how it may overcome some of these problems. It delineates the main approaches to cross-case analysis, (one of the key steps in successful multi-case research,) and reviews the comparative advantages of inductive and deductive approaches to pursuing this. The chapter then proceeds to describe a practical application of multi-case research to the MEGAPROJECT cost action investigation into megaproject design and delivery. This application acts as a lens through which to explore the potential benefits that a multi-case approach may bring to PM research and ways in which operational difficulties may be overcome.

## What is Case Research?

As with many linguistic terms, definitions of what a 'case study' specifically is abound. A useful definition, developed and used by Kathleen Eisenhardt (1989) is that: 'The case study is a research strategy which focuses on understanding the dynamics present within single settings.'

This interpretation is mirrored by Flyvbjerg (2011): '[The case is] An intensive analysis of an individual unit (as a person or community) stressing developmental factors in relation to environment.'

These definitions both identify a case study as the investigation of a particular phenomenon in reality, although their reasons for such an investigation differ. In the former definition, such an investigation is undertaken in order to illuminate and help explain a particular point or theory being made. As such, the case study is designed to reinforce an existing argument. In the second instance, a priori assumptions about what information should emerge from the case study are absent. This illustrates an interesting point within case study research; that hypothesis can be both tested (when a hypothesis is developed prior to the case study research and evidence is sought through such research) as well as developed (when patterns emerge through looking at the information within the case studies).

Yin (2003) proposes that a case study is an empirical inquiry that investigates a contemporary phenomenon within its real-life context, especially when the boundaries between phenomenon and context are not clearly evident. He states that the case study inquiry copes with the technically distinctive situation in which there will be many more variables of interest than data points.

One of the benefits of case study research is that it allows researchers to investigate questions and causal relationships in situations where controlled experiments cannot be conducted. Also, the context and totality of complex phenomena may not lend themselves to dissection into their component parts, because various aspects are deeply interconnected. As such, the entire situation must be viewed holistically if it is to be understood.

## Perceived Weaknesses of Case-Based Research Approaches

Case study research has its critics. These criticisms focus on:

- a lack of methodological rigour is often seen when case study approaches are used. At one time, this resulted from a lack of methodological guidance but, in the last 30 years, much research has been done to set protocols and standards of quality for conducting these types of exercises;
- the idea that case study theories and results cannot be generalised as there are too many variables at play;
- case study investigations where massive amounts of low-quality information are produced;
- the lack of standards or definitions for professional competence in conducting case studies;
- researcher selection bias may incorrectly estimate the magnitude of causes on effects (but this is not, however, unique to case study research and exists across all types of investigative inquiry); and
- the inability to know the statistical significance of particular variables on particular outcomes due to low sample sizes.

In these complex situations, it is difficult to identify which factors impact with which results. In these cases, the theories are more summaries of a particular case than a theory with predictive qualities for other contexts.

## Multi-Case Research

One of the ways in which the problems of single-case research approaches can be ameliorated whilst still retaining the benefits of the approach is through the use of multiple cases. Multiple-case approaches add confidence to the findings. As Miles and Huberman (1994) state:

> By looking at a range of similar and contrasting cases, we can understand a single-case finding, grounding it by specifying how and where and, if possible why it carries on as it does. We can strengthen the precision, the validity and the stability of the findings. We are following a replication strategy. If a finding holds in one setting and, given its profile, also holds in a comparable setting but not in a contrasting case, the finding is more robust.

> With multiple-case studies, does the issue of generalizability change? Essentially, no. We are generalising from one case to the next on the basis of a match to the underlying theory, not to a larger population. Nevertheless, the multiple-case sampling gives us confidence that our emerging theory is generic, because we have seen it work out, and not work out, in predictable ways.

Multiple-case designs have distinct advantages and disadvantages in comparison to single-case designs. The evidence from multiple cases is often considered more compelling, and the overall study is therefore regarded as being more robust. A definition which begins to bridge the gap between single and multiple-case studies is that of one used by Flyvbjerg from Abercrombie, Hill and Turner (1984), whereby:

> The detailed examination of a single example of a class of phenomena, a case study cannot provide reliable information about the broader class, but it may be useful in the preliminary stages of an investigation since it provides hypotheses, which may be tested systematically with a larger number of cases.

Thus, while individual cases can illustrate instances of a particular phenomenon and help uncover suspected causal connections, we cannot derive theory from them. In order to do this, we must mobilise further case studies in the attempt to asymptotically approach *theoretical saturation*. This is the point at which the addition of cases to the portfolio under investigation is deemed unlikely to contribute further to the confirmation or disconfirmation of a particular hypothesis. Frankly, this is something of a judgment call, or perhaps better called an instinct felt by the case study analyst when they feel that both confirming and disconfirming evidence has been fully explored. Intriguingly, one expert in multi-case study analysis has proposed that theoretical saturation is usually reached when around seven to nine case studies are used (Eisenhardt, 1989).

Additionally, it should be noted here that even when theoretical saturation is suspected, statistical data about the likeliness of a particular cause leading to a particular effect cannot be necessarily be extrapolated. As a result of this caution should be exercised when trying to generalise the results of single or multiple-case analysis too far. Multiple-case confirmation of a particular theory will allow for some generalisation, particularly when the theory accounts for both confirming and disconfirming evidence. Naturally, however, this means that the findings of the analysis of each case study should be incorporated into the theory. This will likely have the effect of making the theory applicable to only a well-defined set of contextual conditions.

The use of multi-case approaches goes some way to resolving the issues of 'quality' referred to in the previous sub-section. Using multi-case can improve internal and external validity. In terms of internal validity, for explanatory or causal studies seeking to identify causal relationships and not spurious relationships, multiple cases in an investigation allow cause and effect relationships to be investigated within a case portfolio. The degree to which a 'cause' or event actually happened, as with all empirical investigations, is inferred rather than undoubtedly known. Other causes must be considered as well as the degree to which an event occurred, before moving forward with analysis.

More cases mean more exemplars of events from which to infer causal linkages. In terms of external validity, it is still important to note that case study research is not generalisable to a population or universe. Case study results are, however, useful when attempting to verify a theory in a particular context or set of contexts, but not about all other cases in the same field. For example, in the case of a complex project, a case may allude to the theory that those companies which do not invest in the local community to a certain predefined degree have greater local resistance and incidence of failures against predefined benchmarks. If theory is supported in a particular instance, the theory can be used to identify other cases with similar dynamics and see if it still holds true. A lack of conflicting evidence further strengthens the evidence base supporting the theory but does not, it must be said, prove it.

It is worth noting that multiple-case study analyses require extensive resources to implement. Resultantly, it is important that they are well designed in order to ensure they are completed using available means. This requires that the data to be captured within each case study, the selection of cases and the quality of the finished case portfolio, are all well thought out and have protocols which are tightly followed. Every part of the case study portfolio should have a specific purpose.

Given the resource-intensive nature of multi-case research, the method may employ the use of 'secondary data'. In an investigation using secondary data:

> the individual or group that analyses the data is not involved in the planning of the experiment or the collection of the data. Such analysis can be done based upon information that is available in the statistical information in the published articles, the data available in the text, tables, graphs, and appendices of the published articles, or upon the original data (Church 2002).

Cowton (1998) states that there are several advantages (such as cost and availability) – although some disadvantages – in the use of secondary data but:

> as a general rule it seems to be the case that researchers are not as aware as they might be of the potential of secondary data for providing valuable insights into a whole range of questions in a costeffective manner [...] Two particularly valuable features of secondary data seem worthy of reiteration: first, the possibility of 'eavesdropping', providing unobtrusive access to sensitive situations or to the past, [...] second, the way in which secondary data not only facilitate the pursuit of the empirical research agenda but also expand it as researchers perceive in datasets interesting research issues or novel avenues of enquiry.

There is a provenance of PM research using secondary data (Locatelli and Mancini, 2012).

## Cross-Case Analysis in Multi-Case Research

### DEFINITIONS OF CROSS-CASE ANALYSIS

Barratt, Thomas and Choi (2011) define 'cross-case analysis' as the act of comparing and contrasting the patterns emerging from a range of cases. It is one for the key tool in the process of theory building from case studies (Eisenhardt, 1989). Cross-case analysis is used to extend the knowledge above the single case prompting new questions, seeking new dimensions, measuring alternatives, creating models, and constructing ideal types and utopias (Stretton, 1969). Cross-case analysis is fundamental to understand 'how' relationships may exist among discrete cases, accumulate knowledge on the original case, refine or develop concepts (Ragin, 1997) and build or test theory further (Eckstein, 2002).

### INDUCTIVE VERSUS DEDUCTIVE APPROACHES

Before conducting the analysing process it is to be decided whether an inductive or a deductive approach (or both) will be used. These approaches influence particularly the pattern-spotting philosophy. The criteria for selecting between these approaches could be the nature of the research problem, the research design and the research aim.

The inductive approach intends to 'develop new theory from the observation of empirical reality' (Gill and Johnson, 2002). Thus, the researcher commences analysis by exploring. The identified relationships are examined in the context of each case. For high qualitative results of an inductive approach, it is essential to try to use different lenses in order to shape new constructs. This can be achieved when these new constructs are tested and revised against the evidence of each of the cases over and over again. Meanwhile, the deductive approach 'entails the development of a conceptual and theoretical structure that is then tested by observation' (Gill and Johnson,

2002). Thus, the researcher starts with some propositions derived from existing literature or from the analysis of the research problem. This approach basically intends to test general explanations by checking each of the cases for evidence. Furthermore, it aims to give more detailed and fine-grained explanations than the available knowledge is able to do.

The difference between the inductive and deductive approach will be explained here in the context of the MEGAPROJECT investigation (which is described in more detail in the next section). The aim of this research project was to understand the cross-sectoral performance of European megaprojects. A multi-case study was conducted to investigate this. As megaprojects could be considered in the same milieu of 'normal' projects, existing PM theory could be used as the starting point in a deductive approach to cross-case analysis. Thus, when pattern-spotting across cases, firstly, available theories would be addressed and propositions derived from these. These theoretical propositions would then be examined against the experience of each megaproject case. Subsequently, explanations for 'normal' projects would be used to identify the causes and effects for the performance of megaprojects. The logic of this approach is presented in Figure 29.3.

An inductive approach would start without consideration of PM theory and would focus on the megaproject cases themselves. When the analysis of cases revealed patterns, new theoretical explanations would be postulated and then compared with already existing PM theory in order to enrich the new emerging theory further. This logic is presented below (Figures 29.1, 29.2 and 29.3).

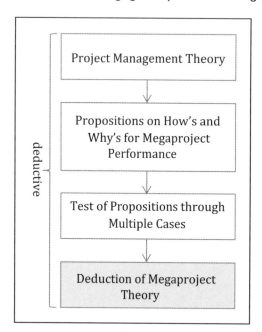
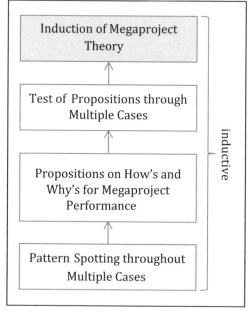

**Figure 29.1    Examples for deductive and inductive approaches in cross-case learning**

Current literature highlights the benefits of using a more inductive approach to theory generation (Locke, 2007) especially in terms of their sensitivity to institutional issues though this is balanced by pleas for a more 'pluralist' approach (Piekkari, Welch and Paavilainen, 2009). However it may be erroneous to focus on the dichotomy between an 'inductive' and 'deductive' approach. As Parke (1993) states:

> In reality, of course, there is no competition, but rather an essential continuity and inseparability between inductive and deductive approaches to theory development.

Indeed the reality (and desirability) of the case research activity is recognised as a 'cycling' of inductive–deductive approaches in a wide variety of diverse contexts.

## APPROACHES TO CROSS-CASE ANALYSIS

Two of the most widely used approaches to cross-case analysis are provided by Yin (2003) and Eisenhardt (1989). It should be noted that cross-case analysis only forms part of the whole multi-case approach recommended of each of the authors.

Yin's process to case study analysis comprises three phases: firstly, the selection of an adequate analysis strategy; secondly, the selection of an analysing technique and; finally, considerations on how to ensure high qualitative research results (Figure 29.2). This approach directs the user first to choose between the general strategic directions of the intended use of the expected results. This general strategy will influence the way of dealing with the cases and the choice of techniques for the analysis.

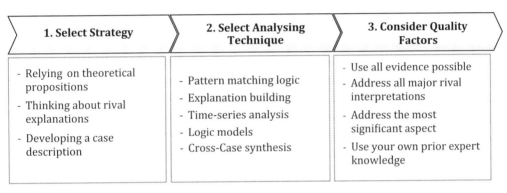

| 1. Select Strategy | 2. Select Analysing Technique | 3. Consider Quality Factors |
|---|---|---|
| - Relying on theoretical propositions<br>- Thinking about rival explanations<br>- Developing a case description | - Pattern matching logic<br>- Explanation building<br>- Time-series analysis<br>- Logic models<br>- Cross-Case synthesis | - Use all evidence possible<br>- Address all major rival interpretations<br>- Address the most significant aspect<br>- Use your own prior expert knowledge |

**Figure 29.2    Adapted from Yin's (2003) approach to analyse multiple cases**

Choosing the pattern matching logic – one of the techniques for cross-case analysis – enables the researcher to test whether predicted patterns match with the data from the cases. The explanation-building technique can be used when a phenomenon is trying to be explained through multiple cases. This process starts with an initial theoretical statement or proposition which is to be confirmed and if necessary revised by the first case, followed by all the others. Time-series analysis is used in order to understand the phenomenon studied in a temporal context. This context might be a simple or a complex one, describing clear or ambiguous developments. With 'logic models' – which are akin to pattern matching logic – events are described as cause–effect–cause–effect–patterns. Logic models are also used to test the observed results against theoretically predicted ones. The last technique is the cross-case synthesis and this is of particular interest in multi-case studies as it includes a 'side-by-side' comparison of the cases' content.

The last steps of Yin's approach to analyse multiple cases is 'a quality gate' which reminds the researcher to consider several aspects. First, the strength of evidence is absolutely crucial to the quality of results. Therefore, all possible sources of evidence should be used. Second, good results hold up with rival interpretations. These should be mentioned and explained or refuted if necessary. Third, high-quality case studies focus on the most significant aspect of the phenomenon analysed. This is not easy to keep in mind as various other aspects might emerge during the analysing process. And, last but not least, the researcher's knowledge and experience might enrich the results and should therefore be allowed to contribute.

The other popular approach to cross-case analysis provided by Eisenhardt (1989) describes five steps which include first, analysing within-case data; second, searching for cross-case patterns; third, shaping hypotheses; fourth, enfolding literature; and fifth, reaching closure (Figure 29.3).

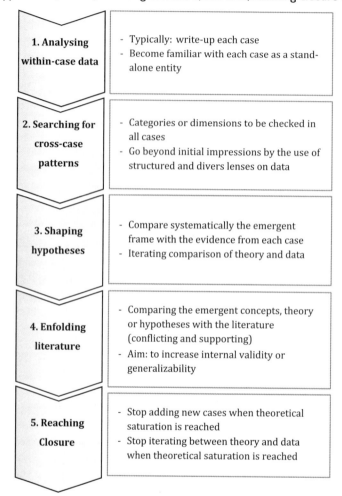

**1. Analysing within-case data**
- Typically: write-up each case
- Become familiar with each case as a stand-alone entity

**2. Searching for cross-case patterns**
- Categories or dimensions to be checked in all cases
- Go beyond initial impressions by the use of structured and divers lenses on data

**3. Shaping hypotheses**
- Compare systematically the emergent frame with the evidence from each case
- Iterating comparison of theory and data

**4. Enfolding literature**
- Comparing the emergent concepts, theory or hypotheses with the literature (conflicting and supporting)
- Aim: to increase internal validity or generalizability

**5. Reaching Closure**
- Stop adding new cases when theoretical saturation is reached
- Stop iterating between theory and data when theoretical saturation is reached

**Figure 29.3    Adapted from Eisenhardt's (1989) approach to learn across multiple cases**

Eisenhardt (1989) emphasises in the first step the need to write-up each case in order to understand each of the cases before relating them to each other. Then, the search for cross-case patterns can be initiated by selecting interesting categories or dimensions which play a role in the problem that is addressed. They could first be checked within similar groups among the whole sample of cases and then across the total sample, in order to go beyond initial impressions. Similarities and difference between cases could lead to further insights as well as the arranging of data by sources.

The third step, shaping hypothesis, is a crucial point and basically consists first, of sharpening the constructs by an iterative comparison of emerging frames and the data and, second, of verifying these constructs with the proper evidence of the analysed cases.

'Enfolding literature', as the fourth step, relates results or hypotheses to the literature. It is important to relate them to both supporting and conflicting literature. Thus, the research enriches existing knowledge and increases its own validity.

The last step, reaching closure, comprises realising that no more cases should be added and the analysis of cases can cease, as no further insights are likely to be arrived at.

In terms of learning across cases, Yin's and Eisenhardt's approaches to case study analysis provide a systematic and easy-to-follow instruction for researcher. However, their approaches reinforce the understanding that case study research in general and the analysis process specifically is a skill that needs to be trained and developed by application.

## Using a Multi-Case Approach in Project Management (PM) Research: The MEGAPROJECT investigation

The MEGAPROJECT investigation was a multidisciplinary, multi-country, multicultural and multi-sectoral European research project investigating the design and delivery of megaprojects. The investigation had two primary research questions:

- Why do megaprojects perform in the way that they do?
- What can we do to make them perform better?

Underlying these research questions was the premise that megaprojects have common experiences regardless of the sector in which they operate.

The researchers undertaking the MEGAPROJECT investigation comprised a large multidisciplinary and multicultural group with very disparate levels of research experience. The researchers from 22 European countries include professors, doctoral researchers, consultants and practitioners from disciplines as diverse as Civil Engineering, Construction, Architecture, Project and Programme management, Town Planning, Economics, Transport Studies and Management, Contract Management and Law, and Production and Operations Management. This diversity in the researchers investigating MEGAPROJECT was compounded by their dispersal across Europe during the course of the project.

## The Multi-Case Research Approach Utilised in the MEGAPROJECT Investigation

The design of the MEGAPROJECT investigation approach was highly reliant on the concepts and processes outlined in Yin (2003). The unit of analysis of the investigation was taken to be a megaproject. This was interpreted as a large infrastructural project that had a total budget of a minimum of the region of one billion dollars or 0.75 billion Euros. The boundaries of the megaproject were delineated through a systemic consideration which also was employed in creating the protocol template.

The decision to pursue a multi-case approach (rather than using a single case) was almost one of necessity given the premise of the MEGAPROJECT investigation, namely that common experiences exist in megaprojects regardless of the sector in which the megaproject operates. The investigation thus employed a sampling logic consistent with this proposition: the sample of cases in the MEGAPROJECT portfolio aimed to include as many sectors as possible. Megaprojects were therefore included in the portfolio from sectors including power generation (nuclear, conventional and renewable), transport (rail, air, sea and road), water provision and flood protection.

Fundamental to ensuring the quality of the research (especially in terms of construct validity and reliability) was the development of a protocol for the investigation. The demands on the transparency and usability of this protocol were significant given the highly disparate group of researchers that used it. The case protocol comprised two elements:

- instructions on the data collection processes to be used in the investigation; and
- a standardised template in which to capture and codify the data.

These elements were co-designed by the investigation's researchers in a workshop and then piloted in selected case scenario. The results of the pilots were feedback to a core team of researchers that amended the protocol and communicated the revised version to the rest of the investigations researchers. Data collection processes involved the use of secondary data that originated either from previous primary research investigations undertaken by the researchers or from publically available data such as government reports, trade press articles and so on. The template utilised systemic thinking to categorise the megaproject (Checkland, 1981; Jenkins 1981). It used the constructs of actors (or system elements) linked together by relationships and engaged in activities that join together into transformation processes. This bounded megaproject system was judged to operate in a wider environment (political, legal and economic) and to possess emergent properties (viewed both in terms of cost, time and performance of the megaproject and the degree to which it satisfied its stakeholders' requirements). The data gathered by the researchers was used to complete the template and used footnotes at the end of the template to indicate the source of each data item. The completed templates were then made available to all of the researchers in the Action via an open-access website and in a searchable format in what was termed the MEGAPROJECT Case Portfolio. The investigation founded its approach to analysis of the cases on the principle of triangulation. Gill and Johnson (2002) define this as follows:

> Triangulation, in social science research methodological terms, allows for verification of postulated relationships through several different approaches performed by different researchers at different points in time arriving at the same conclusions.

Subgroups of researchers were created to use different approaches to analysing the cases to identify emergent themes that could be postulated as impacting on megaproject design and delivery performance. These subgroups employed both inductive and deductive approaches to pattern-spotting across the Portfolio. Some subgroups followed the process proposed by Eisenhardt (1989), others utilised a semantic-based approach to ratifying deductively generated propositions. The themes that were generated by the subgroups were then brought together at a workshop in which they were grouped into meta-themes and ordered in terms of the impact on megaproject performance using a Delphi exercise undertaken by all of the researchers in the MEGAPROJECT investigation.

## Reflections of the Outcomes of the Multi-Case Investigation

Through the triangulation exercise, the following emergent meta-themes were identified as substantively impactive on megaproject management performance:

- managing external stakeholders;
- creating appropriate governance and structure;
- shaping and responding to the political and regulatory environment.

In the context of this chapter, it is important to understand how these themes are different than those that would have arisen from considering a singular case. Firstly, their extendibility is greater as they have been found across megaproject sectors in Europe rather than one particular situation in one sector in one country. This gives confidence to the users of the outcomes of the MEGAPROJECT research (many of whom are practice-based) that considering these meta-themes in designing and delivering a wide range of European mega-projects is appropriate. Secondly, the evidential support from a wide variety of cases enabled a much richer and nuanced exposition of the meta-theme. This included the ability to both *literally* replicate case situations but also to *theoretically* replicate situations (Yin, 2003).

The MEGAPROJECT Project also provides the opportunity to learn from the operational aspects of multi-case research. As has been discussed previously in this chapter, multi-case research is resource intensive and, of necessity, may involve many researchers and potentially the use of secondary data. The success of the MEGAPROJECT template in inculcating a uniform approach to case creation was instrumental to the efficacy of a multi-case research approach. The template enabled a highly disparate group of researchers to work together under the auspices of a single investigation. This suggests that a similar approach to multi-case protocol implementation may meet with equal success (assuming that the case template was well-designed). The use of secondary data did not prove problematic either but it did entail the creation of a very specific 'glossary' for the terminology used in the project to ensure a consistent interpretation of the constructs under investigation.

## Acknowledgements

The authors gratefully acknowledge the support of the ESF COST Action MEGAPROJECT TU1003.

## Tips and Questions

### TIPS FOR STUDENTS

- Face the resource challenges that you will encounter in undertaking multi-case research. Have a realistic understanding that you can undertake this kind of research.
- Think hard about the kind of 'template' you devise to capture your case data. Make sure that it is easy to communicate to both your research team and the people who will be providing you with data.
- Think through what you are going to do if you don't reach a point of theoretical saturation.

### TIPS FOR SUPERVISORS

- Ensure that the student has a well thought through strategy for pattern-spotting prior to starting any data collection.
- Students (and others!) seem to find deductive pattern-spotting approaches much simpler than inductive ones. Ensure that your student makes full use of both techniques.

### QUESTIONS

1. Is inductive or deductive pattern-spotting best for multi-case investigations? Think of exemplar case investigation research questions and decide which you would use and in which context. (Or would you use both?)

2. What advantages does multi-case research bring over single-case investigations?
3. How would you know that you had reached 'theoretical saturation'?
4. Compare and contrast Yin's and Eisenhardt's approach to multi-case research in this project context or one similar and familiar to you.
5. Reflect on the MEGAPROJECT multi-case investigation. What lessons does this have for your own research investigation?

# References

Abercrombie, Ni., Hill, S. and Turner, B. S. (1984). *Dictionary of Sociology*. Harmondsworth, UK: Penguin.

Barratt, M., Choi, T. Y., and Li, M. (2011). Qualitative case studies in operations management: Trends, research outcomes, and future research implications, *Journal of Operations Management*, 29(4), 329–342.

Checkland, P. B. (1981). *Systems Thinking: Systems Practice*. New York: Wiley.

Church, R. M. (2002). The effective use of secondary data. *Learning and Motivation*, 33(1), 32–45.

Cowton, C. J. (1998). The use of secondary data in business ethics research. *Journal of Business Ethics*, 17(4), 423–434.

Eckstein, H. (2002). Case study and theory in political science. In Gomm, R., Hammersley, M. and Foster, P. (eds), *Case Study Method: Key Issues, Key Texts*. London: Sage Publications, pp. 119–163.

Eisenhardt, K. M. (1989). Building theories from case study research. *The Academy of Management Review*, 14(4), 532.

Flyvbjerg B. (2011). Case study. In Denzin, N. K. and Lincoln, Y. S. (eds), *The Sage Handbook of Qualitative Research*, 4th Edition. Thousand Oaks, CA: Sage, Publications, Chapter 17, p. 314.

Gill, J. and Johnson, P. (2002). *Research Methods for Managers*. London: Sage Publications.

Hillebrand, B. and Biemans, W. G. (2004). Links between internal and external cooperation in product development: An exploratory study. *Journal of Product Innovation Management*, 21(2), 110–122.

Jenkins, G. (1981). The systems approach. In Jenkins, G. M. The systems approach, in *Systems Behaviour*, 3rd edition, edited by Open Systems Group. London: Harper & Row.

Koners, U. and Goffin, K. (2007). Learning from postproject reviews: A cross-case analysis. *Journal of Product Innovation Management*, 24(3), 242–258.

Locatelli, G. and Mancini, M. (2012). Looking back to see the future: Building nuclear power plants in Europe. *Construction Management and Economics*, 30(8), 623–637.

Locke, E. A. (2007). The case for inductive theory building. *Journal of Management*, 33(6), 867–890.

Miles, M. B. and Huberman, A. M. (1994). *Qualitative Data Analysis*, 2nd edition. Thousand Oaks, CA: Sage Publications.

Nitithamyong, P. and Skibniewski, M. J. (2011). Success factors for the implementation of web-based construction project management systems: A cross-case analysis. *Construction Innovation*, 11(1), 14–42.

Parkhe, A. (1993). 'Messy' research, methodological predispositions, and theory development in international joint ventures. *Academy of Management Review*, 18(2), 227–268.

Piekkari, R., Welch, C. and Paavilainen, E. (2009) The case study as disciplinary convention: Evidence from international business journals. *Organizational Research Methods*, 12(3), 567–589. doi: 10.1177/1094428108319905.

Ragin, C. C. (1997). Turning the tables: How case-oriented research challenges variable-oriented research. *Comparative Social Research*, 16(1), 27–42.

Stretton, H. (1969). *The Political Sciences: General Principles of Selection in Social Science and History*. London: Routledge and Kegan Paul.

Yin, R. K. (2003). *Case Study Research: Design and Methods*, 3rd edition. Thousand Oaks, CA: Sage Publications..

# 30

# Project Management Research in Post-Conflict Societies: Challenges and Complexities Identified in Kosovo

James Earnest and Carolyn Dickie

*When writing this chapter, we wanted to talk about experiences in the field and provide useful advice on how to organise and conduct research in complex war-torn societies.*

The effects of war limit the effectiveness of institutional aspects of peace-building and reconstruction. Organisations and individuals doing empirical research in PM in war-torn societies should aim to capture information on processes, structures and systems for enhancement of the society's future. The most important challenge for PM researchers is how to conduct field research in such complex, unsettled settings. This chapter highlights the importance of increased awareness of complexities in war-torn civil societies, which can be used to enhance experience and maximise potential with aid agencies, multilateral institutions and non-governmental organizations (NGOs), and identifies the experience of the practical challenges of conducting research on how reconstruction projects are planned and implemented. The chapter concludes with implications to assist researchers and academics in a better understanding and to be able to respond to the complex challenges of reconstruction and development activities between local, national and external actors in post-conflict situations.

At the end of this chapter, the reader can:

*   identify obstacles and challenges in a society transitioning from civil war to establish a new form of government;
*   select a research method that includes a wide range of the society's stakeholders;
*   examine a range of significant issues relevant to both researchers and supervisors.

Keywords: community, complexity, design, ethics, flexibility, research methods

## Background: Post-War Economic Recovery and Project Management Research

Worldwide there are 37 countries – primarily in Asia, Africa, Middle East, the Balkans and beyond – involved in conflict or in the process of post-conflict reconstruction and long-term development (Voetsch and Myers, 2005). Though societal challenges driven by conflict do not provide an easy sinecure for rebuilding and reconstruction, donors provide funding and grants for a broad range of projects and programmes considered the key building blocks for the development of infrastructure projects in post-conflict societies. Consequently it is argued that, for academics and students to undertake successful research in complex societies, important questions need to be answered in relation to the structure and impact of research, the identifying of internationally accepted PM processes and techniques, and the effectiveness of current practices applied in post-conflict infrastructure projects.

The challenge for researchers is to develop a 360-degree type approach to stakeholders to enable rebuilding of post-conflict societies and project implementation of reconstruction projects that develop the overall economic independence of the conflicted societies. Broad-based research is required in the area of post-conflict PM processes because post-conflict research is still in its infancy, and international development organisations and practitioner bodies have a limited understanding of the dynamics of PM methodology in post-conflict settings.

Despite a growing emphasis by aid agencies to promote local participation and consultation, practitioners need assistance from researchers to adopt PM research methods to promote sustainability embedded in the development and management of projects (Grevelman and Kluiwstra, 2010). This will occur only when sound, basic research involving all relevant stakeholders is undertaken and common understanding and shared goals developed.

The impact of war on a nation significantly affects the domestic capacity and integrity of the state to build, legislate and promote economic growth, to improve education and health, and to achieve higher living standards. This limits personal, organisational and societal well-being by damaging physical infrastructure such as public utilities and the communication network. The concept of managing post-conflict reconstruction (PCR) and developing projects with internationally accepted PM processes are comparatively new and developing fields of study (Lukic, 2010).

A significant challenge for researchers is to determine which type of research method is most suitable for a proposed study. From the plethora of methods, a mixed methods approach with opportunities to use a number of research types and strategies is advisable. To provide guidance and practical advice for those undertaking research in post-conflict societies, researchers seeking to reform institutions and rebuild post-conflict societies should understand the dynamics of effective approaches in their efforts to collect data from the field.

The mixed methods approach can maximise the collection of data, assist by amplifying comparative analysis and promote the veracity of results in the quantitative (Bryman and Bell, 2011) and qualitative (Tashakori and Teddlie, 2003) aspects of the study. Traditional quantitative criteria of internal validity, external validity, reliability and objectivity can be balanced with the alternative qualitative criteria of credibility, transferability, dependability and confirmability.

To underscore the broader participation and engagement of key stakeholders there are a number of particularly important requirements (exercises) in post-conflict research for students, for example:

- researchers need to accept and reflect on the complexities of post-conflict societies prior to entering the field;

- organisations and aid agencies that establish management plans/standards of their own and implement projects need to be aware of their own particular challenges other than research;
- the rationale for the collection and analysis of data should be chosen at the earliest stages of the research;
- due to time constraints, use of a pilot study as a preliminary trial of the research before the phase of formal data collection is advisable;
- the researcher should not only choose the most appropriate research methodology but also have an execution plan in detail – the use of local research assistants will ensure that the data collection can be expedited within a manageable timeframe;
- it is essential that researchers share and discuss the ethical issues specific to the culture and location of their work and develop collective ethical standards for the study;
- in post-conflict societies, research respondents can be biased towards political points of view due to cultural, political and social interaction between conflicting communities, an ongoing challenge for researchers;
- the dynamics that shape the development and implementation of projects should be addressed so the researcher is aware of any relationships between corruption and economic developments in the complex, yet fragile society;
- respondents' guaranteed and demonstrated anonymity is needed to facilitate candid responses so participants do not feel exposed in any way by the project team on the basis of their involvement in the research.

## Choosing Appropriate Research Methodology in Post-Conflict Settings

In practice, there are many obstacles and challenges to obtaining high-quality data in every research project; however, these can be compounded in conflict settings. In the first instance, researchers need to have a sound understanding of the typology of mixed methods research (Creswell and Plano Clark, 2007). Regardless of the research method chosen, there is an obligation on the researcher to ensure the approach applied is of the utmost professional standard (Ford, Mills, Zachariah and Upshur, 2009). Consequently, the usual philosophical assumptions associated with research, that is, ontological, epistemological, methodological and axiological, need to be addressed carefully to differentiate among various perspectives of research. In post-conflict research environments there is added pressure on researchers to resolve issues and explain:

- the research environment;
- the objectives of the research;
- the types of information being sought; and
- the applications of the research.

There are many types of research design, and no single ideal research methodology can contribute specifically to the way in which data about a phenomenon should be gathered, analysed and used. Research design is underpinned by the notion of 'fitness for purpose'; the purpose of the research leads to a decision on the methodology and design of the study (Cohen, Manion and Morrison, 2007: p. 78). There are many research methods used to extract information in different contexts, none of which is essentially better than the others.

Generally, it is assumed that by combining both qualitative and quantitative methods the data collected is more comprehensive and a better analysis of the research problem and questions can be achieved than by using either method alone (Brewer and Hunter, 1989). Patton (2002) argued emphatically that the results from different methods could produce quite different interpretations. Thus, the challenge in a post-war conflict environment is to determine the appropriate strategy to be applied through the use of mixed methods evaluations that combine qualitative and quantitative data-gathering techniques and maximise the variety of feedback from research participant stakeholders in each given situation.

Triangulation, explanatory and exploratory research are three well-known types of mixed methods (Creswell, 2002). Nevertheless, mixed methodology is not intrinsically superior to single method research, nor is it an easier way to conduct a study. In effect, mixed methods research:

- must be well designed;
- must be carefully conducted;
- must be appropriate to the major research question;
- may be more time-consuming and costly;
- uses more resources; and
- requires the researcher to have a knowledge and skills, with both quantitative and qualitative research.

A case study approach draws together different forms of data about the same phenomena, processes and events in more than one way (Velde, Jansen and Anderson, 2004). Case studies have been used widely in management research to review processes which are uncertain, and events that are often unknown and/or entail change. Multiple case studies also can be used to examine the organisation's processes and practices in extreme situations where changes occur over time (Druckman, 2005; McCutcheon and Meredith, 1993). Hartley (2004) suggested that case study methodology often focused on the processes of change and was suitable to analyse complex organisational processes. At the same time, using a case study gives the researcher an opportunity to explore social processes in-depth and to develop a better understanding of research questions as they unfold in complex social settings.

By providing a better understanding of the research topic that has significant socio-economic policy implications in a post-war environment, case studies allow for process (how projects are managed), contextual (post-conflict) and longitudinal (dealing with processes) analysis. In the case of Kosovo's socio-economic development, many organisations demonstrated a tendency to use their own crafted, idiosyncratic organisational processes to implement projects. In order to investigate such dynamic practices, a case study approach may be determined to be the most appropriate.

In a post-conflict society, the case study approach gives an ideal opportunity to study a problem in depth within an acceptable time frame (Bell, 2005). Also, the case study approach allows for the practice of selecting and applying a data collection technique in the same way as in any other research process (Veal, 2005). Stake (1994) posited that not all case studies were qualitative and Yin (1994) noted that a case study may be limited to quantitative evidence and should not be viewed always as qualitative. Thus, case studies can be based on both qualitative and quantitative evidence. In the context of the post-war societies, the case study research method provides a greater opportunity than other available methods to obtain a holistic, actual view of an empirical inquiry (Gummesson, 1988).

By focusing on the infrastructure projects' reconstruction development in one of the newest nations in the world (Kosovo), use of the case study revealed certain challenges inherent in project design and management so that new design elements could be developed and tested in other post-conflict societies. Although 'project-based management' processes have not been tested in a post-conflict environment, Druckman (2005) and Veal (2005) highlighted that a case study method can be used to confirm whether or not the theory was suited for adapting to a complex setting. Outlined by George and Bennett (2005, p. 19), case studies can 'achieve a high level of conceptual validity and have powerful advantages in the heuristics identification of new variables and hypotheses through the study of deviant or outlier cases and in the course of field work'.

Drawing on knowledge and practical experience through project work and field trips to build an effective post-conflict PM approach depends on the deliberation and choices made in conducting research. However, post-conflict economic recovery depends largely upon the nature of the enquiry and maximising benefits from available information. In the acquisition of high-quality data from research in complex and volatile task environments with economic stagnation, increased threats to security and unforeseen risks, there are many obstacles and challenges to persons undertaking research in development and reconstruction projects.

In general, for many years researchers have chosen case study methods across a wide variety of academic disciplines. Crowe et al. (2011) posit that a case study approach is particularly relevant to allow in-depth, multifaceted exploration and understanding of complex issues. However, regardless of the research methodology chosen, there is an obligation to ensure the approach applied is of the highest professional standard (Ford et al., 2009).

The PM process review conducted in Kosovo was an exploratory study designed to identify how well the infrastructure reconstruction projects had been established, planned, organised, executed and controlled by donors, multilateral agencies and development organisations. Developing and completing successful research in PCR settings depends on the researcher's ability to recognise the complexities of cognitive, technical, cultural, organisational, personal and political environments, and to respond by coordinating peace-building operations in an effective manner. Using a detailed case study approach to the interviews and survey data, the Kosovo study was aimed not only to determine the strengths and weaknesses of the current PM reconstruction processes, but to establish the differences of opinion within project teams related to project planning and implementation in their wider sense.

The process review had several essential activities for researchers (see Figure 30.1 overleaf):

- prepare a good review of literature of the conflicted society/country;
- conduct a pilot study before embarking on the full-scale study;
- identify and select appropriate case studies;
- obtain a list of relevant agencies prior to travelling in the field;
- prepare a contingency plan if there is a risk of continuing hostilities or difficulty in obtaining data;
- ensure ethics clearances are completed before going into the field, to save time and avoid bureaucratic procedures; and
- clearly map out research questions.

## Design Project Management Research in Post-Conflict Societies: Why Do It?

Despite recognition of PCR needs, no clear paradigm had emerged with standard strategies to underpin the research and conceptualisation of PM processes required for successful operation in PCR (Lukic, 2010), Though there has been much research done on peace-building and peace-keeping by scholars, policy makers and field practitioners (Baranyi, 2005; Knight, 2003). Further, there has also been considerable debate by international peace-keeping researchers to go beyond the current paradigms and develop strategies and long-term processes to achieve durable peace, good governance and promote sustainable development through local community participation in post-conflict societies (Knight, 2003).

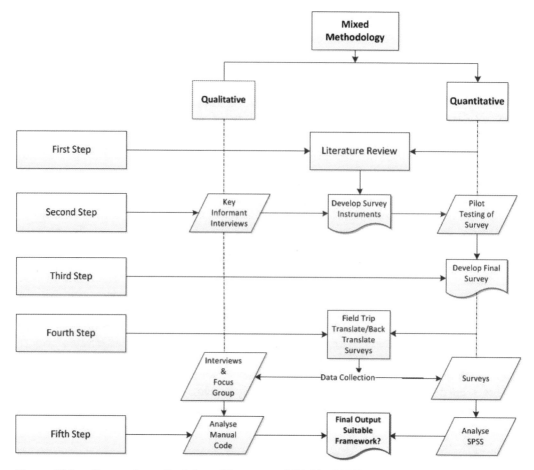

**Figure 30.1    Research methodology (Earnest and Dickie, 2012)**

In addition, there is a limited body of empirical literature available that deals with international development in PM (Lukic, 2010). A related issue is that few post-conflict countries have an Ethics Review Board (Ford et al., 2009). In the absence of specific ethical frameworks developed to guide research practices and organisational behaviour in humanitarian emergencies (Black, 2003), researchers have the demanding task of examining collective ethical standards of a post-conflict society and developing ethical standards for their project and the needs of the environment with which they are faced.

Community participation is a key component of development strategy, but consultation demands significant time and resources (Brown, 2005; Engel, 2003). Members of civil society are seldom included in the decision-making processes; though often they are seen as partners in the implementation of development projects. To achieve sustained growth and development, beneficiaries must be engaged systematically in the planning and decision-making processes throughout the lifecycle of the project (Gennip, 2005; World Bank, 2006).

To a great extent, much of the infrastructure in PCR regions suffers from low-quality design or sub-standard construction (Barrett, 2008). In post-conflict situations, there is an evident lack of funds to support local institutions to meet their objectives and discharge their responsibilities to the community (Grey-Johnson, 2006), and in an environment of scarce funding, projects are operated according to the priorities of the donors rather than the development needs of the local community (Evans-Kent and Bleiker, 2003).

With multiple projects to administer, skilled people are scarce and agencies usually have difficulty meeting the resource requirements necessary to execute project planning and implementation (Brautigam and Knack, 2004; Youker, 1999). The competing demands for material, human and institutional resources raise a number of key issues and challenges which should be taken into account when researching, designing and implementing PCR projects. An effective framework needs to be implemented for the application of reconstruction projects and programmes using an approach that is flexible, while continuing to meet the needs of the civil society.

Due to a lack of coordination and information exchange between agencies in post-war societies, very often projects are duplicated. Furthermore, organisations take over projects for which they do not have adequate training, competencies or experience. For example, development agencies that specialise in water projects also compete for donor funding in psychosocial or housing projects (Evans-Kent and Bleiker, 2003). Similarly, due to the minimal involvement of state institutions in a post-conflict society often there can be limited management capacity, poor emphasis on manpower development and training, and a lack of established management or technical standards. The situation is made more complicated by bureaucratic systems that cause delays in implementing projects and programmes (Brown, 2005).

Issues related to civil participation in the design of post-conflict reconstruction projects are reflected in a significant issue for researchers; what data analysis strategies, including associated use of computer software, are most appropriate for assisting in the accurate interpretation of the research data? Recently, Saldana (2013) presented an enhanced list of coding methods on the analysing of visual and mediated data. The list included strategies for coding of participants' responses by means of first and second cycles of the transition process with further explanation of data analysis and writing after the second cycle. The issue of coding is critical for maximising research participants' information and its correctness as shown in a range of research covering K-12 education, higher education, the arts, human development, social sciences, business, technology, government and social services and health care. Saldana's (2013) approach fits closely to that of Lofland, Snow, Anderson and Lofland (2006: p. 121) who outline nine major units of social organisation, all of which are relevant to post-conflict reconstruction.

In moving from codes to themes in the data, the researcher needs to carefully consider topics revealed in the data, such as:

* cognitive aspects or meanings;
* emotional aspects or feelings; and
* hierarchical aspects or inequalities.

In addition to examining PM, researchers are recommended to consider the Lofland et al. (2006: pp. 144–467) recommendation for examining how a participant agency interacts and interplays with structures and processes, plus causes and consequences observed in the data.

## Why Conduct Research in War-Torn Societies?

In addition to supporting the reconstruction development projects of the community and helping rebuild the fragile economy, doing research in a post-conflict society provides a unique challenge and reward to the researcher. The researcher is not able to process participants and their responses from a distance; in fact, it is in being a participant researcher assisting in developing relationships among stakeholders that is fundamental to the researcher's success. Critically, the researcher listens to the voices of the affected social groups and also the voices of development practitioners who work with the community (Maroun, 2008), provides relevant feedback and facilitates the coordination of research findings and development practices.

There are billions of dollars invested in the development of 'hard' and 'soft' projects, with most 'hard' projects being engineering projects. Organisations do have their own PM processes (Rathmell, 2005) but most project implementation staff do not have the required competence to understand the standards and the processes. Thus, there is limited research undertaken in the light of internationally accepted PM standards and processes even though doing research does help researchers influence the design of standards on how to plan and implement projects in different post-conflict societies. Moreover, the researcher's influence can extend to donors to reconstruction efforts; the latter are happier to fund projects if they are guaranteed of organisations having structured systems/processes to ensure they make effective contributions.

Doing research in such an environment can be complex and time consuming for any researcher who does not have experience of working in a post-conflict situation. The researchers should be fully aware of the limitations of post-war reconstruction and the lack of infrastructure (telecommunication, health, electricity, housing and transport) available during the conduct of the research.

Given the historical and environmental pressures in a post-conflict society, the scope of a longitudinal study is not feasible for most researchers. In the case of research related to PM for reconstruction, quantitative studies are feasible. However, given the special needs of a post-conflict community, researchers are advised to consider the value of a mixed methodology with the benefits arising from the collection of both quantitative and qualitative data. It is important to listen to both the voices of the community (qualitative) and project managers (quantitative) to develop PM standards best suited to the society.

Another challenge for researchers interacting with project managers and project staff in a post-conflict society is their need to be quite conversant with PM standards. While use of PM jargon can be complicated and may not be well understood by research or reconstruction developers, the task of the researcher is to assist in the development of terminology that is commonly understood by all participants.

## Practical Considerations to do Research in Post-Conflict Reconstruction and Development

In the absence of a clear PM framework that can act as a reference point for countries emerging from conflict, their future depends increasingly on the effective implementation of idiosyncratic projects and programmes. The complication is that, in a society, the stakeholders have more complex questions and demand more detailed answers from those doing research in development projects. Thus, following the experience of researching in Kosovo, the following tips are recommended for consideration when doing research involved in PCR planning and development.

## Conclusion and Implications

Whilst it is always a challenge in a post-conflict society to maximise the impact of peace-keeping missions, researchers have a unique opportunity to examine and promote PM concepts that, used comprehensively, can facilitate the achievement of social and infrastructure reconstruction and rehabilitation. Grounded in the nuances of working in a complex environment, with almost non-existent regulatory challenges and rapid changes that affect day-to-day operations, researchers with an understanding of PM can provide practical information on ways to plan and implement 'people-centred' projects that promote a good work environment in the complex workplace.

While post-conflict states undergo reconstruction and development in order to improve the life of people, provision of facilities and good governance in their countries, researchers have skills and strategies to influence international development experts and national, regional and local developers to address the question of how a 'PM approach' to reconstruction processes in a post-conflict society differs from PM in peaceful countries. As further research in project/programme management processes in post-conflict societies is undertaken there will be an increase in the number of research methods, issues and challenges available to ensure that research in such complex societies will be successful.

## Tips and Exercises

TIPS FOR STUDENTS

- Plan to be flexible, with a detailed contact list of key agencies and organisations, to maximise face-to-face contact with participants.
- Leave a detailed daily plan with a second person so that the researcher's availability is traceable in the case of conflict or emergency evacuation being required; similarly, an up-date of daily movement and progress should be registered with the supervisor who can receive up-loaded documents for placement in a secure storage site.
- Travel with a local research assistant to check safety and security, and use an interpreter from the same community as the participant when in a rebel area or conflict-prone community.
- Conduct of interviews or focus group discussions should avoid having more than one interest group represented otherwise, in conflicted areas, participants may not answer questions honestly for fear of being marginalised later.
- Approval for the conduct of the research needs to be arranged and confirmed thoroughly and clearly; for example, even when participants have signed a consent form, data should not be collected from field/project staff without the prior approval of a Country Director or Head of Project. Similarly, because unapproved photography of government properties and infrastructure may lead to a fine or arrest, prior approval is essential for the use of photographs of projects, completed or otherwise.

TIPS FOR SUPERVISORS

- Ensure the researcher has adequate personal insurance despite having anticipated potential pitfalls and obstacles.
- Ensure, for reasons of safety and to keep abreast of possibly substantial risk factors, that the researcher registers with an agency or organisation that coordinates international staff.
- Ensure that the researcher has appropriately prepared and completed contracts for employment of local research assistants/drivers/interpreters and for personal accommodation.
- Ensure local dialect surveys are cross-checked by different translators for accuracy and clarity of content.

## EXERCISES

1.  Fieldwork should be done in teams of at least two people. Partner with another researcher and prepare a detailed itinerary for a hypothetical field trip; include the names of potential contact organisations, phone numbers and dates of visits.
2.  Prepare a field safety plan. Given that post-conflict locations can be fluid, complex and challenging, identify a number of persons from colleagues and the research team from whom you could seek advice. What types of advice may be most useful in helping you reflect on the situation and adjust your safety plan accordingly?
3.  Identify a country where you might do field research and familiarise yourself with the society's cultural, moral, religious and legal values. Choose a post-conflict society and prepare a list of potential problems (that is, obstacles and difficulties). Consider possible solutions and discuss these with your supervisor.

## References

Baranyi, S. (2005). Fragile States and Sustainable Peace Keeping. NSI Policy Brief. North-South Institute.

Barrett, J. (2008). After the war: The risks and growing insurance demand in post-conflict region. *Risk Management*, 38–42.

Bell, J. (2005). *Doing Your Research Project: A Guide for First-time Researchers in Education, Health and Social Science*, 4th edn. England: Open University Press.

Black, R. (2003). Ethical codes in humanitarian emergencies: From practice to research? *Disasters*, 27(2), 95–108.

Black, R. (2003). Ethical codes in humanitarian emergencies: From practice to research? *Disasters*, 27(2), 95–108.

Brautigam, D.A. and Knack, S. (2004). Foreign aid, institutions, and governance in Sub-Saharan Africa. *Economic Development and Cultural Change*, 52(2), 255–285.

Brewer, J. and Hunter, A. (1989). *Multimethod Research: A Synthesis of Styles*. Newbury Park, CA: Sage Publications.

Brown, R. H. (2005). Reconstruction of infrastructure in Iraq: End to a means or means to an end? *Third World Quarterly*, 26(4–5), 759–775.

Bryman, A. and Bell, E. (2011). *Business Research Methods*, 3rd edn. Oxford, UK: Oxford University Press.

Cohen, L., Manion, L. and Morrison, K. (2007). *Research Methods in Education*, 7th edn. New York: Routledge.

Creswell, J. W. (2002). *Research Design; Qualitative, Quantitative and Mixed Methods Approaches*. Thousand Oaks, CA: Sage.

Creswell, J. W. and Plano Clark, V. L. (2007). *Designing and Conducting Mixed Methods Research*. Thousand Oaks, CA: Sage.

Crowe, S., Cresswell, K., Robertson, A., Huby, G., Avery, A. and Sheikh, A. (2011). The case study approach. *BMC Medical Research Methodology*, 11(100), doi:10.1186/1471-2288-11-100.

Druckman, D. (2005). *Doing Research: Methods of Inquiry for Conflict Analysis*. Thousand Oaks, CA: Sage Publications.

Earnest, J. and Dickie, C. (2012). Post-conflict Reconstruction: The complexity and challenges of planning and implementing infrastructure projects in Kosovo. PhD Thesis, Curtin University, Australia.

Engel, E. R. (2003). Reaching for stability: Strengthening civil society-donor partnership in East Timor. *Journal of International Affairs*, 57(1), 169–181.

Evans-Kent, B. and Bleiker, R. (2003). Peace beyond the State? NGOs in Bosnia and Herzegovina. *International Peacekeeping*, 10(1), 103–119.

Ford, N., Mills, E. J., Zachariah, R. and Upshur, R. (2009). Ethics of conducting research in conflict settings. *Conflict and Health*, 3(7), 1–9.

George, A. L. and Bennett, A. (2005). *Case Studies and Theory Development in the Social Sciences*. Cambridge, MA: MIT Press.

Gennip, J.V. (2005). Post-conflict reconstruction and development. *Development,* 48(3), 57–62.

Grevelman, L. and Kluiwstra, M. (2010). Sustainability in project management: A case study on Enexis. *PM World Today,* 12(7), 1–19.

Grey-Johnson, C. (2006). Beyond peacekeeping: The challenges of post-conflict reconstruction and peacebuilding in Africa. *UN Chronicle,* 43(1), 8–11.

Gummesson, E. (1988). *Qualitative Methods in Management Research.* Bromley, UK: Chartwell-Bratt.

Hartley, J. (2004). Case Study Research. In C. Cassell and G. Symon (Eds), *Essential Guide to Qualitative Methods in Organisational Research.* London: Sage.

Knight, W. A. (2003). Evaluating recent trends in peacebuilding research. *International Relations of the Asia-Pacific,* 3(2), 241–264.

Lofland, J., Snow, D., Anderson, L. and Lofland, L. H. (2006). *Analyzing Social settings: A Guide to Qualitative Observation and analysis,* 4th edn. Belmont, CA: Thomson Wadsworth.

Lukic, T. (2010). Regional Project Management Capacity Assessment: A study of the Project Management Capacity in the Western Balkans. USAID Competitiveness Project. Belgrade, Serbia.

Maroun, N. (2008). *The Meaning of Community Participation in Post-conflict Societies: Ethnography of the Challenges of Inter-religious Reconciliation in Lebanon.* ProQuest.

McCutcheon, D. M. and Meredith, J. (1993). Conducting case study research in operations management. *Journal of Operations Management,* 11(3), 239–256.

Patton, M. Q. (2002). *Qualitative Research & Evaluation Methods,* 3rd edn. Thousand Oaks, CA: Sage.

Rathmell, A. (2005). Planning post-conflict reconstruction in Iraq: What can we learn? *International Affairs,* 81(5), 1013–1038.

Saldana, J. (2013). *The Coding Manual for Qualitative Researchers,* 2nd edn. Thousand Oaks, CA: Sage.

Stake, R. E. (1994). Case Studies. In N. K. Denzin and Y. S. Lincoln (eds), *Handbook of Qualitative Research.* Thousand Oaks, CA: Sage.

Tashakori, A and Teddlie, C. (2003). *Handbook of Mixed Methods in Social and Behavioral Research.* Thousand Oaks, CA: Sage.

Veal, A. J. (2005). *Business Research Methods: A Managerial Approach.* NSW, Australia: Pearson Education.

Velde, M., Jansen, P. and Anderson, N. (2004). *Guide to Management Research Methods.* Oxford, UK: Blackwell Publishing.

Voetsch, R. J. and Myers, C. (2005). Operation Urgent: Project Management in Conflict and Post-Conflict Countries. Paper presented at the PMI Global Congress Proceedings, Toronto, Canada.

World Bank. (2006). *Community-Driven Development in the Context of Conflict-Affected Countries: Challenges and Opportunities.* Social Development Department, Environmentally and Socially Sustainable Development Network. Washington, DC: World Bank.

Yin, R. K. (1994). *Case Study Research: Design and Methods,* 2nd edn. Thousand Oaks, CA: Sage.

Youker, R. (1999). Managing international development projects – Lessons learned. *Project Management Journal,* 30(2), 6–7.

# 31

# Complexities of Oil and Gas Exploration in the Middle East

Lawrence Monteilh

*The purpose for this chapter is to address a maturity model that reflects the complexities in the  oil and gas exploration industries in the Middle East. The key to information gathering encompasses industry and country knowledge operating in their organisational settings. The data introduced will inform students with concepts to build awareness for cultural sensitivity while gathering research information. As a comprehensive model, considerations for culture, risk and ethical challenges will be advanced in the research processes.*

At the end of this chapter, the reader can:

* identify cultural considerations in select regional studies;
* improve their understanding of the value and benefits of qualitative case study research;
* improve their preparation techniques for research protocol and information gathering;
* familiarise themselves with web-based ethnography.

Keywords: project management maturity model, culture, risk (complex, political), mixed method research, case study research, ethnography, ethical challenges

## Introduction

The project management maturity (PMM) model concept is realizing increased popularity among education and business. Just as the business environment demands efficiency in controlling cost and time to complete projects, PMM models offer the opportunity to identify critical steps to accomplish the organizational goals in education and business (Demir and Kocabas, 2010).

The purpose of this chapter is to show the connection between independent researches from a portfolio perspective contributing to the maturity model. It will be well noted to understand the features of project portfolio management as having the capability of providing a guide to implementation and sustained development of robust capabilities as the foundation for the study of Killen and Hunt (2013). Based on findings from the literature and multiple-case study, a capability maturity model is proposed to assist in the development of capabilities that are intended to evolve and stay relevant in dynamic environments. As we address maturity models designated for the oil and gas industry in the Middle East, the relevancy factor amplifies as we find it appropriate to develop a model that can sustain the variables in our target industry.

Limitations of PMM and associated models have been disclosed within the confines of managing undefined projects. These projects tend to lack defined parameters, process repetition, reasonable outcomes and expectations advanced by the study of Pasian, Sankaran and Boydell (2012). Recognition of these environments can be difficult to detect. Well-defined projects for study and research are critical.

The exploration of the oil and gas industry in the Middle East encompasses elements of company involvement, cultural influence and trust in working conditions. As researchers we will want to be aware of our soft skills and methods for data collection.

The complexity of the exploration industries operating in the Middle East certainly have responsibility and awareness for health and safety coupled with organizational culture. Seven project business organizations represented diverse organisations and diverse practices informed by habits and intuitive behavior as noted by Roberts, Kelsey, Smyth and Wilson (2012). Literature suggests the need for organisational maturity towards a safety culture. Noted is a methodology informed by ethnography using case-based analysis with seven project business organisations. Health and safety was not top priority for the cases. Reality sets in and student researchers must retain the awareness that good performance may well be aligned with organisational process and effective operations, and not an elevated need to build in the health and safety features.(Kelsey and Smyth, 2012).

Literature also resides in the development of proposing a method to transfer knowledge and skill sets based on technique. A skills transfer management maturity model has been addressed to reflect capability evaluating skills management. Studies evolve on methods to convert extracted knowledge into practical knowledge as noted by Toshihiro, Masakazu, Kota and Kazuhiko (2012).

The model involves the recognition phase, transfer phase and evaluation phase. Few studies exist that focus on methods to convert basic knowledge into practical aspects and ultimately filtering to the learners. As this chapter progresses through the elements to accommodate the complexities of the oil and gas industry in the Middle East, key factors such as cultural considerations and risk analysis of complex projects will be addressed as the research methodology process converges to encompass these factors.

## Cultural Considerations – Middle Eastern Countries

Leadership culture in this region as recognized and reported by Sheldon (2012) has been shaped over centuries through a variety of factors, such as reputation, family and religion, which continue to influence decision making. These factors need attention and must be studied to be successful in the information gathering processes for research students and supervisors. The Middle East consists of 20 countries with different religions, and a variety of ethnic and linguistic groups. These different cultures are in the region of study for this chapter. The region is also the birthplace of Judaism, Christianity and Islam, has evolved from the same tradition and continues to be monotheistic, as displayed and presented in Global Connections: The Middle East (2013).

# Risk in Complex and Politically-Sensitive Case Study Research

Dealing effectively with risks in complex projects is difficult and requires management interventions that go beyond simple analytical approaches. This is one finding of a major field study into risk management practices and business processes of 35 major product developments in 17 high-technology companies. Almost one-half of the contingencies that occur are not being detected before they impact project performance. Yet, the risk-impact model presented in this chapter shows that risk does not affect all projects equally but depends on the effectiveness of collective managerial actions dealing with specific contingencies as reported by Thamhaim (2013). The results of this study discuss why some organizations are more successful in detecting risks early in the project lifecycle, and in decoupling risk factors from work processes before they impact project performance. The field data suggest that effective project risk management involves an intricately linked set of variables, related to work process, organizational environment and people. Some of the best success scenarios point to the critical importance of recognizing and dealing with risks early in their development. This requires broad involvement and collaboration across all segments of the project team and its environment, and sophisticated methods for assessing feasibilities and usability early and frequently during the project lifecycle. These factors are critical as the findings lean towards the organisational structure of the oil and gas industry companies.

The top exploration companies operating in the Middle East depend on the project managers to implement and monitor the processes. This requires specific managerial actions, organisational conditions and work processes for fostering a project environment anchored in effective cross-functional communication and collaboration among all stakeholders. We can envision this as being an important condition to early risk detection and effective risk management in complex project situations (Thamhaim, 2013).

Advancing the purpose of this chapter we find it appropriate to examine key challenges associated with conducting politically-sensitive research within a workplace setting. Well noted by Rebeiro and Mol (2012), strategic partnerships can be developed to address these challenges. Organizational case study research can enter into a 'political minefield', as reported by Lilleker (2003) the logistics of interviewing or securing instruments from those within the political process may result in serious obstacles and the information acquired does not always serve the intended purpose of the study. Rebeiro and Moll (2012) offer key methodological principles from the literature on qualitative case study research: noting the value of outlining the research, addressing the challenges that may emerge, collecting data and monitoring participant authenticity and ultimately communicating the research findings. 'Courage, collaboration and clear communication with stakeholders at all levels of the organisation are critical to the success of workplace based case study research' (Rebeiro and Moll, 2012).

Contrasting views on case study research are disclosed by Radlay and Chamberlain (2012) where criticism is made of the idea that a case is merely an instance or a methodological option, whereas attention should be redirected to the study of the case as being central to issues concerning – in this chapter the social elements of the oil and gas industry stakeholders. Salient to this chapter also are the findings that produce three reasons for approaching case study research in this manner. First, case study research imbeds the basics in procedure to collecting information. Second, communication among professionals involves storied accounts so that cases are made, not found. Third, as a result of communicating experience, individuals can be understood as 'cases' (Radlay and Chamberlain, 2012).

This chapter rightfully has a focus on the student researchers. The value and benefit of involving students in active learning enhances focus on research. By extension, encouraging open and honest dialogue about the challenges, struggles and failures research supervisors experience in their own research efforts, this process tends to generate a reciprocal learning environment (Pfeffer and Rogalin, 2012).

## Mixed Method Research Strategies

Mixed method studies have emerged from the paradigm wars between qualitative and quantitative research approaches to become a widely used mode of inquiry as recognised and reported by Terrell (2012). Well noted also is that mixed methods can provide an investigator with many design choices which involve a range of sequential and concurrent strategies. Mixed methods research is becoming increasingly important in several scientific areas.

The analysis of prevalence rates is a new line of research that has emerged in mixed methods research, and this methodological approach has only been applied carefully in a handful of journals as reported by Lopez-Fernandez and Molina-Azorin (2011). Also noteworthy to this chapter is the work of Bartholomew and Brown (2012) providing a methodological review to explore how researchers use mixed methods in culture-specific psychological research. Mixed methods allow the student researcher and supervisor the opportunity to approach the culture aspects and the other complex political-sensitive issues in developing the PMM model. This is a model that embraces the elements of the specific oil and gas exploration industry, with country focus in the Middle East, and the organizational setting of the project manager to implement and monitor the operations.

Scant explicit guidance currently exists on how to teach mixed research courses as studied by Onwuegbuzie, Frels, Leech and Collins (2011). This study amplifies the nexus between the chapter objectives with the oil and gas exploration industry in the Middle East which warrants the direct quotes from the teacher and student pedagogical outcomes as related to this chapter with the student researchers and supervisors. A combination of pedagogical approaches and student learning perceptions were addressed in a mixed research specific course. As Onwuegbuzie et al. (2011) advised, 'This investigation involved the use of a fully mixed concurrent dominant status design and a mixed sampling design that involved a combination of concurrent, identical, sequential, nested, and multilevel sampling.'

Instructors from eight institutions teaching mixed research courses were selected by case sampling. Doctoral students enrolled in mixed research provided by one of the instructors based on quantitative (number of research methodology courses taken) and quantitative (mixed methodological dissertation research proposals and reflective research journals). A three-dimensional model for categorizing and organizing pedagogical approaches used in mixed research courses emerged. The findings were, as reported by Onwuegbuzie et al. (2011), students who had prior research methodology courses excelled in presenting quality mixed methodological dissertation research proposals. The majority of students (91.7 per cent) reported a positive experience related to the mixed method research study.

## Web Ethnography and Case Study Research

Ethnography versus Case Study Research, as noted by White, Drew and Hay (2009), questioned why research is framed as a series of case studies rather than ethnography. This inquiry further led to the approaches to data collection, analysis and truth claims. Prior and Miller (2012) report traditional ethnography focuses on identifiable cultural groupings of individuals. This chapter, with focus on the oil and gas industry personnel, engages in a process of observation and participant interviews. Student researchers explore the effects of the social dynamic with the industry. Some of the data-gathering techniques may involve electronic methods. Conceivable to envision some or all of the data-gathering techniques may involve electronic techniques. Student researchers in the area of the study residing in the Middle East can take on the observation contact processes.

Web ethnography (also known as netnography, webnography, online ethnography and virtual ethnography) involves the application of ethnographic **research** methods to specific online communities through the observation and analysis of online dialogue. Caution is noted that web ethnography is appropriate only where interactions between group members occur online through the virtual community (White, Drew and Hay, 2009). Web ethnography is not appropriate where the majority of interaction of the organisational personnel is conducted offline. Differing online cultural groups warrants caution in the design of ethnographic studies (Prior and Miller, 2012).

Ethnography has the distinction of conducting research on-site into the daily observations of the cultural group under study. In this naturalistic setting data can be collected over an extended period of time. The process is inductive and a long-term commitment is required (Biklen, 2011).

The online ethnography approach was developed in the study reflected in Decision Analyst (2012) and provides the framework to accommodate the goals imbedded in the online qualitative methodology. Extending the culture considerations as we have described earlier with ethnic and religious concerns, the habitual activities are not upset. Online self-paced entries into a recounting of activities will provide the qualitative depth accounts of exclusive and collective assessments. The opportunity for photos as optional to highlight work-sites is also an instrument that can enhance clarity in definition.

This method of open expression can easily become a safe method of transmitting long-held and sheltered opinions. Care needs to be assured that the participants will be comfortable with the questions and format of the Inquisitions. This Online Forum needs care in developing to gather carefully the detailed responses and comments from the variety of participants. This Online Panel approach will allow for special subsets (such as technology companies, government entities, displaced residents, logistics companies and project managers), all identified as uniquely interesting via the online quantitative survey as first-hand concept acceptors and observers. The methodology employing online ethnography will realise the value and in-depth analysis of respondents at virtually all levels in concert with the behaviour that compliments their decisions.

## Tips and Exercises

### TIPS FOR STUDENTS

- Identify the target countries for the study. Get familiar with the variety of cultures, oil and gas industry companies operating in those select regions.
- Review the features of case study, qualitative, ethnography and mixed method research techniques to accommodate the oil and gas industry in the regions selected.
- Throughout the research process retain the elements of the PMM model. Specific to the oil and gas exploration industry, it is important to recall the contributions of the targeted countries.

### TIPS FOR SUPERVISORS

- Ensure the student research team members are thoroughly cognizant of the cultures that are expected to respond to the surveys.
- Develop concepts for identification of target organizations and participants within.
- Engage teams of student researchers to identify the Middle Eastern countries for the study.

- Revisit and amplify the complexity and challenges inherent in the oil and gas exploration industries.

## EXERCISES

1. Describe the approach and processes anticipated to develop the research strategy to address the complexities in the oil and gas exploration operations in the Middle East with your selected regions.
2. Explain the meaning and value of ethnographic studies within the framework of qualitative case study research. How will this be used in your study?
3. Discuss critical features of your research and the steps involved to address complexity theories of culture and political sensitivity.
4. Describe how you intend to use the case study and mixed method research to accomplish your goals in this study. Address areas of concern that you anticipate.

# References

Bartholomew, T. T. and Brown, J. R. (2012). Mixed Methods, Culture and Psychology: A Review of Mixed Methods in Culture-Specific Psychological Research. *International Perspectives in Psychology*, 1(3), 177–190.

Biklen, D. P. (2011). Research that Matters: Qualitative Research in the Service of Social Transformation. *Journal of Ethnographic & Qualitative Research*, 6(1), 1–13.

Decision Analyst (2012). Online Ethnographic Marketing Research. Retrieved October 4 2012 from: http://www.decisionanalyst.com/Service/Ethnography.dai?=CPC9zqXh471CFcKPPAodRHkA_A.http://www.decisionanalyst.com/Services/ethnography.dai

Demir, C. and Kocabas, I. (2010). Project Management Maturity Model (PMMM) in Educational Organizations. Procedia. *Social and Behavioral Sciences*, 9, 1641–1645. DOI: 10.1016/j.sbspro.2010.12.379.

Global Connections: The Middle East. (2013). Culture a Rich Mosaic. Retrieved 9 September 2012 from: http://www.pbs.org/wgbh/globalconnections/mideast/themes/culture/index.html. Accessed: 9 Sept 2012.

Killen, C. and Hunt, R. A. (2013). Robust Project Portfolio Management: Capability Evolution and Maturity. *International Journal of Managing Projects in Business*, 6(1), 131–151.

Lilleker, D. G. (2003). Interviewing the Political Elite: Navigating a Potential Minefield. *Politics*, 23(3), 207–215.

Lopez-Fernandez, O. and Molina-Azorin, J. F. (2011). The Use of Mixed Methods Research in Interdisciplinary Educational Journals. *International Journal of Multiple Research Approaches*, 5(2), 269–283.

Morse, J. M. and Mitcham, C. (2002). Exploring Qualitatively-derived Concepts: Inductive–Deductive Pitfalls. *International Journal of Qualitative Methods*, 1(4), 1–18.

Onwuegbuzie, A. J., Frels, R. K., Leech, N. L. and Collins, K. M.T (2011). A Mixed Research Study of Pedagogical Approaches Student Learning in Doctoral-level Mixed Research Courses. *International Journal of Multiple Research Approaches*, 5(2), 169–199.

Pasian, B., Sankaran, S. and Boydell, S. (2012). Project Management Maturity: A Critical Analysis of Existing and Emergent Factors. *International Journal of Managing Projects in Business*, 5(1), 146–157.

Pfeffer, C. and Rogalin, C.L. (2012). Three Strategies for Teaching Research Methods: A Case Study. *Teaching Sociology*, 40(4), 368–376.

Prior, D. and Miller, L. (2012). Webethnography. *International Journal of Market Research*, 54(4), 503–520.

Radlay, A. and Chamberlain, K. (2012). The Study of the Case: Conceptualizing Case Study Research. *Journal of Community & Applied Social Psychology*, 22(5), 390–399.

Rebeiro, K. and Moll, S. (2012). Navigating Political Minefields: Partnerships in Organizational Case Study Research. *Work*, 43(1), 5–12.

Roberts, A., Kelsey, J., Smyth, H. and Wilson, A. (2012). Health and Safety Maturity in Project Business Cultures. *International Journal of Managing Projects in Business*, 5(4), 776–803.

Sheldon, G. (2012). A Primer of Middle Eastern Leadership Culture. *Journal of Strategic Security*, 5(4), 99–117.

Terrell, S. R. (2012). Mixed Methods Research Methodologies. *Qualitative Report*, 17(1), 254–280.

Thamhaim, H. (2013) Managing Risks in Complex Projects. *Project Management Journal*, 44(2), 20–35.

Toshihiro, I., Masakazu, O., Kota, I. and Kazuhiko, K. (2012). Analysis of a Knowledge-Management-Based Process of Transferring Project Management Skills. *Campus-Wide Information Systems*, 29(4), 251–258.

White, J., Drew, S. and Hay, T. (2009). Ethnography versus Case Study: Positioning Research and Researchers. *Qualitative Research*, 9(1), 18–27.

## Suggested Reading

Barratt, M., Choi, T.Y. and Mei, L. (2010), Qualitative Case Studies in Operations Management: Trends, Research Outcomes, and Future Research Implications. *Journal of Operations Management*, 29(4), 329–342.

Barth, M. and Thomas, I. (2012). Synthesizing Case-Study Research – Ready for the Next Step? *Environmental Education Research*, 18(6), 751–764.

Baxter, P. and Jack, S. (2008). Qualitative Case Study Methodology: Study Design and Implementation for Novice Researchers. *The Qualitative Report*, 13(4), 544–559.

Cameron, R. (2009). A Sequential Mixed Model Research Design: Design, Analytical and Display Issues. *International Journal of Multiple Research Approaches*, 3(2), 140–152.

Christ, T.W. 2013. The Worldview Matrix as a Strategy when Designing Mixed Methods Research. *International Journal of Multiple Research Approaches*, 7(1), 110–118.

Eto, S. and Kyngas, H. (2008). The Qualitative Content Analysis Process. *Journal of Advanced Nursing*, 62(1), 107–115.

Greaves, S. (2012). A Primer of Middle Eastern Leadership Culture. *Journal of Strategic Security*, 5(4), 85–99.

Hara, K., Uwasu, M. and Kurimoto, S. (2013). Mapping Research Activities and Technologies for Sustainability and Environmental Studies – A Case Study at University Level. *Journal of Environmental Studies and Sciences*, 3(1), 42–48.

Heit, E. R. and Caren, M. (2010). Relations between Inductive Reasoning and Deductive Reasoning. *Journal of Experimental Psychology*, 36(3), 805–812.

Heng-Yu, K., Lahman, M. K. E., Hsin-Te, Y.. and Yi-Chia, C. (2008). Into the Academy: Preparing and Mentoring International Doctoral Students. *Educational Technology Research & Development*, 56(3), 365–377.

Hitchcock, J. H., Nastasi, B. K. and Summerville, M. (2010). Single Case Designs and Qualitative Methods: Applying a Mixed Methods Research Perspective. *Mid-Western Educational Researcher*, 23(2), 49–58.

Houghton, C. E., Casey, D., Shaw., D. and Murphy, K. (2010). Ethical Challenges in Qualitative Research: Examples from Practice. *Nurse Researcher*, 18(1), 15–25.

Houghton, C. E., Casey, D., Shaw, D. and Murphy, K. (2013). Rigor in Qualitative Case-Study Research. *Nurse Researcher*, 20(4), 12–17.

Hynes, G. E. (2012). Improving Employees' Interpersonal Communication Competencies: A Qualitative Study. *Business Communication Quarterly*, 75(4), 466–475.

Iwakabe, S. and Gazzola, N. (2009). From Single Case Studies to Practice Based Knowledge: Aggregating and Synthesizing Case Studies. *Psychotherapy Research*, 19(4/5), 601–611.

Jackson, L. L., Campbell, N. S. and Horvath, B. (2013). Is No Upgrade a Downgrade? *Journal of the International Academy for Case Studies*, 19(3), 45–50.

Lee, B. and Cassell, C. (2013). Research Methods and Research Practice: History, Themes and Topics. *International Journal of Management Reviews*, 15(2), 123–131.

Marais, H. (2012). A Multi-Methodological Framework for the Design and Evaluation of Complex Research Projects and Reports in Business and Management Studies. *Electronic Journal of Business Research Methods*, 10(2), 64–76.

Miller, P. J. and Cameron, R. (2011). Mixed Method Research Designs: A Case Study of Their Adoption in a Doctor of Business Administration Program. *International Journal of Multiple Research Approaches*, 5(3), 387–402.

Rose, W. R. and Cray, D. (2013). Validating and Enhancing a Strategy Transformation Model Using Case Study. *Global Business & Management*, 5(1), 32–53.

Salehi, K. and Golafshani, N. (2010). Commentary: Using Mixed Methods in Research Studies – An Opportunity with its Challenges. *International Journal of Multiple Research Approaches*, 4(3), 186–191.

Sangasubana, N. (2011). How to Conduct Ethnographic Research. *Qualitative Report*, 16(2), 567–573.

Shannon, P., Kim, W. and Robinson, A. (2012). Implementing a Service Learning Model for Teaching Research Methods and Program Evaluation. *Journal of Teaching in Social Work*, 32(3), 229–242.

Sharp, J. L. Mobley, C. and Hammond, C. 2012. A Mixed Methods Sampling Methodology for a Multisite Case Study. *Journal of Mixed Methods Research*, 6(1), 34–54.

Shurden, M., Shurden, S. and Cagwin, D., (2008). A Comparative Study of Ethical Values of Business Students: American vs Middle Eastern Cultures. *Journal of College Teaching & Learning*, 5(8), 27–34.

Snyder, C. (2012). A Case Study of a Case Study: Analysis of a Robust Qualitative Research Methodology. *Qualitative Report*, 17(26), 1–21.

Taber, K. S. (2012). Prioritizing Paradigms, Mixing Methods, and Characterizing the 'Qualitative' in Educational Research. *Teacher Development*, 16(1), 125–138.

Unluer, S. (2012). Being an Insider Researcher while Conducting Case Study Research. *Qualitative Report*, 17(58), 1–14.

Valter, K. and Akerlind, G. (2010). Introducing Students to Ways of Thinking and Acting Like a Researcher: A Case Study of Research-Led Education in the Sciences. *International Journal of Teaching and Learning in Higher Education*, 22(1) 89–97.

Vissak, T. (2010). Recommendations for Using the Case Study Method in International Business Research. *Qualitative Report*, 15(2), 370–388.

Webber, M., Lunch, S. and Oluku, J. (2013). Enhancing Student Engagement in Student Experience Surveys: A Mixed Methods Study. *Educational Research*, 55(1), 71–86.

Welch, C., Piekkari, R., Plakoyiannaki, E. and Paavilainen-Mantymaki, E. (2011). Theorising from Case Studies: Towards a Pluralist Future for International Business Research. *Journal of International Business Studies*, 42(5), 740–762.

Zivkovic, J. (2012). Strengths and Weaknesses of Business Research Methodologies: Two Disparate Case Studies. *Business Studies Journal*, 4(2), 91–99.

# PART VI
# WRITING AS A
# FUTURE RESEARCHER

Anticipating future needs of book readers is always an immediate challenge for any book writer (or editor). When considering IT or systems, these challenges can become especially difficult. Knowing that the reading of this book would start in 2015, I asked colleagues for examples of how PM research could be enabled by IT. These chapters are their responses.

What I find especially interesting – and this is an indication of the exceptional talents of these academics – is that the issues they raise were done several months ago (with specific case details being added later). I know that the information in these chapters will be helpful to researchers, but I hope even more that the anticipatory nature of their authors will inspire them.

- Gibbons and Zolin discuss how social network analysis can be valuable as a research tool to understand how work processes contribute to projects as they become larger and more complex. They provide details on how you can determine if social network analysis can help answer research questions.
- Williams, Ferdinand and Croft also look at social network analysis to examine stakeholder interaction and the impact of that on project success. A community event is used as an example.
- Richardson describes the value of ePortfolios as an enabler for PM researchers and a strategic tool for both supervisors and candidates. Many details are provided for readers to consider in the development of their own tool.

# 32

# Studying Relationships in Project Management Through Social Network Analysis

Deborah E. Gibbons and Roxanne Zolin

*Network studies can be both challenging and rewarding. We hope that this chapter reduces some of the initial challenges and helps readers to find the rewards from conducting their own network research.*

Successful project management depends upon forming and maintaining relationships between and among project team members and stakeholder groups. The nature of these relationships and the patterns that they form affect communication, collaboration and resource flows. Networks affect us directly, and we use them to influence people and processes. Social Network Analysis (SNA) can be an extremely valuable research tool to better understand how critical social networks develop and influence work processes, particularly as projects become larger and more complex. This chapter introduces foundational network concepts, helps you determine if SNA could help you answer your research questions, and explains how to design and implement a social network study.

At the end of this chapter, the reader can:

- understand foundational concepts about social networks;
- decide if SNA is an appropriate research methodology to address particular questions or problems;
- design and implement a basic social network study.

Keywords: social networks, network study design, collection of network data, network analysis methods

Networks affect nearly everything that we do, from buying a sandwich to coordinating an engineering project, and networks affect us. The opinions that our colleagues share, the films that our friends watch and the foods that our family eats help shape our preferences and behaviours. The patterns of relationships around us help shape our career opportunities, and the networks of ties among co-workers and coordinators help shape the quality and timeliness of complex projects. Increasing use of the Internet and social media applications is making social networks even more visible and relevant. Better understanding of these networks and how they work can help project managers become more successful. If you believe that, 'it's not just what you know, but who you know,' you will realise that understanding social networks is important for project managers.

For a researcher, analysis of networks that are directly or indirectly related to PM may yield practical and theoretical insights that are not discoverable through other means, but getting started in network analysis can be daunting. Social network studies look beyond individual attributes that can be analysed using traditional multivariate methods, and they look beyond direct relationships between pairs of actors. Social network studies can be extremely broad yet detailed, as they examine systems of interrelated entities, concepts and activities. They consider the placement of the actors in the larger social network and the structure of the network itself.

Social network data collection can be difficult, and analyses must avoid reliance on standard statistical assumptions. Unique analysis methods have been developed over decades to accommodate the cross-level and interdependent nature of the data. For a novice, network analysis methods may be as confusing as the results are (potentially) enlightening.

In this chapter, you will become familiar with distinct types of social relations and the kinds of influences that they often have. We will introduce you to basic techniques for measuring networks among people, projects and organisations. We will discuss methods for recording network data, identify some common types of network statistics and compare graphs of a network that is shown from various points of view. You will not come out the other side as an expert, but you will be equipped to assess the value of applying network analysis to your research question(s), and you will know the general steps that are required to do it appropriately.

## Understanding Social Networks

Social network studies integrate socio-psychological theories with mathematical analytic methods to yield insights about relationships, the patterns they form when aggregated, and the effects they have on participants and the world around them. Sociologists have used network graphs and analysis methods to represent and quantify patterns of relationships among people for decades, but broad use of SNA in organisational studies began to flourish around the year 2000. Because social networks are ubiquitous and influential, network analysis has become popular for assessing patterns of relationships and their effects. To be successful, social network studies require careful planning prior to data collection, and they require careful analysis using statistical methods that have been designed to accommodate the unique properties of network data.

Figure 32.1 shows the network of resource-sharing ties among members of public health programmes within one of the United States. Each circle represents a person, and each line represents a relationship that includes moderate-to-extensive sharing of resources. We will refer to this network graph as we continue through the chapter.

Both qualitative and quantitative information can be used to represent a network of relationships, generally by identifying attributes of each relationship within the network, and aggregating them. Quantitative values can then be assigned to dyadic relationships, to positions of actors within the networks, and to the networks themselves. After a network has been quantified, many measurements can be taken to characterise its structure and the positions of people within that structure. In addition, relations between the network structure and other variables of interest may be tested. Graphs of the networks, often coloured to highlight attributes of members or their relationships, can provide clear visual representations of system-wide patterns.

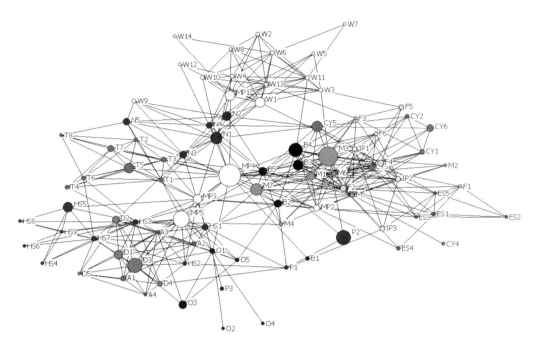

**Figure 32.1**  **Network of resource-sharing relationships in a public health department**

## Types and Levels of Social Networks

Relationships of all types can be studied using SNA, including those that occur among members of a PM team, contractors and subcontractors, competing or collaborating groups, and community or governmental organisations, in fact any stakeholder organisations. You may be most familiar with social networks composed of friends or colleagues, but we can also use network analysis methods to study relationships among concepts, tasks and places, or to map and analyse the structures that enable information or goods to move from one point to another.

Data may be collected and analyses may be conducted at many levels because our basic unit of analysis can be individuals, groups, organisations, nations or even coalitions of nations. These units interact within multidimensional systems, which may be defined as collections of individuals and organisations operating within definable boundaries, wherein they contribute or receive resources. Network theory and analysis give attention to systems within systems, acknowledging that the perspective we take and our location within a system will affect the view that we see. Available analytical methods can help us find and explore distinct effects that occur at various levels of aggregation in a system.

At each level of aggregation in a system, we can address dyadic, group or structurally defined relationships. Dyadic data represent the relationships between pairs of entities (called dyads). The entities are frequently people, and their relationships may commonly include friendship, co-worker status, advisory relations or competition. Dyadic data can also be collected on non-human entities, such as partnerships between hospitals, resource dependencies between government agencies and contractors, or information-sharing between consortium members. Groupwise data represent common membership or identity in a clearly defined collective, such as a project team, a professional association or a particular organisation. Sometimes groupwise data may also be defined by adversarial memberships or identities, such as opponents of a particular group, which may be relevant if you wish to study adversarial stakeholder organisations. Groupwise data can be collected for groups of people, groups of organisations, groups of nations or any other collective.

Structurally defined relations are created among entities by the system in which they are embedded, not by the direct relationship between them. For example, two people who play the same role in an organisation are similar along some dimensions within that system, and two teams that work for the same project manager occupy similar positions in the organisational network for that project. To the extent that two entities occupy similar positions within a network, they are likely to have many of the same advantages and disadvantages. If they are aware of each other, their similarity may lead them to bond or to compete. Structurally defined relations can arise as two entities play the same or complementary roles, collaborate with the same or similar co-workers, complete the same kinds of tasks, or spend their leisure time with the same or similar friends. Two entities may occupy similar positions in one type of network, but not in another. Imagine an accountant and an engineer who have the same friends but work for different organisations. They are structurally similar in their friendship network, but not in their professional networks.

## Consequences of Social Networks

Social networks form channels for transmission of ideas, attitudes and resources among members. People obtain emotional and material support through their ties to others, and organisations find partners, customers and opportunities through theirs. Both the nature (for example, collaboration, advice-sharing, trust) and structure (for example, density, clustering, centralisation) of a network can impact associated individuals, groups and organisations, often in important or dramatic ways. Social networks can:

*   influence self-efficacy and motivation;
*   alter career paths;
*   create commitment and improve group performance;
*   instill and change professional values;
*   diffuse resources, ideas, and practices;
*   promote norm-setting;
*   enforce ethical interactions;
*   develop social capital;
*   support innovation;
*   foster organisational adaptation;
*   enhance organisational survival.

Effects of social networks are sometimes overlooked. The fundamental attribution error is our tendency to overestimate the influence of personal factors when explaining behaviour, and to underestimate the influence of contextual or environmental factors (Ross, 1977; Ross and Nesbit, 1991). Hence the study of social networks within context can have important implications for project managers and researchers. Alongside the nature and structure of the network, population characteristics and requirements of a project are likely to have strong effects on work processes and outcomes. Structures that support some activities may inhibit others, so network studies must be tailored to address the information and activities that are most relevant to the setting and the research questions. For example, the appropriate balance of within- to between-group ties depends on the task, so field research is needed to determine which conditions demand more or less direct connection, and to understand how the optimal pattern of connections may change through the life of a project. It is usually safe to assume that networks are having some effect on processes within and among groups and organisations, but we need a well-designed study to discover the nature, timing, and cause(s) of that effect.

## Designing a Network Study

Your first task in designing a study of social networks in PM is to identify a few interesting and important research questions. If you have had experience with PM, you may have observed processes that were affected by social networks, or perhaps you observed glitches that might have been avoided if communication or collaboration had been better. Do any of these observations raise questions about how or why the project unfolded as it did? If you have read others' accounts of positive or negative experiences with project work, perhaps you wondered about formal versus informal channels for resource-sharing, cooperation, or problem-solving. Did you see glimpses of network effects that might deserve a closer look? Can you identify the kinds of relationships or patterns of interaction that seemed to be useful, detrimental or missing? Are the roles of some kinds of networks or patterns of interaction unknown? Have the roles of other kinds of networks or patterns of interaction been identified but not explained? When crafting your research question(s), try to specify the types of relationships (information, trust, resource-sharing and so on), unit(s) of analysis (people within groups, ties among groups and so on), and particular processes (communication, coordination, resource-sharing and so on) that could be important.

## Fine-Tuning Your Research Questions

Your research questions must be novel, and they should pertain to a process or linkage that has the potential to affect real organisations or people. For example, you might ask how, when or why particular network structures affect different aspects of project completion. Focusing on individuals within social networks, you might ask whether and how specific aspects of individuals' networking patterns help them and their group to work more effectively or efficiently. Questions that address changing relationships, network growth or effects of the networks over time could lead to especially insightful research outcomes.

## Finding Your Opportunity to Contribute to Theory and Practice

When you have a short list of questions that interest you, the next step is to conduct a thorough search to determine which aspects of your research terrain have been addressed by other researchers. Think about their work as a panorama of insights, and try to fit your ideas into that scene. Do you see places where nobody has addressed your questions, or where someone has found an effect without explaining how or why it happens? These are your opportunities to contribute to theory and practice in PM.

## Deciding if a Network Study is Appropriate for Your Research Questions

Social network studies are appropriate to address questions that involve patterns of relationships, resource flows or communication. Research questions about individuals' attitudes or behaviours towards others do not require a network study; for these questions, you can probably use more traditional (and easier) methods. Research questions about individuals' positions within a set of relationships, about patterns of relationships, about interactions between individual and relational factors, or about system-wide interactions are excellent candidates for a network study. Before jumping into a network study, you might benefit from reading a book that summarises a variety of prior studies. Kilduff and Krackhardt (2008) integrated social and individual views of organisational processes to yield insights about cognitive and behavioural phenomena as they interact and evolve with interpersonal networks in organisations. We recommend their book as an introduction to several perspectives on the convergence of individual factors and networks in organisations.

SNA is complicated by the relatedness of the data. For example, if Alice knows Bob and Bob knows Charlie, there is a greater than random probability that Alice knows Charlie. Because the data are not independent, we cannot use statistical methods that assume independence between datapoints. If you intend to conduct a network study, you will need to learn new approaches for data analysis. Several excellent books are available on this topic, including the long-standing go-to reference by Wasserman and Faust (1994). Hanneman and Riddle (2005) have produced a very useful introductory guide to network methods, which is available free of charge from Hanneman's website. We strongly recommend that you read Hanneman and Riddle's book before trying to design a network study. You might also browse the available analysis packages, watching for a good balance between user-friendliness and analytical power.

## Approaches to Network Research

We recommend three approaches to network research that are best done in combination: qualitative, quantitative and network graphing. Qualitative inquiry seeks to understand the actions, attitudes and causal relations from the perspectives of participants and observers, but it lacks statistical validity. Quantitative analysis seeks to identify exact patterns of interaction and to test causal relationships between network attributes and project processes or outcomes. Quantitative analysis delivers precise statistics and supports hypothesis-testing, but it often cannot explain why the observed relationships exist. Network graphing integrates qualitative and quantitative information into visually expressive pictures that enable viewers to quickly understand key attributes of the participants, their relationships and measures of interest. All of these approaches complement each other, and a few qualitative insights can go far towards explaining quantitative results.

To obtain a general understanding of the networks and participants' thoughts about them, you might begin with qualitative inquiry. This could include observations of the way people interact, unstructured interviews that allow people to steer the conversation, or focus groups that discuss the roles of networks in supporting or damaging the project work. Useful qualitative inquiry could also include examination of organisational documents or participation in a work team. An investment in qualitative research as you are formulating your study can help you explore concepts and refine the questions that you hope to answer. Investment in qualitative research alongside or after your quantitative analysis can help you explain how and why your statistical results have occurred.

Quantitative analysis of network effects depends on collection of precise data about the participants, their relationships and the processes or outcomes of interest. The core data most often come from surveys, but sometimes it is more useful or more practical to obtain network data by tracking email, web postings, phone calls or other direct, objective measures of actual interactions. Supplemental data may also need to be obtained from organisational records. Because the success of a network study depends on accurate representation of an entire set of relationships, it is important to correctly define the boundaries of the system you will be studying, and to realistically assess the likelihood that you can convince the majority of people within that system to participate in a survey. Ideally, when measuring a social network, we would like to obtain a response from every member, but realistically, we hope to obtain responses from at least 80 per cent of the people in each group that composes the network. Results of a quantitative network analysis include descriptive, correlational and predictive statistics about attributes of the network and individual, group-level or system-wide outcomes.

Network graphs can provide informative, sometimes dramatic, overviews of the relationships and attributes within a social system. By highlighting issues of interest, whether causes or effects of the network structure, a good network graph can reveal complex relationships to nearly any audience. Network graphs enable visual comparisons of selected subsets of the network, and they allow scrutiny of distinct portions or attributes of the social system.

## Data Collection Strategies

Network studies measure aspects of individual entities, groups, teams or clusters, and aggregate those measures to understand complete systems. In general, our goal is to measure all of the relationships in the network, not to obtain samples from various strata or roles. This distinguishes network studies from other kinds of organisational research that can be accomplished with participation from a smaller percentage of the entities within a system.

Some research questions may be addressed using records of contracts, cooperative agreements, financial statements, email streams, or project reports as source data for constructing the relevant networks. If you cannot answer your research questions using these or other non-human data sources, you probably need to ask people about their interactions and relationships. The most common and cost-effective approach is to develop an electronic survey that captures each person's responses directly. If you are surveying people who do not have private access to computers at work, you might use paper surveys for the sake of confidentiality, but this increases the processing time and expense.

To measure entire networks, a researcher needs strong support from leaders and full participation by the majority of people within the system. A clear explanation of the goals and methods of the study, as well as the types of information that will be reported, can help you recruit the necessary support and participation. It is especially important to decide in advance how you will report the attributes and identities of the participants. Studies of networks among groups, project teams, departments or organisations sometimes name the groups or organisations in the final reports, but studies that map personal relationships among individual people should usually be designed to protect participants' confidentiality. This can be challenging in a network study because the researcher must know the identities of all respondents in order to locate them in the overall network. Thus, participants in a network study can be given confidentiality, but not anonymity. This distinction is important to make clear to participants when you invite them to join the study, and it is important that you, as the researcher, take adequate steps to replace personal identifiers with generic labels before you begin to analyse the data.

The decision about what kinds of labels to use should be made during the planning stage, and it should be shared with potential participants before they are asked to complete a survey or interview. For example in the study that produced Figure 32.1, participants were identified by labels that indicated their programme membership. People knew before completing the survey that their responses would be included in graphs that show the patterns of relationships within and among programmes in their state, and they knew that their names would never appear in any report.

Network surveys tend to be long because each person is asked to report his or her relationship, possibly along multiple dimensions, with many other people. When measuring organisational networks, then, we want to encourage everyone to participate by streamlining the process for them. If possible, without compromising the quality of your study, measure your non-network variables with short scales to limit the number of questions each person must answer. Talk to project leaders about what they want to know, and find ways to make the results of the study valuable for them. Tell participants how the results will be used. If feasible, offer incentives, such as free food, a map of the network or insights for respondents about themselves and their organisation(s).

When personal identities are hidden, you can allow each participant to obtain his or her ID number directly from you. This lets them find their own position in the network graphs that you include in your report, so it is a fairly easy way to give feedback to each participant. You may also let each participant use the survey to provide feedback to you and to co-workers. If you think that network members would like to express their thoughts confidentially, build some open questions into the survey to allow for this. Then aggregate the comments, without any identifiers, and include them with your report. People who might not be willing to complete a lengthy network survey to help a researcher will often complete a slightly longer survey that gives them a voice among their co-workers.

Large networks or networks with unknown membership present unique data challenges. If the network that you want to understand is very large, you may need to parse it into smaller groups. For example, you might ask people about all of their relationships with immediate co-workers, and then ask them to report their main relationships with people outside their group. If the network is very large, you might analyse the networks within a few exemplary groups or you might drop the individual level of analysis and focus on the network among groups. For very large systems where it would not be practical or necessary to map the entire network, you might consider measuring the immediate networks around a sample of key entities. All of these decisions depend on your research question(s), but regardless of the level of analysis, you will need to convert your survey results into matrices that represent your networks.

## Data Management and Analysis

Network data files can be large and confusing, so you will benefit if you develop a logical system for coding data and labelling variables. Plan your data management in advance, map out the steps and keep careful records. Because network data are aggregated from all participants' responses, there is a lot of clerical work, and it is easy to make mistakes. Double-check at each step, before a small error has a chance to become a large problem.

### CONVERTING SURVEY RESULTS INTO NETWORK MATRICES

If you can identify relationships among people, groups or tasks, you can build a network matrix. For example, if Lee obtains support for a project from Pat, Pat obtains support from Lee, and Kim obtains support from both Lee and Pat, we could represent those relationships using zeros and ones as shown in Table 32.1. Notice that the person named on the row is always the sender of the relationship, the focal person. In this case, the row person obtains support from the column person. This orientation is standard practice in network research: each row holds data about the row-person's perceptions, actions, dependencies or feelings towards the people named at the top of each column. When you have recorded everyone's relationships, row by row, you have created a network matrix.

**Table 32.1**  **Network matrix in which row-person obtains project support from column-person**

| | | Alter | | |
|---|---|---|---|---|
| | Row obtains support | Lee | Pat | Kim |
| Ego | Lee | X | 1 | 0 |
| | Pat | 1 | X | 0 |
| | Kim | 1 | 1 | X |

If the relationship that you are studying involves multiple levels of interaction, extents of resource-sharing, or anything else that has amounts or strengths, you can represent the intensity of the relationship in a similar matrix. For example, you might ask in a survey, 'How much do you rely on each person listed below for support on Project A?' Given options of none, minimally, moderately or extensively, we could create a matrix that contains values from zero to three (Table 32.2). If Lee relies extensively on Pat for support, Pat relies minimally on Lee, and Kim relies moderately on both Lee and Pat, we could aggregate that information in the following matrix.

**Table 32.2**  **Network matrix showing intensity of relationships**

| Row obtains support | Lee | Pat | Kim |
|---|---|---|---|
| Lee | X | 3 | 0 |
| Pat | 1 | X | 0 |
| Kim | 2 | 2 | X |

## WORKING FROM A NETWORK MATRIX TO CREATE A GRAPH

We usually show directed relations between people by drawing arrows from each focal person, sometimes referred to as 'Ego,' to the receiver(s) of the relation, sometimes referred to as 'Alter(s)'. The same approach is used to graph relations between other kinds of entities, so once you learn to graph a network of people, you can use the same methods to graph other networks. Network matrices can be translated directly into network graphs (also called sociograms) by placing lines or arrows between all pairs of entities that have a relationship. The thickness of these lines can show the intensity of each relationship, and colouring is sometimes used to indicate the nature (for example, friendship, information-sharing, collaboration) of the relationship. When we graph weighted network data, we need to make some judgments about which relation(s) to show and how to represent the weightings (Figure 32.2). For example, if we want to graph the 'project support' relationships among Lee, Pat and Kim, we have at least three options, as follows. Unweighted, weighted in each direction and average-weighted relations.

If the presence or absence of a relationship is key, we can use unweighted arrows to show the directed ties. This approach allows us to focus on the pattern of ties or clustering of entities within the network. If the intensity of each person's participation in a relationship is key, we may want to use separate arrows that are weighted in each direction. Finally, if the overall extent of a relationship is key, we may average the relationship intensities from Ego to Alter and from Alter to Ego, and weight our arrows to indicate this average. Additional approaches, which may be appropriate under some circumstances, include using the minimum or the maximum value that

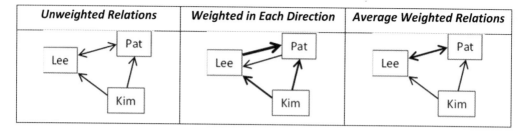

**Figure 32.2**    **Unweighted, weighted in each direction and average-weighted relations**

participants reported for each relationship. These decisions should be driven by the theory and practical concerns that you are trying to address.

## ANALYSING NETWORK DATA

Network analysis will probably seem difficult at first because of the heavy math and enormous variety of analytical possibilities. Network data require distinct analysis methods that do not rely on the assumptions that are common to standard statistics. Because of this, we recommend that you read an introduction to network analysis methods before you begin processing your data. Several non-parametric methods have been developed that enable us to calculate correlations among network variables and to test hypotheses about cause and effect. You may also need to calculate baseline measures about your network(s), including some indicators of members' centralities and clustering patterns, and additional measures that specifically address your research questions. Several software packages, such as UCINET (Borgatti, Everett and Freeman, 2002), are available to analyse network data, so you will not need to become a statistician to conduct a network study. You will, however, need to become familiar with the network analysis methods that are required for your study, and you should know how the software is calculating your network measures so that you can interpret the results correctly.

Depending on your research question(s), you may test hypotheses about individual attributes and network measures at the individual or network level. If your research questions pertain to individuals, you can extract the individuals' network measurements (for example, how central each entity is) and use them in traditional statistical analyses. If your research questions pertain to relationships or network attributes, you can convert individuals' statistics into pairwise measures (for example, difference in scores between both entities, or similarity or dissimilarity on particular attributes) and use them in network-based analyses.

## Reporting Activities

As with any research, you should explain how you collected your data, describe key attributes of the participants and context, and if you use a survey or interviews, report the questions that you asked. If you ask questions that are intended to converge around single concepts, you will outline the process that you used to combine responses into scales or indices, and report standard reliability statistics.

Many of your readers will not be familiar with network studies, so it will be valuable to explain how the relationship data in your study were aggregated to build network matrices. Explain any weightings on the intensity of relations, and tell the readers how you converted those weightings into numbers. Outline your statistical methods and state clearly which statistics pertain to individuals and which pertain to pairs, groups or whole networks. Finally, use audience-friendly tables to report the descriptive statistics and results of hypothesis tests.

## Designing Network Graphs that Make Your Results Stand Out for Readers

You can make the key findings of your network study more accessible to readers with creative graphs. For example, the people represented in Figure 32.1 had previously been asked to increase collaboration among programmes. This graph helps them to see the pattern of resource-sharing among programmes, and to identify the programmes that are not adequately integrated into the system. In this graph, the colour and label of each circle tell us which programme the person works in, such that the colouring enables us to quickly spot members of the same programme, but when the graph is printed in black and white, the label is available to help discern among shades of grey. The size of each circle shows the extent to which each person occupies a gatekeeping position within this network, such that larger circles denote people whose positions give them greater ability to act as resource bridges between others. By presenting these individual, relational and network-level data together, we have summarised key results in a single graph that readers can readily understand. Alongside our textual explanation, the graph increases our ability to communicate key attributes of the network.

Care must be taken in the way a network is positioned on a page, because the orientation of the graph can change the perceptions of the viewer. For example, in Figure 32.1 it is clear that subgroups exist within the network. If the network were placed in a different orientation on the page, those subgroups may not be as clearly visible. For this reason, it is a good idea to work iteratively between your graphs and your statistics, making sure that insights that appear in the graphs are supported by statistical tests, and that statistical findings are appropriately revealed in the graphs. As a network researcher, your task is to discover which aspects of the individuals and structure are relevant to important issues, and to make that information accessible to readers. An informative graph enables readers to discover the results in an intuitive and fun format, and it makes your work more memorable and potentially more valuable to people who read your report.

## Conclusion

Stakeholder relationships are increasingly recognised as critical to success in PM. SNA methods allow you to investigate effects of project network structures on individual, team, organisational, and project processes and outcomes.

This chapter has presented foundational concepts about social networks and provided some guidelines to help you design and implement a basic social network study. By using the techniques that we have outlined in this chapter, you can begin to explore systems of relationships and their consequences. With careful, step-by-step analysis of network data, you will be able to expand your perspectives and discover interesting and potentially important information about the interactions between social factors and project performance.

## Tips and Exercises

### TIPS FOR STUDENTS

- Before launching a network study, we suggest that you conduct some mini-studies of your own project relationships and network(s), and that you define the variables that you must measure to address your most interesting research question(s).
- Try to specify the types of relationships (information, trust, resource-sharing and so on), unit(s) of analysis (people within groups, ties among groups and so on), and specific processes

that you believe are relevant to your question. What individual variables should you measure? Do you need to measure levels of intensity in the relationships? If so, can you define those levels in a way that will allow you to represent them in a network matrix? What environmental conditions might affect your study? How can you control for those conditions?

- Make a list of people with whom you have working relationships. What kinds of resources do you get from them? What kinds of resources do you provide for them? Are the two lists different? How do these relationships affect the efficiency or effectiveness of your work?
- Think of a research question that could be studied using SNA. Why is this question worth the time and energy that you would need to invest to answer it? What would academics find interesting about it? How might the answers provide practical insights about PM?

## TIPS FOR SUPERVISORS

To help your graduate students conduct successful social network studies, we recommend that you pay particular attention to the following:

- Ensure that the student has clearly identified a social network research topic, and that the types of relationships, possible levels or strengths of relationships, and network boundaries have been carefully defined.
- Confirm that the student has a good plan for collecting the data. This should include careful evaluation of survey or interview instruments, firm commitment from the organisation(s) that will participate and safeguards to protect the confidentiality of respondents.
- If you lack experience with network analysis methods, connect the student with an expert who can guide the analyses and critique the student's interpretations of results.

## EXERCISES

Following are some exercises that might help you think more deeply about the possible attributes of relationships and the different kinds of patterns that might affect the work that people do.

1. Map the social network within one of your classes or another group where you are a member. To keep the exercise manageable, try to choose a group that has fewer than 20 people. Based on your own experience, guess which people have worked together on a task or project. Put this information into a chart like the example given earlier in this chapter. Now think about each person in the group, and guess which other(s) that person trusts with sensitive information. Put this information into a second chart.
2. When you have both charts completed, arrange the names on a page and create a graph of the relationships (hint: look online for free software that enables you to import your data from the charts and convert those data into a network graph). Use colours to distinguish between relation types. For example, you might draw blue lines to indicate 'worked together' and red lines to indicate, 'trusts the other person'.
3. As you create your map, you may notice that the two kinds of relations tend to overlap but some people may have worked with someone they don't seem to trust, and other people may trust someone with whom they haven't worked. Further, you may need to use arrows to show the direction of the trust relations.
4. While working together is by nature reciprocal (if Alice has worked with Bob, then Bob has worked with Alice), trust is by nature directed. Alice may or may not trust Bob regardless

of whether or not Bob trusts Alice. What else do you notice about these two kinds of relations? Do you see a pattern of work cooperation or trust among people who share social attributes (educational background, sex, ethnicity) or environmental factors (studying for the same exams, mentored by the same advisor, living in the same building)? What other patterns do you see?

# References

Borgatti, S. P., Everett, M. G. and Freeman, L. C. (2002). *Ucinet for Windows: Software for Social Network Analysis.* Harvard, MA: Analytic Technologies.

Hanneman, R. A. and Riddle, M. (2005). *Introduction to Social Network Methods.* Riverside, CA: University of California, Riverside (published in digital form at http://faculty.ucr.edu/~hanneman/).

Kilduff, M. and Krackhardt, D. (2008). *Interpersonal Networks in Organizations: Cognition, Personality, Dynamics, and Culture in Organizations.* Cambridge: Cambridge University Press.

Ross, L. D. (1977). The intuitive psychologist and his shortcomings: Distortions in the attribution process. In L. Berkowitz (Ed.), *Advances in Experimental Social Psychology* (Vol. 10, pp. 174–221). New York: Academic Press.

Ross, L. and Nisbett, R. (1991). *The Person and the Situation: Perspectives of Social Psychology.* New York: McGraw Hill.

Wasserman, S. and Faust, K. (1994). *Social Network Analysis: Methods and Applications.* Cambridge: Cambridge University Press.

# 33

# Social Network Analysis Applied to Project Management

Nigel L. Williams, Nicole Ferdinand and Robin Croft

*Despite the potential of SNA to create new insights in PM, little guidance exists to support new researchers. This chapter intends to provide some practical guidance to new researchers seeking to explore the technique using free tools for data collection and analysis.*

This purpose of this chapter is to provide an illustration of how SNA can be used in project management research. As a knowledge-based discipline, project management is driven by interactions between individuals. SNA can help understand the nature of these interactions and their effect on project success. While it can be used in conjunction with other methodologies, SNA is of particular value when seeking to evaluate complex outcomes such as stakeholder benefits. Using an example of a programme aimed to generate social benefits, this chapter presents an approach for PM students to begin exploring SNA using data available from online social networks.

At the end of this chapter, the reader can:

* understand the advantages of using SNA;
* understand how to collect and process social network data;
* be able to apply a simple SNA to analyse social benefits.

Keywords: Social Network Analysis, programme evaluation, Twitter

## Social Network Analysis (SNA) Applied to Project Management (PM)

In the past few decades, success measures of project and programme activities have widened time, cost (on budget) and scope (quality) to incorporate team, organisation and stakeholder benefits (Atkinson, 1999; Baccarini, 1999; Schwalbe, 2004). While the early conceptualisations of project success lent themselves to a deductive approach, stakeholder benefits are difficult to define and evaluate. This challenge is magnified at the programme level, defined as a group of projects managed in a coordinated manner to achieve strategic outcomes (Lycett, Rassau and Danson, 2004). In the private sector, these outcomes can be translated into financial or business benefits. Public sector programmes, however, may be staged by governments and NGOs for the development of social capital (Atkinson, 1999; Diallo and Thuillier, 2005) or patterns of relationships between individuals that enable collective action. The development of social capital is increasingly being used as a basis to evaluate a range of public projects from festivals, environmental initiatives, energy generation projects, education and infrastructural improvements (Ika, Diallo and Thuillier, 2012).

## What are Social Networks?

Interactions between individuals form the building blocks of social institutions. Aggregated, these interactions form social networks within families, communities, organisations or countries that transmit information, distribute resources, coordinate activities and manage social norms. They are represented as maps also known as sociograms consisting of nodes and connectors. Nodes represent individuals or groups such as families, cities, companies or countries. Connectors are ties between nodes (Borgatti, Mehra, Brass and Labianca, 2009) that can be classified into:

- Similarities: Nodes may share physical or mental characteristics.
- Interpersonal Relationship: Nodes may have family, interest or knowledge bonds.
- Interactions: Nodes may engage in joint activity such as communication.
- Flow: Nodes may share resources such as energy or information.

While the study of these networks began in the 1800s, recent advances in IT have made it easier to collect and analyse social network data. Researchers currently apply the approach to generate new insights into management. In the domain of project management, SNA has been used to understand project team communications (Chinowsky, Diekmann and O'Brien, 2009), subcontractor management and information management (Park et al., 2010).

## Social Network Analysis (SNA) and Programme Evaluation

SNA has particular strengths in evaluating public programmes based in rural or urban settings since stakeholders are not monolithic, but may contain many subgroups with their own particular interests and perspectives (McLeod, Doolin and MacDonell, 2012). Previously, researchers have employed a range of inductive and deductive approaches to evaluate. For inductive approaches, Smith (2009) utilised semi-structured interviews to evaluate the social benefits accruing to peripheral communities from development projects related to the 2007 Tour de France. Focus groups have also been deployed individually (Sacha, Deborah and Katie, 2005) and combined with other qualitative approaches have also been utilised in this domain. An integrated interview and content analysis of documents were used to examine stakeholder perceptions of social impact as a result of events in three US cities (Misener and Mason, 2006).

Quantitative approaches have also been utilised to evaluate perceptions of programme success. Gursoy, Kim and Uysal (2004) utilised a mail survey to examine the perceptions of a social impact in a particular group of stakeholders for a public programme. Beyond surveys, content analysis has also been used to identify social impacts. Using the assumption that media reports represent social reality, these were analysed to identify success of public health programmes (Miller and Solomon, 2002) and economic development (Dai, Bao and Chen, 2010). Table 33.1 below presents an overview of stakeholder evaluation approaches for programmes.

However, all of these approaches face limitations when evaluating programme success. Communities, even though they share a similar geographic region, are generally heterogenous, not

**Table 33.1**     **Stakeholder evaluation approaches for programmes**

| Evaluation Method | Conventional Usage in Programme Evaluation | Previous applications | Strengths | Possible Limitations |
|---|---|---|---|---|
| Survey | Stakeholder analysis Participant Motivations Economic activity | Canada (Rollins and Delamere, 2007) | Quantitative findings may be seen as more credible to some stakeholders Low cost per response Multiple options for distribution | May ignore relevant segments of population Relatively low response rates |
| Focus Group | Identify and explore attitudes, beliefs and sentiments around programme | Sri Lanka (Schulenkorf and Edwards, 2005) | Useful in particular stakeholder group settings Broad exploration of issues Possible disclosure and ethical issues | Difficult to determine validity of findings Relatively expensive |
| Interview Structured Interview Unstructured Interview | Identify and explore attitudes, beliefs and sentiments around programme | UK Chalip (2004) | Rich data Honest feedback Allows for broad exploration of issues Possible disclosure and ethical issues | Relatively expensive Time consuming |
| Content Analysis | Type, range and volume extent of media coverage Sentiment of media coverage | China (Dai et al., 2010) | Viewed as objective Wide coverage Deep exploration of issues | Resource intensive Relatively slow |

homogenous (Esteves, Franks and Vanclay, 2012). As a result, various groups within the community may hold entirely different views of programme benefits and costs. Qualitative approaches enable deep exploration of the phenomenon and can build a holistic view of the phenomenon that incorporates the views of various subgroups. However, they are resource intensive and require research expertise to produce valid findings. As a result, the analysis is based on a relatively small subset of the community, the validity of which can be called into question. Quantitative approaches such as surveys have the benefit of standard constructs and data collection instruments that can be applied to a range of settings. However, response rates can relatively low and, for some populations, they may not accurately evaluate programme success (Gursoy et al., 2004). Content analysis overcomes these limitations by analysing media and other documents, but it can be expensive and relatively slow (Dai et al., 2010).

    SNA can overcome these limitations and recent technological advances have made it easier to collect and analyse this data. Researchers have used email exchanges and webpages in past work to understand the underlying patterns of interactions (Borgatti and Li, 2009). Unlike other sites, a significant amount of personal identity information is revealed and they provide users with not only information, but platforms for sharing resources and building connections (Grabowicz, Ramasco and Eguiluz, 2012). Researchers have begun to use these networks to uncover new insights since social connections between individuals are explicit and can be directly evaluated. Due to their heavy usage, they are of particular value in understanding issues in projects and programmes that have a large number of stakeholders.

## Ethical Challenges of Research Using Social Networks

Unlike data gathered from other types of research, digital data can be easily traced to respondents. The possibility of exposure requires researchers to explicitly address issues of privacy and security. The nature of social networks as interconnected platforms makes it possible for researchers to obtain data on not only the topic being researched, but relational, location and other information of related individuals. While it may not be possible to eliminate this risk entirely (Bowes, Dawson and Bell, 2012) researchers have begun to create guidelines for operating in online settings. Since technology is changing rapidly, researchers have suggested a bottom up approach that follows a principled rather than a prescriptive review of research questions, data and disclosure (Neuhaus and Webmoor, 2012). Possible ethical issues are to be resolved at each level but not necessarily used as templates for future activities. For PM research, due to the heterogeneity of stakeholders and complex issues in some domains of activity, it may be appropriate to focus on visible, online data such as public postings rather than implicit connections such as friend or follower relationships.

## Social Network Application Example

The following section shows how SNA can be applied to understand issues in Programme management. It uses the case of the Love Luton festival, an event programme consisting of a number of projects, staged in July 2012.

### PROGRAMME DESCRIPTION: LOVE LUTON FESTIVAL

The Luton Festival (Council, 2012) started to cohere as a concept in 2011 as local government officials and councillors considered two major opportunities on the cultural landscape for 2012: London was to be the venue for the Olympic Games, and the council was keen to be nominated as one of the Torch Relay staging posts (where the relay would stop overnight and restart the next day); The Diamond Jubilee celebrations were to include the creation of three new cities, and Luton was keen to be nominated as one of these. The town already had a thriving annual carnival which regularly attracted audiences of 150,000 or more: the council had built on the success of the Luton Carnival with a policy of promoting festivals throughout the borough. The concept of the Luton Festival was intended to create a large-scale cultural attraction, complete with international headline acts. A programme manager was appointed, as were outside agencies to handle ticketing, marketing, public relations and market research. The council itself set up a cross-departmental team to handle most of the internal functions, including safety and sponsorship.

It was decided to merge the proposed new festival with the highly successful Luton Carnival, the Asian Mela Festival and other longer-running cultural events. To help ensure success, the festival was timed to coincide with the Torch Relay's arrival in the town. The original Luton Festival, a week of free concerts in the town centre, was replaced by a weekend event, largely in local parks and – for headline events at least – ticket only. It was hoped that the large historic audiences of the carnival would support the newer festival format. A decision was made to book two major headline acts, Olly Murrs and The Wanted: both acts had a track record of sell-out events, and so the council was able confidently to predict that the festival would cover its costs. The final programme design is below (Figure 33.1).

The following social benefits were expected for the festival: improved social cohesion in the local community, raising the public profile of the town, and encouraging long-term tourism.

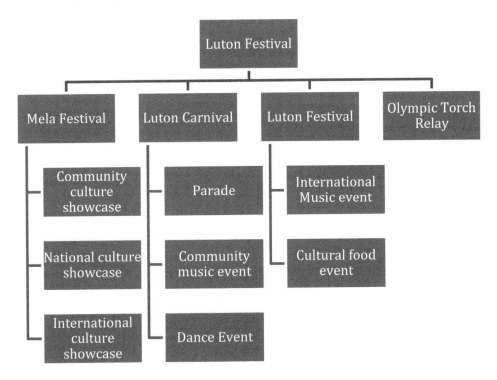

**Figure 33.1    Example of Luton Festival programme design**

## IDENTIFY PROGRAMME SUCCESS TO BE ANALYSED

Festival programmes are staged to catalyse the building of connections between groups (Misener and Mason, 2006) or intra- and inter-community ties (Woolcock and Narayan, 2000). The first, also known as bonding social capital, is based on relationships within similar members of a community. The second, also known as bridging social capital, is based on relationships between communities, such as visitors and tourists (Table 33.2). However, social impacts are not only positive, but can be negative as well. For example, community subgroups can clash, resulting in reduced community cohesion (Dimeo, Armstrong and Giulianotti, 2001).

These advantages make the use of social network data useful for evaluating programme success of festivals and, for this research, we chose to analyse postings on Twitter, a micro-blogging service. Like other social networks, Twitter has a significant user base, ensuring that a large number of opinions would be captured. However, unlike other social networks, most Twitter postings or 'tweets' are public by default (Castillo, Mendoza and Poblete, 2011). Finally, Twitter updates can be sent from a wide variety of devices, ensuring that updates are sent immediately. By eliminating the delay between observation and communication, Twitter updates may be more authentic as less

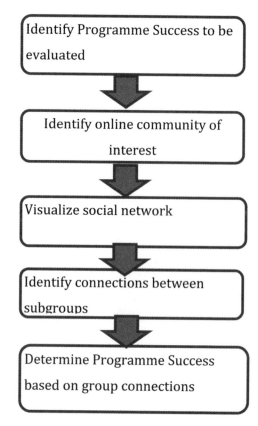

**Figure 33.2**    **Overview of social network analysis methodology**

**Table 33.2**    **Possible social impacts of public festivals**

| Positive Impacts | Description |
|---|---|
| Improved image among non-residents | A positive experience by visitors can result in positive media and word of mouth, improving the image of the region. |
| Intercultural interaction | International festivals provide the space for cultures to share and exchange traditions. |
| Socialising opportunities | International festivals provide both a new community (visitors) and more opportunities to interact in the form of events. |
| Community pride | Community pride can be enhanced as visitors and international performers come to the destination and interact with locals. |
| **Negative** | |
| Increased use of public services | International festivals attract visitors from outside the community who may use public services. Due to the increased demand, locals may either have less access or face delays in accessing public services. |
| Behavioural problems from drug and alcohol consumption | Consumption of alcohol and drugs can lead to aggressive behaviour by visitors. |
| Crime | Related to the above. |
| Worsen relationships between local residents | Host communities are not homogenous and differing groups can have different views of visitors. These differences can cause conflict between the groups. |

rationalisation and information processing is done by the user (Vega, 2011). It is also an inclusive medium as ownership of an expensive device is not required, unlike other social networks that need powerful smartphones or laptops. Further, Twitter allows anonymous postings, unlike other social networks that mandate the use of real names. In this way, privacy of participants can be preserved, reducing ethical risks.

## IDENTIFY COMMUNITY OF INTEREST (COI)

Next all Twitter postings using those designations were archived. Twitter messages or postings are limited to a length of 140 characters and contain usernames preceded by an @ symbol and a hashtag preceded by a # symbol. The latter helps users to identify postings on Twitter and form a useful way of curating discussions on a particular issue (Gechev, 2012). The event used the hashtag #lutonfestival and all tweets using this designation were archived using a Google template (Hawksey, 2012). Monitoring began one month before the festival and was closed one month after the event on August 6. The data was then exported to Excel to identify and remove duplicate tweets. After processing, 26,000 tweets were left for analysis.

These tweets were then filtered in Excel to identify replies between users (nodes) within the hashtag. While Twitter has a number of possible connections in the form of lists, followers or following relationships, these do not necessarily represent active engagement or interaction with a given topic (Clavio and Walsh, 2013). However, replies (using the @ symbol) that is, a response to another user's comments requires deliberate action (Boyd, Golder and Lotan, 2010). As such, they represent active engagement of Twitter users with an area of interest, or a Community of Interest (COI) (Kwak, Lee, Park and Moon, 2010). By focusing on explicit conversation and defined narratives, the risk of involving casual or accidental postings is minimised, preserving the privacy of those participants.

## VISUALISE SOCIAL NETWORK

We then utilised an Excel-based template, NodeXL (Hansen, Shneiderman and Smith, 2010) to visualise the clusters of relationships that exist within the community of replies. While the replies under a hashtag indicate a COI, groups within that community may have alternate perspectives on particular issues due to demographic or other characteristics (Sparrowe, Liden, Wayne and Kraimer, 2001). These clusters are identified as subgroups in which individuals have a greater degree of connectivity with each other than others (Carrington, Scott and Wasserman, 2005) within the overall COI (Clauset, Newman and Moore, 2004). Twitter profiles of members within the subgroup were reviewed to identify the characteristics of each group. Usernames were then replaced to ensure that identities were not traceable. To understand how these groups were connected, we used the vertex grouping function in NodeXL to simplify the appearance of these communities. This visualisation enables us to understand the nature and extent to which sub communities were connected (Figure 33.3).

## IDENTIFY CONNECTIONS BETWEEN MAJOR SUBGROUPS

NodeXL generated a list of actors in each subgroup. The actors in each subgrouping were identified and their interests determined from their profile description on Twitter and content of their tweets. This was used to classify the grouping below (Figure 33.4).

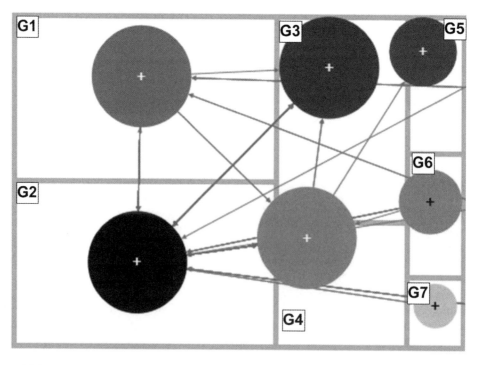

**Figure 33.3    Illustration of network example for sub-communities**

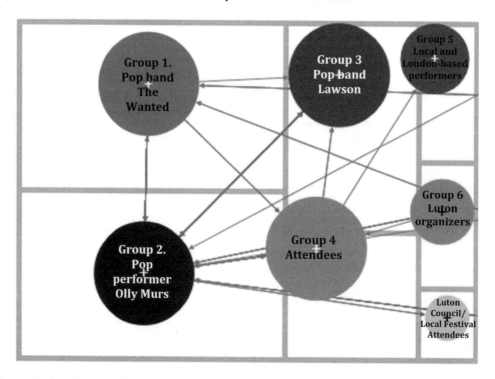

**Figure 33.4    Network illustration example of subgroup connections**

## DETERMINE PROGRAMME SUCCESS FROM SOCIAL NETWORK ANALYSIS (SNA)

An analysis of the scale and connections between subgroups can indicate if objectives were achieved. The dominant subgroups (1–3) were based around national performers, indicating that Objective 2 may have been achieved. Groups 4–7 was comprised of attendees and local stakeholders and there were no direct linkages between them, indicating that Objective 2 was not achieved. The SNA did not reveal direct connections between attendees and visitors, indicating that direct intercultural interaction that can support Objective 3 may not have occurred.

## Tips and Exercises

### TIPS FOR STUDENTS

- Public projects are useful avenues for testing potential applications of SNA as a large amount of data is available on stakeholders, resources and outcomes. Researchers can therefore create projects that examine any or all of these issues using this data.
- Use tools that are free or open source, such as NodeXL that is an Excel plugin or Guelphi. They are generally used by early stage researchers and supported by a large online community that can provide assistance.
- A key benefit of using public data is that it can be opened for review. Share your datasets and analyses to contribute to the research community and benefit from the input of additional researchers.

### TIPS FOR SUPERVISORS

- For students, SNA offers an opportunity to examine project, programme and portfolio outcomes from a new perspective.
- Begin with data from social networks. Data from public communication provides an ideal starting point as relationships are explicit (replies and so on) and exists in a digital form to be collected and analysed. For supervisors, this helps reduce the challenge of finding data that is current and of interest to students.
- Peer learning. There is also the added benefit of peer learning as students can freely exchange datasets without seeking special permission and verify or extend the work of other students.
- Apply techniques to other networks. Once students are comfortable with SNA using social media, they can begin examining other networks such as citations (for knowledge communities) or news articles for common terms. Finally, it provides an opportunity for supervisors to discuss ethics and privacy concerns that have emerged in the last few years using low-risk, observed data. Students can gain an enhanced understanding of these issues as they go on to become researchers in their own right.

### EXERCISES

1. Identify possible research questions that are linked to project or programme design, delivery or outcomes.

2. Identify a public programme for analysis.
3. Perform analysis using simple tools, for example, the ones discussed in this chapter.
4. Compare interpretations to previous research.
5. Identify domains in which the analysis could be improved.

# References

Atkinson, R. (1999). Project management: Cost, time and quality, two best guesses and a phenomenon, its time to accept other success criteria. *International Journal of Project Management, 17*(6), 337–342.

Baccarini, D. (1999) The logical framework method for defining project success. *Project Management Journal, 30*(4), 25–32.

Borgatti, S. P. and Li, X. (2009). On social network analysis in a supply chain context. *Journal of Supply Chain Management, 45*(2), 5–22.

Borgatti, S. P., Mehra, A., Brass, D. J. and Labianca, G. (2009). Network analysis in the social sciences. *Science, 323*(5916), 892–895.

Bowes, A., Dawson, A. and Bell, D. (2012). Ethical implications of lifestyle monitoring data in ageing research. *Information, Communication and Society, 15*(1), 5–22.

Boyd, D., Golder, S. and Lotan, G. (2010). *Tweet, tweet, retweet: Conversational aspects of retweeting on Twitter.* Paper presented at the System Sciences (HICSS), 2010 43rd Hawaii International Conference on. System Sciences

Carrington, P. J., Scott, J. and Wasserman, S. (2005). *Models and methods in social network analysis*: Cambridge University Press.

Castillo, C., Mendoza, M. and Poblete, B. (2011). *Information credibility on Twitter.* Paper presented at the Proceedings of the 20th international conference on world wide web.

Chalip, L. (2004). Beyond impact: A general model of sport event leverage. In B. Ritchie and D. Adair (eds.), *Sport Tourism: Issues, Interrelationships and Impacts.* Clevedon: Channel View.

Chinowsky, P. S., Diekmann, J. and O'Brien, J. (2009). Project organizations as social networks. *Journal of Construction Engineering and Management, 136*(4), 452–458.

Clauset, A., Newman, M. E. and Moore, C. (2004). Finding community structure in very large networks. *Physical review E, 70*(6): 066111.

Clavio, G. and Walsh, P. (2013). Dimensions of social media utilization among college sport fans. *Communication and Sport, September 2014, 2*(3), 261–281.

Council, L. B. (2012). Love Luton Festival 2012. Retrieved: 19 March 2013, from http://www.luton.gov.uk/Leisure_and_culture/Events%20services/Love%20Luton%202010%20Festival%20Weekend/Pages/default.aspx.

Dai, G., Bao, J. and Chen, X. (2010). Event impacts assessment: A model based on media content analysis of Expo'99 Kunming and World Expo 2010 Shanghai. *Journal of China Tourism Research, 6*(2), 183–201.

Diallo, A. and Thuillier, D. (2005). The success of international development projects, trust and communication: an African perspective. *International Journal of Project Management, 23*(3), 237–252.

Dimeo P (2001) 'Team loyalty splits the city into two': Football, ethnicity and rivalry in Calcutta. In: Armstrong, G., Giulianotti, R. (eds). *Fear and loathing in world football*, First ed. Global Sport Cultures, Oxford, UK: Berg Publishers, pp. 105–118.

Esteves, A. M., Franks, D. and Vanclay, F. (2012). Social impact assessment: The state of the art. *Impact Assessment and Project Appraisal, 30*(1), 34–42.

Gechev, R. (2012). Event marketing. In, N. Ferdinand and P. Kitchin (eds) *Events Management: An International Approach.* London: Sage Publications, p. 113.

Grabowicz, P. A., Ramasco, J. J. and Eguiluz, V. M. (2012). Dynamics in online social networks. *Dynamics On and Of Complex Networks*, Volume 2, 3–17. arXiv preprint arXiv:1210.0808.

Gursoy, D., Kim, K. and Uysal, M. (2004). Perceived impacts of festivals and special events by organizers: An extension and validation. *Tourism Management, 25*(2), 171–181.

Hansen, D., Shneiderman, B. and Smith, M. A. (2010). *Analyzing social media networks with NodeXL: Insights from a connected world.* Morgan Kaufmann.

Hawksey, M. (2012). Twitter Archiving Google Spreadsheet. Retrieved 1 June 2012 from http://mashe.hawksey.info/2012/01/twitter-archive-tagsv3/.

Ika, L. A., Diallo, A. and Thuillier, D. (2012). Critical success factors for World Bank projects: An empirical investigation. *International Journal of Project Management, 30*(1), 105–116.

Kwak, H., Lee, C., Park, H. and Moon, S. (2010). *What is Twitter, a social network or a news media?* Paper presented at the Proceedings of the 19th international conference on world wide web.

Lycett, M., Rassau, A. and Danson, J. (2004). Programme management: A critical review. *International Journal of Project Management, 22*(4), 289–299.

McLeod, L., Doolin, B. and MacDonell, S. G. (2012). A perspective-based understanding of project success. *Project Management Journal, 43*(5), 68–86.

Miller, P. A. and Solomon, P. (2002). The influence of a move to program management on physical therapist practice. *Physical therapy, 82*(5), 449–458.

Misener, L. and Mason, D. S. (2006). Creating community networks: Can sporting events offer meaningful sources of social capital? *Managing Leisure, 11*(1), 39–56.

Neuhaus, F. and Webmoor, T. (2012). Agile ethics for massified research and visualization. *Information, Communication and Society, 15*(1), 43–65.

Park, H., Han, S. H., Rojas, E. M., Son, J. and Jung, W. (2010). Social network analysis of collaborative ventures for overseas construction projects. *Journal of Construction Engineering and Management, 137*(5), 344–355.

Rollins, R. and Delamere, T. (2007). Measuring the social impact of festivals. *Annals of Tourism Research, 34*(3), 805–808.

Sacha, R., Deborah, E. and Katie, S. (2005). Methodological considerations in pretesting social impact questionnaires: Reporting on the use of focus groups. Proceedings of 'International Event Research' Conference. Sydney, Australia, July, 2005

Schulenkorf, N. & Edwards, D. C. 2010, 'The role of sport events in peace tourism' in O. Moufakkir and I. Kelly, (eds), *Tourism, Progress and Peace.* UK: CABI, pp. 99–117.

Schwalbe, K. (2004). *Information Technology Project Management* (4th edition). Boston, MA: Course Technology.

Smith, A. (2009). Spreading the positive effects of major events to peripheral areas. *Journal of Policy Research in Tourism, Leisure and Events, 1*(3), 231–246.

Sparrowe, R. T., Liden, R. C., Wayne, S. J. and Kraimer, M. L. (2001). Social networks and the performance of individuals and groups. *Academy of Management Journal, 44*(2), 316–325.

Vega, E. L. (2011). *Communities of Tweeple: How communities engage with microblogging when co-located.* Virginia Polytechnic Institute and State University.

Woolcock, M. and Narayan, D. (2000). Social capital: Implications for development theory, research, and policy. *The World Bank Research Observer, 15*(2), 225–249.

# 34

# The Electronic Portfolio – A Research Enabler

Tracey Richardson

*This chapter brings together my three passions: PM, an academic environment and advancing the electronic portfolio.*

The traditional research process is riddled with inefficient and frustrating challenges. This chapter presents the electronic portfolio (ePortfolio) as a contemporary strategy enabling both the PM researcher and the supervisor to better manage the complex process. The ePortfolio is an Internet-based repository of the research effort. It becomes the single source of a real-time, work-in-progress and provides a 'one-stop-shop' for any reviewer. This strategy includes a reflective component, developing the PM 'lessons learned' mindset, by having the researcher document the process. The ePortfolio is flexible tool that can be designed to fit any PM research methodology.

At the end of this chapter, the reader can:

- evaluate the electronic portfolio (ePortfolio) as a PM research strategy;
- articulate your vision for a PM research ePortfolio;
- list important criteria and considerations for a research ePortfolio.

Keywords: research strategy, reflection, electronic portfolio, digital identity, grants

## Introduction

This book presents fresh research methods for the ever-changing field of PM. While the topics, approaches and results may be very different, the processes of data collection, organisation, analysis and interpretation maintain alignment. Whether your research's purpose focuses on an academic requirement, a grant submission or a scientific journal, the research effort culminates in publication to be critiqued by peers, supervisors or grant administers. Considering the complexity related to standardised research processes and the vast volume of information generated, the following question is posed. How can PM research processes be enhanced to effectively catalogue progress, share work activities, generate quality feedback and improve researcher efficiency?

This chapter is a primer for research enthusiasts and future researchers. It presents a contemporary approach to breathe new life into a very traditional process. This is not a recipe for a new methodology; rather, it explores the traditional process challenges and proposes a solution to document 'research' as a dynamic process, not just a static publication. It proposes a solution fundamental to all research efforts: How do we display our progress and simultaneously share the work in order to receive the best feedback? The ePortfolio is a contemporary solution enabling both the researcher and the supervisor to better manage a complex process.

## A Review of Portfolio Literature

The portfolio has been recognised for decades in the fields of art, architecture and photography as a repository for a professional's growth and expression (Paulson and Paulson, 1991a; Barrett, 2007). While there are variations to purpose and definition, common portfolio characteristics include student selected artefacts that are classified and organised in a manner which exhibits growth and development (Campbell et al., 2001; Ring and Foti, 2003). Traditionally, the portfolio was a leather bound jacket containing hard copies of one's work. These hard copies provided evidence of subject matter expertise gained through the educational experience (Paulson and Paulson, 1990; Paulson and Paulson, 1991b; Adamy, 2004). Upon graduation, the portfolio became a collection of work products that represented the student's expertise and was suitable for presentation to prospective employers.

As technology advanced, the transition from the traditional leather bound portfolio to digital medium was a natural evolution. Conceptually, the electronic portfolio (ePortfolio) became popular as the need to showcase one's accomplishments transitioned from a physical presentation to an electronic medium. This transition provided a platform that is current, portable and instantaneously accessible by any reviewer with Internet access.

A review of the portfolio and ePortfolio literature reveals a list of benefits which include: student selection, revision and reflection of artefacts (Barrett, 2007; Diller and Phelps, 2008); instant access and currency of student progress (Hewett, 2004); increased computer applications (MacDonald et al., 2004; Batson, 2002); instant tracking and sorting of student data (Wilhelm, Puckett, Beisser and Wishart, 2006); increased communication between the student and faculty (Barrett and Garrett, 2009; Penny Light, Chen and Ittelson, 2012; Tsai et al., 2004); and greater outcomes transparency (Barrett, 2007; Diller and Phelps, 2008; Penny Light, Chen and Ittelson, 2012).

The ePortfolio construct is becoming more widely accepted within the halls of higher education as institutions incrementally recognise the many benefits of the new medium. ePortfolios are being implemented successfully to document and assess student learning outcomes, for curriculum assessment, accreditation and professional recognition. Technology is maturing, providing organisations with vetted processes from a variety of vendors. The blend of higher education's attitude and the accessibility of technology, makes the timing right to consider the ePortfolio and its usefulness to the research process.

## A Strategy to Enable the Research Process

Whether you are working on a PM dissertation, grant or journal submission, the process is typically regimented regarding format and content. Requirements may vary, but the common themes of literature review development, data collection, analysis and interpretation are constant. When faced with complex research projects, early challenges include formulating strategies to manage the research process itself.

The following examples illustrate how the ePortfolio construct provides a virtual organisation of the process. The illustrations presented here represent the use of an ePortfolio through the lens of the traditional deliverable: the publication. The ePortfolio is a flexible tool that can be designed to fit any research methodology (Figure 34.1).

## The ePortfolio

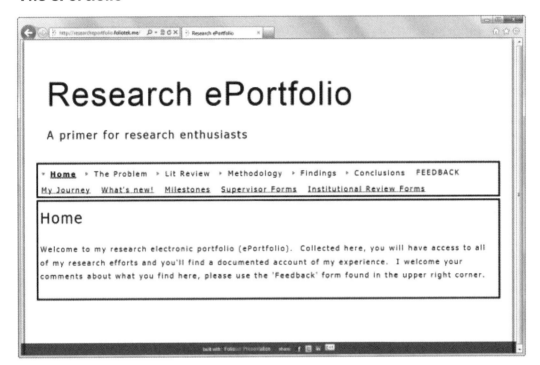

**Figure 34.1    Research ePortfolio – home**

## THE EPORTFOLIO – A COMMUNICATION AND RELATIONSHIP ENABLER

As a primary description, the ePortfolio is a website. And like every website, anyone with access to the Internet and the direct link to the page, can view the work. The researcher's link is private and visibility to its contents is granted by way of an email invitation. The researcher's ePortfolio is made public only if the researcher chooses to 'share' the link with the public domain.

The researcher maintains full ownership of the contents, and once populated with the researcher's work, the ePortfolio becomes a repository of the research effort. A fundamental challenge for the PM researcher centres on keeping supervisors and reviewers on task with the most current version of the progress. The ePortfolio becomes a single source of real-time work-in-progress and provides a 'one-stop-shop' for the researcher to communicate with reviewer(s) during advising sessions. Additionally, the ePortfolio construct provides reviewers with access to original source documents. In this example, the ePortfolio enables communication to be more efficient because research efforts are housed in a single location and can be accessed by anyone invited to participate by the researcher.

If the research project is a collaborative effort, the ePortfolio becomes a space where co-creators work simultaneously. This collaborative approach builds better relationships between co-authors and reviewers. Additionally, the ePortfolio structure adds efficiency to the process (see Figure 34.2). Instant access to the researcher's work allows the author(s) to more easily obtain reviews by and collaborations with outside experts.

## THE EPORTFOLIO – ENABLING AN ACTIVE RESEARCHER

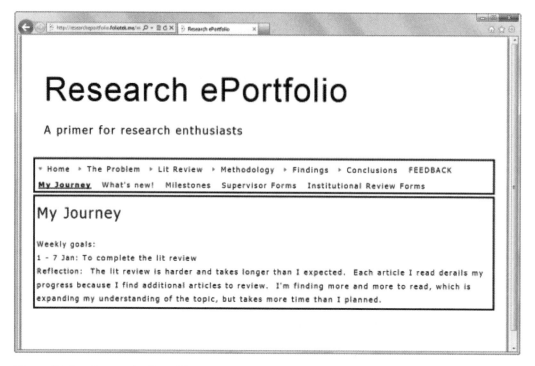

**Figure 34.2    Research ePortfolio – my journey**

The traditional research model focuses on a sound methodology leading to a quality publication. While publication is the tangible result of a researcher's effort, it is the experience of progressing through the research process that develops the researcher's competencies. In the traditional research model, the researcher's reflection on the research process is not intentionally documented. Experiential-based learning is the foundation of how the next generation of researchers will be developed and the practice of self-reflection is recognised as a powerful growth catalyst to learning through self-critique.

This reflective practice documents the researcher's journey and gives the researcher an active voice describing the rationale behind decision making and direction. By encouraging this voice, the researcher becomes an active participant in the process and, as a result, may be better prepared to articulate research findings in an oral defence. Many of tomorrow's researchers are already actively documenting their life experiences through social media. Adding a similar reflective practice into a contemporary strategy is a natural inclusion into tomorrow's research model.

## THE EPORTFOLIO – ENABLING KNOWLEDGE MANAGEMENT AS THE VIRTUAL ORGANISER

**Figure 34.3    Research ePortfolio – portfolio construct**

## Visual Organisation of Chaos

Perhaps the greatest challenge to any research effort is organising and cataloging the volumes of information in a manner that is efficient and manageable. Many an aspiring researcher has been paralysed because of a lack of organisation. The ePortfolio construct provides a visual organisation to a process that can feel overwhelming (see Figure 34.3). As an example, researchers can become overwhelmed when compiling a literature review as the effort often results reviewing in countless articles, journals, and other periodicals representing an in-depth study of the topic. The traditional approach to collection and organisation may be reams of paper stacked in piles in a researcher's work space.

In a contemporary strategy, electronic libraries house the most current literature and searches result in digital sources. The ePortfolio provides a place to collect all of the electronic documents. Not only can the researcher collect the sources, but as technology advances, the electronic documents can be cataloged and searched for topic or theme. The ePortfolio allows the researcher to begin the research process in an organised manner. The ePortfolio is not limited to just articles but can also accept video testimonies, audio files, analytic tables, and any resource that can be digitised.

## A key to opening transparency in research

Another challenge to the traditional process is the lack of transparency. In the traditional approach, the researcher may not have an infrastructure to share the collection of research results for review. As described above, the ePortfolio is the repository for collections of digital artefacts. As an example, if the researcher cites a study in their literature review, and if the supervisor wants to read that study in its original context, that study is accessible to the supervisor because it is stored in the ePortfolio. Not only does having all of the sources at the reviewers' finger tips enhance reviewer satisfaction related to convenience, it supports academic integrity as the researcher is transparent in sources and citations.

## Holistic look at the researcher's efforts and results

Instant access to the work-in-progress, the source documentation, and the documented reflection of the researchers approach, transforms the supervisor's role. By having access to all of the sources in the literature review, the supervisor can get a sense of the quality and quantity of sources the researcher selected. By reviewing the researcher's personal account, the supervisor can get a sense of direction and motivation to continue, allowing the supervisor to hone in on the issues. Using an ePortfolio may not make the process easier but it could make it more efficient and increase the quality of the review.

Often in pursuit of the current research 'problem', other potential research topics present themselves. Herein lies the opportunity to collect these ideas and share them with colleagues as an incubator for future research. These ideas can be stored and later revisited. Since the source documentation is housed in a single location and remains accessible, exploring the idea begins with a level of effort already complete.

## The ePortfolio – enabling engagement

The traditional research process can be daunting, isolating, and lonely. The researcher must be self-motivated to continue working when they feel there is little support. The ePortfolio has a built in feedback mechanism that provides any reviewer a space to comment on the research effort. Not only does this provide the space for the feedback, but it becomes a record of communications between researcher and supervisor. The researcher can expand the outreach by inviting peers, subject matter experts, and research support groups, but a note of encouragement from a family member may be a little needed motivation to continue evaluating the next set of ANOVA results. The ePortfolio presents an opportunity to shift from a process of isolation to a process of collaboration and involvement.

## Criticism: Not without consequences

This chapter presents the ePortfolio as a strategy to enable research. To implement such a strategy, a number of assumptions must be agreed upon. First and foremost, all parties must be willing to accept the ePortfolio as a strategy. All parties must be willing to learn the technology. Keeping the ePortfolio current may be an added level of workload to an already strapped set of limited resources. Additionally, when placing any information on the Internet, how do we keep our intellectual property safe? When considering the Human Subject process, how do we maintain the integrity of our work when we are trying to be transparent? This contemporary approach provides a solution to many of today's challenges, but it could create a new list of challenges for tomorrow.

## Tips and Questions

### TIPS FOR STUDENTS

Additional resources about ePortfolios and their use in academics and industry:

- The International Journal of ePortfolio: http://www.theijep.com/
- JISC eLearning: http://www.jisc.ac.uk/whatwedo/programmes/elearning/eportfolios.aspx
- The Association for Authentic, Experiential and Evidence-Based Learning: http://www.aaeebl. org/
- ePortfolios Australia: http://eportfoliosaustralia.wordpress.com/
- Electronic Portfolio Action and Communication (EPAC): http://epac.pbwiki.com/
- http://electronicportfolios.com/
- Explore the many vendors of ePortfolios
    - Digication: http://www.digication.com/
    - eFolioWorld: www.efolioworld.com
    - Desire2Learn: www.desire2learn.com
    - LiveText: www.livetext.com
    - Foliotek: www.foliotek.com
    - Epsilen: www.epsilen.com
    - PebblePad: www.pebblepad.co.uk
    - Taskstream: www.taskstream.com
    - Marhara: https://mahara.org/ (open source)

### TIPS FOR SUPERVISORS

- Direct students to additional resources about ePortfolios and their use in academics and industry.
- Discuss the safekeeping of Intellectual property and digital identity.
- Encourage reflection on the PM profession and is termed 'lessons learned.' How might reflection about your personal research journey be captured and later used within an ePortfolio?

## QUESTIONS

1.  Review the literature on the uses of the ePortfolio. How is it being used in academics? How is it being used by the practitioner?
2.  Develop a communications plan for your research effort.
3.  Perform a Risk Analysis on your research project. When creating your risk response plan, could the ePortfolio be a strategy to mitigate a negative risk? Could the ePortfolio be a strategy to enhance or exploit a positive risk?
4.  How do you protect your intellectual property once you place it online?

# References

Adamy, P. (2004). Strategies for enhancing assessment with electronic portfolios. *Journal of Computing in Higher Education*, 15(2), 85–97. doi:10.1007/BF02940931.

Barrett, H. (2007). Researching electronic portfolios and learner engagement: The REFLECT initiative. *Journal of Adolescent & Adult Literacy*, 50(6), 436–449. Retrieved from http://ezproxy.libproxy.db.erau.edu/login?url=http://search.proquest.com/docview/216921003?accountid=27203.

Barrett, H. and Garrett, N. (2009). Online personal learning environments: Structuring electronic portfolios for lifelong and life-wide learning. *On the Horizon*, 17(2), 142–152. doi:10.1108/10748120910965511.

Barrett, H. C. (1998). Strategic questions: What to consider when planning for electronic portfolios. *Learning & Leading with Technology*, 26(2), 6–13.

Batson, T. (2002). The electronic portfolio boom: What's it all about. *Campus Technology*, 11.

Campbell, D. Cignetti, P. Melenyzer, B. Nettles, D. and Wyman, R. (2001). *How to Develop a Professional Portfolio: A manual for teachers*. Boston, MA: Allyn and Bacon.

Diller, K. and Phelps, S. (2008). Learning outcomes, portfolios, and rubrics, oh my! Authentic assessment of an information literacy program. *Portal: Libraries and the Academy*, 8(1), 75–89. Retrieved from http://ezproxy.libproxy.db.erau.edu/login?url=http://search.proquest.com/docview/ 216166132?accountid=27203.

Hewett, S. (2004). Electronic portfolios: Improving instructional practices. *TechTrends*, 48(5), 24–28. Retrieved from http://ezproxy.libproxy.db.erau.edu/login?url=http://search.proquest.com/ docview/874024718?accountid=27203.

MacDonald, L., Liu, P., Lowell, K., Tsai, H. and Lohr, L. (2004). Part one: Graduate student perspectives on the development of electronic portfolios. *TechTrends*, 48(3), 52–55. Retrieved from http://ezproxy.libproxy.db.erau.edu/login?url=http://search.proquest.com/docview/873896588?accountid=27203.

Paulson, L. F. and Paulson, P.R. (1990, August). *How do portfolios measure up? A cognitive model for assessing portfolios. Revised*. Presented at the Annual Meeting of the Northwest Evaluation Association, Union WA. Retrieved from http://www.eric.ed.gov/PDFS/ED324329.pdf.

Paulson, F. L. and Paulson, P. R. (1991a). *The ins and outs of using portfolios to assess performance. Revised*. Expanded version of paper presented at the Join Annual Meeting of the National Council of Measurement in Education and the National Association of Test Directors. Chicago, IL. (April, 1991).

Paulson, F. L. and Paulson, P. R. (1991b). *The making of a portfolio*. Retrieved from http://www.eric.ed.gov/PDFS/ED334251.pdf.

Penny Light, T., Chen, H. and Ittleson, J. (2012). Documenting learning with eportfolios.

Ring, G. and Foti, S. (2003). Addressing standards at the program level with electronic portfolios. *TechTrends*, 47(2), 28–32. Retrieved from http://ezproxy.libproxy.db.erau.edu/login?url= http://search.proquest.com/docview/223122970?accountid=27203.

Tsai, H., Lowell, K., Liu, P., MacDonald, L. and Lohr, L. (2004). Part two: Graduate student perspectives on the development of electronic portfolios. *TechTrends*, 48(3), 56–60. Retrieved from http://ezproxy.libproxy.db.erau.edu/login?url=http://search.proquest.com /docview/873895925?accountid=27203.

Wilhelm, L., Puckett, K., Beisser, S., Wishart, W. Merideth, E. and Sivakumaran, T. (2006). Lessons learned from the implementation of electronic portfolios at three universities. *TechTrends*, 50(4), 62–71. Retrieved from http://ezproxy.libproxy.db.erau.edu/login?url=http://search.proquest.com/docview/223120624?account id=27203.

# PART VII
# BENEFITTING FROM EXPERIENCE: SUPERVISORS AND PUBLICATIONS

It's ironic, really … the two (arguably) most important dimensions of your research project will never be accompanied by formal instruction. Managing the relationship with your supervisor and generating publications are constants throughout your research project. You will feel the pressure *from* both and it's your responsibility to establish a track record *with* both that will serve you during the first research project and, in all likelihood, throughout the rest of your research career.

The remaining chapters of this book are entirely devoted to the personal perspectives of academics experienced with both the supervision of PM researchers and support of their publications. Each chapter has its own style, voice and orientation. You will read an interview, an allegory, a long list of mistakes to avoid and instructions to follow.

In previous sections, I've introduced the chapters to give you a sense of what you will read. In this section, I will simply introduce the speakers and leave it to them to speak for themselves.

# 35

# The Voice of Experience:
# An Interview with
# Lynn Crawford

The following is an abbreviated transcript from a conversation with Dr Lynn Crawford in preparation for this book. It took place in June, 2013 in Utrecht, Netherlands. In sharing this conversation with you, I made the same decision as I did with other chapters and removed myself as best I could as interpreter. With Lynn, this decision was even easier – she's a very clear speaker! But I have removed some text for the sake of brevity or where the core of either a question or response was buried. I've also restructured the material somewhat to connect themes that arose in our conversation to relevant chapters in the book. Each of these steps was taken to increase the usability of the text.

**BP: What do you look for in a Master or PhD candidate in PM?**
LC: I'm looking for somebody who can ask questions rather than endeavour to prove a solution. But more specifically … with Master students, people who have achieved certain academic gradings and people who want to learn. You don't want, on a post-experience Master's course, people who will avoid all lessons. Supervisors are looking for people who want to learn.

With PhD students, it's people who have a commitment to do research … who have a vision that there's something they want to achieve and see a PhD as the best way of helping them achieve that vision. I don't like people who join the PhD programme and then within six months start asking what their research should be. I want someone coming to a PhD programme knowing from the start what they want to be researching. It may change slightly as they do the literature, but I want someone who has a vision of what they want to achieve.

**BP: How do you find that vision in a research proposal?**
LC: I have candidates complete a research template when they apply for the programme. It is a three-page document that states the problem, identifies what they see as research objectives, the literature that they think they might look at and how they might solve the problem. You know, it's just a three-page document, but it can actually change substantially as they do the literature search and develop their 20-page research proposal.

**BP: Do you have any concerns about this step?**
LC: My greatest concern when somebody comes to do a PhD is not to have somebody who wants to learn. Someone who, as Miles Shepherd would say, 'who is there, not for a qualification, but as a

seeker of truth.' That's what you're looking for, people who are seeking the truth. So, the thing that really concerns me when people come and want to do a PhD, and this can be the problem of the vision, or of actually wanting to prove a solution they have already developed to a problem they have already identified. I've seen that a lot with practitioners who want to give credibility to their solution and that is something, as a supervisor, you have to break down.

**BP: That sounds important.**
LC: That is hugely important, and particularly because most of the candidates for doctorates in PM are practitioners, and for the majority of them, that's how they come to it.

I'd like to relate this back to their initial documents. Ideally they're thinking of a problem – rather than a solution they are trying to prove – so I'm looking in that initial document or somewhere nearby for their ability to formulate a question or questions and to understand what that means. I'm also then looking for their ability to reference and cite on the basis of good literature.

**BP: What qualifies as suitable literature?**
LC: Well, practitioners read the practitioner magazines. Industry magazines, for example, have their place but should not be considered good literature. That's what they are used to, so they need guidance on how to look for peer review journal articles and avoid tabloid, potboiler and popular books.

They also might use edited books, like the *Oxford Handbook*, which we know was very carefully edited. You can have the odd magazine, article, newspaper article, you know, where it actually makes a point because it can have relevance if you're trying to say that this is the practitioners' view of the world.

**BP: What characteristics do you look for in your student's reference list?**
LC: Beyond the peer-reviewed articles and suitable books, I'm looking for currency. With any doctoral student I have, I tell them to go back, and even just before it goes to the examiners, just go back and check if there's anything else come out. On the other end of the currency is making sure that there are seminal articles. I want to make sure that they've not just taken the current article but they've actually gone back to the origins.

**BP: What if they are not grasping these basics?**
LC: You send them to the Library, and you make them speak to the Librarian. You send them to a student learning support resource, so there's reinforcement for what you're saying to them. Very often with students, they won't listen to the supervisor. Goodness knows why, but they won't, or somehow they just don't hear it, so you triangulate, and you try and get the message across in some way. At the end of the day, they fail. They have to fail.

**BP: That's a harsh lesson.**
LC: Actually, it's not a harsh lesson. It means you haven't learned the lesson despite being given as much support as you possibly can.

**BP: What do you look for in a, I don't want to say successful, but in an effective literature review. Is effective the right word?**
LC: Effective is a reasonable word because it's an effective literature review if they have managed to define boundaries … because they can't read everything. I have known students who have spent their whole time reviewing the literature and never got anywhere, because they see it as little adventure. They think, 'Oh, that's good,' and just keep wandering on really looking at the daisies. So, you've got to find a logical way of bounding what reviews you're going to do. The exciting thing is

when they actually find literature, fields of the literature that actually go together, build towards a good theoretical framework, a good research question and good methodology.

**BP: I think that searching for good literature on methods is something students delay or don't see as part of their initial search where they focus on the subject domain.**
LC: The literature review should include the methodology as well as the subject matter you're dealing with and the theoretical framework.

**BP: That nicely bridges to my next topic ... can you explain what a conceptual model or theoretical framework is? The readers of this book will be facing the challenge of making one.**
LC: There could be so many different answers to that question. I think the practical answer is, that you've done the literature review, you've identified certain concepts and you've identified what you believe should be the relationship between them. This could be cause and effect or something else, but you are showing influence ... whatever it is. From that, you make a pictorial summary that is, in effect, a visual interpretation of your research proposition. The next logical step is to explain how you are going to test it through a methods strategy.

**BP: Can you elaborate further on how the model reflects or proposes a methods strategy?**
LC: The model is a bridge between the student's view of the world, or a map of those parts of the world that are shown to be relevant to the research question. So, for me, it provides the bridge between that and the research design, not so much methodology, but research design. So, a student has these concepts and hypothesising certain relationships between those concepts. The next logical question is ... how are you going to test that?

**BP: And the answer to that question is the basis for your research design.**
LC: Yes, but only the basis. You have to choose methods that would be seen to be valid under your own research circumstances. You can take the same conceptual model and have different research designs.

**BP: Can you speak about your view of quantitative, qualitative and mixed methods as it pertains to PM research?**
LC: Mixed methods are by far my preferred option but it depends on the nature of what it is you're investigating. Qualitative methods concern me slightly it is, by its very nature, subjective and I think that the researcher is bipartisan. They are looking for particular themes, and therefore, are in danger of influencing. It's a case of what they see, and what we see is always influenced by what we're looking for.

With quantitative work, I'll see certain things that I might want to test with a wider population. But PM is about people's opinion, so it might not be truly quantitative. Scales of 1 to 5, for example, will be used and assumed to be objective when, in fact, it's subjective. That's one of my major concerns about this kind of research – people go ahead and do all kinds of detailed quantitative work on issues that can be purely subjective.

Let's use a simple example, if we count the number of chairs in this room, that's objective, but as soon as we start to try and look at anything to do, for instance with the people in the room, or any reason why they might do something, or anything they think is important, then it becomes subjective. Yes, think about the amount of research in PM, it's based on what project managers think is important.

**BP: I'd appreciate your thoughts on the relative merit of a mixed methods strategy in PM research. Do you think there's a need to pay increasing attention to a mixed methods strategy? Is that something that you would recommend your students to more actively consider?**

LC: I think it's really interesting. It's getting on towards 20 years since Mingers and Gill (1997)[1] produced a book on mixed methodology and the paradigm wars, and it's interesting because we've progressed now. There was a time where if you used a positivist approach, we used quantitative methodology, you didn't need to justify your methodology at all, you just did it because that was accepted. If you did anything in qualitative, you had to spend a large part of the thesis actually justifying that methodology. And if you mixed your methods, your research design, would be considered unjustifiable, in effect. What's the phrase ... It would be considered as paradigmatically incommensurable.

That's what Mingers and Gill (1997) were fighting, and what the paradigm wars were all about. I think what's interesting now, is that a mixed strategy is accepted. It's more likely that if you do something quantitative, an examiner is going to say, 'Why didn't you also do something qualitative?' Or if you do something qualitative, they're going to say, 'Well, why didn't you do something quantitative?' So, I think in a way, the safe option today for a PM PhD is to use mixed methods – but then you come to the question about justifying that.

**BP: Let's talk about interviewing. You most often access, I think, senior project manager's and project sponsors, I think the readers of this book might be a little intimidated because they are Master's and PhD students arranging those interviews. I'd appreciate your thoughts on arranging and conducting interviews.**

LC: It's good if you can establish some credibility to begin with, so try not to make a cold-call if you're going to senior people. I would say in this day and age, it's increasingly difficult because there is so much more research being done. So people are being pestered a lot, so you need to be asking them to talk about something that is of interest to them. Engage them and explain how there would be some benefit to them in having that conversation.

Focus groups are another interesting technique but you've got to get buy-in from the organisation. If they can see that there is a benefit to them of having an assortment group of people brought together to discuss a certain thing, and you're seen, in effect, as the facilitator, that can help. Again, this is more and more difficult to achieve. People are busier and they're being asked more and more often so it's less novel and less prestigious than it used to be, to be asked to participate in a research project.

**BP: How much attention do you think should be paid to the ethics of PM research?**

LC: I think in many ways it's over done.

**BP: Really?**

LC: Yes, but let me be clear. I am an absolute believer in ethics applications because they're a good discipline because they make the researcher really think through what they're doing, and very briefly. Probably in a way, we'd like a research student to do an ethics application instead of a proposal when they apply. If you can nail that, then you can do it. But then, their life becomes so easy as soon as they ask, for example, is the identity of the interview subject likely to be known to anyone, including the researcher?

---

1    Mingers, J. and Gill, A. (Eds) (1997) Multimethodology: Theory and Practice of Combining Management Science Methodologies. Chichester: Wiley.

**BP: Of course.**

LC: Yes, but you're there, of course, and you are going to be able to identify them. Even though 'de-identified,' I'm probably still going to remember the interview. So, there's a bit of nonsense in there and most of the research that's done in PM is not exactly going to harm.

**BP: Not unless we're really creative.**

LC: I don't think people get it wrong all that often. And I do think it's extremely beneficial in terms of the credibility of what you're doing, and giving a sense of confidence to the interview subject.

**BP: Can you describe a current project where you applied for ethics approval?**

LC: Research that I'm currently doing relies on data that is available in the public domain, but we applied for ethics approval in order to be able to take what we'd found to the organisations concerned and just get them to look at it to tell us whether in fact, we'd correctly interpreted it. In order to do so, we have to get a 'gatekeeper letter,' and we can't get a gatekeeper letter.

**BP: So that's why you need an insider contact, I guess?**

LC: We have informally spoken to insider contacts, but we can't refer to that as part of the methodology, because the ethics approval, without a gatekeeper letter, means that we can't, and because we asked for the gatekeeper letter, the response was, 'No, we've got too many things going on, we can't speak to anyone.' It we don't mention that, because of all the material we had is in the public domain, then we can actually mention everything, including the name of the organisations.

**BP: So, ethics is difficult to manage, but ultimately of questionable value?**

LC: No, I think it has very good value and very good aspects of value to it, but more and more, I think, it is becoming challenging. Things used to be relatively easy because there weren't that many people doing it. Organisations have become a lot more sensitive, both to the impact that it might have, and to the time that it's going to consume.

**BP: Just a couple of more questions. Do you see certain methods dominating PM research or emerging as critically important?**

LC: I think there's a limit to the number of things you can actually do. When people talk about novel methods, how novel can you get? It's also a practical thing. It's very hard to experiment without that having ethic, you know, in controlled groups, but they're all standard methods. How novel can you get is my question? I want to do more and more research using secondary data. Well, there's so much stuff out there and it's not going to cause anybody any harm to use it, why not use it?

**BP: Yes, which makes the literature review techniques that much more important.**

LC: Yes.

**BP: Do you think there are certain methods that are more suitable to certain industries? Can you offer guidance to research students who will be face with these different options?**

LC: I think, in particular if you're dealing with the defence industry and certain parts of government and so on, you will find that there are huge security barriers to data collection and publication. For instance, I did work with the New South Wales Police, and really couldn't accomplish anything, so that's the danger. You've got to bear in mind that to work in an area where you're going to be able to publish, and so, anything to do with the military, would again have that kind of problem. In those cases, you should rely on secondary or publicly available sources. You know, interviews, if you're dealing with an industry where people like talking, then it's easy to give interviews – but you've got to think about how pressed are they for time. How senior or junior are the people that you wanted to speak to and what forces are at work there? Other than that, I don't think I can make any generalisation.

**BP: I think one generalisation you just alluded to, or suggested, was that certain industries are predisposed to communicating in a certain way, and depending on that type of communication, a method might be more or less appropriate.**
LC: Yes, but I think with everything it's got to be contextual.

**BP: You've started this interview by saying that some of the students that you've encountered are practitioners who come with the agenda to prove something they have experienced, so...**
LC: They mostly come like that. The best come with this problem that they've encountered in practice, which they want to investigate, but there are some who have encountered a problem in practice, they've come up with the solution, and they want to prove that's right and build its credibility. Even when they do with the best of intent, because they really do think, you know, 'I've got this model, and it's really great, so I'm going to prove that this is a good model,' and it can sometimes be really ... that's fine, it's fine to come like that, and some of them really get it when you say, 'That's great, now come back to me when you've got a question.'

**BP: On a very practical level, what advice would you give to students in scheduling their time and identifying resources after their lit review is done? What advice would you give them when they're actually collecting data, analysing it and writing it up?**
LC: My advice would be, schedule periods of no less than three weeks at a time just dedicated to this. Then you can go off and do other things in between. Thinking that you can do this by working in the nights or one night at a time, because you're like a machine, is unrealistic for most. Machines have tool up and tool down time, and so when you're doing this, you've got to get into it, you've got to start to get into the literature and so on. You've got to have time to think about it. It's good to have a deadline, so if you've got commitment to return to work, or something, you can schedule yourself appropriately.

You've got to manage your supervisor, and the best students manage their supervisor really well. So, just don't go missing for long periods of time and then dump something on their desk. Have an agreement with them that you're going to produce something, not the whole thing, for them in a particular point in time, and then make that a deadline and get their commitment around that deadline. You know, like, give them a moral obligation that you're doing this and you need ... So, set yourself deadlines so you can't let it all slide.

And as far as collecting the data is concerned, if you can get anyone to help you, that's good, or build it in to your life, somehow or another.

**BP: Let's finish with the challenge that all students face ... writing a good question. What are the characteristics do you think, that make up a good research question?**
LC: Simplicity. A good clear simple question that you can repeat numerous times when writing up your doctorate, to remind you and the reader. That's what you're doing. I think that's it, it needs to be good, clear, simple, and obviously, relevant.

**BP: A good clear simple answer ... you walk the talk, clearly. On behalf of my readers, thanks enormously.**

# 36

# Supervisors and Their Sociological (and Sometimes Seemingly Illogical) Imagination

Spike Boydell

*In this chapter, I explore the sociological imagination of the research supervisor and their influence on the methods, designs and practices for research into PM. I achieve this through creative non-fiction by using a dialectic approach in the tradition of an allegory. I draw on the interactions between a PM research scholar (we will call her Charlie) and her supervisory team as the basis for our allegorical investigation, as observed through the autoethnographic reflections of the lead (or primary) supervisor.*

At the end of this chapter the reader can:

* perceive the research journey from the other side, that is, the perspective of the supervisor rather than that of the doctoral scholar;
* identify the application of creative non-fiction as a research tool. This chapter demonstrates this approach by engaging an allegory, grounded on autoethnographic reflections, to facilitate discussion of methodology;
* feel less isolated in the naïve research discipline of PM through the realisation that the supervisor aspires to help and facilitate the journey, albeit that sometimes (or sadly perhaps often) scholars achieve their goal despite their supervisors.

Keywords: supervisor, scholar, allegory, autoethnography, creative non-fiction, sociological imagination

## Introduction

Our story starts on the fateful day that Charlie walked into my office, sat down across from me and said, 'So who's my supervisor now?' Such an approach was hardly unexpected from Charlie, a full fee-paying international scholar, who suddenly found herself a 'research orphan' after her primary supervisor relocated to another university to take up a promotion, and her co-supervisor retired. The untimely departure of her chosen supervisory team in the relatively early stages of her candidature was understandably unsettling for Charlie. Appropriately, she turned to me, as research chair of her academic School, to resolve the problem, even though she knew my research expertise was not in mainstream PM.

I knew Charlie as a bright and enthusiastic mid-career scholar, fully engaged in her research area. I had heard Charlie socialise her research in Faculty presentations, and knew her to be an active member of our full-time higher degree research cohort. She had an interesting project, aspects of which coincided with my own lived experience. However, if I was going to be involved in her supervision and provide a level of stability (or at least the façade thereof) to her research progression, I was going to have to ensure that she had a research support group of experienced PM researchers around her.

'So Charlie, how about I lead your supervision to keep you on track?' seemed to be the response she was looking for. 'If I'm going to do this, we need to agree a number of ground rules…' And so the journey began. We often speak of the research journey and the doctoral journey, but rarely of the supervisor's journey, role and equally huge emotional and time investment involved in facilitating and supporting a scholar to achieve their research goal – the eventual award of their doctorate. A proud and defining moment for 'one and all'.

I remember telling Charlie that if I was to be her supervisor I could not be her friend, at least not until she was Dr Charlie. I remember she was thrown by this assertion, and I sensed at the time that she did not understand the need from my perspective of setting very clear boundaries. Possibly this is because it is very hard for a research scholar to conceive of the supervisory experience from their early career researcher perspective. But if you are going to do the job of a research supervisor properly, the relationship needs to be grounded on the process and within an environment that allows hard-talking and serious but realistic expectations by all parties.

## Creative Non-Fiction and the Use of Allegory as a Research Tool

Before presenting the sociological imagination of a research journey from a supervisor's perspective it is important to contextualise the methodological approach adopted in this chapter, which combines creative non-fiction with a dialectic approach in the tradition of an allegory. An allegory offers a useful research tool as, whilst it is not opposed to truth, it presents an alternative and creative way of facilitating an audience's sense-making of the complex issues raised (Alvarez and Merchan, 1992). It allows us to move beyond temporal constraints (Lämsä and Sintonen, 2006) to better explore, in this case, a particular supervisory perspective.

Such an approach draws its methodological inspiration from the field of 'creative non-fiction' (an approach that we have previously used to good effect, on issues of the republic in Boydell and Arvanitakis, 2012, and on our carbon constrained world in Arvanitakis and Boydell, 2010). Methodologically such an approach involves the use of a number of possible techniques, including storytelling, allegory, vignettes, and reflections (Vickers, 2010) to make far-reaching and complex questions more accessible (Arvanitakis, 2008).

By using such a creative approach, which is grounded on the autoethnographic reality of the supervisor, this chapter is able to present these issues in a way that is not only accessible but also grounded in the lived experience (Dillow, 2009). This is something that is rarely achieved by standard approaches to academic writing and research, but one happily engaged with and elaborated upon in another chapter in this book (see Nugapitiya et al., Chapter 20).

Echoing Vickers (2010), this approach challenges the concept that there is only one objective form of enquiry or knowledge (Stanfield II, 1994). Rather, the approach adopted herein attempts to promote a pluralist method of forming knowledge that mirrors the heterogeneous and complex world we are describing in the supervisor/scholar relationship.

Whilst the allegory shared in this chapter recounts, perhaps inevitably, something of a turbulent journey – of course there are tears, drama, trauma, tantrums, breakups, relocations, volatility and passion … it's a story about a life-changing doctoral journey after all – be reassured that it has a happy ending, since I am now pleased to count Dr Charlie as one of my friends.

## Boundaries

As I said, Charlie was quite shocked when I suggested I could not be her friend until she was Dr Charlie. Managing the boundaries between supervisor and research students presents a number of potential challenges. If you are a friend, and a good friend, you should be able to be honest enough to tell your friend that you disapprove of what they are doing and how they are doing it, but it is up to them whether or not they listen to your advice. If you have clear boundaries it is easier to separate multiple roles during the transformation from student to equal. The supervisor's role is as a facilitator. As with other scholars before her, I had to facilitate Charlie's journey from student to her final goal of becoming Dr Charlie.

There are many traps and potential pitfalls along the journey for both the supervisor and the student as they share an intense intellectual space over an extended period (notionally three years here in Australia, as in the UK). In some cases there can be a mutual intellectual infatuation where boundaries become blurred, and even risk being transgressed if the parties in the unequal relationship become lovers.

The unequal relationship was very explicit when I worked in the Pacific, as all through their adolescence and journey into adulthood students were taught to respect God, their teachers, and their parents, in that order. Each was placed on a pedestal. The reality is that periodically the teachers would fall off the pedestal, occasionally transgressing the moral boundary. Creating perceived equality as friends is far more likely to lead to the intellectual infatuation escalating into something more intimate … Welcome to the world of academic morals 101.

The other boundaries are perhaps a tad boring after that one! They do however require managing quite carefully. The friend card is not the same as the director/manager/coordinator/mentor role. These are clear functions in providing academic leadership and a level of inspiration to a research scholar. The same cannot be said for being an emotional babysitter, surrogate parent or emotional analyst.

It is the role of the researcher to be the analyst of their data, but it is not for the supervisor to be an analyst of either their data or emotions. Relying on the supervisor(s) to be a rock is also a pedestal that can be shattered through illness, a sabbatical, or as in Charlie's case the earlier combined rock crushing of one supervisor taking a position elsewhere (and not taking Charlie with her) and another retiring simultaneously. But don't get me wrong; there is plenty of opportunity within the scholar/supervisor relationship for positive engagement, collaboration and mutual support towards a shared goal of timely completion.

An expectation of the supervisor as editor and ever-patient proof-reader is a grey area. It can work fine when the scholar efficiently takes on board what the supervisors have recommended and is seen to quickly learn from instructions/guidance that does not have to be repeated twice. It can result in some tension, however, when the supervisor thinks the student hasn't been listening and continues to make the same 'silly' mistakes in each draft. This can result in the supervisor having a rather twitchy red pen each time they engage with the manuscript, risking that they become frustrated in the detail (and correcting it) in a way that distracts from the more important supervisor role of guiding the bigger project towards timely completion.

This leads us conveniently towards a discussion on the expectations of the supervisor.

## Expectations

These are much easier to articulate with the benefit of hindsight, grounded as they are on lessons learned from the lived experience of supporting a diverse group of scholars on their respective research journeys, as well as the lessons of those who sadly failed to deliver and parted company with their supervisors. Actually, it becomes quite a long list, and whilst lengthy should provide a certain level of insight for those who aspire to follow in Charlie's footsteps.

Whilst the examples that follow are presented in no particular order, they are all important from the perspective of the scholar in understanding how to maximise the limited time that your supervisor can devote to your specific research project. Ideally, much as Charlie originally did with her initial supervisory team, you should select your supervisors because they are already leaders in a field that you want to understand, so that you can expand and progress a particular research conversation to a new level.

But even the best laid plans have to be adapted or changed on some occasions, and you may end up with different supervisors who bring a different approach to the process, may not be as expert in your specific field and may have different expectations of you. This means you need to be adaptable.

All supervisors will expect you to progress your research in a timely manner. If you are fortunate enough to secure a funded research position or a scholarship to work on a bigger project initiated by the potential supervisor, funding will normally be limited to three years anyway. In Australia, the current federally-funded research-training scheme can offer in a fee waiver for local (national) students. However, there are very clear time restrictions that result in the host university only receiving full payment from the government if the scholar submits to examination within three years (or thereabouts) of commencement, if on a full-time basis.

It goes without saying that any doctoral research scholar should have a hunger for knowledge and an ability to read voraciously, grasping new concepts and ideas quickly, effectively and efficiently. The thesis is not about reading, it is about writing. You need to write consistently and you need to write like an angel!

In the early stages of candidature, when all is said and done, more is usually said than done in terms of writing. I always find this an interesting stage as a supervisor, but also quite often a frustrating one. Given the time constraints I elaborated above, I often try and push prospective research students who aspire to join the specific research conversation of my research Centre to develop a very detailed research plan during the pre-enrolment period.

I know many other supervisors do not do this to the same detail, as they know that quite often by helping prospective students in that pre-enrolment stage they can end up in a situation where the prospective scholar may end up taking the evolved application/project to a more highly regarded university where they have been offered a full scholarship. Whilst this has happened to me on several occasions, those early collaborations in developing a robust proposal have been known to pay dividends in later collaborative journal articles.

Talking of articles, how much should you publish during your candidature? There are many different views on this and it largely depends on how output-oriented you are during your candidature, coupled with how confident you are in your own writing and ability. Inheriting Charlie, as I did, part way through her candidature I prioritised progression of human research ethics clearance, subsequent data collection, analysis, and completion of the draft, with a view to publishing during the examination period (when everything is fresh in the mind, and the anxious scholar needs to be kept occupied!) and afterwards, rather than concurrently with thesis production.

Some amazing scholars out there can produce a near-perfect thesis whilst building up a very strong publication record. One of my colleagues, for example, managed to publish 32 journal articles during his two-year and ten-month doctoral candidacy. One may question how much sleep he had, but he was profoundly disciplined and focused, which combined with a quite exceptional output enabled him to secure a highly competitive and well-funded postdoctoral Fellowship that will lead into a tenured position.

There are different approaches in different faculties to the ownership of academic output in published journal articles that are developed during the doctoral candidacy. My esteemed postdoctoral fellow colleague only added publications with his supervisory team to his impressive track record after he had graduated. Similarly, Charlie collaborated on a few papers with her supervisors that were published after she became Dr Charlie.

Most universities have clear directives/policies on authorship. In Australia, these accord with the Australian Code for the Responsible Conduct of Research, which protects research scholars in the sensitive power relationship that can develop in some research centres and faculties whereby a supervisor may attempt to have their name on a scholar's research without having made any direct written content contribution.

Charlie loves travelling, and during her candidature came up with many cunning ruses to present at global conferences. Conferences are of course one of the perks of being involved in academe as you often get travel to faraway and exciting places where you spend time locked in a hotel conference facility feeling profoundly jetlagged and trying to articulate your research in 15 minutes or less. Whilst you may rarely find time to properly explore the city you are visiting, you do have a chance to network and socialise your research to some hopefully interested audiences. Charlie was very good at this, and indeed it was through this sort of network that she made the contacts that led to her current appointment.

Depending on the state of candidature, conferences can also be a wonderful distraction and the amount of time consumed (and resultant jetlag) can distract from progressing the main thesis in a timely manner. Conferences don't just need to be international, as there are many local professional and academic groups that can help you to socialise your ideas whilst challenging you to take your thinking to a new level.

By taking your thinking to a new level you can fulfil the expectation to contribute in your research discipline (I'm loathe to say contribute to the 'body of knowledge' in a chapter in a book targeted at PM researchers, as PMBoK has all sorts of other meanings that are more about process than research). Much to many scholars' surprise, there is an expectation (which usually becomes a reality) for you to overtake your supervisors in terms of the specific content knowledge in the focused area of your research within the first year of candidacy. This is understandable, given that you are devoting your whole time to the exploration of ideas in that particular space.

Try not to be needy. Learn quickly, and make sure you do not need to be told something twice. Listen, learn to reflect rather than react. With your supervisor's consent, record formal discussions so you can listen back over what was actually said rather than acting on what you think that you may have heard. Be technologically savvy, and ensure you are computer literate and a self-learner in engaging with new research analysis software.

Use a bibliographic referencing tool like Endnote, it will help your productivity and your supervisor's patience. Backup, backup and backup again in multiple locations with clearly dated versions of your research. Technology seems to have a psychic insight into your stress levels, and it is unusual to complete the research journey without at least one serious data meltdown, so at worst you should never lose more than a day's input if you backup fastidiously.

Realise in dealing with your supervisors that patience is providence. Accept constructive feedback. Appreciate that the written word is the only word that will be examined, and as I mentioned above when all is said and done, when it comes to progress often more is said than done ... Which means that after the early 'honeymoon' period of convivial and supportive 'fireside' conversations over a pot of tea, your supervisors will be more interested in meeting to discuss what you have written than discussing what needs to be written. The important adage here is that the spoken word provokes reaction, whereas the written word promotes contemplation.

Where possible, try and remain sane. This of course is a huge expectation! When meeting with your supervisors try not to bring problems to the meeting. Rather, wherever possible, work things through in your own mind beforehand and bring suggested solutions for validation. Understand that supervisors are also human, sensitive and fallible creatures. Try not to cry in meetings; I have not always been successful and on some occasions Charlie was not the only one at fault here ... Not that her supervisors broke down, rather they probably were not sensitive enough to know when to back off.

To help you remain sane, ensure that you look after your physical and mental well-being. Remember to eat, exercise, chill out, stretch, sleep, shower and breathe (although not necessarily in that order).

Forget TV, Facebook, and Twitter for three years, but feel free to take a regular yoga class. I would add that I had interesting responses from the chapter reviewers for suggesting abstinence from Facebook and Twitter, a point that was well made. Whilst acknowledging that Facebook can be a useful networking and communication tool, what I want to highlight is that it can also be a huge distraction (like the incessant flow of 'busy work' emails) that can easily interrupt the 'space' and 'stillness' needed to internalise the big theories and issues you are attempting to master through your research journey.

Limit distractions and avoid opening too many new doors in the corridor of learning (curiously, as Dr Charlie has found, most opportunities will still be there when you are a doctor rather than Ms/Mr). In this regard, realise that 'fabulous' opportunities for guest editorials, conferences in amazing locations, book contracts, reviewing others work, beach/shopping trips, meetings (especially committee work with professional organisations or some other 'worthy' cause) are really just 'fabulous' opportunities for procrastination.

When writing, always write for your examiners (even though you may never get to meet them, but given the small world that is PM research you probably will). Remember that when you go to examination you are not the only person being examined; the examiners are also examining the supervisors. Most examiners will try and pass you (remembering that the options are usually (1) pass with flying colours, (2) make a few changes, (3) try harder and resubmit, or (4) goodbye) even though they may end up wanting to fail your supervisors.

The vast majority of theses that get as far as examination and complete the journey to submission do ultimately pass. Once the examiners' reports come back, after an excruciating wait of two or three months (and sometimes much longer) the first thing to do is to remember to breathe... and then take on board the comments, summarise how you have addressed them, finalise any corrections and get on with the rest of your life.

So, in summary, be output-oriented. Don't panic. Don't procrastinate. Don't melt down. Just get on with it... or as Swami Sivananda (1887–1963) said long before Nike coined it as a marketing phrase, 'Just Do It.'

# Tips

## STUDENTS

- Ask yourself, what do I expect of my supervisor? Make a list of five to ten key points. Leave the list for a day or two before revisiting it, revising and refining it. Use this list as part of your 'contract' with your supervisory team – but make sure you are ready to negotiate. But before you start to negotiate, make sure you also have an equally long list that clearly articulates what you will bring to the partnership.
- Schedule time in a supervisory session to discuss:
  - 'Are our expectations mutually inclusive or exclusive?'
  - 'Can we agree on a shared imagination for the research journey?'
  - 'Should creative non-fiction be added to the PM research toolkit?'

## SUPERVISORS

- Ask yourself what you expect of your scholar and write down these expectations – some supervisors actually write 'contracts'. Usually the process and progress issues are well articulated by the higher degree research policies' host academy, so concentrate on other deliverables including how much time you have to devote to the scholar (which is often very different to how much the university allows or expects).
- Identify what the university expects of you as a supervisor. Try and match this with what the research scholar expects of you. Manage the process. Define the boundaries. Be clear and realistic about your expectations. Provide timely and constructive feedback on all written submissions.

# References

Alvarez, J. L. and Merchan, C. (1992). The role of narrative fiction in the development of imagination for action. *International Studies of Management & Organization*, 22(3), 27–45.

Arvanitakis, J. (2008). Staging Maralinga and looking for community (or why we must desire community before we can find it). *Research in Drama Education: The Journal of Applied Theatre and Performance*, 13(3), 295–306.

Arvanitakis, J. and Boydell, S. (2010). The miner and the activist: An Australian parable for our carbon constrained world. *Journal of Political Ecology*, 17, 59–67.

Boydell, S. and Arvanitakis, J. (2012). Five questions on the republic. *Altitude: An e-Journal of Emerging Humanities Work*, 10.

Dillow, C. (2009). Growing up. A journey toward theoretical understanding. *Qualitative Inquiry*, 15(8), 1338–1351.

Lämsä, A.-M. and Sintonen, T. (2006). A narrative approach for organizational learning in a diverse organisation. *Journal of Workplace Learning*, 18(1/2), 106–120.

Stanfield II, J. H. (1994). Ethnic modeling in qualitative research. In N. K. Denzin and Y. S. Lincoln (eds), *Handbook of Qualitative Research*. Thousand Oaks, CA: Sage Publications, pp. 175–188.

Vickers, M. H. (2010). The creation of fiction to share other truths and different viewpoints: A creative journey and an interpretive process. *Qualitative Inquiry*, 16(7), 556–565.

# 37

# Common Flaws in Project Management Research Reports

Gilbert Silvius

*For a non-experienced researcher, as many students logically are, performing and reporting a research project can be a challenge. Many academic supervisors experience that research reports quite frequently show the same flaws. This chapter aims to prevent these common flaws by presenting and discussing them. Based upon the experience of the author as academic lead of several programmes on PM, the chapter discusses the flaws that research reports often show. The chapter concludes that when students learn that performing and reporting research projects are well-structured and logical processes, the quality of the reports, but also the quality of their studies can improve.*

At the end of this chapter, the reader can:

*   identify common flaws in research reports;
*   understand the logical relationships between different sections of a research report;
*   provide guidance on preventing flaws in research reports.

Keywords: reporting, research, consistency, flaws

## Introduction

Although PM is still not generally considered an academic discipline (Turner, 2006), there is a growing amount of academic work being done on PM. A part of this work is embedded in academic programmes, both on the undergraduate and graduate level. Worldwide, several hundreds of graduate programmes in PM exist, while PM is also a core course in many programmes in general management, engineering, architecture and facilities management.

The academic quality of graduate programmes suggests that students not only need to learn knowledge, but also need to able to challenge existing knowledge and develop new knowledge.

The courses and programmes on PM may therefore include a research component in which the students perform a research project, either as thesis work or as course work. Given the practical nature of PM, these research projects may include studying real-life situations, next to studying literature, in order to apply insights derived from literature and/or to develop new insights. These kinds of studies are usually of a deductive nature. And although deductive studies follow a very structured process, that is reflected in the study's report (Saunders, Lewis and Thornhill, 2012), many students struggle with writing a comprehensive and clear research report.

This chapter discusses the most common flaws in PM research reports that I encounter in my work as a college professor. The chapter is structured as follows. After a brief introduction of the background of this chapter and the author, 13 common flaws in PM research reports will be identified and discussed. These common flaws represent the core content of this chapter and provide guidance for students on how to improve the quality of their research reports. With this guidance, the students can eventually also improve their research projects.

## Background

In my work as lecturer on PM courses in several graduate and undergraduate programmes at different universities, I have assessed probably a thousand research papers and certainly close to a hundred master theses. What strikes me in this is that the students, in their enthusiasm to explain the results of their projects, make unnecessary mistakes. Mistakes that not always have to do with the quality of the work that they have done, but most with the way they report it. And because of this, they get frustrated by the feedback they receive from their professors and supervisors, because this feedback is mainly about 'putting the sentences in the right order'. Well. maybe it is. I've noticed that the structure of many papers is so poor, that it takes the attention away from the findings and conclusions of the study. And yes, well-structured and well-written research reports with meager results tend to get assessed higher than poorly structured reports with spectacular outcomes. Structure is important in research, and this reflects in the criteria we apply to research reports.

This chapter therefore aims to show why the flaws are actually flaws and how they can be prevented. Thereby helping students to write well-structured research reports, and prevent unnecessary mistakes.

## The Flaws

This section will present the common flaws encountered in research papers. Most of the flaws typically relate to deductive studies, as most PM studies are, but other flaws are of a more general nature. The order of the flaws is based on a logical clustering, not on their frequency of appearance.

### NO STRUCTURE

In my work, I have come across papers and research reports that simply showed no structure in terms of headings and sub-headings. And although structure plays a supportive role in research reports, a lack of structure is a major flaw. The function of a structure in a report is not just to improve the readability of the report or the lay-out, the function of structure is to support a storyline. Structure allows the reader to distinct between insights drawn from earlier work and the author's contribution. A logical and clear structure is a necessary condition for any research report.

Developing a structure is not difficult. It does not provide a creative challenge for the author. The structure prescribed in research textbooks, such Saunders et al. (2012), is clear and logical. We are not suggesting that other structures cannot exist, for example in indicative research or design science, but the presented structure suffices.

## NOT A CLEAR RESEARCH QUESTION

A second possible flaw is that of not stating a clear research question. The research question is of crucial importance to the reader, because it may define whether the report is of interest to him or her. The question also logically provides guidance for the research project. The research question should therefore be easily recognisable in the report and be stated as a clear and concise sentence.

A related flaw in research reports is stating the research question fairly late in the report. A research question should normally be provided near the end of the introduction, or immediately after the introduction. In most reports, this would be within the first three pages of the report, preferably within the first two. By not providing the research question in this logical place, the reader is being kept in uncertainty as to what the report actually is about. This is unnecessary, and may sometimes even be annoying. To 'hook your reader early, the introduction to your paper needs to motivate your topic, provide a working definition of your key variable(s), and clearly articulate the paper's contributions' (Webster and Watson, 2002).

Following the flow of the research report, the research question may need to be specified for the empirical part of the study. For example, based the conclusions of the literature review, the specified research question may refer to specific definitions or conceptualisations of the main concepts of the research question.

## MOTIVATING THE STUDY FROM THE ASSIGNMENT OR PERSONAL INTEREST

This mistake is an understandable one, given the setting in which the students are performing their research projects. When a project is part of the course work, many students tend to motivate the research by referring to the assignment that the professor gave them. They, for example, open the report with a statement like, 'This paper reports a case study on PMM in company XYZ, as part of the course work of the course Advanced Methods of Project Management.' This statement may be factually true, however, it is not a motivation that shows the relevance of the study to the potential readers. And that is the flaw. Research and a research question should be motivated from an observed phenomenon, problem or development that is of relevance to an intended target group. This target group may be a group of scientists, professionals, organisations or society as a whole. And this relevance should be 'proven' by referencing sources that state or confirm the observed issue and the concerns it may cause.

Similarly flawed is motivating the research project from the researcher's personal interest. Draft versions of theses may show this personal motivation, as the students are normally free to select a thesis project themselves. In itself, a section on personal motivation can provide relevant background information for the reader, especially in case of participative research. However, also in that case it cannot be the motivation for the research project or the research question.

## UNSTRUCTURED LITERATURE REVIEW

Students are aware that a research report should include a section on literature. However, they quite often seem unaware of the function of critically reviewing literature and therefore fail to provide a logical structure in this section. For the reader, this makes the literature review hard to comprehend, because he/she may not understand why a particular section is relevant to the study.

The literature review should, in a well-structured and accessible way, explore the main concepts of the research question, and their relationships. So, if the research question is stated as 'What is the relationship between concept A and concept B?', for example, 'What is the relationship between organisational culture and project success?', the logical structure of the literature review is to first explore the literature on concept A (in the example: organisational culture), then on concept B (project success) and then on the relationship between the two concepts (what earlier studies provided insight on the relationship between organisational culture and project success?).

Each section within the literature review should explore definitions, conceptualisations, shared insights, conflicting opinions and end with a brief conclusion. These conclusions build up to the definitions, conceptualisations and instruments that will be used in the empirical part of the study.

Optimally, the researcher also introduces this structure of the literature review, thereby guiding the reader through the report.

## SELECTIVE LITERATURE REVIEW

Another potential flaw in the literature review is that of considering only a limited number of sources that are selected on their availability. These students do not seem to understand the reason and relevance of reviewing literature and are just filling the literature section in the report because it is required by the format. In itself, being selective in discussing the literature is probably necessary and justified. Most topics, also in PM, have been discussed in a large number of publications that need not be covered fully. On the contrary, literature reviews should be concise and to the point. This requires the selection to be appropriate. The most influential and relevant theories, perspectives or insights on a topic should be covered. For a student, it may be hard to understand which insights are most influential or relevant. However, several authors provide guidance for this. For example, Webster and Watson (2002) recommend the following approach.

- Start with searching for relevant articles in the leading journals in the field. The major contributions and researchers will most likely seek publication in the leading journals, so therefore it makes sense to start with them. In the field of PM, the number of dedicated journals is limited, with as leading journals the *International Journal of Project Management* (IJPM) and *Project Management Journal* (PMJ), which means that researchers also need to consider journals in other domains such as management, engineering, construction, social sciences and IT.
- A second step should be to examine selected conference proceedings, especially those with a reputation for quality. In the PM field, relevant conferences are the bi-annual research and education conference of the Project Management Institute (PMI), the annual world congress of the International Project Management Association (IPMA), the PM track of the annual conference of the European Academy of Management (EURAM) and the bi-annual IRNOP conference. However, because PM is an interdisciplinary field, relevant studies may also appear in other conferences.

- As a next step, the researcher should go backward by reviewing the citations for the articles and papers found in the first two steps. The number of studies that reference a specific earlier publication or insight is an indication of the influence of this publication/insight.
- Then, the student should go forward by searching for articles that reference the paper he or she found in the previous steps.

Following this systematic search process should ensure that the student finds a relatively complete census of relevant literature. The student can recognise when he or she is nearing completion, when new publications do not add new insights, concepts or perspectives to the body of literature already found.

## NO CRITICAL REFLECTION ON THE LITERATURE

Yet another flaw in the literature section of a research report can be that of lacking a critical reflection. In that case the section shows listings of quotes, definitions or conclusions from literature, without adding the researcher's reflection on how this leads to shared insights or conflicting insights, and eventually theory building. The researcher should not reproduce literature but review it. And based on this review, conclude available insights, conceptualisations, instruments and hypothesis that are relevant to the study.

An important aspect of the review of the literature is that it should be critical (Saunders et al., 2012). For students, being critical may be difficult, because they may feel not knowledgeable or experienced enough to be critical, or they may not understand how they should be critical. Mingers (2000) suggests four aspects of a critical approach:

- critique about rhetoric, meaning appraising or evaluating a problem with effective use of language;
- critique about tradition, meaning questioning the usual perspective with which a problem is approached;
- critique about authority, meaning evaluating the quality of the literature that is reviewed;
- critique about objectivity, meaning recognising in the review that the knowledge and insights found in literature are not value free.

## NOT CONNECTING THE EMPIRICAL STUDY TO THE LITERATURE REVIEW

One of the most common flaws I encounter is that of a lack of connection between the literature review and the empirical work. Meaning that the definitions, insights and models found in the literature review do not reflect in the empirical part of the research. If the section on literature was to be removed from the report, it would not make a difference. The empirical study would not logically follow the literature review in the sense that it used the models and instruments that were provided in the literature. Sometimes the empirical study even introduces models or instruments that did not show in the literature review, or the author introduces a new instrument that is not grounded in literature.

This flaw again shows the misunderstanding students may have about the function of the literature review. Critically reviewing the available literature is a logical and necessary step to understand what insights earlier studies have generated on the definition and conceptualisation of the main elements of the research question and their relationships. It provides the insights and instruments on which the researcher can build his/her work and allows the researcher to build upon earlier work, so that he or she does not have to start from scratch. Without reviewing and utilising earlier studies, research would be practically impossible.

Another important aspect of literature review is that it should strengthen the relevancy of the research question, by pointing out blind spots or omitted perspectives in the literature. And, depending on what insights are found in the literature, it may provide motivation for an explorative study that develops new theory, or a deductive one, that tests or verifies existing theory.

If a research report fails to show the logical connection between the insights derived from literature and the empirical study, this may be an indication that the researcher actually did not consider the literature prior to performing his or her own empirical study. This is a major issue in a research project that threatens the consistency and the quality of the work. Empirical studies that use instruments (questionnaires, interview protocols and so on) which are not grounded in literature are basically beyond salvation as a deductive study. In that case, the student may consider changing the deductive approach to an inductive approach, but the impact of that goes beyond the aim of this chapter.

## UNCLEAR RESEARCH PROCESS

Another flaw in research reports is that of not properly revealing and motivating the research process. A basic principle of research is that it follows a structured process and that this process can be reviewed and assessed by the reader. Students do not always fully apprehend this notion and tend to over-focus on the content of their research project and their findings. Understandable as this may be, it is not up to standard in a research report. The report should properly show and motivate the different steps of the research process – from the sources and selection criteria, to the selection of research strategy and data collection, and the method of analysis.

An argument could be made whether a research report should also mention its underlying theoretical perspective. For academic reasons, I would be inclined to agree with this argument. However, in applied research, as many studies on PM are, we can observe that many publications do not refer to a specific theoretical perspective.

## THE RESEARCH STRATEGY AS A GOAL, NOT AS A MEANS TO A GOAL

Related to the flaw of not properly motivating the choices made during the research process, mentioned above, is that of presenting the research strategy as the goal of the study. It appears as, 'The goal of this project was to perform a case study on...'. Students should understand that the goal of a research project is not to perform a case study, a survey, a focus group discussion or a Delphi study. All of these are research strategies that should be suitable for the research question we ask ourselves. The goal of a research project is to answer a research question, and the research strategy should be selected based upon its appropriateness to answer the research question.

## NO DISTINCTION BETWEEN PRESENTATION OF DATA AND ANALYSIS/ INTERPRETATION OF DATA

Another common flaw is that of not clearly separating the objective presentation of the data found in the study, and the subjective analysis or interpretation of that data. Students tend to assume that the reader is mostly interested in analysis and interpretation. This may be true, however, this does not imply that the 'pure' data from the study should not be presented.

In defence of the students, in some research strategies the raw data are not easily presentable. For example, in qualitative studies based on content analysis of interviews, providing the transcripts of the interviews is not suitable for the main body text of a research report. In that case, adding the transcripts as appendices, or stating that they can be retrieved from the authors, would suffice. However, quantitative studies in general generate very presentable data that should be included in the research report to inform the reader before the author performs his/her analysis. And the structure of the 'results' section of the report should clearly show the distinction between the data as such, perhaps with some observations and explanation but without analysis, and the analysis of the data.

## NON-SYSTEMATIC ANALYSIS OF QUALITATIVE DATA

For many students, the statistical techniques used in the analysis of quantitative data are hard to master. Calculating means, standard deviations and correlation coefficients are usually not an obstacle, but more complex procedures are considered as complicated, especially for less analytical and mathematically talented students. It may be for this reason that a qualitative research strategy appeals to many students. They associate a quantitative strategy with the collection of limited data, interviews and summarised findings, and this is also how they perform their studies.

The flaw I want to highlight here is that of non-systematic analysis of quantitative data. In the study of social systems, such as projects, qualitative research strategies are important for the creation of new insights. Qualitative research is concerned with the meaning rather than the measurement of organisational phenomena (Daft, 1983). What is misunderstood by many students is that qualitative research still requires rigorous procedures. Procedures regarding the collection and also the analysis of data. For example, a frequently used data collection technique in qualitative research is interviews, mostly semi-structured or unstructured. Students also use this technique a lot because it is relatively easy to realise. The procedures for analysing data from unstructured or semi-structured interviews include transcription of the interviews, coding the answers and analysing the content in a structured way. Performing these analyses properly is not an 'easy' process and requires a substantial effort from the researcher. In my experience, students tend to underestimate this process and provide unstructured and non-systematic analysis of their results. One of the reasons for this may be that they are not yet skilled enough to do proper coding and analysis, or that they simply do not make the proper effort.

## NOT ANSWERING THE RESEARCH QUESTION

A research project aims to answer a research question. However, they sometimes actually fail to do so. I have come across reports that show the work the researcher did, but fail to provide an answer to the research question. The reasons for this may be different.

Firstly, in order to be able to answer the research question, the report needs to state the question. This refers to the flaw of 'not a clear research question', mentioned earlier. If the question is not clear, it is basically impossible to answer it clearly.

Another reason for not answering the question is providing a sloppy conclusion. Students may be so enthusiastic about having some interesting results in their study, or about finishing the research report, that they feel the report 'speaks for itself', and they provide an incomplete conclusion. In those cases, the conclusion usually states some obvious statements, repeating lines that have been included in the earlier sections of the report. A proper conclusion should summarise the whole of the findings of the study, both the literature part and the empirical part, and reflect on these findings in an answer on the research question. For the reader this answer should be clearly identified. The conclusion should further also mention the limitations of the study's findings and conclusion, and provide some discussion on the conclusion, relating it to the existing literature/body of knowledge, in order to elaborate on its contribution.

A third reason for not answering the question is that the researcher got deviated along the way of his/her research project. Research projects are just like regular projects in a way that not everything may develop according to the plan that was set out at the beginning of the project. It may happen that, in hindsight, when reflecting on the data collection, analysis and the conclusions, the research concludes that he or she did not answer the planned research question, but answered a modified research question. What students quite often do not understand is that in a research project this is actually not a big problem. When a study is completed, it is reviewed or examined based upon the report as such. The original plan for the study is usually not a part of that review or examination, and so the deviations from the plan are not judged. Therefore it may very well happen that, based upon the reflection on the work that has been done, the research question of the study is modified in order to better cover the work of the study. One could consider this some kind of 'reverse engineering' of the research project in order to make it more consistent. And in research reports, consistency and quality are more important than following the plan that actually is not included in the report.

## ADDING 'FLUFF'

A last flaw that I would like to bring to the attention of students is that of having unnecessary texts or 'fluff', in the research report. One of the first things students tend to ask their professors when they are given the assignment to write a research paper, is, 'How many pages should it be?' And in this question, their concern is not about limiting themselves to a restricted number of pages or words, but about how many pages to fill. They consider writing as their big challenge.

What students need to understand is that, in reporting research, the issue is not to write as much as one can, but to write as little as one can. It is the quality of the report that is important, not the quantity. The report should provide a logical flow, be consistent, be precise and be concise. If the student can do that in 3,000 words, that is fine. If he/she needs 10,000 words, that is also fine. (Of course, for journal or conference papers, other guidelines may apply.)

Any sections or bits of text that do not contribute to a well-flowing, consistent, precise and concise report are unnecessary and should be taken out. They basically correspond that the author has either nothing of interest to say anymore or did not complete adequate research. The author may not like taking out bits of text because he/she probably worked hard on them and is attached to them, but the quality of the report is the main criterion. And that quality is helped by writing lean and to the point.

## How to Prevent These Flaws?

The logical question that follows the discussion of flaws is of course: How to prevent them? And actually the answer to that question is just as logical: By not making them! The directions that research textbooks provide, and the common flaws presented in this chapter, should provide enough practical guidance for students on how to prevent the flaws and write a proper research report.

Perhaps the best advice for students is to simply follow the prescribed structures. Good research is based on a well-structured and rigorous process. That does not mean that doing research is a non-creative and mechanical process. Not at all! Doing research is a very creative process. But what students need to understand is that creativity is not spent on 'fancy' titles, reinventing the wheel or flashy lay-outs. The creativity of research is content-oriented. It is about finding new perspectives, raising new questions and applying new concepts. However, in order to develop this creativity, the researcher has to understand what research is and what has already been done in his/her field of interest. Research is not difficult, but it requires serious effort.

## Conclusion

This chapter set out to create awareness of common flaws in research reports made by students and beginning researchers in the field of PM. It discussed common flaws in PM research reports. Preventing these flaws is relatively easy. The trick is to simply not make them. Numerous textbooks and articles provide more than enough guidance to perform and report a research project properly. Doing research is not difficult, but is disciplined. Following a rigorous and structured process to find an answer to a creative question.

Does this mean that we suggest that research is a mechanical process? Not at all. There is certainly a level of craftsmanship related to research (Daft, 1983), however, this may be too much to ask from beginning researchers and students. Following the analogy of research as a craft, we should keep in mind that professors and academic supervisors should be the 'masters', that pass on the skills of the craft to our 'apprentices', the students. I hope that with this chapter we may have contributed to this passing on of the skill.

## References

Daft, R. L. (1983). Learning the craft of organizational research. *Academy of Management Review*, 8(4), 539–546.

Mingers, J. (2000). What it is to be critical? Teaching a critical approach to management undergraduates. *Management learning*, 32(2), 219–237.

Robson, C. (2011). *Real World Research*, 3rd edition. Chichester: John Wiley & Sons.

Saunders, M., Lewis, P. and Thornhill, A. (2012). *Research Methods for Business Students*, 6th edition. Edinburgh: Pearson Education.

Turner, J. R. (2006). Towards a theory of project management: The nature of the project governance and project management. *International Journal of Project Management*, 24(4), 93–95.

Webster, J. and Watson, R. T. (2002). Analyzing the past to prepare for the future: Writing a literature review, *MIS Quarterly*, 26(2), xiii–xxiii.

# 38

# Publish or Perish? Transforming Your Thesis into a Tangible Product

Darren Dalcher

*What now? You have just completed the longest piece of writing you will probably ever write by yourself. The journey has been long and arduous and you are probably seeking to share the results with others. Turning the completed work into a published book might be one way forward, but it is difficult to grasp all the challenges you might be facing and even more difficult to determine where you might turn for advice. This chapter aims to inform you about the issues you should consider in relation to publishing your dissertation as a book, and to look at ways of managing and simplifying that process. One of the key suggestions is that you need to start planning the transition from dissertation to book as soon as possible and the chapter offers some tangible suggestions to embark on that journey.*

At the end of this chapter, the reader can:

* explain the differences between a dissertation and a book;
* develop strategies for developing your dissertation into a book;
* improve your writing and communication skills;
* put together a publishing proposal;
* recognise the timing and requirements related to the publishing cycle.

Keywords: publish, dissertation, book, writing, publishing proposal, publishing cycle, audience, narrative, writing style

## Research as Unpublished Work

A glance through older manuscripts and books will reveal that a mere half century ago, citing a doctoral dissertation included an indication that it was unpublished. Academic CVs would typically include a short section dedicated to unpublished works produced towards academic qualifications.

The process required to produce the completed dissertation would have been more onerous and would have included a number of steps:

- handwriting each page of text in legible handwriting;
- transferring the handwritten pages to a typist;
- typing of the content;
- collecting the finished pages;
- proofreading each page, and marking the errors;
- retyping of the entire page to remove the errors;
- followed by further cycles of: reading, correcting and typing, until each page was correctly typed;
- paying for the total number of typed pages;
- collating the pages into piles;
- taking the stacked piles to the binders;
- binding;
- checking that pages were bound in the correct order;
- submitting the dissertation to the university.

Corrections following the viva-voce involved a similar process. It is no wonder that only a very small proportion of dissertations, estimated at fractionally under 1 per cent, were ultimately published as books.

## The Urge to Publish

When I was writing up my PhD dissertation, I recall attending a training session that emphasised the fact that most doctoral dissertations would only be read by a handful of people. The figure of five or less readers stuck with me for a long time as it felt like a lot of work for a very meagre return.

However, that is no longer the case for most dissertations. The very fact that you are reading this chapter suggests that you might have an interest in publishing your thesis.

Indeed, having invested three to seven years in a research project, it is only natural that you will wish to share the results with a wider audience. Getting your work published and widely distributed is a chance to make it known to more than that handful of people. It may also mean recognition for your effort, and potentially a promotion opportunity for you, your talents and your findings. Perhaps most important of all it represents an opportunity for recognition of achievement at the highest level of Maslow's Hierarchy of needs by moving from esteem, towards self-actualisation, and proving the fulfilment of your potential.

The advent of Internet and IT technology in general have enabled institutions, and in some cases individual authors, to digitise and offer access to dissertations. Moreover, various databases are currently being created in an attempt to include all 'published' dissertations, so what is available is in a process of transition. Nonetheless, many researchers look to publish their results through a publisher.

Traditionally, many of the published dissertations will have been offered through academic presses run by different universities. Only a small minority would have gone through a commercial publishing house.

However, a trend observed in recent years has seen the growth of specialised publishing houses that only deal with academic dissertations. The emergence of such specialism is entirely underpinned by the wide availability of good quality word processing enabling every student to type, develop, draw, and add charts and statistics to their work. The production process is a do-it-yourself publishing process with the student uploading a final format PDF file that is ready to be printed, entering their personal details, adding a short section of blurb that will become the back cover and selecting the picture or photograph for the front cover. Once formally submitted, the production process will take over, and you will receive one free copy of your book in the post within eight weeks.

The book will be available through online retailers and via print on demand outlets. While there is no cost involved, the process resembles self-publishing, and the author will receive little or no advice other than standard templates and advice files. On the other hand, very little work is needed to transform the dissertation into a published book. It is worth remembering that the published book will resemble an academic dissertation, and not benefit from professional rearrangement, editing and typesetting that can significantly improve the appearance, structure and presentation of the final product. Table 38.1 offers a summary of these characteristics.

**Table 38.1    Differences between a dissertation and a book**

|  | Dissertation | Book |
| --- | --- | --- |
| Topic | Research question or problem | Area of interest |
| Audience | Examiners | Paying readers |
| Author | Student | Expert |
| Authority | Needs proving | Assumed |
| Purpose | Demonstrate capability | Share ideas and information |
| Product | Examination | Commercial book |
| Success measure | Pass examination | Commercial sales<br>Book reviews |
| Attributes | Comprehensive<br>Informed | Authoritative |
|  | Defensive<br>Sequential<br>Supported<br>Research-oriented | Others to be defined in proposal |
| Structure | Process-driven | Subject-centred |
| Constraints | Imposed word limit (max 40–100K words) | Commercial (typical 35–60K words) |
| Language | Academic with disciplinary jargon | Clear and targeted at audience |
| Style | Imposed | Crafted narrative |
| Evidence | Infused with quotes and comparative definitions | As needed |
| References | Every relevant source | As needed |
| Methodology | Essential element:<br>Research design central to story | As needed |
| Conclusions | Conclusions at the end | Insights as identified |
| Story | Highly structured: Heavy signposting | Guiding narrative: Unfolding story |

## Thinking about Your Book

If you are looking to publish, the two main challenges are to find a publisher interested in your book, and to rework your dissertation to meet the expectation of a new audience. The former implies identifying a match with a publisher. The latter suggests a realistic understanding of the difference between your dissertation and the book you are hoping to deliver.

If you are looking to have your work published as a regular book, you will need to identify a publisher, discuss their expectations and look at the quality of their existing books, while considering their reputation and their global influence and marketing ability. You could even look at a number of candidates and compare what they can offer. You could do worse than go to a bookshop and look at some of their published products.

However, before you make contact with publishers it is worth considering why such a low percentage of dissertations have actually been transformed into books. While it is fair to focus on technology as a key game changer and enabler, there are other issues that need to be taken into account. It is worth remembering that publishers will expect you to produce a detailed book proposal, which makes a clear and convincing case for publishing your book idea (this will be explored in a later section of this chapter).

As you can see there are many differences between a dissertation and a book that need to be taken into account. The following paragraphs will address some of these considerations.

**Topic**: Many dissertation topics are simply not suitable as books. Your choice of topic has been derived from a literature search, which identified gaps, and from a desire to focus on an area of work that is challenging and promising. The area is likely to be research-focused, but may not be of primary interest to those not engaged in research. Moreover, the narrow focus of your investigation enforced through the need to identify a particular niche, and refine more specific research questions or hypotheses, will have excluded vast tracts of knowledge and multiple interests. Dissertations will normally offer an intense focus on very narrow phenomena and the question you must ask yourself is whether additional content is needed to offer balanced coverage of your area and topic.

**Audience**: A book proposal will normally identify the topic and the potential audience. In order to make the proposal viable, a book should have a well-defined market. However, you need to consider if your research interests are likely to be of interest to practitioners, researchers, undergraduates or postgraduate students. Most research is too narrowly defined to be useful for teaching. It is also likely to be too specific for practitioners. Identifying an interested audience is an important part of the commissioning process and many publishers are likely to do their own market research by sending drafts of your proposal to prospective members of the community that you propose in order to ascertain the likely levels of interest in your suggested publication. Not surprisingly, your publisher would be seeking reassurance that over five or so years, the book is likely to become viable as a commercial proposition and sell several hundred to several thousand copies. If the likely interest is very small and specialised, you are probably better off talking to academic publishing houses, university presses or to relevant professional associations who may be able to target more specific audiences, professions or skills.

**Writing**: Your dissertations will need to be rewritten using a different style and approach in order to make a convincing publication. During the writing up phase of your research you will have acquired skills of writing in academic style, which is defensive and tightly argued. Many assertions will require the development of support and justification. The structure is likely to be rigid and produce ample evidence regarding the direction of progress in your work. There will also be a significant written emphasis on the process of research which will come through your narrative. The formal writing style encouraged in academic writing may not be suitable to the audience that you identify. The rather cautious approach with multiple justifications and links that is used in academic writing may feel rather laborious to readers seeking advice or following an interest in the subject. It is also worth remembering that readers will be turning to your book because you are an expert in the field; they will be seeking insights, not chains of proof, justification and support. A good book should be understandable, with coherent voice and storyline that capture the readers' interest and imagination.

Once you have a good understanding of the issues, and a good idea about the topic and audience, it might be a good time to initiate the discussion with representatives from various publishing houses. They will have much clearer ideas about the areas that are of interest to their readers and will be able to guide you in positioning your proposal.

## Strategies for Converting Your Dissertation to a Book

Even an award-winning dissertation is not ready to be published as a book. Revising your dissertation into a book will require a significant effort. Having made a significant emotional and time investment in developing the dissertation, many researchers are reluctant to eliminate parts of their work, however you need to be focused on the needs and expectations of your readers. Minimal changes will probably be insufficient to turn your dissertation into a quality book.

The choice you have is whether to do a partial, yet good enough revision to address some of the issues highlighted above which will probably result in a reasonable product. The alternative is to invest the time and effort in addressing the key issues and rewriting your work from scratch. This will result in a significantly superior product but must be traded-off against the time, effort, and willingness to face the work when it is still fresh in your mind.

## Writing for the Right Audience

Effective writing is about communicating a clear message with the audience in mind. Effective communication is concerned with presenting the message in a form that appeals to the target audience and hence extends beyond the delivery of a scientifically accurate and grammatically correct written artefact. In order to communicate effectively an author must have a clear idea as to why he, or she, is writing, what the readers would be expecting and how the connection between the two is to be made. Your dissertation was written for a different audience and purpose, and therefore the writing will need to be restructured to fit the new intention.

Using a communication analogy, some of the background information required in the dissertation may be background noise to the intended readers of your book. Noise needs to be reduced, or eliminated and the next section will make some specific suggestions about which aspects to concentrate on. The references at the end of this chapter include a number of sources that can be used to structure and improve your writing style and approach.

Writing clearly is a crucial skill that develops over time. If you are looking for a minimal set of guidelines, George Orwell offered a simple list of five rules for effective writing:

1. Never use a metaphor, simile or other figure of speech which you are used to seeing in print.
2. Never use a long word where a short one will do.
3. If it is possible to cut a word out, always cut it out.
4. Never use the passive where you can use the active.
5. Never use a foreign phrase, a scientific word or a jargon word if you can think of an everyday English equivalent.

Language however is characterised by its limits as well as its power. Where the rules appear to be insufficient or overly oppressive, authors are encouraged to find their own way of expressing their emerging story. Accordingly, Orwell proposed one final additional rule:

6.  Break any of these rules sooner than saying anything outright barbarous.

## Transforming Your Written Work

Having addressed the need to make the message clear, it is time to turn to the specific areas that are likely to require modification and transformation:

**Literature review**: The literature review forms a significant part of the research dissertation, which underpins your writing and places it in context. The evidence that you have read all the relevant sources, critically surveyed the different perspectives and understood the academic debates is not required: your book will be less dependent on what came before. The literature section can be replaced by a brief background discussion, or potentially be eliminated all together, depending on the orientation and intended readership.

**Structure**: Chapters of a dissertation are structured in a very rigid way, stretching from introduction to literature review, to research methods, findings, evaluation and ultimately to a conclusion which sets the contribution, defines the limitations and concludes about the impact of your work. You will need to remove the academic scaffolding to make your work reader friendly. The book will not require the same kind of division and a number of the chapters can be eliminated or reduced to refocus on the heart of the story and reorganise the material to make it more interesting. The old abstract, conclusion and possibly the introduction are likely to prove redundant.

**Narrative**: The dissertation is normally read as a sequential story that moves from one chapter to the next to describe your research journey. The focus on the process of research is less important to your readers. Your book may benefit from a more creative structure, with alternative routes for different reader communities. The flow of the text can make the separation of ideas more intuitive. Excessive separation and sub-division, which may have existed in your thesis, can thus be eliminated. Only add the details needed for the story rather than all you know. Conclusions should be developed and embellished in the appropriate places as you proceed without waiting for the final chapter.

**Research methods**: Your research design and the choice of methods are crucial for assessing the value of your work, however, they are probably of little relevance to your readers. While readers may be interested in obtaining a general impression of your approach, they are unlikely to seek to engage with the finer details of your research design and the specific architectural components of your methodology.

This is especially the case if your target audience is practitioners, or undergraduate students. Consider removing or reducing the chapter focused on the research process unless it is essential to your proposal. The methodology may fit in your new introductory chapter and set some of the context for the book.

**Writing style**: Dissertations are written in a defensive style with clear signposting. Depending on the intended audience for your book, consider adopting a free-flowing style and speaking with greater authority about your subject. The book needs to be readable and appealing so most of your paragraphs will probably require rewriting. You can reduce the number of citations that were marshalled to support your assertions to enable readers to glimpse the essential elements of your argument. Try to keep the larger picture in view and remember the profile of your audience as you re-contextualise the work from their perspective.

**Support**: Eliminate some of the evidence and quotes which were used to prove and support your assertions. You can still use footnotes to maintain some of the evidence that underpins your story, if that fits with the theme, focus and intended audience for your book. Look at each quotation and ask yourself if it is part of your story, or part of your defensive evidence? If you decide to include some of the underpinning quotes, it may be useful to paraphrase them to fit into your general narrative.

**Repetition**: Dissertation's chapters often start with an introduction, followed by the content and conclude with a summary, which may emphasise the value of your approach or findings. Consider if that structure is needed for your book, and whether the same level of formality in your approach to stating your message is needed. In addition your dissertation is also likely to include repetitions between the introduction, main body and conclusions chapter. This structure is probably redundant in your book, and can be revised and significantly reduced.

**Writing**: Your writing should be free from academic jargon and long complicated sentences which might have featured in your dissertation. Aim the revised writing at your target audience and use your own voice. Read each sentence out loud to identify convoluted writing style. Seek effective simplicity in conveying your ideas and avoid complicating your content. Try to reduce lengthy paragraphs to the essential ideas needed by your audience.

**Beginning and end**: You will also need to write a short introduction to the book aimed at your specific audience. The purpose of the introduction is to capture the attention of the audience. This is a very important chapter as it provides the initial interface with your writing for most readers. It is also worth remembering that online booksellers are likely to make the first pages available to view, so it is certainly worth the effort. A conclusion focused on your new story (not on your contribution and limitations) is also required to round off the writing.

**Additional issues**: Remember to remove all reference to words such as thesis, dissertation, PhD and report and consider others such as research. You will need to look into the acquisition of permissions for using copyright materials and approvals for some quotes and diagrams: authors are responsible for obtaining their own permissions, and there may well be material that was legitimately included and referenced in the dissertation that will need a formal written permission if it is to be commercially published. You can also remove unneeded cross-references to other chapters. In addition, you might want to revisit your diagrams and charts: while they may have worked on a large page, and may have a rudimentary feel in the dissertation, they will become more prominent in your book and may need to be adjusted for size and quality (especially if you consider that e-readers are still not very good at handling diagrams).

**Appendices**: Detailed tables are unlikely to be of major interest to your readers. Consider the role and position of each table. The ones that are not directly relevant to the story can be relegated to the appendices (remember: when you have finished the body of the work to revisit the appendices and consider removing some of the content as the page count is fully costed in commercial publishing). An effective strategy for dealing with the additional material is to include it in the additional resources available online to support your book!

## Putting Together a Publishing Proposal

Most publishers will have standard templates for presenting proposals which you will be expected to complete before your proposal is considered. The proposal is likely to go out to reviewers to establish the level of interest in the topic, your overall approach and the proposed structure.

This is likely to result in feedback and you may be asked to revise your proposal to address the concerns raised by the reviewers and editors.

While each publishing house will have specific requirements the basic templates are essentially similar. A typical proposal will be in the range of four to 15 pages long and cover the following key aspects.

- statement of rationale for your book;
- identification of the target audience;
- list of the unique features of your approach;
- information about the target markets;
- list of main chapters or sections, together with a brief description of each;
- brief review of the competition (that is, other titles on the market, with their relative strengths and weaknesses).

Supplementary material is likely to include:

- brief CV of the proposed author;
- list of other publications, if any;
- sample chapters.

The purpose of the proposal document is to provide a clear statement of the focus and content of your book that will enable the publishers to determine the financial viability of the project. The identification of the specific market and the proposed genre is very important to framing the proposal. The rest of the information is used to establish your credibility as an author, to determine the competition, and to identify the unique selling points and sales hooks that distinguish your proposal from all other offerings. The information combined with market knowledge, experience and business intelligence will play a part in evaluating the business value and assessing the feasibility of your proposal, and thus determine if the project is to be allowed to proceed.

## Time and the Publishing Cycle

If you have published a journal article, you will already be aware that publishing can have a long lead-time. Publishing a book takes significantly longer as the publishers will have multiple checks at the beginning of the process, which can be viewed as quality assurance gates intended to evaluate the quality and feasibility of your proposal and your writing ability.

Many publishers suggest that the effort required to transform a dissertation to a book requires a minimum of 12 months' work, although that period has also been known to exceed five years. It might be useful before we explore the process to gain a better understanding of the publishing process.

A book typically begins its life in the editorial department which is responsible for commissioning titles, identifying authors, negotiating contracts, managing writing projects and handing over completed manuscripts to the editing department, which prepares your manuscript for production. The production department oversees the production process which ultimately results in a bound book. Specific tasks such as copy-editing, cover design, typesetting and printing may be handled in-house or contracted out to specialist companies, often located in other countries. The marketing department will support the promotion and advertising of specific titles and produce and distribute brochures and catalogues.

To gain a better understanding of the decisions made by the publishing house, it might be useful to see how they relate to the publishing cycle, or the different stages in the life of a book. Publishing decisions are underpinned by risks assessed under very uncertain conditions. The unknown factors are typically at their highest during the earlier phases in the publishing cycle.

The initial decision-making hurdle is whether to commission an idea or concept. It is akin to a launch decision for a project, based on an enthusiastic yet unknown author, an appealing concept or idea, and a brief book proposal. It commits the publisher to potentially significant expenses in terms of time, effort, and the costs of development, production and promotion of a title. There are very few trustworthy indicators at this stage, and the publishers are therefore likely to send your proposal to be reviewed by a number of qualified reviewers who will be asked to comment on the value and suitability of your approach and the likelihood that it will make a solid book that they may want to read and pay for. Given the high degree of uncertainty, the use of reviewers is an information-buying strategy that provides added reassurance about a proposed title. If the case appears to support the proposal, the publisher will offer you a contract. From a company perspective, they will be issuing a multitude of contracts in the hope that at least some are successful, and that a few become very successful.

Next, the publishers have to decide on the price of the book and the size of the print runs. Different markets may have different pricing strategies but ultimately the decisions will hinge on the perception of the size of the market, the expectation of sales and the perception of how much the market will be willing to pay for a book of this type, in its proposed format and binding. Different prices and binding types will lead to different sale estimates. The publisher will be keen to predict sale numbers to avoid being left with expensive excess unsold stock. The decisions will determine the size of the print run.

This is one of the areas most changed by technology. Many publishers now issue titles simultaneously as e-books. Indeed, some publishers will only issue e-book editions thereby changing some of the decision patterns.

After the book has been printed and you have a few copies of your title on your bookcase, your initial role is almost over, however the cycle still continues. Once the initial stock has been depleted the publisher will be faced with a decision about the future of the title: They may opt for a traditional litho reprint, or a digital reprint, or decide to offer a paperback of a book previously published as hard cover, or decide to move the book to Print on Demand, which effectively keeps it in print for anyone wishing to purchase a hard copy edition. Note that e-book editions remain available. While publishers have information about the actual sales of the book to date, they need to make a decision based on their perception of future sales and continuing interest in the title.

Once again technology is changing the game. The advent of Print on Demand has enabled most publishing houses to reduce print runs significantly as it no longer constrains sales. Previously many titles would sell out of their first print and whilst there was continued demand, it may not have been sufficient to justify a traditional reprint. These days, a reduced print run helps to manage risk as well as the cost of the inventory storage. Print on Demand involves a modest set up cost to create the initial files and then further costs are entirely linked to sales –which makes it a very attractive proposition for publishers.

The final important decision point is whether to take a book out of print. When the sales fall below a certain level and the stock appears to be lying in warehouses untouched with little prospect of future sales, the publisher may decide to end the cycle. At this point, the company will have accumulated a significant amount of sales data and the ultimate decision will be informed by the detailed performance of the title over the complete cycle, as well as other identified trends in the marketplace. Once again, technology has enabled many companies to reduce the size of the first print runs, but to keep the title in print almost indefinitely.

One observation is that the cycle extends beyond a typical product lifecycle. Decisions surrounding a title persist well into the future. The number of major decision-making points is also surprisingly large. Decisions extend into a number of years, which means that the period of uncertainty is longer than that typically experienced. This might go some way towards explaining the caution taken during the process.

You will have gathered from the description of the decisions that publishing houses are in the business of making money. Nonetheless, they are also in the business of dealing with uncertainty and taking risks. Many of the decisions will be based on potential or actual sales, and the promise of identifying a successful title. Editors have a good understanding of the market and will try to help improve your potential product. Yet, it may feel that the focus is on extending the potential profitability of your packaged ideas.

Leading stakeholders in the process include your publisher, the editors and even the marketing team, which will require extensive information when they try to position the book and ensure it is correctly positioned and advertised. Together they will endeavour to maximise the value, visibility and quality of your product. Publishers have been traditionally portrayed as gatekeepers, and as you will have seen from the publishing cycle described above they have a vested interest in making your book as successful as possible. They are also concerned about their reputation and how the products represent them.

Publishers rely on reviewers during the early phases of the publishing cycle. They may resort to using them during the initial evaluation and return the draft chapters to them for a more informed assessment. The length of the review process should not be underestimated as publishers ultimately rely on the good will of reviewers. Reviewers are asked to comment on quality of the proposal and the text, and possibly on the commercial viability of the venture. The decisions described above also have to be scrutinised by editorial publishing meetings, and the financial details need to be rechecked and approved.

In summary, the length of the production process will depend on three factors. The time it takes you to transform your manuscript into a viable book that is likely to appeal to the publishers, the time it takes the publishers to assess, review and ascertain the feasibility of your proposal so that they can make informed decisions, and the time it takes the production department to deliver the finished product. If the rewriting and restructuring is likely to take you 18 months, it will still need to be followed by copy-editing, typesetting, printing, binding and distribution before you can see the finished product on your bookshelf. Taking the process into account, revising your book may be something that you can work on when you accept your first job, after successfully completing your research. The next section will conclude by suggesting the different ways that you can start to work on your book towards the end of your research, and beyond.

## Useful Tips to Get You Started

The following ten suggestions can be used as tips for developing your proposal and transforming your dissertation into a book. There is no reason to wait until your formal work is submitted for examination. Indeed, it is highly recommended that you consider addressing some of the points as soon as you are ready.

Good luck with your research, writing, and your publishing plans. You should also keep in mind that the dissertation comes first!

### PLANNING

- Find a book you like: while you are reading and discovering new sources for your research, identify books and specific authors that you like. Ask yourself why you like them, and consider if the format or approach might work for your writing. This can be done in parallel with your research, as soon as you identify good writing samples.

- Editors: it is important to meet editors in person and talk to representatives of different publishers. If you are attending a conference go to the exhibition area and talk to the different publishers about your intention to publish. Again this can be done at any stage, including the writing-up phase of your research.
- Publishers: research the publishing houses you are interested in. Look at the type of books they publish and browse through some of their titles to become more familiar with their approach and products. You can also start with your favourite books and see who published them.

## WRITING

- Title: start thinking about the title for the book when you write your dissertation. Academic dissertations have typically uninspiring titles; save your best title for the book.
- Audience: consider your audience carefully. Keep the audience in mind throughout the commissioning and revision phases.
- Expand your audience base: revisions at PhD level are associated with corrections. Rethink revision as an opportunity to expand your potential population of readers to make the book more viable for publishing.
- Revision: rethink what needs to be said, again and again. Be prepared to get rid of some sections that do not fit your developing narrative.
- Avoid overexposure: if you intend to publish your dissertation, you cannot publish too much of it as journal articles. Publishers are increasingly unlikely to commission a text that has already appeared in print. The threshold is probably around 20–25 per cent of the content. The best strategy is to use your best single chapter to establish your reputation, followed perhaps by a further chapter/paper, but be sure to leave sufficient content to justify your book.
- Online presence: avoid the temptation to post your dissertation online. If your university library has a policy of publishing all dissertations online, opt out if you would like yours to be published as a book.
- Write the book that you would like to read.

## Further Reading

The reading list includes a mix of: books aimed specially at PhD students looking to convert their dissertations to books; texts that describe the publishing industry and the processes of commissioning and publishing, and the future of books; titles that offer additional insights into writing books; as well as, style manuals that can be used to improve the quality of your prose and writing style.

Barzun, J. (2001). *Simple & Direct: A Rhetoric for Writers*. Quill.

Becker, H. S. (2008). *Writing for Social Scientists: How to Start and Finish Your Thesis, Book or Article*. University of Chicago Press.

Bullock, A. (2012). *Book Production*. Routledge.

Caro, S. (2009). *How to Publish Your PhD*. Sage Publications.

Chicago (2010). *The Chicago Manual of Style: The Essential Guide for Writers, Editors and Publishers*. University of Chicago Press.

Clark, G. and Phillips, A. (2008). *Inside Book Publishing*. Routledge.

Cook, C. K. (2006). *Line by Line: How to Edit Your Own Writing*. Elsevier.

Cope, B. and Phillips A. (2006). *The Future of the Book in the Digital Age.* Chandos Publishing.

Creswell, J., Rocco, T. and Hatcher, T. (2011). The *Handbook of Scholarly Writing and Publishing.* Jossey-Bass.

Darnton, R. (2010). *The Case for Books.* Public Affairs.

Germano, W. (2005). *From Dissertation to Book.* University of Chicago Press.

Germano, W. (2012). *Getting it Published: A Guide for Scholars and Anyone Else Serious About Serious Books.* Readhowyouwant.

Guthrie, R. (2011). *Publishing: Principles and Practice.* Sage Publications.

Harman, E. Montangnes, I., McMenemy, S. and Bucci, C. (2003). *The Thesis and the Book: A Guide for First-Time Academic Authors.* University of Toronto Press.

Haynes, A. (2010). *Writing Successful Academic Books.* Cambridge University Press.

Johnson, N. F. (2011). *Publishing From Your PhD.* Gower Publishing.

Kitchin, R. and Fuller D. (2005). *The Academic's Guide to Publishing.* Sage Publications.

Lerner, B. (2010). *The Forest for the Trees: An Editor's Advice to Writers.* Riverhead Books.

Luey, B. (2009). *Handbook for Academic Authors.* Cambridge University Press

Luey, B. and Thatcher, S. (2007). *Revising Your Dissertation: Advice from Leading Editors.* University of California Press.

Oxford. (2012). *New Oxford Style Manual.* Oxford University Press.

Rabiner, S. (2005). *Thinking Like Your Editor: How to Write Great Nonfiction – and Get it Published.* W. W. Norton

Ritter, R. M. (2005). *New Hart's Rules: The Handbook of Style for Writers and Editors.* Oxford University Press.

Smith, K. (2012). *The Publishing Business: From p-books to e-books.* AVA Publishing.

Striphas, T. (2010). *The Late Age of Print: Everyday Book Culture from Consumerism to Control.* Columbia University press, 2011.

Strunk, W. (2012). *The Elements of Style.* CreateSpace Publishing.

Sword, H. (2012). *Stylish Academic Writing.* Harvard University Press.

Thompson, J. B. (2005). *Books in the Digital Age: The Transformation of Academic and Higher Education Publishing in Britain and the United States.* Polity Press.

Thompson J. B. (2010). *Merchants of Culture: The Publishing Business in the Twenty-First Century.* Polity Press.

Truss, L. (2009). *Eats, Shoots and Leaves.* Fourth Estate.

Williams, J. M. and Colomb G. G. (2010). *Style: Lessons in Clarity and Grace.* Pearson.

# Index